To Sheila and Lucia

Contents

Design and Analysis
A Researcher's Handbook

Fourth Edition

Geoffrey Keppel
Thomas D. Wickens
University of California, Berkeley

PEARSON
Prentice
Hall

Pearson Education International

Senior Acquisitions Editor: Jayme Heffler
Editor-in-Chief: Leah Jewell
Editorial Assistant: Jennifer M. Conklin
Marketing Manager: Sheryl Adams
Assistant Managing Editor (Production): Maureen Richardson
Manufacturing Buyer: Tricia Kenny
Cover Design: Karen Salzbach
Composition/Full-Service Project Management: Fran Daniele, Preparé

10 9 8 7 6 5 4 3 2 1

ISBN 0-13-127776-6

V   WITHIN-SUBJECT DESIGNS   347

16 The Single-Factor Within-Subject Design   350

17 Further Within-Subject Topics   369

18 The Two-Factor Within-Subject Design   401

19 The Mixed Design: Overall Analysis   432

20 The Mixed Design: Analytical Analyses   449

Preface

This fourth edition of *Design and Analysis* is the result of a collaboration that began informally about 25 years ago, when TDW was spending a sabbatical year at Berkeley and attended GK's seminar on experimental design. We have continued our discussions of research design and statistical analysis over the years. TDW was intimately familiar with the earlier editions of this book, using it as a text in his graduate courses at UCLA and contributing substantially to the second and third editions. Our collaboration on this new revision is the natural extension of our discussions. With our equal participation, we have created an essentially new book. We have rewritten it throughout, reorganized the chapters, and introduced much new material.

Our topic is the analysis of variance, the major statistical method used to analyze experimental data in psychology and the behavioral sciences. It gives the researcher a way to compare the means from a series of sets of scores and to determine whether they differ. More than just identifying overall differences, however, the analysis of variance provides a very specific set of procedures that allow a researcher to express particular questions about the study and to measure and test them. Much of the power and the subtlety of the analysis of variance lies in these analytical techniques, which are necessary both when planning a study and when interpreting its results. Accordingly, we devote over a third of the book to them.

The early part of the book contains a detailed discussion of the foundation block of the analysis of variance—the experimental design with independent groups of subjects, each of whom contributes a single observation to the analysis. We then elaborate this structure by expanding it in several ways—to studies in which the groups are classified in two or more ways, to studies with multiple observations, and to studies with several sources of random variability. By the end of this book, a student or researcher will be able to put these parts together and apply them to the analysis of any complex design. We cover the major designs commonly used in psychological research and present, with numerical examples, the analyses appropriate to them. Where possible, we cover statistical arguments in the context of data analysis and interpretation. For example, when we discuss the statistical assumptions that underlie an analysis, we both give their mathematical form and describe how they relate to experimental procedures. To the extent possible while keeping the size of our book within bounds, we describe and illustrate how the analytical techniques are applied in both simple and complex designs—too many books, in our opinion, fail the reader at this point.

We wrote the book with a particular reader in mind: a student at the advanced undergraduate or beginning graduate level who is about to engage in experimental research, but who has little or no formal mathematical or statistical background. We therefore include a discussion of statistical inference, and we limit our assumption of mathematical skills to basic algebra. We give enough detail in our numerical examples for a reader at that level to follow them and to adapt them to new data. Our reader must also be able to use the quantitative methods as part of an overall research plan. We have, therefore, set our numerical examples in context of plausible, if greatly simplified, research designs, so that we can describe both the statistical analysis and how that analysis serves as an inferential tool.

Although we have structured this book as a text, we also envision a second use. The books from which one learns technical material are those to which one returns to review and apply them. We know (or at least hope) that many of our readers will use this book as the handbook of its title and will return to it over the years when using the analysis of variance. With this application in mind, we have included extensive coverage of the analytical analysis of the larger designs. Indeed, we expect that some of the later portions—Part VI, in particular—will gain their full usefulness only once the reader has had some practical research experience.

The earlier editions of this book emphasized the computational aspect of the analysis of variance. Since they were written, the accessibility of computer programs has greatly increased. Quite sophisticated and comprehensive packages of statistical programs are available for use on personal computers without great expense. A researcher now will use a computer for any major analysis. We have considerably modified this edition of the book to accommodate this change. Thus, we have added Chapter 9 on computer applications, and we have completely rewritten our treatments of unequal sample sizes and the analysis of covariance (Chapters 14 and 15) to emphasize the conceptual basis of these techniques. Our treatment of the multifactor designs has likewise been adjusted to be concordant with computer use. The changes here have let us emphasize the principles of the analysis instead of the arithmetic. On the other hand, we have kept our discussions of statistical software general and have not focused on any particular statistical package. Different laboratories are, quite appropriately, committed to different programs. Moreover, the programs differ too much from one to another and change too frequently for us to tie our discussion to a single program or package. A description of a computer package that is *nearly* current can be extraodinarily confusing to a learner. We suggest that an instructor supplement our treatment with examples of whatever computer programs are locally available.

Notwithstanding the importance of the computer, we feel strongly that real facility with the statistical methods comes only when one understands how they work, an idea that is gained from both computer applications and hands-on calculation. Without experience with the actual computation (at least of the simpler designs), a user's skills are brittle—he or she has little ability to go outside the standard analyses or to notice and accommodate unusual characteristics of the data. With the greater flexibility that comes from understanding the techniques well, a researcher can direct the analysis performed by a software package, is more able to use them appropriately, and is not restricted to the particular approach favored by the software developers. Real data sets require this flexibility.

This book is intended for use in a one-semester course or a two-quarter sequence in experimental design and statistical analysis—for a shorter course, an instructor might treat just the single-factor and two-factor designs (Chapters 1–13 and 16–20). The material we cover constitutes what we feel graduate students should master as they become skilled in experimental research.[1] We have found that most students require little supervision in working through the early chapters, so that instructors do not have to duplicate our presentation in their lectures. Instead, we expect that each instructor will supplement this material with topics that suit his or her particular style and interest, for example, by developing the statistical theory more deeply, amplifying the problems of experimental design, or explaining the local computer programs.

We prepared this book using the LaTeX system for mathematical typesetting, from its initial drafts through the pages you are reading. We recommend this system for a large-scale work of this type. It has allowed us to coordinate both content and format of our book in an efficient way.

We wish to acknowledge some of the individuals who assisted in the production of this book. Our editor Jayme Heffler at Prentice Hall, our production coordinator Fran Daniele of Preparé, and our copy editor Barbara Booth all contributed to the quality of this book. We also acknowledge the American Psychological Association, the Federation of American Societies for Experimental Biology, the MIT Press, and the American Association for the Advancement of Science for permission to reproduce copyrighted data from their publications. Finally, we must acknowledge the support and forbearance of our wives, Sheila Keppel and Lucia Bogatay, to whom we dedicate this edition.

To end on a more personal note, we have found the process of preparing this revision both exciting and stimulating. Although we share a common view of the research enterprise, we came to this collaboration with somewhat different goals, strengths, mathematical skills, and writing styles. Establishing a common ground, in both content and style, has been a fascinating, if occasionally frustrating, process. Although our views were not always initially concordant, we are happy to report that no disagreements arose that could not be completely resolved by sharing an order of *moules frits* and a bottle of *rosé* at a local restaurant.

Geoffrey Keppel
Thomas D. Wickens
Berkeley, California

---

[1]Which is not to say that other methods, such as multiple regression, multivariate analysis, and the analysis of categorical data, should not be included in such a course. They are important with other types of data and in other domains, and they are particularly relevant to nonexperimental studies.

Part I

INTRODUCTION

A science is built on a large body of reliable facts and information. As most of you have discovered, or soon will discover, these facts are not easy to come by. They are established through many hours of patient observation, recording, and analysis of the behavior generated during the observation periods. This book focuses on the analysis of data obtained from **designed experiments**. In their simplest form, these experiments consist of two treatment conditions. The subjects in both of these conditions are treated identically, except for one feature that is different. Some aspect of the performance of the subjects in the two treatment conditions is measured and recorded after the treatment has been administered. Because everything else is the same, any difference between the two conditions must have been *caused* by the experimental treatment. This property of designed experiments is often referred to as the "gold standard" of science. In Chapter 1, we describe the important features that must be considered in the design of an experimental study.

The remainder of this book deals with the **analysis of variance**, a body of statistical techniques that was developed as a method of analysis for designed experiments. Its name derives from the idea of dividing the total variability of the scores in an experiment into systematic sources of variability that reflect the experimental manipulations and unsystematic sources that are not influenced by these manipulations. As you will see, there are many forms of experimental designs, but they all can be analyzed in this fashion. For example, the relationship among the conditions in an experiment may be quantitative or qualitative and may be simple or multidimensional. The groups themselves may be chosen in many ways. One quantity may be measured once for each subject, or several observations with their own organization may be made. Each of these variants leads to a somewhat different form of the analysis of variance. This book discusses many of these forms.

1

Experimental Design

An experiment consists of a carefully worked-out and executed plan for data collection and analysis. Treatment conditions are chosen to focus on particular features of the testing environment. An appropriate source of subjects is established. These conditions are administered to subjects in such a way that observed differences in the average values can be unambiguously attributed to the differences among the various treatment conditions. In essence, a well-designed experiment permits the inference of *causation*. This chapter describes a number of important features of experimentation. Many of these points will be amplified throughout the remainder of the book. We will consider throughout the interdependent problems of experimental design along with our presentation of the formal statistical procedures.

1.1 Variables in Experimental Research

The basic requirements of an experiment are simple: Differential treatments are administered to different groups of subjects (or repeatedly to the same subjects), and performance of some sort measured and recorded following the administration of the treatments. In this section, we will elaborate on this relatively simple idea.

The Independent Variable

In the simplest experiment, a researcher creates two equivalent groups of subjects and treats them differently. Frequently these groups are created by some operation performed by the researcher, such as forming a control group and an experimental group, but they can also be defined by preexisting characteristics, such as female and male subjects. The critical difference between the groups is called the **independent variable**. Once these groups have been defined, some form of behavior is observed and measured for each subject. The research question concerns how the average value of this measured behavior depends on the group classification. We will refer to an independent variable in a number of ways, as a **manipulated variable**, a **treatment variable**, or a **factor**.

As an example, suppose we have a single condition consisting of

SATIATED ADULT RATS given FOOD reward for solving a HARD maze.

In addition to the potentially critical features of this treatment condition, written in uppercase letters, we could list other features as well, such as the characteristics of the testing room, the apparatus and the experimenter, the time of testing, and so on. What can we conclude from studying subjects in this single condition? Very little, except to describe the situation. We can infer nothing about the relative importance of the various characteristics in influencing the speed with which the maze is learned. Now let's add a second condition:

SATIATED ADULT RATS given FOOD reward for solving an *EASY* maze.

Although this condition suffers from the same problem as the first when the behavior of the subjects is considered alone, the purpose of the experiment springs into focus when we *compare* the two treatment conditions. More specifically, the critical difference between the two conditions is the difficulty of the maze, and any difference observed between the two conditions will be attributable to this particular difference (hard versus easy). Maze difficulty is the independent variable, and the pair of conditions constitutes an experiment. We could have created additional two-group experiments simply by varying one of the other critical features and holding the others constant, in which case the treatments might be food and water, satiated and hungry, or rat and hamster.

Most experiments consist of more than two treatment conditions. If we were interested in comparisons among species in a given learning task, for example, we might design an experiment in which various types of animals are represented, such as rats, hamsters, and mice. The choice of animal would be dictated by our substantive questions. If we were interested in the effects of food deprivation on learning, we would probably include several treatment conditions varying in the amount of time the animals have been without food, such as 0, 12, 24, and 36 hours.

Types of Independent Variables

It is useful to classify independent variables into different types. We will consider three categories based on the fundamental nature of the manipulation.

The first type of manipulation, **qualitative independent variables** or **categorical independent variables**, represents variations in *kind* or in *type*. Experiments designed to study different methods for teaching reading or of different kinds of drugs are examples of qualitative independent variables. So is the study mentioned above that compares rats, hamsters, and mice. When the qualitative independent variable involves more than two conditions, it can be viewed as a collection of miniature two-group experiments within the context of the larger experiment. Suppose an experiment is designed to study the effects of different rewards on the speed of learning. Rats that have been deprived of food and water are assigned to one of the following three conditions:

- Condition 1: food reward for solving the maze,
- Condition 2: water reward for solving the maze,
- Condition 3: food and water for solving the maze.

A comparison between conditions 1 and 2 concentrates on the relative effects of food and water as rewards for learning, and a comparison between conditions 1 and 3 focuses on the addition of water to the food reward. A comparison between conditions 2 and 3 permits a similar determination of the effects of the addition of food to the water reward. Most experiments involving a qualitative independent variable can be analyzed as a set of smaller, more focused experiments, a topic we will discuss in detail in Chapter 4.

A second type of manipulation, **quantitative independent variables** or **continuous independent variables**, consists of variables that represent variation in *amount*—amount of food deprivation, variations in dosage, loudness of the masking noise, length of the learning task. Variables of this sort usually include treatment conditions that define the range of values of interest to the researcher and several intermediate conditions to provide a picture of the effects of the variable between the two extremes. The effects of quantitative independent variables are usually analyzed differently from those produced by qualitative manipulations. Here, researchers concentrate on the overall relationship between the variation of the independent variable and changes in behavior. The goal of the analysis is to determine the nature or shape of this relationship. Suppose that the independent variable is the number of hours of food deprivation and that we will be measuring the trials required to learn a difficult maze. How are we to describe the relationship? Presumably we will find an increase in performance as the animals become more hungry. But will the increase occur steadily as the number of hours increases, or will there be no effect at first, then a steady increase? Will very high levels of deprivation lead to poorer performance? Specialized procedures known as *trend analysis* are available that permit us to distinguish among these (and other) possibilities. We will discuss them in Chapter 5.

A third type of independent variable is encountered when researchers are interested in the systematic variation of characteristics that are intrinsic to the subjects. Variables of this sort are variously referred to as **classification variables, subject variables, organismic variables**, and **individual-difference variables**. Examples of this type of study are the effect of accidental damage to different areas of the brain on learning and the effect of gender on solving arithmetic problems. Classification variables are created by selecting or classifying subjects on some natural dimension. A manipulation of this sort does not constitute a true experiment since the administration of the "treatments" is obviously not under the control of the experimenter. In an experiment, the independent variable is the only feature of the situation that is allowed to vary systematically from condition to condition. It is this characteristic of an experiment that permits us to infer that a particular manipulation caused systematic differences in the behavior observed among the different groups. But when a classification variable is involved, the subjects may also differ systematically from group to group in characteristics other than the classification variable. Thus, the inferences that can be made regarding a classification variable are weaker than those that can be made from an experimental variable. The statistical procedures in this book allow us to say (or not to say) that the groups differ, but the nature of the design does not let us know why. For example, female and male subjects differ in many ways—physiological, cultural, experiential, psychological, etc. A researcher can find that females and males differ on a particular dependent variable, but cannot easily say which of the many differences between the sexes causes the effect.

Studies in some fields of psychology examine naturally occurring groups that have received different treatments. For example, an organizational psychologist may compare the incentive systems used in two different factories, or a health researcher may compare the relative effectiveness of two diet programs administered in different clinics. Although these studies have much in common with an experiment—in particular, two different treatments are compared—they lack a critical component of a true experiment. The treatments are applied to naturally occurring groups (the factories or the clinics), and these may differ for various other reasons than the particular treatment. Differences in productivity or in weight loss may have been influenced by other factors, such as the kind of person who works at a particular factory or attends a specific clinic. Studies of this sort are called **quasi-experiments** or **nonrandomized experiments**. As with the classification factors, the difficulties are not with the statistical methods per se, but with the interpretation of their outcome. When using a quasi-experimental factor, a researcher must try to establish that the groups do not differ on whatever incidental characteristics there may be that also affect the final scores.

The Dependent Variable

Suppose we have completed the first steps in an experimental investigation: the development of a meaningful hypothesis, the choice of the subjects, and the selection of an experimental design. We must now decide on the particular aspect of the behavior we will observe and how we will measure this behavior.

Even the behavior of a subject in an apparently simple experiment may be measured in many ways. Suppose a researcher is interested in how two groups of students are influenced by different forms of argument in favor of a proposal to require all undergraduate students to take a comprehensive examination at the end of their senior year. The effect of the arguments could be measured by the extent to which the students approved of the proposal, by the extent to which they thought it beneficial, by the thoughts they had while listening to the arguments, by which of the specific points from the argument they could remember, and so on. Each of these possibilities measures a somewhat different aspect of the behavior and constitutes a different potential dependent variable. The researcher must decide which one (or ones) of these to use. Very often the researcher will use several different measures to ensure as complete a description as possible of the phenomenon under study. In this book, we will emphasize the **univariate** procedures that look at one dependent variable at a time. There are also **multivariate** methods that look simultaneously at several dependent variables, which, for the most part, we will leave to advanced study.

A successful dependent variable should not be limited by the range of its values. A **floor effect** occurs when many subjects receive scores close to the minimum possible value, and a **ceiling effect** occurs when many subjects receive scores close to the maximum possible value. The limitations imposed by these restrictions will sharply reduce the sensitivity of the dependent variable. Suppose, for example, that subjects study a list of 10 words under three different levels of incentive, low, medium, and high. On a subsequent recall test, the average recall is 5, 9, and 9.5 words, respectively. Clearly, the low motivation resulted in poorer recall, but we cannot say much about the other two conditions. Both are near the limit of 10 words, and there is no room for them to differ appreciably. The researcher should have used a longer list of words or a more difficult test, so that the scores were not close to the performance limit.

Nuisance Variables

In any research situation, there are many factors that influence the value of the dependent variable other than the treatment of interest. These characteristics constitute **nuisance variables**. They cause the scores to differ, but they are not of interest in the particular study. For example, in the experiment with the word recall, some word lists are easier to recall than others, and subjects tested in the morning may be fresher and recall more words than those run late in the day. These variables could be of interest to some other researcher, who could manipulate them separately, but as they affect the study of incentive, they are simply in the way.

The presence of nuisance variables can have two types of effect. First, if they are systematically related to the treatment conditions, a situation known as **confounding**, they can alter the apparent effects of the treatments. This is what makes quasi-experiments so hard to interpret. Second, even if they have no systematic relationship to the independent variable, their accidental, or nonsystematic, effects will increase the variability of the scores and obscure whatever treatment effects there may be. A researcher must consider both possibilities.

Consider a study designed to examine the effects of three experimental treatments—call them t_1, t_2, and t_3. For convenience in setting up the equipment, the experimenter decides to run all subjects in one condition before turning to the next. As a result, condition t_1 is run in the morning, t_2 in the afternoon, and t_3 in the evening. The nuisance variable *time of day* is now confounded with the experimental treatment. The confounding can have serious consequences. If rats are the subjects, for example, systematic differences in their performance may arise from where in their diurnal cycles they are run. If the subjects are student volunteers, differences may arise because different types of subject volunteer at different times of day—for example, because of their availability on campus (which in turn depends on their class schedule). In either case, the influences on performance are intertwined with those of the independent variable and cannot be separated.

There are many ways to deal with the effects of nuisance variables. Four are common, and many experiments include combinations of all of them.

1. A nuisance variable can be held to a constant value throughout an experiment, say by running all subjects at the same time of day.
2. A nuisance variable may be **counterbalanced** by including all of its values equally often in each condition, say by running one-third of the subjects from each treatment level in each time slot.
3. A nuisance variable may be included in the design as an explicit factor, known as a **nuisance factor**.
4. The systematic relationship between the nuisance variable and the independent variable may be destroyed by **randomization**. Each subject is randomly assigned to a condition to break any possibility of confounding.

We will discuss all of these approaches, particularly randomization, shortly.

In any study, there is an infinitude of potential nuisance variables, some of them important, most not. In many studies, all four of the strategies we just mentioned are employed. An index of the skill of a researcher is the subtlety with which this is done. Only after considerable experience in research will you acquire the sensitivity to treat nuisance variable well and to identify places where potential confounding may occur.

1.2   Control in Experimentation

Our goal in experimentation is to keep everything about the experimental conditions identical except for the manipulations that we are studying. Unfortunately, the world conspires against us. No two subjects are the same, and the environment is never completely constant. Nuisance variables make the scores we record vary, quite apart from any effect of the independent variable. We can take various measures to minimize the differences and make the groups more comparable, even though perfection is impossible. We have two ends in research design: to eliminate any confounding that will alter the comparisons among conditions and to find ways to minimize the differences among the subjects within each condition.

Control by Design

One way to address these ends is to design the experiment carefully. For the greater part, doing so involves applying the first three of the four principles we listed at the end of our discussion of nuisance variables. To start with, certain features can in fact be held constant across the levels of the experiment. All the testing can be done at the same time, in the same experimental room, by the same experimenter, and with the same equipment and testing procedures. Control of other features of the experiment, though not absolute, is sufficiently close to be considered essentially constant. Consider the mechanical devices that are used to hold various features of the environment constant. A thermostat does not achieve absolute control of the temperature in the room, but it reduces its variation. An uncontrolled room would be subjected to a wider range of temperatures during the course of an experiment than a controlled room, although variation is still present. However, this variation is typically small enough to allow us to view the temperature as constant.

What about the subjects? Can they be held constant across treatment conditions? Sometimes that is possible. Each subject in the study can serve in all the conditions instead of just one. In this way, any differences among subjects apply to all conditions equally, greatly increasing their comparability. There are some limitations, however. For one thing, in some studies a subject cannot provide more than one score. Certain independent variables cause changes in the subject that cannot be undone. Most obviously, a treatment as drastic as removal of brain tissue is irreversible and renders the subject unusable for another treatment. More subtly, whatever may have been learned during the course of a treatment cannot be unlearned, making it impossible to return subjects to their original state. There are a host of things to consider when designs with repeated observations are used, which we will describe in Chapter 17.

Suppose the same subject can be used only once. It is still possible to make the groups more comparable by grouping the subjects into sets based on some nuisance variable and then assigning an equal number of members from each set to each of the experimental groups. This procedure, known as **blocking**, has two effects. First, it renders the treatment groups more comparable by assuring that each has the same distribution of the nuisance variable, and, second, it reduces the variability of the scores within a block. The operation of blocking depends on having a way to classify the subjects, and create a classification factor. However, do not think that all classification factors are used for blocking. Classification variables such as gender or age usually appear in a study because their effect is intrinsically of interest. We will discuss blocking in Section 11.5 and the related **analysis of covariance** in Chapter 15.

Properly designing the study can go a long way towards making the conditions comparable. However, inevitably there are many characteristics that influence the behavior that we cannot control. Subjects vary one from another in ways that we can neither explain nor classify. For these we must take another approach.

Control by Randomization

The second way to address the comparability of the groups is to stop trying to achieve an exact balance and adopt an approach that assures that any differences that remain are not *systematically* related to the treatments. To use this procedure, known as **randomization**, we simply assign each subject to a treatment condition completely at random. If we had two conditions, we might flip a coin to determine the group assignment for each subject. Or, if we were planning to run 75 subjects in a three-group experiment, we could start by writing "Group 1" on 25 index cards, "Group 2" on 25 cards, and "Group 3" on 25 cards. Then we would shuffle the deck to put the cards in a random order. When each subject came in, we would pull a card off the stack and let the number on it determine the treatment that subject would receive. There are more sophisticated methods of randomization, including the use of random-number tables, but conceptually they amount to the same thing.

Consider again the control of the time of testing. Earlier we suggested that all treatments could be administered at the same time or that an equal number of them could be administered at each of the available time periods. Suppose, instead, that we randomly assigned the subjects to the treatments regardless of what time they were tested. A subject tested at 9 AM is equally likely to receive treatment t_1, t_2, or t_3, and the same goes for a subject tested at noon or at 6 p.m. Thus, every subject, regardless of the time of testing, has an equal chance of being assigned to any treatment condition. If we follow this procedure with enough subjects, statistical theory tells us that the *average* testing times for the three treatment groups will be almost equal. Under these circumstances, then, the nuisance variable time will have little or no differential effect.

What about other features of the experimental environment that also change? The grand thing about randomization is that once we have controlled one environmental feature by randomization, we have controlled all others as well. Let's list some of the characteristics of the testing session. The room will be at a certain temperature; there will be a certain humidity; the room illumination will be at a particular level; the noise from the outside filtering into the room will be of a certain intensity; the experiment will be given at a particular time of day, on a particular day, and by a particular experimenter; and so on. All of these factors are controlled simultaneously by random assignment. We do not need to consider each one separately, as we would have to if we tried to control them by design.

Differences among the treatment conditions in the characteristics of the subjects are also controlled by randomization. The subjects who are chosen to participate in an experiment will differ widely on a host of characteristics—intelligence, emotionality, attitude, motivation, background, training, and countless others. Many of these will affect the behavior being studied. Consider one of them, say, the amount of prior experience with the task. When we randomly assign subjects to the conditions, subjects with considerable experience are just as likely to be assigned to one treatment as to another. The same is true for subjects with minimal or moderate amounts of experience. Through randomization, we ensure that in the long run there is a near equivalence of subjects across the different treatments. Moreover, the same argument applies equally well to all the other differences among subjects. All are controlled in the same way. Until the experimenter treats them differently, the only differences among the groups are unsystematic accidents that arise from random assignment. This ability to control for all nuisance variables, environmental or subject-related, anticipated or not, is what makes random assignment an indispensable part of experimental design.

There is a limit to what randomization can do, however. We never can run a sufficiently large number of subjects to guarantee a perfect balancing of every nuisance variable. Some accidental differences among the groups are bound to remain, and our groups will never be exactly equivalent with regard to environmental features or to differences among subjects. However, the fact that randomization is a regular and well-understood process makes us able to anticipate and measure the sizes of these differences and account for them in our inferences. In fact, the statistical procedures that we discuss in this book were specifically created to overcome this problem.

1.3 Populations and Generalizing

Our goal in research is to extend a set of findings beyond the subjects that are tested in any actual experiment. We are not specifically interested in the performance of the 40 people who actually serve in our experiment, but in their performance as representative of what would be obtained from a much larger group of individuals. This group, known as the **population**, may be all laboratory rats, all college students, or even all humans. The subjects we actually test are a **sample** from this population. The link between sample and population depends on how the sample of subjects is obtained. The statistical model we consider in Section 7.1 specifies that our observations come from a **random sample** drawn from a known population. In short, each member of the population is equally likely to turn up in the sample and equally likely to be assigned to each treatment condition. The selection of one subject from the population has no effect on the chance that any other subject is selected. When this property is satisfied, the subjects that we observe—the sample—are comparable to those that we did not—the rest of the population. Because they do not differ, findings based on the sample can be generalized to the population.

As attractive as it is, true random sampling from a population is a statistical ideal that is never attained in practice. The subjects we test are not random samples at all; instead, they are more appropriately described as *samples of convenience*—the animals available in the departmental colony or the subjects who volunteer because our experiment fits with their schedules. Although these groups are part of the population that we want to study, they are not random. Under these circumstances, we have to base a portion of our generalizations on *nonstatistical* grounds. Here we are working from experience, not formal statistics. So, we are happy to accept the fact that students at one college will produce effects that are much like those at a different school or that animals from one breeding stock will perform like those from another. To put it another way, the statistical methods allow us to generalize from our sample to an idealized population from which it could have been sampled, and the extrastatistical generalization lets us conclude that this hypothetical population is similar to the actual population that we want to study. Of course, there are limits to the extent of such nonstatistical generalizations. For example, generalizing results obtained from college students to a population of elderly subjects is often not justified. Concerns like this, in fact, often justify the selection of subject variables as an object of study.

Our distinction, then, is between **statistical generalization**, which depends on random sampling, and **nonstatistical generalization**, which depends on our knowledge of a particular research area. Cornfield and Tukey (1956, pp. 912–913) make this point quite clearly:

> In almost any practical situation where analytical statistics is applied, the inference from the observations to the real conclusion has two parts, only the first of which is statistical. A genetic experiment on *Drosophila* will usually involve flies of a certain race of a certain species. The statistically based conclusions cannot extend beyond this race, yet the geneticist will usually, and often wisely, extend the conclusion to (a) the whole species, (b) all *Drosophila*, or (c) a larger group of insects. This wider extension may be implicit or explicit, but it is almost always present.

We have spoken about generalizing to a population of subjects, but there are other forms of generalization that are possible. Various other aspects of the experimental situation can also be thought of as "sampled" from a larger population. Suppose you are studying how fifth graders solve mathematics problems and can draw them from a number of classes within a school system. You cannot include all the classes in your study, but you would like to generalize your findings beyond those you choose to include. You have, in effect, sampled certain classes from a larger set of them. Or, consider the math problems that your subjects are to solve. There are many possible problems that you might have used, and the ones you actually use are only a sample of these. To take a different example, suppose you wish to compare the memory for active and passive sentences. You can't possibly have your subjects memorize every possible active or passive sentence. Only a few instances must suffice. You are not interested in the difference in memory for these particular sentences, but rather for all sentences in general. The type of generalization that goes on here is quite similar to that involving subjects, as you will see in Chapters 24 and 25.

1.4   The Basic Experimental Designs

The analysis of variance applies to a wide range of designs, from the simple two-group experiment to very complex designs involving many independent variables. One useful feature is that the analysis of the complex designs is built upon that of the simpler ones. In this book, we will cover the most common experimental designs used in the behavioral sciences, taking advantage of their building-block nature. In this final section, we will preview some important classes of designs.

The **between-subjects design** is characterized by the fact that subjects receive only one of the different treatment conditions. Between-subjects designs are simple to understand, easy to design and analyze, and require the smallest number of statistical assumptions. Their main disadvantage is that they are less sensitive than some of the other approaches, and so require a larger number of subjects to be used. The first seven chapters in Part II are concerned with the simplest form of between-subjects design, that with a single independent variable. This material is the foundation on which the remaining procedures are erected.

The opposite of a between-subjects design is a **within-subject design**, in which each subject serves in every treatment condition. By using the same subject in every condition, the groups are made more comparable and the tests more sensitive. Its greater sensitivity makes it a popular choice in the behavioral sciences. The increased sensitivity of the within-subject design is not without costs. The statistical assumptions of the within-subject design are more complicated than those of the between-subjects designs. Moreover, a within-subject design introduces a nuisance variable that is not present in a between-subjects study, namely the order in which the conditions are tested. A researcher must be at pains to control it. We discuss these and other issues for the single-factor within-subject design in Chapters 16 and 17.

So far we have mentioned only designs in which one independent variable is manipulated. Designs with two or more factors are actually much more common in behavioral research, and for good reason. The most frequent is the **factorial design**, in which every level of one factor is combined with every level of the other. A factorial design gives information both about the influence of each independent variable on behavior considered separately and about how the effects of the variables combine. The factorial designs permit us to move beyond a one-dimensional view of behavior to a richer, more revealing, multidimensional view.

The two single-factor designs are the building blocks from which factorial designs are constructed. There are three general possibilities. At one extreme, there is the **between-subjects factorial design**, in which every condition contains a unique sample of subjects. At the other extreme is the **within-subject factorial design**, in which a single sample of subjects serves in every condition. Between these two types are factorial designs with some within-subject factors—the same subjects serve at all levels—and some between-subjects factors—different samples are used at each level. This type of design is usually called a **mixed factorial design**. We will introduce the between-subjects factorial designs in Part III and then look at some of their within-subject and mixed forms in Parts V and VI.

Part II

SINGLE-FACTOR EXPERIMENTS

A two-group experiment was used in Chapter 1 to illustrate the experimental method. At one time, this type of experiment was the modal design in the behavioral sciences. Today, however, we see experiments in which a single independent variable is represented by more than two different treatments, and we find many cases in which two or more independent variables are manipulated concurrently in the same experiment.

The major reason for this increase in the complexity of the designs is that a two-group design can only indicate the presence or the absence of a single difference between treatments, while an experiment with more than two treatment conditions provides for a more *detailed* description of the relationship between variations in the independent variable and changes in behavior. Additionally, as our knowledge increases and more facts are established, our theoretical explanations become increasingly complicated and more elaborate designs are needed to test them. To identify the mechanisms and processes that lie behind any given phenomenon, an experimenter frequently must increase the number of treatments and the number of independent variables that he or she includes in a single experiment.

In Part II, we will consider the analysis of experiments in which there is a single classification of the treatment conditions. By this we mean that the different treatments are classified only one way, on the basis of either qualitative or quantitative differences among the treatment conditions. We will refer to either type of manipulation as a **factor** and to the specific treatment conditions represented in an experiment as the **levels** of a factor. In this book, we will also use the terms **levels**, **treatments**, and **treatment levels** interchangeably.

The general purpose of the single-factor experiment may be illustrated by a simple example. Suppose that a researcher in a consumer-testing agency was asked to compare the relative effectiveness of 10 brands of aspirin and that she had no particular reason to expect any one brand to be better than the other. How might she analyze the results of this experiment? One procedure would be to treat each of the possible two-group comparisons as a different *two-group experiment*. That is, she would compare brand 1 versus each of the remaining 9 brands, brand 2 versus each of the remaining 8 brands, brand 3 versus each of the remaining 7 brands, and so on. There are 45 of these two-group comparisons. Obviously, this sort of analysis would require a considerable amount of calculation. Moreover, she should be concerned with the fact that she is using each set of data over and over again to make these comparisons. Each set is part of nine different comparisons. We cannot think of these comparisons as constituting 45 *independent* experiments; if one group is distorted for some reason or other, this distortion will be present in every comparison in which it enters. Finally, a set of 45 tests is difficult to comprehend or interpret. When a researcher wants to test certain differences between individual groups, there are more direct and efficient ways to do so.

The single-factor, or one-way, analysis of variance allows researchers to consider all of the treatments in a *single* assessment. Without going into the details yet, this analysis sets in perspective any interpretations one may want to make concerning the differences that have been observed. More specifically, the analysis will tell the researcher whether or not it will be worthwhile to conduct any additional analyses comparing specific treatment groups.

We will first consider the logic behind the analysis of variance and then worry about translating these intuitive notions into mathematical expressions and actual numbers.

2

Sources of Variability
and Sums of Squares

We will begin our discussion of the design and analysis of experiments with an example of a simple memory experiment.[1] Suppose you have devised a procedure that you think helps people to learn and remember things. You believe that when people use your procedure, they will learn them faster and remember them longer. Although you believe that this procedure works for you, you also know that others will want more compelling evidence than simply your testimony or the testimony of your friends.

You decide to give people a list of 20 obscure facts to learn and then test them the next day to see how many facts they can recall. To make a convincing case for your method, you compare two groups of people, an *experimental group* in which individuals study your memory procedure and a *control group* in which individuals are given the same amount of time to study something irrelevant to the task, such as a lesson on how to solve fraction problems. Following this study period, all individuals are presented the same set of facts to learn and then are tested the next day. You expect that the experimental group will remember more facts than the control group. Following the procedures described in the last chapter, you assemble 32 subjects, assign them randomly to the two conditions, and run your study.

Table 2.1 gives the results of such an experiment. Each row of the table indicates which of the 20 facts a particular subject recalled, identified by a 0 when the fact was not recalled, and by a 1 when it was recalled. In the right column, the total number of facts recalled by each subject is tabulated. There are 16 totals from each group, each potentially consisting of a number between 0 (recalling no facts) and 20 (recalling all of the facts). A glance at these data is not particularly revealing. There are differences among the subjects (the column on the right) and among the facts (the data within the body of the table), which obscure any overall difference between the two groups. If the data are to convey useful information, they must be summarized.

The place to start is with a picture that focuses on the total number of facts recalled by each subject, disregarding the differences among the facts. Figure 2.1 shows a representation of the data, known as a **histogram**. The abscissa of this

---

[1]This section is based on an example developed by Wickens (1998).

Table 2.1: *Recall of 20 facts by the 32 subjects in the two groups of a memory experiment. Correct recall and failure are indicated by 1 and 0, respectively.*

Subject																					Total

Subject	1	2	3	4	5	6	7	8	9	10	11	12	13	14	15	16	17	18	19	20	Total
\multicolumn Control Group																					
1	0	1	1	1	1	1	1	1	1	1	1	1	1	0	1	1	0	1	0	1	16
2	0	0	1	1	1	0	0	1	1	0	1	1	1	1	1	0	1	0	0	1	12
3	1	1	0	0	0	1	1	0	1	1	1	0	1	1	0	0	0	1	1	0	11
4	1	1	1	1	0	1	0	1	1	1	0	0	1	1	1	1	1	0	1	1	15
5	1	0	1	0	0	0	0	1	0	1	1	0	1	0	0	0	1	0	1	1	9
6	0	0	0	1	0	0	1	0	1	0	0	1	1	1	0	0	0	0	0	0	6
7	1	1	0	1	0	1	0	1	0	1	1	1	1	0	1	1	1	0	0	0	12
8	1	0	1	0	1	1	1	1	1	0	0	1	0	0	1	0	1	1	0	1	12
9	1	0	0	1	1	1	1	0	0	1	1	1	1	1	0	0	1	0	1	0	12
10	1	1	1	0	0	1	0	1	0	0	1	0	1	0	1	0	0	1	1	0	10
11	1	1	1	0	0	1	0	0	0	1	0	1	0	1	0	1	0	1	1	1	11
12	1	1	1	0	0	1	0	0	1	0	0	1	1	0	0	1	0	0	1	1	10
13	1	1	1	1	1	0	1	0	1	1	1	0	1	1	1	0	0	0	0	1	13
14	0	0	0	0	0	1	0	1	1	1	1	1	0	1	0	0	1	1	0	0	9
15	1	0	0	1	0	1	0	1	1	0	0	0	1	0	1	1	1	1	1	0	11
16	0	1	1	1	1	1	1	0	1	1	1	0	0	1	0	1	0	1	1	1	14
Total	11	9	10	9	6	12	7	9	11	10	10	9	12	9	8	7	8	8	9	9	
Experimental Group																					
1	1	1	1	1	0	1	1	0	0	0	0	1	1	1	1	0	0	1	0	1	12
2	1	1	0	1	1	1	0	0	1	0	1	0	1	1	0	0	0	1	1	1	12
3	1	1	0	0	1	1	1	0	0	0	0	0	0	0	1	1	1	1	0	1	10
4	0	1	0	1	1	1	1	1	0	0	0	1	1	0	0	0	1	0	0	0	9
5	1	1	1	0	1	1	1	1	1	1	1	1	1	1	1	0	1	1	0	0	16
6	1	1	0	1	1	1	1	0	1	0	1	1	1	1	1	0	1	1	1	1	16
7	1	1	0	1	0	1	1	1	1	1	1	1	0	1	1	1	1	0	1	1	16
8	1	1	0	1	0	1	1	1	1	1	1	1	1	0	1	1	1	1	0	1	16
9	1	1	1	0	1	1	1	0	1	0	0	0	0	0	0	0	1	1	1	1	10
10	1	0	1	1	1	1	0	0	1	0	1	1	1	1	1	1	1	1	1	1	16
11	1	0	0	0	1	1	0	0	0	1	1	1	0	1	0	1	0	1	1	1	11
12	1	1	1	0	1	1	1	1	1	1	1	1	0	0	1	1	0	1	1	1	16
13	1	0	1	1	0	1	1	1	1	1	1	1	1	0	1	1	1	0	0	1	15
14	1	1	1	1	1	1	1	0	1	0	0	1	0	1	0	0	1	1	0	1	13
15	1	1	1	1	0	1	0	1	0	1	0	0	0	1	1	0	0	1	1	1	12
16	1	1	1	1	1	1	1	1	1	1	1	1	1	0	1	1	1	1	1	1	19
Total	15	13	9	11	11	16	12	8	11	8	10	12	9	9	11	8	10	13	9	14	

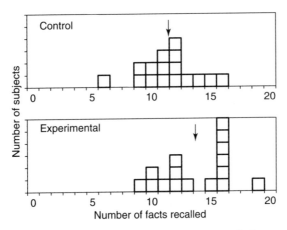

Figure 2.1: Two histograms showing the distributions of the number of facts re-membered for the two conditions of the memory experiment. The arrows mark the means.

graph (the horizontal or X axis) is marked with the number of facts that could be recalled, a range from 0 to 20. For each subject's total, a block is stacked up over the appropriate score on the abscissa. For example, three subjects in the control group remembered 11 facts, so the plot has three blocks above this point. One can easily see from these two histograms, where each distribution of scores is approximately centered or located, how much they spread out from that center, and how much the distributions of the two groups overlap. Like every summary representation, however, this display emphasizes one aspect of the data over others. Here, the overall performance of the individual subjects is apparent, but the identity of the individual subjects and the particular facts they remembered have vanished.

The two most important characteristics of the distributions of scores in Figure 2.1 are their centers and how widely they spread out. The centers reflect the performance levels of the groups as a whole, and their spreads reflect the variability of the totals—how the individual subjects scatter about the center of their respective distributions. The centers of the distributions are commonly summarized either by selecting the middle score in the distribution, known as the **median**, or by averaging the scores to obtain the **arithmetical mean**, or **mean** for short. For the statistical procedures in this book, the mean is the measure of choice. You will recall that the mean for a group, which we will denote by the letter Y with a bar over it, is found by adding up all the scores and dividing by the number of observations. The means of your two groups are

$$\bar{Y}_c = \frac{16 + 12 + \cdots + 11 + 14}{16} = \frac{183}{16} = 11.44,$$

$$\bar{Y}_e = \frac{12 + 12 + \cdots + 12 + 19}{16} = \frac{219}{16} = 13.69.$$

There is a difference of 2.25 facts, favoring the experimental group.

What can you now conclude? Was the special memory activity responsible for the 2.25-fact difference you observed? Unfortunately, you can tell yet. The problem is that the random assignment of subjects to the two conditions does not fully control the influence of nuisance variables, that is, it does not fully equate the groups before the start of the experiment. Specifically, the observed difference between the two group means is influenced jointly by the *actual* difference between the control and experimental treatments and by any *accidental* factors arising from the randomization. The decision confronting you now is whether the difference between the treatment conditions is entirely or just partly due to chance. We will consider, in general terms, the statistical solution to this disturbing problem next.

2.1   The Logic of Hypothesis Testing

Generally, a researcher is not primarily interested merely in describing the performance of the subjects in the different treatment conditions. Instead, the main goal is to make *inferences* about the behavior of subjects who have not been tested in the experiment. Except when studying some special, restricted group (for example, all legislators from a given area), we never test all possible subjects who might have appeared in an experiment, such as all laboratory rats of a particular strain or all college students. Instead, we select samples from these larger groups, administer the experimental conditions, and make inferences about the nature of the population on the basis of the outcome. We refer to these large groups as **populations**. A **sample** consists of a smaller set of observations drawn from the population. Summary descriptions calculated from the data of a sample are called **statistics**, and measures calculated from all the observations within the population are called **parameters**. In most cases, we will use Roman letters to designate statistics and Greek letters to designate parameters.

At this point, we can view the subjects in the treatment conditions as representing samples drawn from different treatment populations. Statistics, calculated on the scores obtained from the different groups of subjects, provide estimates of one or more parameters for the different treatment populations. We are now ready to consider the formal process of hypothesis testing, where we translate the research hypotheses into a set of **statistical hypotheses**, which we then evaluate in light of our data.

Statistical Hypotheses

A research hypothesis is a fairly general statement about the assumed nature of the world that a researcher translates into an experiment. Typically, but not always, a research hypothesis asserts that the treatments will produce an effect. Statistical hypotheses consist of a set of precise hypotheses about the parameters of the different treatment populations. We usually formulate two statistical hypotheses that are mutually exclusive or incompatible statements about the treatment parameters.

The statistical hypothesis we test is called the **null hypothesis**, often symbolized H_0. Its function is to specify the values of a particular parameter (the mean, for example, symbolized as μ and pronounced "mu") in the different treatment populations (μ_1, μ_2, μ_3, and so on). The null hypothesis typically chosen gives the parameters the same value in the different populations:

$$H_0 : \mu_1 = \mu_2 = \mu_3 = \text{etc.}$$

This is tantamount to saying that no treatment effects are present in the population.

Most researchers realize that the null hypothesis is rarely true. Almost any treatment manipulation is bound to produce *some* effect, even if it may be small. You might wonder, then, if the hypothesis is almost always false, why anyone would bother to test it. What researchers really mean by the null hypothesis is a set of differences that are sufficiently small to be considered functionally equivalent to zero, to be treated as if they did not exist.[2] However, we will continue to refer to H_0 in the traditional manner as specifying the absence of treatment differences, realizing that this condition rarely, if ever, holds exactly.

When the actual means obtained from the treatment groups are too deviant from those specified by the null hypothesis, it is rejected in favor of the other statistical hypothesis, called the **alternative hypothesis**, H_1. The alternative hypothesis specifies values for the parameter that are incompatible with the null hypothesis. Usually, the alternative hypothesis states that the values of the parameter in the different treatment populations are *not* all equal. Specifically,

$$H_1 : \text{not all } \mu\text{'s are equal.}$$

A decision to reject H_0 implies an acceptance of H_1, which, in essence, constitutes support of an experimenter's original *research* hypothesis. On the other hand, if the treatment means are reasonably close to those specified by the null hypothesis—the band around zero mentioned above—H_0 is retained and not rejected. This latter decision can be thought of as a failure of the experiment to support the research hypothesis. As you will see, a decision to retain the null hypothesis is not simple. Depending on the true state of the world—the equality or inequality of the actual treatment population means—one can make an error of inference with either decision, rejecting H_0 or retaining H_0. We will have much more to say about these errors.

Experimental Error

The crux of the problem is the fact that one can always attribute some portion of the differences we observe among the treatment means to the operation of chance factors. Every nuisance variable in an experiment that one controls through random assignment of subjects to the treatment conditions is a potential contributor to the results. These influences are called **experimental error**, **error variability**, or **error variance**—we will use these terms interchangeably.

Let's consider some of the components that contribute to the score that we record from each subject.

- *Permanent or stable abilities*. This component remains a constant and is a permanent part of the subject's performance during the study. This component is usually the greatest contributor to a subject's score.
- *The treatment effect*. This component expresses the influence of each treatment condition on the subjects. It is assumed to be identical for all subjects in any given treatment condition. It is absent when H_0 is true.
- *Internal variability*. This component refers to temporary changes in the subject, such as variations in mood, motivation, attention, and so on.

---

[2]Serlin and Lapsley (1985) suggest that a better approach is to establish a band around zero that represents the range of outcomes that are consistent with the absence of a treatment effect.

- *External variability.* This component refers to changes outside the subject that vary from one subject to the next. We mentioned one of these sources in Chapter 1, namely, variations in the testing environment. Another external source is **measurement error**, the fact that, however accurate our instruments, they are not perfect. For example, an experimenter timing some behavior will be faster or slower at recognizing that the behavior has started from one occurrence to the next and so may not start the clock equally quickly. Even automated measuring devices have some measurement error. Another type of external variability arises from variations in the actual treatment conditions. An experimental apparatus cannot be counted on to administer the same treatment to each subject, and an experimenter cannot construct an identical testing environment (the reading of instructions, the experimenter-subject interaction, etc.) for every subject. Finally, there are *measurement mistakes* such as misreading a dial or incorrectly transcribing observations recorded in the laboratory to summary worksheets.

The point is that except for the treatment effect, any given subject's score is a composite of all these components. But because subjects are randomly assigned to treatment groups, they exert an *unsystematic* effect on the treatment conditions. Their influence is independent of the treatment effects.

Experimental Error and Treatment Effects

Suppose you were able to estimate the extent to which the differences you observe among the group means are due to experimental error. You would then be in a position to evaluate the hypothesis that the means of the treatment populations are equal. Consider the scores of subjects in any one of the treatment conditions. In any actual experiment, all the sources of uncontrolled variability we mentioned above will contribute to a subject's score, producing differences in performance among subjects who are given the same treatment. The variability of subjects treated alike, that is, within the same treatment level, provides an estimate of experimental error. By the same argument, the variability of subjects within each of the other treatment levels also offers estimates of experimental error.

Suppose you have drawn random samples from a population of subjects, administered the different treatments, recorded each subject's performance, and calculated the means of the treatment groups. Further assume for the moment that the null hypothesis is true and the population means associated with the treatment conditions are equal. Would you expect the *sample* means you observe to be equal? Certainly not. From our discussion of the use of randomization to control unwanted factors, it should be clear that the means will rarely be exactly equal. If the sample means are not equal, the only reasonable explanation is the operation of experimental error. All the sources of unsystematic variability, which contribute to the differences among subjects within a given treatment condition, will also operate to produce differences among the sample means.

In summary, consider again what can happen by randomly assigning subjects to the treatment conditions. If the assignment procedure is truly random, each subject has an equal chance of being assigned to any one of the different treatments. But this in no way guarantees that the average ability of subjects assigned to these groups is equal. The same applies to the other components of experimental error. There is no reason to expect *any* randomized sources of error to balance out perfectly across the treatment conditions. In short, even when the null hypothesis is true, differences among the sample means will reflect the presence of experimental error.[3]

So far our discussion has considered only the case in which the null hypothesis is true. Researchers almost always hope that it will be false. Suppose there are real differences among the means of the treatment populations. We will refer to these differences as **treatment effects**, a *systematic* source contributing to the differences we observe among the treatment means of an experiment. Does this imply that these latter differences reflect only the differences in the population treatment means? Unfortunately, the answer is "no." The mere fact that the null hypothesis is false does not imply that experimental error has vanished. In short, differences among treatment means may reflect both a systematic component (the treatment effects) and a random or unsystematic component (experimental error).

Evaluation of the Null Hypothesis

You have seen that there are two ways in which experimental error is reflected in the results of an experiment: as differences among subjects given the *same* treatment and as differences among groups of subjects given *different* treatments. We can express these differences as a ratio:

$$\frac{\text{differences among different groups of subjects}}{\text{differences among subjects in the same groups}}.$$

When the null hypothesis is true, you can think of this ratio as contrasting two sets of differences that each reflect the presence experimental error:

$$\frac{\text{experimental error}}{\text{experimental error}}.$$

If you were to repeat this experiment a large number of times on new samples of subjects drawn from the same population, you would expect that the average value of this ratio would be about 1.0.

Now consider the same ratio when the null hypothesis is *false*. Under these circumstances, there is an additional component in the numerator, one that reflects the treatment effects. Symbolically, the ratio becomes

$$\frac{(\text{treatment effects}) + (\text{experimental error})}{\text{experimental error}}.$$

If you were to repeat the experiment a large number of times, you would expect to find an average value of this ratio that is *greater than 1.0.*

You can see, then, that when H_0 is true (that is, the means are equal), the average value of this ratio, obtained from a large number of replications of the experiment, will approximate 1.0, but when H_1 is true (that is, the means are not equal), the average value will exceed 1.0. We could use the value of the ratio to decide whether H_0 is true or false. A problem remains, however, because in any *single* experiment, it is always

---

[3]You may be asking: Why not assign subjects to the groups systematically so that there are no accidental differences among them? The answer is that we sometimes can, to the advantage of our inferences (see our discussion of *blocking* in Section 11.5). But there will always be something else that makes the individuals differ. Ultimately, we still have to fall back on random assignment as our primary method for creating equivalent treatment groups.

possible to obtain a value that is greater than 1.0 when H_0 is true and one that is equal to or less than 1.0 when H_1 is true. Thus, merely checking to see whether the ratio is greater than 1.0 does not tell you which statistical hypothesis is correct.

What researchers will do about this problem is to make a decision concerning the acceptability of the null hypothesis that is based on the chance probability associated with the ratio actually found in the experiment. If the probability of obtaining a ratio of this size or larger just from experimental error is reasonably low, they reject the null hypothesis; if this probability is high, they do not reject it. In the next chapter we will say more about the actual decision rules you use to make this decision.

2.2   The Component Deviations

In the remainder of this chapter, you will see how the abstract notions of variability *between* treatment groups and *within* treatment groups are measured with concrete arithmetic operations. In the next chapter we will use this information to test the null hypothesis.

Suppose we were interested in the effect on reading comprehension of two different therapeutic drugs administered to hyperactive boys. One group of boys serves as a control condition and receives a placebo instead of an actual drug; a second group is given one of the drugs; and a third group is given the other. We will refer to the independent variable, types of drugs, as factor A, and to the three levels of factor A (the control condition and the two drug conditions) as levels a_1, a_2, and a_3, respectively. Let's assume we draw the subjects from a special fourth-grade class and randomly assign $n = 5$ different boys to each of the levels of factor A. One hour after receiving either a drug or the placebo, each boy studies an essay for 10 minutes, then is given an objective test to determine his comprehension of the passage. The response measure is the number of test items correctly answered by each boy. We will denote the score of, say, the third boy in the first group by $Y_{3,1}$, where the second subscript specifies the group and the first the subject's position within the group; in general, we will write the score as Y_{ij} where i stands for the subject and j the group.

Table 2.2 presents data from this hypothetical experiment. The five Y scores for each treatment condition are arranged in three columns. Our first step in the analysis is to compute the mean for each set of scores. We denote the group means

Table 2.2: *Comprehension scores for three groups of 5 boys who received either one of two drugs or a placebo.*

	Control a_1	Drug A a_2	Drug B a_3
Y_1	16	4	2
Y_2	18	7	10
Y_3	10	8	9
Y_4	12	10	13
Y_5	19	1	11

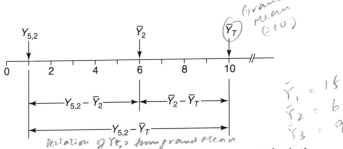

Figure 2.2: Pictorial representation of the component deviations.

by $\bar{Y}$ with a numbered subscript to designate the group, most generally as $\bar{Y}_j$. For these data, the three means are $\bar{Y}_1 = 15$, $\bar{Y}_2 = 6$, and $\bar{Y}_3 = 9$. The grand mean of all three conditions, obtained by taking the average of the three treatment means, is $\bar{Y}_T = (15+6+9)/3 = 10$. As explained above, we cannot conclude that the differences among the group means represent the "real" effects of the different experimental treatments. They could have resulted from experimental error, that is, uncontrolled sources of variability that happened to favor one condition and not another. You saw that the solution to this problem is to compare the differences among the group means against the differences obtained from subjects within each of the individual groups.

For the moment, focus on the worst score in condition a_2, which is $Y_{5,2} = 1$. Consider the deviation of this score from the grand mean $\bar{Y}_T$. This deviation, $Y_{5,2} - \bar{Y}_T$, is represented pictorially at the bottom of Figure 2.2 as the distance between the two vertical lines drawn from the score $Y_{5,2} = 1$ on the left and the grand mean $\bar{Y}_T = 10$ on the right. Now consider the vertical line drawn through the group mean for condition a_2 at $\bar{Y}_2 = 6$. From the figure, it is obvious that the deviation $Y_{5,2} - \bar{Y}_T$ is made up of *two components*. One component is the deviation of the group mean from the grand mean, that is, $\bar{Y}_2 - \bar{Y}_T$, the component on the right. The other component is the deviation of the score from the mean of the group from which it was selected, that is, $Y_{5,2} - \bar{Y}_2$, the component deviation on the left. We can write this relationship as

$$(Y_{5,2} - \bar{Y}_T) = (\bar{Y}_2 - \bar{Y}_T) + (Y_{5,2} - \bar{Y}_2).$$

Traditionally, each of the three deviations has a name:

$Y_{5,2} - \bar{Y}_T$ is called the **total deviation**.

$\bar{Y}_2 - \bar{Y}_T$ is called the **between-groups deviation**.[4]

$Y_{5,2} - \bar{Y}_2$ is called the **within-groups deviation**.

This subdividing of the total deviation, known as **partitioning**, is illustrated with actual numbers in Table 2.3. Substituting $Y_{5,2} = 1$, $\bar{Y}_2 = 6$, and $\bar{Y}_T = 10$ for the symbols in the deviations above, we obtain

$$1 - 10 = (6 - 10) + (1 - 6),$$
$$-9 = (-4) + (-5).$$

Table 2.3 summarizes these calculations for each subject in the experiment.

---

[4] The name between-groups deviation appears to be something of a misnomer, in that the difference $\bar{Y}_j - \bar{Y}_T$ involves only one group's mean. It is possible to develop formulas based on those differences (as we will do in Equation 4.1, p. 61), but here we use the more traditional form.

Table 2.3: Component deviation scores for the data in Table 2.2.

		Total	=	Between	+	Within
Score	Value	$(Y_{ij} - \bar{Y}_T)$	=	$(\bar{Y}_j - \bar{Y}_T)$	+	$(Y_{ij} - \bar{Y}_j)$
			Group a_1			
$Y_{1,1}$	16	(6)	=	(5)	+	(1)
$Y_{2,1}$	18	(8)	=	(5)	+	(3)
$Y_{3,1}$	10	(0)	=	(5)	+	(−5)
$Y_{4,1}$	12	(2)	=	(5)	+	(−3)
$Y_{5,1}$	19	(9)	=	(5)	+	(4)
			Group a_2			
$Y_{1,2}$	4	(−6)	=	(−4)	+	(−2)
$Y_{2,2}$	7	(−3)	=	(−4)	+	(1)
$Y_{3,2}$	8	(−2)	=	(−4)	+	(2)
$Y_{4,2}$	10	(0)	=	(−4)	+	(4)
$Y_{5,2}$	1	(−9)	=	(−4)	+	(−5)
			Group a_3			
$Y_{1,3}$	2	(−8)	=	(−1)	+	(−7)
$Y_{2,3}$	10	(0)	=	(−1)	+	(1)
$Y_{3,3}$	9	(−1)	=	(−1)	+	(0)
$Y_{4,3}$	13	(3)	=	(−1)	+	(4)
$Y_{5,3}$	11	(1)	=	(−1)	+	(2)

Deviations — Total = Between + Within

Thus, the score for each subject can be expressed as a deviation from the grand mean and this deviation can be partitioned into two components, a between-groups deviation and a within-groups deviation. These two component deviations are what we have been after, one quantity that reflects both treatment effects in the population and experimental error (the between-groups deviation), and another that reflects only experimental error (the within-groups deviation). We will now see how these deviations are turned into measures of variability.

2.3   Sums of Squares: Defining Formulas

To evaluate the null hypothesis, it is necessary to transform the between-groups and within-groups deviations into more useful quantities, namely, **variances**. For this reason, the statistical analysis involving the comparison of variances reflecting different sources of variability—in this case, between-groups and within-groups variances—is called the **analysis of variance**. A variance is essentially an average of the squared deviations from the mean. More formally, it is the ratio

$$\text{variance} = \frac{\text{sum of the squared deviations from the mean}}{\text{degrees of freedom}}.$$

The quantity in the numerator is the **sum of the squared deviations from the mean**, usually shortened to **sum of squares** and abbreviated SS. It reflects the degree to which the numbers in a set vary among themselves. When there is no variability, that is, when the numbers are all the same, each deviation from the mean is zero (because the mean is equal to each number in the set), and the sum of the squared deviations (as well as the variance) equals zero. On the other hand, when the numbers in a set are different, they spread out from the mean, and the sum of the squared deviations is a positive value. As the spread increases, both the deviations from the mean and the SS increase.

The quantity in the denominator, **degrees of freedom**, denoted *df*, reflects the number of ways that the deviations are able to vary from each other. The number of degrees of freedom always seems a little mysterious at first—it is slightly fewer than the number of quantities we are summing. We will consider variances and the degrees of freedom in the next chapter. Our concern now is with the component sums of squares.

Let's return to the component deviations developed in Section 2.2. You will recall that the deviation of each subject from the grand mean of the experiment can be divided into a between-groups portion and a within-groups portion. A similar additive relationship holds if we square the three deviations for each subject and then sum the squares over all of the subjects in the experiment. This relationship is fundamental to the analysis of variance:

$$SS_{\text{total}} = SS_{\text{between}} + SS_{\text{within}}. \tag{2.1}$$

Translated into the numerical example from Table 2.3, Equation 2.1 reads, "The sum of the squared deviations of all 15 subjects from $\overline{Y}_T$ may be broken into two components, one obtained by summing all the squared deviations of the individual group means from $\overline{Y}_T$ and the other by summing all the squared deviations of subjects from their respective group means." Now we will translate these words into formulas and numerical values.

Total Sum of Squares

The basic ingredients in the total sum of squares SS_T are the total deviations, that is, the deviations of all the scores in the experiment (Y_{ij}) from the grand mean $\overline{Y}_T$. The SS_T is formed by squaring the total deviation for each subject and summing the results. In symbols,

$$SS_T = \sum (Y_{ij} - \overline{Y}_T)^2. \tag{2.2}$$

As you undoubtedly know, the capital Greek letter sigma, $\sum$, means "the sum of ..." Thus, $\sum (Y_{ij} - \overline{Y}_T)^2$ is read "the sum of the squared deviations formed by subtracting the grand mean of the Y scores from all the Y scores in the experiment." We can calculate SS_T for the numerical example we have been considering by squaring each of the 15 total deviations presented in Table 2.3:

$$SS_T = \sum (Y_{ij} - \overline{Y}_T)^2 = 6^2 + 8^2 + \cdots + 3^2 + 1^2 = 390.$$

Between-Groups Sum of Squares

You saw in Figure 2.2 that one of the components of a subject's total deviation is the deviation of the subject's group mean from the grand mean, $\overline{Y}_j - \overline{Y}_T$. If we square this component and sum the squares for all the subjects in the experiment, we will obtain the between-groups sum of squares. We will refer to this quantity as SS_A, indicating that it is based on the deviations involving the means of factor A. From the between-group deviations listed in Table 2.3,

$$SS_A = 5^2 + 5^2 + \cdots + (-1)^2 + (-1)^2 = 210.$$

A more compact way to express this calculation takes advantage of the fact that the between-group deviation is the same for all subjects in a given group. In this example, the deviation is 5 for a_1, -4 for a_2, and -1 for a_3. We can square these three between-group deviations, multiply the squared deviations by the number of subjects in each group (n), and sum the three products:

$$SS_A = n(\bar{Y}_1 - \bar{Y}_T)^2 + n(\bar{Y}_2 - \bar{Y}_T)^2 + n(\bar{Y}_3 - \bar{Y}_T)^2.$$

Using the sigma notation, this sum of squares is written:

$$SS_A = \sum n(\bar{Y}_j - \bar{Y}_T)^2.$$

When the samples all have the same size (we consider unequal sample sizes in Section 3.5), it is simpler to place the n outside (to the left) of the summation sign, that is, to square and sum the deviations first and then to multiply by n:

$$SS_A = n \sum (\bar{Y}_j - \bar{Y}_T)^2. \tag{2.3}$$

For our numerical example, this formula gives the same value we calculated above:

$$SS_A = (5)[5^2 + (-4)^2 + (-1)^2] = (5)(25 + 16 + 1) = (5)(42) = 210.$$

Within-Groups Sum of Squares

The final sum of squares is the within-groups sum of squares, denoted by $SS_{S/A}$. The subscript S/A is read "S within A," which says that we are dealing with the deviation of subjects from their own group means (i.e within their own groups). In Figure 2.2, the basic deviation involved is $Y_{ij} - \bar{Y}_j$. The first step in finding $SS_{S/A}$ is to obtain a sum of squares for *each group* using these within-group deviations. From Table 2.3,

$$SS_{S \text{ at } a_1} = 1^2 + 3^2 + (-5)^2 + (-3)^2 + 4^2 = 60,$$

$$SS_{S \text{ at } a_2} = (-2)^2 + 1^2 + 2^2 + 4^2 + (-5)^2 = 50,$$

$$SS_{S \text{ at } a_3} = (-7)^2 + 1^2 + 0^2 + 4^2 + 2^2 = 70.$$

In the analysis of variance, the different within-group variances are combined to obtain a more stable estimate of experimental error. Our next step, then, is to add together the separate within-group sums of squares, a process known as **pooling**:

$$SS_{S/A} = SS_{S \text{ at } a_1} + SS_{S \text{ at } a_2} + SS_{S \text{ at } a_3} \tag{2.4}$$

$$= 60 + 50 + 70 = 180.$$

In the form of an equation, the pooled sum of squares is

$$SS_{S/A} = \sum (Y_{ij} - \bar{Y}_j)^2, \tag{2.5}$$

where the summation extends over both the subjects and the groups.

2.4   Sums of Squares: Computational Formulas

Although the defining formulas for the three sums of squares preserve the logic by which the component deviations are derived, they are not convenient for calculation by hand. Instead, it is more practical to calculate sums of squares using formulas that are equivalent algebraically, but much simpler to use.

Notation

Before presenting the different formulas, we should say a few words about our notational system. The basic job of any notational system is to express unambiguously the arithmetic operations in the most complex of designs as well as in the simplest. The system we use in this book is designed specifically to facilitate the calculation of sums of squares in the analysis of variance.

The system has several advantages. Probably the most important is that formulas written in it emphasize the logic of what is being calculated. A second advantage is that it is relatively simple, and it avoids the confusion of subscripts, parentheses, and multiple summation signs used in some other systems. Finally, it makes the common aspects of the calculations in different designs apparent. Quantities that mean the same thing are described the same way. As you will see throughout this book, it works in conjunction with a general analysis scheme that applies to nearly all the designs we will consider. You will come to appreciate this aspect of the system more and more as we turn to the analysis of more complicated designs.

A notational system is essentially a code. The symbols constitute a shorthand for specifying the operations to be performed on a set of data. In the analysis of the single-factor design with independent groups, we need to designate three basic quantities: the individual scores or observations (the **raw data**), the sum of these scores for each treatment condition (the **treatment sums** or **treatment subtotals**), and the sum of all the scores or observations (the **grand sum** or **grand total**).

The Individual Scores. Each subject provides us with a single numerical value that reflects his or her performance on the response measure. As we stated earlier, this basic score or observation is designated by the capital letter Y, with subscripts to indicate the subject number (given first) and the group (given second). We will be consistent in this use throughout this book—that is, the first subscript always refers to subjects and the second always refer to the factor A treatments.[5] When we write Y_{ij}, the letter i stands for the subject and j for the group. Table 2.4 illustrates this notation with numbers from Table 2.2. Here i takes values from 1 to n and j takes values from 1 to a. In Tables 2.3 and 2.4, we have used commas to separate the two numerical parts of the subscript, but from now on we will suppress the comma when it can be done without ambiguity. For example, we will write Y_{23} instead of $Y_{2,3}$ for the second score in the third group, but $Y_{12,3}$ for the twelfth score in that group.

The Treatment Sums. Our first step is to calculate the sums of the scores in each of the treatment groups. These subtotals, or **treatment sums**, are designated by a capital A, which indicates that they are the sums of the scores for the levels of factor A, with a subscript to indicate the particular treatment condition. To designate a treatment sum in general we use the subscript j, writing it as A_j. For the three groups in Table 2.4, the treatment sums for groups a_1, a_2, and a_3 are

$$A_1 = 16 + 18 + 10 + 12 + 19 = 75,$$
$$A_2 = 4 + 7 + 8 + 10 + 1 = 30,$$
$$A_3 = 2 + 10 + 9 + 13 + 11 = 45.$$

---

[5]We have reversed the order of the subscripts from that in previous editions of this book to obtain this consistency and to make our notation conform to that adopted by others.

Table 2.4: An illustration of the notation system.

	Level a_1	Level a_2	Level a_3	
	$Y_{1,1} = 16$	$Y_{1,2} = 4$	$Y_{1,3} = 2$	
	$Y_{2,1} = 18$	$Y_{2,2} = 7$	$Y_{2,3} = 10$	
	$Y_{3,1} = 10$	$Y_{3,2} = 8$	$Y_{3,3} = 9$	
	$Y_{4,1} = 12$	$Y_{4,2} = 10$	$Y_{4,3} = 13$	
	$Y_{5,1} = 19$	$Y_{5,2} = 1$	$Y_{5,3} = 11$	Total
Sums	$A_1 = 75$	$A_2 = 30$	$A_3 = 45$	$T = \sum A_j = 150$
No. of observations	$n_1 = 5$	$n_2 = 5$	$n_3 = 5$	$an = 15$
Means	$\bar{Y}_1 = 15$	$\bar{Y}_2 = 6$	$\bar{Y}_3 = 9$	$\bar{Y}_T = 10$

We use the treatment sums to calculate the **treatment means**, $\bar{Y}_j$, by dividing each treatment sum by the number of scores in that condition. The lowercase letter n_j denotes the number of subjects, or **sample size**, for group a_j. As a formula:

$$\bar{Y}_j = \frac{A_j}{n_j}. \tag{2.6}$$

To refer to specific treatment means, we add a numerical subscript, for example, writing $\bar{Y}_2$ for the mean of the second group. From the data in Table 2.4,

$$\bar{Y}_1 = \frac{A_1}{n_1} = \frac{75}{5} = 15.0, \quad \bar{Y}_2 = \frac{A_2}{n_2} = \frac{30}{5} = 6.0, \quad \text{and} \quad \bar{Y}_3 = \frac{A_3}{n_3} = \frac{45}{5} = 9.0.$$

In much of this book, the sizes of the samples are identical in all groups, in which case we will write the sample size as simply n instead of n_j.

The Grand Sum. The **grand sum** is the sum of all the scores in the experiment, which we designate by T. Computationally, T may be calculated either by summing the entire set of Y scores or by summing the treatment subtotals (A). Expressing these operations in symbols,

$$T = \sum Y_{ij} = \sum A_j.$$

The first summation, $\sum Y_{ij}$, is read, "the sum of all the Y scores," and $\sum A_j$ is read, "the sum of all the A treatment sums." When we turn this sum into a mean (the **grand mean**), the result is designated $\bar{Y}_T$. It is calculated by dividing the sum of all the scores by the total number of scores. With equal-sized groups, this number can be calculated by multiplying the number of scores in each treatment group (n) by the number of treatment groups, which we will designate a. In symbols, the total number of scores is $a \times n$, or an, and the grand mean is

$$\bar{Y}_T = \frac{T}{an}. \tag{2.7}$$

From the numbers in Table 2.4, where $T = 75 + 30 + 45 = 150$, $a = 3$ treatment groups, and $n = 5$ subjects per group,

$$\bar{Y}_T = \frac{150}{(3)(5)} = 10.0.$$

Bracket Terms

Each of the sums of squares is calculated by combining special quantities that we call **bracket terms** (in the previous edition of this book they were called **basic ratios**). Bracket terms are a common step in the computational formulas for sums of squares in the analysis of variance. An important advantage of writing sums of squares with bracket terms is that they preserve the logic of the defining formulas for the sums of squares. We do not expect you to appreciate this particular advantage until we turn to the analysis of more complex designs in later chapters of this book.

All bracket terms have the same form. For the present design, there are three bracket terms, one involving the individual observations (Y), another involving group information—either the treatment subtotals (A_j) or the treatment means ($\bar{Y}_j$)—and the third involving either the grand total (T) or the overall mean ($\bar{Y}_T$). For convenience in presenting computational formulas, we designate each term by putting an identifying letter between a pair of brackets, that is, $[Y]$ for the bracket term based on the Y scores, $[A]$ for the bracket term based on either the treatment sums or treatment means, and $[T]$ for the bracket term based on the grand total or the grand mean. These bracket terms may be read as "bracket Y," "bracket A," and "bracket T," respectively. We will consider first the bracket terms calculated from sums, followed by the bracket terms calculated from means.

Using Sums. Calculating a bracket term involves three simple steps:

1. *Square* all quantities in a given set—the Y_{ij}'s, the A_j's, or T,
2. *Sum* these squared quantities, if more than one is present,
3. *Divide* this sum by the number of scores that went into each of its components.

Let's apply these rules to the three bracket terms. For Y, the first step squares each individual score and the second step sums these squares:

$$\sum Y_{ij}^2 = 16^2 + 18^2 + \cdots + 13^2 + 11^2 = 1{,}890.$$

We will refer to this quantity as the **raw sum of squares**. Each score Y involves only itself, so the third step simply divides this sum by 1 to give $[Y] = 1{,}800$. For the bracket term involving A, the first step squares the group subtotals A from Table 2.4, the second step sums them, and the third step divides by 5 because this is the number of scores that contributes to each A sum. The result is

$$[A] = \frac{75^2 + 30^2 + 45^2}{5} = \frac{5{,}625 + 900 + 2{,}025}{5} = \frac{8{,}550}{5} = 1{,}710.0.$$

The third bracket term is based on the grand total, which must be squared (step one) and divided by the $(3)(5) = 15$ scores that contribute to it (step three):

$$[T] = \frac{150^2}{15} = \frac{22{,}500}{15} = 1{,}500.0.$$

We can combine the three steps to give a single formula for each bracket term:

$$[Y] = \sum Y_{ij}^2, \tag{2.8}$$

$$[A] = \frac{\sum A_j^2}{n}, \tag{2.9}$$

$$[T] = \frac{T^2}{an}. \tag{2.10}$$

Using Means.   Sometimes it is more convenient to calculate bracket terms from means instead of sums. You will need this approach when you want to reconstruct parts of an analysis of variance from someone else's table of data. You could, of course, transform the means back into sums and use the formulas for the bracket terms. But it is easier to work directly with the means.

Bracket terms based on means follow essentially the same three steps described for sums, except that in the final step multiplication replaces division:

$$[A] = n \sum \bar{Y}_j^2, \tag{2.11}$$

$$[T] = an\bar{Y}_T^2. \tag{2.12}$$

The formula for $[Y]$ does not involve means or sums, and so it remains unchanged. Using the means provided in Table 2.4, we find

$$[A] = (5)(15^2 + 6^2 + 9^2) = (5)(342) = 1{,}710.0,$$
$$[T] = (3)(5)(10^2) = (15)(100) = 1{,}500.0.$$

Sums of Squares

All that remains is to use the three bracket terms to find the three sums of squares, SS_T, SS_A, and $SS_{S/A}$. They are combined by addition or subtraction, using an identical form as the three deviations in the defining formulas of Section 2.3. Specifically, the total sum of squares is based on the deviation $Y_{ij} - \bar{Y}_T$, and the computational formula for SS_T combines the bracket terms $[Y]$ and $[T]$ in the same way:

$$SS_T = [Y] - [T]. \tag{2.13}$$

The treatment sum of squares, SS_A, is based on the deviation of the treatment means from the grand mean, $\bar{Y}_j - \bar{Y}_T$, and again the computational formula has the same form:

$$SS_A = [A] - [T]. \tag{2.14}$$

Finally, the within-groups sum of squares is based on the deviation of individual observations from the relevant treatment mean, $Y_{ij} - \bar{Y}_j$, leading to the computational formula

$$SS_{S/A} = [Y] - [A]. \tag{2.15}$$

Substituting the values of the bracket terms that we just found, we obtain numerical values for the three sums of squares:

$$SS_T = [Y] - [T] = 1{,}890.0 - 1{,}500.0 = 390.0,$$
$$SS_A = [A] - [T] = 1{,}710.0 - 1{,}500.0 = 210.0,$$
$$SS_{S/A} = [Y] - [A] = 1{,}890.0 - 1{,}710.0 = 180.0.$$

As a computational check and as a demonstration of the relationship among these three sums of squares, we should verify that Equation 2.1 holds for these calculations:

$$SS_T = SS_A + SS_{S/A} = 210.0 + 180.0 = 390.0.$$

Comment

In our calculations, we will focus almost entirely on the computational versions of the formulas because they are easy to use and can be generated by a simple set of rules. However, you should remember that they are equivalent to the defining versions, which show more closely the logic behind the sums of squares. You can verify for yourself here that the computational formulas produce exactly the same answers as those obtained with the defining formulas. The only time different answers are found is when rounding errors introduced in calculating the treatment means and the grand mean become magnified in squaring the deviations or when too few places are carried in calculating the intermediate bracket terms—a common error when learning to use the formulas. It is not possible to state in advance how many places you need to carry your calculations because that depends on the sizes of both the bracket terms and their differences. If you find that your results have lost accuracy, then you need to go back to the data and carry more figures in your calculations. For example, if you calculated $SS_A = 1{,}738. - 1{,}735. = 3.$ and the data were not really integers, you have been left with only one figure of accuracy. You might find that more accurate calculations gave $SS_A = 1{,}738.31 - 1{,}734.66 = 3.65$, which is an appreciably different result. We will follow these recommendations in our examples.

Exercises

2.1. In an experiment with $a = 5$ treatment conditions, the following scores were obtained.

a_1		a_2		a_3		a_4		a_5	
13	9	7	4	12	11	10	12	13	6
8	7	4	1	4	9	9	7	14	12
8	6	10	7	5	10	15	14	13	10
6	7	5	9	2	8	10	17	8	4
6	10	5	8	3	6	14	12	9	11

a. Calculate the sum of the scores and the sum of the squared scores for each of the treatment groups.
b. Calculate the treatment means.
c. Calculate the sums of squares for each of the sources of variability normally identified in the analysis of variance, that is, SS_A, $SS_{S/A}$, and SS_T. Reserve this information for Problem 3.6 in Chapter 3 and Problem 11.4 in Chapter 11.

2.2. Consider the scores from the memory experiment we presented in Table 2.1 at the beginning of this chapter. Using the total number of facts recalled by the subjects, calculate the SS_A, $SS_{S/A}$, and SS_T. Calculate the same three quantities using the treatment means and the grand mean instead.

3

Variance Estimates
and the F Ratio

We are ready to complete the analysis of variance. The remaining calculations are simple and easy to follow, although their theoretical justification is considerably more complicated. Consequently, we will present the calculations quickly and devote the major portion of this chapter to describing the meaning of the null-hypothesis tests and their consequences. We will conclude by describing what to do when the treatment groups do not have equal sizes.

3.1 Completing the Analysis

The complete analysis of variance is outlined in Table 3.1 in an arrangement called a **summary table**. The first column lists the sources of variance usually extracted from the analysis. The second column gives the three bracket terms that are combined to produce the sums of squares. These combinations are indicated in the third column. To be useful in the analysis, the two component sums of squares are converted to variance estimates, or **mean squares**, as they are called in the analysis of variance. These mean squares are found by dividing the sum of squares by its **degrees of freedom** (abbreviated df), the calculation of which we will consider next. In symbols,

$$MS = SS/df. \tag{3.1}$$

Table 3.1: Summary of the analysis of variance

Source	Bracket Term	SS	df	MS	F
A	$[A] = \dfrac{\sum A_j^2}{n}$	$[A] - [T]$	$a - 1$	$\dfrac{SS_A}{df_A}$	$\dfrac{MS_A}{MS_{S/A}}$
S/A	$[Y] = \sum Y_{ij}^2$	$[Y] - [A]$	$a(n-1)$	$\dfrac{SS_{S/A}}{df_{S/A}}$	
Total	$[T] = \dfrac{T^2}{an}$	$[Y] - [T]$	$an - 1$		

Degrees of Freedom

The degrees of freedom associated with a sum of squares correspond to the number of independent pieces of information that enter into the calculation of the sum of squares. Consider, for example, the use of a single sample mean to estimate the population mean. If we want to estimate the population variance as well, we must take account of the fact that we have already used up some of the independent information in estimating the population mean.

Let's examine a concrete example. Suppose we have five observations in our experiment and that we determine the mean of the scores is 7.0. This sample mean is our estimate of the population mean. With five observations and the population mean estimated to be 7.0, how much independent information remains to estimate the population variance? The answer is the number of observations that are free to vary—that is, to take on any value whatsoever. In this example, there are four, one less than the total number of observations. The reason for this loss of "freedom" is that although we are free to select any value for the first four scores, the final score is then determined by our choice of mean. More specifically, the total sum of all five scores must equal 35, so that the sample mean is 7.0. As soon as four scores are selected, the fifth score is determined and can be obtained by subtraction. Estimating the population mean places a constraint on the values that the scores are free to take. A general rule for computing the degrees of freedom of any sum of squares is:

$$df = \text{(number of independent observations)} \tag{3.2}$$
$$- \text{(number of population estimates)}.$$

The degrees of freedom associated with each sum of squares in the analysis of variance are presented in the fourth column of Table 3.1. We can calculate them by applying Equation 3.2. For factor A, there are a basic observations—the a different sample means. Because one degree of freedom is lost by using the grand mean $\bar{Y}_T$ to estimate the overall population mean μ_T,

$$df_A = a - 1.$$

The degrees of freedom for $SS_{S/A}$ may be found by noting that the within-group sum of squares for any one group (SS_S at a_j) is based on n observations and that one degree of freedom is lost by using the group mean $\bar{Y}_{A_j}$ to estimate the population mean μ_j. That is, df_S at $a_j = n - 1$. When we combine the within-group sums of squares for the a treatment groups, we combine this value a times:

$$df_{S/A} = a(n - 1).$$

Finally, for SS_T, there are an observations, but since one degree of freedom is lost by estimating the overall population mean,

$$df_T = an - 1.$$

As a check, we can verify that the degrees of freedom associated with the component sums of squares add up to df_T:

$$df_T = df_A + df_{S/A}.$$

Substituting the values on the left and right sides, we find that

$$an - 1 = (a - 1) + a(n - 1) = a - 1 + an - a = an - 1.$$

Mean Squares

As we have said, the actual variance estimates are called mean squares (abbreviated *MS*). They appear in the next column of Table 3.1. The mean squares for the two component sources of variance are given by Equation 3.1:

$$MS_A = \frac{SS_A}{df_A} \quad \text{and} \quad MS_{S/A} = \frac{SS_{S/A}}{df_{S/A}}. \tag{3.3}$$

The first mean square estimates the combined presence of treatment effects plus error variance; the second independently estimates error variance alone.

As an example, consider the experiment we presented in Chapter 2 in which $a = 3$ groups, each containing $n = 5$ hyperactive boys, were administered either one of two drugs or a placebo and later given a test of reading comprehension. Using the data from Table 2.4 (p. 28), we found $SS_A = 210.00$ and $SS_{S/A} = 180.00$. Substituting in Equations 3.3, we obtain

$$MS_A = \frac{SS_A}{a-1} = \frac{210.00}{3-1} = 105.00,$$

$$MS_{S/A} = \frac{SS_{S/A}}{a(n-1)} = \frac{180.00}{(3)(5-1)} = \frac{180.00}{12} = 15.00.$$

Confidence Intervals for Treatment Means

Before we use these two mean squares to complete the analysis of variance, we will consider how to establish a plausible range for each population treatment mean, known as a **confidence interval**. These ranges are estimates and as such, are not guaranteed to always include the population mean. But, the procedure we will use to find these ranges specifies the percentage of time we will be successful in bracketing the population treatment means:

$$\text{confidence} = (100)(1 - \alpha) \text{ percent.}$$

By choosing a value of α between 0 and 1.0, we can control our long-term success rate in establishing confidence intervals. To illustrate, if we were to select a relatively low value for α such as $\alpha = .05$, then we would obtain a

$$(100)(1 - .05) = (100)(.95) = 95 \text{ percent confidence interval.}$$

This statement says that 95 percent of the time the range will include the population treatment mean, and 5 percent of the time it will not.[1] You will sometimes find confidence intervals (usually 95%) reported in tables along with the treatment means, and they appear in the output of many of the computer packages. We will discuss the interpretation of confidence intervals further in the next chapter (see p. 75).

The confidence interval for a population mean is given by the formula

$$\bar{Y}_j - t \, s_{M_j} \le \mu_j \le \bar{Y}_j + t \, s_{M_j}, \tag{3.4}$$

where $\bar{Y}_j$ = the mean of the treatment group,

t = a value from Appendix A.2 to be explained in a moment,

s_{M_j} = the estimated standard error of the mean $\bar{Y}_j$.

---

[1]See Estes (1997) for a useful discussion of the application and the interpretation of confidence intervals.

There are two ways that we can estimate the **standard error of the mean**. The simplest and safest method is to base the estimate on the data from condition a_j only. We obtain this estimate by dividing the standard deviation of that group (s_j) by the square root of the sample size:

$$\text{individual } s_{M_j} = \frac{s_j}{\sqrt{n_j}}. \tag{3.5}$$

When the conditions all have the same variability, an assumption we will consider in Chapter 7, a somewhat better estimate is obtained by using information from all the groups. In this case, we estimate the standard error of the mean by

$$\text{pooled } s_M = \sqrt{\frac{MS_{S/A}}{n_j}}. \tag{3.6}$$

The numerator of this ratio is the within-group mean square $MS_{S/A}$ from the overall analysis, which is actually an average of the individual variances for the treatment groups. Where the assumption of equal variance seems satisfied or the sample sizes are so small that the individual variance are very poorly estimated, we can use s_M instead of s_{M_j} in Equation 3.4.

As an example, we will calculate two confidence intervals for the group receiving drug B (a_3) for the current numerical example, the first using an estimated standard error based only on the data for a_3 and the second using one based on the pooled within-groups variance. Equation 3.4 indicates that we need three quantities to find a confidence interval: the group mean $\bar{Y}_j$, the value of t, and the estimate of the standard error of the mean. First we will illustrate the calculation using the data from group a_3 alone. From Table 2.4, we find that the mean for the drug B group is $\bar{Y}_3 = 9.0$ and sample size is $n_3 = 5$. The value of t depends on the level α and the degrees of freedom associated with the standard deviation, which here is $df = n_3 - 1 = 5 - 1 = 4$. Using $\alpha = .05$, we obtain the value $t = 2.78$ from the table of the t distribution in Appendix A.2 at the intersection of the row where $df = 4$ and the column where $\alpha = .05$. The last term is the estimated standard error of the mean, s_{M_j}, which we calculate from the formula for the individual standard error (Equation 3.5). First we find the standard deviation for the drug-B group (s_3), using the deviations in Table 2.3 (p. 24):

$$s_3 = \sqrt{\frac{\sum(Y_{i3} - \bar{Y}_3)}{n_3 - 1}} = \sqrt{\frac{(-7)^2 + 1^2 + 0^2 + 4^2 + 2^2}{5 - 1}} = \sqrt{\frac{70}{4}} = 4.183.$$

Then, using Equation 3.5, the standard error of the mean is

$$s_{M_3} = \frac{s_3}{\sqrt{n_3}} = \frac{4.183}{\sqrt{5}} = \frac{4.183}{2.236} = 1.871.$$

From Equation 3.4, we obtain the two limits of the 95 percent confidence interval:

$$\bar{Y}_3 - t\, s_{M_3} \leq \mu_3 \leq \bar{Y}_3 + t\, s_{M_3},$$

$$9.0 - (2.78)(1.871) \leq \mu_3 \leq 9.0 + (2.78)(1.871),$$

$$9.0 - 5.201 \leq \mu_3 \leq 9.0 + 5.201,$$

$$3.80 \leq \mu_3 \leq 14.20.$$

A confidence interval based on the individual standard error s_{M_j} is appropriate when there is reason to believe that the variance of the scores (and the standard deviation) differ from one treatment population to another. However, if we are willing to assume that these variances are equal, we can obtain a better interval—more accurate and usually narrower—by using the pooled within-groups variance $MS_{S/A}$ and Equation 3.6. We already have the group mean, $\bar{Y}_3 = 9.0$. The value of t is smaller than the one we obtained above because $MS_{S/A}$ has more degrees of freedom than s_j. For this pooled estimate, $df_{S/A} = a(n-1) = (3)(5-1) = 12$, and so, from Appendix A.2, we find $t = 2.18$. Finally, we substitute in Equation 3.6 to get the pooled standard error of the mean:

$$s_M = \sqrt{\frac{MS_{S/A}}{n_j}} = \sqrt{\frac{15.0}{5}} = \sqrt{3.0} = 1.732.$$

From Equation 3.4, we obtain the two limits of the 95 percent confidence interval:

$$\bar{Y}_3 - t\,s_M \leq \mu_3 \leq \bar{Y}_3 + t\,s_M,$$

$$9.0 - (2.18)(1.732) \leq \mu_3 \leq 9.0 + (2.18)(1.732),$$

$$9.0 - 3.776 \leq \mu_3 \leq 9.0 + 3.776,$$

$$5.22 \leq \mu_3 \leq 12.78.$$

You should note that the width of this confidence interval $(12.78 - 5.22 = 7.56)$ is narrower than the one using the individual standard error $(14.20 - 3.80 = 10.40)$. There are two reasons for this difference: a smaller value of t due to the greater number of degrees of freedom and a smaller estimated standard error (1.732 versus 1.871). The advantage due to the smaller t is present for any set of data, but the difference in the relative sizes of the two standard errors depends on whether the variance of the particular group we are examining is larger or smaller than $MS_{S/A}$. Because $MS_{S/A}$ is an average of the groups variances, it will be larger than s_j^2 for some groups and smaller for others.

The F Ratio

The final step in the analysis of variance is the formation of a **test statistic** that allows us to come to a conclusion about the null and alternative hypotheses. This statistic is known as an F **ratio**. The treatment mean square MS_A is divided by the within-groups mean square $MS_{S/A}$, as shown in the last column of Table 3.1. Because the denominator of an F ratio, here $MS_{S/A}$, reflects only error variability, it is called the **error term**. From the arguments advanced in the last chapter, the average value of F is approximately 1.0 when the null hypothesis is true and is greater than 1.0 when the null hypothesis is false. We will return to this argument in the next section, following the completion of the numerical example from the last chapter.

Table 3.2 brings together the results of our earlier calculations. The only remaining step is to find the F ratio:

$$F = \frac{MS_A}{MS_{S/A}} = \frac{105.00}{15.00} = 7.00.$$

The value of F is larger than 1.0, casting doubt on the correctness of the null hypothesis. However, we can't be sure yet; perhaps we could have obtained this value when H_0 was true. Remember that the two mean squares are independent estimates of error variance and will differ by chance. We will discuss how we decide between the two possibilities in the next section.

Table 3.2: Summary table for the analysis of Table 2.4.

Source	SS	df	MS	F
A	210.0	2	105.00	7.00
S/A	180.0	12	15.00	
Total	390.0	14		

Testing the Grand Mean

There is another F test that can be calculated from the quantities involved in the one-way design. The quantity $[T]$ is large when the scores are generally far from zero and small when they are near zero. A test of the hypothesis that the grand mean μ of all the scores is equal to zero is constructed from this term by dividing it by $MS_{S/A}$. Specifically, the bracket term gives the sum of squares, which, because the hypothesis involves only one number (the grand mean), has one degree of freedom:

$$SS_{\text{G.M.}} = [T] \quad \text{and} \quad df_{\text{G.M.}} = 1. \tag{3.7}$$

This sum of squares is formed into a mean square, just as we did for the A effect, and turned into an F ratio:

$$MS_{\text{G.M.}} = SS_{\text{G.M.}}/df_{\text{G.M.}} \quad \text{and} \quad F = MS_{\text{G.M.}}/MS_{S/A}.$$

Continuing with our example of the comprehension scores in Table 2.2, we have from Equations 3.7

$$SS_{\text{G.M.}} = [T] = 1,500.0,$$

from which we obtain the F statistic

$$F = \frac{MS_{\text{G.M.}}}{MS_{S/A}} = \frac{1,500.0}{15.00} = 100.00.$$

This is a large value, and it will lead us to the (hardly surprising) conclusion that the comprehension scores do not come from a population with a mean of zero.

The hypothesis that the grand mean is zero is not very useful in most studies. Usually, when we are measuring the amount of something, all our observations are positive numbers and there is no reason to test whether their mean is zero. We mention the grand-mean test here for two reasons. First, most of the computer programs for the analysis of variance calculate this F statistic, often designated as the *intercept*, and incorporate it into analysis-of-variance summaries such as Table 3.2. Second, there are certain specialized situations where we will need to test a hypothesis of this type. One such situation arises in the analysis of specific questions about a within-subject design, a topic that we will reach in Section 16.2.

3.2 Evaluating the F Ratio

While the F ratio for the treatment effects we calculated in the preceding section brought into question the null hypothesis, we still need to deal with the possibility that it only reflected chance factors. In this section, we will describe how to use a procedure, known as **null-hypothesis significance testing**, to assess the F ratio.

The Sampling Distribution of F

Suppose we had available a large population of scores and drew at random three sets of 5 scores each. You can think of the three sets as representing the results of the experiment we have been examining, except here we know that the null hypothesis is true. Because the scores in every "treatment condition" were randomly drawn from the same population, we know that $\mu_1 = \mu_2 = \mu_3$. Any difference among the sample means reflects only accidents of random sampling, and so the two mean squares, MS_A and $MS_{S/A}$, are independent estimates of error variance.

Now suppose we repeat the random drawing many times, each time forming three groups of 5 scores. For some of these "experiments," MS_A will be larger than $MS_{S/A}$, and for others their order will be reversed. When we compute the value of F for each "experiment," some values will be large and others small. We can group the F's according to size and plot them to get an idea of the variability of the test statistic caused by the random sampling of the scores. Such a distribution is called a **sampling distribution**, in this case of the statistic F. Producing a sampling distribution by repeated random draws is known as **Monte Carlo simulation**. Figure 3.1 shows the Monte-Carlo sampling distribution of F. We had our computer draw three random samples of 5 scores each from a very large collection of normally-distributed numbers and calculate the value of F. We repeated the procedure 1,000 times. The jagged line in the figure is the resulting histogram. From this histogram you can see that small values of F occurred most often and that very few of the simulations gave a value as large as the $F = 7.00$ that we calculated in Table 3.2. This observation implies that obtaining an F of 7.00 or larger is a relatively rare event and that the F we obtained in the numerical example is unlikely to have happened by chance.

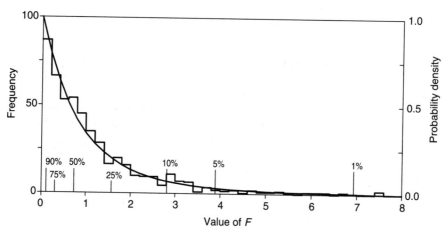

Figure 3.1: *The sampling distribution obtained from 1,000 F ratios, each calculated from three groups of 5 scores randomly drawn from the same population. Four scores with values greater than 8 lie to the right of the plot. The smooth curve is the theoretical F distribution with 2 and 12 degrees of freedom. The percentage points refer to this distribution.*

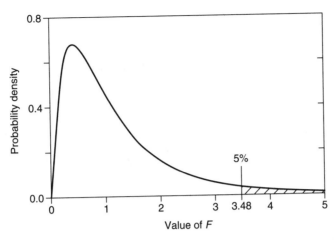

Figure 3.2: Theoretical sampling distribution of $F(4, 10)$.

A Monte Carlo simulation like this helps us understand sampling effects and aids in evaluating testing procedures (we will use them again in Chapter 7). However, we do not need to rely on it for our basic test. The exact distribution of the F statistic when the group means are equal can be derived from statistical theory. This distribution is shown by the smooth curve in Figure 3.1. As you can see, it closely matches the empirical distribution that we found in our Monte Carlo simulation. In effect, the theoretical F distribution is the sampling distribution of F that we would obtain from an infinitely large number of simulated experiments of this sort. Knowing the exact shape of the F distribution lets us determine the value of F that will be exceeded by a given percentage of the experiments when the null hypothesis is true. Several of these values are marked in Figure 3.1. Consider the value $F = 2.81$. Theory tells us that 90 percent of the sampling distribution is less than this value and that 10 percent is greater. If there were no differences between the means, we would expect to obtain a value of F equal to or greater than 2.81 no more than 10 percent of the time. We have located several other values in Figure 3.1.

The F Table

There is not just one F distribution but a family of them. The exact shape of any one of the curves is determined by the number of degrees of freedom associated with the numerator and denominator mean squares in the F ratio. An F distribution with quite a different shape appears in Figure 3.2. It is the theoretical sampling distribution of F (under the null hypothesis) for a study with 5 groups of 3 subjects each, i.e with $df_{num} = 4$ and $df_{denom} = 10$. As a shorthand way of referring to a particular F distribution, we will use the expression $F(df_{num}, df_{denom})$, or here, $F(4, 10)$.

To draw conclusions about an experiment, we do not have to know the exact shape of the F distribution. All we need are the values of F to the right of which certain proportions of the area under the curve fall. These are the percentage points in Figures 3.1 and 3.2. These values are tabulated in the F table in Appendix A.1. A particular value of F in this table is specified by three quantities: (1) the numerator degrees of freedom (represented by the columns of the table), (2) the denominator degrees of freedom (represented by the main rows of the table), and (3) the proportion of area to the right of an ordinate (represented by the rows listed for each denominator degrees of freedom, and labeled by the letter α). The table contains values of F for α of .10, .05, .025, .01 and .001. When we report an F value from the table, we will include the relevant value of α as a subscript, writing $F_\alpha(df_{num}, df_{denom})$.[2]

Consider $F_{.05}(4, 10) = 3.48$, marked in Figure 3.2. This value falls at the intersection of the column at $df_{num} = 4$ and the row at $df_{denom} = 10$ and the entry in the row labeled $\alpha = .05$. The vertical line drawn through this value in Figure 3.2 divides the sampling distribution of $F(4, 10)$ such that 95 percent of the area is to the left and 5 percent is to the right. Some other values found in the same part of the table are $F_{.10}(4, 10) = 2.61$ and $F_{.01}(4, 10) = 5.99$, which indicate that 10 percent and 1 percent of the sampling distribution of $F(4, 10)$, respectively, fall to the right of these points on the abscissa.

We have not included all possible combinations of degrees of freedom in the table. For df_{num}, we have listed the values that a researcher most often needs: consecutive values from 1 to 10, then 12 and 15, which cover most one-way experiments and the factorial designs we discuss later. For df_{denom}, we have listed consecutive values from 2 to 20, then by twos to 30, by fives to 50, and by tens to 120, taking advantage of the fact that the differences between successive rows get smaller as df_{denom} increases, which lets us space the values we list more widely. If you need F for a value of df_{denom} that falls between the ones we give, you can either use the line from the table with df_{denom} smaller than the one you want, or you can estimate the intermediate point. For example, if you wanted $F_{.05}(2, 42)$, you could either use $F_{.05}(2, 40) = 3.23$ or, after noting that $F_{.05}(2, 45) = 3.20$, estimate that $F_{.05}(2, 42)$ is about 3.22. The last row is labeled ∞, and these values apply when df_{denom} is extremely large. As you can see, they are not that far from those for $df_{denom} = 120$.

The Distribution of F When the Null Hypothesis Is False

So far, we have only considered the sampling distribution of F when the null hypothesis is true, that is, when the population means are equal. Obviously, researchers do not intend to conduct many such experiments. They perform an experiment because they expect to find treatment effects. Suppose H_0 were false. What should happen to the F ratio? We have argued that MS_A contains two components—treatment effects and error variance—while $MS_{S/A}$ reflects error variance alone. So, on average, their ratio will be larger than when the null hypothesis is true, and the sampling distribution of the F ratio will be shifted toward larger values (we will show an example in Figure 3.3). It no longer has the standard F distribution we studied above, however. To make the distinction, the standard distribution is known as the **central F distribution**. When the null hypothesis is false, the F statistic is said to have a **noncentral F distribution**, which is denoted by F' instead of F.

---

[2]You should recognize that the letter F is used in three distinct ways in the analysis of variance. First, $F = MS_A/MS_{S/A}$ is the empirical ratio calculated from data; second, the $F(df_{num}, df_{denom})$ distribution is the theoretical form of the sampling distribution of this ratio when the null hypothesis is true; and third, $F_\alpha(df_{num}, df_{denom})$ is a percentile of the F distribution, calculated with respect to its upper end.

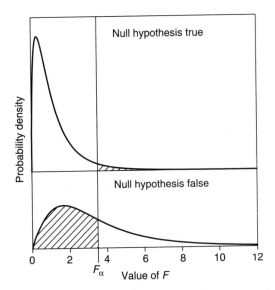

Figure 3.3: *Sampling distributions of the F ratio when the null hypothesis is true (upper panel) and when the alternative hypothesis is true (lower panel). The distributions have 3 and 12 degrees of freedom. The vertical line is the value of $F_{.05}(3, 12) = 3.89$, and the shaded areas represent errors.*

It would be nice to be able to draw the F' distribution and to compare it with a corresponding F distribution. Unfortunately, however, this is difficult to do, because the shape of this distribution depends on the *magnitude* of the treatment effects as well as the numerator and denominator degrees of freedom. Although there is only one central F distribution for any combination of numerator and denominator degrees of freedom, there is a family of noncentral F' distributions, one distribution for each value that the treatment effects may take. All we know, in general, is that the F' distribution is shifted to the right of the F distribution.

Testing the Null Hypothesis

We are now ready to piece together this information concerning the sampling distributions of F to provide a test of the null hypothesis. We start our testing procedure by specifying H_0 and H_1, the null and alternative statistical hypotheses. To review briefly our earlier discussion, the two hypotheses are

$$H_0: \text{all } \mu_j\text{'s are equal,}$$

$$H_1: \text{not all } \mu_j\text{'s are equal.}$$

The null hypothesis we will test states that the means of the treatment populations are equal. We choose this particular null hypothesis because it is usually the only hypothesis that we can state *exactly*. There is no ambiguity in the assertion that the population means are equal; there is only one way it can happen. The alternative hypothesis is a mutually exclusive statement, which generally asserts only that some of the population treatment means are not equal—that is, that some treatment effects are present. This hypothesis is an *inexact* statement. Nothing is said about the actual differences that are in the population.

Suppose we have conducted an experiment and have computed the value of F. What we have to decide is whether it came from the F distribution or from one the F' distributions. Because we are evaluating the null hypothesis, we will turn our attention to the F distribution. Although some values of F are less likely to occur than others, it is still possible theoretically to obtain any value of F in an experiment when the null hypothesis is true. From one point of view our situation is hopeless: If any value of F may be the result of chance factors, then we can never be absolutely certain that the F we observe in an experiment did *not* come from the F distribution. Agreed. However, if we were to take this position, we would never be able to use the experimental method as a way of finding out about the world. We must be willing to risk making a mistake by rejecting the null hypothesis when it is true; otherwise, we could never reject it at all and never learn anything.

Suppose we could agree on a dividing line for any F distribution, where the values of F falling above the line are considered to be "unlikely" and the values of F falling below the line are considered to be "likely." We would then determine whether an observed F falls above or below this arbitrary dividing line. When the F fell above the line, we would conclude that the obtained F is *incompatible* with the null hypothesis. We would reject H_0 and conclude that the alternative hypothesis is true. When the F fell below the line, however, we would conclude that the observed F is *compatible* with the null hypothesis. Under these circumstances, we would retain H_0. By following this set of rules, we will conclude that an independent variable was effective whenever an F is obtained that falls within the region of incompatibility.

Decision Rules

The problem now is to find a way to objectively define the regions of compatibility and incompatibility. When the null hypothesis is true, we can determine the sampling distribution of F. Suppose we find a point on this distribution beyond which the probability of finding F is very small—the probability is represented by the proportion of the total area under the curve that appears beyond this particular point. We will adopt the convention that values of F falling above the dividing line are incompatible with the null hypothesis. Our **decision rule**, then, is to reject the null hypothesis when the observed F falls within this region of incompatibility. We do so, knowing that we will occasionally make the wrong decision.

Suppose we begin to enlarge the region of incompatibility by moving the critical point of transition to the left—toward the larger portion of the curve. As we increase the size of this region, we also increase the chance of observing values from it. Said another way, increasing the region of incompatibility results in the inclusion of F's that are increasingly more *compatible* with the null hypothesis. How big should we make it? In principle, an investigator may pick any probability, so long as the decision is made before the start of the experiment. In practice, however, there is fairly common agreement on a probability of $\alpha = .05$ to define the region of incompatibility for the F distribution.[3] This probability is called the **significance level** of the test.

---

[3]Pollard (1993, p. 458) refers to the tacit agreement as a "shared criterion." See Cowles and Davis (1982) for an interesting discussion of the origins of the 5 percent level of significance.

We are now in a position to state more formally the decision rule that is followed after the calculation of the F ratio. The significance level α defines a **critical value** $F_\alpha(df_{num}, df_{denom})$ that cuts off this proportion at the top of the F distribution. Let's say we have calculated the value $F_{observed}$ from the data. If $F_{observed}$ falls within the region of incompatibility determined by F_α, then the null hypothesis is rejected and the alternative hypothesis is accepted. If $F_{observed}$ falls within the region of compatibility, then the null hypothesis is not rejected. Symbolically, this rule is

$$\left\{ \begin{array}{l} \text{If } F_{observed} \geq F_\alpha(df_{num}, df_{denom}), \text{ then reject } H_0, \\ \text{If } F_{observed} < F_\alpha(df_{num}, df_{denom}), \text{ then retain } H_0. \end{array} \right.$$

There is often confusion about the exact wording of the decision rule in null-hypothesis testing. The problem is that the null hypothesis is a very precise statement (the μ_j's are equal), but the alternative hypothesis is a vague one (the μ_j's are not equal), so we cannot talk about them the same way. When we fail to reject the null hypothesis, we mean that the null hypothesis is *consistent* with our data. We use the word "retained," rather than "accepted" or "proved," because of the near certainty that the treatment has had at least *some* effect, even if it is so small to be essentially undetectable by our study. For the same reason, we do not say that we have "rejected" the alternative hypothesis, only that our data do not support it. In contrast, when there are large differences between the means and the F is significant, we believe that *some form* of the many outcomes subsumed under the alternative hypothesis is almost certainly true. This is why we are much happier in saying that we "reject" the null hypothesis and "accept" the alternative hypothesis. We will consider the issue of proving statistical hypotheses again in Section 8.5.

We will illustrate the decision rule with the F we calculated earlier in this chapter (see Table 3.2). In this example, $df_{num} = 2$ and $df_{denom} = 12$. If we set $\alpha = .05$, the critical value of F, which we find in the tabled values of the F distribution (Table A.1 of Appendix A), is 3.89. The rejection region consists of all values of F equal to or greater than 3.89. The decision rule is

$$\left\{ \begin{array}{l} \text{If } F_{observed} \geq 3.89, \text{ then reject } H_0, \\ \text{If } F_{observed} < 3.89, \text{ then retain } H_0. \end{array} \right.$$

Since the F obtained in this example exceeded this value ($F = 7.00$), we would conclude that treatment effects were present in this experiment. Although not of particular interest, we also calculated an F for the null hypothesis $\mu_T = 0$. For this test, the critical value is $F_{.05}(1, 12) = 4.75$. Because the observed value of $F = 100.00$ exceeded this value, we would conclude that the overall mean was greater than zero.

Other Significance Levels. Although most researchers adopt $\alpha = .05$ as their personal significance level, you will see other probability levels reported in the research literature. Results that are significant at the $\alpha = .01$ or $.001$ levels may be reported as such. Some researchers may note results at the 10 percent level as well. To illustrate using the F test in Table 3.2, the critical value of F with 2 and 12 degrees of freedom at $\alpha = .01$ is 6.93 (see Table A.1), so we could have reported this result as

$$F(2, 12) = 7.00, \quad p < .01.$$

This statement indicates that the observed F falls in the top 1 percent of the theoretical distribution and that the null hypothesis would be rejected by any researcher who had adopted a significance level equal to 1 percent or larger. The main problem with this practice is that it tends to reinforce the false belief that a finding significant at $p < .01$ is somehow "better," "stronger," or "larger" than a finding significant at $p < .05$. As you will see in Chapter 8, comparisons of strength are more appropriately made by obtaining some measure of *effect magnitude* rather than by comparing significance levels.

Many statistical computer programs eliminate the need for an F table by reporting the probability of a result greater than $F_{observed}$ under the null hypothesis. These programs calculate the exact proportion of the sampling distribution of the F statistic falling at or above $F_{observed}$. For example, the F we calculated in Table 3.2, $F = 7.00$, has an exact probability of $p = .009666$. Armed with this information, all one needs to do is to compare this value to whatever level of significance one is using, and reject H_0 when the exact probability is smaller than that level. We can state the decision rule quite simply, without specific reference to F; for example, if $\alpha = .05$, the rule is

$$\begin{cases} \text{If } p \leq .05, \text{ then reject } H_0, \\ \text{If } p > .05, \text{ then retain } H_0. \end{cases}$$

We want to emphasize that however you report a statistical test, you should choose your significance level *before* the start of an experiment. Alternative ways of reporting probabilities do not change this fundamental point. Some researchers make a practice of announcing their significance level before they present the results of an experiment in a research article, allowing them to report the outcome of statistical tests simply as "significant" or "not significant." Doing so avoids the potential confusion created when different significance levels appear among a string of statistical tests.

Another mistake that is all-too-often made is to interpret the probability p as the probability that an effect is present or that the results will be replicated by another study.[4] All that the exact probability provides is a quantitative measure of evidence against the null hypothesis. It should not be used to imply either the strength of a treatment effect or the probability of a successful replication, still less the probability that the effect is "really there."

Comment

Dissatisfaction with hypothesis testing has been expressed ever since the concept was introduced early in the last century. There is a substantial (and tendentious) contemporary literature on the topic. Some individuals support the procedure; others take such extreme stands as recommending that the procedure be "banned" from the journals altogether.[5] There are reasons to be concerned. The paradoxes of hypothesis

---

[4]Such statements are the domain of **Bayesian statistics**, an area that has recently received much attention in the statistical literature (e.g., see Carlin & Louis, 2000). However, the Bayesian techniques are not yet developed to the point where they are practical alternatives to the techniques we describe in this book. In any case, most of the design issues that we discuss do not depend on the type of inference used.

[5]An excellent summary of the discussion of the vices and virtues of hypothesis testing is given by Nickerson (2000). Because Nickerson includes a comprehensive bibliography, we will not cite individual articles here.

testing and its possibilities for abuse are manifold: Why do we test the null hypothesis when we know that it is rarely true and that some differences, even if small, probably result from *any* treatment manipulation? Why do researchers evaluate the null hypothesis using an unvarying significance level of 5 percent? Certainly some results are interesting and important that miss this arbitrary criterion. Should not a researcher reserve judgment on a result for which $p = .06$, rather than turning his or her back on it? Another problem is the ease with which null hypothesis testing can be (and often is) misinterpreted. Many researchers treat the exact p value associated with $F_{observed}$ as a measure of the size of the observed treatment effect or the probability that an effect is present, although it is neither of these.

We believe that these concerns and misunderstandings should not obscure the useful aspects of hypothesis testing. Any procedure that takes limited data about a variable phenomenon and arrives at an assertion about scientific truth is based on many assumptions, all of which are open to question and to misuse. This problem is magnified when that assertion is a dichotomous, yes-no, decision. What is essential is to understand what the test of a null hypothesis does and does not provide. Fundamentally, it serves the important function of allowing a researcher to decide whether the outcome of an experiment could have reasonably happened by chance. Thus, it provides a filter to prevent us from wasting our time talking about things that may well be unstable or irreproducible. It helps us to get others to pay attention to our findings. However, a hypothesis test does not complete the task of inference. In particular, it does not tell us *what* we have found. Suppose the null hypothesis has been rejected. It is still necessary to interpret the outcome and to reconcile it with the body of findings that led us to do the experiment. The rejected null hypothesis does not prove the results agree with the original theory. On the other hand, suppose it had been retained. It is still necessary to think about the outcome. One of the persistent errors among beginning users of hypothesis tests is to cease thinking about the data at this point—in effect, to accept the null hypothesis as true. All the treatment means from a study convey information, and even though we may be appropriately cautious when reporting an effect, the pattern of values we found should influence our understanding. Perhaps the effect we were looking for was present but smaller than expected; perhaps our study was less sensitive than we intended. Or perhaps our initial research hypothesis was completely wrong. The lack of significance itself does not sort out these possibilities.

To close our discussion of null-hypothesis testing, we offer five suggestions that we feel will help you to eliminate its most common abuses.

1. Never lose sight of your data. Plot them, with measures of variability, and study the result. Use confidence intervals (p. 34) to establish reasonable ranges for your effects. Keep asking yourself what your numbers mean.

2. Remember that not all null hypotheses represent interesting or plausible outcomes of the experiment (the hypothesis that the grand mean is zero is often an example) and that their rejection is not inevitably informative.

3. Remember that the null-hypothesis test only gives information about how likely the sampling operations are to have produced your effect. Do not confuse the

significance level with the size of an effect or the probability that another study can replicate it (we discuss proper procedures in Chapter 8).

4. When you find a significant effect, ask what it means. Use the effect-size measures (Chapter 8) to assess its magnitude and the test of contrasts and subsidiary hypotheses (Chapters 4 and 5) to interpret it.

5. Always interpret your results in the context of other studies in the field. Remember that theoretical understanding is an incremental process in which no study stands alone, but each extends and refines the others.

3.3   Errors in Hypothesis Testing

The procedures we follow in hypothesis testing do not guarantee that the decision rule will produce a correct inference. Regardless of whether we decide to reject the null hypothesis or not, there is some chance that the state of affairs in the real world is different. That risk is the price of limited knowledge. In this section, we will look more closely at the types of errors we could make.

The types of correct or erroneous outcomes of an inference are defined in Table 3.3. There are two states that "reality" can take, corresponding to the rows of the table. Either the population treatment means are equal (H_0 is true) or they are not (H_0 is false). And there are two conclusions that we may make, corresponding to the columns. Either we reject H_0 or we retain it. As the table shows, there are two circumstances in which we make the correct decision: (1) if we retain H_0 when the population means are the same and (2) if we reject H_0 when the population means are not the same.

There are also two complementary circumstances in which we make an error: (1) if we reject H_0 when the population means are equal and (2) if we retain H_0 when they are not. These two sorts of error are given special names. A **Type I error** occurs when H_0 is true, but we nevertheless reject it, and a **Type II error** occurs when H_1 is true, but we nevertheless retain H_0. The probabilities of making incorrect decisions under these two circumstances are conventionally denoted by α and β, respectively. For this reason, Type I and Type II errors are sometimes known as α **errors** and β **errors**, respectively. The probability of a Type I error is the same as the significance level of the test, as the use of the letter α suggests. When thinking about these quantities, you should be careful to note that α and β are *conditional* probabilities. That is, α is the probability of error *given that H_0 is true*, and β is the probability of error *given that H_0 is false*. The failure to keep these definitions clear is an important source of conceptual mistakes in applying the null hypothesis tests.

It helps to illustrate the two types of error using the distributions of the F statistic. The upper panel in Figure 3.3 shows the theoretical distribution of F when the null hypothesis is true—when there are no treatment effects and the population means are equal. The region of rejection is the range on the abscissa extending to the right of the critical value at F_α, which is marked by the vertical line in Figure 3.3. The shaded area under the curve represents the probability of making a Type I error, and, by the way the critical value was determined, is equal to α. The unshaded area to the left of F_α represents the probability of making a correct inference and is equal to $1 - \alpha$. The lower panel represents a particular instance of the theoretical distribution of F

Table 3.3: The two types of error in hypothesis testing.

Population state	Decision	
	Reject H_0	Retain H_0
Means equal (H_0 true)	Incorrect decision: Type I error	Correct decision
Means unequal (H_1 true)	Correct decision	Incorrect decision: Type II error

when the null hypothesis is false—when the population means have values that are not equal and so treatment effects are present.[6] The distribution we've drawn is a noncentral F distribution, which we mentioned on page 40. It is more spread out and more symmetric than the F distribution. The probability β is determined from this distribution. The critical value of F remains at the value F_α determined by the level of α, but the different placement and shape of the alternative-hypothesis distribution changes the size of the areas on either side of the critical value. In this distribution, the shaded area to the left of F_α represents the probability β of making a Type II error, and the unshaded area to the right of F_α represents the probability of correctly rejecting the null hypothesis.

The probability of correctly rejecting a false null hypothesis is so important that it is given a special name. The **power** of a test is the probability of rejecting the null hypothesis when a specific alternative hypothesis is true. It is the probability that a test of the null hypothesis will lead to the conclusion that the phenomenon under study exists. Power is the complement of the probability of making a Type II error:

$$\text{power} = 1 - \beta. \tag{3.8}$$

Thus, the less likely is a Type II error, the greater the power and the greater the sensitivity of the test. It is important to give a study as much power as possible, and these important matters are the topic of Chapter 8.

How can we control the two types of errors? First, we must realize that complete control is not possible. We cannot avoid the risk of committing some sort of error, as long as we must make our decisions in the face of incomplete knowledge. We can, however, try to minimize the chance of an error. It is true that we directly control the Type I error probability in our selection of the significance level, and that by setting a rejection region we are taking a calculated risk that a certain proportion of the time (for example, $\alpha = .05$) we will obtain F's that fall into the rejection region when the null hypothesis is true. But we must reconcile ourselves to the fact that Type I errors will not disappear no matter how small we make the rejection region. And we must understand the relationship between these errors and the Type II errors.

What about Type II errors? One way to control them is to increase the size of the rejection region. In Figure 3.3, suppose we increased α to .10. Doing so moves the vertical line at F_α to the left and increases the shaded area in the top distribution.

---

[6]The exact shape of this distribution is determined by a number of factors, including the specific pattern of differences among the μ_i's assumed in the population. Remember that the alternative hypothesis H_1 is general and includes many other possibilities besides the specific alternative hypothesis on which this noncentral distribution is based.

This change has the opposite effect on the shaded area in the bottom distribution. It shrinks as the unshaded area expands. The chance of a Type II error would thus be reduced and power would be increased. We have a trade-off: Increasing the chance of a Type I error decreases the chance of a Type II error, and decreasing the chance of a Type I error increases the chance of a Type II error.[7] Every researcher must strike a balance between the two types of error. When it is important to discover new facts, we may be willing to accept more Type I errors and thus enlarge the rejection region by increasing α. But when we want to avoid Type I errors—for example, not to get started on false leads or to clog up the literature with false findings—we may be willing to accept more Type II errors and decrease the rejection region. As we will discuss in Chapter 6, striking the right balance is particularly important when we plan to run several statistical tests.

The best way to control Type II error is not through a trade-off with Type I error, but through the proper design of the study. Many aspects of the design affect the power, and throughout this book we will consider how powerful experiments are designed. For the time being, we will just mention two useful ways to decrease Type II error (or increase power). One is to add to the number of observations in each treatment condition, and the other is to reduce error variance with a more precisely controlled experiment. Both operations increase the accuracy with which we measure the means, and hence the degree to which we can trust differences in their sample values.

An Empirical Illustration of Type I and Type II Errors

We have found that students seem to understand the meaning of Type I and Type II error and of power better with an empirical demonstration of these concepts. In one demonstration, each member of a class of 45 students was given the same set 30 scores. The mean of these scores was $\bar{Y}_T = 9.0$ and their standard deviation was 4.01. Each student randomly divided the 30 scores into two groups of $n = 15$ each and calculated the means in Table 3.4. What would we expect to find? While we would not expect the two means for each student to equal the overall mean of 9.0, we might expect the *average* of the two sets of means to come reasonably close to that value. As you can see, only student 11 reported means of 9.0 for the two groups; all the others reported a difference between them. In most cases, the difference between the two means were small, but in some, they were substantial: Student 43, for example, found a difference of 4.14 and student 35 found a difference of -3.20. In spite of this variation, the overall difference between the two groups is remarkably small; the means of the two sets of means differed by only $9.20 - 8.80 = .40$. The random assignment of subjects seems to have worked. While marked discrepancies between the two groups were found at the student level, these differences tended to balance out when the "experiments" from all 45 students were combined. This is a demonstration of how random assignment works. It does not guarantee equality of an individual experiment, but the process approaches equality in the long run.

---

[7]While changes in the probabilities of Type I and II errors are in opposite directions—one increases while the other decreases—they do not change by the same amount. Wickens (1998, Figure 12.9) illustrates the relationship between the two error probabilities, α and β.

Table 3.4: *Results of 45 sampling experiments created by randomly assigning 30 scores to two groups of 15 scores each.*

Student No.	$\bar{Y}_1$	$\bar{Y}_2$	F_0	F_1	Student No.	$\bar{Y}_1$	$\bar{Y}_2$	F_0	F_1
1	9.40	8.60	0.28	2.13	24	7.87	10.13	2.43	13.13
2	9.67	8.33	0.80	1.24	25	8.07	9.93	1.61	10.91
3	9.07	8.93	0.01	3.58	26	9.33	8.67	0.19	2.39
4	8.27	9.73	0.97	8.99	27	8.13	9.87	1.37	10.24
5	9.20	8.80	0.07	2.95	28	8.73	9.27	0.12	5.46
6	9.47	8.53	0.38	1.89	29	8.33	9.67	0.80	8.41
7	9.47	8.53	0.38	1.89	30	8.67	9.33	0.19	5.90
8	9.53	8.47	0.50	1.66	31	9.20	8.80	0.07	2.95
9	9.60	8.40	0.64	1.44	32	9.80	8.20	1.16	0.89
10	9.33	8.67	0.19	2.39	33	8.47	9.53	0.50	7.34
11	9.00	9.00	0.00	3.92	34	9.47	8.53	0.38	1.89
12	10.53	7.47	4.80	0.00	35	7.40	10.60	5.31	19.92
13	10.00	8.00	1.86	0.46	36	9.80	8.20	1.16	0.89
14	10.40	7.60	3.89	0.02	37	8.60	9.40	0.28	6.35
15	9.80	8.20	1.16	0.89	38	10.13	7.87	2.43	0.25
16	9.40	8.60	0.28	2.13	39	7.60	10.40	3.89	16.69
17	9.13	8.87	0.03	3.26	40	8.20	9.80	1.16	9.60
18	9.20	8.80	0.07	2.95	41	10.07	7.93	2.13	0.35
19	8.73	9.27	0.12	5.46	42	8.47	9.53	0.50	7.34
20	10.07	7.93	2.13	0.35	43	11.07	6.93	10.14	0.76
21	8.87	9.13	0.03	4.65	44	10.27	7.73	3.11	0.11
22	8.33	9.67	0.80	8.41	45	10.20	7.80	2.76	0.17
23	9.73	8.27	0.97	1.06	Mean	9.20	8.80		

Each student conducted an analysis of variance on their randomly generated data. The F's are given in the column labeled F_0. How many of the 45 F's would we expect to be significant? Because the way the students formed their groups made the null hypothesis true, we would expect the proportion of significant F's to equal about α. With a 5 percent significance level, we should expect somewhere between two and three F's to be significant—more precisely, $(.05)(45) = 2.25$. The F table gives the critical value of $F_{.05}(1, 28) = 4.20$. By this criterion, three of the F's are significant (those of students 12, 35, and 43), quite close to what we would expect. In short, the procedure for evaluating the null hypothesis worked as it is supposed to work.

Following these calculations, each student created a true treatment effect with his or her data by adding 3 to each score in the second group. Now the null hypothesis is false, and there is a 3-point difference between the two groups in the population. What will the F tests conducted on the new data reveal? An inspection of these F's, given in the column labeled F_1 of Table 3.4, shows that the number of significant values increased, as we would expect. They also reveal a relatively dismal state of affairs, however, with only 16 of the F's achieving significance and 29 of them not. If we translate these numbers into proportions, we find that

$$\text{power} = 16/45 = 0.356 \quad \text{and} \quad P(\text{Type II error}) = 29/45 = 0.644.$$

It is instructive to see why the artificial treatment effect did not produce a significant F in more cases. Consider student 12. Random assignment gave an advantage of 3.06 items to the first group, which almost perfectly balanced the treatment effect of 3 items the student bestowed on the second group ($F = 0.00$). In fact, none of the students for whom the first mean exceeded the second in the null condition obtained a significant F. Type II errors occurred instead, because the chance factors associated with random assignment worked against the treatment effect the students introduced into their experiments. We can also see that occasionally random assignment *augmented* the treatment effect, producing larger values of F. Consider student 35, whose random assignment resulted in a 3.20–point advantage to the second group. This advantage, when combined with the 3 points added to the second group, produced an $F = 19.92$! All of the 16 significant F's were found by students for whom the second group had a distinct advantage.[8]

This simple demonstration shows how the chance variation introduced by random assignment leads to Type I or Type II errors. A given experiment was more or less likely to show a difference depending on how the random assignment happened to come out. True treatment effects could be either masked or augmented. It also illustrated how the sampling effects tend to balance out when we consider many experiments—in the long run the means were about right, as was the proportion of experiments that incorrectly rejected a true null hypothesis.

The demonstration illustrates another important aspect of hypothesis testing. The power depends on the nature of the alternative hypothesis that happens to be true. Suppose each student had added 0.1 to the scores in group a_2 instead of 3. The three studies that found significance when the null hypothesis was true would remain significant following the addition of 0.1, and nothing else would change. On the other hand, if 20 had been added instead, all of the studies would have been significant. Thus neither power nor the probability of a Type II error is a unique number associated with a statistical test. They also involve the particular alternative to the null hypothesis. Problem 3.3 uses these scores to illustrate another property of hypothesis tests, the trade-off between the α level and the power.

3.4   A Complete Numerical Example

Now that we have looked at each step of the one-factor analysis of variance, let's work through a numerical example from start to finish. Suppose a team of researchers is interested in the effect of sleep deprivation on the ability of subjects to perform a vigilance task in which they located objects moving on a radar screen. They arrange to house the subjects in the laboratory so that they will have control over their sleeping habits. There are $a = 4$ conditions, namely, 4, 12, 20, and 28 hours without sleep, and $n = 4$ subjects are randomly assigned to each of the treatment conditions. The subjects are well trained on the vigilance task before the start of the experiment.

---

[8]It is interesting to note that student 11, who randomly created perfectly matched groups, failed to obtain a significant F ($F = 3.92$), which shows that this "experiment" was not sufficiently sensitive to detect the 3-point treatment effect, even when the groups were identical at the start.

Table 3.5: *Number of errors in a vigilance task by sleep-deprived subjects, with summary calculations.*

	Hours without sleep			
	4 hr.	12 hr.	20 hr.	28 hr.
	a_1	a_2	a_3	a_4
	37	36	43	76
	22	45	75	66
	22	47	66	43
	25	23	46	62
Sum (A_j)	106	151	230	247
Mean ($\bar{Y}_j$)	26.50	37.75	57.50	61.75
Raw sum of squares ($\sum Y_{ij}^2$)	2,962	6,059	13,946	15,825
Sums of squares (SS_j)	153.00	358.75	721.00	572.75
Degrees of freedom (df_j)	3	3	3	3
Variance (s_j^2)	51.000	119.583	240.333	190.917
Standard deviation (s_j)	7.141	10.935	15.503	13.817
Std. error of mean (s_{M_j})	3.571	5.468	7.752	6.909

They are scored on the number of failures to spot objects on a radar screen during a 30–minute test period. The scores for each subject are presented in Table 3.5.

After arranging the scores into groups, it is wise to closely examine the data, looking for problems that might affect their interpretation or analysis. In Chapter 7, we will consider the assumptions on which the analysis of variance is based, describe how to check for their violation, and discuss how you might cope with any violations that you find. The computer software packages, which we mention in Chapter 9, are very helpful here. For the moment, we just note that you should look over your data for scores that might have been incorrectly recorded. Nothing stands out here.

Next, you summarize the data. At the bottom of Table 3.5 are a number of useful summary statistics, including the mean and several measures of the variability of the groups.[9] Although most of these latter quantities will be familiar from elementary statistics, we summarize their calculation in the following equations:

$$\text{Sums of squares } (SS_j) = \sum Y_{ij}^2 - A_j^2/n,$$

$$\text{Degrees of freedom } (df_j) = n_j - 1,$$

$$\text{Variance } (s_j^2) = SS_j/df_j,$$

$$\text{Standard deviation } (s_j) = \sqrt{s_j^2},$$

$$\text{Standard error of mean } (s_{M_j}) = s_j/\sqrt{n}.$$

---

[9] A word about rounding. It is very important to carry a sufficient number of places in your calculations, particularly when the calculations involve subtraction, as in finding the sums of squares from the bracket terms. There is no easy rule to tell you how many places to use—a safe plan is to use as many as your calculator will carry. However, because you may want to reproduce portions of the calculations in our tables, we base any continuing calculations on the intermediate results as we present them. As you will notice, when we are planning to use a result in a later step, we usually give one or two more places than we would ordinarily report in writing up the research.

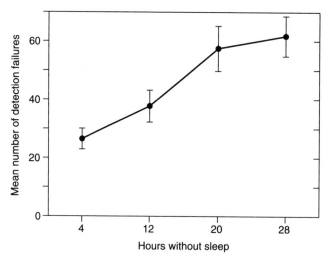

Figure 3.4: The average number of failures as a function of hours of sleep depriva-tion. The vertical bars extend above and below the mean by one standard error of the mean.

You can verify these calculations in Table 3.5. They are also easily obtained from computer programs for the analysis of variance.[10] You will note that we have calcu-lated separate standard errors of the mean, as is conventional when summarizing data, rather than the combined standard error of the mean based on $MS_{S/A}$ (Equation 3.6).

Once you have obtained this summary information, you should plot it, as we have done in Figure 3.4. The vertical lines at each point, known as **error bars**, extend upward and downward by one standard error of the mean. They give a feeling for the accuracy with which each mean is estimated.[11] Now examine the means and standard errors for any interesting outcomes or patterns. Here we see that the average number of failures increases steadily with the number of hours of sleep deprivation. There ap-pears to be some increase in the variability with the amount of deprivation, although, as we will discuss in Section 7.4, the amount of data is too small to definitively sup-port this indication. After taking note of our observations, we turn to the analysis of variance.

The steps in the analysis are summarized in Table 3.6. The upper half of the table details the operations for calculating the bracket terms $[Y]$, $[A]$, and $[T]$, and the lower half presents the summary table of the analysis of variance. From the formulas

---

[10]When you are writing up your results, you should present summaries of this information in the text, tables, or figures. In its *Publication Manual*, the American Psychological Association states that researchers must report sufficient statistical information so that readers can corroborate or enlarge upon the analyses reported in a study (American Psychological Association, 2001). The information on means, sample sizes, and variability of the groups is necessary, and, as a convenience, the error term $MS_{S/A}$ from the overall analysis.

[11]For large samples, you can think of the range marked out by the error bars as a confidence interval calculated at the 68 percent level or as the interval that is likely to contain the mean of a replication about half the time; for the difference in these interpretations, see Estes (1997).

Table 3.6: Summary of the analysis.

Calculation of the bracket terms

$$[Y] = \sum Y_{ij}^2 = 37^2 + 22^2 + \cdots + 43^2 + 62^2 = 38{,}792$$

$$[A] = \frac{\sum A_j^2}{n} = \frac{106^2 + 151^2 + 230^2 + 247^2}{4} = \frac{147{,}946}{4} = 36{,}986.500$$

$$[T] = \frac{T^2}{an} = \frac{(106 + 151 + 230 + 247)^2}{(4)(4)} = \frac{(734)^2}{16} = \frac{538{,}756}{16} = 33{,}672.250$$

Summary of the analysis of variance

Source	SS	df	MS	F
A	3,314.250	3	1,104.750	7.34*
S/A	1,805.500	12	150.458	
Total	5,119.750	15		

* $p < .05$

---

in Section 2.4 (see p. 30), we combine the bracket terms to obtain the sums of squares as follows:

$$SS_A = [A] - [T] = 36{,}986.500 - 33{,}672.250 = 3{,}314.250,$$
$$SS_{S/A} = [Y] - [A] = 38{,}792 - 36{,}986.500 = 1{,}805.500,$$
$$SS_T = [Y] - [T] = 38{,}792 - 33{,}672.250 = 5{,}119.750.$$

We check our calculations by assuring that they sum up properly. The sum of the between- and within-groups sums of squares should equal the total sum of squares SS_T:

$$SS_A + SS_{S/A} = 3{,}314.250 + 1{,}805.500 = 5{,}119.750 = SS_T.$$

The remainder of the analysis uses the formulas in Table 3.1. The sums of squares we have just calculated are entered in Table 3.6. The degrees of freedom associated with the different sums of squares are

$$df_A = a - 1 = 4 - 1 = 3,$$
$$df_{S/A} = a(n - 1) = (4)(4 - 1) = 12,$$
$$df_T = an - 1 = (4)(4) - 1 = 15.$$

We also check these values by summing:

$$df_A + df_{S/A} = 3 + 12 = 15 = df_T.$$

The between-groups and within-groups mean squares are formed by dividing the relevant sum of squares by the corresponding degrees of freedom. Specifically,

$$MS_A = \frac{SS_A}{df_A} = \frac{3{,}314.250}{3} = 1{,}104.750,$$

$$MS_{S/A} = \frac{SS_{S/A}}{df_{S/A}} = \frac{1{,}805.500}{12} = 150.458.$$

The F ratio is obtained by dividing the first mean square by the second:

$$F = \frac{MS_A}{MS_{S/A}} = \frac{1{,}104.750}{150.458} = 7.34.$$

The results of each of these steps are entered in the summary table. We will assume that the α level has been set at $p = .05$ before the start of the experiment. In order to evaluate the significance of the F, we locate the critical value of F at $\alpha = .05$ and $df_{\text{num}} = 3$ and $df_{\text{denom}} = 12$. The F table in Appendix A.1 gives $F_{.05}(3, 12) = 3.49$. Because $F_{\text{observed}} = 7.34$ exceeds this value, we reject the null hypothesis and conclude that the independent variable has produced an effect. The result of the statistical test is indicated by an asterisk in the summary table.

In Section 2.3 (see p. 26), you saw that the within-groups sum of squares is in effect the sum of the individual sums of squares for the treatment groups; that is, $SS_{S/A} = \sum SS_S$ at a_j. The within-groups mean square, which is based on $SS_{S/A}$, can also be viewed as a composite or pooled source of variance. More specifically, the error term for the analysis of variance with equal-sized groups is literally an average of the variances of the separate groups (s_j^2):

$$MS_{S/A} = \frac{\sum s_j^2}{a}. \tag{3.9}$$

As an example, we can calculate the average within-groups variance with the variances presented in Table 3.5:

$$MS_{S/A} = \frac{51.000 + 119.583 + 240.333 + 190.917}{4} = \frac{601.833}{4} = 150.458.$$

This value is identical to the value we calculated with the standard formulas. Viewing the error term as an average of the group variances emphasizes the point that each group produces an estimate of experimental error for each condition, and that these estimates are combined to provide a more stable estimate of experimental error for the entire experiment.

3.5   Unequal Sample Sizes

Most experiments are planned to have the same number of subjects assigned to each treatment condition. This is the wisest way to proceed: Equal sample sizes guarantee that each treatment condition contributes equally to the analysis of a study, as the logic of our experimental designs usually requires. Moreover, as we discuss in Chapter 7, equal sample sizes reduce any problems associated with violations of the assumptions underlying the analysis of variance.

However, unequal sample sizes occur for a variety of reasons. Perhaps a researcher assigns different numbers of subjects to the treatment conditions, either inadvertently or because the groups are unequal when the supply of subjects dries up at the end of the term. Another cause of unequal samples is the need to assign subjects in groups. For example, the researcher may have available several classes, sections, or other groups, each containing a different number of subjects, and must assign all members of each group to the same treatment. Factors defined by a classification variable, such as age or gender, may have intrinsically unequal sample sizes. Similarly, researchers using a quasi-experimental design to study existing groups of individuals who have been treated differently in the past—different incentive systems in a factory, different medical treatments in a hospital, or different therapies in a psychological clinic—rarely obtain equally sized groups. Finally, there can be attrition or subject loss during the course of an experiment, through experimenter mistakes, malfunctioning equipment, or the failure of subjects to complete the requirements of the study. You should be aware that many of these reasons, especially the loss of subjects and the use of intact groups, complicate the inference, and may even compromise it, issues that we mentioned in Chapter 1 and will discuss further in Section 7.2. Regardless of any problems of interpretation, however, most researchers are still interested in determining whether the group means differ, so we turn now to the testing procedure.

Analysis of Variance

A complete treatment of the analysis of unequal groups is complex. There are several ways to conduct the analysis—we describe a more general approach in Chapter 14. However, in a single-factor design, the presence of unequal groups does not seriously complicate the analysis. The approach we used for equal samples may be adapted to unequal samples with only minor changes.

First, some changes in notation. We will use n_j to represent the number of observations in treatment condition a_j. The total sample size is $N = \sum n_j$, and the grand mean $(\bar{Y}_T)$ is the mean of all the Y_{ij} scores; that is,

$$\bar{Y}_T = \frac{\sum Y_{ij}}{N} = \frac{T}{N}. \tag{3.10}$$

Let A_j be the sum of the Y scores in group a_j. The mean of this group is

$$\bar{Y}_j = \frac{A_j}{n_j}. \tag{3.11}$$

Just as in the equal-sample case, the total sum of squares is partitioned into a between-groups portion and a within-groups portion. The defining formulas for these three sums of squares are:

$$SS_A = \sum n_j (\bar{Y}_j - \bar{Y}_T)^2, \tag{3.12}$$

$$SS_{S/A} = \sum (Y_{ij} - \bar{Y}_{A_j})^2, \tag{3.13}$$

$$SS_T = \sum (Y_{ij} - \bar{Y}_T)^2. \tag{3.14}$$

The primary difference between these formulas and those that apply to studies with equal sample sizes is in the formula for the treatment sum of squares SS_A (Equation 2.3). With unequal sample sizes each squared deviation must be multiplied by n_j before the summation takes place, while with equal sample sizes the multiplication by n can take place either before or after the summation.

The computational formulas for calculating the sums of squares also require a change to accommodate the unequal sample sizes. These changes occur in the bracket terms we add and subtract to calculate the three sums of squares. The bracket term $[Y]$ remains unchanged:

$$[Y] = \sum Y_{ij}^2.$$

The bracket term $[T]$ is unchanged if we recall that $N = an$ with equal sample sizes. More specifically, the formulas for calculating $[T]$ with sums or means are

$$[T] = \frac{T^2}{N} \quad \text{and} \quad [T] = N\bar{Y}_T^2.$$

This leaves only the bracket term $[A]$ to be modified. It is revised to move the sample sizes n_j within the summation signs:

$$[A] = \sum \frac{A_j^2}{n_j} \quad \text{and} \quad [A] = \sum n_j \bar{Y}_j^2.$$

There are $a - 1$ degrees of freedom for the groups. The number of within-groups degrees of freedom is the sum of the individual degrees of freedom for each group:

$$df_{S/A} = \sum(n_j - 1) = N - a.$$

The remainder of the analysis proceeds as usual, through the mean squares, the F ratio, and the test of significance.

For a numerical example, consider the data in the top portion of Table 3.7. This table also contains the information we need to summarize the data and run the analysis (calculated using the equations on p. 51). We also need the grand mean $\bar{Y}_T$, which we calculate using Equation 3.10:

$$\bar{Y}_T = \frac{T}{N} = \frac{101}{13} = 7.769.$$

You should note that $\bar{Y}_T$ is not obtained by averaging the treatment means. With equal sample sizes, either way of calculating $\bar{Y}_T$ produces the same answer. With unequal sample sizes, these two definitions are not equivalent. Here the mean of the three treatment-group means is $(7 + 10 + 5)/3 = 7.333$.

In addition to the preliminary squaring and summing, we have also included in Table 3.7 the calculation of the three bracket terms and the completed analysis summary table.[12] You may also calculate SS_A using the defining formula Equation 3.12:

$$\begin{aligned}
SS_A &= (3)(7.0 - 7.769)^2 + (6)(10.0 - 7.769)^2 + (4)(5.0 - 7.769)^2 \\
&= (3)(-.769)^2 + (6)(2.231)^2 + (4)(-2.769)^2 \\
&= 1.774 + 29.864 + 30.669 = 62.307,
\end{aligned}$$

which is the same as the value in Table 3.7, except for rounding error. We complete the analysis by calculating the mean squares and the F ratio. The treatment and within-groups mean squares are obtained in the usual manner:

$$MS_A = \frac{SS_A}{df_A} = \frac{62.308}{3 - 1} = 31.154 \quad \text{and} \quad MS_{S/A} = \frac{SS_{S/A}}{df_{S/A}} = \frac{24.000}{10} = 2.400.$$

---

[12] We calculated the bracket terms $[A]$ and $[T]$ using sums. Except for rounding error, we obtain the same information from the means:

$$[A] = \sum n_j \bar{Y}_{A_j}^2 = (3)(7.0)^2 + (6)(10.0)^2 + (4)(5.0)^2 = 147.0 + 600.0 + 100.0 = 847.0,$$

$$[T] = N\bar{Y}_T^2 = (13)(7.769)^2 = (13)(60.357) = 784.641.$$

Table 3.7: A one-way analysis of variance with unequal sample sizes.

Data and summary statistics

	a_1	a_2	a_3	
	5	12	3	
	9	10	6	
	7	10	5	
		8	6	
		11		
		9		Total
Sum (A_j)	21	60	20	$T = 101$
Sample size (n_j)	3	6	4	$N = 13$
Mean ($\bar{Y}_j$)	7.0	10.0	5.0	
Raw sum of squares ($\sum Y_{ij}^2$)	155	610	106	$[Y] = 871$
Sum of squares (SS_{A_j})	8.0	10.0	6.0	$SS_{S/A} = 24.0$
Degrees of freedom (df_{A_j})	2	5	3	$df_{S/A} = 10$
Standard deviation (s_j)	2.000	1.414	1.414	
Std. error of the mean (s_{M_j})	1.155	0.577	0.707	

Calculation of the bracket terms

$$[Y] = 871$$

$$[A] = \frac{21^2}{3} + \frac{60^2}{6} + \frac{20^2}{4} = 147.0 + 600.0 + 100.0 = 847.0$$

$$[T] = \frac{101^2}{13} = 784.692$$

Summary of the analysis of variance

Source	SS	df	MS	F
A	$[A] - [T] = 62.308$	2	31.154	12.98*
S/A	$[Y] - [A] = 24.000$	10	2.400	
Total	$[Y] - [T] = 86.308$	12		

*$p < .05$

We can now calculate the F ratio:

$$F = \frac{MS_A}{MS_{S/A}} = \frac{31.154}{2.400} = 12.98.$$

With $df_{\text{num}} = a - 1 = 2$ and $df_{\text{denom}} = N - a = 10$, this value is significant.

With equal sample sizes, the error term $MS_{S/A}$ may be calculated simply by averaging the a group variances, as we demonstrated with Equation 3.9. This cannot be done with unequal sample sizes, however, because each group contributes to the $MS_{S/A}$ in proportion to its degrees of freedom. Larger groups have a greater influence on $MS_{S/A}$ than do smaller groups. We can, however, calculate $MS_{S/A}$ by summing the individual within-group sums of squares (as we did in Equation 2.4, p. 26) and dividing by the sum of the degrees of freedom. To illustrate, we have included these sums among the summary information calculated in Table 3.7. As you can see,

$$MS_{S/A} = \frac{\sum SS_S \text{ at } a_j}{\sum df_S \text{ at } a_j} = \frac{24.0}{10} = 2.40. \tag{3.15}$$

Comment

The method we have just presented is widely recommended by applied methodologists and is equivalent to the one implemented by most statistical software programs. Other approaches have been proposed, however, that adapt the equal-groups analysis to unequal groups. One possibility is to average the sample sizes and use that value for all groups when calculating SS_A; another is to drop subjects at random from the more populous groups until all sample sizes are the same. We will not discuss these approaches because they have less power than the method we have described, and so are not currently advocated.

As we noted, the calculations involved in conducting a one-way analysis of variance with unequal groups are not much different from those in the equal-sample case. This similarity should not obscure the fact that the analysis of unequal samples is a more delicate procedure, in the sense that the inferences are more sensitive to violations of the assumptions. It also raises some substantial issues of interpretation, particularly in more complex designs. We will return to these matters at several points.

Exercises

3.1. Find the critical values of F for the following situations: **a.** $F(4, 30)$ at $\alpha = .05$; **b.** $F(1, 120)$ at $\alpha = .001$; **c.** $a = 7$, $n = 5$, $\alpha = .10$; and **d.** $a = 3$, $n = 9$, $\alpha = .01$.

3.2. In an experiment comparing the rate of learning following a brain lesion, the number of trials to learn a T-maze was measured for three groups of $n = 4$ rats. Group a_1 had a lesion in one location of the brain, group a_2 in another location, and group a_3 was a sham-operated control (that is, without a lesion). The number of trials to criterion for the three groups were:

a_1		a_2		a_3	
21	18	30	40	20	19
27	30	27	35	16	33

a. Calculate the means and standard deviations for each group.
b. Plot the means, with their error bars.
c. Estimate 90 percent confidence intervals for the means of the three groups. (Using the pooled standard error in your calculations.)
d. Is there a difference among the groups? What are you able to conclude? Save your calculations for Problem 8.2 in Chapter 8.

3.3. Suppose α had been equal to .10 for the simulations in Table 3.4, what would have happened to the observed error rate and the power? What if $\alpha = .01$?

3.4. Occasionally you will want to reconstruct parts of someone else's analysis, either to verify some of the calculations or to conduct additional tests. This is relatively simple if you have available the treatment means and some measure of variability such as the group standard deviations. Suppose you wanted to compare the results of the experiment reported in Table 3.5 (p. 51) with another study that included only the first three conditions (4 hr., 12 hr., and 20 hr.). Perform an analysis of variance on these three groups, using only the means and standard deviations.

3.5. Consider the following set of scores:

a_1		a_2		a_3	
8	4	9	1	2	7
0	2	4	8	0	7
9		8		5	

a. Calculate the mean and standard deviation for each of the groups.
b. Perform an analysis of variance on these data.
c. What can you conclude from this study?

3.6. Complete the analysis of variance of the data presented in Problem 2.1 in Chapter 2.

3.7. An experiment is conducted with $n = 5$ subjects in each of the $a = 6$ treatment conditions; in the following table, the means are given in the first row and the sums of the squared Y scores in the second:

	a_1	a_2	a_3	a_4	a_5	a_6
$\bar{Y}_{A_j}$	3.0	2.0	5.0	7.0	5.0	4.0
$\sum Y_{ij}^2$	65	35	130	275	150	102

a. Perform an analysis of variance in the usual manner.
b. Calculate 95 percent confidence intervals for the population means. (Use the $MS_{S/A}$ to estimate the pooled standard error s_M.)

3.8. An experimenter conducts a study in which material is learned in environments with various degrees of distraction and later is recalled. A sample of students is obtained and randomly taken to one of three locations: a quiet room, an outside location on campus, and a noisy street intersection (conditions a_1 to a_3, respectively). Because of accidents of scheduling, the sizes of the groups varied. Each group listened to a tape recording of a story. The next day, each subject returned to the testing room and was asked to recall as many facts as possible from the story. The number of facts recalled were as follows:

a_1		a_2		a_3	
13	17	10	7	11	3
14	16	13	13	4	4
		8	10	8	
		9			

a. Calculate the means and standard deviations for each group.
b. Plot the data, with appropriate error bars.
c. Perform an analysis of variance on these data.
d. Estimate the 95 percent confidence interval for each group, using the grouped standard error s_M.

4

Analytical Comparisons Among Treatment Means

In the analysis of most multigroup experiments, a researcher wants to do more than simply conduct the F test we covered in the last two chapters. As you may have realized, this test only demonstrates the presence of differences among the groups. It does not describe the form or the nature of those differences. The means of three or more groups can exhibit many possible patterns, each of which would be interpreted differently. To analyze an experiment fully, we need to test hypotheses about these specific patterns. By selecting the hypothesized patterns carefully, it is usually possible to directly express and test the specific theoretical questions that motivated the experiment in the first place. These focused tests are fundamental to the design and construction of any study, and a good experiment tests them precisely.

We will consider the comprehensive examination of the data from a single-factor experiment in three different chapters. This chapter focuses on the analysis of experiments in which the independent variable involves *qualitative* differences among the treatment conditions. The interest here is in isolating and assessing meaningful comparisons between specific treatment conditions. Chapter 5 concentrates on the analysis of experiments with a *quantitative* independent variable. In this case, we examine the mathematical nature of the relationship between the amount of the independent variable and the behavior. Chapter 6 considers the complications resulting from these additional analyses and offers recommendations for a plan of analysis to deal with them. We will return to all these issues in subsequent chapters.

4.1 The Need for Analytical Comparisons

An **analytical comparison** refers to a comparison between two or more treatment conditions that are components of a larger experimental design. In some circumstances, analytical comparisons are undertaken following a significant F test conducted on the entire experiment. In other circumstances, they are conducted *instead of* the overall F test, in which case they are often referred to as **planned comparisons**.

The Composite Nature of SS_A

The between-groups sum of squares SS_A was defined by Equation 2.3 (p. 26) in terms of the deviation of the group means from the grand mean:

$$SS_A = n \sum (\bar{Y}_j - \bar{Y}_T)^2.$$

An algebraically equivalent form of this equation shows that SS_A reflects the degree to which the group means differ from one another:

$$SS_A = \frac{n}{a} \sum_{\text{pairs}} (\bar{Y}_j - \bar{Y}_k)^2, \tag{4.1}$$

where j and k are two different levels of factor A, and the summation is over all *unique* pairs of $\bar{Y}_j$ and $\bar{Y}_k$ (there are $a(a-1)/2$ of these pairs).

To illustrate, consider the data presented in Table 2.4 (p. 28). There were three levels of factor A and $n = 5$ observations per group. The three means were $\bar{Y}_1 = 15$, $\bar{Y}_2 = 6$, and $\bar{Y}_3 = 9$. There are only three unique differences, for example,

$$\bar{Y}_1 - \bar{Y}_2, \quad \bar{Y}_1 - \bar{Y}_3, \quad \text{and} \quad \bar{Y}_2 - \bar{Y}_3.$$

Substituting these differences into Equation 4.1 gives

$$SS_A = \tfrac{5}{3}[(15-6)^2 + (15-9)^2 + (6-9)^2]$$
$$= (1.667)[9^2 + 6^2 + (-3)^2] = 210.$$

This value is identical to the one obtained in Chapter 2 from the original formula.

Thus, the between-groups sum of squares *averages* the differences between the different pairs of means. As such, it cannot provide unambiguous information about the exact nature of the treatment effects. Because SS_A is a composite, an F ratio based on more than two treatment levels is known as an **omnibus** or **overall** test. The omnibus test is a blunt instrument that only partially addresses the needs of the researcher. The test assesses the *overall* or *average differences* among the treatment means, while a researcher's interest often concerns *specific differences* between means.

The Omnibus F Test

The analysis of the preceding chapters guides us in drawing inferences about differences among the treatment means. With a nonsignificant omnibus F, we are prepared to assert that there is insufficient evidence to reject the null hypothesis and that any differences we have observed among the means are reasonably accounted for by experimental error. Normally, we would stop there. Why analyze any further when the differences can be presumed to be chance differences?

In contrast, a *significant* F allows, if not demands, a further analysis of the data. By accepting the alternative hypothesis, we conclude that differences among the treatment means are present. But which differences are the real ones and which are not? The alternative hypothesis is inexact and, consequently, so must be our conclusion. Suppose, for example, we are examining the following four means: 5.25, 4.90, 5.10, and 10.50, and that the F from the single-factor analysis is significant. What can we conclude? Simply that the four population means are not equal to one another. Nothing is said about *particular* differences among the means. An inspection of the four means suggests that the treatment effects are not spread equally over them—the fourth group deviates from the first three, and these three do not deviate greatly from one another. The omnibus analysis does not locate the source (or sources) of the effects. All it does is indicate that somewhere there are differences among the means.

Planned Comparisons

Most research begins with the formulation of one or more research hypotheses—statements about how behavior will be influenced if such and such treatment differences are manipulated. Experiments are designed specifically to test these hypotheses. Most typically, it is possible to design an experiment that provides information relevant to *several* research hypotheses. Tests designed to shed light on these questions are planned before the start of an experiment and clearly represent the primary focus of analysis. The generality of the omnibus F test makes it an inefficient way to study these specific effects. Thus, most researchers form, or at least imply, an analysis plan when they specify their research hypotheses and design experiments to test them. This plan can be expressed by a set of specific comparisons among the group means, chosen to focus on the research questions. As you will see in Chapter 6, these planned comparisons typically are examined directly, without reference to the significance or nonsignificance of the omnibus F test.

4.2   An Example of Planned Comparisons

We will illustrate the use of planned comparisons by describing an experiment reported by McGovern (1964). In her study, college students first memorized an artificial vocabulary list, then received a second task that interfered with their recall. Finally, they were tested for their memory of the original list. In part of her study, she included $a = 5$ treatment conditions receiving second tasks that interfered with different components of memory. For the sake of simplicity, we will call these memory components A, B, and C. In the upper portion of Table 4.1, we have listed the five conditions and indicated which of the memory components McGovern predicted would be interfered with by the second task, a "yes" for interference and a "no" for no interference. Thus, McGovern predicted that in the control condition a_1, the second task would produce no interference with any of the memory components. In conditions a_2 and a_4, the second task would interfere with one of the memory components—A for condition a_2 and C for condition a_4. The other two conditions were predicted to interfere with two components, A and B for condition a_3 and B and C for condition a_5,

McGovern's study is particularly well-suited to illustrate the use of planned comparisons. Her treatment conditions were designed to provide evidence for the operation of interference with the three hypothesized components of memory. Some of the planned comparisons possible with this design are presented in the lower portion of Table 4.1. The first two comparisons contrast the no-interference or control condition (a_1) with two of the interference or experimental conditions. The first comparison (Comp. 1) is indicated by a + for a_1 and a − for a_2, indicating these two groups are compared. By comparing the yes's and no's in these columns in the upper portion of the table, you can see that the only difference between a_1 and a_2 is the hypothesized interference effect with component A. If such interference is present, we would expect to find better memory performance for a_1 than for a_2. For the second comparison, a_1 versus a_4, any difference between these two conditions implicates the hypothesized

Table 4.1: *An example of planned comparisons from the McGovern (1964) study.*

	a_1	a_2	a_3	a_4	a_5
Memory	Interference with				
Components	Memory Components				
A	No	Yes	Yes	No	No
B	No	No	Yes	No	Yes
C	No	No	No	Yes	Yes
	Comparisons				
Comp. 1:	+	−			
Comp. 2:	+			−	
Comp. 3:		+	−		
Comp. 4:				+	−

interference with component C. Again, if such interference is present, we would expect to find better memory performance for a_1 than for a_4.

The last two comparisons in Table 4.1 involve contrasts between two experimental conditions. Comparison 3 consists of a contrast between a_2 and a_3. Both conditions involve interference with A, but only a_3 involves the additional interference with B, which, if present, would lead us to predict better memory in a_2. Comparison 4 consists of a contrast between a_4 and a_5. Both conditions involve interference with C, but only a_5 involves the additional interference with B. Thus, we would predict better memory in a_4.

Not every possible comparison yields an unambiguous finding like those we have just discussed. With $a = 5$ conditions, there are 10 different comparisons between pairs of conditions.[1] The four comparisons listed in Table 4.1 represent the planned comparisons of *primary* interest because they all focus on the operation of interference with a single memory component. None of the six remaining comparisons share this property with the four we have discussed. A comparison between a_1 and a_3, for example, involves the possible joint interference effects of A and B, while a comparison between a_1 and a_5 involves the possible joint interference effects of B and C.

The McGovern study demonstrates the analytical possibilities of experimentation—that is, creating an experimental design that yields several focused comparisons that are central to the main purposes of the experiment. Quite obviously, these are *planned* comparisons that would be tested directly. We have also indicated that not all the comparisons between pairs of conditions are equally vital or important. Some are of secondary interest and others are uninterpretable. Finally, we need to highlight two important advantages of including these planned comparisons in single study rather than testing each contrast in a separate experiment: efficiency and comparability of groups. A single, comprehensive, experiment is usually more efficient since

---

[1]You might want to enumerate them: a_1 versus each of the remaining four conditions, a_2 versus each of the remaining three conditions, a_3 versus each of the remaining two conditions, and a_4 versus the last remaining condition, a_5.

some groups are used in several contrasts. Comparisons between contrasts are less ambiguous because all groups were formed under a common randomization scheme and all testing occurred within the same experimental context, circumstances that generally do not hold when separate experiments are conducted.

4.3   Comparisons Among Treatment Means

In most of this chapter, we emphasize procedures that answer questions about differences between *two means*. Many questions, like those in Table 4.1, compare the means of two treatment conditions. Comparisons that pit one group mean against another are called **pairwise comparisons**. Less commonly, our questions will involve averages of two or more treatment means. To illustrate, return to the example from Table 2.2 (p. 22) in which hyperactive boys were given a test of reading comprehension one hour following the administration of either an inert substance (control) or one of two therapeutic drugs (drug A or drug B). Suppose the researcher was interested in answering the following four specific questions from this study:

1. Does the control group (a_1) differ from the drug-A group (a_2)?
2. Does the control group differ from the drug-B group (a_3)?
3. Do the two drug groups differ from each other?
4. Do the two drug groups, taken together, differ from the control group?

The first three questions involve differences between pairs of group means. The fourth question also specifies a difference between two means, but one of them is a group mean (the control group) and the other is an average of two group means (the combined drug conditions). Any comparison that involves an average of group means is a **complex comparison**. As you will see, both means in a complex comparison may be averages of several groups.

All four questions may be conceptualized as "miniature experiments" that we create from the overall design, as we illustrate in Table 4.2. The three pairwise comparisons consist of three two-group experiments with $n = 5$ boys assigned to each group. The fourth comparison is a different kind of two-group experiment in that one of the "groups" is created by combining the two drug conditions. Because each of these questions is based on a comparison between two sets of subjects, either as a single group or as a combined group, the degrees of freedom associated with these comparisons are the same as any two-group experiment, namely, $df = 1$. For this reason, we will often refer to such comparisons as **single-df comparisons**. Usually, we would not conduct these comparisons as separate analyses of variance—each with a different error term based on the specific grouping of scores—although that approach may be appropriate when certain assumptions are violated (see Section 7.5). We present them here as a heuristic way to think of comparisons, not as the way to analyze them.

Not every question reduces to a comparison between two means, however. One common exception is found in the analysis of experiments with a quantitative independent variable in which the point of the analysis is to look at the *shape* of the function that relates the independent variable to the dependent variable. We consider this approach in Chapter 5. Another example are composite contrasts that test theoretical predictions derived from a number of separate single-df comparisons combined in a single test, as we discuss in Section 4.6. A final exception are experiments in which

Table 4.2: Comparisons between means as miniature two-group experiments.

Question 1

Control	Drug A
16	4
18	7
10	8
12	10
19	1

Question 2

Control	Drug B
16	2
18	10
10	9
12	13
19	11

Question 3

Drug A	Drug B
4	2
7	10
8	9
10	13
1	11

Question 4

Control	Drugs	
16	4	2
18	7	10
10	8	9
12	10	13
19	1	11

researchers want to test the significance of subsets of three or more means, simply asking whether the means differ among themselves. For instance, suppose we have $a = 4$ treatment conditions, one control condition and three experimental conditions. It might make sense to ask two questions: (1) Does the control condition differ from the combined experimental conditions—that is, is there a general or average experimental effect? (2) Do the experimental groups differ among themselves? In the first case, we have a single-*df* comparison between two means (the control mean versus the average of the three experimental means), and in the second case, we have a comparison among the subset of three experimental means (a three-group analysis derived from the larger $a = 4$ design). We will consider the first type of comparison now and the second type in Section 4.7.

Linear Contrasts

To test the significance of single-*df* comparisons, we need to write each one as a null hypothesis asserting that the effect is absent. Consider the four questions above. The first three questions involve pairwise comparisons. Each null hypothesis asserts that the difference between a pair of means is zero:

$$H_{01}\colon \mu_1 - \mu_2 = 0,$$
$$H_{02}\colon \mu_1 - \mu_3 = 0,$$
$$H_{03}\colon \mu_2 - \mu_3 = 0.$$

The fourth question compares the control group with the average of the two experimental groups. It is represented by the null hypothesis

$$H_{04}\colon \mu_1 - \frac{\mu_2 + \mu_3}{2} = 0.$$

These four null hypotheses have a common form: One group mean (or an average of group means) is subtracted from another group mean (or average of group means).

For analysis purposes, it is convenient to represent this difference as a **linear contrast** (or **contrast** for short), which we will denote by the Greek letter psi (ψ, pronounced "sigh"). It is formed by multiplying each group mean μ_j by a number c_j, known as a **coefficient**, that describes its role in the contrast, then summing the products:

$$\psi = c_1\mu_1 + c_2\mu_2 + \text{etc.} = \sum c_j\mu_j. \tag{4.2}$$

The only restriction placed on a contrast is that the coefficients sum to zero:

$$\sum c_j = 0. \tag{4.3}$$

We will often write the coefficients of a contrast as a set, using curly braces.

Let's return to the four hypotheses (or questions) that we mentioned above. The first of these (H_{01}) refers to the difference between μ_1 and μ_2. It is expressed by a contrast with the coefficient set $\{+1, -1, 0\}$:

$$\psi_1 = (+1)\mu_1 + (-1)\mu_2 + (0)\mu_3 = \mu_1 - \mu_2.$$

The next two questions (H_{02} and H_{03}) also specify differences between means:

$$\psi_2 = (+1)\mu_1 + (0)\mu_2 + (-1)\mu_3 = \mu_1 - \mu_3,$$

$$\psi_3 = (0)\mu_1 + (+1)\mu_2 + (-1)\mu_3 = \mu_2 - \mu_3.$$

These sets of coefficients are $\{+1, 0, -1\}$ and $\{0, +1, -1\}$, respectively. The fourth question (H_{04}) involves all three groups and refers to the contrast

$$\psi_4 = (+1)\mu_1 + (-\tfrac{1}{2})\mu_2 + (-\tfrac{1}{2})\mu_3 = \mu_1 - \frac{\mu_2 + \mu_3}{2}.$$

The coefficients for this comparison are $\{+1, -\frac{1}{2}, -\frac{1}{2}\}$. Using these contrasts, all four questions refer the same null hypotheses:

$$H_0 : \psi = 0.$$

There are several reasons to express comparisons in terms of contrasts—that is, by Equation 4.2. First, the procedure is general; it can compare the means of two groups or it can evaluate complicated comparisons involving many groups. Second, special sets of coefficients are available, particularly for experiments that have a quantitative independent variable. Third, the statistical tests follow a fixed procedure, involving the calculation of sum of squares and an F ratio. Fourth, as you will see in Section 4.5, the independence of two or more contrasts is readily determined by comparing their coefficients. We will be able to ascertain when a set of planned comparisons cleanly extract all the information available in a set of means. Finally, the contrasts can be extended to express questions about designs with two or more independent variables. We will consider the contrasts in Chapter 13.

Many contrasts can be written for an experiment, but only a few are actually tested. These are the comparisons that express meaningful questions. Technically, there is an infinite number of logically different and valid contrasts possible for any experiment with three or more groups. Because the only constraint on the choice of coefficients in a contrast is that they sum to zero (Equation 4.3), a perfectly valid contrast for the McGovern experiment is

$$\psi = (0.42)\mu_1 + (-0.26)\mu_2 + (-1.13)\mu_3 + (0.73)\mu_4 + (0.24)\mu_5.$$

Although the coefficients of this contrast sum to 0, we would not consider it because it does not express an interesting question. In short, the *logical* constraint that a contrast makes sense greatly restricts the number of comparisons that are actually tested.

You should always examine your comparisons carefully to ascertain that they allow an unambiguous conclusion. Generally this means that only one critical difference exits between the two treatment conditions. The four comparisons we considered in Section 4.3 all satisfy this logical requirement—the control versus each of the drug conditions, drug A versus drug B, and the control versus the combined drug conditions. But, what about the comparison

$$\psi_5 = \mu_2 - \frac{\mu_1 + \mu_3}{2} = 0?$$

This contrast compares one of the drug groups (a_2) with an average of the control group (a_1) and the other drug group (a_3). What is the logical basis for combining these two particular groups? You may be able to think of experiments in which this combination makes sense, but not here. Without a justification for combining groups a_1 and a_3, the comparison is useless.

All complex comparisons deserve special scrutiny. You should remind yourself why you are combining groups and consider what the comparison will reveal. Look back at H_{04}, in which the control group was compared with the average of the two drug groups. Although it appears to answer a relatively straightforward question, we still must determine whether it makes logical sense to combine the drug groups. In some studies, the conclusion would be "yes," in others "no." The critical criterion against which we must evaluate a comparison—complex or not—is, as always, whether the comparison yields interpretable information.

Constructing Coefficients

The set of coefficients for a contrast is obtained from the null hypothesis that we want to test. Consider an experiment with five treatment conditions. The null hypothesis for a pairwise comparison, states that

$$H_0 : \mu_j - \mu_k = 0,$$

where μ_j and μ_k are means of different groups. Coefficients for these comparisons are

$\quad$ +1 for one of the groups in the comparison,

$\quad$ −1 for the other group,

$\quad$ 0 for the groups not entering into the comparison.

As a matter of convenience, we prefer to assign these coefficients so a positive value of ψ reflects the direction of the difference we predict and a negative value reflects an outcome opposite to our expectation. Thus, if we predicted that group 2 would be better than group 4 in an experiment with $a = 5$ groups, the coefficients would be {0, +1, 0, −1, 0}, while if we predicted the reverse, they would be {0, −1, 0, +1, 0}. The outcome of the test does not change, but the sign of ψ is a reminder of the success or failure of our prediction.

To illustrate the construction of coefficients for a complex comparison, let's consider a null hypothesis involving the difference between a single group (a_1) and an average of two groups (a_3 and a_5):

$$H_0 : \mu_1 - \frac{\mu_3 + \mu_5}{2} = 0.$$

The coefficients for this comparison are

$+1$ for the single group to the left of the minus sign,

$-\frac{1}{2}$ for the two groups to the right of the minus sign,

0 for the two groups not included in this comparison,

or, as a set, $\{+1, 0, -\frac{1}{2}, 0, -\frac{1}{2}\}$. As another example, suppose we wanted to compare the average mean for groups 2 and 4 with the average mean for groups 1, 3, and 5. The null hypothesis for this complex comparison is

$$H_0: \frac{\mu_2 + \mu_4}{2} - \frac{\mu_1 + \mu_3 + \mu_5}{3} = 0.$$

The coefficients are

$+\frac{1}{2}$ for the two groups to the left of the minus sign,

$-\frac{1}{3}$ for the three groups to the right of the minus sign.

The coefficients set for this comparison is $\{-\frac{1}{3}, +\frac{1}{2}, -\frac{1}{3}, +\frac{1}{2}, -\frac{1}{3}\}$.

Calculating the value of a contrast or entering coefficients into a computer is more convenient when the coefficients are all integers. Fractional coefficients can be eliminated by multiplying each coefficient by the lowest common denominator of the coefficients. This change does not alter either the meaning of the contrast or its statistical test. To illustrate, consider the first example. The lowest common denominator is 2. Multiplying each of the coefficients by 2 turns the coefficient set

$$\{+1, \quad 0, -\frac{1}{2}, \quad 0, -\frac{1}{2}\} \quad \text{into the set} \quad \{+2, \quad 0, -1, \quad 0, -1\}.$$

Similarly, for the second set, the lowest common denominator of $\frac{1}{3}$ and $\frac{1}{2}$ is 6, and multiplying the coefficients by this value turns

$$\{-\frac{1}{3}, +\frac{1}{2}, -\frac{1}{3}, +\frac{1}{2}, -\frac{1}{3}\} \quad \text{into} \quad \{-2, +3, -2, +3, -2\}.$$

Either set of coefficients represents the same basic question, and the choice between sets is purely a matter of convenience and personal preference.

Although it is easier to calculate with integer coefficients, there is some value in keeping all contrasts comparable in size. To this end, some authors recommend that the coefficients be scaled so that the sum of the positive coefficients equals 1 and the sum of the negative coefficients equals -1. Contrasts for which this holds are said to be in **standard form**. To put a contrast in standard form, you add up the positive coefficients and divide all the coefficients (positive and negative) by this value. As you can see, the contrasts we derived directly from averages (those with fractions) are in standard form, while those with integers are not. We are not dogmatic here: use the form that you understand best and makes your work the clearest.

The Sums of Squares for a Comparison

How do we evaluate the significance of a contrast? The observed value of the contrast, which we denote by putting a "hat" on ψ, is obtained by replacing the population means μ_j with the sample means $\bar{Y}_j$:

$$\hat{\psi} = \sum c_j \bar{Y}_j. \tag{4.4}$$

Table 4.3: Numerical example of two comparisons on three groups.

	Treatment Levels		
	Control	Drug A	Drug B
	a_1	a_2	a_3
Means	15	6	9
Comparison 1	0	+1	−1
Comparison 2	+1	−½	−½

This observed contrast is easily converted into a sum of squares:

$$SS_\psi = \frac{n\widehat{\psi}^2}{\sum c_j^2},$$ (4.5)

where n = the number of subjects per treatment condition,

$\widehat{\psi}$ = the difference between the two means being compared,

$\sum c_j^2$ = the sum of the squared coefficients.

The denominator of Equation 4.5 adjusts the size of the sum of squares so that it does not depend on the overall magnitude of the coefficients.

To illustrate these calculations, we will use data from Table 2.4 (p. 28). In this example, there were $a = 3$ groups (control, drug A, and drug B) and $n = 5$ subjects per group. We will focus on two comparisons, a comparison between the two drug groups and a comparison between the control group and an average of the two drug groups. Table 4.3 presents the means for the three groups again, along with the coefficients of the two comparisons.

Using Equation 4.4, we can calculate the values of the two comparisons. For the first contrast, we find a difference favoring drug B over drug A:

$$\widehat{\psi}_1 = \sum c_j \overline{Y}_j = (0)(15) + (+1)(6) + (-1)(9) = 0 + 6 - 9 = -3.$$

We convert this difference into a sum of squares by substituting it into Equation 4.5:

$$SS_{\psi_1} = \frac{n\widehat{\psi}_1^2}{\sum c_j^2} = \frac{(5)(-3)^2}{(0)^2 + (+1)^2 + (-1)^2} = \frac{45}{2} = 22.50.$$

The observed value of the second contrast is

$$\widehat{\psi}_2 = (+1)(15) + (-\tfrac{1}{2})(6) + (-\tfrac{1}{2})(9) = 15 - 3 - 4.5 = 7.5.$$

The positive difference of 7.5 indicates that the boys in the control group scored higher on the test of reading comprehension than the boys in the combined drug groups. If significant, this finding will certainly bring into question the use of these drugs to treat hyperactivity in these boys. Converting this difference into a sum of squares, we find

$$SS_{\psi_2} = \frac{n\widehat{\psi}_2^2}{\sum c_j^2} = \frac{(5)(7.5)^2}{(+1)^2 + (-\tfrac{1}{2})^2 + (-\tfrac{1}{2})^2} = \frac{281.25}{1.5} = 187.50.$$

Table 4.4: The analysis of variance of the contrasts in Table 4.3.

Source	SS	df	MS	F
Treatment (A)	(210.00)	(2)		
Comparison 1	22.50	1	22.50	1.50
Comparison 2	187.50	1	187.50	12.50*
Within (S/A)	180.00	12	15.00	
Total	390.00	14		

* $p < .05$

Evaluating a Comparison

We now can test the significance of the contrasts. In Table 4.4, the two sums of squares are integrated into the original summary table. Because each comparison has one degree of freedom, $MS_\psi = SS_\psi/1 = SS_\psi$. An F ratio is formed by dividing the comparison mean square by the error term from the overall analysis;[2] that is,

$$F = \frac{MS_\psi}{MS_{S/A}}. \tag{4.6}$$

The F is evaluated in the usual manner by comparing it with the value listed in the F table, with $df_{num} = 1$ and $df_{denom} = a(n-1)$, in this case $F_{.05}(1, 12) = 4.75$.

The two F tests are shown in Table 4.4. They provide statistical justification for the observations offered in the last section: There is no evidence that the two drugs differentially affect reading comprehension (comparison 1), and there is clear evidence that, considered jointly, the two drugs disrupted the boys' performance (comparison 2). The advantage of this analysis is the additional information it provides. If we had looked at the overall F ratio, as we did in Chapter 3, we would have rejected the null hypothesis and concluded only that the three treatment means were not the same. Now we can pinpoint the locus of the differences that contribute to the significant omnibus F.

Unequal Sample Sizes

The procedures we have just described require the same number of subjects in each treatment condition. There are times, however, when the sample sizes are not equal (see Section 3.5). Let n_j indicate the number of subjects in group a_j. For any values of n_j—the same or different—the sum of squares is

$$SS_\psi = \frac{\widehat{\psi}^2}{\sum(c_j^2/n_j)}. \tag{4.7}$$

You can verify that the formula with equal sample sizes (Equation 4.5) is obtained from the formula for unequal sample sizes (Equation 4.7) by substituting n for n_j and simplifying the expression.

As a numerical example, we will use the data from Table 3.7 (p. 57). The means $\overline{Y}_j$ for the $a = 3$ groups are 7.00, 10.00, and 5.00, based on sample sizes n_j of 3, 6,

---

[2]The use of $MS_{S/A}$ as the error term is justified when the population treatment variances are equal. We will discuss the evaluation of contrasts with unequal variances in Chapter 7.

and 4, respectively. Suppose we want to test the null hypothesis that the average of the means of groups a_1 and a_3 equals the mean of group a_2:

$$H_0 \colon \tfrac{1}{2}(\mu_1 + \mu_3) - \mu_2 = 0.$$

This hypothesis leads to a complex comparison with the coefficient set $\{+\tfrac{1}{2}, -1, +\tfrac{1}{2}\}$. Using the more convenient set of integers $\{+1, -2, +1\}$, we find

$$\widehat{\psi} = (+1)(7.00) + (-2)(10.00) + (+1)(5.00) = -8.00.$$

Substituting in Equation 4.7, we obtain

$$SS_\psi = \frac{(-8.00)^2}{\dfrac{(+1)^2}{3} + \dfrac{(-2)^2}{6} + \dfrac{(+1)^2}{4}} = \frac{64.00}{.333 + .667 + .25} = \frac{64.00}{1.25} = 51.20.$$

The F test for this comparison is calculated the same way as with equal sample sizes. Substituting $MS_\psi = 51.20$, which we just calculated, and $MS_{S/A} = 2.40$ from Table 3.7 (p. 57) in Equation 4.6, we find:

$$F = \frac{MS_\psi}{MS_{S/A}} = \frac{51.20}{2.40} = 21.33.$$

With $df_{\text{num}} = 1$ and $df_{\text{denom}} = 10$, this value is significant ($F_{.05} = 4.96$).

4.4 Evaluating Contrasts with a t Test

We have developed the analysis of single-df comparisons within the framework of the analysis of variance, converting contrasts into sums of squares and F ratios. This approach emphasizes the continuity between the focused and omnibus analyses. Another approach to the evaluation of contrasts is the t test, a procedure that you have probably encountered in an earlier statistics course. You need to be aware of this alternative approach because some researchers prefer it, and because many statistical software programs analyze single-df comparisons this way. It also is more easily adapted to groups with unequal sample sizes or variances. Where either the F test or the t test can be used, they always lead to the same conclusion.

The t Test

As you may recall, the t test for the hypothesis that the mean of a single group of n scores is equal to a value μ_0 is conducted by finding the observed difference between the sample mean $\overline{Y}$ and μ_0 and dividing by the standard error of the mean:

$$t = \frac{\overline{Y} - \mu_0}{s_M}. \tag{4.8}$$

The standard error of the mean, s_M equals $s/\sqrt{n}$ (Equation 3.5, p. 35). Appendix A.2 gives critical values for the t statistic, which depend on the significance level α and the number of degrees of freedom in the variance, which here is $n - 1$.

The t statistic is also used to test the null hypotheses that a contrast in the analysis of variance is equal to zero. The test statistic now is the observed value of the contrast divided by an estimate of its standard error:

$$t = \widehat{\psi}/s_{\widehat{\psi}}, \tag{4.9}$$

in which the standard error equals

$$s_{\widehat{\psi}} = \sqrt{MS_{S/A} \sum (c_j^2/n_j)}. \tag{4.10}$$

With equal sample sizes, the standard error has a simpler form:

$$s_{\widehat{\psi}} = \sqrt{\frac{MS_{S/A} \sum c_j^2}{n}}. \tag{4.11}$$

Let's apply this test to the second comparison in Table 4.3, which contrasts the control mean with the average of the means for the two drug conditions. We need the following information to calculate t:

- the value of the contrast: $\widehat{\psi} = 7.50$,
- the sample size: $n = 5$,
- the overall error term: $MS_{S/A} = 15.00$,
- the sum the squared coefficients: $\sum c_j^2 = (+1)^2 + (-\frac{1}{2})^2 + (-\frac{1}{2})^2 = 1.5$.

Substituting these quantities in Equation 4.11, we find the standard error:

$$s_{\widehat{\psi}} = \sqrt{\frac{MS_{S/A} \sum c_j^2}{n}} = \sqrt{\frac{(15.00)(1.5)}{5}} = \sqrt{4.50} = 2.121.$$

The t statistic (Equation 4.9), then, is

$$t = \frac{\widehat{\psi}}{s_{\widehat{\psi}}} = \frac{7.50}{2.121} = 3.536.$$

We compare this value to the critical value of the t statistic from Appendix A.2 with $df_{S/A} = 12$. At $\alpha = .05$, the critical value is 2.18, and we conclude that the control group scored higher on the reading comprehension test than did the combined drug groups.

It is important to note that we arrive at exactly the same conclusion with either the F test or the t test. Moreover, we can translate from one statistic to the other by using the fact that when F is based on $df_{num} = 1$ and $df_{denom} = df_{S/A}$, and when t is based on $df_{S/A}$, then

$$F = t^2 \quad \text{and} \quad t = \sqrt{F}.$$

From the value of t we just calculated, we find that $t^2 = 3.536^2 = 12.50$, exactly the same as the value we calculated for F in Table 4.4. Because the two tests are algebraically equivalent, the conclusions are interchangeable: If the t is significant, then F is significant; if t is not significant, then F is not significant.

Up to this point, we have framed the null hypothesis H_0 as the *absence* of an effect—that is, as an assertion that the population treatment means are equal (e.g., $H_0: \mu_1 = \mu_2$) or the contrast is zero ($H_0: \psi = 0$). We can also test null hypotheses that specify outcomes other than the absence of an effect. Suppose, that a standard drug treatment is known to decrease feelings of depression in a clinical population by 2 points relative to a placebo condition. Any new drug should be evaluated with respect to this value. In statistical terms, you want to test the hypothesis $H_0: \psi = 2$, not H_0: $\mu = 0$. This null hypothesis would be rejected only if the difference between the new drug and the placebo was incompatible with $\psi = 2$.[3]

Hypotheses of this more general sort—that ψ is equal to some value ψ_0—are evaluated by a extension of the t statistic. It is only necessary to include the hypothesized value in the numerator:

$$t = \frac{\widehat{\psi} - \psi_0}{s_{\widehat{\psi}}}. \tag{4.12}$$

When $\psi_0 = 0$, Equation 4.12 is identical to Equation 4.9. All other terms in Equation 4.12 are the same, and the t statistic is evaluated in the usual fashion. We will return to this use of the t statistic when we discuss confidence intervals.

Directional Hypotheses

The alternative hypotheses we have considered so far are nondirectional, in the sense that differences between two means in either the positive or negative direction are incompatible with the null hypothesis. That is, with H_0: $\mu_1 = \mu_2$ and H_1: $\mu_1 \neq \mu_2$, the null hypothesis will be rejected whenever F falls within the rejection region, which incudes both $\mu_1 > \mu_2$ and $\mu_2 > \mu_1$. This type of alternative hypothesis, which is most common in psychology, is called a **nondirectional hypothesis** or an **omnidirectional hypothesis**.

When tested with a t statistic, a test with a nondirectional hypothesis is sometimes known as a **two-tailed test**. The "tails" in this case refer to the two rejection regions used in conjunction with the t test, shown by the two shaded areas on the t distribution in the upper-left portion of Figure 4.1. Because a value of t can be either positive or negative depending on the direction of the difference between the two means, the rejection region is located in *both* tails of the t distribution, with one-half of the significance level ($\alpha/2 = .025$) located in the extreme positive portion of the t distribution and the other half in the extreme negative portion. Consider the corresponding F distribution on the right. The F test deals with *squared* values, which treat positive and negative values equivalently, so there is only one rejection region with an area of $\alpha = .05$. Half of the F's in this region are produced by positive differences between the two means and half by negative differences. The critical values directly relate to each other. For example, the critical value of t for the example in the preceding section was $t(12) = 2.18$ for $\alpha = .05$, while the corresponding value of F is $F(1, 12) = [t(12)]^2 = 2.18^2 = 4.75$, the same value found in the F table.

In contrast to a nondirectional alternative hypothesis that allows differences in either direction, it is possible to choose an alternative hypothesis that specifies a particular direction of the outcome. If we wished to show that the mean of group a_1 was greater than that of group a_2, we would test the hypothesis pair

$$H_0: \mu_1 \leq \mu_2,$$
$$H_1: \mu_1 > \mu_2;$$

---

[3]Null hypotheses like this are not common in the behavioral sciences. A two-group study in which one group was given the old drug and the other was given the new drug would be more convincing, because it would assure that the testing conditions were the same.

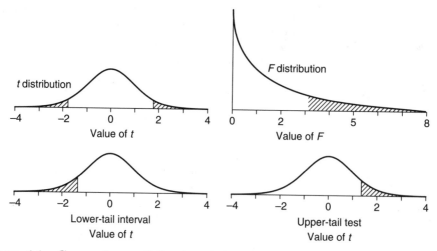

Figure 4.1: *Comparisons of the* t *and* F *distributions for nondirectional tests (above) and of the* t *distribution for directional tests (below). The distributions are drawn with 12 degrees of freedom in the error, and the tests are at* $\alpha = .10$ *to make the areas easier to see.*

and if we were interested in showing the reverse, we would test the hypothesis pair

$$H_0 \colon \mu_1 \geq \mu_2,$$
$$H_1 \colon \mu_1 < \mu_2.$$

Note that in both cases, we have put the relationship we want to show as the *alternative* hypothesis. Because the direction of the outcome is important in these hypotheses, we refer to them as **directional hypotheses**. In either case, if the results came out in the unexpected direction—with $\bar{Y}_1$ below $\bar{Y}_2$ in the first case and above it in the second—we would retain the null hypothesis regardless of how large the difference between the two means might be.

A t test with a directional hypothesis is **one-tailed test** because it has a single rejection region located in the positive or the negative tail. The two possibilities are depicted in the lower part of Figure 4.1. As you can see, the entire rejection region is located in either the positive or negative extremes of the t distribution. We concentrate the entire $p = \alpha$ chosen for the study in either the positive or the negative tail rather than spreading the equally in the two tails.[4]

Directional tests are best suited for applied research in which the purpose of a study is to compare a new or different treatment (a new therapy, drug, or teaching method) with an established one, with an eye toward adopting the new treatment only if it improves on the one currently in use. Here a researcher will not care that the directional test only detects differences in the "positive" direction. A new treatment that is no different from the present one is just as useless as one that is worse. Both would be treated the same way, namely dropped from consideration. However, direc-

---

[4]If you want to test these hypotheses with an F test, then you would pick a critical value based on *twice* your α (e.g., $\alpha = .10$ instead of $\alpha = .05$), but only reject the null hypothesis when the observed means are in the direction specified by the alternative hypothesis.

tional tests are not well suited to basic or theoretical research. Generally, theories are only temporary explanations, tentative ideas about cause and effect. A significant effect in a predicted direction might provide positive support for one theory, while a significant effect in the negative direction can either be evidence against that theory or support for another. Both directions are important. Given the transitional nature of theoretical research, we usually can justify only nondirectional tests. Conducting a directional test under these circumstances is equivalent to adopting a more liberal significance level—for example, $\alpha = .10$ rather than $.05$—which is why many journal editors question research that is based largely on directional tests.

Confidence Intervals for a Contrast

We introduced confidence intervals for the population treatment means μ_j in Section 3.1. Similar intervals may be constructed for contrasts. These interval estimates consist of a range of values for ψ, and they are constructed in such a way that they are expected to include the population difference a certain percentage of the time. This percentage or *confidence* is given by the expression

$$\text{confidence} = (100)(1 - \alpha) \text{ percent.}$$

Most commonly, researchers use $\alpha = .05$, which defines 95 percent confidence intervals, but other values are popular.

The formula for a confidence interval for a contrast is similar to the one for a population mean (Equation 3.4, p. 34):

$$\widehat{\psi} - t\, s_{\widehat{\psi}} \leq \psi \leq \widehat{\psi} + t\, s_{\widehat{\psi}}. \tag{4.13}$$

The standard error $s_{\widehat{\psi}}$ is the same one that we used for a t test—Equation 4.10 when the samples have unequal size or Equation 4.11 when they are equal.

As an example, we will return to the experiment with hyperactive boys and calculate the 95 percent confidence interval for the significant difference we found between the control condition and the combined drug conditions. The means are $\overline{Y}_1 = 15$ for the control group and $\overline{Y}_2 = 6$ and $\overline{Y}_3 = 9$ for the two drug groups. We will use the standard form of this contrast, which expresses the contrast in terms of the means rather than some multiple of the means, to construct a confidence interval. Thus, we calculate $\widehat{\psi} = (1)(15) + (-\frac{1}{2})(6) + (-\frac{1}{2})(9) = 7.50$. From the t table, we find $t(12) = 2.18$, $\alpha = .05$. The final quantity in Equation 4.13 is the standard error of the contrast, which we found to be $s_{\widehat{\psi}} = 2.121$ when we conducted the t test in Section 4.4. We now substitute these values into Equation 4.13:

$$7.50 - (2.18)(2.121) \leq \widehat{\psi} \leq 7.50 + (2.18)(2.121)$$

$$7.50 - 4.62 \leq \widehat{\psi} \leq 7.50 + 4.62$$

$$2.88 \leq \widehat{\psi} \leq 12.12.$$

We have described the confidence interval above as a range that, over many studies, will include the true value of the parameter as often as indicated by the confidence level (for example, 95 percent of the time). Another interpretation is also useful: A confidence interval is the set of values of ψ that are not rejected by hypothesis tests based on the data. Thus, a 95 percent confidence interval indicates that every value included in the interval will be retained by a hypothesis test at $\alpha = 0.05$ and every value outside it will be rejected. Applying this interpretation to the most common null hypothesis, we would retain $H_0 \colon \psi = 0$ when a confidence interval included 0 and reject it when the interval did not. As we indicated in Section 4.4, however, a null hypothesis need not be 0, which is why a confidence interval is particularly useful—it provides a decision rule for testing *all* hypotheses about ψ:

$$\left\{ \begin{array}{l} \text{If } \psi_0 \text{ falls within the confidence interval, then retain } H_0 \colon \psi = \psi_0, \\ \text{If } \psi_0 \text{ falls outside the confidence interval, then reject } H_0 \colon \psi = \psi_0. \end{array} \right.$$

A confidence interval is particularly valuable when we want to say something about ψ after we have rejected the hypothesis that $\psi = 0$, or when we are trying to relate our findings to those of other investigators. Suppose other research had suggested a 15-point difference between the control and the combined drug conditions. A glance at the confidence interval for this difference ($2.88 \leq \psi \leq 12.12$) tells us, without further calculation, that that value is inconsistent with our data. We reject the hypothesis that $\psi = 15$ using the same standards of evidence that we used to test the hypothesis that $\psi = 0$.

4.5   Orthogonal Contrasts

A central concept underlying the analysis of variance is the fact that a sum of squares can be subdivided into separate and independent components. We already saw one example when we partitioned SS_T into the between-groups and the within-groups sums of squares, SS_A and $SS_{S/A}$. In general, we can divide any sum of squares into as many independent sums of squares as there are degrees of freedom. We also considered how we can extract meaningful contrasts out of the omnibus analysis. However, we have said nothing about the relationship between the various contrasts that we might examine in our analysis of an experiment. In this section, we consider a special relationship between two comparisons known as **orthogonality**.

The Definition of Orthogonality

The valuable property of orthogonal contrasts is that they reflect *independent* or *nonoverlapping* pieces of information. Orthogonality is established by applying the following rule: Two contrasts, $\psi_1 = \sum c_{1j}\mu_j$ and $\psi_2 = \sum c_{2j}\mu_j$, are **orthogonal** whenever the sum of products of the two sets of coefficients is zero:[5]

$$\sum c_{1j}c_{2j} = 0. \tag{4.14}$$

Again consider our example with the hyperactive boys. Two of the contrasts we considered as possible comparisons on page 64 were a pairwise comparison between the two drug conditions ($c_{1j} \colon \{0, +1, -1\}$) and a complex contrast between the control and the combined drugs conditions ($c_{2j} \colon \{+1, -\frac{1}{2}, -\frac{1}{2}\}$). Are they orthogonal? We will organize the calculation of Equation 4.14 in a little table:

	a_1	a_2	a_3
c_{1j}	0	$+1$	-1
c_{2j}	$+1$	$-\frac{1}{2}$	$-\frac{1}{2}$
$c_{1j}c_{2j}$	0	$-\frac{1}{2}$	$+\frac{1}{2}$

---

[5] A dictionary defines *orthogonal* as "perpendicular" or "at right angles." As this definition suggests, there is a geometric metaphor that underlies the analysis of single-*df* contrasts. We don't use this metaphor here, but you can look at Wickens (1995) for a discussion.

First, we enter the coefficients of the two contrasts in the rows, then we calculate the product of the coefficients for each treatment condition and write these beneath the box. Finally, we sum them and check whether the sum of products equals zero; in this case they do: $0 - \frac{1}{2} + \frac{1}{2} = 0$. We have shown that these two contrasts are orthogonal.

In contrast, consider two contrasts that are not orthogonal, such as pairwise comparisons between the control condition and each of the drug conditions. Let the contrasts ψ_3 and ψ_4 compare the control group to the first and second drug groups, respectively. The coefficients for these contrasts are c_{3j}:$\{+1, -1, 0\}$ and c_{4j}: $\{+1, 0, -1\}$. Although these two comparisons both express meaningful questions, they are not orthogonal, as we discover by substituting their coefficients into Equation 4.14:

$$\sum c_{3j}c_{4j} = (+1)(+1) + (-1)(0) + (0)(-1) = 1 + 0 + 0 = 1.$$

Orthogonality is a relationship between two contrasts ($\sum c_{1j}c_{2j} = 0$). If you have a set of three or more contrasts, you must verify that this rule holds for each pair of contrasts. With three contrasts, there are three relationships to check (ψ_1 to ψ_2, ψ_1 to ψ_3, and ψ_2 to ψ_3), and with four contrasts, there are six. If all contrasts in a set are orthogonal to one another, they are said to be **mutually orthogonal**.

Orthogonality and the Analysis of Variance

One reason for the importance of orthogonal contrasts is that they provide a simple way to understand the effects in an analysis of variance with several groups. The first important point to notice is that there is a limit to the number of mutually orthogonal contrasts that can be constructed from a set of means:

> There can be no more mutually orthogonal contrasts than the degrees of freedom associated with the omnibus effect.

If we have three means, we can write only two orthogonal contrasts, while if we have four means, we can construct sets of three mutually orthogonal contrasts, and so on.

The second important point is that any set of $a - 1$ mutually orthogonal contrasts completely expresses the variability of the means in the omnibus effect. This fact has an important consequence: The sums of squares for the contrasts in a complete orthogonal set add up to the sum of squares for the omnibus effect; that is,

$$SS_A = \sum SS_\psi. \tag{4.15}$$

We can demonstrate this property for the experiment with $a = 3$ conditions and the two orthogonal comparisons presented in Table 4.4 simply by showing that

$$SS_A = SS_{\psi_1} + SS_{\psi_2} = 22.50 + 187.50 = 210.00.$$

Let's see what happens when the $a - 1$ comparisons are *not* mutually orthogonal. Suppose we compare the control group with each of the drug groups using the data in Table 4.3. We showed above that the corresponding contrasts, ψ_3 and ψ_4, were not orthogonal. Their values are

$$\widehat{\psi}_3 = \bar{Y}_1 - \bar{Y}_2 = 15.00 - 6.00 = 9.00,$$
$$\widehat{\psi}_4 = \bar{Y}_1 - \bar{Y}_3 = 15.00 - 9.00 = 6.00.$$

Now we find the sums of squares, using Equation 4.5:

$$SS_{\psi_3} = \frac{n\widehat{\psi}_3^2}{\sum c_{3j}^2} = \frac{(5)(9.00^2)}{(1)^2 + (-1)^2 + (0)^2} = 202.50,$$

$$SS_{\psi_4} = \frac{n\widehat{\psi}_4^2}{\sum c_{4j}^2} = \frac{(5)(6.00^2)}{(1)^2 + (0)^2 + (-1)^2} = 90.00.$$

The sum of these two sums of squares is $202.50 + 90.00 = 292.50$, which greatly exceeds the omnibus sum of squares $SS_A = 210.00$ given in Table 4.4.

Only orthogonal contrasts are assured of having their sums of squares add up to SS_A.[6] In this sense, the sum of squares obtained from a set of a treatment means is a *composite* of the sums of squares associated with $a - 1$ mutually orthogonal contrasts. A detailed analysis involving a properly constructed set of orthogonal contrasts is an efficient way to examine the results of an experiment. But efficiency is not everything, and researchers will form incomplete sets of orthogonal contrasts and sets including nonorthogonal contrasts when they are dictated by the nature of the questions they want to ask of their data. We will pursue this point in the next section.

Before moving on, we should mention one easy way to construct a set of $a - 1$ orthogonal contrasts. To begin, you compare the first group to the average of the other $a - 1$ groups. In all other contrasts you ignore the first group by giving it the coefficient $c_1 = 0$. For the second contrast, you compare the second group to the average of all the higher-numbered groups, again giving it the coefficient $c_2 = 0$ in any further contrasts. You continue this process, comparing each successive group to the average of the later ones until you reach a comparison between the last two groups. For example, with four groups this process yields three contrasts:

$$\psi_1 = \mu_1 - \frac{\mu_2 + \mu_3 + \mu_4}{3}, \qquad \text{or} \quad c_{1j}: \{1, -\tfrac{1}{3}, -\tfrac{1}{3}, -\tfrac{1}{3}\},$$

$$\psi_2 = \mu_2 - \frac{\mu_3 + \mu_4}{2}, \qquad \text{or} \quad c_{2j}: \{0, 1, -\tfrac{1}{2}, -\tfrac{1}{2}\},$$

$$\psi_3 = \mu_3 - \mu_4, \qquad \text{or} \quad c_{3j}: \{0, 0, 1, -1\}.$$

You can verify that these contrasts are mutually orthogonal. They are known as **Helmert contrasts**. Some computer programs automatically construct and test them. Of course, whether they make any sense will depend on your particular study.

Orthogonality and Planned Comparisons

We noted in Section 4.1 that planned comparisons are a desirable adjunct to the omnibus F test. But do the planned comparisons need to be mutually orthogonal? The answer depends on the questions and the study.

Consider again the four comparisons we listed in Table 4.1 for McGovern's study on interference in memory, given again in the upper portion of Table 4.5. Comparison 1 focuses on a loss of the A memory component, comparison 2 on a loss of the C component, and comparisons 3 and 4 focus on a loss of the B component. Each of

---

[6]When the sample sizes are unequal, the the sums of squares of orthogonal contrasts (calculated by Equation 4.7) may not add up to SS_A. We will discuss the reason for this fundamental nonadditivity in Section 14.4.

Table 4.5: Tests of mutual orthogonality for the contrasts in Table 4.1.

Treatment condition

	a_1	a_2	a_3	a_4	a_5	Sum
			Comparisons			
Comp. 1 (c_{1j})	+1	−1	0	0	0	0
Comp. 2 (c_{2j})	+1	0	0	−1	0	0
Comp. 3 (c_{3j})	0	+1	−1	0	0	0
Comp. 4 (c_{4j})	0	0	0	+1	−1	0
		Tests for Orthogonality				
Comp. 1 vs. 2 $(c_{1j}c_{2j})$	+1	0	0	0	0	+1
Comp. 1 vs. 3 $(c_{1j}c_{3j})$	0	−1	0	0	0	−1
Comp. 1 vs. 4 $(c_{1j}c_{4j})$	0	0	0	0	0	0
Comp. 2 vs. 3 $(c_{2j}c_{3j})$	0	0	0	0	0	0
Comp. 2 vs. 4 $(c_{2j}c_{4j})$	0	0	0	−1	0	−1
Comp. 3 vs. 4 $(c_{3j}c_{4j})$	0	0	0	0	0	0

the four comparisons qualifies as a contrast—that is, the coefficients sum to zero, as shown in the last column on the right. Now we test for orthogonality between all different pairs of comparisons. In the bottom part of Table 4.5, we have calculated the products of the coefficients from each pair of contrasts. For example, the first row gives the products formed from the coefficients of contrasts 1 and 2 $(c_{1j}c_{2j})$. The sums of these products are on the right of the table. These sums reveal that three pairs of contrasts are orthogonal (1 and 4, 2 and 3, and 3 and 4) and three pairs are not orthogonal (1 and 2, 1 and 3, and 2 and 4).

We have established that as a set, the comparisons are not mutually orthogonal. This result implies that these comparisons do not divide the SS_A into tidy independent pieces of information, which would have been true had the set of comparisons been mutually orthogonal (Equation 4.15). On the other hand, orthogonality is only one of several considerations in the selection of contrasts. In the present example, the fact that each comparison tests for the loss of a single memory component overrides the need for orthogonality.

Let's return to our original question: Do planned contrasts need to be orthogonal? We would say "no," but with some qualification. You should strive to look at orthogonal comparisons whenever you can, but not to the extent of ignoring substantively important comparisons. Some important questions simply are not orthogonal, and that fact should not stop us from looking at them. Attaining a proper balance is important here. Too many nonorthogonal contrasts will clutter up your analysis and make it difficult to understand, but ignoring meaningful contrasts will make your discussion less direct and to the point.

4.6 Composite Contrasts Derived from Theory

Sometimes when we have particular expectations for the sequence of means in a multi-group experiment, we want to see whether the data agree with them. The values of these hypothesized means may come from a previous study or may be derived from a theory. This type of analysis is somewhat different from those we have discussed above. Before we discuss it, however, we will consider the simpler problem of constructing a set of contrast coefficients to test for a particular pattern of means.

Contrast Coefficients that Match a Pattern

Suppose we have hypothetical values for the means of two or more groups, and we want to find the contrast ψ that is most sensitive to that particular pattern. The coefficients c_j for this contrast are found from a simple principle:

> The most sensitive contrast to a pattern of means is the one whose coefficients reflect the same pattern.

To obtain these coefficients, all we do is start with values that duplicate the exact patterning of means that we want to detect. Then, we make sure that they obey the fundamental rule for contrast coefficients, that they sum to zero. In more detail, the steps we follow are

1. Use each predicted mean as a starting coefficient.
2. Subtract the average of these means from the predicted means so that they sum to zero.
3. Optionally, simplify the coefficients by multiplying or dividing all of them by the same number to turn them into integers or to give the contrast standard form.

First, we will show that this procedure works for a two-group comparison. Suppose we predict that a control group will score higher than an experimental group. We start by assigning numbers that reflect this expectation, say means of 10 for the control group and 5 for the experimental group (ignore for the moment any other groups not relevant to this comparison). We can't use these numbers as coefficients because their sum is 15 not 0. We solve this problem by subtracting their average, which is $(10 + 5)/2 = 7.5$, from each of them:

$$c_1 = 10 - 7.5 = 2.5 \quad \text{and} \quad c_2 = 5 - 7.5 = -2.5.$$

Now $\sum c_j = 0$. For convenience, we can turn these coefficients into integers by dividing each one by 2.5, giving us the familiar values of $c_1 = +1$ and $c_2 = -1$. The coefficients for groups not entering into this comparison are 0. If you look over these calculations, you can see that the particular starting points (10 and 5) were not critical. What was important was that we choose different values for the two groups.

Now consider a more complex prediction involving several groups. Suppose for our study of hyperactive boys, we predicted that both drugs would increase reading comprehension on the test, and that drug A would increase performance more than group B, say by 7 points instead of 2 points. Both of these values are relative to the control group. We start the process by choosing a convenient value for the control group mean, for example, 10 (this value actually does not affect our result). We would then expect means of 10, 17 and 12 for the control, drug A, and drug B groups, respectively. These values are our starting point in constructing customized coefficients. In step 2, we subtract their average, $(10 + 17 + 12)/3 = 13$, to get

$$c_1 = 10 - 13 = -3, \quad c_2 = 17 - 13 = +4, \quad \text{and} \quad c_3 = 12 - 13 = -1.$$

These coefficients are maximally sensitive to the hypothesized pattern. If the actual means are such that drug A is 7 points above the control and drug B is 2 points above, then SS_ψ will equal SS_A, fully capturing the observed variability among the three groups. Problem 4.6 demonstrates of this property.

Contrasts As Theoretical Predictions

Generally, we create custom coefficients from theoretical considerations. The theory that underlies a study, or a review of previous results, tells us that certain patterns are particularly interesting. That is how the predictions for the hyperactive boys would have arisen. Sometimes the theory is not this complete or specific. Consider the predictions by McGovern that we summarized in Table 4.1. Each column in the upper portion of this table indicates which of the three memory components is affected by the second list. You can see that condition a_1 has no interference, conditions a_2 and a_4 have one interference component, and conditions a_3 and a_5 have two interference components. If the interference from each memory component is roughly the same and their combined effect is the sum of their separate effects, then we could make a composite prediction that

$$\mu_1 > \mu_2 \approx \mu_4 > \mu_3 \approx \mu_5.$$

Several writers have argued that custom coefficients should be used in the analysis of a study such as this to see whether this order appears in the data.[7] They feel this analysis is more closely linked to the theory than a set of separate contrasts.

How do we use such a prediction? To support our theory, the results of a study need to have two characteristics. First, the observed pattern of means should agree with the theoretically-derived expectation. This would tell us that we found what we were looking for. But statistically significant agreement with the pattern we predicted is not all we need. In addition, we need to know how *well* the predicted pattern matched the outcome—whether unexpected or unanticipated differences may also be present. We must look at both aspects.

Let's see how the composite prediction based on the McGovern experiment is translated into a set of coefficients and how we can determine whether unanticipated factors remain to be identified. First, we consider whether the data are concordant with the predicted pattern. We do this by constructing a custom contrast, which we will call ψ_{fit}, that is sensitive to the predicted pattern of means. We will test the null hypothesis that $\psi_{\text{fit}} = 0$, hoping to reject it and conclude that $\psi_{\text{fit}} > 0$. If we do so, our predictions are supported. Assuming that the control mean was about 10 and that each interference component reduced that value by about 2 gives us the predicted means

$$\mu_1=10, \quad \mu_2=8, \quad \mu_3=6, \quad \mu_4=8, \quad \text{and} \quad \mu_5=6.$$

When you apply the procedure for finding custom coefficients to these means, you will discover that these values will be detected by a contrast with the coefficient set $\{6, 1, -4, 1, -4\}$ (see Problem 4.5):

$$\psi_{\text{fit}} = 6\mu_1 + \mu_2 - 4\mu_3 + \mu_4 - 4\mu_5.$$

---

[7]See, for example, Rosnow and Rosenthal (1995) and the commentaries by Abelson (1996), Petty, Fabrigar, Wegener, and Priester (1996) and Rosnow and Rosenthal (1996). An excellent discussion of the procedure is in Levin and Neumann (1999).

This contrast does not look like any of the conventional forms we presented above, but it embodies our particular predictions about the study. If we can reject the hypothesis that it is zero, then we know that the means agree, in some part, with our predictions. Our next job is to determine just how well the prediction fits.

A theoretical prediction in a multigroup experiment involves many distinct aspects. With the five groups in the McGovern experiment, there are 10 different pairwise comparisons that could be written, and the theory makes assertions about all of them. It is possible that ψ_{fit} may be significantly different from zero (a good thing), yet for the theory to fail badly in some important respects. For example, we might find that even though the data looked something like the prediction, our assumption that $\mu_2 \approx \mu_4$ or that $\mu_3 \approx \mu_5$ was wrong. We need a way to look for such failures of our expectations. If we find them, then we would need to qualify the theory or reject it altogether. What we need is a second test that determines the extent to which the theory *fails*. We obtain it by looking at the variability of the means that is *not* accounted for by ψ_{fit}. More specifically, we calculate the omnibus sum of squares SS_A and the sum of squares SS_{fit} for our custom contrast, and then take the difference between them:

$$SS_{\text{failure}} = SS_A - SS_{\text{fit}}. \tag{4.16}$$

This difference reflects any variation among the means that is not part of our composite prediction. If SS_{failure} is small, then the theory is in good shape; if SS_{failure} is large, then something is wrong with it.

We will illustrate the difference between fit and failure with a simple example. Suppose we had a theory that predicted the pattern of means $\mu_1 = 12$, $\mu_2 = 9$, and $\mu_3 = 9$. As you can verify, this pattern leads to the contrast $\psi_{\text{fit}} = 2\mu_1 - \mu_2 - \mu_3$. Now consider two outcomes of an experiment. In the first, the means exactly agree with the predictions: $\bar{Y}_1 = 12$, $\bar{Y}_2 = 9$, and $\bar{Y}_3 = 9$. These values lead to $\widehat{\psi}_{\text{fit}} = 6$. In the second, the means are $\bar{Y}_1 = 12$, $\bar{Y}_2 = 6$, and $\bar{Y}_3 = 12$. Again $\widehat{\psi}_{\text{fit}} = 6$, but clearly these means are far less concordant with the theory than the first set. The difference in outcome is reflected by SS_{failure}, which is small (actually zero) in the first case but substantial in the second.

We test SS_{failure} in the same way that we test any other effect. The degrees of freedom are obtained by subtraction:

$$df_{\text{failure}} = df_A - df_{\text{fit}}. \tag{4.17}$$

Here, the omnibus sum of squares has $a - 1$ degrees of freedom and $df_{\text{fit}} = 1$, so $df_{\text{failure}} = (a - 1) - 1 = a - 2$. We divide the sum of squares by its degrees of freedom to get a mean square, then calculate an F ratio as usual:

$$MS_{\text{failure}} = \frac{SS_{\text{failure}}}{a - 2} \quad \text{and} \quad F_{\text{failure}} = \frac{MS_{\text{failure}}}{MS_{S/A}}.$$

Our hope here is that the result will not be significant, so that we can conclude that nothing other than that predicted by the theory is contributing to the differences among the means.

You will notice that the strategy of testing MS_{failure} we just described is quite different from the way we usually use hypothesis tests. Instead of hoping to reject the null hypothesis, we want to *retain* it. When you use this approach, you must keep some cautions in mind. The first is, of course, that we can never prove a null hypothesis to be true. A significant F_{failure} tells us that our theory is in trouble, but a nonsignificant value does not tell us that it is true. Second, the test is not informative unless it has enough power. Lack of power here is a serious problem. Particularly in a large experiment, in which the data are generally in agreement with our predictions, the power of the test of failure may be quite low for interesting alternatives to the theory.[8] The solution is not to stop after looking at F_{failure}, but also to investigate specific hypotheses that represent to important ways that the theory could be incorrect. For example, we could test the McGovern data to see whether groups a_2 and a_4 differ and whether groups a_3 and a_5 differ using the contrasts

$$\psi = \mu_2 - \mu_4 \quad \text{and} \quad \psi = \mu_3 - \mu_5.$$

You will note that these contrasts are orthogonal both to ψ_{fit} and to each other, so they pick up distinct parts of the variability of SS_{failure}. They are much more specific than the overall failure test, and they are also much easier to interpret.

Let us summarize our recommendations for the use of composite contrasts derived from theory. First, you should determine ψ_{fit} and show that it is significantly nonzero and in the correct direction. Next, you should subtract its sum of squares from SS_A and establish that the remaining variation, SS_{failure}, is not significant. Finally, you should follow up this result by testing contrasts orthogonal to ψ_{fit} that probe the particular places where the theory is vulnerable. You will also need these tests to determine what went wrong when the test of SS_{failure} is significant. The combination of these tests—one significant and the others not, provides the best support for theoretical predictions.

4.7 Comparing Three or More Means

Occasionally an analysis plan will include the examination of a subset of three or more means that are part of a larger experimental design. Studies with control or baseline conditions are common examples. Suppose we were interested in the effects of different incentives on the solving of problems by fifth-grade students. Groups receiving three forms of incentives are included—verbal praise (a_1), monetary reward (a_2), and extra credit (a_3)—in addition to a control group (a_4) receiving no incentives. Certainly, we would want to test the three incentive conditions against the control condition, either separately or combined. We also might want to compare just the three incentive groups to see whether the rewards differed in effectiveness. Then, depending on the outcome of this analysis, we would conduct additional comparisons to analyze the results of this experiment fully. In the absence of any strong theoretical reasons to favor one incentive condition over another, however, an omnibus test involving the three incentive groups is appropriate.

The statistical hypotheses for this test are as follows:

$$H_0: \mu_1 = \mu_2 = \mu_3$$
$$H_1: \mu_1, \mu_2, \text{ and } \mu_3 \text{ are not all equal.}$$

---

[8]In Chapter 5 we will see an example of this phenomenon in our trend analysis of the data in Table 5.1. We discuss ways to estimate and to control power in Chapter 8.

The simplest way to create a sum of squares to test this hypothesis is to ignore the control group and treat the three incentive groups as if they constituted an independent experiment. A between-groups sum of squares captures the variability among these means. More specifically, there are three conditions in this calculation (levels a_1, a_2, and a_3). The treatment sums are A_1, A_2, and A_3, the new grand sum is $T' = A_1 + A_2 + A_3$, the effective number of groups is $a' = 3$, and the sample size is still n. The computational formula for the sum of squares representing variation among these three conditions (Equation 2.14, p. 30, with substitutions) is

$$SS_{A_{123}} = \frac{A_1^2 + A_2^2 + A_3^2}{n} - \frac{(T')^2}{a'n},$$

where the subscript "123" refers to the set of means in the analysis. The degrees of freedom are 1 less than the number of means being compared; that is, $df_{A_{123}} = a' - 1 = 2$. The mean square is formed in the usual way, and the overall $MS_{S/A}$ from the original analysis serves as the error term, just as it did in the test of contrasts:

$$MS_{A_{123}} = \frac{SS_{A_{123}}}{df_{A_{123}}} \quad \text{and} \quad F = \frac{MS_{A_{123}}}{MS_{S/A}}.$$

The critical value of F is found in Appendix A.1 using 2 degrees of freedom for the numerator and those of $MS_{S/A}$ for the denominator (i.e. based on 4 groups, not the 3 being compared).[9] Problem 4.4 gives an example of this analysis.

This type of analysis is appropriate when the formation of subgroups makes logical sense. If the F *is* significant, we treat this finding as we would any omnibus test and probe further to determine in what ways the incentive conditions differ among themselves. Any further tests involving the control group would include the individual experimental means. On the other hand, if the F is *not* significant, we might (with suitable caution about accepting null hypotheses) average the three incentive conditions and compare this combined mean with the mean for the single control condition.

Exercises

4.1. An experimenter is investigating the effects of two drugs on the activity of rats. Drug A is a depressant, and drug B is a stimulant. Half of the subjects receiving either drug are given a low dosage, and half a high dosage. The experimenter also includes a control group that is given an injection of an inert substance, such as a saline solution. In total, 5 groups are formed, each containing $n = 4$ rats assigned randomly from the stock of laboratory rats on hand. The animals are injected, and their activity is observed for a fixed period. The activity scores for the animals and the average activity scores follow:

Control		Drug A				Drug B		
a_1		Low a_2		High a_3		Low a_4		High a_5
10	13	8	16	12	10	18	11	21	17
17	20	12	19	7	3	15	22	26	28

[9]On a computer, you would run an ordinary analysis-of-variance program with the data restricted to the groups that you want to compare (for example, groups 1, 2, and 3). You will need to construct the final F test by hand, using the error term from the full analysis.

a. Perform a one-way analysis of variance on these data.
b. Construct a set of coefficients that will provide the following comparisons:
    i. Control versus the combined experimental groups.
    ii. Drug A versus drug B.
    iii. Low versus high dosage for drug A.
    iv. Low versus high dosage for drug B.
c. Show that these four comparisons are mutually orthogonal.
d. Find the sums of squares associated with these comparisons and test their significance.
e. Verify that the sum of the comparison sums of squares equals the SS_A.

4.2. In Section 4.2, we described McGovern's memory experiment and a set of planned comparisons that could be used to analyze the data. Assume that the experiment was conducted with $n = 16$ subjects in each of the five treatment conditions. The means obtained on the response measure were

a_1	a_2	a_3	a_4	a_5
16.8	12.6	7.6	9.8	7.2

Assume that $MS_{S/A} = 12.50$.

a. Conduct the four planned comparisons indicated in Table 4.1 (p. 63). What conclusions do you draw from this analysis?
b. The comparisons in this set are not mutually orthogonal (see Table 4.5, p. 79). Show that the sum of the comparison sums of squares does not equal the SS_A.

4.3. In Table 4.2, we represented four single-df comparisons. Using these data, conduct the following analyses:
a. For comparison 3 (Drug A versus Drug B), conduct an analysis of variance for this $a = 2$ "miniature experiment," using the computational formulas in Table 3.1 (p. 32). Note that the treatment sum of squares you obtained is equal to the value we calculated as a single-df comparison on page 69 using Equation 4.5.
b. Conduct an analysis of variance for the data relevant to comparison 4 (Control versus Drugs). Because this miniature experiment contains unequal sample sizes ($n_1 = 5$ and $n_2 = 10$), you will need to use the formulas presented in Section 3.5. Again, you should find that the treatment sum of squares equals the value we calculated on page 69.
c. You may have noticed that while the treatment sums of squares obtained from these miniature experiments are identical to those calculated with Equation 4.5, the error terms and resulting F ratios are not. Why did this happen?

4.4. The experiment in Section 4.7 was concerned with the effects of different incentives on the solving of problems by fifth-grade students. There were three incentive groups, verbal praise (a_1), monetary reward (a_2), and extra credit (a_3), and a no-incentive control group (a_4). The experiment was conducted with $n = 10$ children. The response measure consisted of the number of problems solved in 20 minutes. The following treatment means were obtained:

a_1	a_2	a_3	a_4
4.8	5.3	4.7	3.2

Assume that $MS_{S/A} = 4.11$.

a. Determine whether the three incentives were differentially effective in influencing the number of problems solved.

b. Conduct a single-df comparison between the control condition and the combined incentive conditions.

c. Is the omnibus F based on all four conditions significant? Is this finding compatible with the conclusions you drew from the other two analyses? Explain.

4.5. On page 81 we presented a set of coefficients for a composite contrast based on a number of theoretical predictions derived from the McGovern study. First, construct this set of coefficients for yourself, and then use the information in Problem 4.2 to test the hypotheses of fit and failure for this composite contrast.

4.6. This problem illustrates that a set of custom coefficients is maximally sensitive to the hypothesized pattern of means on which the set is based. In Section 4.6, we constructed the set of coefficients $\{-3, 4, -1\}$ to reflect a particular expected patterning of average reading scores for a control and two drug groups (A and B).

a. Suppose you obtained the same means we used to construct the coefficients (10, 17, and 12). Assuming that $n = 10$, calculate SS_A, then $\widehat{\psi}$ and SS_{fit} to see how well the custom coefficients captured the variability among the group means.

b. Now subtract 5 from each of the means, which changes the numbers but not the specific patterning. Again, calculate SS_A and SS_{fit} and compare the two results.

c. Now try a set of means that deviate slightly from the predicted pattern: 11, 16, and 13. What can you say now about the relationship between SS_A and SS_{fit}?

d. Finally, let's try an outcome in which the means for the two drug conditions are reversed: 10, 12, and 17. What does the analysis of SS_A and SS_{fit} now reveal? What has happened to the value of $\widehat{\psi}$?

4.7. This problem is based on an experiment reported by Levin and Neumann (1999), in which they demonstrated the value of testing composite hypotheses. Subjects were asked to identify certain visual targets presented under conditions designed either to speed up or to slow down correct identification by a certain amount. On the basis of theory, they predicted that subjects in conditions designated with a single $+$ in the table below (a_2 and a_3) would speed up relative to a control (a_4), whereas subjects in conditions designated with a single $-$ (a_5 and a_6) would slow down. They also predicted that subjects in the condition with $++$ (a_1) would speed up by twice as much subjects in a condition with a $+$, and subjects in the condition with $--$ (a_7) would slow down by twice as much as subjects in a condition with a single $-$. The average speed of responding to a correct target, referred to as the average reaction time, is also presented in the table. We will assume that $MS_{S/A} = 30.85$ and that there were $n = 49$ subjects in each condition.

	a_1	a_2	a_3	a_4	a_5	a_6	a_7
Predicted effect	$++$	$+$	$+$	0	$-$	$-$	$--$
Mean reaction time $\overline{Y}_j$	543	552	547	554	559	558	565

a. Conduct an overall analysis of variance on these data. What can you conclude? Did the data correspond to the predictions? Remember that a smaller reaction time is a faster response.

b. Create a custom hypothesis on the basis of the prediction, assuming that a plus and a minus speed up or slow down reaction time by the same degree relative to 0 and that two pluses and two minuses have twice the effect as a single plus or minus. What is the relationship among the means and what coefficients would you use to reflect this relationship?

c. Test the hypothesis that $\psi_{fit} = 0$. What can you conclude from this test?

d. Test for any failure of the theory to predict differences in mean reaction time.

e. What additional tests are important in an evaluation of the theory?

5

Analysis of Trend

The procedures in Chapter 4 dealt with the detailed analysis of experiments with a qualitative independent variable. Most of those analyses compared two means, either group means or averages of group means. The analyses summarized in Table 4.5 (p. 79) of the McGovern experiment (the effect of five different interfering tasks on three components of memory) showed how a multilevel study is treated as a set of two-group experiments. However, when a *quantitative* independent variable is manipulated, we typically use another approach, known as **trend analysis**.

The treatment levels of a quantitative independent variable represent different amounts of a single common variable, and are ordered or spaced along a single dimension. Examples of quantitative independent variables are the number of hours of food deprivation, different dosage levels of a particular drug, rates of stimulus presentation, and the intensity of the unconditioned stimulus in a conditioning experiment. In analyzing this sort of experiment, we are less interested in comparing one treatment mean with another than in plotting the entire set of treatment means on a graph and looking at the overall *shape* or *trend*. We are usually interested in the functional relationship between the levels of the independent variable and the mean scores on the dependent variable. We pay attention to the entire set of means at once, not to pairs of groups.

Two related, but different, purposes are served by a trend analysis. The most common is *descriptive*: Following a significant omnibus F test, a researcher attempts to find the simplest mathematical way to describe the relationship between the independent variable X and the dependent variable Y. Generally, a researcher will start the analysis by determining whether the simplest function—a linear, or straight-line, function—is present, and following that assessment by looking at more complex mathematical functions. The second purpose is *theoretical*: to test as planned comparisons theoretical predictions concerning the underlying nature of the relationship between X and Y. We will give illustrations of both research strategies.

5.1 Analysis of Linear Trend

We will introduce trend analysis with a numerical example that shows how we apply the contrast-testing procedure from Chapter 4 to investigate trend. We will then consider in more detail how to conduct the analysis and the different ways to use it in research.

A Numerical Example

Consider an experiment designed to test the proposition that subjects learn better when training is distributed or spaced over a period of time than when the training is massed all at once. We could investigate this question with just two groups, one group that receives massed training and another that receives training at spaced intervals. However, this study would allow only a restricted glimpse of the phenomenon. We could say nothing about spacing longer or shorter than that used. Instead we could conduct a more comprehensive study that included conditions with several different spacings. It would provide information about the *form* of the relationship between learning and the degree of distributed training, giving a much clearer picture of the spacing phenomenon.

The subject's task is to track a spot moving in a random path around a computer screen, using a control stick to position a circle over it. Each subject has 10 one-minute practice trials learning how to track the spot. The independent variable is the time between practice trials: For one group the trials immediately follow another (0 seconds spacing—the massed condition); for a second group there is a 20-second pause between trials, for a third group there is a 40-second pause; and for the fourth group there is a 60-second pause. Twenty minutes after the last practice trial, each subject is given a single 30-second test trial, and the dependent variable is the number of seconds that the subject is able to keep on the target. Suppose $n = 5$ subjects are randomly assigned to each of the four groups. The scores, with some summary statistics, are given in the top part of Table 5.1, and the means are plotted in Figure 5.1. Although there is a general tendency for the tracking scores to increase with the spacing, this is true only up to a point (40 seconds), after which they drop. A trend analysis investigates these observations in a systematic fashion.

Typically, we would start by conducting a standard analysis of variance to see whether the variation among the treatment means is significant. This analysis is summarized in the lower parts of the table, and the overall $F = 11.07$ is significant. Having found that there are differences to explain, we turn to the trend analysis.

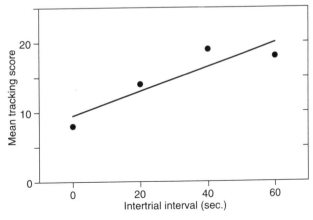

Figure 5.1: Tracking as a function of intertrial interval.

Table 5.1: *Tracking in four groups with different intertrial intervals:* **Overall** *analysis.*

Data and summary statistics

	Intertrial interval (A)			
	0 sec.	20 sec.	40 sec.	60 sec.
	a_1	a_2	a_3	a_4
	4	18	24	16
	6	13	19	17
	10	15	21	13
	9	11	16	23
	11	13	15	21
Sum (A_j)	40	70	95	90
n	5	5	5	5
Mean ($\bar{Y}_j$)	8.00	14.00	19.00	18.00
$\sum Y_{ij}^2$	354	1,008	1,859	1,684
s_j	2.915	2.646	3.674	4.000

Bracket terms

$$[Y] = \sum Y_{ij}^2 = 354 + 1{,}008 + 1{,}859 + 1{,}684 = 4{,}905$$

$$[A] = \frac{\sum A_j^2}{n} = \frac{40^2 + 70^2 + 95^2 + 90^2}{5} = 4{,}725.000$$

$$[T] = \frac{T^2}{an} = \frac{(40 + 70 + 95 + 90)^2}{(4)(5)} = 4{,}351.250$$

Summary of the analysis of variance

Source	SS	df	MS	F
A	$[A] - [T] = 373.750$	3	124.583	11.07*
S/A	$[Y] - [A] = 180.000$	16	11.250	
Total	$[Y] - [T] = 553.750$	19		

* $p < .05$

Testing for Linear Trend

The analysis usually begins with the simplest mathematical way to describe a set of numerical data: a straight line. In addition to plotting the four means in Figure 5.1, we have drawn a straight line through them. This particular line is the best fit to these data, in the sense that it minimizes the discrepancies between the value of $\bar{Y}_j$ at each level and the corresponding value on the line.[1] The straight line is known as a **linear function**, because it rises or drops at the same rate along the extent of the

---

[1] More technically, the line was found by minimizing the sum of squared deviations between the treatment means $\bar{Y}_j$ and corresponding points on the line. We will discuss this **least squares criterion** in Chapter 15. We will show how to find this line later in this section.

independent variable. The data plotted in Figure 5.1 are moderately well described by a linear function. However, the linear function does not fit the data perfectly. We will consider this observation after we complete our discussion of linear trend.

Calculating the Linear Trend Coefficients. The test for linear trend is an application of the tests of single-df comparisons in the last chapter. More specifically, we start with a set of coefficients, which in this case reflects linear trend; next, we determine the degree to which these coefficients describe the relationship among the means in our experiment; and finally, we test the significance of this relationship. What coefficients should we use? Because a linear trend implies a difference between the two end points, we could simply assess their difference, using the coefficients $\{-1, 0, 0, 1\}$. Alternatively, we could use sets that concentrate on other differences that are also implied by the presence of linear trend—for example, $\{-1, -1, 1, 1\}$ or $\{0, -1, 1, 0\}$. In each case, we would expect to find a significant contrast if linear trend is present.

A better way of assessing linear trend is to use a set of coefficients that mimics a straight line. We can do this by creating a set of customized coefficients, using the steps we explained on pages 80–81. We start with a set of temporary coefficients (X_j) that reflect a linear function—for example, the group numbers $\{1, 2, 3, 4\}$ or the actual values for the independent variable $\{0, 20, 40, 60\}$. We will use the latter set. These temporary coefficients are not satisfactory because they do not satisfy the criterion that contrast coefficients must sum to zero (Equation 4.3), that is, $\sum X_j = 0 + 20 + 40 + 60 = 120$. We correct this problem by subtracting from each value of X_j the mean of the entire set of values, $\bar{X} = {}^{120}\!/_4 = 30$. The result is a set of valid coefficients that do sum to zero. We will refer to the deviations of the values of X_j from their mean by x_j. For the four conditions, we obtain the values

$$x_1 = X_1 - \bar{X} = 0 - 30 = -30,$$

$$x_2 = X_2 - \bar{X} = 20 - 30 = -10,$$

$$x_3 = X_3 - \bar{X} = 40 - 30 = +10,$$

$$x_4 = X_4 - \bar{X} = 60 - 30 = +30.$$

Because these deviations sum to zero, they are acceptable as contrast coefficients. To reduce this set of coefficients to a set of smaller integers that are easier to use, we divide each coefficient by 10, obtaining the set $\{-3, -1, 1, 3\}$. We will use these for the linear trend coefficients.[2] If you plot either set of coefficients on a graph (the four conditions on the X axis and the values of the coefficients on the Y axis), you will see that the values of the coefficients form a straight line.

At this point, we need to say a word on notation. We use x_j for the deviations of the X_j from their mean $\bar{X}$. Although we could use these values as the coefficients in a trend analysis, we prefer to reduce them to more convenient numbers and call those c_j. Either set gives the same sum of squares. When the coefficients have been reduced to the smallest integers, we will designate them by c_{1i}, where the 1 means that they are the coefficient of *linear* trend. We will consider the coefficients for higher-order trend

---

[2]Do not confuse the different uses of the word *linear* in this discussion. One is the definition of ψ as the sum or *linear combination* of the group means weighted by coefficients. The other refers to a specific mathematical function—a *linear function*—for which the group means $\bar{Y}_j$ are related to the values of X_j by a straight line.

components shortly. You won't want to go through these calculations each time you decide to investigate linear trend. The set of linear trend coefficients we constructed above, along with those for other numbers of treatments, is given in Appendix A.3.

Before leaving the linear trend coefficients, we want to call your attention to two points. First, as a way of assessing the rise or fall of a set of means, the linear trend contrast is preferable to contrasts based on pairwise comparisons such as those given by the sets $\{-1, 0, 0, 1\}$ or $\{0, -1, 1, 0\}$. They are more sensitive to the presence of linear trend because they give progressively more weight to the treatment conditions located farther away from the center of the independent variable. The other sets of coefficients only incidentally represent the full extent of the linear trend. Second, the coefficients in Appendix A.3 are appropriate only when there are equal intervals between successive levels of the independent variable. They are appropriate for our example because the levels 0, 20, 40, and 60 are equally spaced (20 seconds between each level), but would not be usable if the levels were 0, 15, 30, and 60 or 0, 10, 45, and 60, because the spacing is uneven. Under these circumstances, you would need to construct your own coefficients using the actual values for the independent variable, as we have illustrated.[3]

Completing the Analysis.   We can now return to the numerical example. From here on, the analysis duplicates the analysis of single-df comparisons considered in the last chapter. We use the linear trend coefficients in conjunction with the general formula for single-df comparisons (Equation 4.5) and calculate a sum of squares that reflects the degree to which the variation among the treatment means follows the straight line. The first step is to calculate $\widehat{\psi}$ using the observed treatment means and the linear trend coefficients c_{1j}:

$$\widehat{\psi}_{\text{linear}} = \sum c_{1j}\bar{Y}_j$$
$$= (-3)(8.00) + (-1)(14.00) + (1)(19.00) + (3)(18.00) = 35.00.$$

We next substitute the relevant values into Equation 4.5 (p. 69):

$$SS_{\text{linear}} = \frac{n\widehat{\psi}_{\text{linear}}^2}{\sum c_{1j}^2} = \frac{(5)(35.00)^2}{(-3)^2 + (-1)^2 + 1^2 + 3^2} = 306.25.$$

Finally, we test the significance of this comparison with an F statistic:

$$F = \frac{MS_{\text{linear}}}{MS_{S/A}} = \frac{306.25}{11.25} = 27.22.$$

The F has $df_{\text{num}} = 1$ and $df_{\text{denom}} = 16$. It is significant ($F_{.05} = 4.49$).

The test just conducted is not sensitive to whether the points go up or down, only to the amount of linear trend. If the means had been 18, 19, 14, and 8, instead of the other way around, we would have obtained $\widehat{\psi}_{\text{linear}} = (-3)(18) + (-1)(19) + (1)(14) + (3)(8) = -35.00$ instead of 35.00. When both $\widehat{\psi}_{\text{linear}}$ and the coefficients are squared in Equation 4.5, we obtain exactly the same $SS_{\text{linear}} = 306.25$. You can also verify that changing the sign of the coefficients makes no difference, so that you obtain the same sum of squares with the coefficient $\{3, 1, -1, -3\}$. To determine the direction, simply look at a plot of the means.

---

[3]Most statistical programs can properly analyze experiments with unequal intervals, but you will probably have to modify the default behavior of the program.

Plotting the Regression Line

What do we discover from this analysis? The significant F_{linear} indicates that the data exhibit an overall linear trend, that is, there is a tendency for learning to increase at a constant rate as the time between successive trials increases from 0 to 60 seconds. Given this outcome, most researchers would plot this linear relationship in a graph, as a visual summary of this finding, as we have done in Figure 5.1. The formula for this line is called a **linear regression equation**:

$$\bar{Y}'_j = b_0 + b_1 X_j. \tag{5.1}$$

Here $\bar{Y}'_j$ is the mean for level a_j as predicted by the trend analysis when X_j is a value of the independent variable. The two quantities b_0 and b_1 are known as the **intercept** and the **slope**, respectively. The intercept b_0 is the point at which the line crosses the ordinate of the graph, that is, the value of $\bar{Y}'$ when $X = 0$, and the slope the size of the change in $\bar{Y}'$ when X changes by one unit:

$$b_1 = \text{slope} = \frac{\text{change in } \bar{Y}'}{\text{change in } X}.$$

We will discuss the linear regression equation in more detail in Section 15.1. For the moment, we just need to calculate values for the intercept and slope. The calculation uses the deviations x_j, the group means $\bar{Y}_j$, and the overall means $\bar{X}$ and $\bar{Y}_T$:

$$b_1 = \frac{\sum x_j \bar{Y}_j}{\sum x_j^2}, \tag{5.2}$$

$$b_0 = \bar{Y}_T - b_1 \bar{X}. \tag{5.3}$$

From our calculations on page 91, the deviations x_j are -30, -10, 10, and 30. Substituting these values and the means from Table 5.1 in Equations 5.2 and 5.3 gives us the slope and intercept:

$$b_1 = \frac{(-30)(8.00) + (-10)(14.00) + (10)(19.00) + (30)(18.00)}{(-30)^2 + (-10)^2 + 10^2 + 30^2}$$

$$= \frac{350}{2,000} = 0.175,$$

$$b_0 = 14.75 - (0.175)(30) = 14.75 - 5.25 = 9.50.$$

The linear regression equation, written in terms of the independent variable X_j—the intertrial interval, expressed in seconds—is

$$\bar{Y}'_j = 9.50 + 0.175 X_j.$$

We can use this equation to obtain predicted values for the four points in the experiment. Substituting the four values of X_j, we get

$$\bar{Y}'_1 = 9.50 + (0.175)(0) = 9.50 + 0.00 = 9.50,$$

$$\bar{Y}'_2 = 9.50 + (0.175)(20) = 9.50 + 3.50 = 13.00,$$

$$\bar{Y}'_3 = 9.50 + (0.175)(40) = 9.50 + 7.00 = 16.50,$$

$$\bar{Y}'_4 = 9.50 + (0.175)(60) = 9.50 + 10.50 = 20.00.$$

In a design like this, where intermediate values of X_j, such as 15 seconds, could have been included, it is helpful to draw the regression line on our graph. To draw this line, we need only connect two of our predicted points. Usually the points from the most extreme groups are good choices [here (0, 9.50) and (60, 20.00)], but another handy choice is the intercept $(0, b_0)$ and the means $(\bar{X}, \bar{Y}_T)$ [here (0, 9.50) and (30, 14.75)]. As a check, you should plot one of the intermediate points to be sure the line passes through it. Many researchers draw the regression line even when intermediate values have no meaning. They simply want to display the linear relationship on a graph, to show how well the straight line describes the data.

Evaluating the Linear Fit

Having detected a significant linear trend, we need to determine if this linear function provides a complete summary of the relationship between X and Y or if a more complicated mathematical function is needed. We raised a similar question in Section 4.6 (see pp. 81–83), where a test of a theoretical pattern of the treatment means was followed by an assessment of the variation missed by that ordering (F_{fit} and F_{failure}, respectively). We use the same approach here. The linear function corresponds to the fitted model, and the extent to which it fails is obtained by subtracting its sum of squares from that of the overall effect (Equations 4.16 and 4.17):

$$SS_{\text{failure}} = SS_A - SS_{\text{linear}} \quad \text{with} \quad df_{\text{failure}} = df_A - df_{\text{linear}}.$$

The analysis is completed with the usual F test:

$$MS_{\text{failure}} = \frac{SS_{\text{failure}}}{df_{\text{failure}}} \quad \text{and} \quad F_{\text{failure}} = \frac{MS_{\text{failure}}}{MS_{S/A}}.$$

How does our numerical example fare? Applying the equations above, we find

$$SS_{\text{failure}} = 373.75 - 306.25 = 67.50,$$

$$df_{\text{failure}} = 3 - 1 = 2,$$

$$MS_{\text{failure}} = \frac{67.50}{2} = 33.75,$$

$$F_{\text{failure}} = \frac{33.75}{11.25} = 3.00.$$

With $df_{\text{num}} = 2$ and $df_{\text{denom}} = 16$, this result is not significant ($F_{.05} = 3.63$).

In addition to a test of this remaining, or residual variation, it is often revealing to examine this information in a graph. To do this, we simply calculate the discrepancy between the actual group means and the group means specified by the regression equation, that is, $\bar{Y}_j - \bar{Y}_j'$, and plot them in the graph. Using the values that we calculated previously, the differences are

$$\bar{Y}_1 - \bar{Y}_1' = 8.00 - 9.50 = -1.50,$$

$$\bar{Y}_2 - \bar{Y}_2' = 14.00 - 13.00 = 1.00,$$

$$\bar{Y}_3 - \bar{Y}_3' = 19.00 - 16.50 = 2.50,$$

$$\bar{Y}_4 - \bar{Y}_4' = 18.00 - 20.00 = -2.00.$$

These residual values are plotted in Figure 5.2. They appear to have a simple pattern—a curve that first rises, then falls. Although the test of SS_{failure} suggested that these deviations do not vary more than could be accounted for by accidental variation, many researchers would want to test for the possibility of curvature, regardless of the outcome of the F_{failure} test. We will investigate this possibility next.

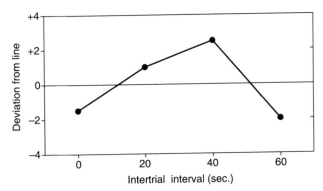

Figure 5.2: Differences in learning between the group means ($\overline{Y}_j$) and the group means associated with the linear regression equation ($\overline{Y}'_j$).

5.2 Analysis of Quadratic Trend

Research in the behavioral sciences focuses on a test for linear trends for good reasons: Linear trend is easier to interpret than complex relationships and it occurs frequently in nature. This does not mean that complex trends are not of interest to researchers, however, as we will illustrate in Section 5.4. Although the test for residual variation that we just described suggested that an exploration for higher-order trends might be fruitless—the F_{failure} was not significant—most researchers would continue the analysis to determine whether the underlying relationship between the independent and dependent variables has any curve in it.[4] We have already noted the apparent reversal of the learning scores between 40 and 60 seconds, which might be important to verify. The plot of the residuals in Figure 5.2 also suggested a possible reversal of trend, with a systematic rising and falling with increases in the intertrial interval.

A function that is not straight is necessarily curved. In its simplest form, it will either be curved so that the opening of the curve is upward or, like Figure 5.2, so that the opening is downward. Such functions are said to be **concave up** or **concave down**, respectively—a shape like Figure 5.2 is also described as having an **inverted U** shape. A nonlinear function that shows this type of curvature is the **quadratic function** (some other functions are considered on p. 107). It has a single concavity or bend. The equation for a quadratic function is

$$Y = b_0 + b_1X + b_2X^2. \tag{5.4}$$

Because we have already looked at the linear part of this function (b_1), the focus of our analysis here is on the significance of the quadratic coefficient, b_2. If this coefficient is zero, the third term vanishes, leaving the linear function, $Y = b_0 + b_1X$, as the mathematical function relating X and Y. There is no quadratic trend. On the other hand, if b_2 has some value other than zero, the term remains and we have a quadratic function. Returning to our numerical example, we have already determined that the linear component is significant. The question now is whether a quadratic term (b_2X^2)

---

[4]To anticipate our discussion in Chapter 6, we would generally suggest that a test for linear trend and a test for curvature are important enough to treat them as planned comparisons.

is needed in the equation to describe the outcome more adequately. This question is answered by assessing the significance of the quadratic component independently of the linear component.

The heart of the analysis is a set of specialized coefficients for quadratic trend that is sensitive to the presence of curvature, but not influenced by linear trend. The quadratic coefficients are constructed to be *orthogonal* to the coefficients for linear trend. For experiments with between $a = 3$ and $a = 10$ groups, Appendix A.3 gives sets of such of coefficients. They are constructed so that each one is orthogonal to the others, hence they are known as **coefficients of orthogonal polynomials**. To use Appendix A.3, we find the set appropriate for our experiment ($a = 4$) and read out the relevant coefficients, namely c_{2j}: $\{1, -1, -1, 1\}$. We can check that they are orthogonal to the linear trend coefficients we used in Section 5.1 (which were c_{1j}: $\{-3, -1, 1, 3\}$) by calculating

$$\sum(c_{1j})(c_{2j}) = (-3)(1) + (-1)(-1) + (1)(-1) + (3)(1) = -3 + 1 - 1 + 3 = 0.$$

Both sets of trend components reflect their respective mathematical properties in idealized form. The linear trend coefficients exhibit a perfect linear trend, a steady rise of two units from -3 through 3, and the quadratic trend coefficients exhibit a perfect quadratic trend, a falling of two units downward and a rising of two units upward. It does not matter that the coefficients reflect a trend opposite to that exhibited by the data because, as we have seen in the last section, the sum of squares does not depend on the sign of ψ.

As with the analysis of linear trend, the sets of trend coefficients in Appendix A.3 are based on equal spacing of the levels of the independent variable. If you have unequal intervals, you must construct sets of orthogonal trend coefficients that are appropriate for the particular spacings of the levels represented in your experiment. We will discuss this matter briefly on pages 105–106.

Testing for Quadratic Trend

The procedure for testing the quadratic trend is identical to that for linear trend. We start with the quadratic coefficients $\{1, -1, -1, 1\}$ from Appendix A.3. Next, we estimate the contrast using Equation 4.4:

$$\widehat{\psi}_{\text{quadratic}} = \sum c_{2j}\overline{Y}_j$$
$$= (1)(8.00) + (-1)(14.00) + (-1)(19.00) + (1)(18.00) = -7.00.$$

We then use Equation 4.5 to find the sum of squares:

$$SS_{\text{quadratic}} = \frac{n\widehat{\psi}^2_{\text{quadratic}}}{\sum c^2_{2j}} = \frac{(5)(-7.00)^2}{(1)^2 + (-1)^2 + (-1)^2 + (1)^2} = 61.25.$$

Finally, we test the significance of this comparison by forming an F ratio:

$$F = \frac{MS_{\text{quadratic}}}{MS_{S/A}} = \frac{61.25}{11.25} = 5.44.$$

With a critical value of $F(1,16) = 4.49$ at $\alpha = 05$, we conclude that in addition to an upward rise (the linear component), the function also displays a downward concavity.

At this point, you may be wondering why the $F_{\text{quadratic}}$ is significant even though the F_{failure} we evaluated following the discovery of a significant F_{linear} in Section

5.1 was not. An explanation of this apparent conflict is that the residual variation evaluated by F_{failure} is an average of all remaining orthogonal trend components. In this case, the significant quadratic trend component was masked by averaging it with the remaining nonsignificant variation. We will return to this matter in Section 5.3.

Evaluating the Quadratic Fit

If we are attempting to find the simplest function that describes our data, we would want to know now whether there is any significant residual variation remaining beyond the linear and quadratic components. We use the same strategy that we used for the linear trend (p. 94). To find F_{failure} here, we subtract both linear and quadratic effects from SS_A,

$$SS_{\text{failure}} = SS_A - SS_{\text{linear}} - SS_{\text{quadratic}} = 373.75 - 306.25 - 61.25 = 6.25,$$

and from the degrees of freedom,

$$df_{\text{failure}} = df_A - df_{\text{linear}} - df_{\text{quadratic}} = 3 - 1 - 1 = 1.$$

We can now calculate

$$F_{\text{failure}} = \frac{MS_{\text{failure}}}{MS_{S/A}} = \frac{6.25}{11.25} = 0.56.$$

Clearly, no trend components beyond the quadratic are present. We conclude that the relationship between tracking performance (Y) and intertrial interval (X) is quadratic in form, with a significant linear component.

Plotting the Quadratic Equation

Because we have found the quadratic component to be significant, we know that the function is more complicated than the linear regression equation that we calculated above (Equation 5.1). The function that we should plot is quadratic:

$$\overline{Y}_j' = b_0 + b_1 X_j + b_2 X_j^2. \tag{5.5}$$

To use this equation, we must determine values for the coefficients b_0, b_1, and b_2.

Calculating the values of the quadratic regression coefficients by hand is a tedious and error-prone process. We suggest instead that you use one of the many multiple regression programs available for small computers. The idea is the following: For each group determine the values for the three variables X_j, X_j^2, and $\overline{Y}_j$. Now enter these numbers as data and use the program to regress $\overline{Y}_j$ onto X_j and X_j^2. The output is the correct regression equation.[5] For our example, the numbers that go into the program are

	X_j	X_j^2	$\overline{Y}_j$
a_1	0	0	8.00
a_2	20	400	14.00
a_3	40	1,600	19.00
a_4	60	3,600	18.00

---

[5]The same answer is obtained from an analysis of the individual scores Y_{ij} when the sizes of the groups are equal, but not when they are unequal—we discuss the difference in Section 14.3. The function found from the means is more appropriate for experimental designs. If you need to do the calculations by hand, you can look up the formulas for two-predictor regression and apply them to these values and obtain the same answer.

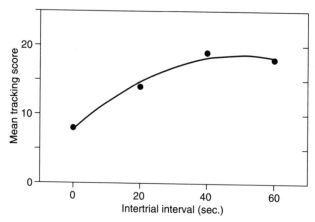

Figure 5.3: The quadratic regression function $\overline{Y}'_j = 7.750 + 0.437X_j - 0.004375X_j^2$ **fitted to the data from Table 5.1.**

The result is the equation

$$\overline{Y}'_j = 7.750 + 0.437X_j - 0.004375X_j^2. \tag{5.6}$$

It is plotted in Figure 5.3. As you can see, its value at the tested levels of X closely match the actual treatment means. We can calculate these values exactly from the regression equation. For example, the predicted mean at the second experimental point ($X = 20$) is

$$\overline{Y}'_{X=20} = 7.750 + (0.437)(20) - (0.004375)(20^2) = 14.740.$$

The equation also provides estimates of the tracking performance for intertrial intervals other than those that were actually tested; for example, the value at the nonexperimental point $X = 10$ is

$$\overline{Y}'_{X=10} = 7.750 + (0.437)(10) - (0.004375)(10^2) = 11.683.$$

You will note that we have drawn the line only for points within the range of X values actually tested. We can be fairly sure that the function applies to this range, but not so sure outside of it. Values of X less than 0 are, of course, meaningless for the design under consideration, and extrapolation to ranges above 60 seconds is risky. The fitted function is starting to turn downward at the right end, but we have no assurance that it will continue to do so at longer intervals.

5.3 Higher-Order Trend Components

The linear function $Y = b_0 + b_1 X$ and the quadratic function $Y = b_0 + b_1 X + b_2 X^2$ are the ones most commonly encountered in research. We characterized the first component as capturing the tendency for the function to rise or fall over the range of X and the second component as capturing the tendency for the function to be curved. After testing these components, many researchers stop. They are using trend analysis as a descriptive device, and these tests answer their questions. The two tests are commonly treated as planned comparisons (which we will discuss in Section 6.2) that are routinely examined when a quantitative independent variable is involved. Their use does not depend on either the significance of the omnibus F test nor on the test of failure to fit following the test for linear trend.

The quadratic function implied by the tests for linear and quadratic trend does not exhaust the patterns that are possible from a set of four or more means. When F_{failure} is significant after including the quadratic term, we know something more is going on. What to do about it is less clear. The conventional approach is to stick with polynomial equations. After the quadratic comes the **cubic function**,

$$Y = b_0 + b_1 X + b_2 X^2 + b_3 X^3, \tag{5.7}$$

and following that is the **quartic function**,

$$Y = b_0 + b_1 X + b_2 X^2 + b_3 X^3 + b_4 X^4, \tag{5.8}$$

and so on. These functions allow more complicated shapes than the linear or quadratic function. The cubic function can rise, level out (or even reverse), then rise again. Each of these equations has a corresponding trend contrast that determines whether a power of X of that order is needed. For example, if you found that a test of the cubic trend contrast gave a significant result, you would know that fitting the data required a polynomial of at least the complexity of Equation 5.7—i.e. one that included a term involving X^3. You will find that these trend contrasts are tested by several of the computer packages.

We should point out, however, that the higher trend components are frequently less useful to the behavioral researcher than are the linear and quadratic components. Many behavioral studies do not have a theoretical basis strong enough to support questions any more complex than those tested by the linear and quadratic trends— that is, slope and curvature (we will see an exception in Figure 5.6). Once those components have been tested, tests of the other components give little further information. Compounding this is the fact that the form implied by any of the polynomial equations is very specific. The quadratic equation in Equation 5.4 has a particular curved form—a parabola—and there are many other curved functions that don't exactly agree with it. Even though these functions may be equivalent from a researcher's point of view, they can give different results from a trend analysis. One function will require a cubic equation, and another will not. A set of data that curves, then levels out, is a common example of this problem. Suppose we had continued the spacing experiment with conditions at 80 and 100 seconds, and the tracking scores remained at about 18 seconds. The hypothesis of curvature is still important, but a quadratic function like Equation 5.4 could be rejected in favor of some higher function, such as a cubic or quartic. The particular values of the trend coefficients would tell us little in themselves, however. For these reasons, we suggest that you not be too quick to turn to these higher components. If your *questions* only concern slope and curvature, then stop with the quadratic.

Testing for Higher-Order Trends

That being said, how should you investigate these complex trend components? Mathematically, the only restriction to the number of possible orthogonal trend components is the number of treatment conditions. When $a = 2$, only a linear trend can be tested; when $a = 3$, linear and quadratic trends are testable; when $a = 4$ linear, quadratic, and cubic trends; and when $a = 5$, linear, quadratic, cubic, and quartic trends. We stated the equivalent restriction in Section 4.5, when we pointed out that the maximum number of mutually orthogonal comparisons is one less than the number of treatment conditions; that is, to $df_A = a - 1$.

Because the trend contrasts are mutually orthogonal, each can be tested without interfering with each other. However, it is better to concentrate on the simpler components and resort to the complex ones only if necessary. One approach is to work upwards from the simple regression equations to the more complex higher ones. Start by testing the linear and quadratic components. Then look at the unexplained variability by calculating and testing $SS_{failure} = SS_A - SS_{linear} - SS_{quadratic}$, as described on page 97. If this test is significant, it implies that you need at least a cubic function (Equation 5.7) to describe your data. So you calculate and test the cubic trend component. Regardless of whether that test is significant, you conduct another test of the unexplained variablity, this time subtracting the linear, quadratic, and cubic sums of squares from SS_A. If this test is significant, you need to go on to the quartic function (Equation 5.8). You continue this process until no more variation is available to be fitted, either because $F_{failure}$ is small or because you have extracted $a - 1$ components.

The actual calculations follow the steps we outlined for the analysis of the linear and quadratic components—all that changes is the set of coefficients. Appendix A.3 gives sets of coefficients for components ranging in complexity from linear to quartic for experiments in which the number of equally spaced treatment conditions ranges from 3 to 10. More extensive listings can be found in books of statistical tables, such as Beyer (1968), Fisher and Yates (1953), and Pearson and Hartley (1970).

We will illustrate the test for cubic trend with our numerical example, even though a test for fit indicates that it was not necessary. We first need the cubic coefficients c_{3j}, which we determine from Appendix A.3 to be $\{-1, 3, -3, 1\}$. Substituting in Equations 4.4 and 4.5, we find

$$\widehat{\psi}_{cubic} = (-1)(8.00) + (3)(14.00) + (-3)(19.00) + (1)(18.00) = -5.00,$$

$$SS_{cubic} = \frac{(5)(-5.00)^2}{(-1)^2 + 3^2 + (-3)^2 + 1^2} = 6.25.$$

The statistic $F_{cubic} = 6.25/11.25 = 0.56$ is not significant. Because $a = 4$, we can only extract three trend components—linear, quadratic, and cubic. We have already calculated sums of squares for the first two, finding $SS_{linear} = 306.25$ and $SS_{quadratic} = 61.25$. Together, we have fully accounted for the variability among the group means, and there is no residual variability to detect. We can see this by showing that the sums of squares combine to equal SS_A:

$$SS_{linear} + SS_{quadratic} + SS_{cubic} = 306.25 + 61.25 + 6.25 = 373.75 = SS_A.$$

5.4 Theoretical Prediction of Trend Components

The most satisfying use of trend analysis is one that is theoretically motivated. We will consider a few examples in this section. The first is the research by Sternberg on the amount of time subjects require to search through a memorized list to see whether or not it contains a particular item (e.g., Sternberg, 1966). Sternberg's theory was simple: The time it takes to correctly identify an item as part of the memorized list

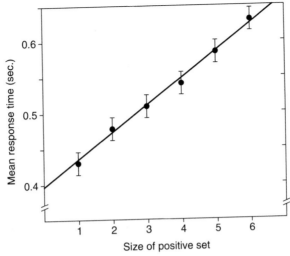

Figure 5.4: Response time as a function of the number of items in a memorized list. Redrawn with permission from S. Sternberg, High-speed scanning in human memory, Science, 1966, 153, 652–654. Copyright 1966 by AAAS.

should be directly related to the length of the list—a linear function. His findings, which have been replicated numerous times, are illustrated in Figure 5.4. There is an unequivocal straight-line relationship between the time to respond and the number of items in the memorized list, and nothing else.

Another example of the theoretical prediction of trend is the classic study of stimulus generalization reported by Grant (1956). He classically conditioned a physiological response (change in skin resistance) to a training stimulus, a 12-inch circle. Once the response was conditioned, subjects were randomly assigned to $a = 7$ different groups, each of which was tested with a different generalization stimulus. One group was tested with the original circle (12 inches), three were tested with smaller circles (diameters of 9, 10, and 11 inches) and three were tested with larger circles (diameters of 13, 14, and 15 inches). For theoretical reasons, Grant expected to find both linear and quadratic components relating the independent variable (size of the testing stimulus) to the dependent variable (the response to the test stimulus). He predicted that subjects would tend to respond more vigorously as the size of the testing circle increased (the linear component). His main interest, however, was in stimulus generalization. He predicted that the response would be greatest for subjects for whom the testing stimulus was the training stimulus itself (the 12-inch circle) and would taper off for subjects tested with circles increasingly different in size (the quadratic component). Figure 5.5 shows his results. Statistical analysis (see Problem 5.1) revealed that only the quadratic trend component was significant. We have drawn the best-fitting linear and quadratic functions on the plot. As you can see, the trend analysis supported the predictions of stimulus generalization that motivated the study.

Our final example is a study reported by Hayes-Roth (1977). Subjects learned a set of propositions of the form "Alice bought the cat before Jane sold the painting" (actually, nonsense syllables were used instead of nouns). After correctly responding

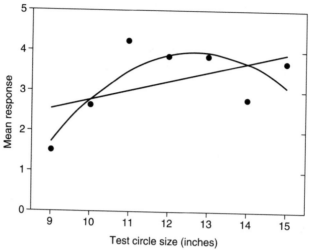

Figure 5.5: *Response to a test circle of various sizes after training with a 12-inch circle (after Grant, 1956). The best fitting linear and quadratic function are shown.*

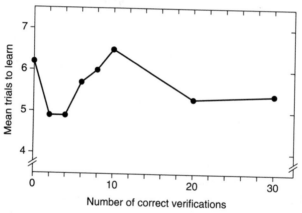

Figure 5.6: *A complex function requiring higher-order trend components. From B. Hayes-Roth, Evolution of cognitive structures and processes, Psychological Review, 1977, 84, 260–270. Copyright 1977 by the American Psychological Association. Adapted by permission.*

to the propositions a predetermined number of times (0, 2, 4, 6, 8, 10, 20, or 30 times), they were given a new, but related, set of propositions to master. Hayes-Roth proposed a theory that predicted a complex relationship between the trials to learn the new set of propositions (the dependent variable) and the number of correct responses given to the first set (the independent variable). She predicted two changes in direction in the function, a characteristics that requires at least a cubic equation. A trend analysis of her results (plotted in Figure 5.6) showed that a function more complex than quadratic was necessary.

Each of these examples demonstrates a different aspect of trend analysis. For both Sternberg and Grant, the linear and quadratic tests were planned comparisons, but they served different purposes. Sternberg's theory predicted only a linear function, with the quadratic test serving as a test of deviations from the theory. For Grant, the test of the quadratic component was his central prediction. The Hayes-Roth study tested the complex trend component predicted by her theory. In her study, the linear and quadratic components formed the baseline against which she found additional components.

5.5 Planning a Trend Analysis

The specific levels chosen to represent a quantitative independent variable have a large influence on the effectiveness of the study. In this section, we consider some factors that determine how they are chosen.

Spacing the Intervals

Suppose we conduct an experiment in which we include five points on some stimulus dimension. We probably would include two groups at the extremes of the dimension, because they give the widest span for the effect of the independent variable to manifest itself. But how should we locate the other three groups? Our first reaction might be to space them equally between the two extremes. Equal intervals are the best choice when we have no particular idea of the shape of the function or when we expect the effects to appear throughout the range. Both the Sternberg and Grant experiments (Figures 5.4 and 5.5) are examples.

In contrast, when we expect important changes to occur in one part of the function, we should choose the conditions to provide detailed information about the area of greatest importance and less detailed information about areas where less change is expected. Hayes-Roth's study (Figure 5.6) illustrates the point. She expected much of the effect of the independent variable would occur between 0 and 10 correct verifications and that changes would be less dramatic further out. Quite sensibly, she clustered more groups in the lower range than the higher.

Let's consider another example in which the theory being investigated dictated the spacing of the groups. The researcher here (Elliott, 1976) was interested in how the annual variation in the amount of daylight affects the reproductive activity of certain animals. He exposed different groups of male golden hamsters to various light-dark cycles, ranging from total darkness (0 hours of light) to total lightness (24 hours of light), for several months. At the end of the time, the hamsters' testes were weighed. Theoretical considerations suggested that periods of about 12 hours should be of considerable importance, so Elliott used an uneven spacing of the independent variable (hours of light), with more values close to this duration. Figure 5.7 shows his results. As you can see, there was little or no change in the average weight between 0 and nearly 12 hours of light, then an abrupt increase, followed by little or no change between 12 and 24 hours. What Elliott did was to concentrate his efforts on collecting data in and around the values where he expected a dramatic change in average weight to occur. He needed only a few other conditions away from that point to establish the stability of the weight in those ranges.

Beyond demonstrating the use of unequal intervals, Elliott's study makes the point that trend analysis is not always the best way to analyze an experiment with a quantitative independent variable. The underlying relationship between his independent and dependent variables is not reasonably described as polynomial. A more illuminating

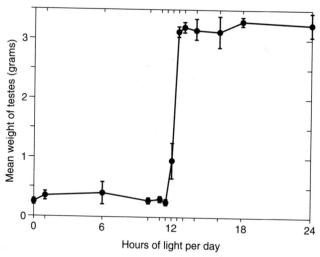

Figure 5.7: Mean weight of the testes of golden hamsters as a function of the number of hours of light per 24 hour period. A trend analysis is uninformative here, and the points have simply been connected. Adapted from Figure 7 in Elliott, 1976, Federation Proceedings, 35. Reproduced with permission of Federation of American Societies for Experimental Biology, permission conveyed through Copyright Clearance Center, Inc.

approach would be to evaluate the outcome with a set of tests that collectively evaluate the different aspects of the theory underlying the research. Suppose his study included $a = 9$ treatment conditions:

- Conditions a_1 to a_3 are spaced between 0 and 11 hours of light (say, at 0, $5\frac{1}{2}$, and 11 hours).
- Conditions a_4 to a_6 are concentrated around the duration when most change is expected (say, at $11\frac{1}{2}$, 12, and $12\frac{1}{2}$ hours).
- Conditions a_7 to a_9 are spaced between 13 and 24 hours of light (say, at 13, $18\frac{1}{2}$, and 24 hours).

Elliott's theory suggested we should observe three major findings: (1) a low and relatively constant weight for the shorter periods of light (0–11 hours), (2) a rapid increase in weight for the next hour or so, and (3) a stability of this increased weight between 13 and 24 hours.

Each of these predictions can be evaluated by a different and orthogonal statistical test. The expectation of a constant weight for the shorter periods is assessed with an omnibus F testing the hypothesis

$$H_{01} : \mu_1 = \mu_2 = \mu_3.$$

This hypothesis can be tested by the procedure we described in Section 4.7. Similarly, the expectation of a constant weight for the longer periods can be assessed with an omnibus F testing the hypothesis

$$H_{02} : \mu_7 = \mu_8 = \mu_9.$$

For the theory to be supported, both of these null hypotheses need to be *retained*. A test of the prediction that the testes weigh less during the periods of relatively shorter periods of light than for the longer periods could be established by rejecting

$$H_{03}: \frac{\mu_1 + \mu_2 + \mu_3}{3} = \frac{\mu_7 + \mu_8 + \mu_9}{3}.$$

Finally, the rapid increase in weight between the short and long periods of light could be evaluated by an omnibus F test involving the relevant conditions,

$$H_{04}: \mu_4 = \mu_5 = \mu_6,$$

or, even better, by a test for linear trend also based on these conditions. At the expense of orthogonality, we might choose to include in this trend analysis the two conditions at the beginning and end of the expected rapid increase in weight, giving us five points, a_3 through a_7, spaced at half-hour intervals.

Trend Coefficients for Unequal Intervals

The trend coefficients in Appendix A.3 are derived for groups that are *equally spaced* on some continuum. In our numerical example, a difference of 20 seconds separated each successive level of the independent variable, creating the values of 0, 20, 40, and 60 seconds. Other examples of equally spaced intervals are exposure durations of 50, 250, and 450 milliseconds; noise levels of 20, 50, and 80 decibels; and drug dosages of 1, 2, and 3 grains. However, using the tabled coefficients when the intervals are *not equal* will distort the trend analysis.

Suppose, we conduct a memory experiment in which subjects are tested at different times after exposure to some learning material. One group is tested immediately after exposure (0 seconds), and other groups are tested 15 seconds, 30 seconds, 60 seconds, 3 minutes, or 5 minutes after exposure. Hypothetical results of this experiment are presented in the upper portion of Figure 5.8. As you can see, the amount remembered decreases rapidly at first (between 0 and 60 seconds) and levels off over the longer time delays (between 1 and 5 minutes)—this was why unequal intervals were used. But suppose we tested with the coefficients in Appendix A.3. Their use is tantamount to assuming that the spacing of the groups is even. We have replotted the data this way in the lower portion of Figure 5.8. You can clearly see that the forms of the two functions are different and that the second analysis would miss the curvature of the data. Of the two, the function of interest to the researcher is the one that preserves the actual spacing of the X_j values.

To analyze the data we cannot use the equal-interval coefficients in Appendix A.3, but must construct sets of trend coefficients appropriate for the actual spacing of the groups. It is relatively easy to derive the linear trend coefficients by matching the coefficients to the pattern we expect, following the procedure described on pages 80–81. Simply pick numbers that agree with the actual spacing, then adjust them to sum to zero. For the delays after exposure mentioned in the last paragraph, start with the actual sequence of times of 0, 15, 30, 60, 180, and 300. To keep the numbers small (it doesn't change the answer), express them in 15-second units, as 0, 1, 2, 4, 12, and 20. The average of these six numbers is $39/6 = 13/2$, and subtracting this value from each of them gives the coefficients for linear trend: $\{-13/2, -11/2, -9/2, -5/2, 11/2, 27/2\}$. We could multiply each coefficient by 2 to create integer values.

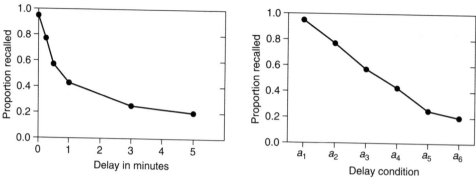

Figure 5.8: Upper graph: Intervals spaced according to actual time values. Lower graph: Intervals spaced evenly.

Finding quadratic coefficients is more difficult because of the need to make them orthogonal to the linear coefficients, and we do not have space to describe the procedures here. If you need these coefficients, you can consult one of the first two editions of this book (Keppel, 1973, 1982) or one of several other advanced texts (e.g., Kirk, 1995, Appendix D; Myers & Well, 1991, Appendix 7.2). Conveniently, many computer programs will accommodate unequal intervals, typically by using the General Linear Model testing procedures described in Chapter 14.

The Number of Intervals

When the object of an experiment is to study trend components, you should include a reasonable number of intervals—at least five—so the underlying relationship between the independent and dependent variables is finely traced. Consider the Hayes-Roth study in Figure 5.6. If she had reduced the number of levels between 0 and 10 correct responses (her independent variable), she would have lost the detailed curvature of the underlying relationship.

This example illustrates another reason to include enough intervals, namely, the detection of higher-order trend components. An experiment that includes relatively few treatment conditions can only detect lower-order trends. With three conditions, Hayes-Roth would not have been able to detect the complex function in Figure 5.6, because she would only have been able to measure the linear and quadratic components. Even when you expect to find only lower-order trends, you should include enough points to convince yourself (and others) that there are no higher-order components. When only linear trend is present in an experiment with five or more well-chosen conditions, you can be confident that the basic relationship is a straight line, as Sternberg's study illustrates (Figure 5.4).

In short, a researcher planning to study a quantitative independent variable should consider the goals of the study carefully. The choice of conditions depends upon the purpose of the study. Sometimes the only intent is to determine if the function rises (or falls) and whether it bends. The theory is simply not strong enough to interpret the higher-order components, so there is little point in testing them. Even if significant, they would not answer a useful question. For these studies fewer conditions are needed—perhaps four or five. On the other hand, when the detailed form of the function is important, a substantial experiment is required. It must both provide convincing evidence of any linear or quadratic trend and give a reasonable opportunity to detect higher-order trends should they be present.

Other Functional Forms

The approach we have described emphasizes fitting functions of polynomial form— straight lines, quadratics, cubics, and so forth. Although these functions are good choices when your questions concern such things as ascending or descending direction or the presence of curvature, they are not always appropriate. There are several reasons to be interested in other mathematical functions. Quantitative theories sometimes predict a form for the data that is not a polynomial. For example, certain types of relationships are better described by an *exponential function* such as $Y = ae^{bX}$ or a *logarithmic function* such as $Y = a + b \log X$. In particular, the polynomials cannot describe data that level off as X_j becomes large.

For example, consider the amount of material that is retained in a memory experiment such as that plotted in Figure 5.8. It drops off rapidly at first, then more slowly, and it can never be less than zero, no matter how long testing is delayed. But suppose we do a trend analysis and fit it with a quadratic equation. The parabolic form of the quadratic function is concave upwards—bowl shaped—and for very large values of delay, it would predict that recall should get better, quite unlike the real behavior. For such data, the polynomials make sense only if they are confined to a limited range. You can see this problem in Figure 5.3, where the fitted function begins to turn downward on the right. We would not expect, had we included conditions with much longer intertrial intervals (say several minutes), that tracking performance would fall below zero, the way the function would do. For example, when we calculate $\overline{Y}'_j$ for a two-minute intertrial interval using the quadratic function we fitted to these data (Equation 5.6), we get the impossible predicted value

$$\overline{Y}'_{X=120} = 7.75 + (0.437)(120) - (0.004375)(120^2) = -2.81.$$

If we had wished to express the effect of intertrial interval over this large a range, we would need to do it another way. The polynomials also may predict values out of the acceptable range of a dependent measure, as when they predict a proportion that is less than zero or greater than one.

How to fit a nonpolynomial function in general is complicated and goes beyond the approaches we discuss here. The analysis is relatively easy when we only need to transform the values of the X_j. For example, we can fit and test the logarithmic function $Y = a + b \log X$ (which often arises in perceptual studies) by performing an ordinary trend analysis using $\log X_j$ instead of X_j for the values assigned to the groups. For other functions, the analysis is either more complicated than the simple trend analysis in this chapter, or a trend analysis cannot be applied at all. Other procedures, known as **nonlinear regression**, are required.

In summary, for studies that do not involve a very wide range of the numerical X variable or a complicated theory, most questions about the form of the relationship can be answered by trend analysis. The "basic" questions of ascent, descent, or curvature, which we have emphasized in this chapter, are treated as well by trend analysis as by more complex analyses. Most of the studies in the behavioral sciences are of this type.

However, in a few more complicated cases, you will need use nonlinear regression or some other model fitting procedure. You may want to seek technical help.

5.6   Monotonic Trend Analysis

You have seen how we can determine which degree of polynomial—linear, quadratic, cubic, and so on—describes the results of a quantitative manipulation. However, sometimes only the order of the conditions is meaningful, not the specific numerical values of X_j assigned to the groups. You may know that one condition has more of something and another less, but not how much. Ordered categories also arise when a researcher has manipulated a quantitative independent, but cannot trust the scaling properties of the numbers assigned to the treatment levels. In effect, the researcher does not know which of the situations in Figure 5.8 holds. Under these circumstances, an analysis based on orthogonal trend coefficients is hard to justify. Still, most researchers would want to know whether the sequence of group means ascends or descends.[6]

Suppose we were interested in the effects of different forms of feedback on the speed with which children can complete a problem-solving task. Five conditions are created, two consisting of positive feedback (mild and moderate praise), two consisting of negative feedback (mild and moderate criticism), and a control condition with no feedback. An obvious set of predictions is that praise will decrease solution time relative to the control, while criticism will increase it, and that this effect will be less for mild than for moderate praise or criticism. We would expect to find that solution times would be ordered such that

$$\mu_{\text{mod. praise}} < \mu_{\text{mild praise}} < \mu_{\text{none}} < \mu_{\text{mild crit.}} < \mu_{\text{mod. crit.}}.$$

However, we really have no theoretical or empirical basis for determining the actual spacing of these conditions on the X axis of a graph. Should we use equal intervals or unequal intervals and, if the latter, how should the conditions be spaced? We have only predicted the rank order of the conditions. This type of prediction is called a **monotonic hypothesis** because it only asserts that the relationship between the independent and dependent variables is a **monotonic function**. All you know is that as the independent variable X increases, the dependent variable Y changes only in one direction, either up or down. You don't know how much.

How should we analyze such a study? One approach would be to assign coefficients as if the groups had equal spacing and proceed with a standard analysis of linear trend. After all, whatever spacing the true function has, it should have some characteristics of an ascending or descending straight line. The trouble with this approach is that the linear trend coefficients are less than optimally sensitive to some forms of monotonic function. Consider the problem-solving example. The means might look like

$$10, 11, 12, 15, 25, \quad \text{or} \quad 5, 15, 16, 17, 18, \quad \text{or} \quad 5, 15, 16, 17, 25.$$

All three sets of means are monotonic, but the shapes of the functions are very different. The evenly spaced coefficients would not be equally sensitive to each of them. In fact, these coefficients are most sensitive to a set that increases regularly, say

$$10, 12, 14, 16, 18.$$

---

[6]For a good discussion of this approach, including ancillary testing strategies, see Braver and Sheets (1993).

What we want is a set of coefficients that is as sensitive as possible to *any* of these sequences.

A solution to this problem was discovered by Abelson and Tukey (1963). They determined the sequence of coefficients that works best under the least favorable pattern of treatment means—what they called the "maximin solution." Their maximin coefficients are complicated, but there is a simple approximation to them. Start with the set of linear trend coefficients given in Appendix A.3, then modify them to place more weight on the end coefficients, which are the ones for the means that are most affected by any monotonic trend. Specifically, you apply the **linear-2-4 rule**:

> *Quadruple the two extreme linear trend coefficients, double the next two coefficients, and leave the remaining coefficients unchanged.*

Let's apply this rule to the problem-solving example. There were five means, and the monotonic hypothesis asserts that $\mu_1 < \mu_2 < \mu_3 < \mu_4 < \mu_5$. For five groups, the linear trend coefficients are $\{-2, -1, 0, 1, 2\}$. Applying the linear-2-4 rule gives the set

$$\{(4)(-2),\ (2)(-1),\ 0,\ (2)(1),\ (4)(2)\} \quad \text{or} \quad \{-8, -2, 0, 2, 8\}.$$

If we find that the sum of squares for a contrast with these coefficients is significant, then we have evidence for the presence of an increase or decrease over the range of the conditions.

In some studies, we want to both look for monotonic trend and to identify whether that trend displays curvature—a bending up or down. The first part is answered by the monotone trend analysis. For the second part, we suggest that you look at the quadratic trend component, using coefficients obtained from Appendix A.3. As you can easily verify, the quadratic component is orthogonal to the monotonic trend contrast and thus picks out the portion of the variability that is most interpretable.

Exercises

5.1. In Section 5.5, we described an experiment reported by Grant (1956) in which he predicted the emergence of linear and quadratic trend components (see p. 102). Subjects were trained to respond to a 12-inch visual stimulus and then were tested on stimuli of different sizes (9, 10, 11, 12, 13, 14, and 15 inches); the response measure was the degree to which subjects responded on the first test trial. There were $n = 14$ subjects in each group. The means he obtained from the $a = 7$ groups were

9 in.	10 in.	11 in.	12 in.	13 in.	14 in.	15 in.
1.52	2.64	4.28	3.86	3.86	2.79	3.70

The within-groups mean square was 5.80.

a. Conduct an analysis of the linear and quadratic trends.

b. The linear and quadratic regression functions derived from this analysis are plotted in Figure 5.5 (p. 102). Calculate the two regression equations and compare your answer with the predicted group means plotted in the figure.

5.2. Suppose the means from an experiment with $a = 6$ equally spaced independent groups with $n = 10$ scores are

$$6, \quad 3, \quad 3, \quad 4, \quad 10, \quad 17.$$

The mean square error is $MS_{S/A} = 21.83$.

a. Can you detect a upward or downward linear trend?

b. Is the function curved?

5.3. Theorists have postulated a complicated relationship between anxiety level and performance on a complex task. To investigate the nature of this relationship, an investigator measured the backward memory span (a rather difficult task) of subjects, who were given special instructions designed to create various degrees of anxiety. There were six sets of instructions, from low anxiety instructions in a_1 through anxiety intermediate levels, to high anxiety instructions in a_6. There were five subjects in each of the anxiety levels. The span lengths obtained were as follows:

a_1		a_2		a_3		a_4		a_5		a_6	
1	1	2	1	3	2	3	2	4	2	3	3
0	1	1	2	4	5	5	5	3	4	2	4
1		2		3		3		3		2	

a. Perform an overall analysis of variance on these data and draw appropriate conclusions.

b. Conduct a trend analysis using the fit-failure procedure beginning with the linear component and ending when the test of the residual variability $F_{residual}$ is no longer significant. Again draw conclusions.

c. Suppose you questioned the assumption that the levels of anxiety were equally spaced and decided to test for the presence of monotonic trend. Is a monotonic trend present? Does it completely describe the outcome of this study?

5.4. It is often found in motor-skill research that practice that varies in nature is more effective than practice that is all of one type. One such experiment looks at the efficacy of practice in basketball free-throw shooting using practice with balls of different weight. One group of six subjects practices free throws using a standard weight ball. A second group practices using two balls of different weights, and a third practices with balls of four different weights. After four weeks of practice sessions, each subject was given 10 chances to shoot free throws using a ball with a weight that had not been used before. The number of successful shots was recorded:

1 ball		2 balls		4 balls	
7	4	5	8	10	10
2	7	6	7	6	9
3	8	6	8	6	7

a. Is there a significant effect of the number of training balls and the mean number of free throws made?

b. Conduct a trend analysis on these data, including tests for both linear and nonlinear effects, taking into consideration the unequal intervals.

6

Simultaneous Comparisons and the Control of Type I Errors

In the preceeding chapters, we have emphasized that the planning of an experiment includes the development of a research plan that includes tests of specific hypotheses. But a comprehensive analysis of an experiment does not stop with the evaluation of these planned tests. Researchers will usually search for interesting, but unexpected differences that may influence the interpretation of the study or form the basis for a new experiment. Although these separate tests increase the precision of the conclusions, they also increase the chance that at least one of them is wrong. Simply put, the probability of at least one error among several tests is greater than the probability of an error on an individual test. To control these errors is the problem of **simultaneous testing** or of **simultaneous comparisons**.

As you have seen, there are two types of error that can be made with any statistical test of a null hypothesis: rejecting a true null hypothesis (a Type I error) or not rejecting a false one (a Type II error). These types of error trade off with each other in the sense that any change in the chance of Type I errors results in an opposite, but not necessarily an equivalent, change in the chance of Type II errors. Because the null-hypothesis testing procedure is asymmetrical, with exact null hypotheses (no differences are present) and general alternative hypotheses (some differences are present), Type I errors are easier to analyze. Although a researcher surely wants to limit the chances of both types of error over a set of tests, Type I errors are more readily controlled. This chapter emphasizes the control of Type I error, with Type II errors playing a role only in the choice of control method. We consider power and the control of Type II errors in Chapter 8.

Many procedures have been developed to deal with simultaneous tests. Each is applicable in a slightly different circumstance. The computer packages present you with a confusingly large number of alternatives.[1] An important step in distinguishing among them is to understand the different ways that contrasts are used in the typical experiment. We look at several possibilities in the next section, and will organize our later discussion around those distinctions.

6.1   Research Questions and Type I Error

We will begin with some definitions. Researchers are often interested in a set of related hypotheses or research questions, and intend to test all of them. We refer to this set as a **family of tests**. This family may be small or large. A small family might contain only the linear and quadratic trend contrasts; a large family might contain every comparison between pairs of means. We define the **familywise Type I error rate** α_{FW} to be the probability of making *at least* one Type I error in the family of tests when all the null hypotheses are true:

$$\alpha_{FW} = \Pr(\text{at least one Type I error given all } H_0\text{'s are true}).$$

In the final stages of data analysis, when we are looking for unanticipated and interesting findings, we need to work with the very large (in fact, infinite) family of all possible tests that could be made while analyzing an experiment. We will refer to the error rate for this family as the **experimentwise error rate** and denote it by α_{EW}. The distinction between familywise and experimentwise error is a useful one. We devote most of this chapter to procedures designed to control Type I error for smaller families of related tests and discuss the control of experimentwise error in Section 6.5.

The Type I error (or any type of error, for that matter) accumulates over a family of tests. Suppose we evaluate each test at the α significance level. The probability of avoiding a Type I error on each test, therefore, is $1-\alpha$. The only way to avoid making a familywise error entirely is to avoid a Type I error on every test. If we could assume that the tests were independent of each other, then we could calculate the probability of no Type I errors as the product of avoiding a Type I error on each of them. If the family consists of c tests, then

$$\Pr(\text{No familywise errors}) = \underbrace{(1 - \alpha)(1 - \alpha)\ldots(1 - \alpha)}_{c \text{ times}} = (1 - \alpha)^c.$$

The familywise error probability, α_{FW}, is the probability of one or more Type I errors. We can calculate it by subtracting the probability of no errors from 1:

$$\alpha_{FW} = 1 - \Pr(\text{No familywise errors}) = 1 - (1 - \alpha)^c. \tag{6.1}$$

For example, with $c = 3$ independent tests and the individual error set at $\alpha = .05$, the familywise Type I error rate is

$$\alpha_{FW} = 1 - (1 - .05)^3 = 1 - (.95)^3 = 1 - 0.857 = 0.143.$$

As Equation 6.1 makes clear, the familywise error rate α_{FW} is always greater than the Type I error rate α for an individual test. This latter quantity is known as the **per-comparison error rate**, which we will denote by an unsubscripted α.

---

[1]The situation is complicated by a lack of common nomenclature. Procedures tend to be identified by the name of their originator, so that techniques that are almost identical may have completely different names. The fact that some procedures were invented independently by different workers further complicates the situation.

A look at Equation 6.1 reveals that any change in the size of the per-comparison error rate α also changes familywise error rate α_{FW}. For example, if you set $\alpha = .01$ for $c = 3$ independent tests, the familywise error rate falls below 5 percent:

$$\alpha_{FW} = 1 - (1 - .01)^3 = 1 - (.99)^3 = 1 - 0.970 = 0.030.$$

Thus, if you were interested in limiting the familywise error to 5 percent for these tests, you could do so by setting α to some intermediate value between $\alpha = .05$ ($\alpha_{FW} = 0.143$) and $\alpha = .01$ ($\alpha_{FW} = 0.030$). By reducing the chance of a Type I error on every test (assuming the omnibus null hypothesis is true), you also reduce the chance of making a Type I error within the family of tests. This idea of controlling familywise error by reducing per-comparison error α underlies all of the procedures we consider.

Many schemes to correct the familywise error rates have been devised. They differ in the size and nature of the family that is to be investigated and the status of the research questions. Our goal here is to introduce you to the most common methods and to give you a basis for choosing among them. Because the appropriate way to control familywise error depends on the role of a given test in the general plan of analysis, we will look first at how analytical comparisons are used in the typical experiment, then turn to the specific techniques used to control familywise error.

We will roughly distinguish among three parts in the analysis of the typical experiment.

1. *Testing the primary questions.* Experiments have a purpose. They are generally undertaken to answer a few specific questions, as we illustrated in Chapter 4 and Chapter 5. The McGovern experiment outlined in Table 4.1 (p. 63) focused on detecting interference with three different memory components, and the Grant study summarized in Figure 5.5 (p. 102) was designed to detect increasing trend and a reversal of the response. Most experiments involve only a few such contrasts, often only one or two and never more than the degrees of freedom for the effect. Because these questions are the principal point of the study, they are best considered in isolation. Each is a major reason why the study was conducted, so each is tested as the unique member of its family. To give these tests the maximum power, their per-comparison error rate is fixed at α, and no other adjustment is made.

2. *Looking at special families of hypotheses.* Sometimes a researcher's planned questions identify families of related hypotheses rather than a few central or primary questions. One example is trend analysis, where the family is the set of polynomial contrasts; another is the comparison of a set of experimental conditions to a single control; a third is the set of all comparisons between pairs of groups. These sets of hypotheses are less focused than planned questions, but they are limited in size. A researcher wants to look at all members of the family. The sensible approach here is to control the Type I error by fixing α_{FW} for the family. Where several families of contrasts are to be studied, they are often treated as separate entities, each given its own allocation of familywise error.

3. *Exploring the data for unexpected relationships.* Finally, a researcher may want to examine all of the data, looking for *any* interesting or suggestive relationship among the groups. The pool of potential tests in this case is the entire collection of contrasts that could be written. Any contrast that can be measured might

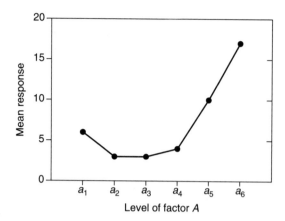

Figure 6.1: Means from an experiment with six equally-spaced groups

turn up in this exploratory analysis. Neither a specific question nor a limited family is identified. Over this experimentwise family, it is necessary to hold α_{EW} to an acceptable level.

The boundaries between these three situations are not sharp, and not every study involves all three parts. It is not always clear when a set of planned comparisons merges into a family of related questions, nor when a planned family becomes so large that it effectively encompasses all possible contrasts. For example, the set of all pairwise comparisons is clearly identified but is often treated as a exploratory analysis. In spite of any fuzziness, however, we can usually identify at least two of these situations, often all three, in most studies. They serve as a guide to a researcher's choice of a particular method for evaluating simultaneous comparisons.

It is not necessary to actually calculate test statistics for all the members of a family to be in a situation bounded by that family. Often by looking at the data we can see that certain possibilities do not need to be tested. A glance at Figure 6.1, for example, indicates that most of the trend resides in the linear and quadratic components and that higher-order effects can be ignored. However, the fact that we don't test a contrast does not mean that we would not have done so had it appeared likely to be present. If Figure 6.1 had shown a rise, a fall, and another rise, then we would certainly have examined the cubic trend. All such potentially interesting comparisons are part of the relevant family regardless of whether they are tested formally or informally.

Another situation in which the consideration of potentially relevant contrasts occurs is during the third, or exploratory, phase of the data analysis, where researchers sift through their data looking for anything that might be interesting. The resulting comparisons clearly are unplanned, but detecting their presence has a high priority for most researchers. Because this post-hoc search could, potentially, find *any* effect, every conceivable contrast is part of the family, even though only a few are formally tested.

As might be expected, the stringency with which the error rate should be controlled differs in the three situations. Planned tests bring the largest amount of extrastatistical information to the analysis—theoretical predictions and relevant findings in the research literature—and so command the highest priority. A researcher knows from the start that he or she will investigate these questions and that they support the strongest inferences. Researchers generally do not exercise familywise error control over these high priority tests. At the other extreme, the exploratory or post-hoc phase uses the least external information and supports the weakest inferences. In between, the nature of the relevant family determines the level of error control needed.

Two other principles commonly influence the choice of a method of error control. First, it is more acceptable to adopt a test that is too stringent than one that is too weak. Researchers are more likely to be criticized for treating a set of related hypotheses as if they were separate planned questions than for combining several planned questions into a small family and applying some form of familywise control. As a result, many researchers adopt somewhat larger families than necessary, even at a cost in power.

Second, there is no reason why the familywise rate α_{FW} or experimentwise rate α_{EW} should obey the same conventions that apply to the per-comparison rate α. Standards, such as the 5 percent significance level for a single test, need not be the same as those used for a family or for the entire experiment. A less strict level for α_{FW} can be justified when the family is large. Increasing α_{FW} is most justified in an exploratory analysis where the family ranges over the entire experiment. The larger value is a compromise that gives the individual statistical tests more power, achieved by tolerating more overall error. A 10 percent experimentwise rate is often used, even by investigators who would never drop their standards below the 5 percent level for a planned test.

You should be aware that simultaneous testing is more open to variation and more visibly influenced by opinion than are many parts of statistics. Whether a contrast is planned or post hoc, hence how it is tested, depends on the underlying motivation for the research. Moreover, a researcher's choice of method is influenced by his or her individual degree of conservativeness and tolerance for Type I error or worry about loss of power. There are standards and conventions for familywise and experimentwise error control, particularly with respect to publication, but they are not always consistent, particularly over different research domains.

6.2 Planned Comparisons

For clearly planned tests, familywise error correction is generally deemed unnecessary. The questions these contrasts express are interesting in isolation, and they are tested that way. If an experiment is designed to investigate a particular hypothesis, then no post-hoc selection of comparisons is involved in testing it. The proper procedures are those discussed in Chapter 4; nothing new is required. There are a few places where differences of opinion or alternative strategies arise, however.

One source of differing opinions concerns orthogonality. Some writers have argued that when more than one planned comparison is to be tested, they should be mutually orthogonal and that when nonorthogonal comparisons are present, they should be treated as a family and subjected to familywise error correction. We believe this assertion is unnecessarily strong. Certainly, orthogonal comparisons should be used where possible. Orthogonality helps keep the hypotheses logically and conceptually separate, making them easier to interpret. It also allows a researcher to obtain a residual sum of squares by subtraction and to present the results as an additive breakdown of the omnibus effect, a form easy to communicate to a reader. Thus, when formulating a set of planned comparisons for testing, you should strive for orthogonality. The very process of developing an orthogonal set of contrasts forces you to think about your design and to clarify how your questions relate to each other. However, you should not let a quest for orthogonality force you into testing hypotheses that are confusing or meaningless. When the point of a particular design cannot be expressed by orthogonal planned contrasts, then nonorthogonal ones should be used.[2]

The real danger with planned comparisons, particularly nonorthogonal ones, is the temptation to pick too many. The number of mutually orthogonal comparisons is limited by the number of groups (i.e. by df_A), but the number of nonorthogonal ones is not. Planning per se is not the real point here; it is the conciseness and separability of the questions. It is not satisfactory to say, "I planned to compare every mean with every other mean," and then use this statement as a justification for ignoring control of a sizable familywise error. Researchers simply don't design experiments with this many separable questions. Often an investigator who feels the need to test a large set of contrasts to achieve the primary goals of an experiment has not taken the time to identify the key questions underlying the research or to put them in testable form. One or two well-tailored contrasts are almost certainly more effective than a larger, but vague, collection. Where several similar contrasts are needed, it is better to treat them as a small family and apply an appropriate correction, as described in the next section. There is room to quibble about whether a contrast is planned or not, but the distinction is for the most part clear.

Another issue concerns the relationship between the omnibus F test and the planned tests of contrasts. Some authors have suggested that any form of contrast should only be tested when the omnibus F statistic indicates that there is a difference among the groups.[3] However, to examine truly planned contrasts in this manner seems both unduly cautious and a violation of the principles of research design. When an experiment has been designed to investigate a particular planned contrast, it should be tested, regardless of the significance of the omnibus F statistic. After all, that is the point of the study.

It is possible for the omnibus F test not to be significant, while the test of a planned comparison is. Suppose the major point of a study is to determine whether treatment conditions a_1 and a_2 differ. The researcher adds a third condition a_3 to find out where it falls relative to the two main groups. Nine subject are used in each group. The study produced means of 8, 20, and 12, with $MS_{S/A} = 150$. Without showing the details, we find with these numbers that $F = MS_A/MS_{S/A} = 336/150 = 2.24$, which does not reach the critical value of $F_{.05}(2, 24) = 3.40$ and is not significant. But the real point of the study is the planned comparison $\psi = \mu_1 - \mu_2$. The observed value is $\widehat{\psi} = \bar{Y}_1 - \bar{Y}_2 = 8 - 20 = -12$. Using Equation 4.5 (p. 69), we find

$$SS_\psi = \frac{n\widehat{\psi}^2}{\sum c_j^2} = \frac{(9)(-12)^2}{2} = 648 \quad \text{and} \quad F = \frac{MS_\psi}{MS_{S/A}} = \frac{648}{150} = 4.32.$$

---

[2]Some computer packages automatically impose orthogonality on any set of contrasts. This may not be what you intend. Always be sure you know what your program is doing!

[3]Strictly, requiring an omnibus F test first makes this procedure a form of sequential testing, which we discuss in Section 6.4.

This statistic exceeds its critical value of $F_{.05}(1, 24) = 4.26$ and is significant. In a situation like this, where the extra group is incidental, it makes more sense to ignore the omnibus F test and test the planned comparison.

6.3 Restricted Sets of Contrasts

The remainder of this chapter describes several procedures for controlling the Type I error rate. Our discussion is divided into three parts. In this section, we consider the small families of hypotheses that come up in the middle stage of our ideal analysis procedure. In Section 6.4, we treat the important problem of pairwise comparisons, that is, of comparing each mean to all the others. Finally, in Section 6.5, we look at error control for exploratory analyses, where the set consists of all contrasts that can be extracted from an experiment.

The types of tests we have in mind in the present section come from relatively small families—for example, an assessment of the differences between a control condition and each of the experimental conditions, a series of orthogonal trend components examined for descriptive purposes, or a coherent set of planned comparisons of secondary interest. Generally these methods are more applicable when the number of tests does not exceed the number of degrees of freedom of the effect, although this limit is not a strict requirement.

The Bonferroni Procedure

The most widely applicable familywise control procedure for small families is the **Bonferroni correction**. It is very general and applies to any sort of test, including statistical procedures other than the analysis of variance.

The basis for the Bonferroni correction is the relationship between the per-comparison and the familywise error rates for a family of c independent tests (Equation 6.1):

$$\alpha_{FW} = 1 - (1 - \alpha)^c.$$

We can't apply this formula directly, because our tests are almost never mutually orthogonal. For example, the set of contrasts comparing each of several experimental groups to a control group are not orthogonal because the same control group is used for each. However, it turns out that independent tests have the largest familywise error, and so, for any set of tests,

$$\alpha_{FW} \leq 1 - (1 - \alpha)^c. \tag{6.2}$$

Some algebra (which we won't show) applied to the right-hand side of this equation shows that it is always less than the number of tests times their error rate. Hence,

$$\alpha_{FW} < c\alpha. \tag{6.3}$$

This very simple relationship is known as the **Bonferroni inequality**. It is so useful that we will restate a more general version of it in words:

> *The familywise error rate is always less than the sum of the per-comparison error rates of the individual tests.*

How do we use the Bonferroni inequality? If we want to control the familywise error rate to be no greater than some number α_{FW}, we simply pick a per-comparison rate that equals this value divided by the number of tests:[4]

$$\alpha = \alpha_{FW}/c. \tag{6.4}$$

Suppose we want to hold the familywise error rate for a set of $c = 7$ contrasts to $\alpha_{FW} = .05$. All we must do is set the per-comparison error rate to $\alpha = .05/7 = 0.0071$.

There are two ways to implement the Bonferroni procedure, one that uses the descriptive level (the "p value") of the tests, the other that uses the test statistic itself. When descriptive p values are available, say from a computer output, the correction is applied by comparing it to the revised significance level of α_{FW}/c. Any test for which p is less than this value is declared significant:

$$\begin{cases} \text{If } p_{\text{observed}} \leq \alpha_{FW}/c, \text{ then reject } H_0, \\ \text{If } p_{\text{observed}} > \alpha_{FW}/c, \text{ then retain } H_0. \end{cases}$$

For example, suppose a computer program reports $p = 0.0131$ for one test in a family of $c = 6$ tests, and you wish to control the familywise Type I error probability to $\alpha_{FW} = .10$. You simply compare the reported p value to the Bonferroni level of $\alpha = .10/6 = 0.0167$ and reject the null hypothesis because it is smaller. Alternatively, you reach the same conclusion by multiplying p_{observed} by c and checking that it is less than α_{FW}:

$$c\, p_{\text{observed}} = (6)(0.0131) = 0.0786 < \alpha_{FW} = .10.$$

The other approach to the Bonferroni correction, which is necessary for hand calculation, uses a critical value of the t or F test statistic for the adjusted per-comparison rate. In most cases, the proper significance level cannot be found in the conventional tables—in our current example, we need the 0.0167 significance level. There are three ways to determine the correct value. One is to use a computer program that calculates critical values of F or t, the second is to use one of several approximation formulas (see, for example, Hays, 1994, or Keppel, 1991, pp. 167–168), and the third is to use a special purpose table. Tables of Bonferroni-corrected critical values of t are provided in many texts or books of tables. We will not present one here, however, because the Šidák-Bonferroni tables that we describe below are superior.

Another example shows how easy and flexible the general Bonferroni principle is to use. Suppose the researcher who collected the data in Figure 6.1 decides to conduct a trend analysis, looking at the linear and quadratic contrasts and a composite test for higher-order trend based on $SS_{\text{higher}} = SS_A - SS_{\text{linear}} - SS_{\text{quad}}$. The first two tests are simple contrasts; the third has $df_A - 2 = 5 - 2 = 3$ degrees of freedom. Suppose the error rate is to be held to 10 percent for this family of three tests. To do so, the per-comparison error rate can be set to $\alpha = \alpha_{FW}/3 = .10/3 = 0.033$. The correction is straightforward, except that a computer program will probably be necessary to obtain the p values. The Bonferroni approach can be used in a more subtle way here. Some statisticians have advocated dividing up α_{FW} in accordance with the importance of the test. The researcher may feel that the linear and quadratic tests are more important

---

[4]When applied to the analysis of variance, the Bonferroni strategy is sometimes called **Dunn's test**, after Dunn (1961), although this name is now losing favor.

than the residual test and want to give them more power. By evaluating them at the
.04 level and the residual at the .02 level, the Bonferroni principle still controls the
overall familywise error rate to $.04 + .04 + .02 = .10$.

The Bonferroni procedure is handy and easy to apply, but it has the limitation
that it is based on an inequality. It overcorrects, especially when the number of tests
is large. In other words, the actual familywise Type I error rate is always less than the
value of α_{FW} that was used to construct the test (known as its **nominal value**). We
know that when α is too small, the power suffers. We can improve things by making
a less extreme, and more accurate, adjustment.

The Šidák-Bonferroni Procedure

One way to increase the power of the tests over that of the Bonferroni adjustment is
to base the correction on the relationship in Equation 6.2 instead of that in the more
conservative Equation 6.3. The resulting significance level is equal to

$$\alpha = 1 - (1 - \alpha_{FW})^{1/c}. \tag{6.5}$$

It is smaller than the Bonferroni value, so the tests are slightly more powerful, although
still conservative unless the tests are independent. This approach was suggested by
Šidák (1967), and the procedure is usually identified as the **Šidák-Bonferroni correction** (the letter Š is pronounced "Sh"). For any value of α_{FW}, Equation 6.5 is
solved for α, and that value is used for the individual tests. In other respects, the
procedure works exactly like the Bonferroni procedure.

Appendix A.4 gives the information you need to conduct this test. The columns
of the table refer to the number of comparisons in the family. The first row gives
the per-comparison α to be used for the individual tests. For example, with four
comparisons at the $\alpha_{FW} = .05$ level, the individual tests are evaluated at the 1.274
percent level. This value is not a large change from the $\alpha_{FW}/c = .05/4 = .0125$ level of
the Bonferroni tests, but it is some improvement. You compare the p values reported
by a computer to this number. Here, the null hypothesis is rejected for any of the four
comparisons for which $p < 0.01274$. The remainder of the table is used to perform
the test if you are not using a computer. It contains critical values of the t statistic at
the given α levels, with the rows indexed by the number of degrees of freedom in the
error term. For example, if the error term were based on $df_{\text{error}} = 40$, then the critical
value for each of the tests would be $t_{\text{crit}} = 2.61$. Because the t statistic is used here,
you will either have to test the contrast with a t test, as discussed in Section 4.4, or
square the tabled value to turn it into the equivalent F_{crit}.

One reason to use the t statistic in the tables is that it lends itself to the construction of confidence intervals (Equation 4.13, p. 75). When you construct a set
of c intervals from Appendix A.4, using the t_{crit}, you have the appropriate degree of
confidence (based on α_{FW}) that they are all satisfied *simultaneously*.

Dunnett's Test

The Bonferroni and Šidák-Bonferroni procedures are easy to use when only a few comparisons are being tested. However, in special circumstances there are procedures with
greater power. We will mention one of these, **Dunnett's test** (Dunnett, 1955), which
is used whenever one group (most commonly the control group) is being compared to

all the other $a-1$ groups (most commonly the experimental groups). The test statistic is the standard t used in the uncorrected, Bonferroni, or Šidák-Bonferroni procedures, but it is compared to a critical value, which we denote t_{Dunnett}, obtained from the specialized tables in Appendix A.5. The particular value of t_{Dunnett} is determined by the total number of groups (including the control), the degrees of freedom for the error term, and α_{FW}. For example, with four experimental groups, one control group, and $n = 10$ subjects per group, the critical value of t at the 10 percent level is $t_{\text{Dunnett}} = 2.22$ (five groups and 45 degrees of freedom). The critical value for the Šidák-Bonferroni procedure on these four tests is 2.30, giving it slightly lower power. Problem 6.2 provides an example of this test.

The comparisons tested in Dunnett's test are all between pairs of means, $\bar{Y}_j - \bar{Y}_c$, where c denotes the standard or control group. Because there are $a - 1$ of these comparisons, it is easier to find a critical value for the difference instead of actually calculating t for each pair of means. This critical difference, D_{Dunnett} is found by setting t to t_{Dunnett} in the formula for a t test (Equation 4.9, p. 71) and solving for the contrast. After some algebra,

$$D_{\text{Dunnett}} = t_{\text{Dunnett}} \sqrt{2MS_{S/A}/n}. \qquad (6.6)$$

Any pair of means that differs by more than this amount is judged to differ significantly. Incidentally, this formula can be used to find critical differences for planned or Šidák-Bonferroni tests by replacing t_{Dunnett} by critical values from the ordinary t table or the Šidák-Bonferroni tables (Appendix A.2 and Appendix A.4, respectively).

6.4   Pairwise Comparisons

Researchers often want to examine all pairwise comparisons, that is, to compare each group with every other group, a family containing a total of $a(a - 1)/2$ comparisons. For example, there are $(5)(5 - 1)/2 = 10$ pairwise comparisons among $a = 5$ groups. Although the Bonferroni or Šidák-Bonferroni procedures can be used here, the large number of comparisons force them to use smaller α values (producing lower power) than techniques specifically developed for this situation. We will discuss three of these in detail, covering procedures that are both widely applied and conceptually different from each other, and note some variants more briefly. For details of these other methods, see Seaman, Levin, and Serlin (1991) or Toothaker (1991).

Tukey's HSD Procedure

The simplest way to control the familywise error rate over the entire set of pairwise comparisons is known as **Tukey's procedure** (proposed in an influential, but unpublished, paper), or sometimes as the **honestly significant difference** (**HSD**) procedure.[5] The easiest way to perform this set of tests is to compare the observed difference between each pair of means to a critical difference D_{Tukey}. This critical value is the product of the standard error of the mean s_M and a quantity q_a found in the table of the **Studentized range statistic** (Appendix A.6):

$$D_{\text{Tukey}} = q_a s_M = q_a \sqrt{MS_{S/A}/n}. \qquad (6.7)$$

---

[5]There is also a Tukey (b) procedure, related to the Newman-Keuls test (see below), which we do not recommend. Another variant of Tukey's procedure applies to complex contrasts.

Table 6.1: Mean comfort ratings for five different headache remedies.

	a_1	a_2	a_3	a_4	a_5
	16	10	9	9	11
	11	5	3	12	9
	22	8	4	12	10
	8	12	8	4	13
	15	0	8	5	13
	6	16	6	10	12
	16	8	13	7	11
	15	12	5	12	18
	12	10	9	9	14
	11	6	7	8	12
Means ($\bar{Y}_j$)	13.20	8.70	7.20	8.80	12.30
Std. Dev. (s_j)	4.59	4.42	2.90	2.86	2.50

Analysis of variance

Source	SS	df	MS	F
A	264.920	4	66.230	5.22 *
S/A	571.000	45	12.689	
Total	835.920	49		

* $p < .05$

To use the Studentized range table you need to know the number of groups in the study, designated by the subscript attached to q_a, the value of df_{error}, and the desired level of error control α_{FW}. Any pair of groups whose means differ by more than this amount is significantly different.

As an example, suppose a researcher wants to determine whether there are any differences among $a = 5$ remedies for headaches. Students with headaches reporting to a health clinic are randomly assigned to the five conditions ($n = 10$ per condition). Eight hours after taking the remedy, the students rate their feeling of physical comfort on a scale from 0 (severe discomfort) to 30 (normal comfort). Table 6.1 gives the data, with the summary statistics and omnibus analysis of variance. Given the absence of any theoretical expectations, this experiment is ideally suited to a systematic examination of the 10 pairwise contrasts. We will use Tukey's test to control the familywise error over these 10 contrasts at $\alpha_{FW} = .05$.

The first step is to calculate D_{Tukey}. We start by looking up the Studentized range statistic in Appendix A.6 for $a = 5$ groups with $df_{S/A} = 45$ and $\alpha_{FW} = .05$. The tabled value is $q_5 = 4.02$. Then using Equation 6.7, we calculate the critical difference:

$$D_{\text{Tukey}} = q_a \sqrt{MS_{S/A}/n} = 4.02\sqrt{12.689/10} = 4.02\sqrt{1.269} = 4.53.$$

Any pair of means farther apart than this value is significantly different.

Table 6.2: *Differences between means for the data in Table 6.1, with the results of three testing procedures. The superscripts t, p, and h label differences that, respectively, are significant by the Tukey HSD test, an ordinary test as a planned comparison, and by the Fisher-Hayter test.*

		a_3	a_2	a_4	a_5	a_1
	$\overline{Y}_j$	7.20	8.70	8.80	12.30	13.20
a_3	7.20	—	1.50	1.60	$5.10^{t,p,h}$	$6.00^{t,p,h}$
a_2	8.70		—	0.10	3.60^{p}	$4.50^{p,h}$
a_4	8.80			—	3.50^{p}	$4.40^{p,h}$
a_5	12.30				—	0.90
a_1	13.20					—

For any pairwise procedure, it is convenient to enter the actual differences in a triangular table. The rows and columns of this table correspond to the groups, and the table entries are the pairwise differences. Table 6.2 gives this table, in which we have (for reasons we will explain later) also ranked the groups in the order of ascending means. You can see immediately that only two differences are significant, $\overline{Y}_1 - \overline{Y}_3 = 6.00$ and $\overline{Y}_5 - \overline{Y}_3 = 5.10$. We have marked these with the superscript t (for Tukey). For comparison, pairs that are significant by an uncorrected test at $\alpha = .05$ are marked by p (a planned comparison); we found them from Equation 6.6 using the standard t instead of t_{Dunnett}:

$$D_{\text{Planned}} = t_\alpha(df_{S/A})\sqrt{2MS_{S/A}/n} = 2.01\sqrt{(2)(12.689)/10} = 3.20.$$

Now six differences are significant. The more stringent error control in Tukey's test reduced the number of significant differences by four.

You will sometimes (particularly in computer output) find the results of a set of pairwise comparisons represented as sets of equivalent means. These groupings, known as **equivalent subsets**, contain means that are not statistically different from one another. By listing these subsets, the results of a set of pairwise comparisons can be summarized concisely. One way to show these subsets is by listing the groups in order of their means, and then drawing lines under the equivalent subsets. For the Tukey comparisons in Table 6.2, this representation is

$$\underline{a_3 \quad \underline{a_2 \quad a_4 \quad a_5 \quad a_1}}\ .$$

To determine whether any two means are different using this diagram, you locate the two groups in question and check whether they are covered by a single line. For example, groups a_2 and a_5 do not differ because the second line covers them both, while groups a_3 and a_5 do differ because no one line covers them.

To construct one of these diagrams, you first list the groups in order of their means (as we did in Table 6.2), then test the most extreme groups first. In our example, the most extreme pair of groups is a_3 and a_1. These do differ significantly, so they are not members of an equivalent subset. We now look at the pairs that are the next most distantly separated and span four groups, namely the pair a_3 and a_5 and the pair a_2 and a_1. The first of these pairs is still significant, but the second pair is not. Because

a_2 and a_1 do not differ significantly, they are members of an equivalent subset, which we indicate by drawing a line under them:

$$a_3 \quad \underline{a_2 \quad a_4 \quad a_5 \quad a_1} \quad .$$

Note that the means of the groups within this underlined subset can never differ significantly—any pair within the subset (e.g., a_2 and a_5 or a_4 and a_5) must differ less than the groups at the end (a_2 and a_1), and these were not significantly different. We continue the testing procedure by looking at the pairs that span sets of three groups. Two of these sets (the pair a_2 and a_5 and the pair a_4 and a_1) fall within the equivalent set we just found, and won't differ significantly. The third pair (a_3 and a_4) falls outside the equivalent set and needs to be checked further. The difference between these means is not significant, which indicates that they are members of another equivalent subset, and we add a line under them:

$$\underline{a_3 \quad a_2 \quad a_4} \quad a_5 \quad a_1 \quad .$$
$$\underline{}$$

If necessary, we could go on to look at the adjacent pairs (a_3 and a_2, etc.), but the diagram shows that all of these are already included in an equivalent subset and need not be checked further.

You may see these subsets presented in another form. In it, members of the same equivalent subset are marked by a superscript or other symbol. For example, the results shown by the line diagram above are indicated by

$$a_1^b, \quad a_2^{ab}, \quad a_3^a, \quad a_4^{ab}, \quad a_5^b.$$

Here the superscript a refers to those groups covered by the first line above, and the superscript b those covered by the second line. Any two groups that share a superscript are not significantly different, while any two groups that do not have a common subscript are significantly different. Thus, a_1 and a_3 are significantly different because they have different superscripts, b and a, respectively, while a_1 and a_5 are not significantly different because they share the superscript b.

How do we interpret the results of this analysis? If your interest is in determining which pairs differ significantly, you can locate them in Table 6.2. Only the pairs (a_1, a_3) and (a_5, a_3) differ. If you want to establish the most effective treatment, the equivalent subsets are more revealing. The second band drawn below the ordered treatment conditions indicates that none of the four best headache remedies (a_1, a_5, a_4, or a_2) emerged as significantly more effective than the others.

When the sample sizes are unequal or the variances are heterogeneous, Equation 6.7 should not be used. Under either of these circumstances, the best solution is to replace $MS_{S/A}/n$ in Equation 6.7 with a value that takes into account the unequal samples or the unequal variances. For unequal samples sizes, Kramer (1956) suggests replacing the n in Equation 6.7 with a special average of the individual sample sizes, called the **harmonic mean** and written $\tilde{n}$. For example, to compare group a_1 with n_1 subjects to group a_2 with n_2 subjects, we calculate the harmonic mean of their sample sizes by[6]

---

[6]The reciprocal of a harmonic mean ($1/\tilde{n}$) is the average of the reciprocals of its parts ($1/n_j$).

$$\tilde{n} = \frac{2}{1/n_1 + 1/n_2}.$$

This number is used in place of n in Equation 6.7. Each pair of groups has a different critical difference because of different combinations of sample sizes. This analysis is in agreement with the analysis of unequal samples in Section 3.5.

When the variances are heterogeneous, the critical differences must take into account the actual variances of the particular groups being tested. The common standard error of the mean, $MS_{S/A}/n$, is replaced by an average of two squared standard errors of the individual groups being tested (Games & Howell, 1976). The critical difference, again for groups a_1 and a_2, is

$$D_{\text{Tukey}} = q_a \sqrt{\tfrac{1}{2}(s_{M_1}^2 + s_{M_2}^2)} = q_a \sqrt{\tfrac{1}{2}(s_1^2/n_1 + s_2^2/n_2)}. \tag{6.8}$$

The degrees of freedom needed to find q_a in Appendix A.6 are obtained from Equation 7.13 below. Subject to the cautions we mention in Section 7.4 in the unequal-variance case, this approach offers a satisfactory way to deal with heterogeneity of variance. You will find these methods in many computer packages, frequently identified by the names of their authors.

The Fisher-Hayter Procedure

Tukey's procedure is the simplest way to test the pairwise differences and is the one that is most applicable to any pattern of effects. It exerts tight control over familywise error, holding the actual α_{FW} error close to the nominal one. It achieves its error control by setting a relatively high criterion for rejecting null hypotheses. However, raising the rejection criterion makes it harder to detect whatever pairwise differences that may be present. For this reason, several other procedures have been developed that attempt to increase the power of the tests. Increases in power always come at some cost; here it is at the expense of greater complexity and a less conservative or weaker control of familywise Type I error. This development reflects the more general problem in experimentation of finding a reasonable balance between a concern about rejecting true null hypotheses and having sufficient power to reject false ones. We will look at two such procedures designed for testing the complete set of pairwise comparisons.

The **Fisher-Hayter procedure** uses a sequential approach to testing. Sequential tests control the familywise error rate by applying a series of steps, each of which depends on the outcome of the previous step. We pass from one test in the sequence to the next, continuing only as long as we continue to reject the null hypothesis. When a difference fails to be significant, we stop. The earlier tests serve as "gatekeepers" for the later tests, so that error control in the later tests can be relaxed. By continuing the testing procedure only when differences are likely to be present, a smaller value of the critical difference can be used, increasing the power without compromising the familywise error rate.

The Fisher-Hayter procedure involves two steps. The first is the omnibus F test to see whether there are any differences among the means. If that null hypothesis is rejected—and only if it is—the second stage uses a Studentized-range test, almost like that in Tukey's procedure, to check for significant differences between pairs of means. The difference is that when the omnibus test is significant, we know that some differences among the means are present, so a smaller critical difference is used in the second stage.[7] More formally, the two steps are

1. Conduct an omnibus test for the difference among the a means at the α_{FW} level. If this test does not indicate differences among the means, then stop. If it does, then go on to Step 2.

2. Test all pairwise comparisons using the critical difference D_{FH} obtained from the Studentized-range table with $a - 1$ groups:[8]

$$D_{\mathrm{FH}} = q_{a-1}\sqrt{MS_{S/A}/n}. \tag{6.9}$$

If you look at the Tukey tables, you will see that q_{a-1} is always smaller than q_a, so the Fisher-Hayter critical difference is smaller than that of Tukey's test (Equation 6.7), giving it greater power. This sequential structure is a good description of a researcher's behavior in post-hoc testing—you don't go on to look for effects unless the omnibus analysis is significant.

We illustrate the procedure by applying it to Table 6.1. The first step of the Fisher-Hayter procedure uses the summary of the omnibus analysis. Taking $\alpha_{FW} = .05$, the omnibus F test is significant, which permits us to continue to the second step. Now we calculate the critical difference D_{FH}. With 5 groups, we look for the Studentized range statistic q_{a-1} in the column labeled 4 in the 5 percent table of Appendix A.6, obtaining $q_4 = 3.77$. Entering this value in Equation 6.9 and using the mean square from the omnibus analysis,

$$D_{\mathrm{FH}} = q_{a-1}\sqrt{MS_{S/A}/n} = 3.77\sqrt{12.689/10} = 3.77\sqrt{1.269} = 4.25.$$

Each of the pairwise contrasts in Table 6.7, including the extreme contrast, is compared against this critical difference; those for which equality can be rejected are marked with the superscript h. Because the critical difference for the Fisher-Hayter procedure ($D_{\mathrm{FH}} = 4.25$) is smaller than that for the Tukey procedure ($D_{\mathrm{Tukey}} = 4.53$), we find that two pairs differ significantly that did not before. In the equivalent-subset notation, these results are summarized by the diagram

$$\underline{a_3 \quad a_2 \quad a_4 \quad a_5 \quad a_1} \quad .$$

The Fisher-Hayter procedure provides excellent control of Type I error, a fact that has been demonstrated in several simulations studies (Ramsey, 1993; Seaman et al., 1991). In their summary of simultaneous testing procedures, Seaman et al. conclude that " ... we would be hard-pressed to find a more suitable practical alternative than the [Fisher-Hayter] procedure" (p. 585). We suggest that you use this procedure, particularly when making calculations by hand.

---

[7]The procedure is actually a modification by Hayter (1986) of an earlier sequential procedure proposed by Fisher (1951). In **Fisher's procedure**, which is also known as the **Least Significant Difference** (or **LSD**) test, the second-stage tests are conducted like ordinary planned comparisons. In many realistic situations, Fisher's procedure does not control error well and should be avoided.

[8]If sample sizes or variances are unequal, adjustments such as Equation 6.8 are made.

The Newman-Keuls and Related Procedures

In the Fisher-Hayter procedure, passing an initial gatekeeper test (the omnibus F test) allowed the subsequent tests to be conducted with a less stringent critical difference than that in the standard Tukey procedure. This idea is extended in the **Newman-Keuls procedure** (Keuls, 1952; Newman, 1939; also sometimes called the **Student-Newman-Keuls procedure** and abbreviated **SNK**) to allow a whole series of gatekeeper tests. The result is a procedure that has greater power than the others, but at the not-inconsiderable cost of greater complexity and substantially less accurate error control. Nevertheless, the procedure continues to be popular among researchers and to be included in many software packages, which is why we describe it here, even though we ultimately recommend against its use.

To understand how the Newman-Keuls procedure works (although you will probably employ a computer program to use it), think back to the way that we constructed the equivalent subsets for Tukey's procedure (pp. 122–123). The Newman-Keuls procedure works the same way except that the criterion changes along with the size of the subset being examined. In particular, when comparing two groups that define a subset of k groups in the ranking of the means, the critical difference is given by

$$D_{\mathrm{NK}_k} = q_k \sqrt{MS_{S/A}/n}. \tag{6.10}$$

Because q_k declines with k, the critical difference is smaller for smaller sets, making the hypothesis of the equality of the means easier to reject. As in the Tukey procedure, once an equivalent subset has been identified, no further tests are conducted on any pair of groups within it. Because the critical differences change in size, keeping the tests ordered in this way is required to make the procedure internally consistent.

To see this procedure in action, again consider Table 6.2. The first comparison involves the two most extreme groups, a_3 and a_1. These groups span a subset of $k = 5$ groups, so the critical value used to test the difference between them is

$$D_{\mathrm{NK}_5} = q_5 \sqrt{MS_{S/A}/n} = 4.02\sqrt{12.689/10} = 4.53.$$

The actual difference ($\bar{Y}_1 - \bar{Y}_3 = 6.00$) exceeds D_{NK_5}, so these groups are not part of an equivalent subset. We now examine the next smaller subsets with a range of $k = 4$; there are two of them, determined by the pairs (a_3, a_5) and (a_2, a_1). They are tested with a new critical difference:

$$D_{\mathrm{NK}_4} = q_4 \sqrt{MS_{S/A}/n} = 3.77\sqrt{12.689/10} = 4.25.$$

Both the differences (5.10 and 4.50, respectively) exceed this criterion, and we reject the two corresponding null hypotheses ($\mu_5 = \mu_3$ and $\mu_1 = \mu_2$). Because we have not yet identified an equivalent subset, we look at pairs that span sets of $k = 3$ groups: (a_3, a_4), (a_2, a_5), and (a_4, a_1). The critical difference for these comparisons is

$$D_{\mathrm{NK}_3} = q_3 \sqrt{MS_{S/A}/n} = 3.43\sqrt{12.689/10} = 3.86.$$

Of these three-group spans, only the difference $\bar{Y}_1 - \bar{Y}_4 = 4.40$ is significant, and we reject the null hypothesis that $\mu_4 = \mu_1$. The other two differences, $\bar{Y}_4 - \bar{Y}_3 = 1.60$ and $\bar{Y}_5 - \bar{Y}_2 = 3.60$, are not significant and we retain the null hypotheses that $\mu_4 = \mu_3$ and $\mu_5 = \mu_2$. These last tests identify two equivalent subsets:

$$\underline{a_3 \quad a_2 \quad a_4 \quad a_5 \quad a_1} \quad .$$

Finally, we look at the four two-step pairs and find that only one does not already fall into one or both of these equivalent subsets, namely the pair (a_5, a_1). The critical difference for this one permissable comparison is

$$D_{\mathrm{NK_2}} = q_2 \sqrt{MS_{S/A}/n} = 2.85\sqrt{12.689/10} = 3.21.$$

The result is not significant, and we draw the final line to complete the analysis:[9]

$$a_3 \quad a_2 \quad a_4 \quad a_5 \quad a_1 \quad .$$

Obviously, the Newman-Keuls procedure is much more complex than the other procedures. On the positive side, the changing sequence of criteria gives it more power, which makes it attractive to many researchers. On the negative side, this increase in power often comes with an increase in the familywise Type I error rate. Monte Carlo studies show that when only some of the group means differ (a state of affairs that is more common than not in research), the error rate for the pairs that do not differ is considerably greater than the nominal α_{FW}, in some cases as much as double the value it should be (Ramsey, 1981, 1993; Seaman et al., 1991). What goes wrong is that rejecting the false null hypotheses lets the critical differences shrink too rapidly. In many typical studies, a researcher who is trying to control the error rate to .05 with the Newmann-Kuels test has an actual error rate much closer to 10 percent for those pairs of means that do not differ.[10]

There is a better solution to the inflation of the error rate in the sequential tests than to tolerate an unknown increase in α_{FW}. Ryan (1960) suggested a modification of the Newman-Keuls procedure in which the critical difference shrinks a little less rapidly as k decreases. With further improvements by Einot and Gabriel (1975) and Welsch (1977), the procedure holds the error rate close to its nominal level, even when some of the population means differ and some do not. The steps in this **Ryan-Einot-Gabriel-Welsch (REGW)** procedure are complicated enough that we will not describe how it works. However, it poses no difficulties for a computer, and it is now an option in some of the packages. It is substantially superior to the Newman-Keuls procedure.

Recommendations

We have presented several ways to test the complete set of pairwise differences. They differ in their complexity and in the degree to which they maintain the familywise error at the chosen value of α_{FW}. Tukey's procedure, which uses a single criterion for all differences is the most accurate in its control of familywise Type I error. Use it

---

[9]If we had applied the last critical range to all the two-step pairs, we would have rejected equality for the difference $\bar{Y}_5 - \bar{Y}_4 = 3.50$. But because a_4 and a_5 fall in the equivalent set from a_2 to a_5 (which we established in an earlier step), we cannot treat them as different. If we did not respect the sequential nature of the Newman-Keuls test, we would obtain the incoherent result that μ_2 does not differ from μ_5 but that μ_4, which falls between them, is different from μ_5.

[10]The Newman-Keuls procedure is particularly inadvisable with significance levels such as .10 or .20, where the inflated familywise error is unacceptably high. Another multiple-step method to avoid is the **Duncan procedure**, which many programs provide. It inflates the Type I error rate even more than the Newman-Keuls—for example, Seaman et al. (1991) found them to be over three times larger than their purported level.

when you want a simple, easily defensible, procedure that maintains the familywise error within the chosen level.

The sequential procedures are more subtle. On the one hand, they have greater power, but on the other, they control the familywise error less well when only some of the groups have different means. The Fisher-Hayter procedure achieves a modest increase in power without much weakening of its error control. We recommend it. Although the Newman-Keuls procedure fails to control the familywise error rate at the chosen level, it is too well entrenched in practice to ignore. However, we do not recommend that you use it, and when you see it in research reports, you should take account of its weaker level of familywise error control when you interpret the findings. If you want the increase in power associated with this type of sequential testing and the Ryan-Einot-Gabriel-Welsch procedure is available on your computer, you can use it with more confidence that your familywise error rate is properly controlled.

6.5   Post-Hoc Error Correction

The final step in any analysis is exploratory: The data are examined for findings not anticipated in the planning stage. Perhaps there is a comparison that became relevant only after the anticipated analyses were conducted and assimilated. Perhaps the researcher looks at the means, notes where the large differences are, and tests these differences for significance. These completely post-hoc analyses are generally subjected to the most stringent error control for potential cumulative Type I errors, and for good reason. The family of tests under examination here is potentially infinite, and is still quite large if we include only contrasts that express potentially interesting comparisons. Although only the contrasts that appear the largest may actually be tested, all contrasts are evaluated implicitly if not explictly. We need a procedure that controls the experimentwise error α_{EW} over the family of all possible contrasts.

The procedures we discussed earlier do not apply here. The Bonferroni-type corrections in Section 6.3 are useful only with small families of tests; otherwise the value of the per comparison α, which diminishes with the number of comparisons c, becomes so small that significance is never attained. The tests for all pairwise comparisons in the last section are more useful, but with the exception of an extension of Tukey's procedure that we have not described, they do not allow for complex comparisons. We need a way to control the error rate over the set of all possible contrasts, both simple and complex. Among the procedures designed to simultaneously test all possible comparisons, one stands out.

Scheffé's Procedure

Of all the error correction procedures, Scheffé's procedure (Scheffé, 1953, 1959) allows the broadest range of possible contrasts. For any contrast ψ, we begin by calculating F_ψ, the test statistic for the null hypothesis $\psi = 0$, just as we would for a planned test (Equation 4.6, p. 70). Ordinarily, we would evaluate this test statistic against the criterion $F_\alpha(1, df_{S/A})$ obtained from the F tables in Appendix A.1. Scheffé's procedure replaces this critical value by

$$F_{\text{Scheffé}} = (a - 1)F_{\alpha_{EW}}(df_A, df_{S/A}). \qquad (6.11)$$

The value of $F_{\alpha_{EW}}(df_A, df_{S/A})$ in this formula, also obtained from Appendix A.1, is the one that would be used to test for an *omnibus* effect at the α_{EW} level. Note that it uses $df_{num} = a - 1$ instead of $df_{num} = 1$. Unless there are only two groups (and only one comparison), the value of $F_{\text{Scheffé}}$ is larger than the uncorrected value. For example, with $a = 5$ groups and $n = 10$ subjects per group, the incorrect criterion $F_{.05}(1, 45)$ is 4.06, but Scheffé's critical value at the same level of significance is

$$F_{\text{Scheffé}} = (a - 1)F_{\alpha_{EW}}(df_A, df_{S/A}) = (5 - 1)F_{.05}(4, 45) = (4)(2.58) = 10.32.$$

This substantially larger value makes the test take account of the many possible contrasts that could have been tested.

Scheffé's procedure is easy to apply when the contrast has been tested by a t test instead of an F. The Scheffé critical value for the t statistic is equal to the square root of Equation 6.11:

$$t_{\text{Scheffé}} = \sqrt{F_{\text{Scheffé}}} = \sqrt{(a - 1)F_{\alpha_{EW}}(df_A, df_{S/A})}. \tag{6.12}$$

For example, applied to a study with 5 groups of 10 subjects each, we take the square root of the value we calculated above, giving $t_{\text{Scheffé}} = \sqrt{10.32} = 3.21$. Approaching the problem through the t test lets one accommodate unequal sample sizes and heterogeneous variances, as we will discuss in Section 7.5.

The way that the Scheffé criterion is chosen links it closely to the omnibus test:

> When the omnibus F is significant, there is at least one contrast ψ that is significant by Scheffé's criterion; when the omnibus F is not significant, no contrast is significant by Scheffé's criterion.[11]

This connection between the omnibus test and the corrected test for the contrast is an attractive feature of Scheffé's procedure. However, it is a strong requirement, and the test is very conservative, with less power than the other methods.

Because it controls error over the set of all simple and complex contrasts, Scheffé's procedure is poorly suited to an examination of pairwise differences alone. Applied to our example of the headache remedies, it finds that only the largest of the differences ($\overline{Y}_1 - \overline{Y}_3 = 6.00$, for which $F = 14.19$) exceeds the Scheffé criterion of $F_{\text{Scheffé}} = 10.32$. We do not recommend using it for a study such as this one, where the emphasis is on pairwise differences. The Scheffé test is more appropriate for an experiment where complex comparisons involving post-hoc relationships among many groups are easier to postulate. Look back at the McGovern experiment (Section 4.2, especially Table 4.1, p. 63). Here the groups differed in various complex, but meaningful, ways. Although we introduced this study to show how the structure of the design leads to theoretically motivated contrasts, you can imagine that if the observed pattern of means differed from the initial expectations, an ingenious researcher could devise other interpretations. These ideas would suggest new contrasts, probably involving several groups, that should be tested. Such discoveries are how new psychological theory evolves. However, because these explanations are post hoc, it is advisable to apply the type of control implied by Scheffé's procedure.

---

[11]You may wonder whether there is a way to find a contrast that is significant by Scheffé's criterion, given a significant omnibus F. There is. Simply determine a custom contrast based on the observed pattern of the means, in the manner we described in Section 4.6. Whether it represents a useful or interpretable combination is another matter.

The error protection provided by the Scheffé procedure is severe, and it is common for researchers to adopt an increased α_{FW} for such tests (perhaps one greater than $\alpha_{FW} = .10$). However, doing so results in an increased chance of a false finding, particularly because the temptation to pounce on *any* significant contrast and devise an interpretation for it is so strong. We suggest that unusual post-hoc results be given most credence when they are consistent with the general pattern of results from both the current study and previous work. You should put only a little faith in an inconsistent and isolated post-hoc finding. It is often best to suspend judgment concerning unexpected but exciting findings, especially those frustrating results that are significant by an uncorrected test but not when subjected to post-hoc correction. This strategy allows you to maintain your standards for evaluating post-hoc comparisons, while not ignoring something that could become a major contribution. The best course is to try to replicate the finding, either by repeating the original study or by conducting one that is designed to take a more accurate or comprehensive look at the novel result.

Exercises

6.1. The contrasts in Problem 4.1 were tested as planned comparisons with no control of familywise Type I error. Use the .10 level for the following tests:
a. Evaluate each contrast using the Bonferroni procedure.
b. Evaluate each contrast using the Šidák-Bonferroni procedure.
c. Suppose, instead, that these tests were *not* planned. Evaluate each contrast using the Scheffé procedure.

6.2. Another possible family of contrasts for the example in Problem 4.1 is the set comparing the control against each of the other four groups.
a. Evaluate these contrasts using the Dunnett procedure and the .05 level for all tests.
b. By way of comparison, use Equation 6.6 with the standard t statistic to evaluate them without correction.

6.3. As one more analysis of the example from Problem 4.1, let's consider some of the correction procedures for pairwise comparisons. (Use the .05 level for all tests.)
a. Use the Tukey method to evaluate the pairwise contrasts from Problem 4.1.
b. Use the Fisher-Hayter method to evaluate these pairwise contrasts.
c. Compare the results to those using a Scheffé correction.

6.4. An article reports a one-way analysis of variance (with equal sample sizes) by the summary statement "$F(4, 20) = 4.5$, $p < 0.01$" and the graph in Figure 6.2.
a. Which pairs of means actually differ from each other? Make post-hoc comparisons at the .05 level using the Fisher-Hayter method.
b. Suppose the independent variable was quantitative with equal spacing between the levels. Perform a complete analysis of trend using a Šidák-Bonferroni adjustment and the .05 level.

6.5. You have run an experiment with four groups and 11 subjects per group. An analysis of variance gives a significant result. You wish to test a comparison ψ, so you calculate its F ratio and obtain $F = 7.0$.
a. Assume that you planned the experiment to test this contrast. What is the critical value for F at the 0.05 level? Is it significant?

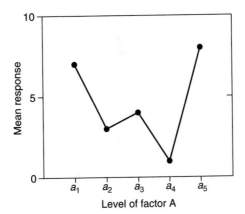

Figure 6.2: A plot of the results of a five-group study (see Problem 6.4).

b. Assume that you noticed this effect when you were looking through the data after completing the study. Test the contrast using Scheffé's method at the .05 level.

c. Explain the discrepancy between the two answers. Why should a result be significant or not depending on when you decide to look at it?

7

The Linear Model
and Its Assumptions

In Chapters 2 and 3 we took a commonsense approach to the development of the F test. The procedure has, however, a much more formal mathematical basis, known as a **statistical model**. This model is a mathematical description that idealizes the process of experimentation. It provides the machinery to derive the properties of the statistical tests, such as the form of the F distribution. It is not necessary to go into the technical details of the model in this book, but some idea of it will help you to appreciate the assumptions that underlie the analysis of variance and to recognize the problems that arise when they are violated. We describe it in the first section below.

Like the mathematical models in every area of statistics, the model for the analysis of variance is an idealization. Real data always deviate from it to some degree. A researcher needs to understand the most likely violations, their effects on the analysis, and ways to avoid them. Depending on their size and nature, these violations can have negligible effects or can seriously compromise the tests. We will discuss these topics in Sections 7.2 and 7.3. One characteristic of many sets of data is a particular problem: different variability in the different treatment groups. In the final section, we discuss how to discover and circumvent this problem.

7.1 The Statistical Model

To explain the model for the analysis of variance, we need to introduce some statistical terminology. A **random variable** is a mathematical device used to represent a numerical quantity whose value is uncertain and that may differ each time we observe it. For example, recall the Monte Carlo simulations in Figure 3.1 (p. 38). Each of these simulations gave a different value of F. So, thinking of the simulations as a whole, F did not have a single value. It had a collection of values, and every time we started a simulation we could not say what value F would have until the sampling process was complete. We were not completely ignorant about its value, however. We knew that some values of F were likely (the small ones), some were unlikely (the large ones), and some were impossible (those less than zero). We can capture this idea by saying that F is a random variable, and that its value is determined by its

probability distribution. We showed this distribution by the smooth theoretical function in Figure 3.1, which is technically known as a **density function**.

How does this idea apply to the analysis of variance? Consider the score Y_{ij} of subject i who received treatment j. Before that score actually materializes in an experiment, its value is uncertain. So, mathematically we can treat it as a random variable. To indicate the uncertainty or random character of this score, we will write it as Y_{ij} instead of Y_{ij}. The random variable Y_{ij} describes the *potential* values of the dependent variable that could occur, while Y_{ij} is the *actual* value of the dependent variable that is observed. Just calling a score a random variable does not tell us much, however. The statistical model asserts what form the probability distribution of Y_{ij} has. To specify this distribution, we need to do two things. First, we must relate it to the independent variable in the experiment, that is, to the treatment groups. Second, we must describe the random part of the probability distribution—which scores are likely and which are not. The first of these tasks is fairly straightforward; the second, and its consequences, will occupy most of this chapter.

The Linear Model

To begin our description, we separate the systematic and random aspects of the model by writing the score Y_{ij} as the sum of the mean μ_j for the treatment group and a random variable E_{ij} that describes how a subject's score varies about that mean:

$$\mathsf{Y}_{ij} = \mu_j + \mathsf{E}_{ij}, \tag{7.1}$$

The mean μ_j is a fixed number, determined by the experimental condition, and the **experimental error** E_{ij} is a random variable.

Now consider the mean μ_j. How does it relate to the treatment condition a_j? It is helpful to think of it as composed of two parts, the overall average of the means, known as the **grand mean** μ_T, and the deviation of the treatment mean from this value, $\alpha_j = \mu_j - \mu_T$, known as the **treatment effect**:

$$\mu_j = \mu_T + \alpha_j. \tag{7.2}$$

Although we can think of the two parts of the model separately, you will often see Equations 7.1 and 7.2 combined as a single equation:

$$\mathsf{Y}_{ij} = \mu_T + \alpha_j + \mathsf{E}_{ij}, \tag{7.3}$$

where Y_{ij} = the ith observation under treatment a_j,
μ_T = the grand mean of the treatment populations,
α_j = the treatment effect for treatment a_j,
E_{ij} = experimental error.

This description is known as a **linear model**, the word *linear* indicating that it is a sum of quantities. This model does for the random variable Y_{ij} what we did for the observed scores Y_{ij} when we partitioned the total deviations into the between-groups and within-group deviations (Figure 2.2, p. 23 and Table 2.3).[1]

---

[1]We mention two pieces of terminology that are not central here, but that come up later. First, the separation of Y_{ij} into a fixed treatment effect and a random error makes it a **fixed-effect model**. We will consider random-effect models in Chapters 24 and 25. Second, because the grand mean μ_T is defined as the average of the μ_j, Equation 7.2 is known as a **means model**.

A benefit of using the linear model to describe a score is that our null hypothesis is associated with a single term of the model. When all the α_j are zero, the group means are identical. Instead of a null hypothesis about the means,

$$H_0\colon \mu_1 = \mu_2 = \mu_3 = \text{etc.},$$

we can write a statement about the treatment effects:

$$H_0\colon \alpha_1 = 0,\ \alpha_2 = 0,\ \alpha_3 = 0,\ \text{etc.}$$

This hypothesis is more compactly written by asserting that the sum of the squared treatment effects is zero:

$$H_0\colon \sum \alpha_j^2 = 0.$$

At this point you won't see much difference between these three versions of the null hypothesis, but the advantage of the forms that use α_j will become apparent when we discuss factorial designs in Part III and particularly when we describe the general linear model in Chapter 14.

The Experimental Error

The second task in describing the model is to specify the nature of the experimental error, that is, how the scores of the individual subjects vary around the means of the treatment conditions. In the linear model (Equations 7.1 and 7.3), this variablity is represented by the random variable E_{ij}. The properties of this random variable are determined by a series of assumptions.

The first two assumptions are the most fundamental:

- **Independence.** The value of E_{ij} is independent of its value for all other subjects. In simpler terms, this assumption says that what one subject does has no effect on any other subject's performance.
- **Identical distribution (within group).** The distribution of E_{ij} is the same for every subject in a treatment group. Stated another way, until the study is conducted, we know no more about one subject's score than about another's.

We like to think of this pair of assumptions as the **random sampling assumptions** because they are likely to be satisfied when we have randomly sampled our subjects from a larger population or have randomly assigned them to groups. The probabilistic equivalence of the subjects within each of the groups is then assured—there is no a priori way to distinguish one subject's score from another.

The third assumption also concerns identical distribution of the error, but this time with respect to the different groups:

- **Identical distribution (between groups).** The distribution of E_{ij} is the same for all treatment groups.

This assumption, as you will see below, is much more vulnerable to being violated than the first two. What it implies is that the groups differ only in their means (the μ_j). There are, of course, many ways in which the error distributions could differ— variance, skew, shape, etc.—and any such difference violates this assumption. Of these characteristics, by far the most important is the variance. When we focus on the variance, the assumption of identical distribution between groups becomes simpler:

- **Homogeneity of variance.** The variance of the random variable E_{ij} is the same for all groups.

This variance is denoted by σ^2_{error} (the lower-case Greek letter sigma). We will have much to say about this assumption in Sections 7.3 and 7.4.

The final assumption concerns the shape of the distribution of errors:

- **Normal distribution.** The random variable E_{ij} has a normal distribution centered around a mean of zero.

The normal distribution here is undoubtedly familiar to you from introductory courses. As we will discuss below, its most important characteristics are that its distribution is smooth, unimodal, and symmetrically arrayed about its mean. You should note that this assumption is more specific than the assumption of identical distributions, which simply states that the distributions are identical, not what shape they must take. Mathematically, we need the assumption of normally distributed error because it justifies the use of the F distribution to evaluate an observed F statistic.

Normal distributions depend on only two quantities, their mean and their variance. As a result, when the assumption of normal distributions holds and the random variable E_{ij} is centered around a mean of zero, the only way that the error distributions can differ is in their variance. Because of that fact, when we make the normal-distribution assumption, we can substitute the assumption of homogeneity of variance for that of between-group identical distribution.

Expected Mean Squares and the F Ratio

In light of the model, let's reconsider the logic of the F test. At the end of Section 2.1 (see p. 21), we stated informally that our test would be based on the ratio

$$\frac{\text{(treatment effects)} + \text{(experimental error)}}{\text{experimental error}}.$$

In Chapter 3 we wrote the test statistic as the ratio

$$F = \frac{MS_A}{MS_{S/A}}$$

and compared it to the theoretical F distribution. We can use the linear model to justify this approach.

The properties of a statistical test are governed by its behavior over a long series of identical experiments. Having a mathematical model allows statisticians to determine the sampling distribution of the sums of squares, the mean squares, and the F ratio. For many purposes, such as determining the relationship of the calculations to the null hypotheses, it is sufficient to look at the long-term average of these quantities, as expressed by their average values, rather than at their full probability distribution. In these theoretical calculations, the average is called the **expected value**, which is the term used to describe the mean of a random variable. We will denote it by the letter E, together with the quantity whose average is being expressed (don't confuse it with the random error E_{ij} of the linear model). Finding the expected values of the mean squares, or **expected mean squares**, tells us which terms of the linear model influence the numerator and which the denominator of the F ratio.

The within-groups mean square $MS_{S/A}$ in the denominator is the simpler of the two. Its magnitude is affected only by the variability of the scores around their average value for their particular group. In terms of the linear model of Equation 7.3, this variability comes only from the experimental error E_{ij}. Some statistical calculation (which we will spare you) shows that the expected value of the within-groups mean square is exactly equal to the error variance, σ^2_{error}, which we assumed was the same for all the treatment conditions. Stated in symbols:

$$E(MS_{S/A}) = \sigma^2_{\text{error}}. \tag{7.4}$$

The expected value of the treatment mean square in the numerator of the F ratio is a little more complicated. It is influenced by three factors, sample size n, the size of the treatment effects α_j, and the amount of experimental error σ^2_{error}. Another set of statistical calculations shows that the expected treatment mean square is

$$E(MS_A) = n\,\frac{\sum \alpha_j^2}{a - 1} + \sigma^2_{\text{error}}. \tag{7.5}$$

The first term is the product of the number of subjects per group and the sum of the squared treatment effects divided by the degrees of freedom, and the second term is the error variance.

Having the expected mean squares lets us discuss the evaluation of the null hypothesis in mathematical terms. The null hypothesis, as we wrote it earlier, states that $\sum \alpha_j^2 = 0$. When this hypothesis holds, the first term in Equation 7.5 vanishes and the two expected mean squares are the same size: $E(MS_A) = E(MS_{S/A})$. The actual values of the two mean squares will generally not be equal because they derive from different aspects of the data—differences among the means and differences among subjects within groups—but on average they will be. When the null hypothesis is false, $\sum \alpha_j^2$ is positive and $E(MS_A)$ is greater than $E(MS_{S/A})$. This difference increases both with how much the null hypothesis is violated (i.e. with the magnitude of the α_j) and with the sample size n. Now consider the F ratio. When the null hypothesis is true, its numerator and denominator have, on average, the same size and $F \approx 1$. When the null hypothesis is false, the numerator is, on average, larger, more so when the differences between groups are large or when the sample size is large.

Violations of the Assumptions

We stated five assumptions about the distribution of the experimental error. These assumptions are part of the mathematical model, which, as we said, is an idealization that is never exactly satisfied by data. How seriously should we take them? If the assumptions are violated, then the F we calculate from our data might not have the F distribution we use to decide whether to reject the null hypothesis. Fortunately, research has shown that the F test is insensitive to some violations. When it is, we say that the F test is **robust** to those violations. What we need to know is which aspects of the F test are robust and which are not—when can we ignore the assumptions, and when is their violation serious enough to compromise our statistical test?

Not surprisingly, individual researchers (and statisticians) differ in their concern for these violations. Some ignore them, some feel that they invalidate the standard analyses, and most fall in between—as in any other human endeavor, there are optimists and pessimists. Wherever you fall on this spectrum, it is important for you to understand how the assumptions may fail and to know how to look for these failures and what their consequences are. We feel strongly that a close examination of the data and a consideration of the assumptions of the statistical design are important parts of any analysis. You cannot simply assume that things will work out well, nor can you leave the checking of the assumptions to a computer program (although the programs can help you check them). You should acquire the habit of looking at how well your study satisfies the assumptions of the analysis, and you should keep them in mind when interpreting your results and those of others.

Substantially violating the assumptions of the analysis of variance can have one of two types of effects. Some violations, particularly those affecting the randomness of the sampling, compromise the entire set of inferences drawn from the study. Others, such as concerns about the distributional shape, affect mainly the accuracy of the statistical tests themselves—their Type I error probability and their power. The two categories of violations should not be confused. Clearly, the first category needs to be taken very seriously. We will discuss the consequences of violating the random-sampling assumptions in Section 7.2 and the ways for dealing with violations of the distributional assumptions in Sections 7.3 and 7.4.

7.2 Sampling Bias and the Loss of Subjects

From the researcher's viewpoint, all the inferential statistical techniques, including the analysis of variance, are founded on the idea that there is some population of subjects from which we have obtained a sample. In Chapter 1, we discussed some issues relating to the definition of that population. The ideal, of course, is to draw the sample randomly, so that each member of the population is equally likely to appear. However, it is impossible to realize this ideal in any actual research situation. The samples we obtain are never perfectly random. In this section, we consider some consequences of this imperfection.

We can view the kind of problems that can arise in terms of the loss of subjects. Two types of loss are possible. One occurs before the experiment proper begins. When the sample is obtained, not all members of the population are equally likely to appear in it. The other occurs after the sample has been drawn. For one reason or another, a subject originally assigned to one of the conditions is unable to complete the study or to provide satisfactory data. Either the exclusion of subjects from the sample before the experiment or the loss of data during the experiment can threaten its integrity.

Exclusion of Subjects from the Experiment

A failure of random sampling before the data are collected implies that the population of interest has not been sampled evenly. Potentially the subjects from whom data are recorded may give a biased picture of the population as a whole. For example, if the subjects who are less competent at a task are also less likely to appear in the sample, then the sample means $\bar{Y}_j$ tend to be greater than the true population means μ_j. You should keep the possibility of such biases in mind when interpreting a study and generalizing it to other populations.

Many users of the analysis of variance, particularly in experimental settings, are less interested in overall population means than in differences among the treatments that define the groups. Here we are on much more solid ground. When the assignment to groups has been made randomly, any bias in recruiting the subjects applies equally to all groups. Differences among the groups are due to their treatments, not to the exclusion of subjects.

Where dangers arise are in **nonexperimental designs**—that is, studies in which the groups constitute natural populations, to which random assignment is impossible. The analysis of variance can tell us that the groups differ, but it cannot tell us why. Consider a study of college students that includes groups of men and of women. We find a difference between the two group means: $\overline{Y}_{\text{men}} \neq \overline{Y}_{\text{women}}$. But in understanding these means, we must consider whether we have recruited different portions of the actual population of men and women at the college. If the samples of men and women were biased in different ways, that alone could account for the difference we observe between the two means. Our concern would be greater if we found that, for example, it was much easier to recruit women for the study than men. The potential for bias of this type is one of the reasons that studies using preexisting groups are more difficult to interpret without ambiguity than those where random assignment is possible. Conclusions about such factors are frequently controversial.

Faced with these concerns, researchers sometimes try to find evidence that no differential sampling bias has occurred. To do this, it is necessary to find some ancillary quantity that might be related to the scores and then try to show that it does not differ among the groups. For example, studies in which a clinical population is compared to a group of nonclinical control subjects often start by showing that the two groups do not differ in such things as age, education, and so forth. Although an analysis such as this is essential, you should note that it depends on *accepting* a null hypothesis, and as such, can never lead to as clear an outcome as the more usual rejection strategy. At the least, it adds a step to the logical chain that leads to a conclusion.[2]

When differences among the initial samples are suspected, it may be possible to apply some form of statistical correction to ameliorate the situation. Like the demonstration of equivalent groups we described in the preceding paragraph, this approach also depends on the availability of some ancillary variable that can be used to "adjust" the scores. Sometimes the new factor can be introduced as a blocking factor (as we discuss in Section 11.5); other times the analysis of covariance is used (see Section 15.7). As we describe there, either of these two approaches is fraught with danger, and must be used carefully. In our view, even though the corrections used in these analyses often are better than nothing, no statistical adjustment can entirely eliminate differential sampling biases.

Loss of Subjects

What are the consequences of losing subjects after the groups have been formed? Suppose we have used random assignment to create treatment groups with equal numbers of subjects, but subjects are lost or their data become unusable. The researcher now has an **unbalanced design**, one with unequal sample sizes, and must face two problems, one minor and one serious. The minor problem is that the calculations needed to analyze the design are more complex. For a one-way design, we showed the overall analysis with unequal groups in Section 3.5 and the test of analytical comparisons in Section 4.4. The calculations for unbalanced designs with more than one factor

---

[2]It is also possible to try to match the groups on these quantities before the study starts. Such matching is common in clinical research.

are harder, but modern computer programs can perform them using the approach we discuss in Chapter 14. The more serious problem is that the loss of subjects potentially damages the equivalence of groups that were originally created randomly.

Examples of Subject Loss.   There are many reasons for data to be lost or subjects to be discarded from an experiment. In animal studies, subjects are frequently lost through death and sickness. In a human study in which testing continues over several days, subjects are lost when they fail to complete the experimental sequence. For example, in a memory study requiring subjects to return a week later for a retention test, some subjects will not appear, perhaps because of illness, a scheduling conflict, or simple forgetfulness. Subjects are also lost when they fail to reach a required performance criterion, such as a certain level of mastery—those who cannot perform the task are not included in the analysis. Suppose we are interested in the time that subjects take to solve a problem. Those subjects who fail to solve it cannot contribute to the analysis and must be eliminated.

When observations are lost or unavailable for some reason, we should ask what effects the exclusion has on the results. The most important questions here are whether the loss depends on the *behavior* of the subject and whether the loss threatens the assumption of equivalent groups. For example, consider the time-to-solve measure mentioned above. The subjects who are lost from this study are those whose solution times (if they could eventually solve the problem) are greater than those of subjects who solve within the time limit. Can we still assume that the groups contain subjects of equivalent ability? If roughly the same number of subjects fail to reach the criterion in all of the conditions, then we may still be able to assume equivalency. Although the groups would contain slightly better problem solvers than the original population, the critical assumption of equivalent groups would be largely intact. We would, however, need to make clear that our conclusions applied to a population from which poor problem solvers had been excluded. On the other hand, when different proportions of subjects are lost, we cannot convincingly assume that the resulting samples are equivalent. Groups with a greater proportion of lost subjects would contain, on average, better problem solvers. Contrast this case with the situation when the loss is due to the occasional malfunctioning of the experimental equipment. Such losses are unrelated to the behavior of the subjects and thus pose no threat to the assumption of equivalent groups. With random loss, the inferences are not affected.

Ignorable and Nonignorable Loss of Subjects.   It is useful to classify any loss of subjects in terms of its effect on the assumption of equivalent groups (see Schafer & Graham, 2002, for a recent discussion of these issues). Following a scheme proposed by Little and Rubin (1987, 2002), we will call a loss that does not disturb the random formation of the groups **missing at random** or **ignorable** and one that does, **missing not at random** or **nonignorable**. When the loss is ignorable, the chance that a subject's data are lost is independent of what these data would have been had the loss not occurred; when it is nonignorable, the chance that a subject's data are lost is related to the score the subject would have obtained, had we been able to make the observation. So, with malfunctioning equipment the losses are unrelated to the unrecorded score, and the loss is ignorable. Inferences based on such data are unaffected by the loss. In contrast, consider the solution-time example. The only subjects who fail to provide scores are those that would have had long solution times. This is a nonignorable loss. Because the high scores are missing, the observed mean time $\bar{Y}_j$ is less than the population value μ_j. More seriously, this bias is greater for groups that received a hard problem, where more subjects failed to solve within the time limit, than it is for an easy problem, where most subjects solved. The comparison between groups is contaminated.

Faced with subject loss, a researcher must decide whether it is random, that is, whether it is ignorable or nonignorable. The answer depends on what causes the subjects to leave the experiment, and this can be almost impossible to know for certain. For example, consider a memory experiment in which each subject is tested either 15 minutes or 2 days after learning. Fifty subjects are randomly assigned to each condition. Of the 50 subjects in the 15-minute condition, all are available for the retention test. However, only 38 of the 50 subjects in the two-day group return for the final test. Whether this loss is ignorable depends on why the subjects did not show up. If the failure was because of an unanticipated scheduling conflict or illness, then it is random and in the same category as equipment failure or an experimenter's error. If the subjects who failed to return were mostly poorer learners who were dissatisfied with how they were doing, then it would not be. The delay group would have a greater proportion of the better subjects than the 15-minute group, and we would overestimate the mean of the two-day group.

Let's take another example. Regrettably, in animal studies, particularly those involving a physiological manipulation, the animals in highly stressful conditions (such as operations, drugs, high levels of food or water deprivation, or exhausting training procedures) are sometimes unable to complete the study. If this were the case, only the strongest and healthiest animals would give valid data. The difficult or more stressful conditions would contain a larger proportion of healthy animals than the less severe conditions. Thus, a potentially critical selection factor—health of the animals—may make this loss nonignorable.

Sometimes it is possible to solve the problem of nonignorable loss by taking corrective action. A useful strategy is to make the same selection pressures apply to all groups. In the memory experiment, we could require that *all* subjects return after two days, even those who had already received the 15-minute test. The data from any subject in the short retention condition who failed to show up later would also be discarded. In an animal study, we could apply similar stresses to animals in all conditions so as to equalize the chance that an animal would be dropped.

If the drop-out rates cannot be equalized, it may still be possible to make the groups more equivalent by artifically excluding some members of certain groups. Suppose that in the study that measured time to solve a problem, 5 of 20 subjects in one condition had failed to solve within the time limit, while all of the 20 subjects in the other condition had solved. To make the groups more comparable, we could drop the 5 slowest solvers from the second condition, so that each group included the 15 fastest solvers. For this technique to work, it is necessary to assume that the subjects whose data are discarded are those who would have failed to complete the study had they been assigned to the condition that produced the failures. This assumption may be questionable, but it must be made before any meaningful inferences can be drawn from data adjusted in this manner. It is usually preferable to assuming that all losses are ignorable and making no correction at all.

We should reemphasize that the critical problem with nonignorable subject loss is the interpretation of the results, not any imbalance in the sample sizes (with which it has sometimes been confused). When subjects have been lost nonignorably, we can still perform an analysis of variance and it can still show that the means differ, but we will have trouble interpreting that result. You can see that the sample sizes per se have nothing to do with the problem by considering what would happen if you ran additional subjects to make up for the ones who were missing, so that all the groups ended up the same size. The new subjects would still be affected by the same selection biases as the original ones, and the problems of interpretation would still remain. Do the different sample means imply differences in the population or are they simply the consequence of uneven loss of subjects? We would not know.

Clearly a loss of subjects should be of paramount concern to the experimenter. You have seen that when the loss is related to the phenomenon under study, randomness is destroyed and a systematic bias may be added to the differences among the means. This bias cannot be disentangled from the treatment effects. You must solve this problem before you can draw meaningful conclusions from your experiment. However, if you can be convinced (and, crucially, you can convince others) that the subject loss has not resulted in a bias, then you can go ahead to analyze the data and interpret your results unequivocally.

7.3 Violations of Distributional Assumptions

We turn now to the assumptions associated with the *distribution* of the scores. In terms of the linear model of Equation 7.3, these assumptions describe the random variable E_{ij} that expresses the random part of the model. Violations of these assumptions are less catastrophic than violations of the random-sampling assumptions. They do not affect the equivalence of the groups, but can alter the accuracy of the tests. In this section, we discuss how these assumptions come to be violated, the consequences of their violation, and what you can do about it. We have organized our discussion according to the individual assumptions, but you should be aware that this division is artificial. In reality, the assumptions are interconnected. Events that violate one of them almost always violate one or more of the others.

Methodologists and applied statisticians have approached the study of the violation of assumptions both mathematically and by conducting Monte Carlo studies like the one we described in connection with Table 3.1 (p. 38). In either approach, the distribution of F is examined when one or more of the assumptions is violated in some way. To use a Monte Carlo study to check out one of the assumptions, we have a computer draw groups of scores for which the null hypothesis is correct but the assumption in question is wrong, and then run an analysis of variance. We repeat the process many times, and we find the proportion of the "experiments" for which H_0 is rejected. If the violation is not critical, then this proportion is essentially the same as the α we used to perform the test, i.e. the **nominal significance level**. We then say that the test is **robust** with respect to this violation of the assumptions. If the actual proportion of rejections does not equal the nominal alpha level, then the test is sensitive to this violation. When the observed proportion exceeds the nominal α level, the violation of the assumption has given the test a **positive bias** and that it is **liberal** with regard to Type I error; when the proportion is less than the nominal level, it has a **negative bias** and is **conservative**.

Independence of the Scores

The first assumption of the analysis of variance is that the random part of an observation (i.e. the random variable E_{ij}) is independent of the random part of every other observation, both those in the same group and those in other groups. Independence here means that knowing the value of one observation tells us nothing about what value any of the other observations will take.

Independence can be violated in many ways. The most obvious way is when one subject knows what another has done and lets that information influence his or her response. Thus, whenever subjects are tested in small groups, care should be taken to be sure that they cannot, even inadvertently, be aware of each other's behavior. Another type of violation occurs when subjects are chosen from small natural classes that are likely to respond similarly, say a person and his or her friend, or two rats from the same litter. Here the link is not overt—one rat does not peek at the other rat's response—but occurs because they are more similar to each other from the start than they are to other animals. Similar associations are created when subjects are tested in groups, and all the members of a group may be affected, advantageously or adversely, by incidental things such as minor variation in the experimental procedures (see Section 6.3 of Stevens, 2002 for a discussion of this problem). A more subtle failure of independence occurs when the data are collected over time and the response taken at one time influences that taken at the next. For example, in some studies the scores are ratings assigned by the experimenter or a judge. Unless great care is taken, it is easy for the judge's rating of one subject to influence his or her rating of the next by contrasting their two performances.

How can we tell when independence is violated? Before stating the study, take a critical look at the detailed procedure. Consider the nature of the subjects, the random assignment procedure, and the conditions of testing. In a well-designed experiment, there are few opportunities for violations of the independence assumption. But one must be vigilant, for it is all too easy for opportunities for dependence to slip in. We emphasize that this examination is best conducted in advance—it is far easier to plug the loopholes before the data are collected than to try to fix them after it is too late.[3]

Violations of independence, if substantial, can be quite serious. The independence of observations is not a statistical nicety but a basic requirement of experimental design. When the observations are not independent, the mathematical model is likely to underestimate the true variability of the results, leading to tests that are biased toward rejection of null hypotheses (Scariano & Davenport, 1987). These biases affect the estimates of the mean squares, and, as a result, their effect often *increases* with the

---

[3]The assumptions that underlie multiple regression theory are similar to those of the analysis of variance, and in that domain a wide variety of qualitative and graphical techniques have been developed to check assumptions. Some of these are relevant to the analysis of variance. We will discuss a few of these below; you can find others in most books on multiple regression (e.g., Pedhazur, 1997). The packaged computer programs can produce many of them.

sample size. Large samples do not cure dependencies in the data. As should be clear, the assumption of independence is fundamental to the entire statistical enterprise. Independence is best approached in the original design, through careful experimental procedures, tight control of the design, random assignment of subjects to the treatment groups, and by being especially careful whenever group testing is used. There are few ways to recover from dependent observations after the data have been collected.

Identical Within-Group Error Distribution

The second and third assumptions of the statistical model state that the random part E_{ij} of every score has the same distribution. This assumption does not say that the scores are the same—that would surely be unrealistic—but that the probability distribution of E_{ij} does not depend on either j (the particular group) or i (the particular subject). Every subject's error component comes from the same distribution. We examine the within-group assumption first, and will look at the between-group aspects later.

The most common violation of the within-group identical-distribution assumption in experimental studies occurs when the population contains subgroups of subjects with substantially different statistical properties. Several examples illustrate the range of problems that can arise. Suppose a study is designed that uses samples of college students as subjects and that a systematic difference exists in the population between the average scores of the men and the women. As a result, the samples contain members from the two distinct subpopulations with different means and, perhaps, different variances. Changes in distribution can also be created by outside events— college students tested at the start of the term may be different from those tested just before final exams, and political opinions recorded before an election may be different from those recorded after it. Even when the subjects are homogeneous, changes in the experimental procedure can create changes in distribution. Perhaps the equipment changes as it ages, or the researcher becomes more skilled in executing the procedure. Subjects run by different research assistants may have different distributions.

A failure of the identical-distribution assumption has two types of effect on the analysis. One effect is on the interpretation of the results. When the samples are a mixture of subpopulations whose means are different, a sample mean is not an estimate of the mean of any of these subpopulations, and, if the subpopulations are sufficiently different, then it may not be a good description of any individual. For example, the sample mean in a study where the scores of men and women differ greatly does not describe either the men or the women. The other effect involves the statistical tests. For one thing, a distribution that is a mixture of several subpopulations with different properties usually does not satisfy the normal-distribution assumptions, a topic that we will discuss later. More critically, because the study contains a systematic source of variability that is not taken into account (the difference between subpopulations), the error term is inflated and the power of the test is reduced. A very small value of F, one much less then 1, is sometimes an indication that the error term has been inflated by a mixture of subgroups with different properties.

Where they can be identified, many failures of identical distributions can be corrected by introducing additional factors into the design. For example, if there appear to be gender differences in the scores, a gender factor can be added. We discuss these designs in Part III. When the distributions shift over time in a simple way, we can use analysis of covariance (Chapter 15). Both approaches reduce the size of the error term and, consequently, increase the power of the tests.

Normally Distributed Error

The last of the distributional assumptions states that the individual scores in each treatment population have a normal distribution. Clearly, this assumption is an idealization—among other things, scores from a normal distribution can take any value from $-\infty$ to $+\infty$, although real measurements never have this range. Surveys of actual data sets (e.g., Micceri, 1989) indicate that most of them deviate appreciably from normality. We need to know whether violations of the normality assumption affect the tests.

The normal distribution, the shape of which is determined by a mathematical formula, is characterized by three properties:

- *Unimodality.* The normal distribution has a single central peak, or *mode*, not two or more distinct modes.
- *Symmetry.* The normal distribution is symmetrical about this central peak.
- *Moderate spread.* The normal distribution has the often-illustrated "bell-shaped" form. Its distribution function is neither too concentrated in the center, nor too spread out in the tails. This characteristic is sometimes referred to by the formidable term **mesokurtic**, which, from its Greek roots, means medium-bulging.

Both the asymmetry and the spread of the distribution are measured by numerical coefficients known as the **skew** and the **kurtosis**, respectively. These indices are 0 for a normal distribution and can be positive or negative for non-normal distributions.[4] Figure 7.1 shows a normal distribution, a pair of skewed distributions, and a pair of distributions with different amounts of kurtosis. Most computer packages will calculate them and may even test whether these values deviate from those of a normal distribution. However, these tests are untrustworthy, because they can pick up deviations from normality that have no impact on the test of means. So we suggest that, while you may want to use the measured skew and kurtosis to give descriptive pictures of the distributions, you do not pay much attention to the tests.

The simplest way to check for these characteristics in your data is to construct a histogram of your scores and look at its shape. From this plot, you can spot obvious deviations from normality, like multiple modes, the presence of extreme scores, and skewed distributions. You must not be led astray by the bumps and irregularities that come from sampling variation, however. Particularly when the samples are small, empirical distributions can look quite irregular, even when the actual population is nearly normal. When there do not seem to be appreciable differences among groups in the shapes of their histograms, a better overall picture is obtained by estimating the random variable E_{ij} for each subject by subtracting the observed group mean from the observed score:

$$\text{estimate}(\mathsf{E}_{ij}) = E_{ij} = Y_{ij} - \bar{Y}_j. \tag{7.6}$$

---

[4]Some programs may give the kurtosis of the normal distribution as 3 instead of 0.

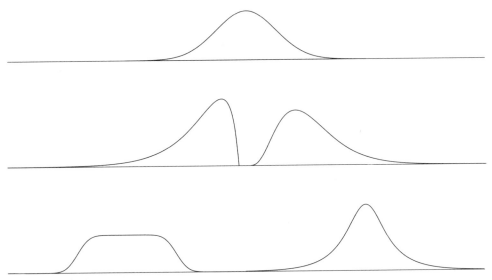

Figure 7.1: A normal distribution (top) and four non-normal distributions, all with the same variance. The first two non-normal distributions are asymmetrical, with skew coefficients of −1.5 on the left and +1.0 on the right. The second two are symmetrical (skew coefficients of 0), but with a kurtosis of −1 on the left and +2.5 on the right. These distributions are said to be platykurtic and leptokurtic, respectively.

This deviation, or **residual**, is then plotted in a histogram of the residuals E_{ij} for all groups at once. Most computer programs can construct some version of this plot and also offer a variety of other residuals and diagnostic plots.

The assumption of the normal distribution is the foundation on which the F distribution is based. Thus, when it fails, the sample statistic $F = MS_A/MS_{S/A}$ might not have the theoretical F distribution used to obtain the critical values in Appendix A.1. However, the situation is much improved by the fact that the hypotheses we want to test concern the means $\overline{Y}_j$, and the sampling distribution of a mean is always much closer to normal than is that of the original scores. In fact, an important theoretical result, known as the **central limit theorem**, states that as the size of the sample increases, the mean comes to have a normal distribution. Consequently, once the samples become as large as a dozen or so, we need not worry much about the assumption of normality. Simulation studies using a wide variety of non-normal distributions show that the true Type I error rates deviate little from their nominal values, and when they do, it is often in a conservative direction (Clinch & Keselman, 1982; Sawilowsky & Blair, 1992; Tan, 1982). The one place where appreciable deviation from the nominal values occurs is when the underlying distribution is skewed and the sample sizes are unequal. In this case, the Type I errors are asymmetrical, with the mean of the smaller group tending to deviate in the direction of the skew. Tests of directional hypotheses (see p. 73) are inaccurate and should be avoided.

Although the F test is robust with regard to violations of the normality assumption, you still need to be on the lookout for the presence of aberrant scores, or **outliers**, that seem to come from a completely different population. These abnormal scores tend to have a disproportionate influence on the mean and to inflate the variance. Outliers are relatively easy to spot. You can think of them as scores that fall outside the range of most of the other data, say more than three standard deviations from the mean. The more comprehensive computer packages contain procedures for identifying them. What is more difficult is to decide what to do with them. You should examine these extreme scores in detail to see if something, other than just being extreme, makes them exceptional. Often they turn out to be errors made when copying the data. Alternatively, a subject may have failed to follow instructions or refused to cooperate. Experimenter error, such as giving a subject the wrong treatment, also can produce outliers. After identifying the problem, or when the score is palpably absurd, it is appropriate to exclude an outlier from the analysis (but you should note this fact when you describe your study). However, any distribution of data is likely to contain some extreme scores. Real data often are a little more scattered than a normal distribution—the technical term is **overdispersed**. These observations are a valid part of the distribution and should be included in the analysis.[5]

The treatment of non-normality varies with the way in which the assumption is violated. Several ways that the data can deviate from normality are relatively easy to spot—multiple modes, extreme scores or outliers, and asymmetrical or skewed distributions. The discovery of multiple modes is usually the easiest to deal with. They suggest that the data are a mixture of two or more underlying distributions, which implies that the assumption of an identical distribution of the random variable E_{ij} for all subjects is violated. The presence of subpopulations is best treated by identifying the source of the heterogeneity (for example, gender) and including it as an explicit factor in the design.

Another way to deal with data that are not normal is to abandon the analysis of variance and to switch to a form of testing that does not depend on the normality of the scores. There are several procedures, known collectively as **nonparametric tests**, that examine null hypotheses about location under weaker distributional assumptions. For data from independent groups, as we discuss here, the relevant null hypothesis is that the medians of the distributions are the same,[6] and the alternative is that some of the medians differ. If the groups differ only in that their distributions are shifted left or right relative to each other, then this hypothesis can be tested by the **Kruskal-Wallis test** or its two-group equivalents, the **Mann-Whitney U test** and the **Wilcoxon rank sum test**. When the underlying distributions are substantially skewed or have many extreme scores, these tests are less sensitive to distributional differences and have greater power than does the standard analysis of variance.[7]

---

[5]Some data analysts suggest routinely **trimming** the data—that is, excluding the most deviant scores from all treatment conditions. We do not recommend such a wholesale exclusion of data. Throwing out extreme scores that are actually part of the distribution reduces the error mean square and gives the F test a positive bias.

[6]The median, you will recall, is the score that divides a distribution such that half of the scores are smaller than it and half are larger. Without getting into details, when the number of scores is odd, the median is the value of the middle-most score, and when the number of scores is even, it is the average of the two scores in the middle.

[7]Space limitations prevent us from describing the nonparametric tests here. You can turn to any of several good books on the subject, all of which cover much the same ground (psychologists often

However, before switching to a nonparametric test, you should be aware of their limitations. First, the nonparametric tests have their own set of underlying assumptions. Although these are weaker than those of the standard analysis of variance, they must still be satisfied. Second, although these tests protect you against violations of the distributional assumptions, they do not solve the difficulties of sampling bias associated with random assignment. Finally, they are most useful for the one-way designs and are much less so for the complex experimental designs that we discuss later in this book.

Between-Group Differences in Distribution—Homogeneity of Variance

We turn now to the far more serious problem of differences in the shape of the distribution among the groups. The assumption states that these distributions do not differ. It is helpful to distinguish between differences in variance—the scores in one group vary about their mean more than do those of another—and differences in other characteristics such as the skew or the kurtosis. By far the most serious problem is the presence of differences in the variability. We can pass over differences in skew or kurtosis quickly. They pose no problem unless the sample sizes are tiny or unequal. The remarks on page 145 still hold. The only real problem arises when the direction of the skew differs among groups and the samples are small. In that case, when a Type I error occurs, it is more likely to be that sample means are displaced in the direction of the skew than one in which they are displaced the other way.

In contrast to the skew and kurtosis, differences in the variances do pose serious problems. Let's consider why we might find such differences among the groups. The first thing to realize is that the assumptions refer to *population* differences in variance, not those we observe in the samples. Although each sample variance s_j^2 is an estimate of the corresponding population variance σ_j^2, they need not be identical. Even when the populations from which we drew our subjects have the same variance, the sample variances are rarely identical, and we should expect moderate differences among the observed variances, particularly with small samples. These accidental differences do not concern us, as they are accurately accommodated by the statistical procedures that lead to the F test.

Of more concern to the researcher are *systematic* causes of heterogeneity. These typically arise in one of three ways:

1. Groups that are defined by a classification factor, such as gender or socio-economic level, can have intrinsically different variances.

2. Experimental manipulations can produce differences in variance as well as differences in the group means.

3. With some measures, such as response times, the variability of a score is related to its size. Groups with many large scores have greater variances than groups with many small scores.

The first of these is the simplest to explain. Natural groups of subjects can differ in variability just as they can in average size. Consider two examples. First, young children may have a more diverse collection of approaches to solving a problem than

---

cite Siegel & Castellan, 1988; a more comprehensive treatment is Hollander & Wolfe, 1999). Most of the computer packages can apply them.

do older ones, who have already encountered instances where similar problems were solved. The wider variety of strategies employed by the younger children results in a more variable distribution of scores. Second, a clinical population may differ in variance from a set of normal controls, as a result of whatever characteristics make it a clinical population. Which group is the more variable here depends on the particular population that is being studied and how the controls were chosen.

The second systematic cause of differences in variance arises when the treatment itself affects subjects differently, producing differences among the group variances. The experimental manipulation can consolidate or scatter subjects within a group by making them behave more similarly or more disparately. For example, a stressful condition might lead some subjects to buckle down and try harder and others to give up, increasing the variance of that group relative to a less stressful condition. The floor effects and ceiling effects that we mentioned on page 5 have the effect of compressing the range of scores and creating differences in variance.

The third source of variance differences is more intimately tied to the scores than to the treatments. Observations that are bounded or restricted at one side of the scale (often by zero) frequently have greater variability the farther they are from that boundary or point of restriction. Data that are counts of events have this characteristic. For example, the number of nerve impulses recorded in a fixed interval or the number of speech errors made while reading a given text have greater variability when the number of impulses or number of errors is large than when it is small. Response latency—the time that a subject takes to make a response—also has this property: Conditions leading to long latencies usually have larger variances than conditions leading to shorter latencies. For example, the variability of subjects solving problems will almost certainly be greater for the groups that take more time to solve them. With any of these measures, a manipulation that changes the mean also changes the variance, producing a situation in which the variances are related to the means.

Having seen that differences in variance can arise in many types of study, we need to consider their effects on the analysis.[8] It used to be thought (based on an investigation by Box, 1954b) that the F test was relatively insensitive to the presence of variance heterogeneity, except when unequal sample sizes were involved (for an excellent review of this older literature, see Glass, Peckham, & Sanders, 1972). However, more recent work, summarized by Wilcox (1987), has shown that even with equal samples, substantial differences in variance bias the F test positively. The null hypothesis is rejected too often.

To demonstrate the effects of heterogeneity of variance, we conducted the series of Monte Carlo simulations in Table 7.1. The table shows three sets of simulations, separated by horizontal lines. The four right-hand columns give the proportion of 100,000 simulated experiments that were rejected at different nominal significance levels. The first four rows give the properties of three-group analyses with $n = 10$ subjects per group, no differences between the means, and, except in the first row, different variances. In the first row, the variances are homogeneous, and you can see that the obtained or actual alpha levels are almost exactly equal to their nominal

---

[8]The effects of heterogeneity of variance on the analysis of variance is sometimes called the **Behrens-Fisher problem** after early workers.

Table 7.1: Monte Carlo significance levels estimated from sets of 100,000 simulated experiments with various combinations of heterogeneity of variance, sample size, and number of groups.

Number of Groups	Sample Size	Pattern of Variances	Nominal significance level α			
			.10	.05	.025	.01
3	10	1,1,1	.100	.050	.026	.010
3	10	1,2,3	.104	.054	.029	.013
3	10	1,4,9	.112	.063	.037	.018
3	10	1,9,25	.116	.069	.041	.022
3	5	1,4,9	.116	.066	.038	.019
3	10	1,4,9	.112	.064	.036	.018
3	15	1,4,9	.111	.062	.035	.017
3	25	1,4,9	.107	.061	.035	.017
3	50	1,4,9	.107	.060	.035	.017
3	10	1,4,9	.110	.060	.036	.018
6	10	1,1,4,4,9,9	.123	.073	.044	.023
9	10	1,1,1,4,4,4,9,9,9	.130	.078	.047	.023

values. The next three rows have increasing degrees of heterogeneity of variance, and there is a corresponding increase in the proportion of null hypotheses rejected at each significance level. This positive bias is largest at the smaller significance levels—for example, when the largest variance is 25 times the smallest (a very substantial difference), the actual rejection rates is more than twice the nominal $\alpha = .01$ level.

In the second series of simulations, the degree of heterogeneity is held constant and the sample size changes. From these simulations we see that although there is some improvement with larger samples, the positive bias does not go away, even when n is as large as 50.[9] In the third series, we varied the number of groups, keeping the differences in variability among the groups the same. The positive bias is somewhat larger in the experiments with many groups. In short, the presence of heterogeneity leads to an inflation of the actual Type I error that is reduced, but not eliminated, by an increase in sample size.

The analysis of variance is more susceptible to the problems of unequal variance when the samples do not have equal sizes. We do not have space here to discuss these effects in detail, but you should be aware of a few points. First, the biases we have demonstrated are greater when the sample sizes are unequal than when they are nearly equal. Second, the problem is much more serious when the smaller samples have the greatest variability. Third, tests that use a directional alternative hypothesis are more

---

[9]The row with $n = 10$ replicates a condition from the first series, which is replicated again in the third series. The proportion of rejections are quite similar in the three rows, although not exactly the same. This variability reflects the random behavior of Monte Carlo simulations and gives an idea of how closely you can trust each individual result.

at risk than are those that use the standard omnidirectional alternative hypothesis. Many researchers feel that these facts make it important for a good study to have samples of approximately equal size. We concur with this recommendation.

7.4   Dealing with Heterogeneity of Variance

In this section, we discuss how to test for differences among group variances, then examine several ways to accommodate heterogeneity of variance in the analysis of differences among the means.

Testing the Differences Among Variances

The principal reason that researchers test for differences among variances is to check the assumptions of the analysis of variance. However, there are studies where differences in variance are themselves of substantive interest. We mentioned above that the variance can be greater in a stressful condition than in a less stressful one. Another example occurs in a problem-solving task. In one condition, the instructions may lead all subjects to perform the task in a similar way, producing considerable conformity in the solution times. In another condition, the strategies are less constrained, and much greater variablity occurs. Both sets of differences concern aspects of the behavior that are not measured by a test for differences among the means. The researcher would want to look at the variances quite apart from any concern about the assumptions of the analysis of variance.

The statistical hypotheses evaluated in testing the differences among variances are similar to those evaluated when comparing means:

$$H_0\colon \sigma_1^2 = \sigma_2^2 = \sigma_3^2 = \text{etc.},$$
$$H_1\colon \text{not all } \sigma_j^2\text{'s are equal.}$$

The number of ways to test these hypotheses is surprisingly large. With means, there are only a few commonly-used alternatives to the analysis of variance, which, as we have seen, is fairly robust to violations of the distributional assumptions. The corresponding situation for variances is less satisfactory, so statistical workers have proposed many different testing strategies. Conover, Johnson, and Johnson (1981) describe 56 different tests that could be used, and others have been suggested since that article was published. Happily, we only need to look at a few of them.

We start by reviewing a procedure proposed by Hartley (1950), not because we recommend it, but because you may encounter it. His test statistic, $F_{\max}$, is simply the ratio of the largest group variance to the smallest group variance:

$$F_{\max} = \frac{\text{largest } s_j^2}{\text{smallest } s_j^2}.$$

A large value of $F_{\max}$ indicates the variances differ. Critical values for the $F_{\max}$ statistic have been calculated and tabled (Pearson & Hartley, 1970, 1972). Unfortunately, in spite of its simplicity and of the fact that it is provided by many packaged computer programs, the $F_{\max}$ statistic is unsatisfactory. Its sampling distribution, as reflected in the Pearson-Hartley tables, is extremely sensitive to the assumption that the scores have a normal distribution. It lacks the robustness of the analysis of variance.

Among the many alternatives proposed to the F_{max} test, two stand out in the Conover et al. (1981) survey as both accurate and relatively easy. Both are based on the same simple idea. First, we find a way to measure how much each score deviates from the center of its group (its mean or its median). If the variances are homogeneous, then the average size of these deviations, disregarding their sign, will be about the same for all the groups, while if the variances are heterogeneous, then the deviations will be large in the most variable groups. In this way, a question about variances is turned into a question about average deviations, and that can be investigated with an ordinary analysis of variance.

The better of the two tests is due to Brown and Forsythe (1974a). They measure the deviation of a score from the center of its distribution by the absolute value of its difference from the median of that group, Md_j:

$$Z_{ij} = |Y_{ij} - Md_j| \qquad (7.7)$$

(the two vertical lines indicate to ignore the sign of the deviation). The other version of the test, proposed earlier by Levene (1960), uses the absolute deviation from the mean, $|Y_{ij} - \bar{Y}_j|$. Either procedure works well, but the Brown-Forsythe procedure is slightly more robust.

Table 7.2 shows a numerical example of this procedure, using the data originally given in Table 2.2 (p. 22). The upper part of the table presents the initial calculations. There are three columns for each group. The first of these columns reproduces the original scores, with the median of each group, 16, 7, and 10, marked by a box. In the second column, this median is subtracted from each score. As a check on our calculation, note that each column contains the same number of positive and negative entries, as must be the case unless there are ties at the median. The third column contains the absolute values of these differences, that is, the Z_{ij} of Equation 7.7. We now conduct a standard analysis of variance on the Z_{ij}, treating them exactly as we would any other set of scores. Below the columns of Z_{ij} are the sums of the Z_{ij} and the sums of the squared Z_{ij}—in our standard notation, these are the sums A_j and each group's contribution to the raw sums of squares $[Y]$, respectively. From these values we calculate the three bracket terms:

$$[Y] = \sum Z_{ij}^2 = 65 + 55 + 75 = 195,$$

$$[A] = \frac{\sum A_j^2}{n} = \frac{15^2 + 13^2 + 13^2}{5} = \frac{563}{5} = 112.600,$$

$$[T] = \frac{T^2}{an} = \frac{(15 + 13 + 13)^2}{(3)(5)} = \frac{1,681}{15} = 112.067.$$

We obtain the sums of squares from the bracket terms in the usual fashion (see Table 3.1, p. 32). The results, with the remainder of the analysis, are summarized at the bottom of Table 7.2. The degrees of freedom are $df_A = 2$ and $df_{S/A} = 12$, and the mean squares and F ratio are found as usual. The small value of F gives no evidence for heterogeneity. Thus, we can proceed with an analysis of variance for the differences among the group means without undue concern for the homogeneity assumption.

The goal in the Levene or Brown-Forsythe procedure is different from that in the usual F test. Instead of hoping to reject the null hypothesis (thereby showing differences in variability), we do *not* want to reject it. It is important that the test

Table 7.2: Numerical example of the Brown-Forsythe test for heterogeneity of variance.

Original scores and deviations from the group medians

| | — a_1 — | | | — a_2 — | | | — a_3 — | |
Y_{1j}	$Y - Md$	Z_{1j}	Y_{2j}	$Y - Md$	Z_{2j}	Y_{3j}	$Y - Md$	Z_{2j}
16	0	0	4	−3	3	2	−8	8
18	2	2	7	0	0	10	0	0
10	−6	6	8	1	1	9	−1	1
12	−4	4	10	3	3	13	3	3
19	3	3	1	−6	6	11	1	1
$\sum Z_{ij}$		15			13			13
$\sum Z_{ij}^2$		65			55			75

Summary of the analysis

Source	SS	df	MS	F
A	0.533	2	0.267	0.04
S/A	82.400	12	6.867	
Total	82.933	14		

have sufficient power, so many methodologists recommend conducting it at $\alpha = .10$ instead of .05. Some suggest even larger values.

Testing the Means When the Variances Differ

The conclusion we drew from the Monte Carlo experiments in Table 7.1 was that the actual significance level could appreciably exceed the nominal α level when the group variances were unequal. Under these circumstances, we need a way to adjust or modify our analysis. We will mention four approaches in this section. Although none of them is universally effective, most problems can be solved (or ameliorated) by one of the four.

Use a More Stringent Significance Level.   The simplest response to heterogeneity is to reduce the nominal significance level. Look back at Table 7.1. Although the estimated significance levels were frequently above their nominal values, in no case did the actual error rate for the nominal .025 level exceed the more conventional .05 level. So, unless the situation is far outside the range in the table—more groups and larger variance differences—the Type I error will be kept below the 5 percent level by setting $\alpha = .025$. If your concern is to keep the Type I error under control, then a conservative halving of α is the fastest and simplest way to eliminate concerns about heterogeneity. Because it does not require access to the data, it is easy to apply to the results reported in a published experiment.

   This strategy has a cost, however. Using a more stringent significance level makes it harder to reject a null hypothesis (in the language of Chapter 8, it reduces the power of the test). Reducing the α level is appropriate when there really are differences in variance, because this reduction simply brings the actual Type I error rate back to where it belongs. However, when the variances really do not differ, or they differ by only a small amount, reducing α diminishes the power. This lost power can be restored by adding more subjects. How many are needed can be calculated using the methods that we discuss in Chapter 8. In the type of designs most common in psychology, the difference amounts to about a 20 percent increase in sample size. Thus, when you are designing a study in which unequal variances are a possibility, you might consider reducing α and raising the sample size by this amount.

Transform the Data. A second approach to heterogeneity of variance is to modify the scores themselves in such a way that the heterogeneity is either reduced or eliminated. When this can be done, it is superior to a "blunt-instrument" approach like reducing the significance level. This approach is best when the source of the heterogeneity is related to the nature of the scores themselves. The third of the reasons for heterogeneity (p. 148) was the presence of a fundamental relationship between the size of the scores and their variability. Response times, counts, and proportions all have this characteristic. With these types of measures, we can sometimes stretch or compress the scale on which the responses are measured to remove the heterogeneity. Applying a transformation can do more than just reduce heterogeneity of variance. Data for which a transformation is appropriate are often skewed, and the transformation usually reduces this skew and makes the within-group distributions more nearly normal.

The particular transformation to apply depends on how the scores were generated and the approximate relationship between the group means and variances. Suppose the data are counts of the number of events occurring during an observation interval. Data of this type generally have variances that are roughly proportional to the means. If you have such data, you can apply the transformation

$$Y'_{ij} = \sqrt{Y_{ij} + 1/2}. \tag{7.8}$$

Adding the half improves the transformation when Y_{ij} is small, but makes little difference when it is large, and you may see the transformation written without it. Taking the square root reduces the large scores proportionally more than the small ones, pulling together the observations in the groups with larger means. It is likely to reduce or eliminate the heterogeneity. The procedure is easy to apply: You transform every observation Y_{ij} to the new Y'_{ij} and conduct the analysis of variance as usual.

Table 7.3 illustrates this transformation. The first three columns in the top panel give scores such as might be obtained from counts of the number of errors made by three groups of seven subjects when reading a passage under low, medium, or high levels of stress. From the summary information at the bottom of the columns, you can see that they show the type of heterogeneity that is typical of such a measure. The variability is least in condition a_1, where the fewest errors are made, and greatest in condition a_3 where the most errors are made. A Brown-Forsythe test here is almost significant ($F(2, 18) = 3.53$ against a criterion of 3.55) and certainly would be so if this pattern were found in an experiment with a larger sample size. Because the data are counts, it makes sense to try the square-root transformation in Equation 7.8. The

Table 7.3: Transformation of data by the square root (Equation 7.8).

	Original data			Transformed data		
	Low	Med	High	Low	Med	High
	a_1	a_2	a_3	a_1	a_2	a_3
	5	15	27	2.345	3.937	5.244
	10	7	18	3.240	2.739	4.301
	8	12	24	2.915	3.536	4.950
	8	17	20	2.915	4.183	4.528
	5	8	13	2.345	2.915	3.674
	6	5	16	2.550	2.345	4.062
	7	14	25	2.739	3.808	5.050
Mean	7.000	11.143	20.429	2.721	3.352	4.544
Variance	3.333	20.476	26.286	0.109	0.476	0.327

Analysis of variance of the transformed scores

Source	SS	df	MS	F
A	11.998	2	5.999	19.33*
S/A	5.472	18	0.304	
Total	17.470	20		

* $p < .05$

transformed values are in the right three columns of Table 7.3. The differences among the variances now are smaller, are not related to the means in any simple way, and no longer approach significance by the Brown-Forsythe test ($F(2, 18) = 1.86$). We can now perform an analysis of variance on these transformed data. We don't show the details of these calculations because they are just like the one-way calculations elsewhere in this book, but the result is given at the bottom of the table. The analysis shows that the averages of the transformed scores differ among the groups. What does this analysis tell us about the original scores, which, of course, are the ones that we care most about? For the most part, it supports the same conclusions. Although the transformation changes the scores, it does not change their order. The original and transformed scores are also very highly correlated—for Table 7.3, $r = 0.994$. Consequently, groups that differ on the transformed scores also differ on the original scores.[10] Thus, we suggest discussing the results in terms of the original scores. In our example, we would talk about the number of errors, not their square root.

We will mention two other situations in which transformations are helpful. The first arises when data are generated by the timing of events, for example, the latency or time taken to respond. With such data, the standard deviations (rather than the variances) tend to be roughly proportional to the treatment means. Here a logarithmic

---

[10]It is possible to find exceptions to this assertion, but they almost never occur when a transformation is used in the type of theoretically-motivated circumstance we have described.

transformation is usually superior to the square root:

$$Y'_{ij} = \log(Y_{ij} + 1). \tag{7.9}$$

Like the $1/2$ in Equation 7.8, adding the 1 is only important when the scores are small, so it is sometimes omitted.

The second situation arises when the score Y_{ij} is a proportion—for example, the proportion of correct responses in a given number of attempts. The variance of the sampling distribution of a proportion depends on the true value of the proportion. It is greater when the proportion is near $1/2$ than when it is near 0 or 1.[11] Thus, when the treatment conditions produce differences in the average proportions, the variances also differ. The appropriate transformation to remove the dependency in proportions is[12]

$$Y'_{ij} = 2\arcsine\left(\sqrt{Y_{ij}}\right). \tag{7.10}$$

This transformation is most useful when the study contains some groups with very large or small proportions and some with intermediate values.

Before you apply a transformation, you should check whether it is appropriate for your study. Most important, it should be consistent with the analysis you plan to conduct. Any analysis that depends on the exact spacing between the group means, such as a trend analysis, is altered by transforming the data. For example, a straight-line sequence of means may become curved after a transformation is applied, creating a quadratic component that was not in the original data. Any such analysis should be conducted on the original scores, using the corrections we will describe in Section 7.5. Caution is also needed for the factorial designs described in Part III. As we will discuss in Section 10.5, a transformation can change the size or existence of the interaction. Finally, you should verify that the transformation is consistent with the source and nature of your data (counts, times, or proportions, for example), and that the means and variances (or standard deviations) are related in the appropriate way. We do not advise using a transformation simply because the variances appear to differ, without a theoretical motivation for its use. Such a transformation is usually unconvincing to readers of your research.

Alternatives to the Analysis of Variance. The third approach to heterogeneity of variance is to change the analysis procedure altogether, and use one that allows for differences in variance. Statisticians have developed several tests whose accuracy is less strongly influenced by the presence of heterogeneity of variance than is the standard analysis of variance. Some of the more commonly referenced tests are by Welch (1938, 1951), Brown and Forsythe (1974b), and two versions by James (1951) (see Coombs, Algina, & Oltman, 1996, for a summary of these methods and Johansen, 1980, for a formulation that links them).

---

[11] The variation comes about because the sampling distribution is binomial, a distribution that is described in many elementary books.

[12] The **arcsine**, or inverse sine, in this equation requires you to find the angle whose sine is equal to its argument. It is given in some books of tables and can be calculated with a scientific calculator or statistical package. The arcsine is not defined when a sample proportion is equal to 0 or 1; these values can be replaced by $1/(2M)$ and $1 - 1/(2M)$, respectively, before the transformation is applied, where M is the total frequency in the proportion.

All these tests accommodate unequal variances, although, when the variances are equal, they have less power than the standard analysis. Among them (and others), the best choice according to current research appears to be the second version of James's method, usually known as **James's second-order method** (Alexander & Govern, 1994; Wilcox, 1988; see Coombs et al., 1996, for a review of the voluminous literature leading to this recommendation). Unfortunately, the computational demands of James's procedure are substantial and, as of this writing, it has not been incorporated into the standard statistical software packages (some code to run it with the SAS package is mentioned by Lix & Keselman, 1995). The Welch procedure is more tractable, but is somewhat less accurate.

Emphasize Single-*df* Tests. In Chapters 4 and 5, we described the use of single-*df* contrasts to investigate specific hypotheses. It is easy to accommodate unequal variances into these tests, and the results are more robust than the omnibus tests. Many computer programs automatically test individual contrasts this way. Thus, even when you question the accuracy of your omnibus tests (or decide to use a conservative α level), you can use robust procedures for your planned or post-hoc analyses. In many designs, an analysis that emphasizes the single-*df* contrasts is the most practical and satisfactory approach to heterogeneity. We discuss the details in the next section.

7.5   Contrasts with Heterogeneous Variance

The standard tests of a single-*df* contrast ψ presented in Chapter 4 are severely compromised by heterogeneity of variance. While the omnibus F statistic involves all groups equally, a contrast puts more weight on some group means (those for which the coefficients c_j are large, either positive or negative) and less or none on others (those for which the c_j are small or zero). Consequently, the variability of $\widehat{\psi}$ depends on the variability of the particular groups that are weighted most heavily. The overall $MS_{S/A}$, which was used for the error term in Chapter 4, is not sensitive to the particular coefficients and variances. Fortunately, it is easy to modify the t procedure from Section 4.4 to take different variances into account.[13]

The t statistic for a contrast is calculated by dividing the observed contrast by an estimate of its standard error (Equation 4.9, p. 71):

$$t = \widehat{\psi}/s_{\widehat{\psi}}. \tag{7.11}$$

When homogeneity of variance can be assumed, the standard error $s_{\widehat{\psi}}$ is based on $MS_{S/A}$ (Equation 4.10), which is an average of all the group variances. When the variances differ, however, the standard error must be based on the properties of the groups involved in the contrast—their size n_j and variance s_j^2. Each mean $\overline{Y}_j$ has a sampling variance (i.e. squared standard error) of $s_{M_j}^2 = s_j^2/n_j$ (Equation 3.5, p. 35). The standard error of a contrast is a combination of these variances:

$$s_{\widehat{\psi}} = \sqrt{\sum c_j^2 s_{M_j}^2} = \sqrt{\sum c_j^2 s_j^2/n_j}. \tag{7.12}$$

Now t is calculated by Equation 7.11.

---

[13] An equivalent modification of the F test can be constructed, but we will not describe it because the t procedure is the one implemented by most software packages.

Equation 7.12 uses the variances for the individual groups, and so is more accurate than an average standard error based on $MS_{S/A}$. For example, suppose a study has $a = 3$ groups and we want to compare μ_2 to μ_3. The coefficients for this contrast are $\{0, 1, -1\}$. The variability is

$$s_{\widehat{\psi}} = \sqrt{0^2 s_{M_1}^2 + 1^2 s_{M_2}^2 + (-1)^2 s_{M_3}^2} = \sqrt{s_{M_2}^2 + s_{M_3}^2}.$$

Thus, $s_{\widehat{\psi}}$ is based on the squared standard errors of the two conditions entering into this comparison, and the variability of the remaining group is not involved. For a complex comparison with the coefficients $\{2, -1, -1\}$,

$$s_{\widehat{\psi}} = \sqrt{2^2 s_{M_1}^2 + (-1)^2 s_{M_2}^2 + (-1)^2 s_{M_3}^2} = \sqrt{4 s_{M_1}^2 + s_{M_2}^2 + s_{M_3}^2}.$$

Here all three squared standard errors are used, but in unequal parts. The squared standard error for the first group is multiplied by $c_1^2 = 2^2 = 4$, and those for the other two groups are multiplied by $(-1)^2 = 1$.

There is one further complication. The unequal variances give the test statistic a sampling distribution that differs from a standard t distribution. The critical value must be approximated by entering the t table in Appendix A.2 with a somewhat ungainly special value for the degrees of freedom (Satterthwaite, 1941, 1946):

$$df = \frac{s_{\widehat{\psi}}^4}{\displaystyle\sum \frac{c_j^4 s_{M_j}^4}{n_j - 1}}. \tag{7.13}$$

This value will generally not be an integer, in which case, the next smaller integer is used.

For a numerical example, let's return to the unequal-variance data in Table 3.7 (p. 57). Suppose you wanted to examine the contrast $\psi = \mu_1 - 2\mu_2 + \mu_3$. The means of the three groups are 7.0, 10.0, and 5.0, based on samples of size 3, 6, and 4, respectively, and the corresponding standard errors are 1.155, 0.577, and 0.707. From these, you calculate the observed contrast, the estimated standard error of $\widehat{\psi}$, and the test statistic:

$$\widehat{\psi} = \sum c_j \bar{Y}_j = (1)(7.0) + (-2)(10.0) + (1)(5.0) = -8.0,$$

$$s_{\widehat{\psi}} = \sqrt{\sum c_j^2 s_{M_j}^2} = \sqrt{(1^2)(1.155)^2 + (-2)^2(0.577)^2 + (1^2)(0.707)^2}$$

$$= \sqrt{1.334 + (4)(0.333) + 0.500} = \sqrt{3.166} = 1.779,$$

$$t_\psi = \frac{\widehat{\psi}}{s_{\widehat{\psi}}} = \frac{-8.0}{1.779} = -4.497.$$

The approximate degrees of freedom (Equation 7.13) are

$$df = \frac{s_{\widehat{\psi}}^4}{\displaystyle\sum \frac{c_j^4 s_{M_j}^4}{n_j - 1}} = \frac{(1.779)^4}{\dfrac{(1^4)(1.155)^4}{3 - 1} + \dfrac{(-2)^4(0.577)^4}{6 - 1} + \dfrac{(1^4)(0.707)^4}{4 - 1}}$$

$$= \frac{10.016}{(1)(1.780)/2 + (16)(0.111)/5 + (1)(0.250)/3} = \frac{10.016}{1.329} = 7.536.$$

The next smaller integer is 7, so we compare the observed $t = -4.50$ to $t_{.05}(7) = 2.36$. The result is significant, indicating that the mean for group a_2 (10.0) is greater than the combined means for a_1 and a_3 $(7.0 + 5.0)/2 = 6.0$.

You may want to employ some form of control for Type I error when testing several hypotheses. All the procedures we discussed in Chapter 6 work as before, except that the value calculated from Equation 7.13 replaces $df_{S/A}$ as the degrees of freedom used to enter the appropriate statistical tables. Because the combination of groups is different for each contrast, the approximate degrees of freedom may also differ. With the procedures that require the specialized Šidák-Bonferroni, Dunnett, or Tukey tables, you may have to look up critical values for each contrast. Similarly, Scheffé's procedure can be applied by using Equation 6.12 to obtain a critical value from the F tables with $df_{S/A}$ replaced by this adjusted degrees of freedom (Brown & Forsythe, 1974c). In the Tukey and Fisher-Hayter procedures, the critical difference D also depends on the standard error, and it must be calculated separately for each pair using Equation 6.8 (p. 124).

Exercises

7.1. Examine the data for the numerical example in Section 3.4 (Table 3.5, p. 51) to see if the assumption of homogeneous group variances is met.
a. Use the Brown-Forsythe (1974a) test whether the variances are heterogeneous.
b. On the basis of the arguments in this chapter, how should we proceed?

7.2. In Table 7.3, we summarized an analysis of variance of a set of Y_{ij} that were given a square root transformation. On page 153, we reported the outcome of two Brown-Forsythe tests conducted on the original data and the transformed data. Verify these two F's?

7.3. Because factor A in Table 7.3 is quantitative, a trend analysis is of interest.
a. Why is a test of a linear trend contrast on the transformed scores inappropriate?
b. Conduct the appropriate test using the method in Section 7.5. Is there is any curve in the function?

8

Effect Size, Power, and Sample Size

The results of an experiment are expressed most directly by the values of the sample means. The report of any study should include a description of the pattern of means and estimates of their variability, usually the standard deviations of the scores. However, it is also useful to have an overall measure of the magnitude of the effect that incorporates all the groups at once. Such measures of effect size have come into greater prominence recently, when they have been proposed as adjuncts to the conventional hypothesis tests (or even as alternatives to them). They circumvent some, although not all, of the problems with hypothesis tests that we discussed at the end of Section 3.2 (p. 44). We describe some of these measures in Sections 8.1 and 8.2.

The remainder of this chapter concerns the planning of experiments. It is unwise for a researcher to begin a study unless it is likely to obtain reportable results. An important part of the planning process, one that is now required by many granting agencies, is an analysis of the power of a proposed experiment—the probability that a particular alternative to the null hypothesis will lead to a significant outcome. We discuss how power is calculated, and, of greater value to the researcher, how to determine the appropriate sample size for a projected experiment.

If you read literature in this area, you will discover it is plagued by a disparate collection of procedures, measures, and recommendations (Richardson, 1996, gives some useful history). We will describe a consistent approach to this topic, but will mention in footnotes some alternative that you might encounter.

8.1 Descriptive Measures of Effect Size

An **effect-size measure** is a quantity that measures the size of an effect as it exists in the population, in a way that is independent of certain details of the experiment such as the sizes of the samples used. You might ask why we don't use the F statistic or its associated p value as a measure of effect size. One problem is that when there are differences among the μ_j in the population, a study that uses large samples tends to give a larger value of F and smaller p value than does a study with small samples. Thus, these quantities depend on both the population and the particulars of the study.

A related problem is that a test statistic such as F and its associated p value have no population counterparts. It makes sense to say that the subjects in one group remembered 10 percent more material than those in another group, but not that they remembered $F = 8.75$ more or $p < .01$ more.

Descriptive measures of effect size, other than the means themselves, can generally be divided into two types, those that describe differences in means relative to the study's variability and those that look at how much of the variability can be attributed to the treatment conditions. Each type emphasizes a different aspect of the effect, and each has its place in describing a study. Depending on your needs, you might use either or both of them. We discuss them in turn.

Differences Relative to the Variability of the Observations

The first measure is often known the **standardized difference between means**. Consider the control and drug A groups in the study of hyperactive boys in the example from Chapter 2 (Table 2.2, p. 22). The means of these groups are $\bar{Y}_1 = 15$, $\bar{Y}_2 = 6$, and the sample size $n = 5$. We could say that the effect of the drug here is to reduce the scores by $15 - 6 = 9$ points. Useful as this quantity is, it takes no account of how much variability there is in the scores. Is a 9-point difference large or small relative to the extent to which performance varies from one boy to another?

To obtain a measure of the effect that takes this variability into account, we divide the difference by the standard deviation of the scores:[1]

$$d_{12} = \frac{\bar{Y}_1 - \bar{Y}_2}{s_{12}}. \tag{8.1}$$

(Of course, we use different subscripts when groups other than a_1 and a_2 are involved.) The standard deviation s_{12} in Equation 8.1 is the pooled standard deviation of the two groups. With equal sample sizes, it equals the average of the variances:

$$s_{12} = \sqrt{\frac{s_1^2 + s_2^2}{2}}. \tag{8.2}$$

With unequal sample sizes, we must pool the sums of squares and degrees of freedom separately, as we did when finding the mean square in a similar situation (Equation 3.15, p. 58):

$$s_{12} = \sqrt{\frac{SS_1 + SS_2}{df_1 + df_2}}. \tag{8.3}$$

In our example, the two groups contain the same number of boys, so we can use either formula to calculate s_{12}. After calculating the variances from the data in Table 2.2 and entering them in Equation 8.2, we find

$$s_{12} = \sqrt{\frac{s_1^2 + s_2^2}{2}} = \sqrt{\frac{15 + 12.5}{2}} = 3.708.$$

Substituting this information in Equation 8.1, we find that the effect size is

$$d_{12} = \frac{\bar{Y}_1 - \bar{Y}_2}{s_{12}} = \frac{9}{3.708} = 2.43.$$

---

[1]Do not to confuse this measure with a t test statistic (Equation 4.8, p. 71), in which the divisor is an estimate of the *standard error* of the difference between means.

Thus, the groups differ by more than two standard-deviation units. We could calculate the statistics d_{13} and d_{23} in the same way for the other pairs of groups.[2]

The measure d is quite popular, because it is simple to use and makes good intuitive sense. If any measure can be called simply "*the* effect size," it is this. It is zero when there is no difference between the two means, and increases without bound when the difference becomes large. It is particularly useful in the field of **meta-analysis**, which involves combining the findings from several studies (e.g., Hedges & Olkin, 1988; Rosenthal, 1991). By working with d instead of the actual differences between means, the disparate studies are put on a common basis.

The Proportion of Variability Accounted for by an Effect

The d statistic is a natural measure of effect size when only two groups are involved. When a study involves more than two groups, it is useful to have a single measure that summarizes the effect in the entire experiment. This measure is constructed by considering how the total variability is divided into systematic and unsystematic parts.

You will recall that the sums of squares for the original set of data can be divided into a part associated with the difference between groups and a part associated with error (Equation 2.1, p. 25):

$$SS_T = SS_A + SS_{S/A}.$$

The size of the differences among the groups determines SS_A, which is zero when the means in the experiment are all the same and positive when they are not. To obtain an overall measure of the effect, we can take the ratio of the size of this component to the total amount of variability:

$$R^2 = \frac{SS_A}{SS_{\text{total}}} = \frac{SS_{\text{total}} - SS_{S/A}}{SS_{\text{total}}}. \tag{8.4}$$

This quantity is known as the square of the **correlation ratio**.[3] It is zero when there are no differences among groups and approaches one as the group differences come to dominate the within-groups variability. An equivalent formula, based on the F statistic, is

$$R^2 = \frac{(a-1)F}{(a-1)F + a(n-1)}. \tag{8.5}$$

This formula is often the easiest way to find R^2, particularly from published results (which usually report F's, not sums of squares).[4] Using the analysis summary in Table 3.2 (p. 37) for the data from the hyperactive boys, Equations 8.4 and 8.5 give

---

[2]The effect size d_{12} in Equation 8.1 is sometimes calculated using the pooled standard deviation ($s_{\text{pooled}} = \sqrt{MS_{S/A}}$) instead of one based on the two groups in question. The difference between the two is not large unless the variances are heterogeneous, in which case the individual estimate s_{12} is preferable.

[3]Historically, the correlation ratio was denoted the Greek letter η (eta), which is still used. The modern convention reserves the Greek letters for population quantities.

[4]For this reason, we dislike the convention of reporting small F's by simply writing "$F < 1$." The exact value is much more informative.

$$R^2 = \frac{SS_A}{SS_{\text{total}}} = \frac{210}{390} = 0.538,$$

$$R^2 = \frac{(a-1)F}{(a-1)F + a(n-1)} = \frac{(2)(7.0)}{(2)(7.0) + (3)(4)} = \frac{14.0}{14.0 + 12} = 0.538.$$

Effect-size measures of this type are widely reported. You may find it helpful to think of them in a broader context. The sums of squares are measures of the variability of the scores, so we can express the two parts of Equation 8.4 in words as

$$\text{effect size} = \frac{\text{variability explained}}{\text{total variability}}$$

$$= \frac{\text{total variability} - \text{unexplained variability}}{\text{total variability}}. \tag{8.6}$$

This expression is easily adapted to all kinds of treatment effects, including those in complex experimental designs and those based on procedures other than the analysis of variance.

In a very influential book on power analysis, Cohen (1988) defined some standards for interpreting effect sizes:[5]

- A **small effect** is one that captures about 1 percent of the variance (i.e. $R^2 = 0.01$). These effects tend not to be noticed except by statistical means. In terms of the standardized difference, a small effect has $d \approx 0.25$.

- A **medium effect** captures about 6 percent of the variability (or $d \approx 0.5$). These effects are apparent to careful observation, although they are not obvious to a casual glance.

- A **large effect** captures at least 15 perfect of the variability (or $d \approx 0.8$ or more). It is obvious to a superficial glance.

By these standards, the effect in our example ($R^2 = 0.538$) is very large indeed.

When using Cohen's guidelines, you should avoid any evaluative interpretation of the words "small," "medium," and "large." From a researcher's perspective, a large effect may not be better or more important than a small one. Indeed, the type of effects that need careful research and statistical analysis are the medium and small ones. Large effects, in Cohen's sense, are often widely known and there is nothing to be gained from verifying them. Where the discovery of large effects makes important contributions to psychological theory, they are often introduced and made possible by advances in instrumentation or the introduction of new paradigms instead of statistical analysis. Particularly in mature fields, the medium and small effects are the most often investigated. For example, a survey by Sedlmeier and Gigerenzer (1989) reported that the average study in the *Journal of Abnormal Psychology* produced a "medium" effect, a value that has been found in other areas of research (e.g., Cooper & Findley, 1982). There is some agreement among methodologists that a small effect is roughly the lower limit of what one might call a meaningful effect.[6]

---

[5]Strictly, Cohen defined these standards for the population effect sizes that we discuss in the next section, but in practice they are usually applied indiscriminately to either sample or population values.

[6]For some interesting examples of situations where small effects are important, see Prentice and Miller (1992).

8.2 Effect Sizes in the Population

The effect-size measures d and R^2 are descriptive statistics. However, in most studies we are less interested in describing the sample per se, as in making inferences about the population from which the sample came. We need a definition of effect size expressed in terms of population characteristics.

We can easily write the standardized difference for two groups in population terms by replacing the sample values in Equation 8.1 with corresponding population values. For groups a_1 and a_2, this ratio is

$$\delta_{12} = \frac{\mu_1 - \mu_2}{\sigma_{\text{error}}}. \tag{8.7}$$

With more than two groups, we can use the general formula of Equation 8.6 to define the effect size as the amount by which the total variability is reduced when group membership is known. The total variability is the variance of the scores around the grand mean μ_T, which, in theoretical terms, is the expected value (or long-term average) of the squared difference between Y_{ij} and μ_T:

$$\sigma_{\text{total}}^2 = \text{E}[(Y_{ij} - \mu_T)^2].$$

When group membership is known, this variability is reduced to the variance of the scores around the individual group means, which is the same as the error variance from the linear model:

$$\sigma_{\text{error}}^2 = \text{E}[(Y_{ij} - \mu_j)^2].$$

Substituting these variances into Equation 8.6 gives a measure of effect size known as **omega squared**:

$$\omega^2 = \frac{\sigma_{\text{total}}^2 - \sigma_{\text{error}}^2}{\sigma_{\text{total}}^2}. \tag{8.8}$$

Another way to characterize ω^2 uses the parameters of the linear model in Section 7.1. In that model, α_j is the deviation of the group mean μ_j from the grand mean μ. The variability of the group means around the grand mean is measured by the average of the squares of these deviations:

$$\sigma_A^2 = \frac{\sum \alpha_j^2}{a}. \tag{8.9}$$

A nasty little bit of algebra (which we won't show) determines that the total variability σ_{total}^2 is the sum of this between-group variance and the within-group error σ_{error}^2:

$$\sigma_{\text{total}}^2 = \sigma_A^2 + \sigma_{\text{error}}^2.$$

Using these quantities, Equation 8.8 becomes

$$\omega^2 = \frac{\sigma_A^2}{\sigma_{\text{total}}^2} = \frac{\sigma_A^2}{\sigma_A^2 + \sigma_{\text{error}}^2}. \tag{8.10}$$

This equation shows clearly that ω^2 is the ratio of the variability of the treatment conditions (i.e. σ_A^2) to the total variability (i.e. the sum of the explained and error variability).[7]

---

[7]A related quantity used in much of Cohen's writing (e.g., Cohen, 1988) is $f = \sigma_A/\sigma_{\text{error}}$. You can easily translate this measure to and from ω^2:

$$f = \sqrt{\omega^2/(1-\omega^2)} \quad \text{and} \quad \omega^2 = f^2/(f^2+1).$$

How do the sample statistics d and R^2 relate to their corresponding population quantities δ and ω^2? Surprisingly, not very well. As a result of sampling variability, R^2 tends to be larger than ω^2 and d tends to be larger in magnitude (farther from zero) than δ. In other words, if we take the sample values for d or R^2 at face value, we will *overestimate* the population treatment effects. To help understand why the sample statistics are inflated, suppose there were no treatment effects in the population, i.e. that $\delta = 0$ and $\omega^2 = 0$. However, although the population means are the same, it is unlikely that the sample means will be exactly equal in any given experiment. Thus, we would observe a nonzero value for d and a positive value for R^2, both larger than their true values. A similar bias affects the two statistics when the null hypothesis is false.

Estimation of the population effect sizes is a complicated matter, which we will not explore in detail. Without showing their derivation (see Hays, 1994), we will simply present two formulas that let you estimate ω^2. When the complete analysis of variance summary table is available, the estimate of ω^2 is

$$\widehat{\omega}^2 = \frac{SS_A - (a-1)MS_{S/A}}{SS_{\text{total}} + MS_{S/A}}. \tag{8.11}$$

The same value can be obtained directly from the F statistic

$$\widehat{\omega}^2 = \frac{(a-1)(F-1)}{(a-1)(F-1) + an}. \tag{8.12}$$

The way that these formulas correct for sampling error is most easily seen in the second formula. You will recall that when no differences exist among the groups, the chance value of F is approximately 1. In Equation 8.12, this chance value is subtracted from F everywhere it appears. This adjustment does not appear in the formula for R^2 (Equation 8.5), which is why it is always larger than $\widehat{\omega}^2$. We will always use $\widehat{\omega}^2$ when we are trying to infer population values or to use this information to estimate power and sample size.[8]

When the within-groups variability exceeds the between-groups variability (that is, when $F < 1$), Equations 8.11 and 8.12 give negative values. Of course, the population effect size can not be less than zero. What the negative value tells us is that the within-group error variability has swamped any differences among the treatment conditions that might have been present in the population. Under these circumstances, it is best to set $\widehat{\omega}^2 = 0$. This value does not prove that treatment effects are absent (nothing can do that), only that what differences there are can reasonably be attributed to random variation.

We will illustrate the estimation of ω^2 using the same data for the hyperactive boys we used for the descriptive measures. Both Equation 8.11 and Equation 8.12 give the same value:

---

[8] A similar estimation formula can be written to estimate δ, but it is of less use. As we noted above, an important use of d is for meta-analysis, and there the nature of the procedures makes the descriptive measure appropriate. The correction is most important for the power and sample-size calculations we discuss below, and for them the ω^2 measure is necessary.

$$\widehat{\omega}^2 = \frac{SS_A - (a-1)MS_{S/A}}{SS_{\text{total}} + MS_{S/A}} = \frac{210.00 - (3-1)(15.00)}{390.00 + 15.00} = \frac{180.00}{405.00} = 0.444,$$

$$\widehat{\omega}^2 = \frac{(a-1)(F-1)}{(a-1)(F-1) + an} = \frac{(3-1)(7.00-1)}{(3-1)(7.00-1) + (3)(5)} = \frac{12.00}{27.00} = 0.444.$$

Taking sampling error into account makes this value is considerably smaller than the sample value of $R^2 = 0.538$ that we calculated with the same information.

Effect Sizes for Contrasts

Up to now, we have considered measures of the *omnibus* or *overall* effect size. As we argued in Chapter 4, researchers are often more interested in particular analytical contrasts than in the omnibus effect. Consequently, a measure of effect size for selected contrasts is often more useful as the omnibus measure.

The variability of a contrast $\psi = \sum c_j \mu_j$, comparable to σ_A^2 above, is

$$\sigma_\psi^2 = \frac{\psi^2}{2 \sum c_j^2}. \tag{8.13}$$

This quantity can be incorporated into an effect size in two distinct ways. One measure is based on the proportion of the total variability that the contrast captures. We simply replace σ_A^2 in the left part of Equation 8.10 by the variability of the contrast to obtain

$$\omega_\psi^2 = \frac{\sigma_\psi^2}{\sigma_{\text{total}}^2} = \frac{\sigma_\psi^2}{\sigma_A^2 + \sigma_{\text{error}}^2}. \tag{8.14}$$

We will refer to this quantity as the **complete omega squared**.

The other measure is the **partial omega squared**. It expresses the variability of the contrast relative to itself and the error, rather than to all the variability in the study. To construct it, we replace σ_A^2 in the denominator of Equation 8.10 by the variability of the contrast, σ_ψ^2:

$$\omega_{\langle\psi\rangle}^2 = \frac{\sigma_\psi^2}{\sigma_\psi^2 + \sigma_{\text{error}}^2}. \tag{8.15}$$

We have indicated the partial measure by putting angle brackets around the subscript. Because the partial statistic has σ_ψ^2 in the denominator instead of σ_A^2, it is not affected by the size of any contrasts that are orthogonal to ψ. This property often makes the partial measure more useful than the complete one.

When a study has been completed, the effect size for a contrast in the population can be estimated from the test statistic F_ψ. The formula is quite similar to the one used to estimate the overall ω^2, and the complete and partial measures differ only in their denominators. The complete ω_ψ^2 is estimated by

$$\widehat{\omega}_\psi^2 = \frac{F_\psi - 1}{(a-1)(F_A - 1) + an}. \tag{8.16}$$

Note here the presence of the omnibus test statistic (which we have indicated by F_A) in the denominator. The partial statistic is estimated by

$$\widehat{\omega}_{\langle\psi\rangle}^2 = \frac{F_\psi - 1}{F_\psi - 1 + 2n}. \tag{8.17}$$

Suppose a four-group experiment has obtained means (based on $n = 10$ subjects) of $\overline{Y}_1 = 2$, $\overline{Y}_2 = 6$, $\overline{Y}_3 = 3$, and $\overline{Y}_4 = 11$ are obtained. The overall analysis is

Source	SS	df	MS	F
A	490	3	163.33	10.21*
S/A	576	36	16.00	
Total	1,066	39		

* $p < .05$

Now consider the contrast ψ with coefficients $\{1, -1, 0, 0\}$. A standard analysis finds it to be significant:

$$\widehat{\psi} = \bar{Y}_1 - \bar{Y}_2 = 2 - 6 = -4,$$

$$SS_\psi = \frac{n\widehat{\psi}^2}{\sum c_j^2} = \frac{(10)(-4)^2}{1^2 + (-1)^2 + 0^2 + 0^2} = \frac{160}{2} = 80.0,$$

$$F_\psi = MS_\psi / MS_{S/A} = 80/16.00 = 5.00.$$

The complete effect size for this contrast is estimated from Equation 8.16 to be

$$\widehat{\omega}_\psi^2 = \frac{F_\psi - 1}{(a-1)(F_A - 1) + an} = \frac{5.00 - 1}{(4-1)(10.21 - 1) + (4)(10)} = 0.059.$$

Thus, it accounts for nearly 6 percent of the total variability in the experiment. The estimate of the partial effect size, using Equation 8.17, is considerably larger:

$$\widehat{\omega}_{\langle\psi\rangle}^2 = \frac{F_\psi - 1}{F_\psi - 1 + 2n} = \frac{5.00 - 1}{5.00 - 1 + (2)(10)} = 0.167.$$

The partial omega squared here is, in effect, like the effect size for a study that included only groups a_1 and a_2.[9] Its value is independent of the means $\bar{Y}_3$ and $\bar{Y}_4$ of the other two groups. Changing those means would alter the complete omega squared but not the partial omega square. Under most circumstances, we want an effect measure to behave this way. The effect size for a contrast should not be influenced by the value of any unrelated contrast. For this reason, the partial $\widehat{\omega}_{\langle\psi\rangle}^2$ is typically more useful than the complete $\widehat{\omega}_\psi^2$. We will see this distinction again in our discussion of multifactor designs in Section 11.6.

Recommendations

Although a great deal has been written on the need for including estimates of effect sizes in research reports, there are few conventions either for what should be reported or how to report it.[10] If the calculation of an effect size is not to be an empty ritual, you need to think about what to report. Because every piece of research is different, it is impossible to offer hard-and-fast rules; instead, we present a few guidelines.

To begin, we remind you to report the descriptive statistics—the means and their standard deviations or standard errors—and to give F statistics for any tests, perhaps

---

[9]You can verify this statement by analyzing the means for groups a_1 and a_2 as a two-group experiment using $MS_{S/A} = 16.00$ as the error term (you will get $F = 5.0$) and estimating ω^2 from Equation 8.12.

[10]The most current edition of the *Publication Manual of the American Psychological Association* (American Psychological Association, 2001) mentions a number of measures of effect size without making specific recommendations. The editors do not to distinguish between descriptive measures (for example, R^2 and d) and estimates that take sampling error into account (for example, $\widehat{\omega}^2$), a distinction that we believe is critical.

along with a their error mean square. The effect sizes you report are adjuncts to this information, not substitutes for it.

If you wish to summarize the effects for the experiment as a whole, we recommend that you use $\widehat{\omega}^2$. This index takes the sampling variability into account and so is most relevant to the population you are studying. Because so many other measures are available, you should make it clear *what* you are reporting—don't just say "the effect size was 0.04" and leave a reader to guess whether you are talking about R^2, $\widehat{\omega}^2$, d, or something else. When you are discussing the difference between two groups, you might consider reporting d, because it is widely used and closer to the data than the proportion of variability. However, you should remember that this measure is influenced by sampling error. Cohen's division into large, medium, and small effects is helpful in thinking about how readily an effect stands out from the background variability, but you should remember that this classification says nothing about the practical importance of an effect nor its usefulness to psychology theory.

Finally, remember that specific results are often more useful than overall ones and tests of contrasts are frequently more informative than omnibus tests. The same goes for measures of effect sizes. If you plan to discuss a particular aspect of the results, represented by a contrast, then you should give the effect size for that contrast. When you do so, you will probably find the partial omega squared more useful than the complete statistic.

8.3   Power and Sample Size

In Section 3.3, we discussed two types of errors associated with hypothesis testing and gave the conditional probabilities of these two events the symbols α and β:

$$\text{Type I error:} \quad \Pr(\text{Reject } H_0 \text{ given } H_0 \text{ is true}) = \alpha,$$
$$\text{Type II error:} \quad \Pr(\text{Retain } H_0 \text{ given } H_0 \text{ is false}) = \beta.$$

It is more usual to talk about the **power** of the test instead of the Type II error rate:

$$\text{Power} = \Pr(\text{Reject } H_0 \text{ given } H_0 \text{ is false}) = 1 - \beta.$$

In designing and analyzing any experiment, we attempt to control the size of both types of errors, Type I error by setting the significance level at some low value, and Type II error through choices made when planning the experiment. As you will see, the power of an experiment is determined by the interplay of several factors: the significance level α, the sample size n, and the magnitude or size of the treatment effects ω^2. In this section, we will describe some general issues and then turn to detailed calculations in the remainder of the chapter.

Power calculations are used in two ways in research. By far the most important of these is in the planning stage. A major determinant of the power of a test is the number of observations. By analyzing the power of a proposed experiment, we can find the sample size that is necessary to obtain a given power to detect a particular pattern of means. These calculations would ordinarily be conducted to assure that the experiment has a reasonable likelihood of success. We discuss how they are made in Section 8.4. The other type of power calculation works the other way, starting with an existing design and finding the power of that study to reject the null hypothesis in favor of a particular alternative. These calculations tell us whether that study would be likely to detect that alternative. We describe them in Section 8.5.

Before turning to a closer examination of power, we want to start with a warning. It is very easy to overestimate the regularity of data and thereby overestimate the power of a study and to underestimate the sample size it requires. Even experienced and statistically sophisticated researchers make these errors, as has been well documented in research starting with the publication of the still-important paper by Tversky and Kahneman (1971). To avoid these errors, a power analysis is essential: We need to know ahead of time if our planned study is capable of detecting our anticipated results. If it is, then we can proceed as planned; otherwise, we need to rethink the design of the study.

Determinants of Power

We can control power by changing any of its three determinants: the significance level α, the size of the treatment effects ω^2, and the sample size n. Changing the α level, however, is not an option, because it is set (typically to .05) by the standards in the research domain. Increasing the size of the effect is more promising. The use of stronger manipulations to increase σ_A^2 will increase ω^2, as will decreasing the error variance σ_{error}^2 either through better experimental control or by selecting subjects from a more homogeneous population. Nevertheless, by far the most direct way to control the power of an experiment is sample size, and we will concentrate on it here.

We will illustrate the interplay between power, sample size, and effect size using an experiment with $a = 4$ treatment conditions. Figure 8.1 shows the relationship between power (on the abscissa) and the sample size needed to attain it (on the ordinate) for two significance levels ($\alpha = .05$, and $\alpha = .01$) and three effect sizes ($\omega^2 = .01$, .06, and .15). To determine the sample size n for a particular combination of significance level, effect size, and power, select a value for power, extend a vertical line upward until it intersects the appropriate combination of significance level and effect size, and read the required group sample size on the ordinate.

The dashed lines show the sample sizes needed when the significance level is $\alpha = .05$. Look at the line for small effect sizes ($\omega^2 = .01$). Here, the sample sizes needed to obtain a substantial level of power are outrageously large—about 270 subjects per group to achieve a power of .80 and 350 per group for a power of .90. With medium-sized effects ($\omega^2 = .06$) the corresponding numbers are 45 subjects and 60 subjects group, still surprisingly large. Finally, the sample sizes needed to find a large effect ($\omega^2 = .15$) are more like those we typically find in psychology research journals—namely, $n = 17$ and 22, for powers of .80 and .90, respectively.

Now compare the solid lines for the more stringent significance level of $\alpha = .01$ to the dashed lines for $\alpha = .05$. To achieve power of .80 in an experiment with a medium-sized effect, for example, the sample size must be increased from about 45 per group when $\alpha = .05$ to over 60 when $\alpha = .01$. By making it more difficult to reject false null hypotheses, power is reduced, and to offset this decrease, we must increase the sample size.

What do these numbers tell us? For one thing, you need to have substantial resources in terms of subjects and the cost of testing them—probably more than are available to most researchers—before you can have an appreciable chance of detecting

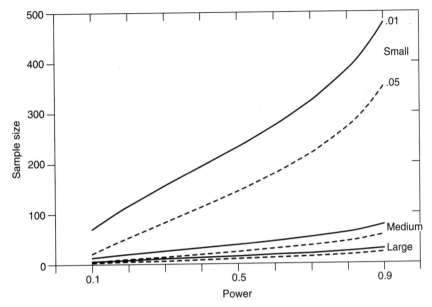

Figure 8.1: *Sample size needed in a four-group study as a function of power, for* $\alpha = .01$ *(solid lines) and* $\alpha = .05$ *(dashed lines), and for three effect sizes.*

a small effect. For another, when you have only a small number of subjects, you are unlikely to detect anything but a large effect. It would be foolish to undertake a study that had only a small chance of finding a result. Psychologists often conduct studies that are underpowered, as has been pointed out by Cohen (1962, 1992) and expanded upon by Rossi (1990), Sedlmeier and Gigerenzer (1989), and others. The tradeoffs involved here are complicated. For example, if you have only a given number of subjects available, are you better off expending them all in one strong study, or in using them over a series of weaker studies where you can refine your procedure and questions as you go along? We won't attempt to answer such questions, for the most productive research course surely depends on the domain in which the research is done. What is clear is that you should know how to choose the sample size that will produce the level of power you want.

8.4 Determining Sample Size

The most important application of power calculation in research is to determine the sample size of a planned experiment. It is easy to become confused by these calculations, however. The number of concepts involved is large, and the calculations can be performed using several seemingly different formulas. To reduce confusion here, we will presentall of our formulas in terms of the effect-size measure ω^2.

It is not necessary to be highly precise in your estimation of sample size. There are so many uncertainties about a projected study that its effect size is never known to within more than about 10 percent. Power calculations need not be more precise than that. Fortunately, rough values give you the essential information. Knowing that you need about 30 subjects per group and that you cannot get by with only 15 is very important, but the difference between $n = 28$ and $n = 30$ is not. You certainly need to know when the study demands more subjects than you have available, but not the exact number.

Steps in Determining Sample Size

We have found that the best way to perform the power calculations correctly is to be systematic. We suggests you follow the following sequence of steps.

1. *Determine the form of the experiment to be analyzed.* So far, we have discussed only the single-factor design, but after completing this book, you will be able to consider a number of design issues at this stage, such as the number of independent variables, the nature of these variables, and the use of subjects in more than one treatment condition.

2. *Decide on the hypothesis test to be conducted.* Choose the null hypothesis to be tested, the type of statistical test to be used, and the Type I error probability α. Your null hypotheses may be of omnibus form, $\mu_1 = \mu_2 = \mu_3 =$ etc., or may concern the value of a contrast.

3. *State the alternative to the null hypothesis that you wish to detect.* This step requires you to find the effect size ω^2 for the desired effect using the formulas in Section 8.1.

4. *Select the desired power.* This value will usually be somewhere between about .50 and .90. When you have a good idea of the effect you are seeking, such as when you are replicating an existing study, you should choose a fairly high level, say at least .80. When you have merely specified the smallest effect that you would find interesting (and hope to find a larger one), you might pick a smaller value, such as .50 or .60.

5. *Combine this information to find the sample size.* We describe these calculations below.

Finding the Size of the Target Effect

Estimates of the effect size for a projected study are usually obtained in one of two ways. Either the researcher has some idea of what the outcome of the study is likely to be, or he or she decides on the smallest effect that is of practical interest. One way to obtain an estimate of the first type is to review the literature and come up with a set of plausible means for your conditions. Another is to find some earlier experiment that you believe to be like yours and use it as a model. These estimates have in common that the projected effect is one you think is likely to occur. The second approach is more useful when you don't have enough information to pick a plausible outcome. You may still be able to decide on the smallest differences among the means that you would care about. In our experiment with hyperactive boys, for example, the researcher could decide that a difference of 3 points on the comprehension test between the control condition and either of the two drug conditions was the minimum effect needed to justify conducting further research with this therapy. A smaller difference, even if significant, would not be practically important.

However you come up with a target effect, translate it into a value of ω^2. When your target effect is expressed as means, you will have to make an estimate of σ^2_{error}, then use Equations 8.9 and 8.10 to obtain ω^2. When your target effect comes from the results of a previous experiment, you should use either Equation 8.11 or Equation 8.12 to correct your estimate for chance differences.

Consider three examples that illustrate this process. Suppose you are planning a three-group experiment which, from the reading of several papers in the literature, you expect to have means of 25, 28, and 16. Because these means do not come from any particular experiment, you can treat them as given exactly (otherwise you would need to correct the effect size for sampling error). In your survey, you noted that the within-groups standard deviation σ_{error} was about 12. From this information, you calculate the effect size. You find the grand mean μ_T, subtract it from the treatment means μ_j to find the effects α_j, and from these calculate σ_A^2 (Equation 8.9). All these calculations are easily done in a little table:

	a_1	a_2	a_3	Sum	Mean
Means, μ_j	25	28	16	69	23
Effects, α_j	2	5	−7	0	
α_j^2	4	25	49	78	26

We listed the means in the first row, and, on their right, summed and averaged them to find the grand mean $\mu_T = 23$. In the next row, we subtracted the grand mean from the treatment means to obtain the treatment effects α_j (these should sum to 0). Finally, in the third row, we squared, summed, and averaged the effects to obtain $\sigma_A^2 = 26$. Now, using Equation 8.10,

$$\omega^2 = \frac{\sigma_A^2}{\sigma_A^2 + \sigma_{\text{error}}^2} = \frac{26}{26 + 12^2} = \frac{26}{170} = 0.153.$$

We are looking for a sizable effect.

As our second example, suppose you planning a study that you know is very similar to one that has already been completed. Exact replications of another study are not very common, but when the resemblance between the two studies is close—the same dependent variable and similar treatments—you can use the first study as a model for yours. Suppose the model experiment had $a = 4$ groups and was run with $n = 25$ subjects per group, and that it found a significant effect with $F = 3.87$. You want to design your study to have a power of .80 to find a similar effect, using an F test at the 5 percent significance level. You can estimate the effect size with Equation 8.12:

$$\widehat{\omega}^2 = \frac{(a-1)(F-1)}{(a-1)(F-1) + an} = \frac{(4-1)(3.87-1)}{(4-1)(3.87-1) + (4)(25)} = 0.079.$$

You will treat this value as the effect you will look for in the new experiment.

It makes most sense to use a previous experiment as a model to determine sample size when that study has found significant results. For the most part, an attempt to "replicate" a study that did not find a significant result is a risky undertaking (unless, as sometimes happens, you hope *not* to find a significant result). The closer the observed F approaches its chance value of approximately 1, the more the observed means are contaminated by sampling error. In the extreme case where F is less than 1 (and we estimate omega squared as $\widehat{\omega}^2 = 0$), the study gives no reliable information about the true means at all. In cases such as these, we suggest that you use the previous study only to obtain an estimate of σ_{error} and postulate a likely or at least interesting effect based on other information.

Finally, suppose you are initiating research in a new area and you plan an exploratory study with $a = 2$ groups. However, you have no real idea of what to expect. You think about what would be the least interesting effect, and decide that you would not care about anything smaller than a four-point difference in your dependent measure. You have conducted a little pilot study of your dependent measure—usually a good idea in a new area—and determine from it that $\sigma_{\text{error}} \approx 10$. The four-point difference between the two groups implies that the effects are two points above the grand mean for one group ($\alpha_1 = 2$) and two below the grand mean for the other group ($\alpha_2 = -2$). Using this information, you find

$$\sigma_A^2 = \frac{\sum \alpha_j^2}{a} = \frac{2^2 + (-2^2)}{2} = 4 \ \text{ and } \ \omega^2 = \frac{\sigma_A^2}{\sigma_A^2 + \sigma_{\text{error}}^2} = \frac{4}{4 + 100} = 0.038.$$

This value of ω^2 represents your estimate of the minimum effect size you wish to detect, which implies that you are really looking for something larger.

Finding the Sample Size

You now need to translate the value of ω^2 into a projected sample size. There are at least three ways to do so. One possibility is to look up the sample size in the table we present next or in the more extensive tables in Cohen, 1988. These tables are limited by the fact that they cannot contain all combinations of sample size and power. When you require more accurate results than the table can provide, you can use the set of charts in Appendix A.7. Finally, there are now available computer programs that can calculate power or sample size. We used one of these (GPOWER, see Erdfelder, Faul, & Buchner, 1996) to construct Table 8.1 below. The programs give you the most accurate result.

Table 8.1 gives the required sample size for tests at the 5 percent level for three levels of power (.60, .80, and .90), effects ranging in size from $\omega^2 = .01$ to .15, and experiments with between $a = 2$ and 8 groups. Using this table is easy: You simply coordinate the power, effect size, and number of groups, then read the sample size directly from the table. Of course, it is only accurate when it contains the particular combination of conditions that match your study. However, often all you want from a power analysis is an indication of whether the sample size falls within your research budget or whether you need to approach your problem from another direction. For such rough estimates, the table is quick and valuable.

To illustrate the table's use, let's look at the sample sizes needed for the three studies we mentioned above. The first was a three-group study with an effect size of $\omega^2 = 0.153$. For this effect size, we can use the table entry for $\omega^2 = .15$. With $a = 3$ groups, a power of .80 is obtained with $n = 20$ (i.e. 60 subjects are needed in all), and a power as great as .90 needs only $n = 25$. These are reasonable numbers, not out of line from those we see in actual experimentation. The second experiment had $a = 4$ groups, and the effect size estimated from a previous study was $\widehat{\omega}^2 = 0.079$. The table entry for $\omega^2 = 0.08$ indicates that $n = 33$ subjects are needed to achieve a power of .80. Finally, for the two-group study with a minimal effect size of $\omega^2 \approx 0.04$ (actually, $\omega^2 = 0.038$), we might decide to adopt a slightly lower power and use the .60 part of

Table 8.1: *Sample size needed to achieve a power of .60, .80, and .90 in a test at* $\alpha = .05$ *for studies with from 2 to 8 groups and effect sizes* ω^2 *from .01 to .15.* *These values were calculated by the program* GPOWER *(Erdfelder et al., 1996).*

ω^2	$a=2$	$a=3$	$a=4$	$a=5$	$a=6$	$a=7$	$a=8$
			Power $=$ .60				
.01	244	207	179	158	143	131	122
.02	122	103	89	79	72	66	61
.03	81	69	59	53	48	44	41
.04	60	51	44	39	36	33	31
.05	48	41	36	32	29	26	25
.06	40	34	30	26	24	22	20
.08	30	25	22	20	18	17	15
.10	24	20	18	16	14	13	12
.12	19	17	15	13	12	11	10
.15	15	13	12	10	10	9	8
			Power $=$ .80				
.01	390	319	271	238	213	194	179
.02	194	159	135	118	106	97	89
.03	128	105	90	79	71	64	59
.04	96	79	67	59	53	48	44
.05	76	63	53	47	42	38	35
.06	63	52	44	39	35	32	30
.08	47	38	33	29	26	24	22
.10	37	30	26	23	21	19	18
.12	30	25	21	19	17	16	15
.15	24	20	17	15	14	12	12
			Power $=$ .90				
.01	522	419	352	306	273	248	228
.02	259	208	175	153	136	123	113
.03	171	138	116	101	90	82	75
.04	127	103	86	75	67	61	56
.05	101	82	69	60	54	49	45
.06	84	68	57	50	44	40	37
.08	62	50	42	37	33	30	28
.10	49	39	33	29	26	24	22
.12	40	32	27	24	22	20	18
.15	31	25	22	19	17	16	14

the table—after all, we hope the effect is larger than our minimum. The table gives $n = 60$, which implies we must commit substantial resources to the study.

Using the Power Charts

Although Table 8.1 is extremely useful, it is limited by the number of entries it contains. If you need sample sizes for levels of power not included in the table or for different effect sizes, you must use another method of calculation. A set of charts that applies to a much wider range of effect size and power was developed by Pearson and Hartley (1951) and is widely reproduced in books on the analysis of variance. Appendix A.7 contains modified versions of these charts, appropriate for tests at the 5 percent level and studies with df_{num} between 1 and 6.[11]

The power charts make use of a quantity known as the **noncentrality parameter** that measures the extent to which the experiment gives evidence for differences among the population means. It is denoted here by ϕ (the Greek letter phi). The charts let us translate power into a value of the noncentrality parameter. Once we have ϕ, we combine it with the effect size ω^2 to calculate the sample size using the equation

$$n = \phi^2 \frac{1 - \omega^2}{\omega^2}. \tag{8.18}$$

The relationship between power and ϕ depends on the degrees of freedom in the analysis. Appendix A.7 contains a separate chart for each value of df_{num}, and each chart contains power functions for several values of df_{denom}. You start by picking the chart and line that applies to your study. You will know df_{num}, and we suggest you start with $df_{denom} = 50$. Next, you find your desired power on the ordinate and extend a horizontal line from that point to the right until it intersects with the power function. From the point of intersection, drop down to the abscissa and read off the noncentrality parameter ϕ. Finally, put this value and the effect size into Equation 8.18 and calculate the sample size. There is one minor complication. You may find when you are done that the sample size you find implies a value $df_{S/A}$ different from the starting value of $df_{denom} = 50$. When that happens, just pick a line based on $df_{S/A}$ and repeat the calculation. In most cases, the change in n will be small.

We can use the charts to recalculate the sample sizes for our three example studies. The first experiment had $a = 3$ groups and an effect size of $\omega^2 = 0.153$. On the chart for $df_{num} = a - 1 = 2$, we draw a horizontal line from our target power of .80 on the ordinate to the function labeled $df_{denom} = 50$ and note that the scale value immediately below this point is $\phi \approx 1.85$. We obtain the sample size from Equation 8.18:

$$n = \phi^2 \frac{1 - \omega^2}{\omega^2} = (1.85)^2 \frac{1 - 0.153}{0.153} = 3.423 \frac{0.847}{0.153} = 18.95,$$

or 19 when we round up to the nearest whole subject. This sample size implies that $df_{S/A} = a(n-1) = (3)(19-1) = 54$, which is close to our starting value of $df_{denom} = 50$. We have used the correct line.

The second experiment involved $a = 4$ groups and had an estimated effect size of $\widehat{\omega}^2 = 0.079$. To determine the sample size needed to attain a power of .80, we use the

---

[11]The Pearson-Hartley charts plot the power on a nonlinear scale that expands the upper end of the power axis. They are more accurate than our charts when the power is near one, but are less so for smaller values.

chart labeled $df_{num} = 3$ and the power function for $df_{denom} = 50$. The value of ϕ that this line associates with a power of .80 is $\phi \approx 1.7$. Equation 8.18 gives

$$n = \phi^2 \frac{1 - \omega^2}{\omega^2} = (1.7)^2 \frac{1 - 0.079}{0.079} = 2.89 \frac{0.921}{0.079} = 33.69,$$

or 34 subjects. With this sample size, $df_{S/A} = 132$, so our use of the power function for $df_{denom} = 50$ was a little off. Redoing the calculations with the line for $df_{denom} \approx 100$ changes the noncentrality parameter to $\phi = 1.68$ and the sample size to $n = 32.9$ or 33 subjects. The impact is very small.

The power charts allow you to find samples sizes for powers other than the three in Table 8.1. Suppose you wished to perform the test in the third example (two groups and a minimum interesting effect of $\omega^2 = 0.038$) with a power of .50. From the chart for $df_{num} = 1$ and the line for $df_{denom} = 50$, we find the noncentrality $\phi \approx 1.42$. Based on this value, the sample size is

$$n = \phi^2 \frac{1 - \omega^2}{\omega^2} = (1.42)^2 \frac{1 - 0.038}{0.038} = 2.016 \frac{0.962}{0.038} = 51.04.$$

This value of n implies $df_{S/A} = 102$, which indicates that we should have used the power function for $df_{denom} = 100$. Returning to the power chart, we find the new values $\phi = 1.40$ and $n = 49.6$. Again, you can see that the refined estimate of ϕ produced only a slight change.

Sample Sizes for Contrasts

The basic analysis of variance is an omnibus procedure. For a study with more than two groups, the overall F statistic tests many simple hypotheses at once. The power of the analysis is different for each component hypothesis. For example, when two means in a three-group design are close together and the third is very different, the power to detect the difference between the two closely-spaced means is much less than that for overall significance. Some of the component hypotheses will be of much greater interest than others. As a practical matter, sample-size calculations should be based on the part of the design where the effects are most important. If discrimination between the two closely-spaced groups is crucial to the research, then the power calculations should be based on that difference, not on the omnibus analysis.

To find the sample size for a component hypothesis, we start by expressing it as a contrast and determining the partial effect size $\omega^2_{\langle\psi\rangle}$ that it will have. When you have information about the population means μ_j and the standard deviation σ_{error}, use Equation 8.15; when you are basing the estimate on F_ψ from a previous experiment, use Equation 8.17. Note that the partial effect size, not the complete effect size, is used. Now you are on familiar ground: You turn to either the $a = 2$ column of Table 8.1 or the power charts for $df_{num} = 1$ in Appendix A.7 and convert the value of this partial omega squared to a sample size.[12]

As illustration, recall that the first of our three examples was a three-group study with population treatment means of 25, 28, and 16, and $\sigma_{error} = 12$. We found that the omnibus test with a power of .80 needed a sample size of 19 or 20 per group. Suppose

---

[12]Sometimes you may want to test a null hypothesis that ψ equals a value other than 0 (the procedure was described with Equation 4.12, p. 73). To find the power or sample size for these hypotheses, you replace ψ^2 in Equation 8.13 by $(\psi - \psi_0)^2$ when calculating σ^2_ψ.

it were critical to detect the difference between the first two groups. Because this is the smallest of the three pairwise differences, we would expect to need more subjects than our estimate for the omnibus effect. This pairwise difference is the contrast $\psi = \mu_1 - \mu_2$. Finding the hypothesized value of this contrast and using Equations 8.13 and 8.17, we estimate the effect size:

$$\psi = \mu_1 - \mu_2 = 25 - 28 = -3,$$

$$\sigma_\psi^2 = \frac{\psi^2}{2 \sum c_j^2} = \frac{(-3)^2}{2[1^2 + (-1)^2]} = 2.25,$$

$$\omega_{(\psi)}^2 = \frac{\sigma_\psi^2}{\sigma_\psi^2 + \sigma_{S/A}^2} = \frac{2.25}{2.25 + 12^2} = 0.015.$$

Table 8.1 gives a sample size between 194 (for $\omega^2 = .02$) and 390 (for $\omega^2 = .01$). The power charts give a more precise value. The values we got from the power table tell us that $df_{S/A}$ will be large and we can safely use the power function with the largest value of df_{denom} (infinity). From this line on the power chart for $df_{\text{num}} = 1$, we obtain $\phi \approx 1.95$ for a power of .80. Entering these values in Equation 8.18,

$$n = \phi^2 \frac{1 - \omega^2}{\omega^2} = (1.95)^2 \frac{1 - 0.015}{0.015} = 3.8025 \frac{0.985}{0.015} = 249.7.$$

About 250 subjects per group are required, a far cry from the sample sizes needed to detect the omnibus effect.

Comments

Power analyses should be an integral part of designing any experiment. It does not make sense to conduct an experiment that is seriously under-powered. You probably won't obtain a significant result, and you won't be able to interpret that outcome. The effect you expected may have been there, but your experiment couldn't detect it. Your study is all too likely to end up in your file drawer of unpublishable research. Finding that the implied sample size is unrealistically large should alert you to redesign your study. Perhaps you can make your treatments more effective, so that the differences between means increase; perhaps you can reduce the variability of the scores through better experimental control or the use of more homogeneous subjects. On the other hand, perhaps you will find that the sample size you require is reasonable, and you can proceed with the study in greater confidence that, significant or not, the outcome will be meaningful.

You should be sure that your expectations regarding sample size are realistic. The functions in Figure 8.1 relating sample size and power are not straight lines, particular the ones for small effect sizes. They imply that it is much harder to increase power by even a few percentage points when it is already high than when it is in the middle or lower part of its range. As a result, a disproportionate amount of resources is required to raise the probability of finding an effect to near certainty—levels of power above .95. A power of .90 is attainable in some designs, but near certainty is not a realistic goal, particularly when the effect you are searching for is small in magnitude. Interestingly, methodologists seem to agree that a power of about .80 is a reasonable value for researchers in the behavioral sciences. It is a sensible compromise between the need for adequate power and the finite resources available to most psychological studies.

8.5 Determining Power

In this section, we briefly consider a second use of power analyses in research, namely, determining the power of an existing experimental design to discover a given effect. In this application, the sample size has already been chosen and the researcher wants to evaluate the power of the experiment as it has been designed. Sometimes the study in question has not yet been performed, and the goal of the analysis is to decide if it has sufficient power to detect an interesting effect. Sometimes the experiment has been conducted, and it is desired to see whether it would have been able to detect a particular effect. We will return to these uses after we have described how the calculations are made.

Calculating the Power of an Experiment

Because the power calculations usually require a wider range of power and effect-size values than the sample-size calculations, it is impractical to present quick tables like Table 8.1. The key equation we need to use the power charts in Appendix A.7 relates the effect size ω^2 to the noncentrality parameter ϕ. We find this equation by solving Equation 8.18 for ϕ:

$$\phi = \sqrt{\frac{n\omega^2}{1 - \omega^2}}. \tag{8.19}$$

Once we have calculated ϕ, we can convert this value to a power by using the appropriate power chart.

To illustrate this form of power analysis, consider again the three-group experiment we mentioned first on page 171 for which we estimated an effect size of $\omega^2 = 0.153$. Suppose you had only 30 subjects, 10 for each group. Rather than going ahead with the study immediately, you check to see if this particular sample size gives the study sufficient power to justify the effort of conducting it. You use Equation 8.19 to estimate the noncentrality parameter:

$$\phi = \sqrt{\frac{n\omega^2}{1 - \omega^2}} = \sqrt{\frac{(10)(0.153)}{1 - 0.153}} = \sqrt{1.806} = 1.34.$$

The power chart for $df_{\text{num}} = 2$ translates this value into the power. Because $df_{\text{denom}} = a(n - 1) = (3)(10 - 1) = 27$, we use the function for $df = 30$. We locate $\phi = 1.34$ on the abscissa, extend a vertical line upward until it intersects the appropriate power function, then extend the line horizontally to the axis, where we read the power to be slightly below .50.

This analysis reveals that when the true means are as hypothesized, the experiment will reject the null hypothesis about half the time. Whether this power is sufficient to go ahead with the experiment depends on how the specific alternative hypothesis was chosen. If the three means are the values that you thought were the most likely to be true, then the design is not very satisfactory. You should search for ways to increase its power. On the other hand, if the three means describe the smallest effect that you would be interested in finding and that the real effect is likely to be larger, then the power may be sufficient to proceed.

As a second example, look at the comparison of the means μ_1 and μ_2 in this same experiment. On page 175, we found that the sample size required to achieve a power of .80 for a test of the contrast $\psi = \mu_1 - \mu_2$ was much greater than that needed for the omnibus effect ($n = 250$ vs. $n = 20$). But suppose the study were conducted with that smaller sample size? What is the power to detect the difference between μ_1 and μ_2? Again we work from the effect size ω^2. In our earlier calculations, we found the effect size for the contrast to be $\omega^2_{\langle\psi\rangle} = 0.015$. Again using Equation 8.19,

$$\phi = \sqrt{\frac{n\omega^2}{1 - \omega^2}} = \sqrt{\frac{(20)(0.015)}{1 - 0.015}} = \sqrt{\frac{0.30}{0.985}} = 0.552.$$

Turning to the power chart for $df_{num} = 1$, we see that power is only about .10, an abysmally small value. Thus, although a study with this sample size has adequate power to detect the omnibus effect, it has very little power to detect the anticipated difference between these two groups. If this difference were important or critical, then the experiment as planned is inadequate. As this example illustrates, it is simply not enough to conduct a power analysis—you need also to consider the specific effects you are interested in detecting.

Comments

You will notice that in our two examples, the effect sizes were determined *before* the experiment was undertaken. Wherever the means 25, 28, and 16 came from in our example, they were not based on information obtained after the study had been conducted. This separation between the effect that is to be found and the study that will look for it is characteristic of power analyses. When planning a study we start with an effect and project to a future study. A power analysis should never be used after a study has been completed, simply as a descriptive measure. It makes no sense to apply the power formulas to a set of observed means, calculating what amounts to the power of the study to find the results it has just found. The calculation is as circular as it sounds. It gives no information that is not better expressed by one of the measures of effect size.[13]

There is one circumstance where power calculations can be made after a study has been completed. When the null hypothesis is retained, a researcher may want assurance that the failure to reject the null hypothesis was not due to a lack of power. A power calculation here can show that had the population means followed some particular pattern other than the observed sample values, the study was likely to have detected it. Consider our three-group example, and suppose that after conducting the study using $n = 20$ subjects per group, the omnibus F test was not significant. We could return to the population means we had originally hypothesized—25, 28, and 16—to see whether the study was likely to have come out significant, had those been the true values. We have already performed these calculations above and found that

---

[13]You should be aware that some of the computer packages include an option to make these after-the-fact calculations. This so-called "observed power" is not meaningful. It is also sometimes suggested that a power analysis be used after a study is complete to determine which values of the means are consistent with the results. By this argument, only those values for which the study has a high power to reject the null hypothesis can be ruled out. However, this use of power analysis is logically inconsistent (Hoenig & Heisey, 2001). If you want to make a statement about plausible outcomes, use a confidence interval.

the study had a fairly high power—about 80 percent. Armed with this information, we can be more confident that the failure to find this result was not just due to low power. Or, to take an example that comes out the other way, we saw that the power of that study to reject the null hypothesis, when in fact $\psi = \mu_1 - \mu_2 = 25 - 28 = -3$, was only about 10 percent. With this finding, we could question the adequacy of this experiment to detect this particular difference between the two means. Another example of these calculations appears in Problem 8.5.

Exercises

8.1. Two groups of 8 subjects were tested for errors in depth perception. Group a_1 was tested after a good night's sleep, and group a_2 was tested after sleep deprivation. Each subject received a score indicating the average error in judgment of distance to a target. The data, with some summary statistics, are

	Rested		Deprived	
	11.8	5.3	13.8	12.3
	8.8	14.8	11.5	12.8
	11.8	16.3	17.0	15.0
	10.0	14.0	15.3	11.5
$\sum Y_{ij}$	92.8		109.2	
$\sum Y_{ij}^2$	1164.7		1518.2	

a. Perform an analysis of variance on these data and draw a conclusion.
b. How large is the difference between the groups, measured relative to their variability? What proportion of the total observed variability can be attributed to the treatment? What is your estimate of this value in the population?
c. Suppose you wished to repeat the experiment, increasing the power but not changing α. Suggest at least two realistic things that you could do.

8.2. In Problem 3.2 of Chapter 3, an experiment was reported in which the rates of learning a T-maze by three groups of rats were compared following different operations: Group a_1 received a lesion in one location of the brain, group a_2 a lesion in another location, and group a_3 a sham operation. Using the data in that problem, estimate omega squared for the following:
a. The overall effect of the three conditions.
b. The partial effects of the following comparisons:
    i. The comparison between the two groups receiving brain lesions.
    ii. The comparison between the control (a_3) and an average of the other two groups.

8.3. Consider two almost identical experiments that have found the same means, $\overline{Y}_1 = 12.3$, $\overline{Y}_2 = 10.6$, $\overline{Y}_3 = 15.3$, and $\overline{Y}_4 = 9.8$. Their analyses of variance are different:

Source	SS	df	MS	F	Source	SS	df	MS	F
A	266.7	3	88.9	2.90	A	266.7	3	88.9	1.32
S/A	1,713.6	56	30.6		S/A	3,763.2	56	67.2	
Total	1,980.3	59			Total	4,029.9	59		

Calculate the squared correlation ratio R^2 and the estimate of ω^2 for the two experiments. Explain why the four values you have found are not the same, even though all calculations are based on the same means.

8.4. Suppose you are preparing to conduct a four-group experiment that you will analyze with an analysis of variance. You expect that your group means will show no less deviation than the set $\mu_1 = 66$, $\mu_2 = 71$, $\mu_3 = 74$, and $\mu_4 = 85$. A plausible guess at the standard deviation is $\sigma_{error} \approx 14$. How many subjects should you choose if you want a power of .9 to detect the following effects at the $\alpha = .05$ level?
a. The omnibus effect.
b. Linear trend.

8.5. A four-group analysis of variance gives the following results:

Source	SS	df	MS	F
A	30	3	10	2
S/A	300	60	5	
Total	330	63		

This result is not significant, and the person who performed the analysis wishes to claim that the null hypothesis can now be accepted. This assertion is based on the notion that in the smallest alternative of interest, the four group means differ by one point (e.g., 9, 10, 11, 12). What is your estimate of the power of the analysis to detect this effect? Is the claim reasonable?

8.6. A four-group experiment with 30 subjects per group gives the means 10.6, 11.8, 9.5, and 12.1. An analysis of variance finds that these means do not differ significantly:

Source	SS	df	MS	F
A	127.8	3	42.6	0.71
S/A	6,925.2	116	59.7	
Total	7,053.0	119		

The experimenter decides to replicate the experiment with a larger sample. What can you say about the sample size needed to replicate this study with a power of .95?

8.7. A researcher performs an analysis of variance and obtains the statistic $F = 1.32$ on 2 and 27 degrees of freedom. He estimates the effect size for his observed means to be $\hat{\omega}^2 = 0.021$, then uses the power charts to find the power of his experiment to detect an effect of this magnitude. His calculation gives a power of less than .10, and so he runs a sample-size calculation and determines that 160 subjects per group would give him a power of about .80 to detect the effect. In his report of the study he states

> A power analysis showed that the experiment lacked sufficient power to detect the pattern of means that was found. Had a sample size of $n = 160$ been used, the groups would have differed significantly.

His calculations are correct, but his interpretation is not. Explain what is wrong with this statement.

9

Using Statistical Software

In no area of statistics has change been so rapid as in computation. The evolution of computers has altered both statistical methods and practice. Changes in the methods are less apparent—although far from absent—in a relatively mature field such as the analysis of variance, but changes in practice are manifold. These days, you will surely use a computer to conduct most of the analyses we discuss here, and it would be foolhardy to approach a large set of data any other way.[1]

A few years ago, the statistical field was dominated by large programs running on central "mainframe" computers; presently, these same statistical packages are better run on individual desktop machines. The distribution of the programs has also changed. It is now feasible to own or lease quite powerful programs for personal use. With the changes in distribution have come changes in marketing. The packaged programs are not static, and their publishers release new versions with additional features and options every few years. This rapidity of change within the field of computation, then, makes it difficult to cover the computer programs in a form that has both generality and applicability.

This chapter discusses the use of statistical software at a relatively general level and, for several reasons, does not attempt to describe how to use any of the software packages in detail. First, the programs change frequently, both in their content and their options, making it impossible for us to provide instructions that will remain current. Second, to be comprehensive enough to be useful, such explanations require a far greater investment in space than is possible here. Software programs are necessarily complex, a state that reflects both the variety of statistical methods and differing demands made by their users. What we will do, then, is to make some higher-level suggestions—in this chapter and scattered throughout this book—that will help you to employ whatever program you use effectively. When you begin working with a particular program, you will want to seek documentation tailored to your particular task and level of experience. Many other books are available to fill this need; they

---

[1]One of the authors recalls a summer job in college during which a five- or six-way mixed analysis of variance (a design we will discuss later) was conducted (and checked!) using a desk calculator. It took two people, working full time, the better part of a week. It would now take at most a few seconds of computer time.

provide tutorials, detailed instructions, and even introductions to data analysis that are particularly directed to one or another program or package.[2]

One reason that we don't emphasize any particular program is that we do not have any idea which one you will use. Any of the major packages, and many of the minor ones, will do all the analyses in this book, and the major ones, such as SPSS (SPSS, Inc., 1999) or SAS (SAS Institute, Inc., 1998), will do more. Which you end up using will depend on what might otherwise be secondary factors, such as their availability and the fact that your colleagues are using them. Do not underestimate the latter factor: Support from somebody who has become proficient with a particular package goes a long way to solve the difficulties that arise understanding the documentation.

9.1   Using the Programs

Two steps are required to use any statistical program. One is to enter the data in a specific format; the other is to identify the particular way these data are to be analyzed. Different programs perform these steps in somewhat different ways, but they have much in common.

Data Format

All programs specify the form in which the data and certain aspects of the design are organized. In many, this information is entered in a two-dimensional "spreadsheet," with each row, line, or "record" containing the data for a single subject. Each column in this grid records the values of a particular independent variable or dependent variable. Many researchers will create this table in an actual spreadsheet program and later transfer (or "import") it to the statistical program. It is a good idea to include in this table columns containing any incidental information about the subject, such as gender, even if that is not part of the analysis you have planned—you can never tell whether it will be useful later, such as in post-hoc blocking designs (see Section 11.5).

For the single-factor design, the minimum information that must be provided for each subject is an indication of the treatment condition (the independent variable) and the subject's score Y_{ij} (the dependent variable). In Chapter 5 we described a study in which subjects practicing a tracking task with different amounts of spacing between the trials. The dependent variable was the score on a later test trial (see Table 5.1, p. 90). Table 9.1 shows a typical way these data might be prepared for a computer. There is one line for each of the $an = 20$ subjects and five columns. The first column, labeled Subj, is the subject number (which the program may provide automatically). The second column (Spacing) specifies the level of the independent variable assigned to each subject—1 for the first level, 2 for the second, and so forth. The information in the next two columns is not actually needed for the analysis. Column 3 (Gen) indicates whether the subject was female or male; we include it here as an obvious example of the sort of subject information that is wise to record in the file. Column 4 (Interval) contains the actual spacing interval for that subject. It, of course, can be determined from the level or group number, but it is convenient to have these values available to facilitate such analyses as the construction of comparisons or the

---

[2]Tabachnick and Fidell (2001) is a very useful treatment of the types of techniques we cover, as they would be applied with several popular software packages. You might also check for Web sites that provide examples and help.

Table 9.1: Data from Table 5.1 as configured in spreadsheet style for input to a computer program.

Subj	Spacing	Gen	Interval	Score
1	1	M	0	4
2	1	F	0	6
3	1	M	0	10
4	1	F	0	9
5	1	M	0	11
6	2	F	20	18
7	2	F	20	13
8	2	M	20	15
9	2	M	20	11
10	2	F	20	13
11	3	M	40	24
12	3	F	40	19
13	3	F	40	21
14	3	F	40	16
15	3	M	40	15
16	4	F	60	16
17	4	F	60	17
18	4	M	60	13
19	4	M	60	23
20	4	F	60	21

calculation of the regression lines. Finally, the `Score` column contains the value of the dependent variable Y_{ij}.

Two further notes about Table 9.1: First, although the arrangement is tidy, there is no need to keep the subjects in a group together, the way we have done in the example. The program does not care about their order. Sometimes it is better to enter the subjects in the order in which they were run in the experiment—the first subject on the first line, the second on the next, and so on. If random assignment to groups had been used—as it should have been—the groups would not be together. Organizing the data by the order of running makes it easier to look for temporal trends or violations of the assumption of independence of the scores (see Section 7.3). Second, the spacing or group variable is a different type of number from those in the `Score` column. It serves only to designate the treatment level and need have no numerical meaning in itself. Thus, it has more in common with the gender variable, which is also unordered. Of course, in this example, spacing does have a numerical interpretation, which is reflected in the `Interval` score, but as far as the program is concerned, it need not. Such variables are often indicated as **nominal** or **categorical**.

The layout in Table 9.1 is easily extended to accommodate larger, more complicated designs. More subjects can be added by adding more rows to the array, and more (or fewer) levels are accommodated by using more (or fewer) values of the independent variable. Because the group assignment of each subject is indicated by the value of this variable, there is no requirement that the samples have equal size. More important, the other designs we will discuss can be fitted into this framework by adding columns to the table. Designs with two or more independent variables, such as those in Part III, are accommodated by using a separate column for the levels of each independent variable. Designs in which each subject supplies more than one score—the within-subject or repeated-measures designs discussed in Part V—are accommodated by using one column for each quantity measured on a subject. Thus, the spreadsheet format has the flexibility to represent the data from all the designs we will consider.

Within the program, it is usually possible to manipulate the data in the rows of the table and to calculate new variables from existing ones. For example, in Table 7.3 (p. 154) we applied the square root transformation $Y'_{ij} = \sqrt{Y_{ij} + 1/2}$ to a set of data to reduce heterogeneity of variance. If the dependent variable in the data table was named `errors` (it was the number of speech errors), it could be transformed by creating a new variable `trerror` using an expression something like

$$\text{trerror} = \text{SQRT}(\text{errors} + 0.5).$$

Calculating new variables will be particularly useful when we come to applying contrasts to the within-subject designs, and we will have much more to say about how it is used when we get to them.

Specification of the Analysis

Even though all the data required for the analysis are available in Table 9.1, a computer program needs to be told what to do with this information before it can proceed with the analysis. To start out, it needs to know what type of analysis to conduct. Next, it must know which column contains the independent variable and which the dependent variable. Finally, there are various options that must be specified, such as the level of α to use in constructing confidence intervals and as part of certain other analyses. How this information is specified will depend on the particular program you are using.

It helps here to understand some of the history of the programs. When larger statistical packages started to appear, control of the program was determined by a short text file containing a series of instructions. These *control statements* determined which analysis the program ran, how the data were used, and what options were chosen. As these programs became available on personal computers, they maintained this structure. Soon, however, they began to introduce some form of *graphical interface* to coexist with the control language. The graphical interface tends to be easier to use, but less flexible, than the control language. At the time of this writing, packages such as SPSS and SAS maintain some form of both, but some aspects of the programs can be accessed only through control statements. The graphical interface is very good for setting up the initial analysis and obtaining the overall picture. When you come to detailed analysis, such as the use of special contrasts, you may have to turn to the control language. Whether or not you specify your design through a control file or a series of mouse clicks, it is wise to be sure that the control statements appear somewhere in your printed output so you can reconstruct exactly what you specified.

Table 9.2: Control language to analyze Table 9.1 using Release 10 of SPSS.

```
1.    UNIANOVA
2.       score  BY spacing
3.       /CONTRAST (spacing)=Polynomial
4.       /METHOD = SSTYPE(3)
5.       /INTERCEPT = INCLUDE
6.       /POSTHOC = spacing ( TUKEY )
7.       /PRINT = DESCRIPTIVE ETASQ HOMOGENEITY
8.       /CRITERIA = ALPHA(.05)
9.       /DESIGN = spacing .
```

9.2   An Example

We will illustrate some of these ideas by following through the analysis of the data in Table 9.1. Because we are not writing a manual for computer usage, we will not offer recommendations as to which program to use, and we certainly will not attempt to explain the graphical interface (which like as not will have changed by the time this book is printed). Instead, we will offer an explanation that is general enough to help you understand the output of whatever program you happen to use. This approach is possible for this material because the analysis of variance is fairly well standardized, so the bulk of the analysis has a common form, regardless of the program used.

For our particular example, we will use Release 10 of SPSS. We hasten to add that our choice of this program was made for the not very profound reason that it was available to us as we were writing this chapter. Another program or version would have served us as well. We began by entering the data in the form, and with the variable names, in Table 9.1. We then used the graphical interface to set up and run the program. We had the program save the control statements so that we could study them more closely. They are given in Table 9.2, with line numbers added so that we can refer to them easily.

Let's go through these statements in detail. The first line, UNIANOVA, contains the name of the particular module of SPSS that we are using. It conducts an analysis of variance (strictly, a univariate analysis of variance, which explains the name). Line 2 has the very important function of specifying the dependent and independent variables, score and spacing, respectively. The remaining lines, those starting with a slash, tell the program more details about what we want it to do. You can ignore lines 4 and 5 (we will mention the Type III sums of squares in Chapter 14, and line 5 simply tells the program that the grand mean can be different from zero). Line 8 says to use the .05 level for any operations that require a significance level. Line 7 tells the program that we want it to calculate (and "print") several things: the descriptive statistics, measures of effect size, and a test for homogeneity of variance. Lines 3 and 6 request two types of analytical analysis, namely, a trend analysis and comparisons of the group means using the Tukey test. Finally, line 9 indicates the particular form of design that is to be used, which at this point is simply a standard one-way analysis of variance, in which the means depend on the variable spacing.

Table 9.3: Selected output from SPSS for Tables 9.1 and 9.2—Overall analysis.

Descriptive Statistics

Spacing	Mean	Std. Deviation	N
1	8.00	2.92	5
2	14.00	2.65	5
3	19.00	3.67	5
4	18.00	4.00	5
Total	14.75	5.40	20

Levene's Test of Equality of Error Variances

F	df 1	df 2	Sig.
.523	3	16	.673

Tests of Between-Subjects Effects

Source	Type III Sum of Squares	df	Mean Square	F	Sig.	Eta Sqr
Corrected Model	373.750[a]	3	124.583	11.074	.000	.675
Intercept	4351.250	1	4351.250	386.778	.000	.960
Spacing	373.750	3	124.583	11.074	.000	.675
Error	180.000	16	11.250			
Total	4905.000	20				
Corrected Total	553.750	19				

[a]R Squared = .675 (Adjusted R Squared = .614)

A portion of the output of the program is given in Tables 9.3 and 9.4. We have reproduced the content of the output but have not tried to maintain details of the typefaces or spacing, and we have omitted many nonessential portions. The first table shows the basic overall analysis. It includes three parts. The first reports the descriptive statistics, namely, the mean and standard deviation of the scores in each group and of the data as a whole. The next portion is the test for homogeneity of variance, the Levene test, which, as you may recall from Section 7.4, is an analysis of variance based on the deviations of the scores from the mean. The program gives a value of $F = 0.523$ for this test, and it has calculated the exact probability of obtaining a value of F this large or larger if the null hypothesis were true, $p = 0.673$. As this value is well above .05, we have no reason to suspect that the variances of the groups are different.

The primary analysis of variance is reported by SPSS under the heading *Tests of Between-Subjects Effects*, meaning that the tested effects are based entirely on the differences among (between) the individual subjects. You will notice several differences between this table and the summary of the analysis of variance in Table 5.1 (p. 90).

For one thing, there are more sources listed here; for another, the labels are unfamiliar. You can figure out what is what by comparing the program's results to those of our previous analysis. Comparing the two tables tells us (correctly) that the three sources you expected to find, A, S/A, and Total, appear here as *Spacing* (the name we gave to our independent variable), *Error*, and *Corrected Total*, respectively. The source labeled *Intercept* is a test of the hypothesis that the grand mean is equal to zero (see p. 37), which is not very interesting here. The source labeled *Corrected Model* is, for this design, the same as the effect of spacing (it will differ for designs with more factors), and that labeled *Total* is simply the sum of the Y_{ij}^2. Ignore for the moment that the sums of squares are labeled *Type III Sums of Squares*; we will explain that in Chapter 14. The remainder of the F table should be familiar. Note that, as for the Levene test, the program calculates the exact descriptive level for the three F tests (*Spacing*, *Intercept*, and *Corrected Model*), which here are so small as to be reported as zero. Because they are all less than α, all the null hypotheses associated with these effects are easily rejected. The measure of effect size reported by SPSS is the R^2 in our discussion of effect size (Equation 8.4, p. 161), indicating that approximately 68 percent of the total sum of squares is associated with the differences among the treatment conditions.[3]

The request for analytical analyses (lines 3 and 6 in Table 9.2) produced a considerable volume of output, of which we reproduce only a few parts in Table 9.4. The first section concerns the trend analysis. Because there are four levels of spacing, three trend coefficients (linear, quadratic, and cubic) can be tested, and the program tests all of them—we give only the output from the linear part.[4] The analysis appears straightforward: The program reports the observed value of the contrast and its standard error. Although it does not give the calculation itself, the ratio of the observed contrast and its standard error is a t statistic (Equation 4.9, p. 71):

$$t_\psi = \frac{\widehat{\psi}}{s_{\widehat{\psi}}} = \frac{7.826}{1.500} = 5.217.$$

This value is significant, as indicated by the descriptive level of .000 in the row labeled *Sig*. As you can verify, this t statistic is the square root of the statistic $F = 27.22$ that we calculated for these data in Section 5.1, a property that always holds when the two statistics are applied to the same contrast. The program also calculates a 95 percent confidence interval for ψ_{linear} (from 4.646 to 11.006). This interval does not include zero, which again shows that the hypothesis that $\psi_{\text{linear}} = 0$ can be rejected.

The last analysis in Table 9.4 is the Tukey test (described in Section 6.4, pp. 120–124). The output includes differences between means and confidence intervals for each pair of means (which we do not show), and a summary of the result using the equivalent subset notation (pp. 122–123). The output identifies two sets of equivalent groups, with group a_1 alone in one subset and the remaining groups in the other. The significance information in the last row refers to a test of significance for differences

---

[3]This program, like many others, does not calculate $\widehat{\omega}^2$, but you can easily determine it from the sums of squares or F statistic using Equations 8.11 and 8.12. The adjusted R^2 is a less substantial correction of a similar sort.

[4]SPSS assumes equal intervals for this analysis; special steps must be taken when the intervals are not equal.

Table 9.4: Selected output from SPSS for Tables 9.1 and 9.2.

Spacing Polynomial Contrast[a]

Linear	Contrast Estimate		7.826
	Hypothesized Value		0
	Difference (Estimate - Hypothesized)		7.826
	Std. Error		1.500
	Sig.		.000
	95% Confidence Interval for	Lower Bound	4.646
	Difference	Upper Bound	11.006

[a] Metric = 1.000, 2.000, 3.000, 4.000

Post Hoc Tests[a,b]

Tukey HSD

	N	Subset	
Spacing		1	2
1	5	8.000	
2	5		14.000
4	5		18.000
3	5		19.000
Sig.		1.000	.076

The error term is Mean Square(Error) = 11.250.
[a] Uses Harmonic Mean Sample Size = 5.000.
[b] Alpha = .05.

among the means in each subset. The first set contains only one group, so the test statistic of 1.000 is vacuous (one mean is not different from itself). The probability of 0.076 for the second subset indicates that null hypothesis of equal means within this subset is not significant (it exceeds $\alpha = .05$).

Contrast Values and Sums of Squares. On closer inspection, Table 9.4 contains a surprise. The linear trend coefficients we used in Chapter 5 (those in Appendix A.3) are $\{-3, -1, 1, 3\}$, but when we apply these values to the means, we obtain $\widehat{\psi}_{\text{linear}} = 35.00$, not the value given by the program. Neither of the calculations is wrong—both lead to the same test statistic and the same conclusions—but their particular values are different. You have to do a little exploring with the numbers to discover what happened. It turns out that the computer adjusts the coefficients so that their squared values sum to 1 before it calculates the value of $\widehat{\psi}$. The original coefficients had $\sum c_j^2 = 20$, so the program, in effect, divides each of them by $\sqrt{20}$. In detail, the program used the coefficient set $\{-0.6708, -0.2236, 0.2236, 0.6708\}$ instead of $\{-3, -1, 1, 3\}$. We did not do the calculations this way in Chapter 5, because the decimal places are an annoyance, but they pose no obstacle to the computer.

Our purpose in pointing out the different calculations is to alert you that software packages differ in the output they provide and the way they do the calculations. Although the tests are correct, some of the intermediate values may be different from the values obtained using the procedures and formulas in this book or, for that matter, from those given by a different program or a different part of the same program.

One reason we bring this matter up here is that sometimes you need to combine the results from several parts of the computer output. For example, in our discussion of theoretical predictions (Section 4.6), we pointed out that it is often useful to determine the variability that is *not* explained by a particular contrast or set of contrasts. Thus, in trend analysis, we used this approach to evaluate whether a straight line is sufficient to describe the relationship between the independent variable and the group means (p. 94). The relevant sum of squares is the difference between the sums of squares for the overall effect and those for the contrasts (Equation 4.16, p. 82). It is essential that these sums of squares are calculated on a consistent basis.

Let's complete the analysis here as we did in Section 5.1. When the sum of the squared coefficients equals 1, the equation for the sum of squares (Equation 4.5) is very simple:

$$SS_\psi = \frac{n\widehat{\psi}^2}{\sum c_j^2} = n\widehat{\psi}^2.$$

Applying this formula to the value of $\widehat{\psi}$ calculated by the computer, we obtain[5]

$$SS_{\text{linear}} = n\widehat{\psi}_{\text{linear}}^2 = (5)(7.826)^2 = 306.231.$$

This value can properly be combined with the sum of squares from the overall analysis to obtain a measure of how much the linear function fails to fit the data:

$$SS_{\text{failure}} = SS_A - SS_{\text{linear}} = 373.750 - 306.231 = 67.519.$$

We found $SS_{\text{failure}} = 67.50$ when we calculated this value in Section 5.1; the difference is attributable to rounding. The remainder of the analysis proceeds as we showed it in Chapter 5.

Before leaving this illustration, we want to make a larger point. There are frequently several different computational approaches to solving a particular problem, and a given computer program may use any one of them. We have presented the analysis of variance in the form we believe is easiest to understand, but it is frequently (and rightly) not the one that a programmer would choose. When you are going beyond the simple results of the significance tests, it is important to verify that the computer's output is what you think it is by applying it to an example whose values you already know and understand.

9.3   Hints, Cautions, and Advice

We will close this chapter with a few observations and suggestions on the use of the software packages.

---

[5]Another way to calculate the sum of squares is to work from the test statistic. Because $F = MS_\psi/MS_{S/A}$, $t^2 = F$, and $df_\psi = 1$, we have $SS_\psi = t^2 MS_{S/A}$. This formula is useful when the program provides t statistics but you don't know what coefficients it used.

- Use a documented or well-established program or package of programs. These have generally been tried and tested by other researchers, and the output they provide will usually be easier to communicate to others.

- Expect to spend some time understanding how to use the program. The documentation supplied with the statistical software is frequently unsatisfactory, even for experienced researchers. You may find it useful to consult one or more of the many supplemental books and manuals that have been published. Seeking help from someone who has used the program is very valuable, but make sure he or she understands what you are asking and that you understand what he or she recommends.

- With an unfamiliar program (or an unfamiliar option of a familiar one), start by running a set of sample data for which you know the answer. We have provided scores for our examples and suggest you use them as test cases. Be sure the analysis conforms to what you expect—the sources of variability, degrees of freedom, etc. Explore the different options.

- Take control of your statistical package. Do not settle on the defaults supplied by the program designers. Find out how to get the program to perform the analysis you want, and, if this is not possible, be ready to make a few calculations by hand. For example, if you want $\hat{\omega}^2$ and the program doesn't calculate it, do it yourself. Also remember that a program may perform analyses several ways, and you, not it, must decide which is relevant to your data. For example, you may find t tests calculated using both the equal- and unequal-variance formulas (Equations 4.10 and 7.12), but you will report only one of them.

- Save a backup copy of your data, particularly if you are using an external program for data entry and manipulation before you transfer it to the statistical package. Everyone we know who has manipulated data with an actual spreadsheet program has at least once sorted the columns incorrectly, mixed up the variable identifications, and had to reenter or reload them.

- Look over the results for errors or inconsistencies. Computer analyses are vulnerable to different sorts of mistakes than hand calculation. If you were doing the calculations yourself, you would spot silly errors like a percentage that was greater than 100 or a subject who recalled 125 items from a 30-word list, but a computer has no way to know about the meaning of these numbers. On the other hand, you are much more likely to make an arithmetic error or drop a term out of an equation than is the computer. Of course, it is important to proofread your data carefully, and you should also look over your output carefully to be sure that the means are approximately what you expect. If the program has a way to check for "outliers," use it to spot typographical errors.

- Do not be surprised if the output contains some things that you do not recognize. Programs often calculate various specialized statistics that are irrelevant to your particular application. Don't feel that you have to use them.

- Create a trail so that you can reproduce the analysis. If you have used a graphical interface to set up the analysis, make sure that the program includes the control language in the output. Having this information will be essential if you need to seek help from a statistical or computer consultant.

- In writing up your results, describe the analysis you have conducted, not the name of the program or option you used. For example, say "a one-way analysis of variance followed by a trend analysis," not "an SAS PROC GLM." Programs often are general, and the same module can analyze the data several ways.

Exercises

We will not give specific exercises here. If you have not already done so, we suggest that you gain access to your local computer package and duplicate analyses reported in the earlier chapters and the numerical parts of the exercises. You should do the same in the following chapters. We also suggest that you get hold of a larger set of real data and apply the programs to it.

Part III

TWO-WAY FACTORIAL EXPERIMENTS

In this part, we will introduce experiments in which treatment conditions are classified with respect to the levels of *two* independent variables. We will continue to assume that subjects serve in only one of the treatment conditions, that they provide only a single score or observation, and that the sample sizes n are equal. In later chapters, we will relax these restrictions and consider designs in which the same subjects receive some or all of the treatment conditions and designs with unequal sample sizes. The designs in this part are the simplest examples of experiments with two independent variables, computationally as well as conceptually, and they serve as the basis for the more complicated designs we consider later.

The most common way by which two or more independent variables are manipulated in an experiment is a *factorial arrangement of the treatments* or, more simply, a **factorial experiment** or **factorial design**. We will use these terms interchangeably. We will refer to the two independent variables as factor A and factor B and to the design itself as an A-by-B factorial. Factorial designs are those in which the independent variables are completely **crossed**, which refers to the fact that the design includes every possible combination of the levels of the independent variables. Suppose, for example, that two variables are both varied in a factorial design—the magnitude of the food reward given to a hungry rat for completing a run through a maze and the difficulty of the maze the rat must learn. There are three levels of food magnitude (small, medium, and large) and two levels of maze difficulty (easy and hard). We create a factorial design by combining each of the three levels of reward with each of the two levels of difficulty to produce the six cells in the following table:

Type of Maze	Reward Magnitude		
	Small	Medium	Large
Easy			
Hard			

We will often refer to a factorial design by the number of levels of the factors involved. In this case, the experiment is a 3×3 factorial design, with the times sign indicating that the levels of the two factors are crossed to produce a total of $3 \times 3 = 9$ treatment combinations.

In comparison with the single-factor design, the factorial has advantages of *economy*, *control*, and *generality*. Factorial designs are economical in the sense that they provide considerably more information than separate single-factor experiments, often at reduced cost of subjects, time, and effort. They achieve experimental control by providing a way to remove important but unwanted sources of variability that otherwise would be part of the estimate of error variance. Finally, factorial designs allow us to assess the generality of a particular finding by studying the effects of one independent variable under different conditions or with different types of subjects. We evaluate this generality by examining the results of a factorial experiment for an *interaction* between the factors.

There are four chapters in Part III. Chapter 10 considers the important characteristics of factorial designs, particularly the concept of interaction, without regard to numerical calculation; Chapter 11 covers the standard analysis of the two-factor experiment; and Chapters 12 and 13 present analytical comparisons that are particularly useful in the detailed analysis of this type of experimental design.

10

Introduction
to Factorial Designs

In a single-factor experiment, the groups are organized along a single qualitative or quantitative dimension. Most interesting experiments are more complicated: They involve two or more independent variables varied within a single study. Factorial designs are created by combining every level of one independent variable with every level of another, as illustrated on page 193.

10.1 Basic Information from a Factorial Design

Factorial experiments are rich with information. They contain information, not only about the effects of the two independent variables separately, but also about the way the independent variables combine to influence the dependent variable.

Simple Effects of an Independent Variable. Suppose we are putting together a reading series for elementary schools and believe that the format of the books will influence reading speed. Two factors we might consider are the *contrast* between the printed letters and the paper and the *length* of the printed lines. Say we chose three contrasts (low, medium, and high) and three line lengths (3, 5, and 7 inches). Combining these two independent variables factorially produces the factorial design on the left of Table 10.1. It involves nine treatment conditions, each formed by pairing a level of contrast with a level of line length.

What is not obvious from a casual examination is that a factorial design contains within it a set of separate *single-factor* experiments. We could create three single-factor experiments as follows: One consists of three groups of children randomly assigned to the different line conditions with the letters printed in *low* contrast. This single-factor experiment studies the effects of line length on reading speed under conditions of low contrast, and, if the manipulation were successful, we would attribute any significant differences to the variation of line length. Two other experiments are exactly like the first except that the letters are printed in *medium* contrast for one and in *high* contrast for the other. These three experiments are depicted on the right of Table 10.1. These experiments are components of the factorial design on the

Table 10.1: A factorial experiment (left) and its interpretation as a set of single-factor experiments (right).

A Factorial Design				Three Single-Factor Designs		

A Factorial Design

Line Length

Contrast	3 in.	5 in.	7 in.
Low			
Medium			
High			

Three Single-Factor Designs

	3 in.	5 in.	7 in.
Low Contrast			

	3 in.	5 in.	7 in.
Medium Contrast			

	3 in.	5 in.	7 in.
High Contrast			

left. Each component experiment provides information about the effects of line length under different conditions of contrast.

We can also view the factorial design as a set of component single-factor experiments involving the independent variable contrast. Each column of the factorial design on the left of Table 10.1 represents a single-factor experiment with three levels of contrast (low, medium, or high), but conducted with printed lines of the same length. The first column is an experiment on the effects of contrast with 3-inch lines; the second and third columns involve the same contrast manipulation with 5-inch and 7-inch lines, respectively.

The results of these component single-factor experiments are called the **simple effects** of an independent variable.[1] Thus, the results of the first component experiment in Table 10.1 (first row) are referred to as the simple effect of line length for low-contrast letters, and the results of the component experiment in the third column on the right are referred to as the simple effect of contrast for 7-inch lines.

One of the advantages of a factorial design is its *economy*. The factorial design contains the equivalent of three single-factor experiments in which line length is manipulated, and three in which contrast is manipulated. If we had to obtain the same information from true single-factor experiments, we would have needed to conduct six separate experiments, each with three groups. These single-factor studies would require a total of $6 \times 3 = 18$ groups. By embedding them in a single factorial design, we obtain the same information from half as many groups.

Interaction Effects. Although it is informative to study the effects of the two independent variables separately in the component single-factor experiments, it important to compare their results. For example, we should determine whether the simple effect of contrast with 3-inch lines is the same as those for 5- and 7-inch lines and whether the simple effect of line length with low contrast is the same as those for

---

[1] They are also called **simple main effects**. We prefer to use the shorter term *simple effects* to distinguish them from another statistical concept, the *main effects*, that we will introduce shortly.

Table 10.2: Cell means contributing to the main effects.

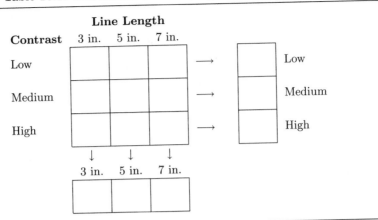

medium or high contrast. A unique feature of the factorial design is the possibility of looking for differences among the results of each set of single-factor experiments. This comparison is called the analysis of **interaction**. There is no interaction when the outcomes of the different component experiments—say, of contrast—are identical at each level of the other independent variable—say, line length. But when the outcomes of the component experiments differ, an interaction is present. We will refer to this outcome as an **A-by-B interaction**.

Main Effects. The **main effect** of an independent variable refers to the *average* of the component single-factor experiments making up the factorial design. The main effect of the contrast variable, for example, refers to the effect of this independent variable when line length is ignored. As illustrated by the arrows in Table 10.2, we obtain this main effect by combining the individual treatment means for the three line lengths to produce new averages that reflect variations in contrast alone. Similarly, we obtain the main effect of line length by averaging the means for the three contrast levels. Main effects are most appropriately interpreted when interaction is *absent*. Under these circumstances, the differences produced by one of the independent variables—contrast or line length—are numerically the same at each level of the other independent variable. This implies that we can safely study the effects of each independent variable separately, in the same way that we would study their effects in two actual single-factor experiments.

Summary. A factorial design produces three types of information. First, the *simple effects* refer to the results of the component single-factor experiments that make up the design. They reflect treatment effects associated with one of the independent variables, with the other held constant. Second, *interaction effects* reflect a comparison of the simple effects. An interaction is present when the component single-factor experiments produce different results; it is absent when the results are the same. Finally, the *main effects* treat the factorial design as two single-factor experiments.

Table 10.3: A hypothetical set of means for the reading experiment that shows no interaction.

	Line Length (Factor B)			
Contrast (Factor A)	3 in. (b_1)	5 in. (b_2)	7 in. (b_3)	Mean
Low (a_1)	0.89	2.22	2.89	2.00
Medium (a_2)	3.89	5.22	5.89	5.00
High (a_3)	4.22	5.55	6.22	5.33
Mean	3.00	4.33	5.00	4.11

10.2 The Concept of Interaction

Interaction is a new concept introduced by the factorial experiment. Main effects have the same meaning as in the single-factor analysis of variance, and they are calculated in exactly the same way. Thus, the principles and procedures in the single-factor analysis of variance—partitioning sums of squares, the logic of hypothesis testing, and planned and post-hoc comparisons—are also involved in more complicated designs. By the same token, the two-factor analysis of variance is a building block for designs involving three or more variables, with the concept of interaction linking them together.

An Example of No Interaction

Table 10.3 presents some hypothetical results for our experiment on reading speed. Assume that equal numbers of children have been randomly assigned to each of the nine conditions and that the values in the table are the average reading scores. We will refer to the contrast variable as factor A and to the three degrees of contrast as levels a_1, a_2, and a_3. Likewise, the line-length variable is factor B and the three line lengths are levels b_1, b_2, and b_3.

The main effect of contrast (factor A) is obtained by summing the three cell means for the three length conditions and then averaging these sums. The last column of the table gives these means for the three contrast conditions. These averages are called the row **marginal means** because they can be written in the margin of the table. Thus, the average reading speed for subjects in the low-contrast condition is found by combining the means from the three length conditions and calculating an average:

$$\overline{Y}_{A_1} = \frac{0.89 + 2.22 + 2.89}{3} = 2.00.$$

This mean represents the average performance of all the subjects in the experiment who received the reading material under low contrast; the specific conditions of factor B (the three line lengths) are unimportant at this point. We can obtain similar averages for the subjects receiving the materials under medium and high contrast. These two marginal means are given in the other two rows.

In like fashion, the marginal averages in the columns give us information concerning the main effect of the different line lengths (factor B). Specifically, the average reading speed for subjects in the 3-inch condition is an average of the means for the three contrast conditions:

$$\overline{Y}_{B_1} = \frac{0.89 + 3.89 + 4.22}{3} = 3.00.$$

This average, with those for the other length conditions, appear as column marginal means in the Table 10.3. Each of these marginal means represents the average performance of all subjects who received the specified length condition, ignoring the particular level of contrast (factor A) that each subject received.

You will usually want to plot the cell and marginal means in a graph. A graphical display often reveals aspects of the data that are less apparent in a table of means. Figure 10.1 shows several ways to plot the means in Table 10.3. First, look at the marginal averages for contrast, which are plotted in the upper left panel. This plot shows that low contrast produces the lowest reading scores and that medium and high contrast produce higher but similar averages. It provides a general description of the overall or main effect of factor A. The graph does not tell us whether the effects of contrast are the same for all line lengths. That question requires the double-classification plot of the cell means in the upper right panel of Figure 10.1. We draw this graph by marking off contrast on the baseline, plotting the cell means, and connecting the points with the same value of line length. The functions for the three component experiments in this graph are *parallel*, which means that the pattern of differences obtained with contrast is exactly the same at each level of line length. Parallel lines indicate that there is no interaction.

We arrive at the same conclusion if we focus on the other independent variable, line length. The graph at the lower left of Figure 10.1 plots the main (or average) effect of factor B. You can see that reading speed increases steadily as the length of the lines increases from 3 to 7 inches. The component single-factor experiments in the three rows of Table 10.3 are plotted in the right-hand graph. Again, the patterns of differences associated with the length variable (factor B) are the same for the three contrasts. The lines are parallel, and there is no interaction.

In the absence of interaction, we usually focus our attention on the main effects—the two sets of marginal means—rather than on the cell means. Since the effects of contrast, for example, do not depend on any particular line length, we can combine the results from the relevant component experiments without distorting their outcomes. A similar argument applies to line length.

An Example of an Interaction

Table 10.4 presents a second set of hypothetical results for the reading example. The same main effects are present; that is, the means in the row and column margins of Table 10.4 are identical to the corresponding means in the margins of Table 10.3. There is a big difference, however, in the simple effects. Figure 10.2 shows plots of the individual means like those on the right of Figure 10.1. Contrast is on the baseline of the left-hand graph and line length is on the baseline of the right-hand graph. In both plots, you can see that the patterns of differences for the simple effects are not the same at all levels of the other independent variable. Thus, an interaction is present.

To be more specific, consider the simple effect of contrast at level b_1—the cell means in the first column of Table 10.4. These three means are plotted in the left-

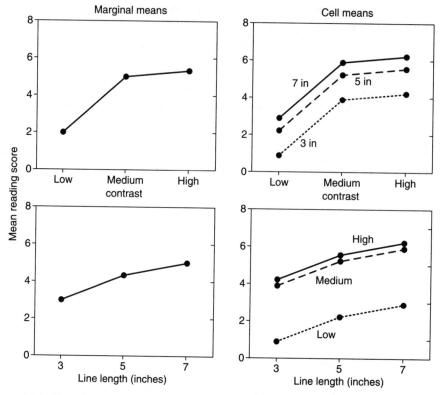

Figure 10.1: Reading scores from Table 10.3 plotted as a function of contrast (upper panel) and as a function of line length (lower panel). No interaction is present.

Table 10.4: A hypothetical set of means for the reading experiment that shows an interaction.

Contrast (Factor A)	3 in. (b_1)	5 in. (b_2)	7 in. (b_3)	Mean
Low (a_1)	1.00	2.00	3.00	2.00
Medium (a_2)	3.00	5.00	7.00	5.00
High (a_3)	5.00	6.00	5.00	5.33
Mean	3.00	4.33	5.00	4.11

Line Length (Factor B)

hand graph of Figure 10.2. The relationship here is positive and linear. For the simple effect for 5-inch lines (the second column), the relationship is not as simple—the function bends away from a straight line. For the 7-inch lines (the third column), there is a clear reversal of the trend, with maximum performance being found with a medium contrast. In short, the three lines are not parallel.

The cell means in the three rows of Table 10.4 are plotted on the right of Figure 10.2. They show an analogous variation in the simple effects. For the simple effect of

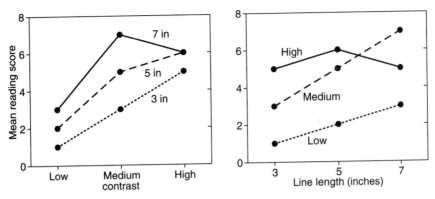

Figure 10.2: Reading scores from Table 10.4. An interaction is present.

line length under low contrast (the first row), the relationship is linear. The simple effect at level b_2 (medium contrast) shows a steeper linear trend. But look at what happens in the high-contrast condition. The relationship in this third component experiment is curved—the reading scores first increase and then decrease with line length. Again, the lines are not parallel.

With either plot, you can see at a glance that the form of the relationship between one independent variable (contrast or line length) and the mean reading score depends on the level of the other independent variable. You can now understand why we are less interested in the main effects when an interaction is present than when it is absent. In either plot, the patterns of differences in the simple effects are not the same as the pattern expressed in the corresponding main effects. The main effects are not representative of the simple effects and, thus, distort the single-factor experiments that make up the factorial design. There was no such distortion in Figure 10.3, where the interaction was absent.

10.3   The Definition of an Interaction

The presence of an interaction indicates that the main effects alone do not fully describe the outcome of a factorial experiment. Instead, the effects of each independent variable must be interpreted together with the level of the other independent variable. We will consider several definitions that highlight different aspects of this important concept.

One definition is stated in terms of the two independent variables:

An interaction is present when the effects of one independent variable on behavior change at the different levels of the second independent variable.

This definition contains a critical point often missed by beginning students, namely, its focus on the *effects* of the independent variables. A common mistake is to think of two independent variables as influencing one another. One independent variable does not influence the other independent variable—that makes no sense. Independent variables influence the *dependent* variable, the behavioral measure under study.

Another definition focuses on the actual pattern of results associated with the independent variables. Depending on the nature of the factor, the pattern may be expressed by a number of comparisons or contrasts, such as those discussed in Chapters 4 and 5. The definition is:

> An interaction is present when the values of one or more contrasts in one independent variable change at the different levels of the other independent variable.

We saw this definition in action when we described Figure 10.2. On the left, we saw different magnitudes of linear trend at the three levels of the contrast variable, and quadratic trend was present only at the highest contrast. We will study this form of interaction in detail in Chapters 12 and 13.

A more formal definition of interaction is in terms of the simple effects, that is, of the effect of one independent variable at a specific level of the other:

> An interaction is present when the simple effects of one independent variable are not the same at all levels of the other:

A related definition focuses on the main, or average, effects:

> An interaction is present when the main effect of an independent variable is not representative of the simple effects of that variable.

Other definitions of interaction are possible. One student created a definition that avoided "statistical jargon" by focusing on the differences observed among the cell means:

> An interaction is present when the differences among the cell means representing the effect of factor A at one level of factor B do not equal the corresponding differences at another level of factor B.

Some methodologists use the term *conditional* to express interaction:

> An interaction is present when the effects of one of the independent variables are conditionally related to the levels of the other independent variable.

A more mathematical way to define an interaction is based on a linear model of the type we described in Section 7.1. We will discuss this definition further when we describe the statistical model for the two-way design in Section 11.4.

Our reason for offering so many definitions of an interaction is to broaden your understanding of the concept and to provide alternative ways to express it. Many students have difficulty in defining interaction correctly and precisely.[2] The concept is essential to understanding factorial designs, both the two-factor design and the multifactor designs we discuss later.

Interaction and Theoretical Analysis

The presence of an interaction usually demands theoretical explanations of greater complexity than when no interaction is present. Consider the two outcomes in Tables 10.3 and 10.4. The main effect of each independent variable was the same in both examples. In the first case, where there is no interaction, the effect of one of the independent variables adds to the effect of the other variable. The combination is simple.

---

[2]Problem 10.2 gives some of the incorrect definitions proposed by graduate students on a final examination.

In the second case, the combination is complex—it will take theoretical ingenuity to explain why the relationship between contrast and reading speed is different for the different line lengths or why the relationship between line length and reading speed is different for the three levels of contrast. The discovery of an unexpected interaction usually puts a strain on the current theories and forces them to be modified.

Some theories, however, are rich enough to predict interactions, and when they do, the detection of this interaction is often the major point of the experiment. A good illustration comes from the program of research conducted by John Garcia, who studied the interplay between different classes of stimuli and reinforcers in a classical conditioning paradigm. In classical conditioning, a previously neutral cue (e.g., a flashing light) is paired with a reinforcer (food reward) that reliably elicits a particular behavior (salivation). Formally, these are called the conditioned stimulus, the unconditioned stimulus, and the unconditioned response, respectively. Conditioning is said to occur when the conditioned stimulus comes to reliably elicit the response, now called the conditioned response, in the absence of the reinforcer.

Garcia suggested (e.g., Garcia, McGowan, Ervin, & Koelling, 1968) that animals are equipped with two independent learning systems, one promoting the identification of cues in the external environment associated with sustenance (food and water) or danger, the other sensitive to serious changes in the animal's internal environment (cues associated with ingested dangers such as poisons and other noxious stimuli that produce illness). He designed a series of experiments that followed the same basic strategy: a gustatory stimulus (the flavor of a food pellet) was paired for one group with an "internal" reinforcer that resulted in sickness (a nonlethal poison) and for another group with an "external" reinforcer (an electric shock). He hypothesized that conditioning would occur only with the internal reinforcer. The other part of these experiments involved two more groups, one receiving a nongustatory stimulus (a flashing light) paired with the internal reinforcer and the other receiving the same stimulus paired with the external reinforcer. Here, he hypothesized the opposite result, namely, that conditioning would occur only with the external reinforcer. The basic design of this experiment is a 2×2 factorial design in which type of conditioned stimulus (flavor and light) is crossed with type of reinforcer (poison and shock). These theoretical expectations are summarized in a simple table, in which "Yes" and "No" indicate whether conditioning is successful:

	Reinforcer	
Stimulus	Poison	Shock
Gustatory (flavor)	Yes	No
Nongustatory (light)	No	Yes

If you assigned numbers to the four cells, say 5 to the "Yes" cells to represent conditioning and 0 to the "No" cells to represent no conditioning, and plot the results, you will see there are no main effects, but that the simple effects go in opposite directions. Garcia and his associates found this pattern in many experimental settings, with different external and internal reinforcers and with different gustatory and nongustatory stimuli, thus confirming their theoretical analysis.

Table 10.5: Eight different outcomes of a two-factor experiment.

(1)	b_1	b_2	$\bar{Y}_A$	(2)	b_1	b_2	$\bar{Y}_A$	(3)	b_1	b_2	$\bar{Y}_A$	(4)	b_1	b_2	$\bar{Y}_A$
a_1	5	5	5	a_1	4	4	4	a_1	7	3	5	a_1	6	2	4
a_2	5	5	5	a_2	6	6	6	a_2	7	3	5	a_2	8	4	6
$\bar{Y}_B$	5	5		$\bar{Y}_B$	5	5		$\bar{Y}_B$	7	3		$\bar{Y}_B$	7	3	

(5)	b_1	b_2	$\bar{Y}_A$	(6)	b_1	b_2	$\bar{Y}_A$	(7)	b_1	b_2	$\bar{Y}_A$	(8)	b_1	b_2	$\bar{Y}_A$
a_1	6	4	5	a_1	5	3	4	a_1	8	2	5	a_1	7	1	4
a_2	4	6	5	a_2	5	7	6	a_2	6	4	5	a_2	7	5	6
$\bar{Y}_B$	5	5		$\bar{Y}_B$	5	5		$\bar{Y}_B$	7	3		$\bar{Y}_B$	7	3	

10.4 Further Examples of Interaction

To broaden your understanding of the interaction of two variables and to provide practice in extracting information from double-classification tables and plots, consider the hypothetical outcomes of several 2×2 factorial experiments. The means for each set of four treatment combinations are presented in Table 10.5, and we have plotted them in Figure 10.3.

You have seen that the means in the margins of a two-factor table reflect the main effects of the two independent variables and that the cell means within the body of the table reflect the presence or absence of an interaction. In this discussion we will assume that if any difference is present between the column marginal means or between the row marginal means, a corresponding main effect is present, and that if the effect of one independent variable changes at the two levels of the other independent variable, an interaction is present—of course, we actually need the analysis of variance to assess the statistical significance the effects. Our eight examples represent each combination of the presence or absence of the two main effects and the interaction. You should note in Figure 10.3 the characteristic form shown by each combination of effects.

Before we begin, let's review the basic definitions.

- A **factorial design** contains the conditions formed by combining each level of one independent variable with each level of another.
- A **simple effect** expresses the differences among the means for one independent variable at a fixed level of the other independent variable.
- A **main effect** expresses the differences among the means for one independent variable averaged over the levels of the other independent variable.
- An **interaction** is present when the simple effects of one independent variable are not the same at all levels of the other independent variable.

The simple effects can be thought of as single-factor component experiments that together make up the factorial design.

The first four examples in Table 10.5 contain no interaction. Notice that in the corresponding four panels of Figure 10.3, the lines expressing the simple effects of A

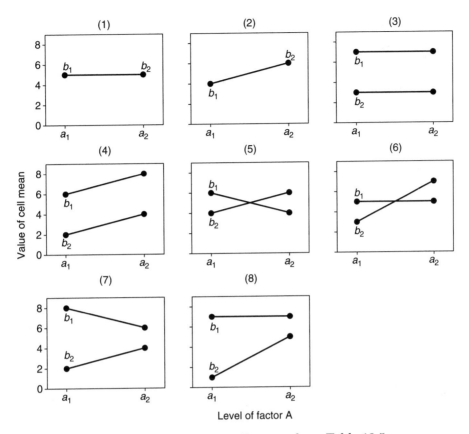

Figure 10.3: Plot of the cell means from Table 10.5.

at levels of B are either superimposed or parallel. This form characterizes the lack of an interaction. The first example shows a completely negative outcome—neither the main effects nor an interaction is present. In the second example, there is only a main effect of factor A, as you can verify by noting that the row marginal means are different $(4 - 6 = -2)$ and that the column marginal means are equal $(5 - 5 = 0)$. You can also verify the absence of interaction by checking that the difference between the two means at level b_1 $(4 - 6 = -2)$ is identical to the corresponding difference at level b_2 $(4 - 6 = -2)$. In the third example, the marginal means show a main effect of factor B $(7 - 3 = 4)$, but no main effect of factor A $(5 - 5 = 0)$. Again, no interaction is present—the difference between the two means at level b_1 $(7 - 7 = 0)$ is identical to the difference at level a_2 $(3 - 3 = 0)$. In example 4, both independent variables have main effects—the differences between the marginal means are $4 - 6 = -2$ for the A main effect and $7 - 3 = 4$ for the B main effect. However, there is no interaction, because the two simple effects of factor A are identical $(6 - 8 = -2$ and $2 - 4 = -2)$, as are the two simple effects of factor B $(6 - 2 = 4$ and $8 - 4 = 4)$.

The last four examples contain $A{\times}B$ interactions. In the corresponding panels of Figure 10.3, the lines for the simple effects are not parallel, a form that characterizes an interaction. The marginal means for example 5 show no difference between the two row means and no difference between the two column means; hence, there are no main effects of either factor. On average, neither factor has an effect, and on this basis someone might conclude that the manipulations were ineffective. But when you look at the cell means, you see that the independent variables produce quite striking effects. When factor A is manipulated at level b_1, a_1 is superior to a_2, but when it is manipulated at level b_2, the effect is reversed. There wasn't a main effect because the two simple effects canceled each other out. This pattern—an interaction without main effects—is sometimes called a **pure interaction**. We saw this type of interaction in Garcia's experiment.

The next two examples illustrate situations in which there is an interaction and one main effect. The main effect in example 6 is revealed in the row marginal means $(4 - 6 = -2)$, but not in the column marginal means $(5 - 5 = 0)$. An interaction is apparent in the plot of the cell means and can be verified by comparing either set of simple effects. In example 7, the situation is reversed; the marginal means indicate a main effect of factor B $(7 - 3 = 4)$ and no main effect for factor A $(5 - 5 = 0)$, and the nonparallel lines indicate an interaction. Finally, in example 8 all three effects are present. There a main effect for both independent variables and an $A \times B$ interaction, as you can see from the nonparallel lines or by comparing either set of simple effects.

10.5 Measurement of the Dependent Variable

A researcher is often faced with the choice between several ways to measure a psychological concept. Not only are there usually several completely different dependent variables available, but there are several ways to implement any of them. Consider something that is certainly familiar to readers of this book, an examination to test a student's knowledge of statistics. There different types of examinations—multiple choice, short answers, problems, essays, etc.—and each of these can be constructed in a variety of ways. These choices may not change the rank order of the students (at least not by very much), but it will change the relative difference between them. For example, if the examination contains many hard questions, then the better students will be relatively spread out at the upper end of the scale and the less proficient students will be clumped together at the bottom. In contrast, if it contains many easy questions, then the bottom students will be well discriminated and the better ones clustered at the top. What we have here is a situation in which we want to measure something (knowledge of statistics), we have a measurement device (the test), and the choice of how that test is constructed determines the particular distribution of the scores. Almost all psychological measurements have similar properties. There is some underlying concept that is to be measured, there are several ways to measure it, and these different ways change the relative differences between the measured individuals.[3]

For the most part, measurement issues did not have a substantial impact on the one-way procedures discussed in Part II. This is because when a null hypothesis in a one-way design holds for one measure, it holds for another, and when it is false for

---

[3]The study of the relationship between something we want to study and the measurements we make of it is known as **measurement theory**. We do not have the space to discuss it in any detail here. Many introductory statistics books cover some of it (Hays, 1994, Chapter 3, has a good discussion). A thorough, although more technical, treatment is Roberts (1979).

one, it is false for another. Things are not so simple for two-factor designs and the interpretation of interaction, however. The choice of how we measure a concept can determine the size and nature of an interaction, and even its presence or absence.

To illustrate the way measurement issues affect an interaction, we'll look at a situation in which the interpretation problem is fairly clear. Suppose we have a 2×2 design comparing the amount learned after 10 or 20 minutes of study for young and older children. Among the many ways we could measure "the amount learned," we decide to use a 60-item test. The test is rather hard, and the average score for the younger children after 10 minutes of study is 8 items and that of the older children is 30. These values are quite far apart on the 60-item scale. Suppose also that the scores from both 20-minute groups are 6 items larger than those of the 10-minute groups:

	10 min	20 min
Younger	8	14
Older	30	36

The two simple effects here exhibit the same 6-point change, so mathematically, there is no interaction. But for us to interpret these equal increases as indicating that age and study time do not interact, we would have to believe that a 6-item change represents the same amount of additional learning at the bottom of the range (the younger children) as it does in the middle (the older children). We might well question this assumption—after all, the young children nearly doubled their scores while the older ones increased theirs by only 20 percent. Moreover, we have no assurance that the same lack of interaction would be obtained if learning were measured in another way, say by the number of questions the children could answer in a 5-minute test period or the time they would take to answer a question based on the studied material. Even though another measure may place the groups in the same order (the older children learn more than the younger, and increasing the study time helps both groups), we cannot tell whether an interaction would be present until we actually performed the study. In a case like this, we cannot trust the comparability of the differences, so the interpretation of the interaction (or its absence) is clouded.

What this example shows is that for the size of an interaction to be precisely interpretable, we need to know that the simple effects—in this case the differences between means—mean the same thing regardless of where they lie in the range of the dependent variable. Strictly speaking, the following principle must hold:

> *The meaning of the difference between two values of the dependent variable does not depend on the size of the scores.*

This statement concerns the relationship between the quantity we want to measure (the amount of learning in the example) and the specific way we measure it (the number of correct answers or the number of answers in the 5-minute period). In measurement theory, dependent variables for which this principle holds are said to be measured on an **interval scale**.[4] On an interval scale, a given difference (like the

---

[4]The concept of an interval scale was introduced into psychology by Stevens (1951). There is a substantial literature (frequently polemical) on the appropriateness of these assumptions on statistical

6-point simple effects) has the same meaning regardless of the particular value of the numbers (8 and 14 or 30 and 36). If we could be sure that our potential dependent variables were all on an interval scale, we could use any of them and reach the same conclusions. However, if we cannot, we need to look more cautiously at the interaction. In extreme cases, such as the differences in the example above, it may be impossible to say whether an interaction really exists or not in more than a superficial way.

Most real situations are not as problematic as our ficticious example. When the means fall in a roughly equivalent range, the presence or absence of an interaction is usually clear. In fact, there are some interactions for which concerns about the scaling of the dependent variable are irrelevant. These are interactions that cannot be eliminated by changing the dependent variable, as long as the order of the means remains the same. Such interactions are said to be **nonremovable**. To determine whether an interaction is nonremovable, we plot the data twice, once with each of the independent variables on the abscissa. If the lines in *either* of these two plots cross, then the interaction is nonremovable—for this reason, a nonremovable interaction is sometimes known as a **crossover interaction**. To illustrate, consider two different outcomes for a $2{\times}2$ factorial study:

$$
\begin{array}{cc|cc}
 & & b_1 & b_2 \\
\hline
a_1 & & 1 & 3 \\
a_2 & & 8 & 4 \\
\end{array}
\quad \text{and} \quad
\begin{array}{cc|cc}
 & & b_1 & b_2 \\
\hline
a_1 & & 1 & 3 \\
a_2 & & 2 & 8 \\
\end{array}
$$

The results for the study on the left are plotted in the top part of Figure 10.4. You can see that the lines cross when the levels of factor A are placed on the abscissa (left plot). This crossover implies that the interaction is nonremoveable. The fact that the lines do not cross when plotted with factor B on the abscissa (right plot) does not alter this conclusion. The means from the other study are quite different. They are plotted in the bottom part of Figure 10.4, and the lines in neither of the two plots cross. The interaction here is a **removable interaction**. There exists *some* equivalent dependent variable that keeps the scores (and the means) in the same order, but for which the factors do not interact. The fact that an interaction is removable does not imply that you should ignore the finding, of course. Some removable interactions are quite convincing, particularly those involving well-established dependent variables. Nevertheless, many researchers consider nonremoveable interactions more compelling and less ambiguous because they are resistant to every possible change in the measurement scale.

Scaling issues of this type also need to be considered whenever transformations are used to reduce the impact of violations of the distributional assumptions, such as heterogeneity of variance, as we discussed in Section 7.4 (see pp. 153–155). For example, we might apply a square root or logarithmic transformation (Equations 7.8 and 7.9) when the groups with the larger means also have larger variances. Because transforming the scores changes the size of the differences between groups, it changes both the sizes of the simple effects and the size of the interaction. It may create or (less often) eliminate a removable interaction. Whenever we apply a transformation

---

analysis. Hand (1996) reviews much of this literature in a balanced way, and Loftus (1978) gives a straightforward discussion of scaling issues in the measurement of learning.

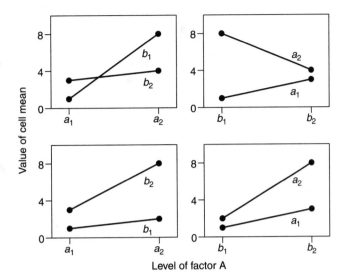

Figure 10.4: *A nonremovable, or crossover, interaction (top) and a removable interaction (bottom). Each set of means is plotted twice, one with factor A on the abscissa and once with factor B.*

to the data from a factorial experiment, and particularly when removable interactions are involved, we should verify that the transformation does not alter the substantive form of our conclusions.

In summary, you can interpret a nonremovable interaction with confidence, but you must be careful with removable ones. You should question the validity of interactions when they depend on simple effects that are widely separated on the response measure (as in our example with study time and younger and older children). When designing a study in which finding an interaction is important, it is advisable to choose a dependent variable for which all the groups fall within a comparable range.

Exercises

10.1. Figure 10.5 shows the population means for nine experiments. For each one indicate whether an A effect, a B effect, and an $A \times B$ interaction is present. Because we have assumed population means, do not worry about sampling error.

10.2. The following definitions of an interaction were given on an examination by graduate students in psychology. Each attempt at a definition fails to define the concept precisely. Identify the flaw in each attempt.

a. Interaction exists when the levels of one independent variable affect the other.

b. Interaction is the influence of independent variables on the dependent variable.

c. Interaction occurs when the effects of one level of an independent variable are different at the different levels of another independent variable.

d. Interaction occurs when the values of one independent variable are dependent on the levels of the other independent variable in a two-factor design.

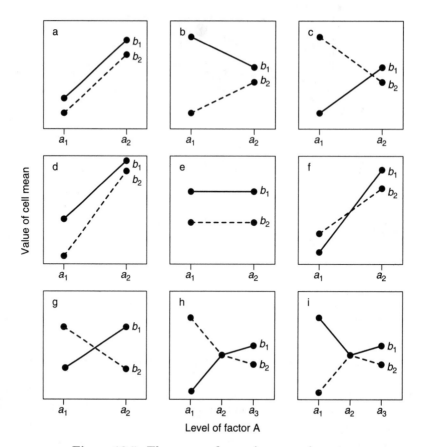

Figure 10.5: The means from nine experiments.

10.3. The six tables below give cell means for a 2×4 factorial experiment. For each example, indicate which effects are present and which are not. Assume that the means are population values and, thus, are error-free.

a.

	b_1	b_2	b_3	b_4
a_1	10	12	14	16
a_2	8	10	12	14

b.

	b_1	b_2	b_3	b_4
a_1	10	14	12	16
a_2	7	11	9	13

c.

	b_1	b_2	b_3	b_4
a_1	10	14	12	16
a_2	12	10	8	14

d.

	b_1	b_2	b_3	b_4
a_1	10	12	14	16
a_2	14	12	10	8

e.

	b_1	b_2	b_3	b_4
a_1	10	12	14	16
a_2	8	9	10	11

f.

	b_1	b_2	b_3	b_4
a_1	12	12	8	8
a_2	8	8	12	12

10.4. For each of the sets of means in Figure 10.5 that shows an interaction, indicate whether that interaction is removable or nonremovable.

11

The Overall Two-Factor Analysis

You saw in Chapter 2 that the total sum of squares could be partitioned into two parts: the between-groups sum of squares SS_{between} reflecting the deviation of the treatment groups from the overall mean and the within-groups sum of squares SS_{within} reflecting the variability of subjects treated alike. In subsequent chapters, we asked more refined questions of the data by dividing the SS_{between} into component sums of squares. The analysis of the factorial experiment follows a similar pattern, except that the SS_{between} is rarely of systematic interest. Instead, we are primarily interested in three components of SS_{between}: (1) a sum of squares SS_A reflecting the main effect of factor A, (2) a sum of squares SS_B reflecting the main effect of factor B, and (3) a sum of squares $SS_{A \times B}$ representing the $A \times B$ interaction. In this chapter, we will consider only designs in which each treatment condition contains the same number of subjects. The analysis of experiments with unequal sample sizes is described in Chapter 14.

11.1 Component Deviations

In this section, we look at how the deviations of the scores from the grand mean of all the data can be divided into parts associated with the various effects.

Design and Notation

The notational system we use is summarized in Table 11.1. The factorial arrangement of the two independent variables, illustrated with $a = 2$ and $b = 3$, appears in the upper portion of the table. There are $ab = (2)(3) = 6$ treatment conditions, each containing $n = 4$ different subjects. We will designate the conditions of factor A by a_1, a_2, etc. and those of factor B by b_1, b_2, etc. The groups formed by combining a level of factor A with a level of factor B are indicated by putting the two treatment indicators together, for example $a_1 b_1$ and $a_2 b_3$. The score of the ith subject in condition $a_j b_k$ is written Y_{ijk}. These scores are arranged in the **data table** in the middle portion of Table 11.1.

A necessary component of the analysis are the sums created by adding the scores Y_{ijk} within a group. These **treatment sums** or **cell totals** are denoted by AB_{jk};

Table 11.1: Design and notation for the two-factor design.

Experimental design

Factor B

Factor A	b_1	b_2	b_3
a_1	$n = 4$	$n = 4$	$n = 4$
a_2	$n = 4$	$n = 4$	$n = 4$

Data table

Treatment Combinations

	a_1b_1	a_1b_2	a_1b_3	a_2b_1	a_2b_2	a_2b_3
	Y_{111}	Y_{112}	Y_{113}	Y_{121}	Y_{122}	Y_{123}
	Y_{211}	Y_{212}	Y_{213}	Y_{221}	Y_{222}	Y_{223}
	Y_{311}	Y_{312}	Y_{313}	Y_{321}	Y_{322}	Y_{323}
	Y_{411}	Y_{412}	Y_{413}	Y_{421}	Y_{422}	Y_{423}
Sum	AB_{11}	AB_{12}	AB_{13}	AB_{21}	AB_{22}	AB_{23}

AB table of sums

Factor B

Factor A	b_1	b_2	b_3	Sum
a_1	AB_{11}	AB_{12}	AB_{13}	A_1
a_2	AB_{21}	AB_{22}	AB_{23}	A_2
Sum	B_1	B_2	B_3	T

for example, AB_{12} is the sum of the $n = 4$ scores in condition a_1b_2. These sums are conveniently assembled in the **AB table** in the lower panel of Table 11.1. We also need the **marginal sums**, found by summing the entries of the AB table over one of the dimensions. Row marginal totals A_j are formed by summing the cell totals in each row, column marginal totals B_k are formed by summing all the cell totals in each column. For example, in Table 11.1, $A_1 = AB_{11} + AB_{12} + AB_{13}$ and $B_2 = AB_{12} + AB_{22}$. The **grand total** T is obtained by summing either set of marginal totals or summing all the Y scores in the data table.

Many different means can be calculated from a factorial design. Each is found by dividing one of the sums by the number of observations that went into it. We will be concerned with four sets of means:

$$\bar{Y}_{jk} = \frac{AB_{jk}}{n}, \quad \bar{Y}_{A_j} = \frac{A_j}{bn}, \quad \bar{Y}_{B_k} = \frac{B_k}{an}, \quad \text{and} \quad \bar{Y}_T = \frac{T}{abn}.$$

We will refer to the means $\bar{Y}_{jk}$ as **group means**, **treatment means**, or **cell means** and sometimes write them generically as $\bar{Y}_{AB}$. The two single-factor means, $\bar{Y}_{A_j}$ and $\bar{Y}_{B_k}$, are **marginal means**, and $\bar{Y}_T$ is the **grand mean**.

Partitioning the Deviations

In Table 2.3 (p. 24), we showed how the deviations from the grand mean are partitioned in the one-way design. The similar partitioning in the factorial design involves a greater number of effects. To begin, think of the treatment means as coming from a single-factor experiment with ab groups. According to Equation 2.1, the total sum of squares can be divided into between-groups and within-groups portions:

$$SS_T = SS_{\text{between}} + SS_{\text{within}}. \tag{11.1}$$

The between-groups sum of squares SS_{between} is based on the deviation of the individual treatment means from the grand mean, $\overline{Y}_{jk} - \overline{Y}_T$. Consider the deviation for the subjects in group $a_j b_k$. This deviation is influenced by three sources of variability: the A main effect, the B main effect, and the $A \times B$ interaction. In words,

deviation of $\overline{Y}_{jk}$ from $\overline{Y}_T = (A_j$ effect$) + (B_k$ effect$) +$ (interaction effect).

The deviations for the two main effects are defined, as they were in the one-way design, by the deviations of the appropriate means from the grand mean:

$$(A_j \text{ effect}) = \overline{Y}_{A_j} - \overline{Y}_T \quad \text{and} \quad (B_k \text{ effect}) = \overline{Y}_{B_k} - \overline{Y}_T.$$

The interaction effect is the part that is left over and can be calculated by subtraction:

$$\text{interaction effect} = (\text{deviation of } \overline{Y}_{jk} \text{ from } \overline{Y}_T) - (A_j \text{ effect}) - (B_k \text{ effect})$$
$$= (\overline{Y}_{jk} - \overline{Y}_T) - (\overline{Y}_{A_j} - \overline{Y}_T) - (\overline{Y}_{B_k} - \overline{Y}_T)$$
$$= \overline{Y}_{jk} - \overline{Y}_{A_j} - \overline{Y}_{B_k} + \overline{Y}_T. \tag{11.2}$$

Thus, we can write the between-group deviation as the sum

$$\overline{Y}_{jk} - \overline{Y}_T = (\overline{Y}_{A_j} - \overline{Y}_T) + (\overline{Y}_{B_k} - \overline{Y}_T) + (\overline{Y}_{jk} - \overline{Y}_{A_j} - \overline{Y}_{B_k} + \overline{Y}_T). \tag{11.3}$$

We can verify that Equation 11.3 is correct by performing the indicated additions and subtractions. There is only one $\overline{Y}_{jk}$ on the right-hand side of Equation 11.3, so it will stay, but $\overline{Y}_{A_j}$ and $\overline{Y}_{B_k}$ will both drop out since each appears once as a positive quantity and once as a negative quantity. The final term, $\overline{Y}_T$, appears three times on the right, twice as a negative quantity and once as a positive quantity. We are left with the same expression, $\overline{Y}_{jk} - \overline{Y}_T$, on both sides of the equation.

So far, we have worked only with the means. Now we include the scores of the individual subjects in the picture. The deviation of the score Y_{ijk} from the grand mean $\overline{Y}_T$ is the sum of the deviation of the group mean from the grand mean and the deviation of the score from the group mean:

$$Y_{ijk} - \overline{Y}_T = (\overline{Y}_{jk} - \overline{Y}_T) + (Y_{ijk} - \overline{Y}_{jk}).$$

Replacing $\overline{Y}_{jk} - \overline{Y}_T$ by its decomposition into individual effects (Equation 11.3) gives us the complete subdivision of the total deviation:

$$Y_{ijk} - \overline{Y}_T = (\overline{Y}_{A_j} - \overline{Y}_T) + (\overline{Y}_{B_k} - \overline{Y}_T) + (\overline{Y}_{jk} - \overline{Y}_{A_j} - \overline{Y}_{B_k} + \overline{Y}_T) + (Y_{ijk} - \overline{Y}_{jk}). \tag{11.4}$$

Thus, the deviation of any subject's score from the grand mean breaks into four components: (1) an A_j treatment effect, (2) a B_k treatment effect, (3) an $A \times B$ interaction effect, and (4) the deviation of the subject's score from his or her group mean.

Each component deviation can be squared and summed to produce a corresponding sum of squares. For example, the sum of squares for the A main effect is based on the terms $(\overline{Y}_{A_j} - \overline{Y}_T)^2$, that for the B main effect is based on $(\overline{Y}_{B_k} - \overline{Y}_T)^2$, and so forth. It can be shown that these sums of squares add up just as the deviations do. The counterpart of Equation 11.4 with the sums of squares is

$$SS_{\text{total}} = SS_A + SS_B + SS_{A \times B} + SS_{\text{within}}.$$

Table 11.2: Steps for determining the sources of variability.

1. List each factor as a source.
2. Examine each combination of factors. If they are all crossed (each combination of levels appears in the design), then include that interaction as a source.
3. When an effect is repeated, with different instances, at every level of another factor, then include that factor in the source after a slash.

We could complete the analysis using the deviations. However, performing the calculations this way is impractical and an easy place to make arithemetic mistakes. So we turn to computational formulas that are easier to use.

11.2   Computations in the Two-Way Analysis

The calculations in the analysis of variance of any design have a common form that lets them be captured in a few sets of principles or rules. Throughout this book, we will list these sets of rules in boxes, so that you can turn to them when necessary. They will give you the tools for any calculations you need to do, and help you to identify which parts of the analysis remain the same across designs.

The computations in the analysis of variance involve four steps. First, we identify the sources of variance that can be extracted (Table 11.2). Second, we determine the degrees of freedom for each of these effects (Table 11.3). Third, we use the degrees-of-freedom statements to construct formulas for the sums of squares for each effect (Table 11.4). These are written with the *bracket terms* we introduced in connection with the one-way design, and part of the process is to construct formulas for them. Finally, we specify the mean squares and F ratios needed for the analysis (Table 11.6).

Identifying the Sources of Variance

Our first set of principles (Table 11.2) consists of the series of steps we use to determine the sources of variance. We have already discussed what these sources are (Equation 11.4), but it is useful to go over them again more formally.

First, following Step 1, we write down all the factors:

$$A, \quad B, \quad \text{and} \quad S.$$

Step 2 tells us to check each combination of factors to see whether they are crossed with each other. Factors A and B are crossed—each level of factor A appears with each level of factor B—so there is an interaction. Neither factor is crossed with factor S, because *different* subjects appear at each level of A or B. Therefore, we expand our list to

$$A, \quad B, \quad A \times B, \quad \text{and} \quad S.$$

In Step 3, we look at each of the four effects to see if it is repeated at the individual levels of another factor. The A, B, and $A \times B$ effects are not repeated. However, a different set of subjects (the levels of factor S) appears in each group, that is, within each combination of factors A and B. We refer to this arrangement by saying that

Table 11.3: Rules for calculating the degrees of freedom.

1. The total number of degrees of freedom, df_T, equals the number of observations less one.
2. The main effect of a factor has degrees of freedom equal to the number of levels of that factor less one.
3. An interaction has degrees of freedom equal to the product of the degrees of freedom of its separate parts.
4. When a source has a slash in its name, multiply the degrees of freedom for the effect or interaction by the number of levels of the factors listed to the right of the slash (or the leftmost slash, if there is more than one).
5. The degrees of freedom for the separate effects add up to df_T.

subjects are **nested within** factors A and B. So we add $/AB$ to the designation of this source, making our final list

$$A, \quad B, \quad A{\times}B, \quad \text{and} \quad S/AB.$$

Going through the steps of Table 11.2 may seem more trouble than it is worth for this simple single-factor design. However, we will need them when we discuss the multifactor designs in Part V and VI.

Degrees of Freedom

The rules for determining the degrees of freedom are listed in Table 11.3. We will discuss the meaning of the degrees of freedom at the end of this section; right now, we'll just apply the rules mechanically.

We start with the degrees of freedom for the total sum of squares. By Rule 1, it equals the total number of observations minus 1:

$$df_T = abn - 1.$$

Rule 2 says that the degrees of freedom associated with each factor equal the number of levels minus 1. This rule gives us the main-effect degrees of freedom:

$$df_A = a - 1 \quad \text{and} \quad df_B = b - 1.$$

For the $A{\times}B$ interaction, Rule 3 gives the degrees of freedom as the product of df_A and df_B:

$$df_{A{\times}B} = df_A \times df_B = (a-1)(b-1). \tag{11.5}$$

The calculation of the degrees of freedom for the within-groups source S/AB is slightly more complicated. The variability for this source involves a separate subject factor within each group. Within group $a_j b_k$, there are n subjects, so that source has $n-1$ degrees of freedom (Rule 2). Because this factor is present in each of the ab treatment conditions, the number of degrees of freedom for S/AB is the product of the number of groups and the number of degrees of freedom for factor S within each group (Rule 4):

$$df_{S/AB} = (\# \text{ of groups}){\times}(df \text{ per group}) = ab{\times}df_S = ab(n-1).$$

You can check that the degrees of freedom for the four sources agree with Rule 5:

$$df_T = df_A + df_B + df_{A{\times}B} + df_{S/AB}.$$

*Table 11.4: **How to find computational formulas from the degrees of freedom.***

Convert the degrees of freedom to computational formulas

> 1. Multiply out the degrees of freedom into single-letter products.
> 2. Replace each set of letters by the equivalent bracket term. The product of all the letters becomes $[Y]$, and the number 1 becomes $[T]$.

Form the bracket terms from the sums

> 1. Square the sums designated by the same letters as the bracket term and add them up.
> 2. Divide the result by the number of scores that contributed to the sums in the original table.

Form the bracket terms from the means

> 1. Square the means indicated by the same letters as the bracket term and add them up.
> 2. Multiply the result by the number of scores that went into the original means.

The agreement tells us we have not miscalculated or left out any terms. When you are working with these rules, it is handy to notice that Rules 2, 3, and 4 parallel the three steps we used in Table 11.2 to identify the sources of variability: first we listed the factors, then the interactions, and finally added the nesting.[1]

Computational Formulas

We can use the degrees of freedom to write the computational formulas for the different sums of squares. As in the one-way design (see Section 2.4), we write the computational formulas for the sums of squares as combinations of bracket terms, $[A]$, $[AB]$, and so on. Table 11.4 tells how to construct these formulas. It has three parts—one that gives a formula in terms of the bracket terms, and two that tell how to calculate the bracket terms. Table 11.5 applies these steps to the two-factor design. At the top of this table, each source of variance and its corresponding degrees of freedom are listed in the first two columns. In the third column, Step 1 is applied, and the different degrees of freedom are multiplied out in an expanded form, with the sets of letters arranged by decreasing numbers of letters.[2] When present, the number 1 is listed last.

Step 2 tells us that each term in these expanded degrees-of-freedom statements—single letters, combinations of letters, or the number 1—corresponds to a bracket term. The sequence of pluses and minuses in these statements indicates how these terms are

---

[1] Rule 4 allows for more than one slash, a condition we will not need until Chapter 25.

[2] You may have forgotten how to multiply the quantity $(a-1)$ by the quantity $(b-1)$. You start by multiplying the -1 in the second quantity times the two terms in the first quantity—that is, $(-1)(a-1)$—which produces $-a$ and $+1$. Next you multiply the b in the second quantity times the two terms in the first quantity—that is, $(b)(a-1)$, which gives ba and $-b$. Finally, you arrange these four products to produce $ab - a - b + 1$.

Table 11.5: Computational formulas generated by applying the rules in Table 11.4.

Forming computational formulas from the degrees of freedom

Source	df	Expanded df	Computational Formula
A	$a-1$	$a-1$	$[A] - [T]$
B	$b-1$	$b-1$	$[B] - [T]$
$A \times B$	$(a-1)(b-1)$	$ab - a - b + 1$	$[AB] - [A] - [B] + [T]$
S/AB	$ab(n-1)$	$abn - ab$	$[Y] - [AB]$
Total	$abn - 1$	$abn - 1$	$[Y] - [T]$

Formulas for the bracket terms

Letter Codes	Bracket Terms	
	Sums	Means
$[A]$	$\dfrac{\sum A_j^2}{bn}$	$bn \sum \bar{Y}_{A_j}^2$
$[B]$	$\dfrac{\sum B_k^2}{an}$	$an \sum \bar{Y}_{B_k}^2$
$[AB]$	$\dfrac{\sum (AB_{jk})^2}{n}$	$n \sum \bar{Y}_{jk}^2$
$[Y]$	$\sum Y_{ijk}^2$	$\sum Y_{ijk}^2$
$[T]$	$\dfrac{T^2}{abn}$	$abn \bar{Y}_T^2$

combined. The last column at the top of Table 11.5 gives the formulas for the sum of squares using the bracket terms. The letter T substitutes for the numeral 1 and the letter Y for abn; otherwise, the translation from the expanded degrees-of-freedom statement to the computational formula is simple and direct. You should also note the correspondence between these formulas and the deviations in Equation 11.4.

Forming the Bracket Terms

We now need to find the values of the five bracket terms for the analysis: $[A]$, $[B]$, $[AB]$, $[Y]$, and $[T]$. One of these, $[Y]$, is based on the scores Y_{ijk} in the data table and the others on the totals found in the AB table of sums or in its marginals. Table 11.4 gives two ways to calculate the bracket terms, one based on the sums and the other on the means. First let's look at the rules that use the sums. In Chapter 2, we squared the sums, added them up, and divided by the number of scores they involved (see pp. 29–30). To calculate $[A]$, for example, you find the A marginal sums, square each entry, and sum them up (Step 1 in the center part of Table 11.4). Then, because an A sum is based on bn observations, you divide the sum by bn (Step 2). We've listed the result in the middle column at the bottom of Table 11.5. The other entries in this column are found the same way. When using these rules, remember that the grand sum T is based on abn observations and that Y refers to the sum of the squared

Table 11.6: Computational formulas for the two-factor analysis of variance.

Source	Computational Formula	df	MS	F
A	$[A] - [T]$	$a-1$	$\dfrac{SS_A}{df_A}$	$\dfrac{MS_A}{MS_{S/AB}}$
B	$[B] - [T]$	$b-1$	$\dfrac{SS_B}{df_B}$	$\dfrac{MS_B}{MS_{S/AB}}$
$A \times B$	$[AB] - [A] - [B] + [T]$	$(a-1)(b-1)$	$\dfrac{SS_{A\times B}}{df_{A\times B}}$	$\dfrac{MS_{A\times B}}{MS_{S/AB}}$
S/AB	$[Y] - [AB]$	$ab(n-1)$	$\dfrac{SS_{S/AB}}{df_{S/AB}}$	
Total	$[Y] - [T]$	$abn - 1$		

scores in the original data table—this sum of squared scores is implicitly divided by 1, which we have not shown in the table.

The rules for bracket terms based on means appear in the bottom panel of Table 11.4. The steps are almost the same as for sums, except that Step 2 now involves multiplication instead of division. The results are shown in the final column at the bottom of Table 11.5. You can see the parallel between the two sets of formulas by comparing the two columns.

The formulas that use sums and those that use means produce the same values. Any differences between them are minor and arise from rounding. In this regard, note that the equations for the sums of squares in Table 11.5 require the bracket terms to be subtracted from each other, so you must be sure to carry enough places in your calculations to ensure that these differences are accurate. In this chapter, we will emphasize the procedure that uses the sums, and illustrate the one based on means (which is particularly useful when performing analyses based on summary data from a previous study) when we discuss the three-way design in Chapter 21.

Completing the Analysis

Table 11.6 summarizes the analysis. We repeat the formulas for the sums of squares in the second column and the degrees of freedom in the third. The fourth column gives the mean squares, found by dividing each sum of squares by its corresponding degrees of freedom. Finally, the F ratios in the fifth column are formed by dividing each effect mean square by the error mean square $MS_{S/AB}$. These F ratios are evaluated using the F table in Appendix A.1 with the appropriate numbers of numerator and denominator degrees of freedom. The logic behind the construction of these ratios is the same as we described for the single-factor design.

More About Degrees of Freedom

When we described how to find the degrees of freedom in Table 11.3, we simply showed how to construct the formulas. It helps to understand their values if we go back to our discussion of the one-way design (p. 33). In it, we gave the general formula:

$$df = \text{(number of independent observations)}$$
$$- \text{(number of population estimates)}.$$

This rule can also be stated in terms of the number of constraints placed on the values that the relevant scores or means are free to take (since each constraint implies a population characteristic that must be estimated):

The number of degrees of freedom for a sum of squares equals the number of different observations used to calculate it minus the number of constraints imposed on those observations.

Table 11.7 illustrates how these constraints operate in a 3×4 design. Let's start with the two main effects. The observations involved are the marginal sums (or means) for the columns and rows. Because we are interested in variation around the grand mean, they are constrained by the requirement that they sum to T (or that the means average to $\bar{Y}_T$). We have symbolized this constraint in Table 11.7 by placing an X in one cell in each margin, specifically cells a_3 and b_4. If you knew all the other entries in that column or row, you could figure out what X was because they must sum to T. For SS_A and SS_B, then, there are, respectively, a and b marginal sums (or means), which are subject to this single constraint; thus,

$$df_A = a - 1 \quad \text{and} \quad df_B = b - 1.$$

The interaction is calculated from sums within the table. How many degrees of freedom do they have? Look at the constraints. For any of the rows, the sum of the cell totals must equal the corresponding marginal total, which we used to find the sum of squares for A. These sums place one restriction on each of the rows; these restrictions are represented by X's in the column at level b_4. Similar restrictions apply to the columns, because the sum of the cells in any column equals the corresponding marginal total. These restrictions are indicated by X's in the row at level a_3. The unrestricted cells, then, represent the degrees of freedom for the $A \times B$ interaction. This rectangle has $a - 1$ columns and $b - 1$ rows, so the total number of cells without X's has the value we gave in Equation 11.5:

$$df_{A \times B} = (a-1)(b-1).$$

The degrees of freedom for the within-groups sum of squares $SS_{S/AB}$ follow the same rule. This sum of squares is calculated from the abn scores in the entire data table. However, these data are subject to the constraints imposed by the sums used

Table 11.7: Sums in a 3×4 design. The constrained cells, indicated by X, determine the degrees of freedom.

	Factor B				
Factor A	b_1	b_2	b_3	b_4	Sum
a_1	AB_{11}	AB_{12}	AB_{13}	X	A_1
a_2	AB_{21}	AB_{22}	AB_{23}	X	A_2
a_3	X	X	X	X	X
Sum	B_1	B_2	B_3	X	T

to calculate the group means. The scores in each group must add up to the total for that group. Because there are ab groups, there are ab constraints. So the within-group degrees of freedom is

$$df_{S/AB} = abn - ab = ab(n-1).$$

We obtain the same result by noting that each individual group has n scores, subject to one restriction: They add up to the group total, and so the n scores have $n - 1$ degrees of freedom. Summing these over the ab groups gives $df_{S/AB}$.

Although the principles in this section are needed to understand the degrees of freedom in complex situations, the rules in Table 11.3 implement these principles automatically for the standard effects in this book. With them, you will always know the computational formulas as well, since you can easily construct them from the degrees-of-freedom formulas using Table 11.4.

11.3   A Numerical Example

We are now ready for a complete numerical example. It concerns a hypothetical investigation of the role of hunger and certain drugs on the learning performance of monkeys. The animals are given a series of oddity problems. Each problem takes the same form: Two identical objects and one different object are presented to the monkey on a tray. There is a hole under each object, and a food reward is placed under the odd object, while the holes under the two repeated objects are empty. The monkey must select the nonduplicated, or "odd," object to get the food. Each animal receives a total of 25 problems, over the course of which the rule "choose the odd object" is to be learned. The response measure Y for each animal is the number of errors in the 25 problems. One of the independent variables (factor A) consists of a control and two drug conditions. The other independent variable (factor B) is determined by how long it has been since the animal had food available, either 1 hour or 24 hours—the "drive level." Thus, the design is a 3×2 factorial. We will suppose that $n = 4$ monkeys are randomly assigned to each treatment combination. The error scores for the individual animals appear in Table 11.8.

Preliminary Analysis

The first step in any analysis is to summarize the scores and plot them to get a glimpse at the results. These calculations, beneath the error scores in the data table, are the same as those presented in Chapter 3 (Table 3.5, p. 51). To illustrate for group a_1b_1,

$$AB_{11} = \sum Y_{i11} = 1 + 4 + 0 + 7 = 12,$$

$$\sum Y_{i11}^2 = 1^2 + 4^2 + 0^2 + 7^2 = 66,$$

$$\bar{Y}_{11} = \frac{AB_{11}}{n} = \frac{12}{4} = 3.00,$$

$$s_{11} = \sqrt{\frac{\sum Y_{i11}^2 - (AB_{11})^2/n}{n-1}} = \sqrt{\frac{66 - 12^2/4}{4-1}} = 3.162,$$

$$s_{M_{11}} = \frac{s_{11}}{\sqrt{n}} = \frac{3.162}{\sqrt{4}} = 1.581.$$

Table 11.8: Errors made by monkeys under three drug conditions and two degrees of food deprivation.

	1-hour deprivation			24-hour deprivation		
	Control (a_1b_1)	Drug X (a_2b_1)	Drug Y (a_3b_1)	Control (a_1b_2)	Drug X (a_2b_2)	Drug Y (a_3b_2)
	1	13	9	15	6	14
	4	5	16	6	18	7
	0	7	18	10	9	6
	7	15	13	13	15	13
AB_{jk}	12	40	56	44	48	40
$\sum Y^2$	66	468	830	530	666	450
$\bar{Y}_{jk}$	3.00	10.00	14.00	11.00	12.00	10.00
s_{jk}	3.162	4.761	3.916	3.916	5.477	4.082
$s_{M_{jk}}$	1.581	2.381	1.958	1.958	2.739	2.041

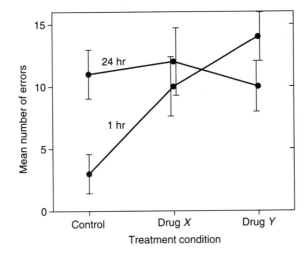

Figure 11.1: A plot of the data in Table 11.8. The vertical lines are error bars extending one standard error of the mean above and below each point. For the drug conditions, they have been slightly displaced so they do not overlap.

Figure 11.1 shows a plot the treatment means. As you can see, there seems to be an interaction of the two independent variables. Relative to the control conditions, the drugs appear to have had little effect on the number of errors committed by the hungry monkeys and a marked effect on those committed by the less hungry monkeys.

Along with the treatment means, we have drawn error bars, which extend one standard error of the mean above and below the treatment mean. For example, the limits of the error bars for the treatment mean for group a_1b_1 are

$$\text{upper limit} = \bar{Y}_{11} + s_{M_{11}} = 3.00 + 1.581 = 4.581,$$

$$\text{lower limit} = \bar{Y}_{11} - s_{M_{11}} = 3.00 - 1.581 = 1.419.$$

These error bars tell us two things. First, they give an idea of how accurately each mean is measured. Second, a comparison of their lengths gives us a rough indication as to whether we expect to have difficulties with heterogeneity of variance. Although we should use the Levene or Brown-Forsythe tests to be sure (see below, p. 228), the lengths of the error bars suggest we have no cause to worry in this regard.

Confidence intervals for the population treatment means are constructed using the methods described in Chapter 3 (see p. 34). For the population mean μ_{jk} of one of the groups, the confidence interval is

$$\overline{Y}_{jk} - ts_{M_{jk}} \leq \mu_{jk} \leq \overline{Y}_{jk} + ts_{M_{jk}}, \tag{11.6}$$

where $\overline{Y}_{jk}$ = the observed treatment mean,

t = a value obtained from Appendix A.2 with $df = n_{jk} - 1$,

$s_{M_{jk}}$ = an estimate of the standard error of the treatment mean,

n_{jk} = the sample size for this group (n if the group sizes are equal).

If we use the common estimate of the standard error (Equation 3.6), then for all groups,

$$s_{M_{jk}} = \sqrt{MS_{S/AB}/n_{jk}}, \tag{11.7}$$

and the value of t is found with $df = df_{S/AB}$.

Confidence intervals for the population marginal means μ_{A_j} and μ_{B_k} are found the same way, except that n in Equation 11.7 is replaced by the number of scores that contribute to these means, which are, respectively, bn and an when the cell sizes are equal:

$$\begin{aligned} \overline{Y}_{A_j} - ts_{M_A} \leq \mu_{A_j} \leq \overline{Y}_{A_j} + ts_{M_A} \quad \text{with} \quad s_{M_A} = \sqrt{MS_{S/AB}/bn}, \\ \overline{Y}_{B_k} - ts_{M_B} \leq \mu_{B_k} \leq \overline{Y}_{B_k} + ts_{M_B} \quad \text{with} \quad s_{M_B} = \sqrt{MS_{S/AB}/an}. \end{aligned} \tag{11.8}$$

The value of t is still based on the degrees of freedom for the error term, $df_{S/AB}$. Problem 11.1 illustrates these calculations. When the sample sizes are not equal, the situation is considerably more complicated, and you should use the computer methods described in Chapter 14.

Sometimes you will want to use a standard error of the mean that is based only on the scores that go into that particular mean, either because you want a confidence interval (or error bar) that reflects the actual measurement accuracy or the cell variances are heterogeneous. For the cell means, $s_{M_{jk}}$ in Equation 11.7 should calculated using the variance s_{jk}^2 for that group instead of $MS_{S/AB}$, and a t statistic with $df = n_{jk} - 1$. For the marginal means, you can average the variances in the relevant row or column to get the standard errors in Equations 11.8 when the group sizes are the same:

$$s_{M_{A_j}} = \sqrt{\frac{1}{bn} \frac{\sum_k s_{jk}^2}{b}} \quad \text{and} \quad s_{M_{B_k}} = \sqrt{\frac{1}{an} \frac{\sum_j s_{jk}^2}{a}}. \tag{11.9}$$

For example, the standard error of the mean $s_{M_{A_1}}$ for the monkey data is

$$s_{M_{A_1}} = \sqrt{\frac{1}{bn} \frac{s_{11}^2 + s_{12}^2}{b}} = \sqrt{\frac{1}{(2)(4)} \frac{(3.162)^2 + (3.916)^2}{2}} = \sqrt{\frac{25.333}{16}} = 1.258.$$

With unequal group sizes, you should turn to Chapter 14.

Table 11.9: Overall factorial analysis of the data appearing in Table 11.8.

Table of AB treatment sums, with A and B marginal sums

	Drive (Factor B)		
Drug	1 hour	24 hours	
(Factor A)	(b_1)	(b_2)	Sum
Control (a_1)	12	44	56
Drug X (a_2)	40	48	88
Drug Y (a_3)	56	40	96
Sum	108	132	240

Summary of the analysis of variance

Source	SS	df	MS	F
A	112.00	2	56.00	3.06
B	24.00	1	24.00	1.31
$A \times B$	144.00	2	72.00	3.93*
S/AB	330.00	18	18.33	
Total	610.00	23		

* $p < .05$

The Analysis of Variance

Numerically, the two-way analysis of variance starts with the table of the AB treatment sums shown at the top of Table 11.9. From it we calculate the row sums A and column sums B in the margins. To avoid errors, it is best to verify that both sets of marginal sums add up to the grand total T, which here is $T = 240$.

Next, we calculate the sums of squares. The first step is to find the bracket terms. Using the sums at the top of Table 11.9 and the formulas in Table 11.6, we obtain:

$$[T] = \frac{T^2}{abn} = \frac{240^2}{(3)(2)(4)} = \frac{57{,}600}{24} = 2{,}400.00,$$

$$[A] = \frac{\sum A_j^2}{bn} = \frac{56^2 + 88^2 + 96^2}{(2)(4)} = \frac{20{,}096}{8} = 2{,}512.00,$$

$$[B] = \frac{\sum B_k^2}{an} = \frac{108^2 + 132^2}{(3)(4)} = \frac{29{,}088}{12} = 2{,}424.00,$$

$$[AB] = \frac{\sum (AB_{jk})^2}{n} = \frac{12^2 + 40^2 + \cdots + 48^2 + 40^2}{4} = \frac{10{,}720}{4} = 2{,}680.00.$$

The final bracket term uses the sums of the squared individual scores that we calculated when we summarized the data:

$$[Y] = \sum Y_{ijk}^2 = 66 + 468 + 830 + 530 + 666 + 450 = 3{,}010.$$

The bracket terms are combined according to the formulas in Table 11.6 to calculate the sums of squares:

$$SS_A = [A] - [T] = 2{,}512.00 - 2{,}400.00 = 112.00,$$

$$SS_B = [B] - [T] = 2{,}424.00 - 2{,}400.00 = 24.00,$$

$$SS_{A \times B} = [AB] - [A] - [B] + [T]$$
$$= 2{,}680.00 - 2{,}512.00 - 2{,}424.00 + 2{,}400.00 = 144.00,$$

$$SS_{S/AB} = [Y] - [AB] = 3{,}010 - 2{,}680.00 = 330.00,$$

$$SS_T = [Y] - [T] = 3{,}010 - 2{,}400.00 = 610.00.$$

These sums of squares are entered in the standard summary table at the bottom of Table 11.9. To check for computational errors, we verify that the component sums of squares add up to SS_T.

The numerical values of the degrees of freedom are found by substitution in the formulas in Table 11.6:

$$df_A = a - 1 = 3 - 1 = 2,$$

$$df_B = b - 1 = 2 - 1 = 1,$$

$$df_{A \times B} = (a - 1)(b - 1) = (3 - 1)(2 - 1) = 2,$$

$$df_{S/AB} = ab(n - 1) = (3)(2)(4 - 1) = 18,$$

$$df_T = abn - 1 = (3)(2)(4) - 1 = 24 - 1 = 23.$$

Again, we verify that the component degrees of freedom add up to df_T.

The mean squares are obtained by dividing each sum of squares by the appropriate degrees of freedom. Finally, each mean square is tested against the within-groups mean square $MS_{S/AB}$, which measures the error variance. The obtained F ratios are compared to $F_{.05}(2, 18) = 3.55$ and $F_{.05}(1, 18) = 4.41$ from Appendix A.1. Here, only the interaction source of variance reaches the .05 level of significance.

11.4   The Statistical Model

As with the single-factor design, the statistical analysis we have just covered is based on a particular statistical model. We describe this model first, along with the consequences of violating its assumptions.

The Linear Model

The core assumptions of the statistical model for a fixed-effect factorial design are the same as those of the one-way design described in Section 7.1. An individual observation is represented by a random variable Y_{ijk}, and this random variable is taken to have a normal distribution, independent of any other observations, with mean μ_{jk} and a variance σ^2_{error} that does not depend on the group. The linear model for the scores in the two designs differ. The one-way model divides the observation into a grand mean μ_T, an effect α_j, and a random part E_{ij} (Equation 7.3, p. 133), while the factorial model divides the effect portion into several parts.

We start by defining the theoretical counterparts of the marginal means $\bar{Y}_{A_j}$ and $\bar{Y}_{B_k}$ and the grand mean $\bar{Y}_T$ as the averages of the group means:

$$\mu_{A_j} = \frac{1}{b}\sum_k \mu_{jk}, \quad \mu_{B_k} = \frac{1}{a}\sum_j \mu_{jk}, \quad \text{and} \quad \mu_T = \frac{1}{ab}\sum_{j,k}\mu_{jk}, \qquad (11.10)$$

the sums being over the indices k, j, and both indices, respectively, as indicated by the subscripts on $\sum$. The **main treatment effects** are the differences between the marginal means and the grand mean:

$$\alpha_j = \mu_{A_j} - \mu_T \quad \text{and} \quad \beta_k = \mu_{B_k} - \mu_T. \qquad (11.11)$$

These quantities express the effects of each factor while ignoring those of the other. The way these parameters are defined makes them sum to zero over their index:

$$\sum \alpha_j = 0 \quad \text{and} \quad \sum \beta_k = 0. \qquad (11.12)$$

When an interaction is present, the α_j and the β_k do not completely express the treatment means. The **interaction effect** is defined, just as for the observed means (Equation 11.2), as the deviation that remains after the main effects are removed:

$$(\alpha\beta)_{jk} = (\mu_{jk} - \mu_T) - \alpha_j - \beta_k$$
$$= \mu_{jk} - \mu_{A_j} - \mu_{B_k} + \mu_T. \qquad (11.13)$$

You should note that $(\alpha\beta)_{jk}$ is a single symbol here, not a product of two terms. With this definition, the $(\alpha\beta)_{jk}$ sum to zero over either index j or index k.

Using these definitions, the linear model underlying the analysis is

$$\mathsf{Y}_{ijk} = \mu_T + \alpha_j + \beta_k + (\alpha\beta)_{jk} + \mathsf{E}_{ijk}, \qquad (11.14)$$

where Y_{ijk} = the random variable corresponding to the score in question,

μ_T = the grand mean of the populations,

α_j = the treatment main effect for condition a_j,

β_k = the treatment main effect for condition b_k,

$(\alpha\beta)_{jk}$ = the interaction effect for condition $a_j b_k$,

E_{ijk} = the random experimental error.

The statistical hypotheses for the main effects and the interaction are stated in terms of these parameters:

$$A \text{ main effect:} \begin{cases} H_0: \text{All } \alpha_j = 0, \\ H_1: \text{Some } \alpha_j \neq 0, \end{cases}$$

$$B \text{ main effect:} \begin{cases} H_0: \text{All } \beta_k = 0, \\ H_1: \text{Some } \beta_k \neq 0, \end{cases}$$

$$A \times B \text{ interaction:} \begin{cases} H_0: \text{All } (\alpha\beta)_{jk} = 0, \\ H_1: \text{Some } (\alpha\beta)_{jk} \neq 0. \end{cases}$$

The expected values of the mean squares used in the analysis of variance are average values, which we could calculate (conceptually and theoretically) from a very large number of identical experiments that differed only in their sample of subjects. For the present design, these expected mean squares are

$$E(MS_A) = \sigma_{\text{error}}^2 + \frac{bn}{a-1}\sum \alpha_j^2,$$

$$E(MS_B) = \sigma_{\text{error}}^2 + \frac{an}{b-1}\sum \beta_k^2,$$

$$E(MS_{A\times B}) = \sigma_{\text{error}}^2 + \frac{n}{(a-1)(b-1)}\sum (\alpha\beta)_{jk}^2.$$

When any of the null hypotheses is true, the second term of the corresponding expected mean square disappears. To round out the picture, the expected within-groups mean square is determined by nothing but the error variability:

$$E(MS_{S/AB}) = \sigma_{\text{error}}^2.$$

As in the one-way case, the logic behind the analysis of variance lies in the construction of ratios that have the form

$$F = \frac{MS_{\text{effect}}}{MS_{\text{error}}},$$

where the expected value of MS_{error} matches the expected value of the MS_{effect} except for the component that reflects the effect being tested. Symbolically,

$$E(MS_{\text{effect}}) = \text{error} + \text{effect}$$

$$E(MS_{\text{error}}) = \text{error}.$$

Under the null hypothesis, the parameters of the tested effect are zero, so the null-hypothesis component ("effect") drops out and

$$E(MS_{\text{effect}}) = E(MS_{\text{error}}).$$

When this happens, the F ratio is distributed as $F(df_{\text{effect}}, df_{\text{error}})$, provided the fundamental assumptions of normality, homogeneity of variance, and independence of the observations are satisfied. Because the expected value of the three effect mean squares equals the expected value of $MS_{S/AB}$ when the corresponding null hypothesis is true, the error term for all three tests is the within-groups mean square.[3]

The Linear Model in a 2×2 Table

In a 2×2 design, the linear model is particularly simple because all the tests have one degree of freedom so are equivalent to contrasts on the means. The means in this design are:

	b_1	b_2	Mean
a_1	μ_{11}	μ_{12}	μ_{A_1}
a_2	μ_{21}	μ_{22}	μ_{A_2}
Mean	μ_{B_1}	μ_{B_2}	μ_T

The marginal means in the first row and column are $\mu_{A_1} = (1/2)(\mu_{11} + \mu_{12})$ and $\mu_{B_1} = (1/2)(\mu_{11} + \mu_{21})$, respectively (Equations 11.10). The grand mean is the average of the four cell means: $\mu_T = (1/4)(\mu_{11} + \mu_{21} + \mu_{12} + \mu_{22})$.

Now we write the parameters of the linear model in terms of the means, using Equations 11.11 for α_j and β_k, and Equation 11.13 for $(\alpha\beta)_{jk}$. For factor A,

---

[3]This error term applies only for the fixed-effect factorial design; we consider factorial designs with random factors in Chapter 24.

$$\alpha_1 = \mu_{A_1} - \mu_T$$
$$= \tfrac{1}{2}(\mu_{11} + \mu_{12}) - \tfrac{1}{4}(\mu_{11} + \mu_{21} + \mu_{12} + \mu_{22})$$
$$= \tfrac{1}{4}(\mu_{11} + \mu_{12} - \mu_{21} - \mu_{22}).$$

A similar calculation for α_2 gives

$$\alpha_2 = \mu_{A_2} - \mu_T = \tfrac{1}{4}(\mu_{21} + \mu_{22} - \mu_{11} - \mu_{12}).$$

The sign of each μ_{jk} in this result is exactly the opposite of what it was in α_1, and so α_2 is equal to $-\alpha_1$. That is as it should be, because the parameters must sum to zero (Equations 11.12). The results for factor B are similar:

$$\beta_1 = \mu_{B_1} - \mu_T = \tfrac{1}{4}(\mu_{11} + \mu_{21} - \mu_{12} - \mu_{22}),$$
$$\beta_2 = \mu_{B_2} - \mu_T = \tfrac{1}{4}(\mu_{12} + \mu_{22} - \mu_{11} - \mu_{21}) = -\beta_1.$$

For the interaction, Equation 11.13 gives us for the first cell,

$$(\alpha\beta)_{11} = \mu_{11} - \mu_{A_1} - \mu_{B_1} + \mu_T$$
$$= \mu_{11} - \tfrac{1}{2}(\mu_{11} + \mu_{12}) - \tfrac{1}{2}(\mu_{11} + \mu_{21}) + \tfrac{1}{4}(\mu_{11} + \mu_{21} + \mu_{12} + \mu_{22})$$
$$= \tfrac{1}{4}(\mu_{11} - \mu_{21} - \mu_{12} + \mu_{22}).$$

The parameters for the remaining three cells are all either equal to this value or its negative:

$$(\alpha\beta)_{21} = \mu_{21} - \mu_{A_2} - \mu_{B_1} + \mu_T = \tfrac{1}{4}(\mu_{21} - \mu_{11} - \mu_{22} + \mu_{12}) = -(\alpha\beta)_{11},$$

$$(\alpha\beta)_{12} = \mu_{12} - \mu_{A_1} - \mu_{B_2} + \mu_T = \tfrac{1}{4}(\mu_{12} - \mu_{11} - \mu_{22} + \mu_{21}) = -(\alpha\beta)_{11},$$

$$(\alpha\beta)_{22} = \mu_{22} - \mu_{A_2} - \mu_{B_2} + \mu_T = \tfrac{1}{4}(\mu_{22} - \mu_{21} - \mu_{12} + \mu_{11}) = (\alpha\beta)_{11}.$$

The importance of these equations is that they show that the effects in a 2×2 table are equivalent to single-df contrasts among the cell means:

$$\left.\begin{aligned}
\psi_A &= \mu_{11} - \mu_{21} + \mu_{12} - \mu_{22}, \\
\psi_B &= \mu_{11} + \mu_{21} - \mu_{12} - \mu_{22}, \\
\psi_{A\times B} &= \mu_{11} - \mu_{21} - \mu_{12} + \mu_{22}.
\end{aligned}\right\} \tag{11.15}$$

The contrasts expressing ψ_A and ψ_B are formed by subtracting the two cell means at one level of a factor from those at the other. The interaction contrast, $\psi_{A\times B}$, may also be written as a difference between the two simple effects of either the rows (factor A) or the columns (factor B) of the 2×2 table:

$$\psi_{A\times B} = (\text{simple effect of } A \text{ at } b_1) - (\text{simple effect of } A \text{ at } b_2)$$
$$= (\mu_{11} - \mu_{21}) - (\mu_{12} - \mu_{22}) \tag{11.16}$$
$$= \mu_{11} - \mu_{21} - \mu_{12} + \mu_{22}.$$

Notice that the parameters of the linear model are just one quarter the values of these contrasts, possibly with the sign reversed; for example, $\alpha_1 = \psi_A/4$ and $\alpha_2 = -\psi_A/4$. Thus, by rejecting the hypothesis that $\psi_A = 0$, we also show that the α_j are nonzero and that an A effect is present. The same holds for the other effects. Some treatments of the analysis of variance emphasize these contrasts heavily.

Assumptions and Their Violation

The assumptions that underlie the model for the two-way analysis of variance are identical to those for the single-factor design. The consequences of violating them are also the same. The independence assumption is fundamental to the analysis and is usually guaranteed by randomly assigning subjects to the treatment conditions and by testing subjects individually. Of the several assumptions concerning the distribution of scores, the assumption of between-group variance homogeneity is most important.

As in Section 7.4 (see pp. 151–152), you can test for heterogeneity of the cell or group variances using either the Levene test or the slightly more robust Brown-Forsythe test. These tests are based on the deviations of the Y_{ijk} scores from the mean or median of the relevant treatment group, respectively. With a factorial design, the test can be conducted in one of two ways. One possibility is to treat the ab groups as if they came from a single-factor design and proceed as in the one-way analysis. Done this way, the test assesses the homogeneity of the entire set of cell variances. A superior approach is to keep the factorial arrangement and test separately the two main effects and the interaction.[4] This approach gives information on how differences in variance relate to the factors of the design. This information is useful when trying to understand why the variances differ—the researcher with the monkeys would be interested to know, for example, if the variances changed with the drug condition (factor A). We will also need it when we determine how the presence of heterogeneity affects the tests of simple effects (pp. 251–253).

The presence of heterogeneity raises two problems for the analysis of a factorial design. The first concerns the actual significance level for the omnibus statistical tests. These are subject to the same inflation of the error rate by a few percentage points, discussed in Chapter 7 (e.g., Table 7.1, p. 149). To deal with this problem, you should consider one of the procedures we discussed there, perhaps no more than adopting a conservative value for the nominal α level. The other consequence of variance heterogeneity is potentially more important. Significant omnibus effects are generally followed up by the types of analytical analysis we will describe in Chapters 12 and 13. These tests focus the analysis on part of the data only. When variance heterogeneity is present, the error term that is appropriate for a test may be either larger or smaller than the pooled error term $MS_{S/AB}$, leading to positive or negative biases, respectively, if $MS_{S/AB}$ is used. Thus, (as we also recommended in Section 7.5) you should use an error term based on the specific groups involved instead of the pooled error term. We will consider these complications when we discuss the tests.

11.5   Designs with a Blocking Factor

With proper planning, the partitioning of variability in a two-factor design can be exploited to add power to what would otherwise be a single-factor design. The key to these **blocked designs** is the introduction of a **blocking factor** into the design. The purpose of this factor is to capture variability that is irrelevant to the effect of interest and thereby reduce the size of the error term. A blocking factor must have

---

[4]Your statistical software programs, if it offers a variance homogeneity test, may only use the one-way approach. You would need to get the program to calculate the required deviations, then use them in a factorial analysis.

two characteristics: First, it must be intrinsic to the subject, and second, it should be related to the dependent variable.[5] It can be a classification or subject variable, such as gender or college major, or it may be based on a quantitative variable, such as age or performance on some test.[6] By including the blocking factor in the analysis, the size of the F ratio is increased, and the power of the test is augmented. Although this increase in power is the primary reason to use a blocked design, it also lets us respond to certain violations of the assumption of homogeneity caused by the presence of subgroups in the population, a problem discussed in Section 7.3.

There are two forms of blocked designs. In a **randomized-blocks design**, the blocking is part of the original study and controls the assignment of subjects to groups. In a **post-hoc block design**, the second factor is created after the data are collected.

The Randomized-Blocks Design

Suppose that a researcher is investigating the effects of four sets of instructional material on how well college students learn a body of quantitative material—for example, statistics. The simplest procedure is to obtain a sample of 60 students, say, and to randomly assign $n = 15$ subjects to each of the four groups to create a completely randomized single-factor experiment. This design and its analysis are summarized in the upper portion of Table 11.10. A critical aspect of this design is the random assignment of subjects to groups, which assures that, except for the accidents of random sampling, the groups are comparable.

Now suppose the researcher realizes there is great variability in the student performance, probably arising from differences in their quantitative skills before the study started. This variability makes $MS_{S/A}$ large and limits the power of the design to detect differences among the instruction conditions. One way to improve power would be to increase the sample size, but that recourse is expensive and may require more subjects than are available. An alternative is to decrease the variability of the scores. Although there isn't anything the researcher can do to make the subject population more homogeneous, it is still possible to reduce the *within-group* variability. What the experimenter can do is to administer a test of generalized quantitative ability to the 60 students before the study begins, rank them according to ability, and divide them on the basis of rank into three equal-sized groups of 20 subjects each. Subjects in these groups, known as **blocks**, are less diverse in quantitative ability than those in conditions of an unblocked design.

In more detail, the top 20 subjects become the first block (b_1), the middle 20 become the second block (b_2), and the bottom 20 become the third block (b_3). Once the blocks are formed, the investigator randomly assigns five members from each block to each of the four treatment conditions and the experiment proceeds as before.

---

[5]In a series of investigations, Feldt (1958) showed that the correlation between a numerical blocking factor and the dependent variable should be at least 0.2 for blocked design to be more powerful than an unblocked one-way analysis and that the optimal cell size n in a blocking study should, roughly speaking, be about 5 when the correlation is 0.2, and that it drops to 4, 3, and 2 for correlations of 0.4, 0.6, and 0.8, respectively (the actual block sizes are a times these values). The optimal cell sizes are slightly smaller when there are more than three levels of the treatment variable.

[6]Of course, classification factors are used for other purposes than reduction of error. More often, they are introduced because a researcher is interested in their effects or their interaction with a treatment factor.

Table 11.10: A comparison of a completely randomized single-factor design and a randomized-blocks design.

Completely randomized (unblocked) design

Instructions (Factor A)

a_1	a_2	a_3	a_4
$n = 15$	$n = 15$	$n = 15$	$n = 15$

Source	df
A	$a - 1 = 3$
S/A	$a(n-1) = 56$
Total	$an - 1 = 59$

Randomized-blocks design

Instructions (Factor A)

Blocks	a_1	a_2	a_3	a_4
b_1	$n = 5$	$n = 5$	$n = 5$	$n = 5$
b_2	$n = 5$	$n = 5$	$n = 5$	$n = 5$
b_3	$n = 5$	$n = 5$	$n = 5$	$n = 5$

Source	df
A	$a - 1 = 3$
B	$b - 1 = 2$
$A \times B$	$(a-1)(b-1) = 6$
S/AB	$ab(n-1) = 48$
Total	$abn - 1 = 59$

This new design is diagrammed in the lower portion of Table 11.10. It now has two crossed factors, one the original instruction manipulation (factor A), the other the new blocking factor (factor B). It is analyzed using the two-factor analysis of variance summarized on the right. This blocking design is known as a *randomized-blocks* design to emphasize the random assignment of subjects from each block to the treatment conditions. We will not illustrate the numerical analysis, which is identical to that we covered in Section 11.3, but give an example in Problem 11.4.

Now let's compare a study that uses blocking to one that does not. When the blocking factor is related to the dependent variable, its use results in an experiment that is more sensitive than the corresponding experiment without blocks. The error term in the completely randomized experiment of Table 11.10, $MS_{S/A}$, reflects the variability of subjects from a population in which the blocking factor varies without control. In contrast, the error term for the blocked design, $MS_{S/AB}$, reflects the variability of subjects from subpopulations in which variation is restricted. By examining the analysis summary, you can see how the blocking arrangement reduces the error variance. For the unblocked design, error variance is what remains once the treatment sum of squares are subtracted from SS_T:

$$SS_{S/A} = SS_T - SS_A.$$

When the blocking factor is introduced, the error variance is further reduced by also subtracting SS_B and $SS_{A \times B}$:

$$SS_{S/AB} = SS_T - SS_A - SS_B - SS_{A \times B}.$$

The total and effect sums of squares, SS_T and SS_A, are presumably almost the same in both designs—the subjects and the treatments have not changed—but the two additional terms subtracted in the blocked design makes the error term smaller.

The randomized-blocks design has two positive side effects beyond the reduction in the error term. The first is that it increases the comparability of the groups by assuring that each one contains the same number of subjects from each block. In our example, the average quantitative ability is likely to be more similar across the treatment groups in the blocked design than it is in the completely randomized design, where there is a greater chance of accidental mismatching. The second side effect is that the design allows any interaction of the two factors to be detected. When the influence of the blocking variable is roughly the same in all groups, this effect is small and has minimal effect on the conclusions. However, a significant treatment-by-blocks interaction indicates that the blocking factor influences the magnitude of the treatment effect. For example, in the study diagrammed in Table 11.10, it may be that one set of instructions is particularly helpful to students with a strong quantitative background and another set to students with a weaker one. Discovering this interaction would help to clarify the influence of the instructions on the task.

When a study has been conducted using blocked assignment of subjects, the blocking factor should be included in the analysis regardless of its statistical significance. Dropping a nonsignificant blocking factor is tempting because it simplifies the analysis—you have a one-factor design instead of a factorial. However, doing so would be proper only if the factor could be proved to have no effect, and, as you know, a null hypothesis can never be proved true. The actual effects of dropping the blocking factor are complicated and depend on the true relationships among the variables, but under many circumstances it can actually decrease the power of the experiment. Our recommendation is that you analyze any blocking factors, be they significant or not.

Post-Hoc Blocking

To use the randomized-blocks design, blocking information must be available on all the subjects *before* they are assigned to the treatment conditions. In many studies this degree of planning is impossible. Often subjects are available for the study only one at a time and cannot be assembled for pretesting and assignment. Sometimes the blocking measure can only be scored after the subject has left the experimental setting. And sometimes the importance of a potential blocking factor only becomes apparent after the data have been collected.

Fortunately, it is still possible to separate out some of the error variability by blocking the subjects after the data are collected. This form of **post-hoc blocking** uses a blocking variable to segregate subjects into homogeneous blocks. In our example, the investigator may need to give the quantitative ability test at the start of each experimental session, when it is too late to use it in the assignment of subjects to treatments. The 60 subjects can still be divided into three group of 20 based on the pretest score and this classification used as a factor in the analysis. As another example, suppose you discover that the distribution of the scores in your study is very spread out (or even bimodal) and note that the spread is due to female subjects scoring higher on the dependent variable than male subjects. This observation has two implications for the analysis: First, the assumption of homogeneity of the individuals within the groups is violated, and second, these gender differences depress F by increasing the within-group variability. You can use gender as a blocking factor by segregating the scores for each group into females and males. The only difficulty with post-hoc blocking is that samples of equal size are rarely attained. However, unless something was badly wrong with your random assignment procedures, the cell sizes will be roughly equivalent. Although you won't be able to apply the equal-samples computational methods in this chapter to such data, you can use the procedures discussed in Chapter 14.

Where the potential blocking information is available as a numerical quantity (like our quantitative ability scores), an alternative to post-hoc blocking is to use a statistical procedure known as the **analysis of covariance**, discussed in Chapter 15. It gives more powerful tests than post-hoc blocking when the correlation between the blocking variable and the dependent variable is substantial. However, the statistical model for the analysis of covariance is more stringent than for a blocked design, and some care is necessary to be sure it is appropriately used.

11.6   Measuring Effect Size

You saw in Section 8.1 how measures of effect size help with the interpretation of an experiment. Most of this discussion applies to the two-factor design. The principal differences arise because variability in a factorial design is divided into four parts (A, B, $A{\times}B$, and S/AB), instead of two (A and S/A).

You can see how the multiple sources of variability complicate the analysis by examining the definition of ω^2 (Equation 8.10, p. 163):

$$\omega^2 = \frac{\sigma_A^2}{\sigma_{\text{total}}^2} = \frac{\sigma_A^2}{\sigma_A^2 + \sigma_{\text{error}}^2}, \tag{11.17}$$

where σ_A^2 is the variability of the treatment means μ_j about the grand mean μ_T and σ_{error}^2 is the variance of the scores around the individual means. The fact that $\sigma_{\text{total}}^2 = \sigma_A^2 + \sigma_{\text{error}}^2$ in the one-way design meant that the two versions of Equation 11.17 are the same. With the multifactor designs, however, σ_{total}^2 involves all the effects, and so the two denominators differ. The two forms lead to different classes of effect-size measures, one that includes all sources of variability in the denominator and one that includes only those sources directly relevant to the effect in question. We encountered a similar problem in Section 8.2 when we discussed effect sizes for contrasts in the single-factor design.

Complete Omega Squared

The first way to define effect size uses the total variability in the experiment as a baseline against which the effect is measured. This **complete omega squared** follows the first part of Equation 11.17:

$$\omega_{\text{effect}}^2 = \frac{\sigma_{\text{effect}}^2}{\sigma_{\text{total}}^2}, \tag{11.18}$$

where σ_{total}^2 is the sum of the variability of all the individual effects,

$$\sigma_{\text{total}}^2 = \sigma_A^2 + \sigma_B^2 + \sigma_{A{\times}B}^2 + \sigma_{S/AB}^2.$$

Each of the three systematic components of the variability is found by averaging a squared parameter of the linear model:

$$\sigma_A^2 = \frac{\sum \alpha_j^2}{a}, \qquad \sigma_B^2 = \frac{\sum \beta_k^2}{b}, \quad \text{and} \quad \sigma_{A{\times}B}^2 = \frac{\sum (\alpha\beta)_{jk}^2}{ab}. \tag{11.19}$$

The fourth quantity, $\sigma^2_{S/AB}$, is the error variance. The parameters needed for these expressions are found from the means by using Equations 11.11 and 11.13.

Usually we are not working with population values, but from the results of an experiment. To take chance differences into account, it is necessary to use estimation equations analogous to Equation 8.12:

$$\widehat{\omega}^2_{\text{effect}} = \frac{df_{\text{effect}}(F_{\text{effect}} - 1)}{df_A(F_A - 1) + df_B(F_B - 1) + df_{A \times B}(F_{A \times B} - 1) + abn}. \tag{11.20}$$

As an illustration, we will use the summary information from our numerical example in Table 11.8 to calculate $\widehat{\omega}^2_A$. From Equation 11.20,

$$
\begin{aligned}
\widehat{\omega}^2_A &= \frac{df_A(F_A - 1)}{df_A(F_A - 1) + df_B(F_B - 1) + df_{A \times B}(F_{A \times B} - 1) + abn} \\
&= \frac{(2)(3.06 - 1)}{(2)(3.06 - 1) + (1)(1.31 - 1) + (2)(3.93 - 1) + (3)(2)(4)} \\
&= \frac{4.12}{4.12 + 0.31 + 5.86 + 24} = 0.120.
\end{aligned}
$$

You can verify that the sizes of the other two effects are $\widehat{\omega}^2_B = 0.009$ and $\widehat{\omega}^2_{A \times B} = 0.171$.

Partial Omega Squared

The complete omega squared relates the estimate of the population treatment component to the sum of all the components specified in the linear model. Thus, for example, ω^2_A is influenced by the size of the other two treatment effects, σ^2_B and $\sigma^2_{A \times B}$. A measure of effect size that does not involve these nonrelevant factors is the **partial omega squared**, obtained from the second part of Equation 11.17:

$$\omega^2_{\langle \text{effect} \rangle} = \frac{\sigma^2_{\text{effect}}}{\sigma^2_{\text{effect}} + \sigma^2_{\text{error}}}. \tag{11.21}$$

Note that, as we did for contrasts (Equation 8.15, p. 165), we use angle brackets in the subscript to distinguish the partial from the complete omega squared. Applied to the A main effect and the $A \times B$ interaction, Equation 11.21 is

$$\omega^2_{\langle A \rangle} = \frac{\sigma^2_A}{\sigma^2_A + \sigma^2_{S/AB}}, \quad \text{and} \quad \omega^2_{\langle A \times B \rangle} = \frac{\sigma^2_{A \times B}}{\sigma^2_{A \times B} + \sigma^2_{S/AB}}.$$

Because the denominator of the partial omega squared is smaller than the denominator of the complete omega squared, $\omega^2_{\langle \text{effect} \rangle}$ is always larger than ω^2_{effect}.

We estimate the partial omega squared from the results of an experiment, using the F ratio and information about the design:

$$\widehat{\omega}^2_{\langle \text{effect} \rangle} = \frac{df_{\text{effect}}(F_{\text{effect}} - 1)}{df_{\text{effect}}(F_{\text{effect}} - 1) + abn}. \tag{11.22}$$

The estimate of the partial effect size for factor A in Table 11.8 is

$$
\begin{aligned}
\widehat{\omega}^2_{\langle A \rangle} &= \frac{df_A(F_A - 1)}{df_A(F_A - 1) + abn} \\
&= \frac{(2)(3.06 - 1)}{(2)(3.06 - 1) + (3)(2)(4)} = \frac{4.12}{4.12 + 24} = 0.147.
\end{aligned}
$$

Again, you should check that the partial statistics for the other effects are $\widehat{\omega}^2_{\langle B \rangle} = 0.013$ and $\widehat{\omega}^2_{\langle A \times B \rangle} = 0.196$. Each of these partial statistics is larger than the corresponding complete statistic that we calculated above.

Descriptive Effect Measures

You will also encounter several purely descriptive measures of effect size in the research literature or computer output. One of these measures is the squared correlation ratio R^2_{effect}. It is defined like ω^2, except that the theoretical variances are replaced by sums of squares. There are both complete and partial forms:

$$R^2_{\text{effect}} = \frac{SS_{\text{effect}}}{SS_{\text{total}}} = \frac{df_{\text{effect}} F_{\text{effect}}}{df_A F_A + df_B F_B + df_{A \times B} F_{A \times B} + df_{S/AB}}, \tag{11.23}$$

$$R^2_{\langle \text{effect} \rangle} = \frac{SS_{\text{effect}}}{SS_{\text{effect}} + SS_{S/AB}} = \frac{df_{\text{effect}} F_{\text{effect}}}{df_{\text{effect}} F_{\text{effect}} + df_{S/AB}}. \tag{11.24}$$

The effect here can be A, B, or $A \times B$. You should remember that R^2_{effect} is a descriptive statistic and does not take account of sampling variability.

The other descriptive measure is the standardized difference between means. To calculate it for any pair of cell means, simply treat the design as if it were a single-factor design with ab groups and apply Equations 8.1 and 8.3 (p. 160). For example, the standardized difference between the means $\overline{Y}_{11}$ and $\overline{Y}_{12}$ is

$$d_{a_1 b_1, a_2 b_1} = \frac{\overline{Y}_{11} - \overline{Y}_{21}}{\sqrt{(SS_{11} + SS_{21})/(df_{11} + df_{21})}},$$

where the sums of squares are those of the individual groups. With equal cell sizes the denominator is the square root of the average of the two variances, $\sqrt{(s^2_{11} + s^2_{21})/2}$. The same formula is used to measure the size of the difference between any two means, although those that come from both different rows and different columns may be hard to interpret because they cut across the factorial structure of the design (but see Section 13.5 for some exceptions).

For differences between two marginal means, say $\overline{Y}_{A_1}$ and $\overline{Y}_{A_2}$, the difference between them is divided by an average of all relevant cell standard deviations. You can calculate this variability by dividing the sum of the within-cell sums of squares for all groups that contribute to the two means by the sum of their degrees of freedom:

$$d_{a_1, a_2} = \frac{\overline{Y}_{A_1} - \overline{Y}_{A_2}}{\sqrt{(\sum SS_{1k} + \sum SS_{2k})/(\sum df_{1k} + \sum df_{2k})}}.$$

Which Effect Statistic Should You Use?

You are undoubtedly asking at this point which effect-size statistic should you use. With regard to the distinction between the estimates of ω^2 and the descriptive measures d and R^2, we can restate our recommendations from Chapter 8: The estimated $\widehat{\omega}^2$ is a more accurate description of the population under study, and so is preferable, both to summarize the effects and to estimate an effect for power calculations. However, the descriptive measure d is normally used in meta analyses and is acceptable if your intent is to focus on two conditions, either from a main effect or in the full design, provided you recognize that it is inflated by the sampling variability. We do not find R^2 particularly useful as a measure of the overall effects of a factorial.

You still have to decide between the complete and the partial measures. You need to consider both the design and the uses to which the effect size will be put. Suppose that you wish to report a measure that will describe the effect of factor A for a particular population. You will want the statistic that gives a value most like the one that you would have found had you investigated that factor separately in a one-way experiment. If factor B in the study is another experimental factor—one that you devised and manipulated—then you would not want its variablity, either as a main effect or in the interaction, to affect your description of the A effect. Thus, you would report the partial statistic $\omega^2_{\langle A \rangle}$. On the other hand, if factor B is a blocking factor included to reduce your error term, then you probably want to report the complete statistic ω^2_A. The blocking factor divides the subject population into groups with less internal variability, but these groups are an artifact of your design and not intrinsic to the population. You should keep the variability associated with the blocking factors in the calculation and use ω^2_A. Effect estimates for use in sample-size calculations are an exception. As we discuss below, you should base them on the partial measure in a design that includes any blocking factor you plan to use.

11.7 Sample Size and Power

Power and sample-size calculations for the two-factor analysis of variance are quite similar to those for the one-factor designs (Section 8.4). The most salient difference is that the study can require a different sample size to detect each treatment effect. In choosing the actual sample size, you need to use the largest value of n among all the effects (assuming that you care about all of them, which is not always the case). This way, power will be sufficient to detect every effect, from the smallest to the largest.

In practice, it is not always possible, or necessary, to make sample-size or power calculations for all the effects. When planning a study, we may only have good information about one factor or only about the main effects and not the interaction. Basing the calculations on the known effects (or on a simple effect, as discussed in the next chapter) can be better than making a wild guess at an unknown effect. Moreover, not all factors are interesting. Researchers usually do not worry about the significance of a factor included for blocking or to distinguish subpopulations, so do not involve it in sample-size calculations except indirectly through the size of the error term.

We can determine sample size two ways, either by using hypothesized population values or information derived from an experiment. We consider these two situations, then briefly discuss estimating power for an already planned experiment.

Determining Sample Size from Population Effects

When using a main effect to determine the sample size for a projected study, you can apply the methods for the one-way design, including the sample size table (Table 8.1, p. 173) and the power charts in Appendix A.7.

Using the Sample-Size Table with a Main Effect. You apply the sample-size table to a main effect the same way you apply it to a one-way design, except for two differences. First, you measure the effect with a *partial* measure, not a complete measure, for example, with $\omega^2_{\langle A \rangle}$, not ω^2_A. Second, the sample sizes that you find will be for all the subjects at a level of whichever factor you use, not for those in one cell.

So, if you are finding sample sizes based on factor A, the table will give you a value for bn, and if you are finding them based on factor B, the table will give you an.

Suppose you are planning a $3{\times}2$ factorial design and expect the marginal means for the three-level factor A will be 25, 27, and 32. You guess that the within-cell standard deviation will be about 8. How big should your samples be? First, you convert this information to a partial omega squared $\omega^2_{\langle A \rangle}$, following the sequence of calculations we used in the example on page 171. Begin by constructing a table containing the effect parameters and their squares, then average the squares to obtain σ^2_A (Equations 11.19):

	a_1	a_2	a_3	Sum	Average
μ_j	25	27	32	84	28.0 $(= \mu_T)$
$\alpha_j = \mu_j - \mu_T$	-3	-1	4	0	
α_j^2	9	1	16	26	8.667 $(= \sigma^2_A)$

Now use Equation 11.21 to calculate the partial omega squared:

$$\omega^2_{\langle A \rangle} = \frac{\sigma^2_A}{\sigma^2_A + \sigma^2_{S/AB}} = \frac{8.667}{8.667 + 8^2} = 0.119.$$

Finally, turn to the entry in Table 8.1 for $a = 3$, $\omega^2 = .12$, and power $= .8$, where you find that you need a sample of about 25 for a test at the 5 percent level. This value is the sample size for the marginal means (bn); the cell or group sample size n is obtained by dividing the tabled value by $b = 2$. The result is a sample size of $n \approx 13$ subjects per cell. One minor correction may be necessary. Table 8.1 was calculated under the assumption that a one-way design was used, and the values it gives slightly underestimate the sample size needed for a factorial design. The safe thing to do is to design this experiment with 14 or 15 subjects per cell.

Using the Power Charts.   If you need values of power or effect size other than those in Table 8.1, you can use the power charts. You also need them if you are basing the calculations on something other than a main effect—an interaction or a contrast, for example. The key equations for all power determinations are those that link the sample size, the size of the treatment effect, and the noncentrality parameter ϕ. The measure of effect size needed for these equations can be written using either the variability parameter σ^2_{effect} or the partial omega squared $\omega^2_{\langle \text{effect} \rangle}$. To be general, we will write the relationship so it gives the total sample size N for the entire experiment:

$$N = \frac{\phi^2(df_{\text{effect}} + 1)\sigma^2_{\text{error}}}{\sigma^2_{\text{effect}}} = \phi^2(df_{\text{effect}} + 1)\frac{1 - \omega^2_{\langle \text{effect} \rangle}}{\omega^2_{\langle \text{effect} \rangle}}, \qquad (11.25)$$

where N = the sample size for the entire experiment (here abn),
$\qquad \phi$ = the noncentrality parameter from Appendix A.7,
$\quad \sigma^2_{\text{effect}}$ = the variability from Equations 11.19,
$\quad df_{\text{effect}}$ = the degrees of freedom for the effect,
$\quad \sigma^2_{\text{error}}$ = the error variance,
$\quad \omega^2_{\langle \text{effect} \rangle}$ = the partial effect size from Equation 11.21.

This equation is equivalent to the more specific equations we presented in Chapter 8.

To see how these equations apply, let's expand the example of a 3×2 factorial above in which we looked at the main effect. Suppose that we can project the full pattern of group and marginal means:

	b_1	b_2	Mean
a_1	34	16	25
a_2	35	19	27
a_3	36	28	32
Mean	35	21	28

Again, we will assume that the within-group standard deviation is about 8. Because we are entertaining hypotheses about the entire experiment, we will need to make sample-size calculations for each effect. These calculations are most easily accomplished in parallel. First, we convert the means into the parameters of the linear model. We begin by subtracting the grand mean from the marginal means to determine the main-effect parameters:

$$\alpha_1 = 25 - 28 = -3, \quad \alpha_2 = 27 - 28 = -1, \quad \text{and} \quad \alpha_3 = 32 - 28 = 4;$$

$$\beta_1 = 35 - 28 = 7 \quad \text{and} \quad \beta_2 = 21 - 28 = -7.$$

Unless we have made a mistake, each set of values will add up to zero. Next, we calculate the interaction parameters using Equation 11.13:

$$(\alpha\beta)_{jk} = \mu_{jk} - \mu_{A_j} - \mu_{B_k} + \mu_T.$$

For example, the interaction parameter $(\alpha\beta)_{32}$ is

$$(\alpha\beta)_{32} = \mu_{32} - \mu_{A_3} - \mu_{B_2} + \mu_T = 28 - 32 - 21 + 28 = 3.$$

The entire set of interaction parameters found this way are

	b_1	b_2
a_1	2	-2
a_2	1	-1
a_3	-3	3

The effects are the averages of the squared parameters (Equations 11.19). We have already found $\sigma_A^2 = 8.667$ above; the other two variances are

$$\sigma_B^2 = \frac{7^2 + (-7)^2}{2} = \frac{98}{2} = 49.0,$$

$$\sigma_{A \times B}^2 = \frac{2^2 + 1^2 + \cdots + (-1)^2 + 3^2}{(3)(2)} = \frac{28}{6} = 4.667.$$

The values of ϕ are taken from the power charts, using 50 as the initial value of df_{error} and power of .80. For the A and $A \times B$ effects, the chart for $df_A = 2$ gives $\phi = 1.9$, while for the B effect, the chart for $df_B = 1$ gives $\phi = 2.0$. Now apply the first part of Equation 11.25 three times:

$$N = \frac{\phi_A^2(df_A + 1)\sigma_{\text{error}}^2}{\sigma_A^2} = \frac{(1.9)^2(2+1)8^2}{8.667} = \frac{693.12}{8.667} = 80.0,$$

$$N = \frac{\phi_B^2(df_B + 1)\sigma_{\text{error}}^2}{\sigma_B^2} = \frac{(2.0)^2(1+1)8^2}{49.0} = \frac{512.00}{49.0} = 10.4,$$

$$N = \frac{\phi_{A\times B}^2(df_{A\times B} + 1)\sigma_{\text{error}}^2}{\sigma_{A\times B}^2} = \frac{(1.9)^2(2+1)8^2}{4.667} = \frac{693.12}{4.667} = 148.5.$$

The $A{\times}B$ interaction requires the largest total number of subjects, so it determines the need for cell frequencies of $n = N/ab = 148.5/6 \approx 25$.[7] With this sample size, the power to detect the $A{\times}B$ effect is roughly 80 percent. For the A and B effects, the power is well above that value.

Using Estimated Treatment Effects

It is at least as common to base sample-size projections on related experiments as to draw them from population values. The easiest way to transfer information from one study to another is to use the estimates of partial omega squared $\widehat{\omega}_{\langle\text{effect}\rangle}^2$, discussed in Section 11.6. If we are only interested in the main effects, we can estimate the size of the relevant partial effect from the original study and use Table 8.1 to estimate the sample size (that is, if its power levels and effect sizes match our needs). If we need a value other than those in the table, we can use Equation 11.25 and the power charts, just as above.

As an illustration, let's return to our numerical example in Table 11.8. The main effect of factor A fell just short of significance ($F_A = 3.06$, against a critical value of $F_{.05}(2, 18) = 3.55$). Suppose we wanted to design a new experiment with sufficient power to detect an effect of the magnitude found in the first study. We have already calculated $\widehat{\omega}_{\langle A\rangle}^2 = 0.147$ (p. 233). All we have to do is to insert this estimate into the second part of Equation 11.25. The value of ϕ from the charts for $df_A = 2$ and $df_{\text{error}} = 50$ (as a trial value) is 1.9. Then,

$$N = \phi_A^2(df_A + 1)\frac{1 - \omega_A^2}{\omega_A^2} = (1.9)^2(2+1)\frac{1 - 0.147}{0.147} = (10.83)\frac{0.853}{0.147} = 62.8,$$

which implies that to achieve a power of 80 percent, we need a sample size of $n = N/ab = 62.8/6 = 10.5$, or about 11 subjects per group. If we wanted to control power for the other effects, we would obtain different sample sizes.

Estimating Power

Power analyses are also used to assess the power of an existing experiment, as we discussed in Section 8.5. For these calculations, we solve Equation 11.25 for ϕ_{effect}:

$$\phi_{\text{effect}} = \sqrt{\frac{N\sigma_{\text{effect}}^2}{(df_{\text{effect}} + 1)\sigma_{\text{error}}^2}} = \sqrt{\frac{N\omega_{\langle\text{effect}\rangle}^2}{(df_{\text{effect}} + 1)(1 - \omega_{\langle\text{effect}\rangle}^2)}}. \qquad (11.26)$$

We then look up ϕ_{effect} in the power charts to find the power.

---

[7]Our trial degrees of freedom of 50 used to obtain ϕ for the $A{\times}B$ effect is not correct. As we did in Section 8.4 (see p. 175), we could redetermine ϕ and recalculate N. Using the power function for $df_{\text{error}} = 100$, we find that $\phi \approx 1.8$, giving a cell size of about 23.

Suppose that the 3×2 experiment considered on page 237 was to be conducted with $n = 5$ subjects per cell. What is the power of this study to detect the hypothesized interaction effect? We start with the value of $\sigma^2_{A \times B}$ that we have already calculated to be 4.667. With $n = 5$ subjects per cell, there are $N = abn = 30$ in the full design. Then, with the left-hand version of Equation 11.26, we find

$$\phi_{A \times B} = \sqrt{\frac{N\sigma^2_{A \times B}}{(df_{A \times B} + 1)\sigma^2_{S/AB}}} = \sqrt{\frac{(30)(4.667)}{(2+1)(8^2)}} = \sqrt{\frac{140.01}{192.0}} = \sqrt{0.729} = 0.854.$$

The error degrees of freedom for the proposed study are $df_{S/AB} = ab(n-1) = 24$, and so we use the power function for 20 degrees of freedom from the charts. From the second chart in Appendix A.7, we find that $\phi_{A \times B} = 0.85$ on the baseline corresponds to a power of about 0.20 on the ordinate. Obviously, the proposed study is underpowered with regard to this effect, and some form of corrective action, such as substantially increasing sample size, should be taken.

Exercises

11.1. A two-variable factorial experiment is designed in which factor A consists of $a = 4$ equally spaced levels of shock intensity and factor B consists of $b = 3$ discrimination tasks of different difficulty ($b_1 = $ easy, $b_2 = $ medium, and $b_3 = $ hard). There are $n = 5$ rats assigned to each of the $ab = (4)(3) = 12$ treatment conditions. The animals are to learn to avoid the shock by solving the discrimination task within a 10-second period. The response measure consists of the number of learning trials needed to reach the criterion of an avoidance of the shock on three consecutive trials. The data are

a_1b_1	a_1b_2	a_1b_3	a_2b_1	a_2b_2	a_2b_3	a_3b_1	a_3b_2	a_3b_3	a_4b_1	a_4b_2	a_4b_3
6	14	15	5	12	14	13	14	16	15	15	17
7	18	18	11	10	17	12	19	18	19	12	15
3	12	14	6	15	15	10	17	19	13	16	19
4	13	13	5	14	11	14	12	11	17	18	14
9	11	15	7	11	14	9	13	14	12	13	16

a. Conduct an analysis of variance on these data. Reserve your calculations for Problem 12.3 in the next chapter.
b. Construct a 95 percent confidence interval for the cell mean μ_{11} and for the two of the marginal means, μ_{A_2} of factor A and μ_{B_3} of factor B. Use $MS_{S/AB}$ to estimate the standard error s_M.
c. Estimate complete omega squared for each of the three factorial effects.
d. Estimate partial omega squared for each of the three factorial effects.

11.2. The following table of data are for a 3×3 design with $n = 4$ subjects per treatment condition.

a_1 b_1	a_1 b_2	a_1 b_3	a_2 b_1	a_2 b_2	a_2 b_3	a_3 b_1	a_3 b_2	a_3 b_3
10	11	9	18	15	19	8	12	11
9	8	7	16	12	16	11	9	7
8	9	8	16	14	18	10	10	8
7	8	9	13	16	20	10	8	7

a. Conduct an analysis of variance on these data.   Reserve your calculations for Problem 12.1 in the next chapter.

b. Estimate complete and partial omega squared for each of the factorial effects.

11.3. To conserve space, journals rarely publish analysis-of-variance summary tables. The most we can expect to find is a table of means and the values of F, sometimes with MS_{error}. At times, however, we wish the researcher had examined certain comparisons of particular interest to us. We can perform these analyses even without a detailed summary of the analysis by reconstructing it. Suppose we had been given the following table of means based on $n = 4$ subjects per cell:

	b_1	b_2	b_3
a_1	11	12	10
a_2	3	10	14

The article reports only that the $A{\times}B$ interaction is significant, with $F = 3.93$, $p < .05$. Reconstruct the entire summary table, including the sums of squares, the degrees of freedom, and the F's.

11.4. Suppose that the data in Problem 2.1 had been collected by 5 different assistants, each of whom ran 2 subjects in each of the $a = 5$ conditions. Instead of simply $a = 5$ treatment conditions with $n = 10$ subjects randomly assigned to each, the design now is blocked, with 5 blocks (assistants) each containing 10 subjects:

Experimenters (B)	\a_1		a_1		a_1		a_1		a_5	
b_1	13	9	7	4	12	11	10	12	13	6
b_2	8	7	4	1	4	9	9	7	14	12
b_3	8	6	10	7	5	10	15	14	13	10
b_4	6	7	5	9	2	8	10	17	8	4
b_5	6	10	5	8	3	6	14	12	9	11

Treatments (A)

a. Analyze the data as a randomized-blocks design.

b. Compare the results of this analysis with the single-factor analysis you completed in Problem 3.6 in Chapter 3. What have you gained from this analysis? What have you lost?

11.5. A 2×3 factorial pilot study with $n = 5$ subjects per group gives the following means:

	b_1	b_2	b_3
a_1	2.7	6.5	7.7
a_2	3.9	2.5	4.5

a. Perform an analysis of variance. Assume $MS_{S/AB} = 14.66$.

b. Although none of the sources of variance is significant, the interaction reflects the pattern of means important to you, so you decide to replicate the study. What sample size would you need to have a power of .80 to detect the main effect of factor B at $\alpha = .05$? Use both the sample-size table (Table 8.1, p. 173) and the power charts in Appendix A.7 to make your estimate.

11.6. A replication of the study that you analyzed in Problem 11.1 is contemplated. Find the sample size required to achieve a power of .95 for factor A in the replication in the following two situations:

a. An exact replication.

b. A replication of factor A in a one-way design in which factor B is fixed at level b_2.

11.7. Two researchers were interested in the possibility that a certain drug adminis-tered after learning would enhance memory for the task 24 hours later.[8] On Day 1, rats were placed in an apparatus, in which they were administered an electric shock if they failed to enter a distinctive adjoining chamber within 30 seconds; each rat was given two chances to avoid the shock. Immediately following training, one group was administered a drug (the experimental condition) and another an inert substance (the control condition). On Day 2, all animals were tested eight more times in the avoidance apparatus (without shock). The dependent variable was the number of avoidance responses in the eight trials. After successfully replicating the facilitating property of the drug in a number of related experiments, the researchers planned a more elaborate series of experiments, designed to pinpoint the locus of the effect of the drug in the brain. They introduced a second independent variable (operation) in which animals either had a particular area of the brain removed surgically or were given a sham (control) operation. The design is a 2×2 factorial in which factor A is the control and drug conditions and factor B is the sham and actual operation. From earlier research in the same experimental setting, the experimenters estimated the a within-cell standard deviation would be about 1.6. They predicted the following outcome:

Drug Conditions	Operation Sham (b_1)	Actual (b_2)	Mean
Control (a_1)	4.2	3.0	3.6
Drug (a_2)	5.8	3.0	4.4
Mean	5.0	3.0	4.0

What sample size do they need to have a power of .80 to find a significant interaction?

---

[8]This problem is based on an actual experiment. We thank Drs. Joe Martinez and Patricia Janak for providing us with this illustration.

12

Detailed Analysis
of Main Effects
and Simple Effects

The factorial design is both an efficient way to study the separate and joint effects of two or more independent variables on behavior and a rich source of analytical comparisons that identify the specific treatment conditions responsible for a significant main effect or a significant interaction. The test for interaction is usually an effective way to begin the analysis, because its outcome influences all the analyses that follow. If the interaction is significant, then less attention is paid to the two main effects, and the analysis tends to focus on the individual cell means and the joint variation of the two independent variables. If the interaction is not significant or is relatively small in size, then attention is directed to the marginal means and the variation of each independent variable considered without reference to the other.

The analysis of any study must return eventually to the actual pattern of means. It never suffices to assert that one factor is significant and another is not, nor that an interaction is or is not present. A detailed description of the substance of the study is always necessary. A large variety of techniques are available to aid the researcher here, the majority of which use the linear contrasts discussed in Chapters 4 and 5. In a given situation, some of these procedures are useful and some are not. This chapter deals with the analysis of individual independent variables, either as main effects, when the other independent variable is disregarded, or as simple effects, when the other independent variable is held constant. In either case, the analyses are functionally identical to the analysis of a single-factor design, except that they are set within the context of the factorial. Chapter 13 looks at procedures that specifically emphasize the two-dimensional structure of the data.

12.1 Interpreting a Two-Way Design

The first step in examining data from a factorial study is to plot the means. A properly chosen picture often makes clear the nature of a set of main effects or an interaction. Line graphs are usually clearer than bar graphs, particularly when exploring the data,

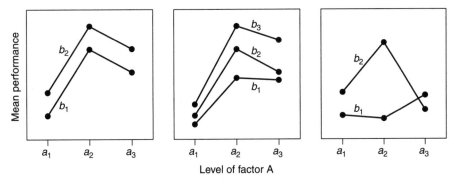

Figure 12.1: Three different outcomes of a two-factor experiment.

because the slopes of the lines emphasize the differences between groups—a series of interleaved bars can be impenetrable, while a set of lines that are not parallel makes an interaction immediately obvious. The picture can appear quite different, depending on which factor is placed on the abscissa, and different plots emphasize different characteristics of the results—something even more evident in the three-factor and higher designs. It is often necessary to try several plots before finding a good representation. The plots provided by the computer statistical packages are helpful, although often they are too rigidly formatted, and they do not substitute for a more carefully designed figure. The process of plotting the cell means yourself forces you to look closely at them and frequently leads to unexpected insights.

The pattern of means from a factorial design can be expressed as main effects, simple effects, interaction components, or various special patterns implied by a theory. Normally we do not apply all of these overlapping explanations to the same set of data. We work with whichever representation expresses the phenomenon under study most clearly. There is no recipe or algorithm, statistical or otherwise, for selecting the most appropriate description. You have to consider why the study was conducted in the first place. You should ask what pattern of means was predicted by the theory that underlies the investigation and think about what pattern of means would violate it. Try to find a way to plot the data that makes these patterns apparent. You should couple this visual analysis with specific tests to determine whether the expected pattern is present and whether other meaningful, but unpredicted, effects also appear.

The predictions of a theory may or may not be perfectly concordant with the division of variability into main effects and interactions, and you should not feel bound to follow the conventional analysis-of-variance structure if another organization is clearer. Nevertheless, let's look at three possible outcomes, illustrated in Figure 12.1, and how they might dictate the subsequent analyses.

1. No interaction is present. The left panel of Figure 12.1 shows two factors that do not interact. Without an interaction, the experiment is, in effect, two individual one-way experiments, conducted simultaneously. Each factor can be interpreted in isolation, using the principles that apply to the analysis of a one-way design. The two-way design is reduced to two one-way effects, and our attention is directed at follow-up tests that investigate analytical questions about the marginal means.

2. An interaction is present, but it is dominated by the main effects. When an interaction is present, the effect of either factor changes with the levels of the other. The simple picture of two main effects is not appropriate, and the two factors cannot be treated completely separately. To investigate the finding, we must consider how the simple effects of one factor differ with the levels of the other. Although the presence of an interaction implies that the simple effects are not the same, we still may not need to interpret each simple effect separately. The interaction in the center panel of Figure 12.1 is relatively small, particularly in comparison with the main effects. We might approach the analysis by trying to understand the main effects first, then see how this pattern is modulated by the other factor. Main effects that dominate the interaction usually represent solid, well-known and often-replicated manipulations—for example, recall performance and the length of the delay between learning and testing, maze performance and the number of training trials, speed of searching a visual display for a target and the complexity of the display. Often a researcher expects to alter only the magnitude of these general findings, not their form.

3. The interaction dominates the main effects. Here, the strategy of viewing interaction as a modulation of a strong main effect is not useful. With a large interaction, as on the right of Figure 12.1, it can be deceptive to look at the marginal effects at all. Try visualizing the main effect of the factor assigned to the baseline by mentally averaging the two means at each level of that factor. The result does not describe either simple effect accurately. The two simple effects differ qualitatively, and this particular manipulation is best understood by looking at the simple effects separately. We would be justified in ignoring the main effects altogether.

The outcome of the test of interaction in the conventional analysis of a factorial experiment leads us to examine either the main effects or the simple effects. When the interaction is small or absent, we examine the marginal means $\overline{Y}_A$ or $\overline{Y}_B$—the simple effects are essentially similar at all levels of the other factor. When the interaction is substantial, we examine the cell means $\overline{Y}_{AB}$ in the form of simple effects. In each case, we effectively eliminate one dimension from the data. When we look at a main effect, we collapse the table of cell means $\overline{Y}_{AB}$ to eliminate a factor by ignoring it; when we look at simple effects, we "slice" the table into separate rows or columns to eliminate a factor by holding it constant. Either way, the two-way design is reduced to one-way configurations. This reduction greatly simplifies the analysis.

12.2   Comparisons for the Marginal Means

The marginal means for either variable are obtained by averaging over the classification of the other independent variable. You can actually think of the two sets of means as coming from two single-factor designs. As you will see, the only change in any formula written for an actual one-way design is in the number of observations contributing to each set of marginal means.

Computational Formulas

Single degree-of-freedom comparisons are used in many places in the analysis of factorial experiments. Although the particular form of the formula for the sum of squares for these comparisons depends on the circumstances, they are all instances of a more general equation. We will start with it:

$$SS_\psi = \frac{N_{\text{mean}}\widehat{\psi}^2}{\sum c^2}, \tag{12.1}$$

where N_{mean} = the number of observations contributing to each mean,
  $\widehat{\psi}$ = the observed value of the comparison,
  $\sum c^2$ = the sum of the squared coefficients used to calculate $\widehat{\psi}$.

As usual, the coefficients of the comparison are restricted to sum to zero: $\sum c_j = 0$.

How does this formula adapt to comparisons involving the marginal means? For $\psi_A = \sum c_j \mu_{A_j}$, we find the observed contrast,

$$\widehat{\psi}_A = \sum c_j \bar{Y}_{A_j}. \tag{12.2}$$

Each mean is based on $N_{\text{mean}} = bn$ observations (n observations in each cell and b levels of factor B over which the averaging takes place), so Equation 12.1 is

$$SS_{\psi_A} = \frac{bn\widehat{\psi}_A^2}{\sum c_j^2}. \tag{12.3}$$

In the case of the main effect of B, the same logic leads us to the equations

$$\widehat{\psi}_B = \sum c_k \bar{Y}_{B_k} \quad \text{and} \quad SS_{\psi_B} = \frac{an\widehat{\psi}_B^2}{\sum c_k^2}.$$

These contrasts, like any other, have one degree of freedom, so their mean squares are the same as their sums of squares. They are evaluated against the error term $MS_{S/AB}$ from the overall analysis:

$$F_{\psi_A} = \frac{MS_{\psi_A}}{MS_{S/AB}} \quad \text{and} \quad F_{\psi_B} = \frac{MS_{\psi_B}}{MS_{S/AB}}.$$

These ratios are compared to the critical values from the F table with $df_{\text{num}} = 1$ and $df_{\text{denom}} = df_{S/AB} = ab(n-1)$.[1]

The choice of error term here warrants some attention. At first glance, you might have thought that because the mean square for a contrast on the marginal means $\bar{Y}_{A_j}$ was calculated by disregarding the B classification, we would do the same thing to obtain the error by pretending that B did not exist and calculating $MS_{S/A}$. This mean square does not represent an estimate of "pure" error variance, however, as the subjects at any level of A differ systematically with regard to factor B—for example, some received a_1 in conjunction with b_1, some in conjunction with b_2, and so on. Only an error term based on the variability within the factorial cells provides an estimate of the true variability of subjects treated alike.[2] As in the one-way analysis, the use of the common error term requires reasonable homogeneity of the within-cell variances. If it is not present, we would need to use a special error term that is based on only the cells that actually contributed to MS_ψ, as we described in Section 7.5.

---

[1] We didn't really need to present the formulas for both factors A and B, because the identification of a particular factor by a letter is arbitrary. From now on, we will usually give only one version.

[2] The situation would be different if the levels of factor B were not chosen systematically, as we will see in Chapter 24.

A Numerical Example

As an example, consider the data in Table 11.8 (p. 221) and suppose that we wanted to compare the control group with the group that received drug Y (the means $\overline{Y}_{A_1}$ and $\overline{Y}_{A_3}$, respectively). For this comparison, the coefficients are 1, 0, and -1 for levels a_1, a_2, and a_3. Summarizing the contrast,

	a_1	a_2	a_3
Coefficients c_j	1	0	-1
Marginal means $\overline{Y}_{A_j}$	7.00	11.00	12.00

We substitute into Equation 12.2 to calculate the value of the contrast, then into Equation 12.3 to calculate the comparison sum of squares:

$$\widehat{\psi}_A = \sum c_j \overline{Y}_{A_j} = (1)(7.00) + (0)(11.00) + (-1)(12.00) = -5.00,$$

$$SS_{\psi_A} = \frac{bn\widehat{\psi}_A^2}{\sum c_j^2} = \frac{(2)(4)(-5.00)^2}{1^2 + 0^2 + (-1)^2} = \frac{200.00}{2} = 100.00.$$

The mean square and the F (using $MS_{S/AB} = 18.33$ from Table 11.9, p. 223) are

$$MS_{\psi_A} = SS_{\psi_A} = 100.00 \quad \text{and} \quad F_{\psi_A} = \frac{MS_{\psi_A}}{MS_{S/AB}} = \frac{100.00}{18.33} = 5.46.$$

The critical value of $F(1, 18)$ at $\alpha = .05$ is 4.41, so the null hypothesis is rejected, and we can conclude that drug Y produces significantly more errors on the discrimination task than found with the control condition.

Contrasts of this type are valuable only when the marginal means contain useful information about the phenomenon being studied. That will most often be the case when no interaction is present or when the main effect in question dominates the interaction—a state of affairs that you can usually recognize by looking at a plot of the data. You may find that only one of the two main effects is large relative to an interaction. In this case, only the larger one will have meaningful contrasts.

12.3 Interpreting the Interaction

Looking at the main effects is satisfactory as long as no interaction is present. When you find one, you need to say something about it, and finding the right approach can be difficult. The remainder of this chapter and all of the next describe the tools you have available for this task.

The first thing to realize is that you will rarely want to interpret the interaction by itself. The conventional tests in the analysis of variance divide the differences among the cell means into the main effects and the interaction. The tests of these effects give us very important information about how we should go about describing the results. However, when we actually try to understand our finding, we have to go back to those means—after all, they most closely represent the behavior we are studying. The presence of an interaction, as revealed by the test of $MS_{A \times B}$, tells us that any conclusions about the means observed for one factor must be tempered by a consideration of the level of the other factor at which they were collected.[3]

---

[3]The distinction between the test of an interaction and its interpretation has been brought into focus by several recent discussions. See, for example, Rosnow and Rosenthal (1989) and the series of articles mentioned in footnote 7 (p. 81).

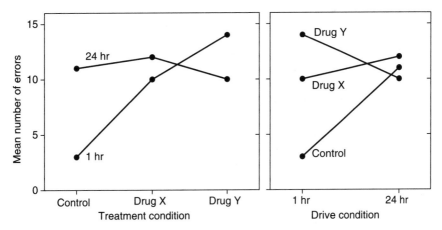

Figure 12.2: Means for the data in Table 11.8 plotted as both types of simple effect.

When our tests have revealed an interaction in our data, we must adjust our interpretation of the means. What this usually implies is that we look separately at the effects of one factor at the individual levels of the other factor—the simple effects—systematically determining which are significant and which are not. When we do so, we are looking at a combination of the variablity expressed by the interaction and by one of the main effects, as we shall show formally later. It is almost essential to start by drawing a graph that shows the simple effects. The statistical procedures you need here, as we describe in the rest of this chapter, can be adapted from those for the one-way designs. In particular, you can look for differences among the means in a specific row or column (Section 12.4) or at contrasts that elucidate the meaning of these differences (Section 12.5).

To be concrete, let's return to the example in Section 11.3, in which monkeys at two degrees of food deprivation (i.e. drive) learned oddity problems in a control condition or after having been given one of two drugs. The overall analysis (Table 11.9, p. 223) found a significant interaction. Figure 12.2 shows the two sets of simple effects, plotted on the left for the treatment conditions given the two drive conditions and on the right for the drive conditions given the three treatment conditions. The presence of an interaction tells us that the lines in each of these figures have different shapes. As a first step, then, we determine which of the simple effects are significant and which are not. Such an analysis might reveal, for example, that the treatment conditions differ only under the 1-hour drive condition (left panel) or that the drive manipulation is effective only for the control condition (right panel).

When a simple effect has more than one degree of freedom, it is a composite of various simple contrasts. The next step is to examine these simple contrasts, just as we turned to an examination of single-df comparisons in a single-factor design when SS_A is a composite effect. For example, a significant simple effect of factor A under the 1-hour drive condition might be followed by a comparison between the means of the two drug conditions or one between either of them and the control condition. The analysis does not stop here, however, as it might in a single-factor design, but continues with a comparison of any significant simple contrast across the levels of the other factor. Such an analysis requires a new statistical test, and the tool here is the **interaction component** or the **interaction contrast**. A hypothesis about an interaction component is like the hypothesis of the overall $A \times B$ interaction, but specialized to refer to a particular contrast, not to the simple effects as a whole. By using them, we can determine exactly the nature of an interaction identified by the omnibus test. We consider interaction components in Chapter 13.

Let us be clear on the strategy we are suggesting. We use the *tests* of interactions, both the omnibus test and the more specific tests of interaction components, to tell us when some characteristic of one factor varies over the levels of another factor. We use the simple effects and contrasts based on them to help us *understand* and *interpret* what the interaction tests tell us.

Selecting a Set of Simple Effects for Analysis

Because they represent partially redundant information, you may not want to analyze both sets of simple effects, although there is no law that prevents you from doing so. Usually, you will choose to analyze the set of simple effects that is the most useful, potentially revealing, or easy to explain. In addition to the substantive interpretation of the findings, we can suggest some heuristic principles that can help with your choice.

- *Choose the factor with the greater number of levels.* The simple effects of the independent variable with the greater number of levels are often the easiest to visualize. In Figure 12.2, the two lines in the left panel look simpler than the three lines on the right. This strategy minimizes the number of simple effects you need to describe.

- *Choose a quantitative factor.* When one of the independent variables is a quantitative manipulation and the other is qualitative, the simple effect of the quantitative factor is frequently easier to describe. You can use the language of trend analysis to describe the simple effects. In Figure 12.2, this principle suggests analyzing the right-hand panel, where each line expresses the numerical function of drive.

- *Choose the factor with the greater main-effect sum of squares.* This choice maximizes the amount of variability that is captured by the simple effects. The analysis of this set may provide more information than the set with the smaller main-effect sum of squares.

- *Choose a manipulated factor.* When one factor is manipulated and the other is a classification or blocking factor, it is usually more revealing to analyze the simple effects of the manipulated variable. Researchers are most interested in how the effects of this factor vary within each level of the nonmanipulated factor. For example, with a gender factor, it usually makes more sense to say how the female and male subjects behaved than to describe female-male differences for each experimental condition.

These principles are suggestions, not rules. Not infrequently, they will contradict each other, as the first two did for Figure 12.2. You can probably think of exceptions to each of them. However, thinking about them will help you find an effective way to describe your study.

Table 12.1: *Means involved in the main effect and the simple effects of factor A at levels of B.*

	b_1	b_2	Mean
a_1	$\overline{Y}_{11}$	$\overline{Y}_{12}$	$\overline{Y}_{A_1}$
a_2	$\overline{Y}_{21}$	$\overline{Y}_{22}$	$\overline{Y}_{A_2}$
a_3	$\overline{Y}_{31}$	$\overline{Y}_{32}$	$\overline{Y}_{A_3}$
Mean	$\overline{Y}_{B_1}$	$\overline{Y}_{B_2}$	$\overline{Y}_T$
	$\downarrow$	$\downarrow$	$\downarrow$
Effect	A at b_1	A at b_2	A

12.4 Testing the Simple Effects

We now turn to the actual mechanics by which the simple effects are tested. We will give the formulas first, then apply them to the data plotted in Figure 12.2, and finally, discuss some issues related to their interpretation.

Computational Formulas

Because the simple effects describe variation along a one-dimensional array of groups, their sums of squares are found like those in a one-way analysis of variance.[4] Table 12.1 illustrates the parallel between the simple effects and the main effect for a 3×2 design. We have drawn boxes around the three sets of A-effect means: the marginal means $\overline{Y}_{A_j}$ on the right and the two sets of simple-effect means within the table of cell means. Consider the main effect of factor A. This main effect is based on variation among the means in the right-hand box; specifically, its sum of squares is constructed from the deviations of the marginal means $\overline{Y}_{A_1}$, $\overline{Y}_{A_2}$, and $\overline{Y}_{A_3}$ from the grand mean $\overline{Y}_T$:

$$SS_A = bn \sum (\overline{Y}_{A_j} - \overline{Y}_T)^2.$$

The multiplier bn arises because that many scores contribute to each marginal mean. We have indicated this main effect in Table 12.1 by the arrow and the letter A in the list of effects at the bottom.

Now consider the simple effects of factor A at b_k. They are based on the deviations within the columns of the table of means. For example, the simple effect of A at b_1 is based on the variation of the cell means $\overline{Y}_{j1}$ within in the box on left. The sum of squares is constructed from the deviations of these cell means $\overline{Y}_{jk}$ from the marginal mean $\overline{Y}_{B_k}$:

$$SS_{A \text{ at } b_k} = n \sum_j (\overline{Y}_{jk} - \overline{Y}_{B_k})^2. \tag{12.4}$$

The number of scores contributing to these means is n, which accounts for the multiplier. Thus, the simple effects of A at b_k express exactly the same type of variation as the main effects, but applied to different means.

---

[4]You can actually use a computer program for a one-way analysis to find the sum of squares by selecting the relevant portion of the data. However, you will need to recalculate the F statistic, replacing the error term supplied by the one-way program ($MS_{S/A}$) with the one from the overall analysis of the factorial ($MS_{S/AB}$).

Although you can use Equation 12.4 to calculate sums of squares for the simple effects, it is computationally easier to use bracket terms. The bracket expression for the simple effects of factor A at any level of b_k is

$$SS_{A \text{ at } b_k} = [A \text{ at } b_k] - [T \text{ at } b_k], \tag{12.5}$$

where the bracket terms are

$$[A \text{ at } b_k] = n \sum_j \overline{Y}_{jk}^2 = \frac{\sum_j (AB_{jk})^2}{n}, \tag{12.6}$$

$$[T \text{ at } b_k] = an\overline{Y}_{B_k}^2 = \frac{B_k^2}{an}. \tag{12.7}$$

These bracket terms are restricted versions of the terms $[A]$ and $[T]$ that we use to calculate the main effect of factor A. The degrees of freedom for each simple effect is one less than the number of cell means involved in the effect:

$$df_{A \text{ at } b_k} = a - 1.$$

The mean squares for simple effects are obtained as usual, by dividing each sum of squares by the appropriate degrees of freedom. The error term for each of these mean squares is the within-groups mean square from the original analysis.

A Numerical Example

We will illustrate these formulas by calculating the two simple effects of factor A for our continuing example. The relevant means are:

	b_1	b_2
a_1	3	11
a_2	10	12
a_3	14	10
Mean	9	11

One way to calculate the sums of squares uses the deviations (Equation 12.4):

$$SS_{A \text{ at } b_1} = n \sum_j (\overline{Y}_{j1} - \overline{Y}_{B_1})^2$$
$$= (4)[(3 - 9)^2 + (10 - 9)^2 + (14 - 9)^2] = (4)(62) = 248,$$

$$SS_{A \text{ at } b_2} = n \sum_j (\overline{Y}_{j2} - \overline{Y}_{B_2})^2$$
$$= (4)[(11 - 11)^2 + (12 - 11)^2 + (10 - 11)^2] = (4)(2) = 8.$$

Identical values are found using the bracket terms. For the simple effect of A at b_1, we'll use means to find the bracket terms. Applying Equations 12.6 and 12.7, then entering the results in Equation 12.5, we get

$$[A \text{ at } b_1] = n \sum_j \overline{Y}_{j1}^2 = (4)(3^2 + 10^2 + 14^2) = (4)(305) = 1{,}220,$$

$$[T \text{ at } b_1] = an\overline{Y}_{B_1}^2 = (3)(4)(9^2) = 972,$$

$$SS_{A \text{ at } b_1} = [A \text{ at } b_1] - [T \text{ at } b_1] = 1{,}220 - 972 = 248.$$

The value is the same as we found with the deviations. For the simple effect of A at b_2, we'll illustrate the calculations with sums (obtained from Table 11.9, p. 223). Using the same sequence of formulas:

$$[A \text{ at } b_2] = \sum_j (AB_{j2})^2/n = (44^2 + 48^2 + 40^2)/4 = 5{,}840/4 = 1{,}460,$$

$$[T \text{ at } b_2] = B_2^2/an = 132^2/[(3)(4)] = 1{,}452,$$

$$SS_{A \text{ at } b_2} = [A \text{ at } b_2] - [T \text{ at } b_2] = 1{,}460 - 1{,}452 = 8.$$

We see that the three methods—deviations, means, or sums—give the same result.

We have found it very useful to summarize an analysis like this in a table that shows both the standard tests and those of the simple effects (Table 12.2). The top part of the table reproduces the conventional effects. The second part, marked off by lines, gives the simple effects, along with their degrees of freedom, mean squares, and F ratios. The F's for the simple effects substantiate statistically what we observed in our visual examination of Figure 12.2, namely, that the drug manipulation is effective only when the animals are relatively satiated.

A similar analysis can be conducted on the simple effects of factor B, which describes the effect of the drive manipulation for the control and two drug conditions (Figure 12.2, right panel). You should have no difficulty applying the analysis to this factor in Problem 12.2.

Variance Heterogeneity

As we noted in our discussion of assumptions in Section 11.4 (see p. 228), the presence of variance heterogeneity brings into question the use of $MS_{S/AB}$ from the overall analysis as the error term for testing the significance of effects based on a portion of the data. You can use the Levene or Brown-Forsythe tests to determine whether heterogeneity is present. We recommend that you keep the factorial structure of the design in either of these tests, as the location of the heterogeneity of variance determines how it affects the tests of simple effects and contrasts. The most serious problems for the analysis of simple effects arise when there is significant heterogeneity associated with the factor held constant—the main effect of factor B for the simple effects of A at b_k and the main effect of A for the simple effects of B at a_j.

Although the data for the monkey study do not show heterogeneity, we can use it as an example to help understand the problem with using $MS_{S/AB}$ as the error term when heterogeneity is present. Suppose that the variance tests revealed heterogeneity for the

Table 12.2: Analysis of Table 11.8, including the simple effects of factor A.

Source	SS	df	MS	F
A	112.00	2	56.00	3.06
B	24.00	1	24.00	1.31
$A{\times}B$	144.00	2	72.00	3.93*
A at b_1	248.00	2	124.00	6.76*
A at b_2	8.00	2	4.00	0.22
S/AB	330.00	18	18.33	
Total	610.00	23		

* $p < .05$

Table 12.3: *Analyzing the simple effect of the drug conditions for the satiated animals when there is concern about variance differences.*

Extracted table of data

	Control	Drug X	Drug Y
	1	13	9
	4	5	16
	0	7	18
	7	15	13
Mean	3.00	10.00	14.00

Analysis of the simple effect

Source	SS	df	MS	F
A	248.00	2	124.00	7.75*
S/A	144.00	9	16.00	
Total	392.00	11		

*$p < .05$

deprivation factor (factor B), with a smaller variance in the food-satiated conditions (b_1) than in the food-deprived conditions (b_2). As a result, any simple effect of the drug factor—A at b_k, or a contrast extracted from it—would be calculated from scores that are either less variable (b_1) or more variable (b_2) than the average of variability expressed by $MS_{S/AB}$. Using $MS_{S/AB}$ as an error term would lead to biased F tests: The simple effect of A at b_1 would be tested with an error term that expresses more variability than the scores under consideration, and the test would have a negative bias. Conversely, the simple effect of A at b_2 would be biased in a positive direction. Similar problems would arise for the simple effects of B at a_j if the main effect of factor A were significant in the heterogeneity test.

The safest solution when this type of heterogeneity appears is to base your error term only on the groups that actually contribute to the simple effect. In essence, you analyze the simple effects as separate single-factor designs. To continue our example, suppose you wanted to test the simple effect of the drug conditions for the satiated animals. You would extract the relevant portion of the data from Table 11.8, as we illustrate at the top of Table 12.3, and perform a one-way analysis on this subset. The lower part of the table summarizes the result. Compared to the complete analysis in Table 12.2, you will notice that the simple effect itself has the same sum of squares but that the error term is different and is based on half as many degrees of freedom. Some power is lost by this reduction in degrees of freedom, but you are protected from a possible bias in the F test due to an inappropriate error term.

The consequences of heterogeneity of variance among the groups being tested by the simple effect—that is, factor A for the simple effects of A at b_k or factor B for the simple effects of B at a_j—are less catastrophic. The tests are subject to the same sort of inflation of α we mentioned in Section 7.3 (see Table 7.1, p. 149). It can be treated by the various solutions that we discussed in Section 7.4, including changing α, transforming the data, and using an alternative test. However, if you emphasize contrasts to interpret the simple effects, you will need to calculate the special error term that we discuss below.

Partitioning of the Sums of Squares

The analysis of simple effects and the conventional analysis of main effects and interaction give us different views of a factorial experiment. The views are, in a sense, complementary, and they both are vital for a good understanding of the study.

The simple effects focus entirely on the effects of one of the independent variables. Thus, the simple effect of A at b_k expresses all the variability of A at a single level of B. When we have calculated the simple effects for all levels of B, we will have captured all the variability among the means related to factor A. In terms of the sums of squares:

$$\text{All variability related to } A = \sum SS_{A \text{ at } b_k}.$$

In the conventional analysis, this same variability is divided between the A main effect and the $A \times B$ interaction, as SS_A and $SS_{A \times B}$, respectively. Adding these two sums of squares gives us a second way to write the variability related to factor A:

$$\text{All variability related to } A = SS_A + SS_{A \times B}.$$

The two expressions are different ways to say the same thing:

$$SS_A + SS_{A \times B} = \sum SS_{A \text{ at } b_k}. \tag{12.8}$$

We can verify this equation using the numerical sums of squares in Table 12.2:

$$SS_A + SS_{A \times B} = 112.00 + 144.00 = 256.00,$$

$$SS_{A \text{ at } b_1} + SS_{A \text{ at } b_2} = 248.00 + 8.00 = 256.00.$$

A similar equation can also be written for the simple effect of factor B:

$$SS_B + SS_{A \times B} = \sum SS_{B \text{ at } a_j}.$$

This analysis also tells us that the simple effects of one factor do not capture any of the main effect of the other factor. This fact should not be a surprise. In creating the simple effects, we look only at the separate rows (or columns) of the table of means, which prevents any differences among the levels of the factor held constant from influencing the sums of squares. For example, the numerical results above do not include $SS_B = 24.00$, which must be added to either side of Equation 12.8 to obtain the total variability among the means of the study.

We now have three ways to partition the between-groups variability of the two-factor design into orthogonal components. The first is the conventional breakdown into two main effects and an interaction, the second is a breakdown into the simple effects of A and the main effect of B, and the third the breakdown into the main effect of A and the simple effects of B:

$$\left.\begin{aligned} SS_{\text{between}} &= SS_A + SS_B + SS_{A \times B}, \\ SS_{\text{between}} &= \sum SS_{A \text{ at } b_k} + SS_B, \\ SS_{\text{between}} &= SS_A + \sum SS_{B \text{ at } a_j}. \end{aligned}\right\} \tag{12.9}$$

All three decompositions are equally valid; they simply partition the variation differently. A common error when working with a factorial analysis of variance is to become so focused on one of these representations that any information provided by the others is overlooked. The following two examples show why all of them are necessary.

1. *Significance of the simple effects and the interaction.* When a simple effect is significant, it tells us that the means in that row or column of data are unequal. An interaction tells us that the simple effects differ. What happens when we find that we can reject the null hypothesis of equal means for one simple effect but not for another? Does it imply that we will find a significant interaction? Surprisingly, it does not.

The phenomenon is illustrated by Table 12.4, which shows the means from a 2×2 factorial study with $n = 10$ observations per group. Assume that $MS_{S/AB} = 60$. The analysis summarized at the bottom of the table (in the same manner as Table 12.2) shows a significant effect of factor A, but no significant B effect or $A \times B$ interaction. Moreover, the simple effect of A is significant for b_1, but not for b_2. Superficially, this difference in the statistical outcome of these two simple-effect tests seems to contradict the lack of a significant interaction because it suggests that the means of the A factor are different at level b_1 but not at level b_2. In reality, there is no contradiction. At both levels of B, the means drop between a_1 and a_2. However, the sizes of these drops are such that the larger drop ($12 - 2 = 10$ points at b_1) is significant, but the smaller drop ($5 - 1 = 4$ points at b_2) is not. To say that these drops differ hinges on accepting the null hypothesis of no A effect at b_2, which we cannot do. If we are interested in comparing the simple effects, we must find an analysis that specifically assesses these differences. The necessary test is for an interaction, which was not significant. A better conclusion here is to say that there is a drop across factor A for both groups (the main effect of A), but that there is insufficient evidence to show that factor B affects the size of this drop, given the sensitivity of the study. The lesson here is fundamental: A difference between simple effects can only be discovered by testing for an interaction, never by different outcomes of separate tests. Confusion here is perhaps the most common error that is made (by both naive and experienced users) when interpreting factorial designs.

2. *Direct interpretation of the conventional effects.* Our second illustration is, in a sense, the reverse of the first. Researchers sometimes concentrate so heavily on the conventional effects (A, B, and the interaction) that they attempt to interpret each of them in isolation. By doing so, they can overlook the meaning of their results. Suppose we conducted a two-factor study looking at the effects of two types of training on an athletic task. The basic design crosses training method A (a_1: no training, a_2: training A given) with training method B (b_1: no training, b_2: training B given). Group a_1b_1 provides a baseline that receives no training; the two groups a_1b_2 and a_2b_1 receive one of the training programs but not the other, and group a_2b_2 receives both. Figure 12.3 shows two possible outcomes for the study. In the left-hand panel, neither training is helpful by itself, but there is an improvement in performance when the athletes receive both. In contrast, the outcome on the right shows that both types of training are helpful and that the two together are no better than either one alone. Only when neither training is given does the performance suffer. Obviously, these two outcomes have very different implications for how one would set up a training program.

Table 12.4: A pattern of means in which the main effect of A is significant at level b_1 of factor B but not at level b_2, yet there is no $A \times B$ interaction.

Cell and marginal means

	b_1	b_2	Mean
a_1	12	5	8.5
a_2	2	1	1.5
Mean	7	3	5.0

Analysis of variance and simple effects

Source	SS	df	MS	F
A	490	1	490	8.17*
B	160	1	160	2.67
$A \times B$	90	1	90	1.50
A at b_1	500	1	500	8.33*
A at b_2	80	1	80	1.33
S/AB	2,160	36	60	
Total	2,900	39		

* $p < .05$

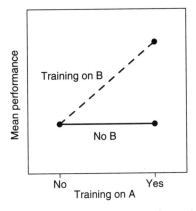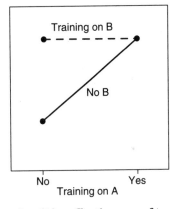

Figure 12.3: Two outcomes from a factorial study of the effectiveness of two training techniques. The dashed lines represent groups receiving training on B and the solid lines groups receiving no training on B.

However—and this is the crucial point—both the main effects and the interaction are identical for the two sets of means.[5] For these two examples, the standard tests provide a start on the analysis (in particular, they establish the presence of an interaction), but the revealing information is only found by examining the simple effects. We will discuss this example further in Section 13.5.

---

[5]To verify this statement, assign numbers to the two sets of cell means that match the patterns in Figure 12.3, assume some value for n, and then calculate the three sums of squares using the fomulas in Table 11.5 (p. 217). You will find the same sums of squares for all three sources in the two designs.

12.5 Simple Comparisons

In Chapter 4 we saw the importance of single-df comparisons in the analysis of one-way designs. Whenever a factor has more than two levels, the omnibus test only tells us that there are differences among the means, not specifically where those differences lie. The tests of the analytical comparisons we used there are just as important when we look at simple effects in factorial designs, which, as we have emphasized, are like little one-way designs. In general, any simple effect with more than one degree of freedom is a composite of elementary effects. Just as in the one-way designs, we will turn to **simple comparisons** among the means within a simple effect, either because they express specific hypotheses that are suggested by theory or because we have found a significant simple effect and wish to better understand its particular form.

The simple comparisons take the form of linear combinations of means, for example,

$$\psi_{A \text{ at } b_k} = \sum_j c_j \mu_{jk}, \quad \text{where} \quad \sum c_j = 0. \tag{12.10}$$

These simple comparisons are amazingly versatile. The coefficients c_j are selected to express meaningful questions, which include pairwise comparisons, comparisons that involve the averaging of conditions, custom comparisons, and trend analysis. We described how such contrasts are chosen in Chapter 4 and Chapter 5, so we will not discuss this point further. The hypothesis we normally want to test is H_0: $\psi_{A \text{ at } b_k} = 0$ against the alternative that it is nonzero. When the null hypothesis can be rejected, we know that the pattern expressed by the contrast is present in the data. In every case, the focus is on the means in a particular row or column of the table of cell means.

Computational Formulas

The contrast in Equation 12.10 acts to select certain groups from the study and forms their means into a linear combination. A test of the hypothesis that this combination is zero is conducted in the same way that we tested the contrasts in a one-way design (Equations 4.4 and 4.5). First we find the observed value of the contrast by substituting the cell means for their population counterparts:

$$\widehat{\psi}_{A \text{ at } b_k} = \sum_j c_j \overline{Y}_{jk}. \tag{12.11}$$

Then we convert this observed contrast to a sum of squares by squaring it, multiplying by the number of scores involved in each mean, and dividing by the sum of the squared coefficients:

$$SS_{\psi_A \text{ at } b_k} = \frac{n\widehat{\psi}^2_{A \text{ at } b_k}}{\sum c_j^2}. \tag{12.12}$$

Each simple comparison has one degree of freedom and is tested against the error term from the omnibus analysis, $MS_{S/AB}$.

These calculations should be modified when the variances are heterogeneous. If so, the overall error term will be affected by groups that are not involved in the calculation. For example, suppose the groups at level b_1 of factor B are less variable that those at level b_2. The combined error $MS_{S/AB}$ will then be too large for $\psi_{A \text{ at } b_1}$ and too small for $\psi_{A \text{ at } b_2}$, biasing the tests of both effects, as we described on pages 251–253. Differences in variance among groups at the same level of factor B are also a problem. The proper thing to do in these cases is to calculate a unique error term for each contrast, using the procedures that we described for the one-way design (see Section 7.5, particularly, Equations 7.11–7.13).

Numerical Examples

Our analysis of the simple effects in Section 12.4, summarized in Table 12.2, revealed a significant effect of the drug manipulation for the satiated animals (factor A at level b_1). This omnibus test does not establish where in particular the differences lie—whether the two drug conditions differ from each other and whether they differ from the control condition. One interesting simple contrast compares the control animals to those given drug X (i.e. group a_1b_1 to group a_2b_1). The relevant means and contrast coefficients for the contrast are

	a_1	a_2	a_3
Cell means $\overline{Y}_{j1}$	3	10	14
Coefficients c_j	1	−1	0

Entering these values into Equations 12.11 and 12.12, we find that

$$\widehat{\psi}_{A \text{ at } b_1} = \sum c_j \overline{Y}_{ABj1} = (1)(3) + (-1)(10) + (0)(14) = -7,$$

$$SS_{\psi_A \text{ at } b_1} = \frac{n\widehat{\psi}^2_{A \text{ at } b_1}}{\sum c_j^2} = \frac{(4)(-7)^2}{1^2 + (-1)^2 + 0^2} = \frac{196}{2} = 98.0.$$

With one degree of freedom, the mean square is also equal to 98.0. The F ratio is formed by dividing $MS_{\psi_A \text{ at } b_1}$ by $MS_{S/AB}$ from the original analysis:

$$F = \frac{MS_{\psi_A \text{ at } b_1}}{MS_{S/AB}} = \frac{98.0}{18.33} = 5.35.$$

This value is significant at the 5 percent level ($F_{.05}(1, 18) = 4.41$), implying that the number of errors increased when drug X was given.

The fact that we did not find a significant simple effect of the drug manipulation for the hungry monkeys (factor A at level b_2) makes it unlikely that any simple contrast involving these cell means will be significant. However, we might still conduct these tests, either as a planned portion of the analysis or as a comparison with the corresponding analyses performed on the satiated monkeys. You can verify that when the same contrast coefficients, $\{1, -1, 0\}$, are applied to the means 11, 12, and 10, they give $\widehat{\psi}_{A \text{ at } b_2} = -1$, $SS_{\psi_A \text{ at } b_2} = 2$, and $F = 0.11$. Not surprisingly, the effect is far from significant.

Our second illustration of a simple contrast is based on a specific prediction concerning the outcome for the satiated animals (b_1). Suppose we have some previous results that suggest that, as compared to the control group, the group receiving drug X would make 15 more errors and the group receiving drug Y would make 12 more errors. In Section 4.6 (see p. 81) we described how to construct a customized set of coefficients that is sensitive to a specific pattern. A pattern of means that expresses the predictions (e.g., 3, 18, and 15) leads to the coefficient set $\{-3, 2, 1\}$, and a test of this contrast shows it to be significant:

$$\widehat{\psi}_{A \text{ at } b_1} = \sum_j c_j \overline{Y}_{ABj1} = (-3)(3) + (2)(10) + (1)(14) = 25,$$

$$SS_{\psi_A \text{ at } b_1} = \frac{n\widehat{\psi}^2_{A \text{ at } b_1}}{\sum c_j^2} = \frac{(4)(25)^2}{(-3)^2 + 2^2 + 1^2} = \frac{2,500}{14} = 178.57,$$

$$F = \frac{MS_{\psi_A \text{ at } b_1}}{MS_{S/AB}} = \frac{178.57}{18.33} = 9.74.$$

This significant outcome tells us that we have found a result rather like the expected pattern. However, as we emphasized in Section 4.6, such support is not sufficient to indicate agreement with the earlier results. We also need to check that other effects are not present, which we do by looking at the sum of squares associated with the remaining variation. We find the residual sum of squares representing the failure of our explanation by subtracting the contrast sum of squares from that for the omnibus simple effect (see Equation 4.16, p. 82):

$$SS_{\text{failure}} = SS_{A \text{ at } b_1} - SS_{\psi_A \text{ at } b_1} = 248.00 - 178.57 = 69.43.$$

The degrees of freedom for SS_{failure} are found from a similar subtraction:

$$df_{\text{failure}} = df_A - df_{\psi_A \text{ at } b_1} = 2 - 1 = 1.$$

The resulting F ratio is not significant:

$$F = \frac{SS_{\text{failure}}/df_{\text{failure}}}{MS_{S/AB}} = \frac{69.43/1}{18.33} = 3.79$$

$(F_{.05}(1, 18) = 4.41)$. Thus, the theoretical prediction does a good job of explaining this particular simple effect.

Simple Contrasts and Interactions

In the numerical example, we found that the control and drug X conditions were significantly different for the satiated (1-hour deprived) animals but not for the hungry (24-hour deprived) animals. You might think that because one of these results is significant and the other is not, they must be different from each other. However, to draw this conclusion without further testing would be to fall into the trap we discussed on page 254. Different outcomes for tests of the simple effects do not guarantee that the $A \times B$ interaction is significant. The same thing is true for the simple contrasts. Finding one simple contrast significant and another not significant does not establish that they differ, just as finding both of them significant does not establish that they are the same. Certainly in the present case, the means look convincing: The difference between the control condition and drug X for the satiated animals $(3 - 10 = -7)$ is much greater than the corresponding difference for the hungry animals $(11 - 12 = -1)$. However, to be sure, we need to explicitly test whether these differences are themselves different. We will discuss this test in the next chapter.

12.6   Effect Sizes and Power for Simple Effects

In most studies that use a factorial design, effect sizes are reported for the overall main effects and interaction (Sections 11.6 and 11.7), and they are used to find the power or calculate sample sizes for a new study. There are also some situations where calculations based on the simple effects are necessary.

Effect Size

We would usually want to report the size of a simple effect when the effect of one factor is especially meaningful at a particular level of the other factor. The effect of two training programs in Figure 12.3 is a good example. Consider the right-hand pattern of means, which showed each procedure had an effect when used alone. If we wanted to discuss the size of the effect for training procedures A, we would not want this estimate to be contaminated by averaging it across conditions in which training procedure B had and had not been used. We would consider only those groups for which procedure B is absent (condition b_1), that is, the simple effect of A at level b_1 in the original design. Similarly, a measure of the effect for the B procedure should use the groups for which A is absent (the simple effect of B at a_1).

In Section 11.6, we described two types of effect-size measures, complete measures in which an effect is expressed relative to all the variability in the study and partial measures in which it is expressed relative to just the error variability and the variability of the effect itself. For studies with manipulated factors, the partial measures were more appropriate. Our recommendation here is the same: You should report partial effect sizes for simple effects and any contrasts derived from them. That way, the values are not affected by whatever other differences among groups are present in the data. We will, therefore, discuss only the partial measures.

Equation 11.21 defined the partial omega squared as the ratio of the variability of an effect to that variability plus the error variability:

$$\omega^2_{\langle \text{effect} \rangle} = \frac{\sigma^2_{\text{effect}}}{\sigma^2_{\text{effect}} + \sigma^2_{\text{error}}}.$$

Applying this equation to each of the specialized effects for factor A, we obtain

main comparison: $$\omega^2_{\langle \psi_A \rangle} = \frac{\sigma^2_{\psi_A}}{\sigma^2_{\psi_A} + \sigma^2_{\text{error}}},$$

simple effect: $$\omega^2_{\langle A \text{ at } b_k \rangle} = \frac{\sigma^2_{A \text{ at } b_k}}{\sigma^2_{A \text{ at } b_k} + \sigma^2_{\text{error}}},$$

simple comparison: $$\omega^2_{\langle \psi_A \text{ at } b_k \rangle} = \frac{\sigma^2_{\psi_A \text{ at } b_k}}{\sigma^2_{\psi_A \text{ at } b_k} + \sigma^2_{\text{error}}}.$$

Corresponding formulas for the other factor are written similarly. The variability of the effects, $\sigma^2_{\psi_A}$, $\sigma^2_{A \text{ at } b_k}$, and $\sigma^2_{\psi_A \text{ at } b_k}$, are calculated like those in a one-way design.

To estimate the partial omega squared for a treatment effect from an experiment, we use the relevant F ratio from the analysis summary:

main comparison: $$\widehat{\omega}^2_{\langle \psi_A \rangle} = \frac{F_{\psi_A} - 1}{(F_{\psi_A} - 1) + 2bn}, \qquad (12.13)$$

simple effect: $$\widehat{\omega}^2_{\langle A \text{ at } b_k \rangle} = \frac{df_{A \text{ at } b_k}(F_{A \text{ at } b_k} - 1)}{df_{A \text{ at } b_k}(F_{A \text{ at } b_k} - 1) + an}, \qquad (12.14)$$

simple comparison: $$\widehat{\omega}^2_{\langle \psi_A \text{ at } b_k \rangle} = \frac{F_{\psi_A \text{ at } b_k} - 1}{(F_{\psi_A \text{ at } b_k} - 1) + 2n}. \qquad (12.15)$$

The only fundamental difference among these equations is in the final term of the denominator, whose value depends on the number of scores that go into the means being tested (bn for a main comparison and n for a simple effect or contrast) and whether an entire effect or a contrast is being tested (a or 2, respectively). By subtracting one from F, these estimates correct for increases in variability that result from sampling error.

As an example, consider the size of the simple effect of the drug manipulation for the satiated monkeys in our numerical example (factor A at b_1). The study had $a = 3$,

$b = 2$, and $n = 4$, so $df_{A \text{ at } b_1} = 2$, and, from Table 12.2, the simple effect of factor A at b_1 was significant with $F = 6.76$. Using Equation 12.14, we obtain

$$\widehat{\omega}^2_{\langle A \text{ at } b_1 \rangle} = \frac{df_{A \text{ at } b_1}(F_{A \text{ at } b_1} - 1)}{df_{A \text{ at } b_1}(F_{A \text{ at } b_1} - 1) + an}$$

$$= \frac{(3 - 1)(6.76 - 1)}{(3 - 1)(6.76 - 1) + (3)(4)} = \frac{11.52}{11.52 + 12} = 0.490.$$

The corresponding simple effect of A at b_2 had $F = 0.22$, which is not large enough to establish any effect magnitude. Equation 12.14 would give a negative value, and so we set $\widehat{\omega}^2_{\langle A \text{ at } b_2 \rangle} = 0$.

As another example, look at a portion of the effect just described. Suppose we are interested in reporting the size of the effect associated with drug X for the satiated animals. For this measure, the effect of drug Y is irrelevant. Thus, we look at the difference between the control group and the group receiving drug X, which we tested as a simple contrast in the last section and found that $F = 5.35$. The partial effect size is calculated using Equation 12.15:

$$\widehat{\omega}^2_{\langle \psi_A \text{ at } b_1 \rangle} = \frac{F_{\psi_A \text{ at } b_1} - 1}{(F_{\psi_A \text{ at } b_1} - 1) + 2n}$$

$$= \frac{(5.35 - 1)}{(5.35 - 1) + (2)(4)} = \frac{4.35}{4.35 + 8} = 0.352.$$

Sample-Size Calculations

The power for a simple effect in a factorial design or its components rarely needs to be calculated. Few studies are sufficiently well specified to make these values useful. On the other hand, sample-size calculations based on portions of a factorial design are necessary when some parts of a proposed study are better specified than others. Both the simple effects and the contrasts discussed in this chapter can be treated as data from a one-way design, which allows the methods we described in Chapter 8 to be used. We do not need any new formulas, but will illustrate the process with two examples.

Our first example is a sample-size projection based on theoretically determined means. Suppose we were interested in a three-level factor A that had previously been studied only in a one-way design. We propose to add a new two-level factor B, which will be the same as in the previous study at level b_1 and different at level b_2. The prior research therefore gives us information about the anticipated simple effect of A at b_1, but not about the main effects or interaction. In planning the study, we can decide to use a sample size that has a good chance (a power of .80) to detect the known effect of A at b_1 and use that value for the entire factorial. We cannot include the B or $A \times B$ effects in our calculations because we don't know yet what they might be. In particular, suppose a review of the literature suggests that at b_1 the means should be about $\mu_{11} = 22$, $\mu_{21} = 26$, and $\mu_{31} = 33$ and that the within-groups standard deviation σ_{error} is about 15. We find the sample size per group exactly as we did in the example of a one-way analysis on page 171. To determine σ^2 for the effect, we average the three means to obtain the marginal mean μ_{B_1}, subtract it to determine the effects (comparable to α_j in the one-way design), square them, and average them. We can perform these calculations in a small table like the one we used before:

	a_1	a_2	a_3	Sum	Mean
Means, μ_{j1}	22	26	33	81	27 $\quad (= \mu_{B_1})$
Effects $(\mu_{j1} - \mu_{B_1})$	-5	-1	6	0	
Squared effects	25	1	36	62	20.67 $(= \sigma^2_{A \text{ at } b_1})$

The mean of the squared effects is the variance $\sigma^2_{A \text{ at } b_1} = 20.67$, and the size of the effect (Equation 8.10, p. 163) is

$$\omega^2 = \frac{\sigma^2_{A \text{ at } b_1}}{\sigma^2_{A \text{ at } b_1} + \sigma_{\text{error}}} = \frac{20.67}{20.67 + 15^2} = \frac{20.67}{245.67} = 0.084.$$

To determine the sample size n, we can use our quick sample-size table (Table 8.1, p. 173). For three groups, an effect size of .08 and a power of .80, the table tells us we need about 38 observations per group. We would use this number for all the groups in the new factorial design.

If we had more specific information about the value of a contrast in one of the simple effects, we could use the one-way formulas to determine sample size. In this case, the effect size we are hoping to find is calculated from Equations 8.13 and 8.15:

$$\sigma^2_\psi = \frac{\psi^2}{2 \sum c^2} \quad \text{and} \quad \omega^2_{\langle \psi \rangle} = \frac{\sigma^2_\psi}{\sigma^2_\psi + \sigma^2_{S/A}}. \tag{12.16}$$

The sum in the denominator of the first equation includes the coefficients of the means defining ψ. The sample size n is found directly from the quick table or from Equation 8.18 (p. 174) in conjunction with the power charts in Appendix A.7. We would use the same formula if we were estimating sample size on the basis of a contrast found in a main effect (ψ_A or ψ_B), but then the sample size we obtained would be that of the marginal mean, i.e. bn when we are looking at a contrast among the A marginal means and an when we are looking at one among the B marginal means.

When sample-size calculations are based on effects measured in a previous experiment, Equations 12.13–12.15 are used to estimate the effect size. For instance, suppose that the researcher who conducted the monkey study is planning a new experiment. Factor A (the drug conditions) will be the same as before, but because the original study found drug effects only with the satiated monkeys, all animals will be tested under that condition. The second factor in the new study will be the type of stimuli used. One set (b_1) is the same as before, the other set (b_2) is much less discriminable than the first set. The two studies have one simple effect in common: The simple effect of factor A under the satiated condition in the original study is the same as the simple effect of A with the original stimulus set in the new study. The researcher can use this simple effect to link the two studies. Suppose the researcher wants to be very sure (power = .95) that the original simple effect will be significant when replicated. First, $\widehat{\omega}^2_{\langle A \text{ at } b_1 \rangle}$ is estimated from the first study using Equation 12.14; we made the calculation above and found the value 0.49. Next, a sample-size calculation is made for this effect, treating it as if it were in a single-factor study. For a test with 2 degrees of freedom and power = .95, the power charts indicates $\phi \approx 2.3$. Then, using Equation 8.18, the required sample size per group is found:

$$n = \phi^2 \frac{1 - \omega^2}{\omega^2} = (2.3)^2 \frac{1 - 0.49}{0.49} = 5.51.$$

About six subjects per condition are needed to detect this simple effect, and this value should be used for all groups in the new study. The fact that we could attain such a high power with so few subjects is a consequence of the large effect in our example; don't expect real data to be so accommodating.

12.7   Controlling Familywise Type I Error

You will recall from Chapter 6 that the familywise Type I error α_{FW} refers to the probability of making at least one Type I error over a set (i.e. family) of statistical tests when all null hypotheses are true. To review, the more statistical tests we perform, the greater the chance of a Type I error somewhere in the set. This increase is the inevitable consequence of conducting many tests. It leaves us with a dilemma: If we ignore α_{FW}, we risk reporting sampling accidents as true findings. But if we keep too tight a control on this probability, by making it more difficult to reject the individual null hypotheses, then we increase the chance of overlooking a real effect (a Type II error). Any analysis must be sensitive to both possibilities.

The problem of controlling familywise error is considerably more complex in a factorial design than in a single-factor design. For one thing, factorial designs typically involve more groups than one-way designs, increasing the number of possible tests. For another, these tests divide up into many more distinct families. In the single-factor design, we saw such well-defined families as the complete set of trend components, all comparisons between a control condition and several experimental conditions, or all possible pairwise comparisons. In the factorial design, each of these families can apply to each separate main effect or simple effect. Moreover, in Chapter 13 we will introduce the set of interaction components, a family unique to factorial designs. Which of these families we actually use depends on the study—which questions are important and how the omnibus analysis came out—but we should be ready to control error for any of them.

First, consider the three principal effects—the two main effects and the interaction. There is a general consensus that these are planned tests and do not require error correction. They are evaluated at a conventional significance level, such as $\alpha = .05$. If there were actually no differences among the cell means, then the experimentwise Type I error rate over these three tests, would be larger than α, somewhere just below the Bonferroni limit of $3 \times \alpha = .15$. However, this level of experimentwise error in a two-factor design is rarely a concern for researchers because the tests are mutually orthogonal and express distinct questions. They are generally treated as planned and thus do not need special error correction.

Main-Effect Comparisons

In the absence of an interaction, attention is usually drawn to one or both of the two main effects. The analysis is treated like two separate single-factor experiments. When either factor has more than two levels, main-effect comparisons may be needed. The two factors are usually treated separately, each with an allotment of familywise error equal to the level of the original tests, (e.g., $\alpha_{FW} = .05$; picking a higher rate can lead to a confusing proliferation of errors if both effects are analyzed). Our discussion in Chapter 6 applies to these analyses. We will review the main points.

- A comparison that is a central planned portion of the study is evaluated without error control.
- For a small set of c meaningful comparisons, such as a few trend components, the familywise error rate can be controlled with the Bonferroni method by taking $\alpha = \alpha_{FW}/c$ (Equation 12.15). The similar Šidák-Bonferroni correction, using the tables in Appendix A.4, is slightly more powerful.
- The set of all pairwise differences between means is most easily tested with the Tukey procedure or its more powerful Fisher-Hayter modification. The Fisher-Hayter procedure starts when the main effect is significant, then tests each pairwise difference using Tukey's procedure based on one fewer mean. In the factorial design, the critical differences for the two factors are

$$D_{\text{FH-}A} = q_{a-1}\sqrt{\frac{MS_{S/AB}}{bn}} \quad \text{and} \quad D_{\text{FH-}B} = q_{b-1}\sqrt{\frac{MS_{S/AB}}{an}}, \qquad (12.17)$$

where q_{a-1} and q_{b-1} are obtained from the Studentized range statistic tables in Appendix A.6 (Equation 6.9, p. 125).
- When the broadest error control is desired—for example, with a large set that includes complex contrasts—the Scheffé procedure is used. The critical value of F is increased (Equation 6.11, p. 128) in the factorial design to

$$
\begin{aligned}
F_{\text{Scheffé-}A} &= (a-1)F_{A,\alpha_{FW}}(df_A, df_{S/AB}), \\
F_{\text{Scheffé-}B} &= (b-1)F_{B,\alpha_{FW}}(df_B, df_{S/AB}).
\end{aligned}
\qquad (12.18)
$$

The Scheffé error control is particularly stringent, but with the strongest standard for identifying an effect—you can be quite sure of any contrast that it finds significant.

Simple Effects

Error control with simple effects is more complicated, primarily because they are used in so many ways. There is no consensual standard for the level of familywise error to use with them. Some researchers argue that a significant interaction justifies the use of uncorrected tests for the simple effects. In effect, they consider the breakdown of the sums of squares into simple effects (Equation 12.9) as a planned family. Others control the error rate over the family of simple effects. The Bonferroni (or Šidák-Bonferroni) procedure is the most practical approach here. For example, by setting α_{FW} to .10 in our 3×2 monkey example, the two simple effects of A at b_k would be evaluated at a per-test rate of $\alpha = .10/b = .10/2 = .05$ or the three simple effects for B at a_j would be evaluated at a per-test rate of $\alpha = .10/a = .10/3 = .033$. The familywise error rate of $\alpha_{FW} = .10$ makes more sense here than, say, $\alpha_{FW} = .05$ (as long as only one of these sets is to be tested), because the families of simple effects subsume a main effect and the interaction that were originally tested separately. In a small design like this, the amount of extra error control required is small (none when the design is divided along the two-level factor), so any loss of power is small.

Error control is more important when a significant simple effect is followed by tests of simple comparisons. The number of such tests can be large, and the interesting ones are frequently determined only after the fact. Because simple effects can be viewed as one-way designs embedded in a factorial, you can use any of the techniques applicable to a one-way design, which we summarized for main-effect contrasts above. The formulas from Chapter 6 apply directly, except that the error term $MS_{S/AB}$ from the factorial design is used instead of $MS_{S/A}$. We suggest you hold the familywise Type-I error rate to the same level that you used for the test of the simple effect. When error control has already been applied to those tests, this approach can lead to per-comparison levels that are not included in standard tables, so it is easiest to work with a computer program that prints out descriptive levels.

With corrections of this type, it is easy to lose sight of the goals of the analysis in an effort to find the "right" value for α_{FW}. There really isn't any. When an interaction is present in a factorial design, there are many ways that the analysis can proceed, each involving different families of tests. Some of these are planned and others are developed after the data have been examined. You need to be flexible, both in picking an analysis strategy and in devising your error-control procedure. Keep in mind that the point of any of these corrections is to protect you from identifying spurious effects, and that the possibility of doing so goes up with the number of tests you conduct. But also remember that the heedless choice of the most stringent error correction can exact unacceptable costs in power. The "right" choice, then, may involve any of the various procedures, consistent with these twin objectives.

Exercises

12.1. Problem 11.2 revealed only a significant main effect of factor A. Conduct the following single-df comparisons involving the marginal means $(\bar{Y}_{A_j})$:

a. Test the pairwise difference between $\bar{Y}_{A_1}$ and $\bar{Y}_{A_3}$.

b. Test the complex comparison involving the difference between $\bar{Y}_{A_2}$ and the average of the other two marginal means, $\bar{Y}_{A_1}$ and $\bar{Y}_{A_3}$.

12.2. Consider the data in the numerical example in Table 11.8.

a. Test the significance of the simple effects of factor B.

b. Show that the total sum of squares associated with the three simple effects equals the sum of SS_B and $SS_{A \times B}$.

12.3. Problem 11.1 revealed a significant $A \times B$ interaction, setting the stage for an analysis of simple effects of either factor (or both factors).

a. Follow the guidelines for selecting a set of simple effects for analysis (p. 248) to assess the simple effects of shock intensity (factor A).

b. The simple effect for the easy discrimination problems (b_1) is significant, so you would be interested in examining single-df comparisons, which in the context of this analysis, are simple comparisons. Test the pairwise difference between the means at levels a_1 and a_4.

c. Factor A is a quantitative independent variable (equally spaced levels of shock intensity), so that the comparison in the previous part simply contrasts the two extreme intensities. A more revealing approach uses trend analysis. For the easy problems, investigate whether the relationship is entirely linear or whether the relationship curves.

12.4. Suppose an experiment is conducted in which three strains of rats are to be compared. One strain was obtained by selectively breeding rats that performed ex-

ceptionally well in a maze-learning task (the "bright" rats); a second strain was obtained by selectively breeding rats that performed quite poorly in the task (the "dull"
rats); a third strain consisted of rats that were bred without regard for maze-learning
performance (the "mixed" rats). One group from each strain was raised under "enriched" environmental conditions, and a second group was raised under "impoverished" conditions. From each strain, $n = 8$ rats were randomly assigned to each
environment. Following six months of exposure to the environment, every rat was
tested in a standard maze. The response measure consisted of the trials needed to
perform the maze without error. The following treatment means were obtained:

Strain	Environment (Factor B)	
(Factor A)	Enriched	Impoverished
Bright	3.50	3.75
Mixed	4.00	7.75
Dull	7.50	11.00

a. Conduct a omnibus analysis of variance, assuming that $MS_{S/AB} = 5.00$.
b. Are the simple effects for the three strains of rats raised in the enriched and
impoverished environments significant? Estimate their partial effect sizes.
c. Is the difference between the bright and mixed strains reared in the enriched
environment significant? Again, estimate the partial effect size.

12.5. The $A \times B$ interaction in Problem 12.4 was not significant. Suppose the researcher decides to repeat the experiment with sufficient power to detect the interaction, assuming that it is present in the population.
a. What sample size is needed to detect the overall interaction with a power of .90?
b. Will this sample size provide the same power for the simple effects examined in
Problem 12.4?

13

The Analysis
of Interaction Components

The pivotal point of the analytical strategy in Chapter 12 was the $A \times B$ interaction. The lack of an interaction led to the analysis of the main effects and perhaps to main comparisons, while the presence of an interaction led to the analysis of the simple effects and simple comparisons. One drawback to this approach is the proliferation of tests when an interaction is found. When we look at a particular simple contrast in two or more rows or columns, we are faced with deciding when their magnitudes differ. However, it is not enough to note that one is significant and another is not. Just as we need the overall $A \times B$ interaction to determine when simple effects differ, we need a statistical test to tell us when simple contrasts are different.

Moreover, except in a 2×2 table, the $A \times B$ interaction is a composite effect with several degrees of freedom. Many different patterns in the data—differences among many different simple effects—can create an interaction of a particular size. We need a focused strategy to interpret the interaction. As you will see, the tests of interaction components discussed in this chapter answer both of these needs.

13.1 Types of Interaction Components

Whenever the omnibus $A \times B$ interaction has more than one degree of freedom, individual components that express precise questions, called **interaction components**, can be extracted. The most exact questions are expressed by single-df interaction components. These minimal components can always be written as contrasts, so we will call them **interaction contrasts**. In this section, we will illustrate the principal types of interaction components and contrasts, leaving the computational matters for later. For the time being, we will not worry about whether these components are planned or post hoc, deferring Type I error control until Section 13.6.

We will introduce the different types of interaction components with a specific example of a 3×3 factorial study. Suppose that 45 fifth-grade schoolchildren are randomly assigned to $ab = (3)(3) = 9$ groups, with $n = 5$ subjects per group. Each child learns a list of vocabulary words in the laboratory and is tested for recall one week later. One of the two three-level factors, call it factor A, determines the type of verbal feedback given during learning:

- a_1: The subjects receive no verbal feedback;
- a_2: The subjects receive positive comments following each training trial;
- a_3: The subjects receive negative comments following each training trial.

The no-feedback condition, a_1, provides a baseline against which the effects of feedback are measured. The second factor, B, determines the type of words on the list:

- b_1: Low-frequency words with low emotional content;
- b_2: High-frequency words with low emotional content;
- b_3: High-frequency words with high emotional content.

This factor embodies two single-factor manipulations (frequency and emotional content) that use the same reference condition b_2 (high-frequency words with low emotional content), a structure that will dictate our choice of contrasts below.[1]

The upper portion of Table 13.1 gives the individual Y_{ijk} scores, the middle portion the mean number of words recalled by each group, and the lower portion the analysis of variance. All three effects are significant at the 5 percent level. Examination of the means shows that two of the groups recalled substantially fewer words ($\overline{Y}_{23} = 4.4$ and $\overline{Y}_{33} = 3.8$) than the other seven (a range between 7.6 and 8.8 words). This difference is a principal source of the interaction: The simple effects of factor A are sizable only at level b_3, and the simple effects of factor B are sizable at a_2 and a_3.

Interaction of a Contrast and a Factor

Suppose we form the same simple contrast $\psi_{A \text{ at } b_k}$ at every level of factor B. The values of these contrasts may vary from one simple effect to another, and some of them may be significantly different from zero and others not. A natural question is whether these differences in the simple contrasts reflect real differences in the population. To answer this question, we need a statistical test. Specifically, we need to determine whether the contrast ψ_A interacts with factor B, that is, we need to investigate the $\psi_A \times B$ interaction.

What contrasts should we look at in Table 13.1? For the first two word types (b_1 and b_2), the type of feedback appears to have little effect on recall, but for the third word type (b_3), recall following either positive or negative feedback (conditions a_2 and a_3) is substantially lower than the baseline condition (a_1). An easy way to examine the differences among the types of feedback is to set up the three pairwise contrasts:

- ψ_{A_1}: A comparison between positive and negative feedback;
- ψ_{A_2}: A comparison between no feedback and positive feedback;
- ψ_{A_3}: A comparison between no feedback and negative feedback.

---

[1]Some researchers would be tempted to add a fourth condition (low-frequency words with high emotional content, assuming such words could be found) to create two crossed factors. Doing so would allow the interaction of frequency and emotional content to be assessed, but it would increase the number of groups to 12, requiring either a larger total N (hence more expense) or smaller cell sizes (hence less power for tests of particular comparisons and greater vulnerability to violation of assumptions). There is no point in elaborating a study unless it is called for by the point of the research.

Table 13.1: *The number of words recalled by fifth-grade children, with group means and an overall analysis of variance.*

Individual scores

a_1b_1	a_2b_1	a_3b_1	a_1b_2	a_2b_2	a_3b_2	a_1b_3	a_2b_3	a_3b_3
7	6	10	7	6	7	7	3	2
7	8	8	8	8	7	7	5	3
9	7	8	9	8	6	10	3	4
10	9	6	10	9	9	7	6	5
9	9	8	10	9	9	9	5	5

Table of means

	Word type (B)		
	Low F	High F	High F
	Low E	Low E	High E
Feedback (A)	b_1	b_2	b_3
None: a_1	8.4	8.8	8.0
Positive: a_2	7.8	8.0	4.4
Negative: a_3	8.0	7.6	3.8

Summary of the analysis of variance

Source	SS	df	MS	F
A	32.933	2	16.467	9.26*
B	72.933	2	36.467	20.51*
$A \times B$	23.334	4	5.834	3.28*
S/AB	64.000	36	1.778	
Total	193.200	44		

* $p < .05$

In formal notation, these are

$$\left.\begin{aligned} \psi_{A_1} &= 0\mu_1 + 1\mu_2 + (-1)\mu_3, \\ \psi_{A_2} &= 1\mu_1 + (-1)\mu_2 + 0\mu_3, \\ \psi_{A_3} &= 1\mu_1 + 0\mu_2 + (-1)\mu_3. \end{aligned}\right\} \tag{13.1}$$

Our description of the effects above indicates that the values of contrasts ψ_{A_2} and ψ_{A_3}, each of which expresses a comparison between the no-feedback group a_1 and one of the feedback groups, should vary with B.

When the contrast being examined is a pairwise comparison, we can see the interaction component by looking at a subtable of the original data. Three 2×3 subtables, corresponding to the contrasts ψ_{A_1}, ψ_{A_2}, and ψ_{A_3}, are shown in the upper part of Table 13.2. Each subtable extracts the appropriate rows from the original table of means. Below each column is the difference between the two rows, which equals the value of $\widehat{\psi}_A$ for that simple contrast. There appears to be at most a small interaction

Table 13.2: Tables of means extracted from Table 13.1 with contrast values. The upper tables contain group means; the lower table shows the no-feedback and pooled feedback conditions.

Three 2×3 subtables of group means

	b_1	b_2	b_3
Pos.	7.8	8.0	4.4
Neg.	8.0	7.6	3.8
$\widehat{\psi}_{A_1}$	−0.2	0.4	0.6

	b_1	b_2	b_3
None	8.4	8.8	8.0
Pos.	7.8	8.0	4.4
$\widehat{\psi}_{A_2}$	0.6	0.8	3.6

	b_1	b_2	b_3
None	8.4	8.8	8.0
Neg.	8.0	7.6	3.8
$\widehat{\psi}_{A_3}$	0.4	1.2	4.2

No-feedback and feedback means, with values of contrast ψ_{A_4}

	b_1	b_2	b_3
No Feedback	8.4	8.8	8.0
Feedback	7.9	7.8	4.1
$\widehat{\psi}_{A_4}$	0.5	1.0	3.9

in the first subtable (whose rows corresponds to the contrast ψ_{A_1}) and substantial interactions in the other two (ψ_{A_2}, and ψ_{A_3}). Each of these interactions captures a portion of the original $A \times B$ interaction.

Our observations also suggest a more complicated interaction component. The primary source of interaction appears to reside in a comparison of the no-feedback condition to the two feedback conditions. This comparison is expressed by a contrast that pits the baseline condition against the average of the two feedback conditions:

$$\psi_{A_4} = \mu_1 - \tfrac{1}{2}(\mu_2 + \mu_3) = 1\mu_1 + (-\tfrac{1}{2})\mu_2 + (-\tfrac{1}{2})\mu_3. \tag{13.2}$$

The bottom of Table 13.2 illustrates this contrast. The first row gives the no-feedback means, the second row gives the average of the two feedback means, and the values of the simple contrasts are in the last row. The fact that these simple contrasts are different suggests an interaction with factor B. This relationship is a $\psi_A \times B$ interaction, but not one that derives directly from a subtable of the original means.

We could also have constructed interaction components based on contrasts involving factor B crossed with factor A. There are two contrasts of interest in our example:

- ψ_{B_1}: A comparison of the recall for low- and high-frequency words with the same (low) emotional content (b_1 and b_2, respectively);

- ψ_{B_2}: A comparison of the recall for words of low and high emotional content with the same (high) frequency (b_2 and b_3, respectively).

In equation form, these contrasts are

$$\left.\begin{aligned} \psi_{B_1} &= 1\mu_1 + (-1)\mu_2 + 0\mu_3, \\ \psi_{B_2} &= 0\mu_1 + 1\mu_2 + (-1)\mu_3. \end{aligned}\right\} \tag{13.3}$$

Each pairwise contrasts implies a 3×2 subtable of means from Table 13.1. Write them out, and you will see that ψ_{B_1} does not appear to interact with type of feedback (factor A), but that ψ_{B_2} does. In each of these subtables, the A effect is crossed with a contrast involving factor B, and so it expresses an $A \times \psi_B$ interaction.

Interaction of Two Contrasts: Interaction Contrasts

The $\psi_A \times B$ or $A \times \psi_B$ interaction component is one portion of the $A \times B$ interaction. When the interacting factor (B or A, respectively) has more than two levels, these interactions are still composites. A more precise interaction effect is created by viewing both factors as contrasts. The resulting **interaction contrast** is formed by crossing the two contrasts.[2] This $\psi_A \times \psi_B$ **interaction** helps us pinpoint the source(s) of an omnibus $A \times B$ effect. These interaction contrasts have one degree of freedom and, as we will see, can be written as a contrast ψ_{AB} on the cell means. Where necessary, we will add subscripts to identify the particular contrasts; for example, $\psi_{A_1} \times \psi_{B_2}$ or $\psi_{A_1 B_2}$.

Many of the most useful interaction contrasts are formed by crossing two pairwise contrasts. The resulting interaction contrast extracts a 2×2 subtable of the original means. Consider the interaction between ψ_{A_2}, which expressed the difference between the no-feedback and positive feedback conditions, with factor B (the second of the three subtables at the top of Table 13.2). Because factor B has three levels, this $\psi_A \times B$ interaction is a composite effect. Within it, we can focus on the emotional content of the words by restricting attention to the high frequency words (b_2 and b_3). We are left with a 2×2 subtable of means:

	Low E	High E
No Feedback	8.8	8.0
Positive Feedback	8.0	4.4

What does the interaction in this subtable tell us? There is little difference between low and high emotional content for the no-feedback condition and a sizable one for the positive feedback condition. Calculating the simple comparisons ψ_{B_2} at a_j supports this observation—the first contrast is small (presumably it would not be significant) and the second is large (presumably it would be significant). A significance test of the interaction contrast would establish whether the difference between the two simple contrasts is supported statistically. We could also describe the interaction in terms of the feedback comparison. Positive feedback has little effect on the recall of the low-emotion words, but an appreciable negative effect on the recall of high-emotion words. Either way, we are examining the $\psi_{A_2} \times \psi_{B_2}$ interaction.

Researchers trying to understand this type of interaction often reduce a large table to a series of pairwise subtables and examine the interaction in each. This strategy is, for interactions, much like looking at the set of pairwise comparisons for main effects. When the two comparisons that make up the interaction contrast express meaningful questions, the $\psi_A \times \psi_B$ interaction usually describes a meaningful aspect of the interaction. We have already seen that the three pairwise contrasts on factor A in Equations 13.1 and the two pairwise contrasts on B in Equations 13.3 are meaningful. Crossing these two sets of single-df comparisons creates six interaction contrasts,

---

[2]For this reason, you may also see interaction contrasts referred to as **interactions of contrasts** or **interacting contrasts**.

Table 13.3: *Interaction contrasts based on Equations 13.1 and 13.3 for a study involving words of different frequency and emotional content.*

		ψ_{B_1}		ψ_{B_2}	
		Low Freq.	High Freq.	Low Emot.	High Emot.
ψ_{A_1}	Positive	7.8	8.0	8.0	4.4
	Negative	8.0	7.6	7.6	3.8
ψ_{A_2}	None	8.4	8.8	8.8	8.0
	Positive	7.8	8.0	8.0	4.4
ψ_{A_3}	None	8.4	8.8	8.8	8.0
	Negative	8.0	7.6	7.6	3.8

each of which is described by a 2×2 subtable of the original data, as shown in Table 13.3. Each of these miniature factorials isolates a different aspect of the overall $A \times B$ interaction. The first column of three tables involves comparisons between words of low and high frequency (ψ_{B_1}), and the three rows of tables correspond to different comparisons in factor A. Thus, the three questions addressed by the interaction contrasts in the first column are:

- Is the difference between positive and negative feedback (ψ_{A_1}) the same for low- and high-frequency words?
- Is the difference between no feedback and positive feedback (ψ_{A_2}) the same for low- and high-frequency words?
- Is the difference between no feedback and negative feedback (ψ_{A_3}) the same for low- and high-frequency words?

A similar set of three questions comes from the second column, except that they compare words of low and high emotional content (ψ_{B_2})

Interaction contrasts can also be formed using complex comparisons in which cell means are averaged. For example, we could determine whether the contrast that compared the baseline condition to the combined feedback conditions, $\psi_{A_4} = \mu_1 + (-\frac{1}{2})\mu_2 + (-\frac{1}{2})\mu_3$, interacted with the lists of low and high word frequency, $\psi_{B_1} = \mu_1 - \mu_2$. This $\psi_{A_4} \times \psi_{B_1}$ interaction contrast answers the question

- Is the difference between no feedback and combined feedback (ψ_{A_4}) the same for low- and high-frequency words (ψ_{B_1})?

13.2 Analyzing Interaction Contrasts

A test of the null hypothesis that an interaction contrast is zero is fundamentally similar to the other single-*df* tests in this book. It begins by calculating a sum of squares and dividing it by the number of degrees of freedom (which equals 1) to produce a mean square. The mean square is then divided by the error mean square, usually based on the overall analysis, to obtain an F ratio that is evaluated for significance. Of these steps, only the first—calculating the sum of squares—is any different from what we have done before.

Testing Interaction Contrasts

When you are testing the interaction of two pairwise contrasts (such as those in Table 13.3), you can calculate the sums of squares by directly applying the formulas for the interaction in a 2×2 design (see Table 11.6, p. 218) to the subtable of means. The result is tested against $MS_{S/AB}$ from the full analysis. This approach is useful when you are exploring your data with a computer. However, we will concentrate here on a more general approach that can be used with any interaction contrast, not just pairwise contrasts.

The key to this approach is to combine the contrasts ψ_A and ψ_B into a single contrast that applies to the entire set of ab groups in the study:

$$\psi_{AB} = \sum c_{jk}\mu_{jk} \quad \text{with} \quad \sum c_{jk} = 0, \tag{13.4}$$

where the sums are over both the subscripts. This interaction contrast is then tested using standard approaches.

Contrast Coefficients.   Suppose we wish to test the interaction of the contrasts

$$\psi_A = \sum c_{A_j}\mu_j \quad \text{and} \quad \psi_B = \sum c_{B_k}\mu_k.$$

We have added an A or a B to the subscripts (retaining the subscripts j or k) to indicate the factor to which they apply, following the notation we used for marginal means. The coefficients c_{jk} of the interaction contrast (Equation 13.4) are the product of the corresponding coefficients of the individual contrasts:

$$c_{jk} = c_{A_j}c_{B_k}. \tag{13.5}$$

A value of c_{jk} is determined for every combination of j and k.

It is often easiest to calculate the coefficients by constructing a table in which the coefficients c_{A_j} are placed on one side of the table (we will choose the left), the coefficients c_{B_k} are placed on the other, and their products are entered in the body of the table. Table 13.4 shows two examples. On the left is the interaction contrast formed from the pairwise comparisons ψ_{A_1} (Equations 13.1) and ψ_{B_2} (Equations 13.3). The entries in the center are the products; for example,

$$c_{32} = c_{A_3}c_{B_2} = (-1)(1) = -1.$$

The resulting interaction contrast, ignoring the five cells with zero coefficients, is

$$\psi_{A_1 B_2} = \mu_{22} - \mu_{32} - \mu_{23} + \mu_{33}.$$

It expresses the same interaction as the 2×2 table at the upper left of Table 13.3. On the right of Table 13.4 are the coefficients for the interaction of ψ_{A_4} (Equation 13.2), which involves three means and compares the no-feedback baseline to the average of the two feedback conditions, and the same pairwise ψ_{B_2}. The resulting interaction contrast involves the means from six of the nine groups.

When using some computer programs, you will need to find the interaction coefficients this way. You calculate the coefficients c_{jk} using Equation 13.5, and give them to the program as a user-defined or "custom" contrast. Then you run the analysis of

Table 13.4: Two examples of finding the coefficients of an interaction contrast.

$c_{A_{1j}}$	$c_{B_{2k}}$ 0	1	-1	$c_{A_{4j}}$	$c_{B_{2k}}$ 0	1	-1
0	0	0	0	1	0	1	-1
1	0	1	-1	$-\frac{1}{2}$	0	$-\frac{1}{2}$	$\frac{1}{2}$
-1	0	-1	1	$-\frac{1}{2}$	0	$-\frac{1}{2}$	$\frac{1}{2}$
	$\sum c_{jk}^2 = 4$				$\sum c_{jk}^2 = 3$		

variance—in some programs it will be as a one-way design with ab groups. Depending on how the program treats the contrast (see our discussion of Table 9.4, p. 188), the sums of squares may not agree with those we calculate below, but the F reported by the program will be correct.

Contrast Values. The observed value of the contrast $\widehat{\psi}_{AB}$ is easy to calculate by applying the coefficients to the group means. For example, the second of the contrasts in Table 13.4 (ignoring the column of zero coefficients), is

$$\widehat{\psi}_{A_4 B_2} = \overline{Y}_{12} + (-\tfrac{1}{2})\overline{Y}_{22} + (-\tfrac{1}{2})\overline{Y}_{32} + (-1)\overline{Y}_{13} + (\tfrac{1}{2})\overline{Y}_{23} + (\tfrac{1}{2})\overline{Y}_{33}$$
$$= 8.8 + (-\tfrac{1}{2})(8.0) + (-\tfrac{1}{2})(7.6) + (-1)(8.0) + (\tfrac{1}{2})(4.4) + (\tfrac{1}{2})(3.8)$$
$$= -2.9.$$

Another way to calculate an interaction contrast is to write it as a contrast applied to the contrast values for the other factor. First, we calculate values of the simple contrast for each level of one of the factors, then we apply the other contrast to them. The b simple contrast values for ψ_A are

$$\widehat{\psi}_{A \text{ at } b_k} = \sum_j c_{A_j} \overline{Y}_{jk}.$$

Now we calculate the contrast of contrast values:

$$\widehat{\psi}_{AB} = \sum_k (c_{B_k})(\widehat{\psi}_{A \text{ at } b_k}). \tag{13.6}$$

This approach gives the same answer as that obtained directly from the means, but is easier to understand when the simple contrasts $\widehat{\psi}_{A \text{ at } b_k}$ are meaningful themselves.

Consider the interaction contrast $\psi_{A_4} \times \psi_{B_2}$, whose value we just calculated. The contrast ψ_{A_4} compares the no-feedback condition to the combined feedback conditions. We calculated values for these simple contrasts in the bottom panel of Table 13.2 and found that feedback produced a smaller reduction in recall for the low-emotion words (1.0 items) than for the high-emotion words (3.9 items). The contrast ψ_B compares these values. Substituting the simple contrasts in $\psi_{B_2} = \mu_2 - \mu_3$ gives the same value that we calculated from directly from the means:

$$\widehat{\psi}_{A_4 B_2} = \widehat{\psi}_{A_4 \text{ at } b_2} - \widehat{\psi}_{A_4 \text{ at } b_3} = 1.0 - 3.9 = -2.9.$$

The Sum of Squared Coefficients. The sum of the squared coefficients, $\sum c_{jk}^2$, is obtained by squaring all ab coefficients and adding the results. These sums are given below each part of Table 13.4. These sums may also be calculated by multiplying the sum of the squared coefficients of the individual contrasts ψ_A and ψ_B:

$$\sum c_{jk}^2 = (\sum c_{A_j}^2)(\sum c_{B_k}^2). \tag{13.7}$$

Again look at the second example in Table 13.4. The squares of the two sets of contrast coefficients (at the left and top of the table) are

$$\sum c_{A_j}^2 = 1^2 + (-\frac{1}{2})^2 + (-\frac{1}{2})^2 = 1.5,$$

$$\sum c_{B_k}^2 = 0^2 + 1^2 + (-1)^2 = 2.0.$$

Equation 13.7 gives the same answer that we found from the c_{jk} directly:

$$\sum c_{jk}^2 = (\sum c_{A_j}^2)(\sum c_{B_k}^2) = (1.5)(2.0) = 3.0.$$

This calculation is faster and less error prone, particularly when (as in Table 13.3) several interaction contrasts are examined. It must be used when the sum of squares are calculated as a contrast of contrasts (Equation 13.6), without finding the individual coefficients c_{jk}. When do use the c_{jk}, comparing the answers obtained from the two approaches lets you check that you have calculated their values correctly.

Completing the Analysis.   However $\widehat{\psi}_{AB}$ is obtained, the corresponding sum of squares is found from the usual formula:

$$SS_{\psi_{AB}} = \frac{n\widehat{\psi}_{AB}^2}{\sum c_{jk}^2}, \qquad (13.8)$$

where $\widehat{\psi}_{AB}$ = the observed value of the contrast, $\sum c_{jk}\overline{Y}_{jk}$,
   n = sample size per group,
   $\sum c_{jk}^2$ = the sum of the squared coefficients.

It has one degree of freedom, and, unless heterogeneity of variances is a concern, it is tested against the mean square from the complete design.

A Numerical Example

We can now complete the analysis of the two interaction contrasts in Table 13.4. For the $\psi_{A_1} \times \psi_{B_2}$ interaction, the observed the contrast value is

$$\widehat{\psi}_{A_1B_2} = \overline{Y}_{22} - \overline{Y}_{32} - \overline{Y}_{23} + \overline{Y}_{33}$$

$$= 8.0 - 7.6 - 4.4 + 3.8 = -0.2,$$

and we already calculated the $\widehat{\psi}_{A_4B_2} = -2.9$ above. Substituting these two values in Equation 13.8 gives

$$SS_{\psi_{A_1B_2}} = \frac{n\widehat{\psi}_{A_1B_2}^2}{\sum c_{jk}^2} = \frac{(5)(-0.2)^2}{4} = 0.050,$$

$$SS_{\psi_{A_4B_2}} = \frac{n\widehat{\psi}_{A_4B_2}^2}{\sum c_{jk}^2} = \frac{(5)(-2.9)^2}{3} = 14.017.$$

The two test statistics are $F = MS_{\psi_{A_1B_2}}/MS_{S/AB} = 0.050/1.778 = 0.03$ and $F = 14.017/1.778 = 7.88$. The first is obviously not significant; the second is. The first finding is part of our justification for combining the two feedback conditions and ignoring the differences in type of feedback, and the second tells us that the effects of feedback depend on the emotional content of the words.

After finding the significant $\psi_{A_4} \times \psi_{B_2}$ interaction, we would want to test the simple contrasts directly.[3] The sums of squares are found by substituting the contrast values from Table 13.2 into Equation 12.12:

$$SS_{\psi_{A_4} \text{ at } b_2} = \frac{n\widehat{\psi}^2_{A_4 \text{ at } b_2}}{\sum c_j^2} = \frac{(5)(1.0)^2}{1^2 + (-\frac{1}{2})^2 + (-\frac{1}{2})^2} = \frac{5.0}{1.5} = 3.333,$$

$$SS_{\psi_{A_4} \text{ at } b_3} = \frac{n\widehat{\psi}^2_{A_4 \text{ at } b_3}}{\sum c_j^2} = \frac{(5)(3.9)^2}{1^2 + (-\frac{1}{2})^2 + (-\frac{1}{2})^2} = \frac{76.05}{1.5} = 50.700.$$

The first of these comparisons is not significant at the 5 percent level, but the second one is ($F = 3.333/1.778 = 1.87$ and $F = 50.700/1.778 = 28.52$, respectively). The researcher can reasonably assert that the feedback effect is largely limited to the high-emotion words.

Variance Heterogeneity

As we mentioned for simple effects (see pp. 251–253), the presence of heterogeneity can lead to biased F tests because $MS_{S/AB}$ is no longer the appropriate error term. Suppose we were testing the interaction contrast formed by crossing the two pairwise comparisons depicted on the left of Table 13.4—a contrast involving only four of the nine treatment groups. With heterogeneous variances—say as indicated by a Levene or Brown-Forsythe test—the variability of the scores for these four groups may be different from the average value $MS_{S/AB}$ calculated from all nine groups.

The solution is to base the calculation only on the groups actually involved in ψ_{AB}. The simplest procedure treats the analysis as a one-way design with ab groups and conducts the t test described in Section 7.5, which uses an error term specially calculated for the particular contrast:

$$t_\psi = \frac{\widehat{\psi}_{AB}}{s_{\widehat{\psi}}} \quad \text{where} \quad s_{\widehat{\psi}} = \sqrt{\sum c_{jk}^2 s_{M_{jk}}^2},$$

and the degrees of freedom are calculated using Equation 7.13.

Effect Size, Sample Size, and Power

Researchers have few occasions to report effect sizes for, or base sample-size determinations on, effects as far removed from the basic analysis as interaction contrasts. Nevertheless, these calculations are simple. The trick is to remember that any single-df comparison can be treated as if it were a comparison in a one-way design with ab groups. As a result, the procedures for contrasts in a one-way design can be used.

If you want a measure of effect size for an interaction contrast, you should calculate the partial statistic, which expresses the size of the observed contrast relative to the error variability without including any other effects. You can use Equation 8.15 (p. 165) for theoretical calculations (except that the error variability is $\sigma^2_{S/AB}$ instead of $\sigma^2_{S/A}$) and Equation 8.17 for an estimate based on data. For an example of the latter, the partial effect size for the interaction contrast $\psi_{A_4 B_2}$ that we tested above is estimated from the observed $F = 7.89$ to be

---

[3]Although we remind you again that the significant interaction only tells us that the two simple contrasts are different, not whether these contrasts themselves are significantly different from zero.

$$\widehat{\omega}^2_{\langle\psi_{A_4 B_2}\rangle} = \frac{F - 1}{F - 1 + 2n} = \frac{7.89 - 1}{7.89 - 1 + (2)(5)} = \frac{6.89}{16.89} = 0.408.$$

When $F < 1$, as it was for the interaction contrast $\psi_{A_1 B_2}$, the estimate is $\widehat{\omega}^2 = 0$.

For sample-size calculations, you follow the procedure described for contrasts in one-way designs (pages 175–176). With a theoretically derived contrast, you first calculate an effect size using Equations 8.13 and 8.15. As applied to the factorial design, these are:

$$\sigma^2_{\psi_{AB}} = \frac{\psi^2_{AB}}{2 \sum c^2_{jk}} \quad \text{and} \quad \omega^2_{\langle\psi_{AB}\rangle} = \frac{\sigma^2_{\psi_{AB}}}{\sigma^2_{\psi_{AB}} + \sigma^2_{S/AB}}.$$

For an effect estimated from another experiment, you use the estimated partial $\widehat{\omega}^2_{\langle\psi_{AB}\rangle}$ as calculated in the preceeding paragraph. Once you have $\omega^2_{\langle\psi_{AB}\rangle}$, you determine the sample size from Equation 8.18 and power from Equation 8.19, in each case making use of the noncentrality parameter and the power charts:

$$n = \phi^2 \frac{1 - \omega^2_{\langle\psi_{AB}\rangle}}{\omega^2_{\langle\psi_{AB}\rangle}} \quad \text{and} \quad \phi = \sqrt{\frac{n\omega^2_{\langle\psi_{AB}\rangle}}{1 - \omega^2_{\langle\psi_{AB}\rangle}}}.$$

13.3 Orthogonal Interaction Contrasts

An interaction contrast is a component of the overall $A \times B$ interaction. This fact gives it several important properties. First, its variability, $SS_{\psi_{AB}}$, is a portion of the omnibus $SS_{A \times B}$. Second, with but one degree of freedom, interaction contrasts are the smallest such components—they can not be subdivided any further. Third, they reflect pure interaction in the sense that they are orthogonal to both of the main effects and any main comparisons. We saw in Section 4.5 that it was possible to divide up a one-way omnibus effect into a set of orthogonal contrasts that completely capture the variability of the overall effect (see Equation 4.15, p. 77). Similarly, sets of orthogonal interaction contrasts can completely capture the entire variability of the $A \times B$ interaction. The number of contrasts in these sets equals the degrees of freedom of the overall interaction, $df_{A \times B} = (a - 1)(b - 1)$. For such a set,

$$SS_{A \times B} = \sum SS_{\psi_{AB}}. \tag{13.9}$$

Many different sets of orthogonal interaction contrasts can be constructed. The simplest way to construct a set is to base it on complete sets of orthogonal contrasts for each of the two factors. We start with $a - 1$ orthogonal contrasts for factor A and $b - 1$ orthogonal contrasts for factor B, then cross each contrast in the first set with each contrast in the second. The result is a set of $(a - 1)(b - 1)$ interaction contrasts, each of which is orthogonal to all the others.

Table 13.5 illustrates this process for a 3×3 experiment in which factor A is quantitative and factor B is not. Suppose that the three levels of factor A are represented by the linear and quadratic trend components, and the three levels of factor B are represented by one contrast that compares condition b_1 to the average of conditions b_2 and b_3 and another that compares conditions b_2 and b_3. The set of orthogonal interaction contrasts are formed by crossing the two sets:

$$\left.\begin{array}{l} \psi_{A_1} = (-1)\mu_1 + 0\mu_2 + 1\mu_3 \\ \psi_{A_2} = (-1)\mu_1 + 2\mu_2 + (-1)\mu_3 \end{array}\right\} \quad \times \quad \left\{\begin{array}{l} \psi_{B_1} = 1\mu_1 + (-\frac{1}{2})\mu_2 + (-\frac{1}{2})\mu_3 \\ \psi_{B_2} = 0\mu_1 + 1\mu_2 + (-1)\mu_3. \end{array}\right.$$

Table 13.5: A complete set of four orthogonal interaction comparisons for a 3×3 design, constructed by crossing two orthogonal comparisons for factor A with two orthogonal comparisons for factor B.

		ψ_{B_1}			ψ_{B_2}		
		1	$-\frac{1}{2}$	$-\frac{1}{2}$	0	1	-1
	-1	-1	$\frac{1}{2}$	$\frac{1}{2}$	0	-1	1
ψ_{A_1}	0	0	0	0	0	0	0
	1	1	$-\frac{1}{2}$	$-\frac{1}{2}$	0	1	-1
	-1	-1	$\frac{1}{2}$	$\frac{1}{2}$	0	-1	1
ψ_{A_2}	2	2	-1	-1	0	2	-2
	-1	-1	$\frac{1}{2}$	$\frac{1}{2}$	0	-1	1

The resulting four interaction contrasts appear in Table 13.5. We can verify that they are orthogonal by applying Equation 4.14 (p. 76) to each pair of contrasts. For example, simply multiply the coefficients for $\psi_{A_2}\times\psi_{B_1}$ by those for $\psi_{A_1}\times\psi_{B_2}$ and show they sum to zero.

When we discussed the relationship between orthogonality and planned comparisons in Section 4.5, we noted that orthogonal contrasts are somewhat easier to discuss because they represent distinct, nonoverlapping portions of an effect. However, they are only sensible if they are meaningful in terms of the design. To form meaningful interaction contrasts, each set of orthogonal contrasts for the two individual factors must make sense. Our example with the words and feedback is a case where orthogonal interaction contrasts do *not* make sense. It is reasonable to divide up factor A (the feedback) into a pair of orthogonal contrasts, one comparing feedback to no feedback, and the other comparing the two types of feedback:

$$\psi_{A_4} = 1\mu_1 + (-\tfrac{1}{2})\mu_2 + (-\tfrac{1}{2})\mu_3 \quad \text{and} \quad \psi_{A_1} = 0\mu_1 + 1\mu_2 + (-1)\mu_3.$$

However, because of the way the word lists were constructed, the two meaningful contrasts on factor B are those of Equations 13.3:

$$\psi_{B_1} = 1\mu_1 + (-1)\mu_2 + 0\mu_3 \quad \text{and} \quad \psi_{B_2} = 0\mu_1 + 1\mu_2 + (-1)\mu_3.$$

These two contrasts are not orthogonal, and no orthogonal set of contrasts makes much sense for factor B. When a nonorthogonal set of contrasts for one factor is crossed with an orthogonal set for another, the resulting interaction contrasts will not be orthogonal. As a result, their sums of squares will not add up to $SS_{A\times B}$, i.e. Equation 13.9 will not hold.

13.4 Testing Contrast-by-Factor Interactions

In Section 13.1 we described two ways to analyze the interaction. In the last two sections, we discussed one of these, namely, the interaction contrast formed by crossing two contrasts. Here, we consider the interaction components formed by crossing one contrast with an intact factor. These interaction components will have more than one

Table 13.6: Means and omnibus analysis of variance for an experiment in which the number of self-administered electrical shocks by rats was studied under five intensities (factor A) to three areas of the brain (factor B).

Table of means

	Brain Area			
Intensity	b_1	b_2	b_3	$\overline{Y}_{A_j}$
a_1	2.2	1.3	2.7	2.07
a_2	3.3	4.7	2.4	3.47
a_3	1.9	7.3	2.5	3.90
a_4	2.3	7.7	3.0	4.33
a_5	2.6	6.2	1.8	3.53
$\overline{Y}_{B_k}$	2.46	5.44	2.48	3.46

Omnibus analysis of variance

Source	SS	df	MS	F
A	43.55	4	10.89	3.29*
B	147.02	2	73.51	22.21*
$A \times B$	100.22	8	12.53	3.79*
S/AB	198.60	60	3.31	
Total	489.39	74		

* $p < .05$

degree of freedom (unless the intact factor has only two levels) and so are less specific than the interaction contrasts.

We start with an example that shows the usefulness of these tests. Consider an experiment in which rats were able to self-administer weak electrical shocks to the brain. The design is a 5×3 factorial with factor A consisting of $a = 5$ shock intensities and factor B of $b = 3$ different areas of the brain. There were $n = 5$ rats per group. Table 13.6 gives the mean number of shocks per minute that the rats received in each condition. The overall analysis shows that all effects are significant. We will concentrate on the significant interaction. In Figure 13.1, we have plotted the data in a form that shows the function relating intensity to the mean number of shocks for each of the three brain areas. These functions differ in several respects. The functions for b_1 and b_3 are nearly flat; that for b_2 climbs steeply and then begins to drop at the highest intensities. As a result, we ask two questions:

- Do the linear (straight-line) functions relating intensity to performance for the three brain areas differ in slope?

- Do the three linear relationships fully capture the $A \times B$ interaction?

As we discussed in Section 5.1, the simplest characteristic of a quantitative relationship is the linear trend, which is expressed for five groups by the contrast:

$$\psi_{A_{\text{linear}}} = (-2)\mu_1 + (-1)\mu_2 + 0\mu_3 + 1\mu_4 + 2\mu_5.$$

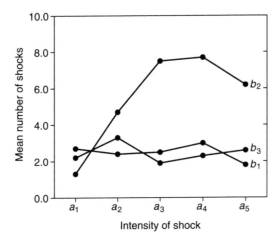

Figure 13.1: A plot of the means in Table 13.6.

Our first question asks whether this contrast varies with B. Formally, we need to test the $\psi_{A_{\text{linear}}} \times B$ interaction. The second question may be answered in either of two ways. As we have emphasized, the most important aspect of a nonlinear relationship is its curvature, and this effect is detected by the quadratic trend component:

$$\psi_{A_{\text{quadratic}}} = 2\mu_1 + (-1)\mu_2 + (-2)\mu_3 + (-1)\mu_4 + 2\mu_5.$$

Thus, we could detect whether the three groups differ in curvature by looking at the $\psi_{A_{\text{quadratic}}} \times B$ interaction. The other way to assess nonlinearity is to look at the part of the interaction that is not captured by the $\psi_{A_{\text{linear}}} \times B$ interaction—an example of the failure-of-linearity approach discussed on page 94. We will illustrate both approaches below.

Computational Procedure

The sum of squares for a $\psi_A \times B$ interaction can be calculated in two ways. They are useful in slightly different circumstances and give different insights into the nature of the interaction. One approach focuses directly on the variation among the simple contrasts. Recall the deviation formula for SS_A in the one-way design (Equation 2.3, p. 26):

$$SS_A = n \sum (\bar{Y}_j - \bar{Y}_T)^2.$$

In this equation the group means $\bar{Y}_j$ are the focus, and their deviation from the grand mean $\bar{Y}_T$ reflects the treatment effects. To write a formula for a contrast-by-factor interaction, we can substitute the value of each simple contrast $\widehat{\psi}_{A \text{ at } b_k}$ for $\bar{Y}_j$ and the main-effect contrast $\widehat{\psi}_A$ (which is the mean of the simple contrasts) for $\bar{Y}_T$. To accommodate the particular values of the coefficients, we must divide by $\sum c_j^2$:

$$SS_{\psi_A \times B} = \frac{n \sum_k (\widehat{\psi}_{A \text{ at } b_k} - \widehat{\psi}_A)^2}{\sum c_j^2}. \tag{13.10}$$

As you can see, this sum of squares quite literally represents the variability among the simple contrasts. You might use this approach if you are conducting the analysis by hand or are working from previously calculated means.

The other approach calculates this sum of squares indirectly, taking advantage of the fact that the sums of squares for a main effect and an interaction add up to the sum of the simple-effect sums of squares (Equation 12.8, p. 253):

$$SS_A + SS_{A \times B} = \sum SS_{A \text{ at } b_k}.$$

The same equation holds when we replace A by the contrast ψ_A:

$$SS_{\psi_A} + SS_{\psi_A \times B} = \sum SS_{\psi_A \text{ at } b_k}.$$

We know how to calculate the sums of squares for a main contrast ψ_A (Equation 12.3, p. 245) and for simple contrasts $\psi_{A \text{ at } b_k}$ (Equation 12.12, p. 256). By rearranging the equation, we produce a formula for the interaction sum of squares:

$$SS_{\psi_A \times B} = \sum SS_{\psi_A \text{ at } b_k} - SS_{\psi_A}. \tag{13.11}$$

This approach is efficient when you find a significant interaction and need to test the simple contrasts to explore its nature. In many computer packages, the contrasts on the right-hand side of Equation 13.11 are easier to specify than the interaction itself, so you may find it convenient to calculate its sum of squares this way.

The degrees of freedom for this interaction are the product of the degrees of freedom for the contrast (df_{ψ_A}) and those for the intact effect (df_B):

$$df_{\psi_A \times B} = df_{\psi_A} \times df_B = (1)(b-1) = b - 1. \tag{13.12}$$

We finish the analysis by calculating the mean square and testing it as usual against the within-cell error, $MS_{S/AB}$.

Numerical Example

Now return to Table 13.6. It is helpful to conduct the calculations systematically, in a table like Table 13.7. First we list the means of the groups and the relevant marginal means, as we have done in the left part of the table. To this table, we add a pair of columns for each interaction component that we want to test. In the first column, we enter the value of the contrast for that row, either a simple contrast or a main contrast. For example, using the linear contrast, the second and fourth rows (group means and marginal means, respectively) are

$$\widehat{\psi}_{A_{\text{linear}} \text{ at } b_2} = (-2)\bar{Y}_{12} + (-1)\bar{Y}_{22} + 0\bar{Y}_{32} + 1\bar{Y}_{42} + 2\bar{Y}_{52}$$
$$= (-2)(1.3) + (-1)(4.7) + (0)(7.3) + (1)(7.7) + (2)(6.2) = 12.8,$$

$$\widehat{\psi}_{A_{\text{linear}}} = (-2)\bar{Y}_{A_1} + (-1)\bar{Y}_{A_2} + 0\bar{Y}_{A_3} + 1\bar{Y}_{A_4} + 2\bar{Y}_{A_5}$$
$$= (-2)(2.067) + (-1)(3.467) + \cdots + (1)(4.333) + (2)(3.533) = 3.798.$$

We find the sum of squares for the interaction component using Equation 13.10:

$$SS_{A_{\text{linear}} \times B} = \frac{n[\sum_k (\widehat{\psi}_{A_{\text{linear}} \text{ at } b_k} - \widehat{\psi}_{A_{\text{linear}}})^2]}{\sum c_j^2}$$
$$= \frac{(5)[(-0.2 - 3.798)^2 + (12.8 - 3.798)^2 + (-1.2 - 3.798)^2]}{(-2)^2 + (-1)^2 + 0^2 + 1^2 + 2^2}$$
$$= \frac{(5)(122.00)}{10} = 61.00.$$

Table 13.7: *Calculation of the linear and quadratic interaction components for Table 13.6.*

	\multicolumn{5}{c}{Original means}	\multicolumn{2}{c}{Linear}	\multicolumn{2}{c}{Quadratic}
	a_1	a_2	a_3	a_4	a_5	$\widehat{\psi}_{A_{\text{lin}}}$	$SS_{A_{\text{lin}}}$	$\widehat{\psi}_{A_{\text{quad}}}$	$SS_{A_{\text{quad}}}$
b_1	2.2	3.3	1.9	2.3	2.6	-0.200	0.02	0.200	0.01
b_2	1.3	4.7	7.3	7.7	6.2	12.800	81.92	-12.000	51.43
b_3	2.7	2.4	2.5	3.0	1.8	-1.200	0.72	-1.400	0.70
$\overline{Y}_{A_j}$	2.067	3.467	3.900	4.333	3.533	3.798	21.64	-4.400	20.74

If use Equation 13.11, we can perform the calculations directly in the table. In the second of the added columns, we enter the sum of squares for each contrast. Again for the second and fourth rows:

$$SS_{\psi_{A_{\text{linear}}} \text{ at } b_2} = \frac{n\widehat{\psi}^2_{A_{\text{linear}} \text{ at } b_2}}{\sum c_j^2} = \frac{(5)(12.8)^2}{10} = 81.92.$$

$$SS_{A_{\text{linear}}} = \frac{bn\widehat{\psi}^2_{A_{\text{linear}}}}{\sum c_j^2} = \frac{(3)(5)(3.798)^2}{10} = 21.64.$$

Finally, we combine this information in Equation 13.10:

$$SS_{A_{\text{linear}} \times B} = \sum SS_{A_{\text{linear}}} - SS_{A_{\text{linear}}} = (0.02 + 81.92 + 0.72) - 21.64 = 61.02.$$

This is the same value we obtained by the other method, except for differences due to rounding—we will use 61.00 in subsequent calculations.

This effect has $df_{\psi_A \times B} = b - 1 = 2$ (Equation 13.12), and the mean square and F ratio are

$$MS_{A_{\text{linear}} \times B} = 61.00/2 = 30.50 \quad \text{and} \quad F = 30.50/3.31 = 9.21.$$

This result is significant at the 5 percent level (against $F_{.05}(2, 60) = 3.15$), so we conclude that the slopes of the lines in Figure 13.1 are not the same. To continue, we would test the significance of the individual simple linear contrasts (and find that linear trend is significant at level b_2, but not at b_1 and b_3).

What about the nonlinear portion of the effect? We could look at the quadratic component or at all the remaining components at once. The test of the quadratic component is usually more powerful. We perform this test simply by using the quadratic contrast in the same type of analysis we just illustrated for linear trend. Using the preliminary calculations in the last two columns of Table 13.7, you can verify that $MS_{A_{\text{quadratic}} \times B} = 31.40/2 = 15.70$ and $F = 15.70/3.31 = 4.74$. This value is significant. A follow-up analysis reveals that the quadratic component is significant at b_2, but not at the other two levels.

Testing for nonlinear effects by looking at all the nonlinear variability at once is sensitive to a wider range of shapes, but it is less specifically attuned to curvature and therefore less powerful. The test itself is easy: All we do is subtract the sum of squares for the linear interaction component from $SS_{A \times B}$:

$$SS_{A_{\text{nonlinear}} \times B} = SS_{A \times B} - SS_{A_{\text{linear}} \times B} = 100.22 - 61.00 = 39.22,$$

which is associated with the corresponding difference in degrees of freedom:

$$df_{A_{\text{nonlinear}} \times B} = df_{A \times B} - df_{A_{\text{linear}} \times B} = 8 - 2 = 6.$$

A test of this residual variation shows

$$MS_{A_{\text{nonlinear}} \times B} = 39.22/6 = 6.54 \quad \text{and} \quad F = 6.54/3.31 = 1.98.$$

In contrast to the test of the quadratic component alone, this result is not significant $(F_{.05}(6, 60) = 2.25)$. You can see from the smaller mean square that this test is attenuated by mixing the quadratic component with the less plausible cubic and quartic parts. When you are only interested in the curvature, we would advocate the more specific approach.

13.5 Contrasts Outside the Factorial Structure

The analyses we have considered so far make use of the factorial structure of the design. The main-effect contrasts, simple contrasts, and interaction components are defined using that structure. Often this approach is the easiest to use and certainly it is the most familiar. However, you should not feel constrained to use it when some other organization of the analysis is simpler to understand or more informative. We will briefly consider three types of contrasts in this section: pairwise contrasts, where the groups are not confined to a single row or column of the table of means; complex contrasts that relate one set of means to another; and contrasts that express patterns of means derived from a theory.

Computationally, these analyses are based on procedures we have already covered. We remarked at the start of this chapter that an $A \times B$ factorial design can be treated as a one-way design with ab groups and that any single-df hypothesis can be thought of as a contrast applied to these groups. The sum of squares for this hypothesis are calculated using Equations 13.4 and 13.8:

$$\widehat{\psi} = \sum c_{jk} \overline{Y}_{jk} \quad \text{and} \quad SS_\psi = \frac{n\widehat{\psi}^2}{\sum c_{jk}^2}. \tag{13.13}$$

There is nothing new here, so we will focus on the coefficients that define the contrast.

Non-Factorial Contrasts

In many factorial designs, it is hard to interpret comparisons between groups that come from different rows and different columns. Because they vary on both factors, the reason for their difference can be ambiguous and difficult to pin down. Thus, it is almost never useful to make pairwise comparisons among all the groups in a factorial design. In certain designs, however, specific comparisons that cross the factorial boundaries are meaningful.

A good example of such a design is the study of two training programs introduced in Figure 12.3 (p. 255). Factor A was the use (a_2) or nonuse (a_1) of training procedure A, and factor B was the use (b_2) or nonuse (b_1) of training procedure B. Table 13.8 gives a set of means for this study, with an analysis of variance (based on $n = 10$ subjects per cell). Suppose we wanted to know whether the two training methods differed in effectiveness. The comparison that tests this hypothesis is between the condition that used method A and not B (group a_2b_1), and the condition that used

Table 13.8: Results from a study of the combination of two training procedures.

Means

	Training B		
Training A	No (b_1)	Yes (b_2)	Mean
No (a_1)	8.20	8.90	8.55
Yes (a_2)	10.20	16.70	13.45
Mean	9.20	12.80	11.00

Analysis of variance

Source	$\widehat{\psi}$	SS	df	MS	F
A		240.10	1	240.10	17.85*
B		129.60	1	129.60	9.64*
$A \times B$		84.10	1	84.10	6.25*
ψ_1	1.30	8.45	1	8.45	0.63
ψ_2	7.60	434.29	1	434.29	32.29*
ψ_3	1.35	12.15	1	12.15	0.90
Between		453.80	3		
S/AB		484.20	36	13.45	
Total		938.00	39		

*$p < .05$

B and not A (group $a_1 b_2$). This contrast is $\psi_1 = \mu_{21} - \mu_{12}$, which cuts across the factorial design. Its observed value is

$$\widehat{\psi}_1 = \bar{Y}_{21} - \bar{Y}_{12} = 10.20 - 8.90 = 1.30.$$

We have entered this value and its sum of squares (calculated from Equations 13.13) in the analysis of variance in Table 13.8. It is not significant.

The same example shows how complex contrasts can arise outside the factorial structure. The means in Table 13.8 appear to show little or no effect of either training condition individually, but a sizeable effect in combination—the idealized pattern in the left panel of Figure 12.3. None of the analyses considered so far tests this particular hypothesis directly. The standard analysis of variance, for example, gives no help in verifying this impression. An analysis of the simple effects in the rows and columns is more useful. This analysis reveals that neither training A nor B by itself is significantly different from no training at all (the simple effects in the first column, $10.20 - 8.20 = 2.00$, and in the first row, $8.90 - 8.20 = 0.70$, respectively), but the combined training is significantly better than either training A or B alone (the simple effects in the second column, $16.70 - 8.90 = 7.80$, and in the second row, $16.70 - 10.20 = 6.5$, respectively). These analyses are not highly focused, however. A more direct approach is to create a single contrast ψ_2 that specifically compares the combination of both training procedures ($a_2 b_2$) to the average of the other three groups:

$$\widehat{\psi}_2 = \bar{Y}_{22} - \tfrac{1}{3}(\bar{Y}_{11} + \bar{Y}_{21} + \bar{Y}_{12}) = 16.70 - \tfrac{1}{3}(8.20 + 10.20 + 8.90) = 7.60.$$

This contrast and its sum of squares are also given in the table. It is significant, implying that the combination is better than the other conditions combined.

We should not stop here. The test of the contrast tells us the dual-training condition exceeds the mean of the other three conditions, but not whether the two single-training conditions and the no-training control are really equivalent. Although this assumption seems reasonable from an inspection of the means in Table 13.8, it should be evaluated statistically. One way is to look at the three contrasts between each pair of means; we examined these above and found none to be significant. Another possibility is to conduct an omnibus test of the three groups that were combined in ψ_2. Following the procedure illustrated in Section 4.7, the sum of squares that measures the variability among the three means (8.20, 10.20, and 8.90, with mean 9.10) is

$$SS_{\text{set}} = n \sum (\bar{Y}_{jk} - \bar{Y}_{\text{set}})^2$$
$$= (10)[(8.20 - 9.10)^2 + (10.20 - 9.10)^2 + (8.90 - 9.10)^2] = 20.60.$$

This value gives $MS_{\text{set}} = 20.60/2 = 10.30$ and $F = 10.30/13.45 = 0.77$, which is not significant, suggesting that neither training procedure is effective by itself. A particularly elegant approach is to investigate a third contrast that compares the two groups that received one training procedure to the control condition that received none, $\psi_3 = (\mu_{21} + \mu_{12})/2 - \mu_{11}$:

$$\widehat{\psi}_3 = \tfrac{1}{2}(\bar{Y}_{21} + \bar{Y}_{12}) - \bar{Y}_{11} = \tfrac{1}{2}(10.20 + 8.90) - 8.20 = 1.35.$$

As shown in the table, this difference is not significant. What makes this approach "elegant" is that the contrasts ψ_1, ψ_2, and ψ_3 are mutually orthogonal. Together they fully account for all the systematic variability in the experiment, just as the conventional analysis does—that is,

$$SS_{\psi_1} + SS_{\psi_2} + SS_{\psi_3} = SS_{\text{between}} = SS_A + SS_B + SS_{A \times B}$$

(the small discrepancy is due to rounding error). The analysis through these non-factorial contrasts is more appropriate to this study than is the partition into conventional factorial effects.

Our purpose in this section has been to suggest that flexibility is necessary when analyzing a factorial experiment. The conventional analysis is often only a preliminary step and sometimes is unnecessary (although most researchers would routinely conduct it). When the nature of the design suggests components of the effect that fall outside the factorial structure of the experiment, you should be ready to analyze them.

Predicted Patterns of the Group Means

Contrasts that fall outside the conventional analysis also occur when they are used to measure agreement with the pattern suggested by a theory. We described this approach for one-way designs on pages 81–83. That discussion also applies to factorial designs. These predictions usually produce contrasts that involve all the groups (or at least most of them), and so they cut across the standard effects by treating the experiment as a one-way design with ab groups.[4]

---

[4]We should note that some controversy surrounds this procedure, particularly as applied to a factorial experiment, and that it can never prove a theory correct. See our discussion earlier and the references in footnote 7 on page 81.

For example, suppose that you have a theory that predicts that the means in a 2×2 design should be ordered $\mu_{11} < \mu_{21} < \mu_{12} < \mu_{22}$. This is a hypothesis about a monotonic sequence, and we can investigate it using the Abelson-Tukey monotonic trend contrasts (Section 5.6). Specifically, support for this predicted ordering would come from finding a substantial value for the contrast[5]

$$\psi_{\mathrm{monotone}} = -6\mu_{11} - \mu_{21} + \mu_{12} + 6\mu_{22}.$$

Only a positive value of this contrast would support the theory; a negative one would indicate that it was drastically wrong.

As we said in Section 5.6 (and in our analysis of Table 13.8), rejecting the hypothesis that $\psi_{\mathrm{monotone}} = 0$ in favor of the alternative that it is positive is only part of what we need to do to support a theoretical ordering of the conditions. It is also necessary to show that other relationships are not present. The best way to do this is to test specific hypotheses that are orthogonal to ψ_{monotone}. The tests of failure to fit (see Equation 4.16, p. 82) can also be used. Specifically, we would calculate

$$SS_{\mathrm{failure}} = SS_{\mathrm{between}} - SS_{\mathrm{monotone}} = (SS_A + SS_B + SS_{A \times B}) - SS_{\mathrm{monotone}},$$

with $df_{\mathrm{failure}} = df_{\mathrm{between}} - df_{\mathrm{monotone}} = (ab - 1) - 1 = ab - 2$, and test it against the usual error term $MS_{S/AB}$. If the result is significant, then the theory that led to the original ordering of the means is incomplete and needs to be expanded.

13.6 Multiple Tests and Type I Error

In our discussion of interaction components and interaction contrasts, we have ignored the problem of Type I error. In fact, the issues of multiple comparisons discussed in Chapter 6 and Section 12.7 are all relevant. We would certainly have an inflated familywise error rate if we were to look at all the potential interaction contrasts and report only those that were significant by some standard criterion. Some sort of adjustment for multiple testing is necessary if we are not to fool ourselves.

Interaction components, particularly interaction contrasts, describe very precise relationships among the treatments. Only a few of them will focus on the precise point of the research in most studies. Those that do are planned comparisons and should be tested without concern for familywise error. It is certainly appropriate to treat a small set of the most relevant tests as planned.

On the other hand, an unrestrained proliferation of interaction contrasts distorts the notion of planning. Not all interaction contrasts are of equal importance, nor are they equally likely to be present. For a post-hoc search of the data, we need some way to reduce the per-comparison error rate and hold the familywise error rate under reasonable control. Based on our discussion of the one-way design in Chapter 6, we can offer some suggestions on how to proceed.

Often a researcher will investigate a significant interaction by dividing the data into the set of 2×2 subtables formed by crossing a large number of pairwise comparisons for both factors and then looking for an interaction in each of them. Error control

---

[5]We obtained this contrast by applying the linear-2-4 rule on page 109. We started with the linear trend contrast with coefficients $\{-3, -1, 1, 3\}$ from Appendix A.3. Then we quadrupled the outside coefficients and doubled the next two to produce $\{-12, -2, 2, 12\}$. Finally, we divided by 2 to remove the common factor.

in this family of interaction contrasts may be achieved with the Šidák-Bonferroni inequality (Section 6.3), which adjusts the per-comparison error α according to the size of the contemplated family of tests. We can calculate the maximum number of these pairwise tables by noting that, at most, there are $a(a - 1)/2$ pairs of groups created from the a conditions of factor A and $b(b - 1)/2$ pairs of groups created from the b conditions of factor B. Multiplying these two values gives the total number of pairwise interaction contrasts in this family. For example, in a 3×3 design, each of the factors yields a total of $3(3 - 1)/2 = 3$ pairs. When we cross the three contrasts ψ_A with the three contrasts ψ_B, we produce a total of nine 2×2 interaction contrasts. The Šidák-Bonferroni tables in Appendix A.4 give us the adjusted per-comparison α for different levels of α_{FW} and the critical value of t for the 9 interaction contrasts in our present example. With a concern for maintaining reasonable power, we could set the familywise error rate at $\alpha_{FW} = .10$. Turning to the table for an overall error rate of 10% and locating the column numbered 9 tests, we find at the top of the column that this set of interaction contrasts will be tested at the $\alpha = 0.01164$ level, which is useful information if you are using a computer program that prints out descriptive probability values.[6] Alternatively, you can find the critical value of t by looking up the tabled entry for the degrees of freedom in the error term. If there were 10 subjects per group, then $df_{S/AB} = 81$, and the critical value of t is about 2.58 (using the $df = 80$ line of the table). We would test the contrast with a t test, using Equation 4.9 (p. 71) and this critical value. If we were working with F tests instead, we would use $F = t^2 = (2.58)^2 = 6.66$. The Šidák-Bonferroni strategy is also appropriate for a complete set of orthogonal interaction contrasts, as in Table 13.5.

This procedure will not work when sifting through data, looking at pairwise and more complex interaction contrasts. Under these circumstances, the number of possible interaction contrasts is so large that the Šidák-Bonferroni inequality is overly conservative. You are better off using the Scheffé criterion applied to the $A \times B$ interaction. Adapting Equation 6.11 (p. 128) for an interaction contrast, the critical value for F over the family of interaction effects is

$$F_{\text{Scheffé}} = df_{A \times B} F_{\alpha_{FW}}(df_{A \times B}, df_{S/AB}). \tag{13.14}$$

Specifically, for a 3×3 design with 10 subjects per condition and $\alpha_{FW} = .10$, this critical value is

$$F_{\text{Scheffé}} = (4)F_{.10}(4, 80) = (4)(2.02) = 8.08.$$

The critical value of t is the square root of this value ($t_{\text{Scheffé}} = \sqrt{8.08} = 2.84$). This value is slightly larger than the one from the Šidák-Bonferroni tables in the last paragraph, but not too much, considering the greatly expanded pool of contrasts.

Exercises

13.1. Problem 12.4 involved an experiment on selective breeding in which one of the independent variables (factor A) consisted of three strains of rats (bright, mixed, and dull) and the other (factor B) consisted of two different environments in which the rats were raised (enriched and impoverished). Factor A lends itself to a number of

---

[6]When the number of contrasts exceeds the values in our tables, you can calculate a significance level using Equation 6.5 on any "scientific" calculator.

meaningful single-df comparisons. For example, a comparison between the bright and dull rats reflects both the positive and the negative effects of the selective breeding, while a comparison between bright and mixed focuses on the positive effects, and a comparison between dull and mixed focuses on the negative effects. If you treat the two levels of factor B as a contrast rather than an intact factor, you can form a different interaction contrast by crossing ψ_B (factor B) with each of these single-df comparisons ψ_A involving the three strains of rats. For each one,

a. Form the relevant 2×2 subtable of means.
b. Calculate the sum of squares for the interaction contrast and test its significance.
c. State in words the nature of the interaction.

13.2. In Section 12.5, we analyzed the simple effects in our numerical example with monkeys solving problems (the data came from Table 11.8, p. 221), and we found that admistering drug X significantly increased the number of errors relative to the control for the satiated monkeys (b_1) but not for the hungry monkeys (b_2). When we summarized these result (p. 258), we noted that the analysis was not complete until we determine whether the two simple effects were actually different. Is this difference significant? What can you conclude?

13.3. Another way to approach the analysis of the data in Problem 13.2 is to consider interaction contrasts directly. Factor A lends itself to several other meaningful contrasts. Use each to form an interaction contrast with the two drive conditions and test each for significance. If an interaction contrast is significant, test the simple effects of ψ_A at b_1 and b_2.

a. Drug Y versus the control.
b. Drug X versus drug Y.
c. The control versus the two combined drug conditions.

13.4. In Problem 12.3, a significant linear effect of shock intensity for the rats learning an easy discrimination task (b_1) was found. Some questions left unanswered by this analysis concerns the possibility of linear effects for the rats given either a medium or hard difficulty task and whether the slopes are the same for all tasks.

a. Test the hypothesis that $\psi_{\text{linear}} = 0$ for the medium and hard tasks.
b. Test the linear contrast-by-factor interaction component.

13.5. Suppose we are interested in the effects of two independent variables on the solving of problems by fifth-grade students, factor A consisting of two levels of problem complexity (simple and complex) and factor B of three levels of incentive (verbal praise, monetary reward, and no specific incentive). Ten children are randomly assigned to each condition. The response measure is the number of problems solved in 20 minutes. The means for the six groups are:

Task (A)	Incentive condition (B)			
	Verbal	Monetary	None	Mean
Simple	14.40	13.20	14.10	13.90
Complex	9.60	11.90	6.40	9.30
Mean	12.00	12.55	10.25	11.60

Assume that $MS_{S/AB} = 15.00$. The interaction in this design is significant ($MS_{AB} = 51.35$, $F = 3.42$), but noting this fact does not complete the analysis. The researcher would go on to test certain interaction comparisons.

a. One important interaction contrast is formed by crossing the two incentive conditions (verbal versus monetary) with the two levels of the task variable (simple versus complex). Test the significance of this interaction. What does it reveal?

b. Given the outcome of the test in part a, the researcher may decide to combine the two incentive conditions (verbal and monetary) and to form an interaction contrast comparing the difference between the combined incentive conditions and the control condition (none) at the two levels of the task variable. What does this test reveal?

c. Because the interaction contrast in part b is significant, the researcher would probably be interested in assessing the significance of the simple comparisons. Determine whether the difference between the combined incentive condition and the control condition is significant for the simple task and for the complex task.

13.6. Consider an experiment in which performance on a task is studied as a function of pretraining. One independent variable (factor A) is the nature of the pretraining, facilitating or interfering, and the other variable (factor B) is the amount of pretraining—3, 6, 9, and 12 trials. The treatment mean (based on $n = 10$) are

Amount of pretraining

Pretraining	b_1	b_2	b_3	b_4	Sum
Facilitating (a_1)	2.9	4.2	4.6	3.5	3.800
Interfering (a_2)	2.4	1.5	1.2	2.0	1.775
Sum	2.65	2.85	2.90	2.75	2.788

Assume that $MS_{S/AB} = 2.400$.

a. Because the $A \times B$ interaction is significant ($F_{A \times B} = 8.247/2.400 = 3.44$) and factor B is a quantitative manipulation, a natural next step is to examine the trend components of the interaction. Test the linear and quadratic interaction components ($A \times \psi_{\text{linear}}$ and $A \times \psi_{\text{quadratic}}$, respectively) and describe what they show.

b. The quadratic component of the interaction in part b was significant. Examine the simple quadratic trend for both types of pretraining(factor A) and describe the results.

13.7. Table 13.8 was analyzed both using the conventional effects and nonfactorial contrasts.

a. Verify the analyses presented in Table 13.8.

b. Demonstrate that the three contrasts in Table 13.8 are mutually orthogonal.

Part IV

THE GENERAL LINEAR MODEL

In the previous chapters, we have primarily considered situations in which the different independent variables were cleanly separated from each other. For example, in the factorial design, the influence of factor A is distinct from the influence of factor B. In particular, knowing how a subject was classified on factor A tells us nothing about how that subject was classified on factor B. Such factors are said to be **orthogonal** to each other, in the same sense that the contrasts in Chapter 4 could be orthogonal. We mentioned there that most pairs of contrasts are not orthogonal (although we did point out that orthogonal contrasts are easier to interpret). In this part, we discuss two types of designs in which the researcher must take account of potential nonorthogonality among the major factors of the design.

The first of these designs is the factorial analysis of variance with groups of different sizes. We emphasized the equal-sample designs in Part II and III because they are the easiest to understand and to analyze and because they are the most resistant to violations of the assumptions underlying the statistical models. However, there are many ways that unequally sized groups can arise. Sometimes accidental loss of subjects is the problem, and sometimes the inequalities are intrinsic to the design. However they arise, these inequalities create associations among the independent variables of the analysis. These associations, in turn, complicate the analysis of variance and its interpretation. We will discuss how to treat these **nonorthogonal** or **unbalanced designs** (we will use either term) in Chapter 14.

In Chapter 15 we discuss an extension of the analysis of variance known as the **analysis of covariance**. In this analysis, some information is available about the value of the dependent variable through an ancillary numerical variable known as a **covariate**. This numerical information is used to improve the quality of the analysis in two ways: by decreasing the size of the mean square against which the effects are tested and by making the groups more comparable. However, the analysis of covariance is subject to the same type of nonorthogonality as the unbalanced factorial design and must be approached in the same way.

The treatment of both these designs is much simpler than it was when the first edition of this book was written. At that time, considerable controversy surrounded both procedures. Hand calculation was necessary, and the resulting algorithms were complicated, difficult to follow, and gave little intuitive understanding of the procedures. Few computer programs were available. This situation has changed. Both the nonorthogonal analysis of variance and the analysis of covariance have been incorporated into the major computer packages, to the extent that their application is almost transparent to the user. The interpretation of the outcome, however, particularly for the analysis of covariance, can still be confusing.

Both the analysis of factorial designs with unequal cells and the analysis of covariance require us to approach to the analysis differently from the more traditional presentation in the earlier chapters. That approach gives the most direct understanding of how the analysis of variance works, what effects can be tested, and the basic logic of the tests. Its extension to unbalanced designs is awkward, however, and its application to the analysis of covariance is far from obvious. Both are better understood through an approach based on what is known as the **general linear model**. This method of analysis is flexible enough that it subsumes the calculations in the analysis of variance, the analysis of covariance, and multiple regression. It gives the same answers for balanced designs as the traditional approach but readily accommodates the unbalanced designs. All the modern computer packages use it. We will discuss this procedure in Section 14.1, then apply it to the two designs.

These two chapters differ from those elsewhere in this book in an important respect. The calculations needed to apply the general linear model are sufficiently complicated that, except for very simple examples, they obscure understanding more than help it. A computer is essential. Accordingly, we will emphasize the conceptual basis of the analysis and will assume that you will use a computer program when you come to apply these procedures to data. You won't find the same sort of "hands-on" calculation that was possible with the traditional approach to balanced designs. However, you will understand the principles by which the general linear model works and the potentials and pitfalls of applying it to unbalanced designs and the analysis of covariance. You will understand what the computer is doing and be able to identify and interpret the output it produces.

14

The General Linear Model and Unbalanced Designs

The ideal for most research designs is to have an equal number of subjects in each group. However, unequal sample sizes are often the reality, even in studies that were planned to have equal samples. Sometimes the source of subjects dries up before the study is complete. For example, the term may end while some groups still need a few more college-student subjects. An unexpected loss of data from illness or equipment failures also can produce unequal groups. The use of classification factors whose levels can only be determined after the sampling has occurred almost always leads to unequal groups. Inequalities of this type are more fundamental to the analysis than those produced by accidents, as the differences in sample sizes usually reflect differences in the underlying population. For example, suppose that after completing an experiment with college students, you might group your subjects by college major into natural sciences, social sciences, and humanities. It is unlikely that you will have equal number of students in these majors, particularly if the sizes of the original populations are different (say your school has fewer natural science majors than social science majors). The problems of unequal samples is further complicated when several classification factors are used, for example, if you also classified the students by gender.

The likelihood of obtaining unequal groups is even greater for nonexperimental designs in which the assignment to groups is out of the researcher's control. For example, a political psychologist who is analyzing a survey and wishes to divide up the respondents by their self-reported race and occupation will surely obtain unequal groups. Traditionally, these types of design have been analyzed by techniques other than the factorial analysis of variance, such as multiple regression. Nevertheless, researchers are often interested in hypotheses that are identical to those of the analysis of variance. For example, the researcher classifying the respondents with respect to race and occupation may wish to know whether the occupational groups differ in average age or in agreement with a political statement and whether these differences interacted with race. Hypotheses like these should be tested with the same statistical procedures as other tests of means.

Section 3.5 described how to test for differences among means in a one-way design with unequal samples. That test was essentially a generalization of the equal-sample procedure. When we consider factorial designs, however, the issues related to sample size are more complex. Not only are there several different computational procedures available, but several distinct null hypotheses can be tested. The whole topic of the analysis of factorial designs with unequal samples has been the subject of considerable debate in the not-so-distant past. Several approaches were developed and their differences hotly argued. Happily, a consensus on how to proceed has now largely been reached. Nevertheless, even within the optimal approach, several choices must be made, and computer programs typically give you several alternatives. For most purposes, one of these is best, and it is this approach that we will discuss.

14.1   The General Linear Model

To analyze experiments with unequal samples, the statistical procedures of the analysis of variance must be given in a more general form. Statisticians have observed that most varieties of the analysis of variance can be expressed in a common way and that this representation also includes related techniques such as multiple regression. This approach is known as the **general linear model**.

An analysis using the general linear model is identical to that described earlier in this book in some respects, but it differs in others. The similar parts are the fundamental questions—the hypotheses about means, interactions, and contrasts—and the overall testing strategy. We still find sums of squares for the effects and for error and, using their degrees of freedom, conduct tests by computing mean squares and comparing them in F ratios. Where the procedures differ is in the logic by which the sums of squares are found. We will illustrate this approach in this section by returning to the one-way analysis of variance and re-analyzing the data we considered there. In this simple situation, we can follow the logic of this approach step by step and see that the final outcome coincides with that described in Section 3.5. Following this example, we will present the analysis of the general linear model in a form that allows it to be extended to more complex designs.

A Numerical Example

The one-way data that we will re-analyze are from the three-group study with unequal samples that we presented in Section 3.5. The first column of Table 14.1 shows those data again, with all the scores in a single column and separated into the three groups by horizontal lines. We want to test for differences among the means of these groups. We will make this test by comparing what happens when the null hypothesis is true to what can happen when it is not.

The first block of three columns in Table 14.1 shows what happens when the null hypothesis is true. Under this hypothesis, the means for the three groups are equal to a single value. Our best guess for this value is the average of all 13 scores:

$$\bar{Y}_T = \frac{\sum Y_{ij}}{\sum n_j} = \frac{5 + 9 + \cdots + 5 + 6}{3 + 6 + 4} = \frac{101}{13} = 7.77.$$

This single value is entered for each subject in the second column of the table. We can measure how well the null hypothesis describes the data by calculating the sum of the

Table 14.1: Data from three groups (from Table 3.7, p. 57) with descriptions fitted under the null hypothesis (first block of three columns) and its alternative (second block).

Group	Y_{ij}	$\bar{Y}_T$	$Y_{ij} - \bar{Y}_T$	$(Y_{ij} - \bar{Y}_T)^2$	$\bar{Y}_j$	$Y_{ij} - \bar{Y}_j$	$(Y_{ij} - \bar{Y}_j)^2$
			Null hypothesis true			Null hypothesis false	
a_1	5	7.77	−2.77	7.67	7.00	−2.00	4.00
	9	7.77	1.23	1.51	7.00	2.00	4.00
	7	7.77	−0.77	0.59	7.00	0.00	0.00
a_2	12	7.77	4.23	17.90	10.00	2.00	4.00
	10	7.77	2.23	4.97	10.00	0.00	0.00
	10	7.77	2.23	4.97	10.00	0.00	0.00
	8	7.77	0.23	0.05	10.00	−2.00	4.00
	11	7.77	3.23	10.43	10.00	1.00	1.00
	9	7.77	1.23	1.51	10.00	−1.00	1.00
a_3	3	7.77	−4.77	22.75	5.00	−2.00	4.00
	6	7.77	−1.77	3.13	5.00	1.00	1.00
	5	7.77	−2.77	7.67	5.00	0.00	0.00
	6	7.77	−1.77	3.13	5.00	1.00	1.00
Sum of squared deviations:				86.28			24.00

squared deviations between the actual scores Y_{ij} and the value $\bar{Y}_T = 7.77$. The next columns of Table 14.1 show the calculation. The third column contains the deviations, the fourth column their square, and their sum (86.28) is below that column. This sum of squares represents the variability of the Y_{ij} scores that cannot be explained by a description of the data in which the group means are the same. We will denote this **unexplained sum of squares** by $SS_{\text{unexp}}^{H_0}$; the H_0 as a superscript means that it refers to the unexplained variability when the null hypothesis holds.

Now we need to decide if the unexplained variability measured by the sum of squares $SS_{\text{unexp}}^{H_0} = 86.28$ is sufficiently large to question the validity of the null hypothesis. To do so, we compare it to a similar sum of squares in which we allow the null hypothesis to be false. This calculation is shown in the last block of three columns. When the null hypothesis can be false, we can let the means depend on the group, and our best guesses are the actual group means. Thus, the first column in this block contains $\bar{Y}_1 = 7$ for the 3 scores from group a_1, $\bar{Y}_2 = 10$ for the 6 scores from a_2, and $\bar{Y}_3 = 5$ for the 4 scores from group a_3. How well do these values describe the data? In the last two columns we have calculated the discrepancies $Y_{ij} - \bar{Y}_j$ and squared them. You can see that the deviations are smaller than they were when we were restricted to the single value $\bar{Y}_T = 7.77$ by the null hypothesis. At the bottom of the table, we calculate an objective measure of the goodness of this alternate description by summing the squared deviations. We write this sum of squares as $SS_{\text{unexp}}^{H_1}$, which indicates that it represents unexplained variability when we allow ourselves the flexibility of the alternative hypothesis. The value of $SS_{\text{unexp}}^{H_1} = 24.00$ is a considerable improvement over the value of $SS_{\text{unexp}}^{H_0} = 86.28$ that we found for the null hypothesis.

Next we ask what sources of variability contribute to these two sums of squares. When we allow the null hypothesis to be false, only the variability of the scores around the means of the individual groups $\overline{Y}_j$ contributes to the sum of squares, and $SS_{\text{unexp}}^{H_1}$ reflects only experimental error. But when we force the null hypothesis to be true, the unexplained variability includes *both* the differences among sample means and the variability of the scores around those means—a mixture of treatment effects and experimental error. Thus, we can measure the variability produced by the treatment effects by taking the difference between the two unexplained sums of squares:

$$SS_A = SS_{\text{unexp}}^{H_0} - SS_{\text{unexp}}^{H_1}$$
$$= (\text{treatment effects} + \text{error}) - (\text{error})$$
$$= 86.28 - 24.00 = 62.28.$$

Except for differences due to rounding, this value is the same as the sum of squares we calculated in Table 3.7.

In Table 14.1, there are appreciable differences among the group means, which is why SS_A is large. But suppose there had been no differences in the population. You would then expect the group means $\overline{Y}_j$ to be close to the overall mean $\overline{Y}_T$. Any variation in the sample means due to the effects of sampling is likely to be small, so $SS_{\text{unexp}}^{H_0}$ would be only slightly larger than $SS_{\text{unexp}}^{H_1}$, and SS_A would be small. To decide whether SS_A is large or small, we need something to compare it to. This standard is the variability of the individual scores around the sample means, which reflects only sampling error:

$$SS_{\text{error}} = SS_{\text{unexp}}^{H_1} = 24.00.$$

Once we have SS_A and SS_{error}, the analysis parallels the one described in Chapter 3. The degrees of freedom for the two unexplained sums of squares are equal to the number of scores ($N = 13$, the number of rows of Table 14.1) less the number of different values used in the predictions (one for the grand mean μ_T in the null hypothesis, and $a = 3$ for the group means μ_j in the alternative):

$$df_{\text{unexp}}^{H_0} = 13 - 1 = 12 \quad \text{and} \quad df_{\text{unexp}}^{H_1} = 13 - 3 = 10.$$

The degrees of freedom for the effect equals the difference between these values:

$$df_A = df_{\text{unexp}}^{H_0} - df_{\text{unexp}}^{H_1} = 12 - 10 = 2.$$

Because the error is calculated from the alternative-hypothesis part of the table, SS_{error} has the same number of degrees of freedom as $SS_{\text{unexp}}^{H_1}$, in this case 10. Now we can calculate the mean squares:

$$MS_A = \frac{SS_A}{df_A} = \frac{62.28}{2} = 31.14 \quad \text{and} \quad MS_{\text{error}} = \frac{SS_{\text{error}}}{df_{\text{error}}} = \frac{24.00}{10} = 2.40.$$

These mean squares are compared in an F ratio:

$$F = \frac{MS_A}{MS_{\text{error}}} = \frac{31.14}{2.40} = 12.98.$$

To evaluate this observed test statistic, we use the standard F distribution, in this case $F_{.05}(2, 10) = 4.10$. The null hypothesis is rejected, implying that the groups differ. Although the calculations were done differently, we obtain exactly the same results as in Section 3.5.

The test of the equality of the means in Table 14.1 is fairly straightforward. However, it is not immediately clear how these methods apply to more complicated designs. The rest of this section describes how to compare the unexplained variability under the null and alternative hypotheses in a more rigorous way. We will then be able to analyze the factorial designs.

The Linear Model

The basis for the analysis of nonorthogonal designs is the linear model in Section 7.1. For the one-way design, that model (Equation 7.3, p. 133) is

$$Y_{ij} = \mu_T + \alpha_j + E_{ij} \quad \text{with} \quad \sum \alpha_j = 0. \tag{14.1}$$

Because it includes a parameter $\alpha_j = \mu_j - \mu_T$ for each group, this model can describe the data under the alternative hypothesis, where treatment effects α_j are present. We call Equation 14.1 the **alternative-hypothesis model**. The null hypothesis for the analysis of variance asserts that the parameters α_j are all equal to zero. When that hypothesis holds, Equation 14.1 turns into the simpler **null-hypothesis model**:

$$Y_{ij} = \mu_T + E_{ij}. \tag{14.2}$$

The two models have a fundamental asymmetry. The null-hypothesis model is correct *only* when the null hypothesis holds, but the alternative-hypothesis model is correct when *either* hypothesis holds. When the null hypothesis it true, both models fit the data; when it is false, the more flexible alternative-hypothesis model fits the data better than the inflexible null-hypothesis model. The two models (unlike the two hypotheses) form a **hierarchical pair**, in which the null-hypothesis model is a special case of the other. This hierarchical relationship is the key to testing the null hypothesis.

Equations 14.1 and 14.2 have the same form. Each is the sum of a systematic portion that expresses the hypothesized relationship among the group means (μ_T for H_0 and $\mu_T + \alpha_j$ for H_1) and a random error E_{ij}. In the general linear model, the systematic portion is always a linear, or additive, function of a set of parameters, and the error is a normally distributed random variable. The linear model for the two-way design (Equation 11.14, p. 225) has this structure:

$$Y_{ijk} = \mu_T + \alpha_j + \beta_k + (\alpha\beta)_{jk} + E_{ijk}.$$

The systematic portion is the sum of the four Greek-letter parameters, and the error is the normally distributed random variable E_{ijk}. Almost all the models in this book have this form.

The observable counterparts of the systematic and unsystematic parts of the linear model for the one-way design are shown in Table 14.1. The columns labeled $\bar{Y}_T$ and $Y_{ij} - \bar{Y}_T$ are estimates of the systematic (μ_T) and random (E_{ij}) portions of the null-hypothesis model (Equation 14.2), and the columns labeled $\bar{Y}_j$ and $Y_{ij} - \bar{Y}_j$ are estimates of the same portions of the less restricted alternative-hypothesis model (Equation 14.1). The F statistic gives a test that compares the unexplained variability of the two models. The advantage of this approach, as Table 14.1 illustrated, is that it does not depend on having equal samples sizes.

Testing by Model Comparison

Now we'll examine how hypotheses are tested using the general linear model.[1] The testing strategy rests on several important ideas. The first of these is the comparison of hierarchical models. When testing any null hypothesis, we construct a hierarchical pair of linear models that differ in whether the effect to be tested is included or not. The two linear models for the one-way design defined above are such a hierarchical pair. The alternative-hypothesis model in Equation 14.1 *allows* the means to differ, and the null-hypothesis model in Equation 14.2 *forces* them to be the same. The models differ by the parameter α_j, and the null hypothesis that we want to test is that $\alpha_j = 0$. Thus, when the null hypothesis is true, Equation 14.1 turns into Equation 14.2. Usually we can write the alternative-hypothesis model first, then strike out the parameter we want to test to produce the appropriate null-hypothesis model.[2] Thus, we create Equation 14.2 by deleting α_j from Equation 14.1. We will illustrate this procedure for the factorial design in Section 14.2.

The second important idea is the concept of unexplained variability. It measures the degree to which a model *does not* agree with the data. We obtain this measure by first fitting the model to the data and then calculating the sum of the squared deviations between the data and the fitted values. We will use the "hat" symbol to indicate the estimates of the scores obtained by fitting a model, for example, $\widehat{Y}_{ij}$. Using this symbol, the sum of squared deviations is:

$$SS_{\text{unexp}} = \sum[(\text{data}) - (\text{fitted value})]^2 = \sum(Y_{ij} - \widehat{Y}_{ij})^2. \qquad (14.3)$$

In the one-way analysis in Table 14.1, $\widehat{Y}_{ij} = Y_T$ for the null-hypothesis model and $\widehat{Y}_{ij} = \overline{Y}_j$ for the alternative-hypothesis model. As we indicated, we will designate the unexplained variability observed under the null-hypothesis model by $SS_{\text{unexp}}^{H_0}$ and that under the alternative-hypothesis model by $SS_{\text{unexp}}^{H_1}$.

The unexplained variability serves two functions. One is to fit models to data. A linear model is fitted to data by minimizing the unexplained variability. Specifically, the **principle of least squares** states that

> *The parameters of any linear model are estimated by choosing the values that make SS_{unexp} defined in Equation 14.3 as small as possible.*

Finding the least-squares solution for a linear model is not difficult in principle, but generally involves a considerable amount of calculation—essentially it amounts to solving a large collection of simultaneous equations. Fortunately, excellent computer algorithms have been developed to perform these calculations, and you need not worry about how they do it.

The other use of the unexplained variability is to construct hypothesis tests. The principle is straightforward:

---

[1]The approach is very general and is applicable to many situation other than the analysis of variance. If you are familiar with the testing strategies in multiple regression analysis, you will note they are applications of the general linear model.

[2]Because eliminating parameters restricts a model, some treatments of this testing strategy refer to the null-hypothesis and the alternative-hypothesis models as the **restricted model** and the **unrestricted model**, respectively.

The sum of squares for the test of a null hypothesis is the difference between the unexplained variability under the null-hypothesis model and that under alternative-hypothesis model:

$$SS_{\text{effect}} = SS_{\text{unexp}}^{H_0} - SS_{\text{unexp}}^{H_1}. \tag{14.4}$$

This difference is always positive because the null-hypothesis model has fewer parameters to estimate and is less flexible than the alternative-hypothesis model. It cannot fit the data better than the alternative-hypothesis model. Large values of the difference are evidence against the null hypothesis. To decide whether a value of SS_{effect} is large enough to reject the null hypothesis, we need a standard, which we will simply call SS_{error}. In most cases, the alternative-hypothesis model specifies all the possible systematic effects, so that what remains after fitting that model is unsystematic variability. In such cases, $SS_{\text{error}} = SS_{\text{unexp}}^{H_1}$.

The third important idea is the number of degrees of freedom associated with a sum of squares. The degrees of freedom for the unexplained variability are calculated directly from the principle we stated in Chapter 3 (Equation 3.2, p. 33). Specifically, the degrees of freedom for the unexplained variability associated with a model are equal to the number of observations (which we have called N) less the number of quantities estimated from the data, i.e., the number of parameters in the model:

$$df_{\text{unexp}} = (\text{observations}) - (\text{parameters}). \tag{14.5}$$

The null-hypothesis model has only one parameter, the common mean μ_T, so

$$df_{\text{unexp}}^{H_0} = N - 1. \tag{14.6}$$

The alternative-hypothesis model has a parameters, one for the grand mean μ_T and $a - 1$ free values of α_j:[3]

$$df_{\text{unexp}}^{H_1} = N - a. \tag{14.7}$$

The degrees of freedom for an effect are calculated by taking the difference between the degrees of freedom of the null- and alternative-hypothesis models:

$$df_{\text{effect}} = df_{\text{unexp}}^{H_0} - df_{\text{unexp}}^{H_1}. \tag{14.8}$$

In the one-way design, the result is our usual value:

$$df_{\text{effect}} = (N - 1) - (N - a) = a - 1.$$

You can see that the equations used to calculate the effect sum of squares and degrees of freedom (Equations 14.4 and 14.8, respectively) are exact parallels of each other.

The final steps of the testing procedure are those of the conventional analysis of variance. The mean squares are found by dividing the sums of squares by their degrees of freedom:

$$MS_{\text{effect}} = \frac{SS_{\text{effect}}}{df_{\text{effect}}} \quad \text{and} \quad MS_{\text{error}} = \frac{SS_{\text{error}}}{df_{\text{error}}}.$$

The test statistic is the ratio of these mean squares:

$$F = \frac{MS_{\text{effect}}}{MS_{\text{error}}},$$

with degrees of freedom $df_{\text{num}} = df_{\text{effect}}$ and $df_{\text{denom}} = df_{\text{error}}$.

---

[3]On first glance, this model seems to have $a + 1$ parameters—the grand mean μ_T and one value of α_j for each group. However, because the α_j sum to zero, we can always find any one of them once we have the $a - 1$ others; for example, with three groups, $\alpha_3 = -\alpha_1 - \alpha_2$. We discussed these constraints when we described the degrees of freedom for a two-way design on pages 218–220.

14.2 The Two-Factor Analysis

We described the general linear model and its use with the one-way design in Section 14.1 so that we could start with something familiar and not too far removed from our earlier treatment of unequal samples in Chapter 3. The principles we developed for this design extend the analysis to designs with more than one factor. When we apply them to data with equal sample sizes, we obtain the same answers as the methods in Part III. Unlike those earlier methods, however, they also work with unequal samples.

We will start our discussion of the two-factor design with an example that illustrates again how unequal frequencies often arise. Suppose a researcher conducts a study in which undergraduate psychology students study common words under one of three different conditions (factor A) and are tested later for their recall. To speed up the study, the researcher has the subjects sign up in groups of up to five subjects, all of whom must be assigned to the same condition. The subjects who sign up for the first session are given treatment a_1, those who sign up for the second session are given treatment a_2, and those who sign up for the third session are given treatment a_3. The researcher goes through this procedure three times, hoping to obtain at least 12 subjects in each condition. However, sometimes three subjects sign up for a session, sometimes four, and sometimes five. In the end, there are 12 subjects in the first condition, 15 in the second, and 10 in the third.

Next, the researcher decides to classify the subjects as male or female, creating a second factor (factor B). The researcher had no control over the gender of the subjects who signed up and could only hope that the frequencies of male and female subjects would balance out over the three conditions. Table 14.2 shows the data that were obtained. The population of students from which the sample was obtained (those students who might have signed up for the study) apparently contained more women than men, and as a result, the sample contains 23 women, but only 14 men. Moreover, they are not distributed evenly over the three conditions, although the differences are not unreasonable for samples of this size.

Before continuing, we have three comments on this example. First, the researcher could have obtained equal samples by recruiting the same number of men and women and randomly assigning one-third of them to each treatment group. Although the analysis then would be cleaner and less vulnerable to heterogeneity of variance, there are practical reasons why many researchers would reject it. The researcher had no direct control of who signed up for the study, so it would be difficult to preselect the groups for equal numbers of men and women. Moreover, the study was completed more rapidly because several subject were run at once, even though the need to assign all subjects in a session to the same condition made the group sizes more variable.[4] Second, many studies include classification factors like the gender factor here. They are important enough to be worth examining, but not central enough to affect the experimental design. Third, you may encounter a recommendation that subjects be randomly discarded from the larger groups until all groups have the same size. We do not advice such a Draconian approach. The smallest group here has only three

---

[4]The possibility that the differences among the sessions was large enough to affect the result is another concern. We will discuss this problem—that of random effects—in Chapter 24.

Table 14.2: Memory retention scores for three treatments (factor A) with the groups divided by gender (factor B).

	Men (b_1)			Women (b_2)		
	a_1	a_2	a_3	a_1	a_2	a_3
	16	21	8	9	22	8
	12	20	18	6	19	10
	9	19	12	15	24	14
	14	15		11	25	7
	17	17		12	19	5
		22		8	19	11
				14	14	8
					26	
					21	
Sum:	68	114	38	75	189	63
n_{jk}:	5	6	3	7	9	7
$\bar{Y}_{jk}$:	13.600	19.000	12.667	10.714	21.000	9.000

subjects, and to reduce all groups to that size would require abandoning more than half the data. The cost in power would be unacceptable and the gains minimal.

The General Linear Model in a Factorial Design

We will start our analysis of Table 14.2 by specifying the hypotheses. There are two populations of subjects, one of men, the other of women. Each subject in these populations can be given any of the three treatments, and we let μ_{11}, μ_{21}, and μ_{31} be the three means for the men under each treatment and μ_{12}, μ_{22}, and μ_{32} be the corresponding means for the women. To look at the treatment effects without regard to the gender factor, we form the averages

$$\mu_{A_1} = \tfrac{1}{2}(\mu_{11} + \mu_{12}), \quad \mu_{A_2} = \tfrac{1}{2}(\mu_{21} + \mu_{22}), \quad \text{and} \quad \mu_{A_3} = \tfrac{1}{2}(\mu_{31} + \mu_{32}). \qquad (14.9)$$

The null hypothesis of no treatment effect (factor A) states that these means are the same, i.e. that $\mu_{A_1} = \mu_{A_2} = \mu_{A_3}$. Similarly, the null hypothesis of no gender effect asserts that $\mu_{B_1} = \mu_{B_2}$, where

$$\mu_{B_1} = \tfrac{1}{3}(\mu_{11} + \mu_{21} + \mu_{31}), \quad \text{and} \quad \mu_{B_2} = \tfrac{1}{3}(\mu_{12} + \mu_{22} + \mu_{32}). \qquad (14.10)$$

Finally, the hypothesis of no interaction states that the simple effect of the treatments for the men, as expressed by the differences among μ_{11}, μ_{21} and μ_{31}, is the same as that for the women, as expressed by the differences among μ_{12}, μ_{22}, and μ_{32}.

To use the general-linear-model approach to test these three hypotheses, we need to construct linear models for which each of the null hypotheses is true. In Section 14.1, the testing procedure for the single-factor design was based on a comparison of a null-hypothesis model in which treatment effects are absent and an alternative-hypothesis model in which they may be present (Equations 14.2 and 14.1, respectively). In the two-factor design, we follow a similar approach but need three pairs of models to compare, one for each of the three hypothesis tests.

A good strategy here is to start with an alternative-hypothesis model that includes all the effects to be tested and simplify it to create the null-hypothesis models. Then each of the three null-hypothesis models is compared with the same alternative-hypothesis model. The starting point is the standard two-factor linear model (Equation 11.14, p. 225):

$$Y_{ijk} = \mu_T + \alpha_j + \beta_k + (\alpha\beta)_{jk} + E_{ijk}. \tag{14.11}$$

Because this alternative-hypothesis model contains all the parameters of the standard two-factor linear model, it is sometimes called the **full linear model** or the **general alternative-hypothesis model**. We now create the three null-hypothesis models by deleting different parameters from this model—in effect, setting them to be equal to zero. For the null-hypothesis model to test for an A effect, we delete the term α_j associated with this effect:

$$Y_{ijk} = \mu_T + \beta_k + (\alpha\beta)_{jk} + E_{ijk}. \tag{14.12}$$

For the null-hypothesis model to test a B effect, we delete β_k from Equation 14.11:

$$Y_{ijk} = \mu_T + \alpha_j + (\alpha\beta)_{jk} + E_{ijk}. \tag{14.13}$$

Finally, to test the interaction effect, we set the $(\alpha\beta)_{jk}$ in the alternative-hypothesis model to zero to produce a null-hypothesis model with no interaction:

$$Y_{ijk} = \mu_T + \alpha_j + \beta_k + E_{ijk}. \tag{14.14}$$

To test the three hypotheses, all four models are separately fitted to the data using the principle of least squares. The alternative-hypothesis model (Equation 14.11) produces estimates $\widehat{Y}_{ijk}$ for the scores that are the same as the appropriate observed group means. The estimates from the other models are all restricted in a way that agrees with the appropriate null hypothesis. Specifically, the null-hypothesis model without α_j (Equation 14.12) produces estimates for which (as we will see numerically below) the marginal A averages are all equal, in accordance with the null hypothesis that $\mu_{A_1} = \mu_{A_2} = \mu_{A_3}$. They may, however, show B or $A{\times}B$ effects. Similarly, the model of Equations 14.13 and 14.14 produce estimates that have, respectively, no marginal B effect and no interaction.

At this point, we follow the general procedure described in Section 14.1. We first determine the unexplained sum of squares for each model by summing the squared deviations between the scores Y_{ijk} and the appropriate estimates $\widehat{Y}_{ijk}$ (Equation 14.3). We then use the four values of SS_{unexp} to calculate sums of squares for the three treatment effects by subtracting the unexplained variability of the alternative-hypothesis model from that of the appropriate null-hypothesis model (Equation 14.4):

$$SS_{\text{effect}} = SS_{\text{unexp}}^{H_0} - SS_{\text{unexp}}^{H_1}. \tag{14.15}$$

The alternative-hypothesis model also provides the sum of squares for the error term used in all the tests:

$$SS_{\text{error}} = SS_{\text{unexp}}^{H_1}. \tag{14.16}$$

The degrees of freedom for these sums of squares can be found from the parameter-counting strategy described in the last section. The number of degrees of freedom for each test is equal to the number of free parameters that have been eliminated from the alternative-hypothesis model in creating the null-hypothesis model. The analysis, which we will not go through in detail, gives values that are the same as those in the ordinary analysis of variance:

$$df_A = a - 1, \quad df_B = b - 1, \quad \text{and} \quad df_{A \times B} = (a - 1)(b - 1).$$

For the error, the number of degrees of freedom equals the number of scores less the number of groups,

$$df_{\text{error}} = N - ab.$$

Numerical Example

It is important to understand the intermediate steps in the analysis of an unbalanced design, even though you will use a computer to analyze your own data and will not need to calculate them yourself. The top part of Table 14.3 gives the means estimated according to the principle of least squares for the four models.[5] For a point of reference, the group means $\overline{Y}_{jk}$ are given as the first column of numbers. The next four columns (labeled by the number of the equation specifying the relevant model) give the estimated values $\widehat{Y}_{ijk}$ that are obtained by fitting each of the models using the principle of least squares. Their values are comparable to those in the second and fifth column of Table 14.1 for the two models in the single-factor design. The first of these columns contains the estimates for the alternative-hypothesis model of Equation 14.11. Because this model includes as many parameters as there are groups, it is able to reproduce the six group means exactly. The remaining three columns contain the estimates for the three null-hypothesis models.

We can now follow the steps set out in Table 14.1—subtracting the appropriate group estimate from each score in that group (i.e. $Y_{ijk} - \widehat{Y}_{ijk}$), squaring the differences, and summing the squares over all subjects to obtain the unexplained sum of squares SS_{unexp}. For example, using the estimates under H_1, we would subtract $\widehat{Y}_{i11} = 13.600$ from each of the $n_{11} = 5$ scores from group $a_1 b_1$, $\widehat{Y}_{i21} = 19.000$ from each of the $n_{21} = 6$ scores from group $a_2 b_1$, and so on. Next, we would square each of these differences and sum them to produce $SS_{\text{unexp}}^{H_1} = 353.295$. Because the means under this model match those of the data perfectly, this model fully accounts for the variation among the different groups. Consequently, the unexplained sum of squares associated with this model reflects only the within-group variation of the scores—the pure error that we referred to as $SS_{S/AB}$ in our earlier treatment—not any failure of this model to reproduce the between-subjects effects.

Each of the null-hypothesis models in Table 14.3 exhibits some degree of failure to fit the group means. The column labeled $H_0(A)$ gives the computer-fitted values for Equation 14.12, which lacks the parameters α_j associated with the A effect. These values do not show a marginal A effect, as we can verify by calculating the three marginal averages (Equations 14.9):

$$\widehat{Y}_{A_1} = \tfrac{1}{2}(\widehat{Y}_{11} + \widehat{Y}_{12}) = \tfrac{1}{2}(17.045 + 13.177) = 15.111,$$

$$\widehat{Y}_{A_2} = \tfrac{1}{2}(\widehat{Y}_{21} + \widehat{Y}_{22}) = \tfrac{1}{2}(13.133 + 17.089) = 15.111,$$

$$\widehat{Y}_{A_3} = \tfrac{1}{2}(\widehat{Y}_{31} + \widehat{Y}_{32}) = \tfrac{1}{2}(18.656 + 11.566) = 15.111.$$

---

[5]Most computer packages for the analysis of variance do not provide this amount of detail. We obtained the least square estimates $\widehat{Y}_{ijk}$ in Table 14.3 using a multiple-regression program.

Table 14.3: Analysis of the four models fitted to Table 14.2. Fitted scores $\widehat{Y}_{ijk}$, with their sums of squares (top panel) and an analysis of variance (bottom panel).

Estimates of the means and deviation sums of squares

	$\overline{Y}_{jk}$	Estimated Scores $\widehat{Y}_{ijk}$ from Equation			
		14.11	14.12	14.13	14.14
		H_1	$H_0(A)$	$H_0(B)$	$H_0(A \times B)$
a_1b_1	13.600	13.600	17.045	12.769	12.520
a_2b_1	19.000	19.000	13.133	18.307	20.820
a_3b_1	12.667	12.667	18.656	11.284	10.823
a_1b_2	10.714	10.714	13.177	11.307	11.486
a_2b_2	21.000	21.000	17.089	21.461	19.786
a_3b_2	9.000	9.000	11.566	9.592	9.789
SS_{unexp}:		353.295	952.990	372.190	410.990

Analysis of variance

Source	SS	df	MS	F
A	599.695	2	299.848	26.31*
B	18.895	1	18.895	1.66
$A \times B$	57.695	2	28.848	2.53
Between	824.975	5		
Error	353.295	31	11.397	
Total	1,178.270	36		

* $p < 0.05$

A comparison of the estimates from this model to those fitted with the alternative-hypothesis model reveals that it has serious problems. An objective measure of this discrepancy is given by the unexplained sum of squares, obtained by subtracting these estimates from the appropriate scores, squaring the result, and summing the squares to produce $SS_{\text{unexp}}^{H_0(A)} = 952.990$. It is almost three times larger than the alternative-hypothesis value of 353.295. The next column gives fitted values based on the model in Equation 14.13, which lacks the parameter β_k. You can verify the absence of a B effect by calculating the marginal averages for b_1 and b_2 (Equations 14.10) to see that they are equal. A comparison of these estimates to those for the alternative-hypothesis model reveals a much closer match than for the first null-hypothesis model, a fact substantiated by the much smaller unexplained sum of squares ($SS_{\text{unexp}}^{H_0(B)} = 372.190$). The final column gives the estimates for the null-hypothesis model that lacks an interaction (Equation 14.14), as you can see by plotting the values in a graph or computing the simple effects. Again the fit is fairly good ($SS_{\text{unexp}}^{H_0(A \times B)} = 410.990$).

Finally, we assemble the analysis of variance. To obtain the sum of squares for the effects, we subtract the unexplained variability for the alternative-hypothesis model from that of the appropriate null-hypothesis model (Equation 14.15):

$$SS_A = SS_{\text{unexp}}^{H_0(A)} - SS_{\text{unexp}}^{H_1} = 952.990 - 353.295 = 599.695,$$

$$SS_B = SS_{\text{unexp}}^{H_0(B)} - SS_{\text{unexp}}^{H_1} = 372.190 - 353.295 = 18.895,$$

$$SS_{A \times B} = SS_{\text{unexp}}^{H_0(A \times B)} - SS_{\text{unexp}}^{H_1} = 410.990 - 353.295 = 57.695.$$

These sums of squares are entered in the summary at the bottom of Table 14.3. The error sum of squares is equal to the unexplained variability under the full alternative hypothesis (Equation 14.16): $SS_{\text{error}} = SS_{\text{unexp}}^{H_1} = 353.295$.

The analysis of variance table in Table 14.3 contains two other rows. One is the total sum of squares. It is the unexplained variability under a model of no differences among groups, $Y_{ijk} = \mu_T + E_{ijk}$. It is calculated essentially as we did for the one-way analysis in the left panel of Table 14.1. We find the mean of all 37 scores ($\bar{Y}_T = 547/37 = 14.784$), square the deviations between the scores and this value, and sum the results to obtain $SS_{\text{total}} = 1,178.270$. The other sum of squares is for the differences among the groups without regard to their factorial classification. This between-group sum of squares is found by subtracting the unexplained variability remaining after all sysematic effects have been removed ($SS_{\text{unexp}}^{H_1}$) from the total sum of squares:[6]

$$SS_{\text{between}} = SS_{\text{total}} - SS_{\text{unexp}}^{H_1} = 1,178.270 - 353.295 = 824.975.$$

The degrees of freedom for this sum of squares is one less than the number of groups, i.e. $df_{\text{between}} = ab - 1$.

Computationally, the rest of the analysis involves nothing new. We have entered the degrees of freedom in the appropriate columns of the summary table, divided the sums of squares by them to obtain the mean squares, and used MS_{error} to calculate the F ratios. The F ratio is significant for the A main effect, indicating that the means for the three treatment groups are not the same, but is not significant for either the B main effect of gender nor the $A \times B$ interaction, implying that there is no evidence that the men and women performed differently, either on average (as a main effect) or in response to the particular conditions (as an interaction).

You would probably be able to find all the numbers in the analysis-of-variance table of Table 14.3 in the output of your computer package. We say "probably" here because programs differ in what they report and because there are several different ways by which the sums of squares can be calculated. What we have shown in Table 14.3 are known as **Type III sums of squares**, or sometimes **SAS Type III sums of squares**, after the computer package that first identified them this way.[7] We will discuss how to interpret tests based on this type of sums of squares in Section 14.3.

Nonorthogonality of the Effects

If you look closely at the sums of squares in Table 14.3, you will notice that they do not add up the way they would in a design with equal samples. The between-group sum of squares (obtained from the six-group analysis) is $SS_{\text{between}} = 824.975$, but the sum of the sums of squares for the three effects is only

---

[6]You can calculate this sum of squares by treating the data as if they had come from a one-way design. From each score Y_{ijk}, subtract the mean $\bar{Y}_{jk}$ of its group. Then square these deviations and sum them to get $SS_{\text{unexp}}^{H_1}$.

[7]You may find this method referred to as the analysis of the **means model** in other sources. Various other terms were used in the older literature.

$$SS_A + SS_B + SS_{A \times B} = 599.695 + 18.895 + 57.695 = 676.285.$$

Likewise, these three effect sums of squares and the error sum of squares do not add up to SS_{total}. Evidently, there is something about the unequal sample sizes that changes the relationships among the sums of squares. In our discussion of nonorthogonal contrasts on page 77, we noted that the sums of squares for a set of $a - 1$ contrasts do not add up to SS_A unless they were orthogonal. Conversely, when the sums of squares do not add up, the contrasts cannot be orthogonal. This lack of additivity means the same thing with unbalanced designs. The unequal group sizes cause the A, B, and $A \times B$ effects to be partially confounded with each other. This nonorthogonality is an intrinsic characteristic of unbalanced factorial designs, and it is why they are also called **nonorthogonal designs**.

There is an important difference between the nonorthogonal contrasts of Chapter 4 and the nonorthogonal effects in an unbalanced factorial design. In the former case, it was the contrasts themselves, and hence the hypotheses about the data that they express, that were not orthogonal. Here, there is nothing nonorthogonal about the hypotheses. As they are defined in terms of the marginal means (Equations 14.9 and 14.10), they are distinct and orthogonal. It is only the unequal amounts of data from the different groups that entangles the effects. That being the case, the tests in Table 14.3 are appropriate, despite their nonorthogonality. Although the *tests* of the main effects and the interaction are not orthogonal in the mathematical sense, the *questions* they ask are.

Some workers have taken the failure of the sums of squares to add up very seriously and have developed testing procedures that give sums of squares that are additive. This approach produces what are called **Type I sums of squares** (in contrast to the Type III sums of squares that we calculated above) or sometimes **hierarchical sums of squares**. Many computer programs have an option to conduct this analysis, and some may do it by default. However, we do not recommend it. The additivity of the sums of squares is obtained at the cost of altering the hypotheses that are tested (Speed, Hocking, & Hockney, 1978; see also Section 8.2 of Wickens, 1995). They do not express the difference between population means, making it difficult to give them a sensible meaning in experimental contexts.

14.3 Averaging of Groups and Individuals

The presence of unequal sample sizes presents a dilemma whenever we combine data from two or more groups. The particular result that we obtain depends on how we choose to interpret the unequal sample sizes and that choice, in turn, affects the hypotheses that we want the analysis of variance to test. These issues affect the way a researcher uses the computer packages.

It is helpful to look at the problem of averaging unequal groups first in miniature, before turning to the factorial design. Suppose you have two tiny groups of data. The first group contains four scores, 5, 7, 9, and 3, and the second group contains two scores, 13 and 15. You are asked to calculate an average score that combines the two groups. There are two ways you could proceed. One possibility is to lump the groups together and average all six scores:

$$\text{average} = \frac{5 + 7 + 9 + 3 + 13 + 15}{6} = \frac{52}{6} = 8.667.$$

The other possibility uses the group structure. The mean of the first group is $\overline{Y}_1 = 6$ and that of the second is $\overline{Y}_2 = 14$. The average of these two group means is

$$\text{average} = \frac{6 + 14}{2} = \frac{20}{2} = 10.000.$$

The two results are considerably different. Which one is correct?

In fact, neither value is intrinsically better than the other. They are simply based on different interpretations of what is being averaged. Suppose the six scores had been sampled from a single population and divided into two groups according to some classification variable. The first calculation then estimates the grand mean of the whole population, taking into account the fact that some categories are more prevalent than others. On the other hand, suppose the two groups had been created by some experimenter-imposed treatment. The second calculation then estimates the grand mean of the two treatments, paying no attention to the different sizes of the groups. Each answer makes sense in its own context.

The two calculations give the individuals and the groups different importance. The first calculation gives each score equal weight and combines them that way. By doing so, it makes the second group less important than the first, because it contains half as many observations. The second calculation reverses the emphasis. It gives equal weight to each group mean and combines them equally. Because the second group contains half as many observations, an observation from that group has twice the influence on the result as an observation from the first group. The difference makes an important point. When we combine groups of unequal size, we can give the *groups* equal importance or we can give the *observations* equal importance, but we cannot do both at once.

The same thing happens when we average the cell means to calculate the main effects in a factorial design. When the groups have unequal sizes, the marginal means, which involve a combination of groups, depend on whether we give equal importance to the individual scores or to the groups. In extreme cases, it is even possible to reach different conclusions, depending on which emphasis is adopted. The example in Table 14.2 shows the difference. Consider condition a_1. Basing the calculation on the individual scores, we find the average by summing the 12 scores (5 from b_1 and 7 from b_2) and dividing by 12:

$$\overline{Y}_{A_1} = \frac{16 + 12 + \cdots + 14 + 17 + 9 + 6 + \cdots + 8 + 14}{12} = \frac{143}{12} = 11.917.$$

If we wish to treat the groups equivalently, then we average the two group means:

$$\overline{Y}_{A_1} = \frac{\overline{Y}_{11} + \overline{Y}_{12}}{2} = \frac{13.600 + 10.714}{2} = 12.157.$$

The results are different. The other conditions show similar disparities. The marginal means calculated from the scores are $\overline{Y}_{A_1} = 11.971$, $\overline{Y}_{A_2} = 20.200$, and $\overline{Y}_{A_3} = 10.100$, and those calculated from the group means are $\overline{Y}_{A_1} = 12.157$, $\overline{Y}_{A_2} = 20.000$, and $\overline{Y}_{A_3} = 10.834$. In some computer programs, the score-based averages are calculated by the descriptive section of the program, while the group-based averages are calculated by the analysis-of-variance program itself and are often identified as **estimated means**, **adjusted means**, or **least-squares means**.

The two sets of means have different interpretations. The first type, which averages the scores, takes into account the fact that apparently there were more women than

men in the college population from which the sample was drawn. It is an estimate
of what we would find were we to apply the treatments to every member of this
population. In contrast, the second type treats every group equivalently, without
regard to the proportion of men and women. These means are the ones that we want
to use when the group sizes are irrelevant to the conclusions of the study. Which set to
use in the example here is clear. The researcher will make a general statement about
the effects of the treatment (and perhaps also about the lack of gender differences)
that is unrelated to the distribution of men and women in the particular university
where the study was conducted. The unequal sample sizes are incidental to this goal.
We made our intent explicit when we stated the null hypotheses in terms of the group
means in Equations 14.9 and 14.10. Another way to see why we want to calculate the
main effects at the group level is to think of what would happen if the study were to
be replicated at a school in which the gender ratio was different. The sample sizes
would change, but the hypotheses about the treatment effects should not. Thus, the
researcher should calculate and test averages of the group means, not averages of the
scores of the individual subjects.

The same principle holds for most psychological research. Usually the focus of a
study is on the properties of the individual—how he or she responds to a particular
treatment or is characterized by some classification factor. Differences in sample size,
whether completely accidental (like the differences between the sizes of the treatment
groups in our example) or a result of properties of the subject population (like the fact
that more women signed up than men) are irrelevant. On this basis, we recommend
that unless you have some particular reason to do otherwise, you base your analysis
on the average of the group means, not on an average of the individual scores.

How does the type of means relate to the analysis of variance? The particular null-
hypothesis and alternative-hypothesis models that are compared determine the type
of mean tested. When the alternative-hypothesis model contains all the parameters
of the model, as it did in the procedure we described in the last section, we obtain
tests that treat the groups equivalently. This is what the Type III sums of squares do.
If your computer program does not explicitly identify what type of sums of squares
it uses, you should try it out on Table 14.2 (or another example for which you know
the answer) and verify that it reports the sums of squares given in Table 14.3. You
should also be sure that when you discuss the main effects, you use the estimated
means—those that weight the groups equally—not those that come from averaging
the individual scores. They are what the tests compare.[8]

It was not necessary to pay attention to the different types of sums of squares
in the equal-sample analysis of variance for the simple reason that all methods of
calculation give the same result. As you can verify by experimenting with a statistical
program, the Type III and Type I sums of squares are identical when the sample sizes

---

[8]In some research areas, particularly those involving sociological or political questions, the sampling proportions in the population are part of the hypotheses, and main effects based on the individual scores should be used. It is possible to perform these tests, although many programs make
it difficult. For example, with Type I sums of squares, the first main effect is tested this way,
but not the others. If you want to weight individuals equally, you need to run the program twice,
once with each independent variable listed first. For those who want to experiment using Table
14.2, the subject-weighted main effect sums of squares are $SS_A = 758.054$, $SS_B = 19.500$, and
$SS_{A \times B} = 57.694$.

are equal (as are two other variants, Type II and Type IV sums of squares, which you are unlikely to use). The tests using these different options also agree with the computational procedures we discussed for equal samples. It is only with unequal samples that differences appear.

The logic behind the recommendations in this section and the previous one sometimes seems confusing. However, the conclusion is simple:

> *Unless you wish your conclusions to depend on the size of the samples, the analysis of variance with unequal sample sizes should use Type III sums of squares. You should interpret them using marginal averages based on the cell means (i.e. the estimated, adjusted, or least-squares means).*

14.4 Contrasts and Other Analytical Analyses

The results from an unbalanced factorial experiment are often followed up with the type of analytical analyses that we described in Chapters 12 and 13. The contrasts and hypotheses that you will test are the same as those for equal samples. In keeping with the principle immediately above, you should formulate the analyses in terms of the cell means and marginal averages based on them—averages that weight the groups equally—and think of them as if there had been no differences in the sample sizes. Probably the hardest thing to do will be to coax your computer program to do the same thing. We will discuss first tests that involve several degrees of freedom, then turn to a more extensive discussion of the single-df comparisons.

The primary situation in which follow-up analyses with multiple degrees of freedom arise is with simple effects. These can be analyzed by selecting out the relevant portion of the data, performing a one-way analysis of variance with unequal sample sizes, then completing the F test by dividing the mean square for the effect by the MS_{error} from the full analysis. For example, suppose we wanted to look at the simple effect of the treatment conditions for the men in our example. We would submit the first three columns of Table 14.2 to the computer and ask for a one-way, three-group analysis. The resulting mean square reported by the computer is $MS_{A \text{ at } b_1} = 57.495$. (If calculating by hand, we would follow the procedures of Section 3.5 to obtain the same mean square.) Instead of using the F ratio from this analysis of the selected data, we would use MS_{error} from the complete analysis in Table 14.3, which has more degrees of freedom:[9]

$$F = \frac{MS_{A \text{ at } b_1}}{MS_{\text{error}}} = \frac{57.495}{11.397} = 5.04.$$

This statistic, on 2 and 31 degrees of freedom, is significant. The same strategy works for contrast-by-factor interactions based on a pairwise contrast—in the present example, say $\psi_A = \mu_1 - \mu_2$. We would isolate the relevant portion of the data as a $2 \times b$ design, analyze it as if it were an unbalanced two-factor design, and recalculate the F statistic using the overall MS_{error}.[10]

---

[9]As in the balanced case, this error term is appropriate unless we had evidence of heterogeneous variances, in which case we would base the error term only on the variances of the groups involved, as described in Section 12.4.

[10]Interaction components based on contrasts involving three or more means are not so easily analyzed. How the different programs deal with the situation varies, and you will have to dig through the documentation to find out what to do.

Now consider single-*df* tests. There are two approaches that you may see, one that gives an F test and one that gives a t. They yield equivalent answers—the F statistic is the square of the t. Because many programs report the t procedure, we will emphasize it in this discussion.

We begin by treating the entire set of ab groups as a one-way design and expressing a single-*df* effect in that context:

$$\psi = \sum c_{jk}\mu_{jk} \quad \text{where} \quad \sum c_{jk} = 0.$$

Doing so simplifies any direct calculation and ensures that the correct error term is used. It is often the easiest way to enter the contrast into the computer program. Many of the contrasts that we discussed in Chapters 12 and 13 are already in this form. For example, in Section 13.2 we expressed interaction contrasts this way so that we could apply the equations for a one-way design. Other types of single-*df* effects can be expressed similarly, as we will illustrate below.

Once we have expressed a contrast in terms of the cell means, we can either supply the c_{jk} coefficients to the computer or analyze it by the t formula on page 72. The relevant equations are Equations 4.9 and 4.10, with MS_{error} substituted for $MS_{S/A}$:[11]

$$t_\psi = \frac{\widehat{\psi}}{s_\psi} \quad \text{with} \quad s_\psi^2 = MS_{\text{error}} \sum \frac{c_{jk}^2}{n_{jk}}. \tag{14.17}$$

When the groups have unequal variances in addition to unequal sample sizes, we need to use Equation 7.12 (p. 156) to find s_ψ and to make appropriate adjustments to the degrees of freedom using Equation 7.13.

In our example, the treatment factor did not interact with gender, so the researcher would be most interested in exploring the A main effect. Suppose the researcher decides to test two contrasts, one that compares the mean of condition a_1 to that of a_3 and one that compares the combination of these conditions to condition a_2. Using integer coefficients these contrasts are:

$$\psi_1 = \mu_{A_1} - \mu_{A_3} \quad \text{and} \quad \psi_2 = \mu_{A_1} - 2\mu_{A_2} + \mu_{A_3}.$$

These contrasts are orthogonal at the level of the marginal means. Before testing them, we must rewrite them using the means of the individual groups—that will let us use Equations 14.17 to find their standard errors s_ψ. The marginal means are averages of the cell means (Equations 14.9), and substituting these averages into the contrasts gives[12]

$$\psi_1 = \mu_{A_1} - \mu_{A_3} = \tfrac{1}{2}(\mu_{11} + \mu_{12}) - \tfrac{1}{2}(\mu_{31} + \mu_{32})$$
$$= \tfrac{1}{2}\mu_{11} + \tfrac{1}{2}\mu_{12} - \tfrac{1}{2}\mu_{31} - \tfrac{1}{2}\mu_{32},$$

$$\psi_2 = \mu_{A_1} - 2\mu_{A_2} + \mu_{A_3} = \tfrac{1}{2}(\mu_{11} + \mu_{12}) - 2[\tfrac{1}{2}(\mu_{21} + \mu_{22})] + \tfrac{1}{2}(\mu_{31} + \mu_{32})$$
$$= \tfrac{1}{2}\mu_{11} + \tfrac{1}{2}\mu_{12} - \mu_{21} - \mu_{22} + \tfrac{1}{2}\mu_{31} + \tfrac{1}{2}\mu_{32}.$$

Now we test the contrasts as in a one-way design. For ψ_1, we find

$$\widehat{\psi}_1 = \tfrac{1}{2}\overline{Y}_{11} + \tfrac{1}{2}\overline{Y}_{12} - \tfrac{1}{2}\overline{Y}_{31} - \tfrac{1}{2}\overline{Y}_{32}$$
$$= \tfrac{1}{2}(13.600 + 10.714 - 12.667 - 9.000) = 1.324.$$

---

[11]For an equivalent F test, we calculate $SS_\psi = \widehat{\psi}^2 / \sum(c_{jk}^2/n_{jk})$ and test it against MS_{error}.

[12]It is easier to multiply these coefficients by 2 to eliminate fractions before entering them in a computer program. The contrast sets then are $\{1, 1, 0, 0, -1, -1\}$ and $\{1, 1, -2, -2, 1, 1\}$.

We find the standard error and the t statistic using Equations 14.17:

$$s^2_{\hat{\psi}_1} = MS_{\text{error}} \sum \frac{c^2_{jk}}{n_{jk}} = (11.397) \left[\frac{(1/2)^2}{5} + \frac{(1/2)^2}{7} + \frac{(-1/2)^2}{3} + \frac{(-1/2)^2}{7} \right]$$

$$= (11.397)(0.0500 + 0.0357 + 0.0833 + 0.0357) = 2.333,$$

$$t = \frac{\hat{\psi}_1}{s_{\hat{\psi}_1}} = \frac{1.324}{\sqrt{2.333}} = 0.87.$$

The critical value is $t_{.05}(31) = 2.04$, so the contrast does not differ significantly from zero. We have no evidence for a difference between these marginal means. The contrast ψ_2 tells a different story, as you can verify by applying the same equations to it:

$$\hat{\psi}_2 = -17.010, \quad s^2_{\hat{\psi}_2} = 5.499, \quad \text{and} \quad t = -7.25.$$

This result is significant, indicating that the combined performance of conditions a_1 and a_3 was significantly lower than the performance of condition a_2.

14.5 Sensitivity to Assumptions

The analysis of data with unequal sample sizes shows the same sensitivity to assumptions as the analysis of data with equal sample sizes. If anything, the tests are more sensitive. We won't go over the assumptions of random sampling, independent observations, and the normal distribution again, as all the remarks we made in Sections 7.3 and 7.4 still apply. However, unequal samples do increase the sensitivity of analyses to heterogeneity of variance.

Several simulation studies of the assumption of homogeneity of variance have been conducted, but so many factors must be explored—sample sizes, variances, types of hypotheses, the other distributional assumptions—that only a fraction of the possible configurations have been studied. You will recall that unequal variances caused the tests involving equal samples to be biased toward giving too many Type I errors (see Table 7.1, p. 149). With unequal samples, the situation becomes more complicated because the direction of the bias (positive or negative) depends on how the differences in sample size correspond to the differences in variance. When the smaller groups are the ones with the larger variances, the tests are biased to give too many Type I errors, while when the larger groups have the smaller variances, the tests are biased to give too few Type I errors (Keselman, Carriere, & Lix, 1995; Milligan, Wong, & Thompson, 1987). These effects are most pronounced when the sample sizes are small or the variances are very heterogeneous.

Your first defense against these problems is not to let them arise. When you think variance heterogeneity is a possibility, you should design your study so that the sizes of the groups are approximately the same. Moreover, because moderately large sample sizes somewhat mitigate the effects of heterogeneity, you should avoid planning a study in which some cells have fewer than 10 subjects per group. If you have no choice but to analyze a study that has both heterogeneous variances and unequal group sizes, then you should be very cautious when interpreting results that are near the borderline of significance. Look at the relationship between sample size and variability, and if you find that the small groups are the more variable, you may want to adopt a more stringent significance level (e.g., $\alpha = .025$). You could also try to apply procedures that take the unequal variances into account. As we mentioned above for single-df contrasts, the standard error s_ψ for the t test can be calculated in a way that accommodates the heterogeneity (Equation 7.12). For the omnibus tests, procedures such as the Welch or James tests are necessary (see Keselman et al., 1995, for information). You will undoubtedly need assistance in using these tests. In the end, you will have to accept the fact that a study with small, unequal samples and heterogeneity of variance will have low power and is likely to give ambiguous results.

Exercises

14.1. Calculate the means of the men and the women in Table 14.2 using the individual scores and the means. For which set is the difference larger?

14.2. In Section 14.4, we described how an analysis of simple effects can be performed with an unbalanced design.
a. Using the data in Table 14.2, verify that $MS_{A\ \text{at}\ b_1} = 57.495$ for the simple effects of the treatment factor A and complete the F test.
b. Calculate the corresponding test for the female subjects.

14.3. Using the data in Table 14.2, calculate the following single-df contrasts:
a. The interaction contrast formed by crossing $\psi_A = \mu_1 - 2\mu_2 + \mu_3$ with $\psi_B = \mu_1 - \mu_2$.
b. The simple contrast ψ_A for the female subjects.

14.4. The following data were originally presented in Table 11.8 (p. 221) as an example of a two-factor experiment with equal sample sizes. In this example, factor A consisted of a control and two drug conditions and factor B consisted of two levels of food deprivation. Suppose a close examination of testing procedure revealed that four of the monkeys had been incorrectly trained. The remaining data appear below with the deleted scores indicated by dashes:

a_1b_1	a_2b_1	a_3b_1	a_1b_2	a_2b_2	a_3b_2
1	13	9	15	6	14
4	—	16	6	—	7
0	7	18	10	9	6
7	15	—	13	—	13

Assuming that the loss of data was entirely random, conduct the overall analysis, using a computer program.

14.5. Conduct the following detailed analyses, using the data in Problem 14.4:
a. Test the main comparison involving the control (a_1) and drug Y (a_3).
b. Analyze the simple effects of factor A at both levels of factor B.
c. Test the simple contrast between the control and drug X (a_1 and a_2) for the monkeys under 1-hour food deprivation (b_1).
d. Test the interaction contrast involving the two drug conditions (drug X versus drug Y) and the two drive conditions (1 hour versus 24 hour).

15

The Analysis of Covariance

In a completely randomized design, subjects are randomly assigned to the experimental treatments. Although this design assures us that there is no systematic bias in the treatment means, it leaves individual differences uncontrolled. It is quite likely that different numbers of good or poor subjects will be assigned to the different treatment conditions. The potential variability produced by these sampling accidents is accommodated in the significance tests through the size of the within-groups error term ($MS_{S/A}$ in the one-way design). However, as we have seen in our discussion of power, this variability limits the sensitivity of the tests. We want to minimize it.

The randomized-blocks design in Section 11.5 is one way to reduce the within-groups variability. In it, blocks of subjects are formed that are more homogeneous than the population at large, and subjects are assigned to the treatments from these blocks. The key requirement is to have some ancillary information related to the dependent variable available for each subject—this information is known as a **concomitant variable** or, in the analysis considered in this chapter, as a **covariate**. The gain in power comes about because variability associated with the concomitant variable is removed from the error term (it appears as the B and $A \times B$ effects; see Table 11.10, p. 230). The error sum of squares, $SS_{S/AB}$, is smaller and the F ratio for the treatment effect is larger than if the blocking factor were not taken into consideration.

The randomized-blocks design requires the concomitant variable to be available from all the subjects before they are assigned to groups. When that information is not available until after the study is completed, in which case, blocks may be formed after the fact. The scores in such post-hoc blocks are less variable than the original unblocked scores, again increasing the power of the tests. When the ancillary information comes from a numerical variable—before or after the experiment—a technique known as the **analysis of covariance** can be used to reduce the variability of the error term by adjusting the scores statistically. When it is appropriate, the analysis of covariance makes more efficient use of the concomitant variable than post-hoc blocking, and increases the power even more.

The principal use of the blocked designs and the analysis of covariance is to increase power. However, they have another advantage. This advantage is easiest to understand in the blocked designs. In a randomized-blocks design, each treatment condition is guaranteed to contain the same number of subjects from each block, making the groups more similar to each other before the treatment is applied than they would be without blocking. This balance is lost when blocked assignment is not used. Post-hoc blocking restores the balance statistically. When the subjects are divided into blocks after the data have been collected, the number of subjects from each block in the different treatment conditions will typically be uneven (think of the gender factor in our example in Table 14.2). But the means that are tested by the Type III sums of squares—the least-squares, adjusted, or estimated means—are calculated *as if* the cells had had equal size. Thus they restore, at least numerically, the balance that could have been obtained from an actual randomized-blocks design. The analysis of covariance does the same thing. As we will discuss in Section 15.3, it produces adjusted means from which the effects of accidents in the assignment of subjects to groups are removed.

When the subjects are randomly assigned to groups, the group means of the co-variate are unlikely to differ much from each other. Nonrandom assignment is another matter. It is impossible to randomly assign subjects when investigating naturally oc-curring classifications, such as children of different ages, college students with different majors, voters from different geographical areas, or patients with different disorders. Because the subjects in these studies come from natural populations, it is quite possible for them to differ systematically on both the dependent variable and the covariate. Researchers sometimes use the analysis of covariance to adjust the means of a dependent variable for differences in the covariate associated with a classification variable. This application of the analysis of covariance is far more delicate and controversial than its use in a randomized design. In our discussion, we will concentrate first on designs with random assignment, in which only accidental differences in the covariate means exist. In Section 15.7, we will return to the analysis of data in which the groups have systematic differences—not random differences—on the covariate.

The computational steps in the analysis of covariance are complicated and make arithmetic mistakes likely. A computer is essential. Because the computation casts little illumination onto how the analysis of covariance works, we will emphasize its conceptual aspects and omit its computational details.[1]

15.1   Covariance and Linear Regression

The analysis of covariance combines the hypothesis-testing procedures for the general linear model from Chapter 14 with the notion of linear regression. We will begin by reviewing regression.

Suppose you have one group of subjects and have collected two numerical scores X and Y from each of them. These could be simple measures such as height and weight, and it is useful to keep some such example in mind when thinking about regression. Also suppose the scores change together, with high scores on one measure tending to be paired with high scores on the other, low scores on one with low scores on the other, and so on. One way to measure the extent to which X and Y vary together is to

---

[1] If you wish to conduct the analysis entirely by hand, you can look at an earlier edition of this book or at books such as Huitema (1980), Kirk (1995), or Winer, Brown, and Michels (1991). Huitema's book is very helpful in understanding the complexities of the design and its alternatives, as is the discussion by Maxwell, O'Callaghan, and Delaney (1993).

Table 15.1: Eight pairs of scores, with calculation of the sums of squares and the sum of products.

			Deviations		Squares and products			
Subj.	X	Y	$X-\bar{X}$	$Y-\bar{Y}$	SS_X	SS_Y	SP_{XY}	XY
1	11	9	3	5	9	25	15	99
2	6	1	-2	-3	4	9	6	6
3	5	2	-3	-2	9	4	6	10
4	8	3	0	-1	0	1	0	24
5	9	5	1	1	1	1	1	45
6	4	2	-4	-2	16	4	8	8
7	9	4	1	0	1	0	0	36
8	12	6	4	2	16	4	8	72
Sum	64	32	0	0	56	48	44	300
Mean	8	4						

calculate the **sum of products**, which is obtained by subtracting the mean from each score, taking the product of these deviations for each subject, and summing them:

$$SP_{XY} = \sum(X_i - \bar{X})(Y_i - \bar{Y}). \qquad (15.1)$$

When X and Y vary together as we described, the deviations $X_i - \bar{X}$ and $Y_i - \bar{Y}$ for most subjects in the sample have the same sign, and SP_{XY} is a positive number. When X and Y are unrelated to each other, SP_{XY} is near zero, and when they deviate in opposite directions (high with low and low with high), it is negative.

Table 15.1 shows the calculations for a small set of scores. The first block of two columns (after the subject numbers) contains the values of X and Y. Their sums and means are given at the bottom of the table. In the next block of two columns, the mean has been subtracted from each score to form deviations. They sum to zero, as they must. The following block of three columns contains the squares and products of these deviations. In the first row, for example, these numbers are $(X_1 - \bar{X})^2 = 9$, $(Y_1 - \bar{Y})^2 = 25$ and $(X_1 - \bar{X})(Y_1 - \bar{Y}) = 15$. The sums at the bottom of these columns are the sums of squares for X and Y and the sum of products, respectively.

Just as there is a computational formula for a sum of squares that does not require the mean to be subtracted from each score, there is a computational formula for the sum of products:

$$SP_{XY} = \sum X_i Y_i - \frac{\left(\sum X_i\right)\left(\sum Y_i\right)}{n}. \qquad (15.2)$$

This equation is easier to use than the definition in Equation 15.1. In the last column of Table 15.1 the products of the original scores X and Y are calculated and summed. Then using Equation 15.2,

$$SP_{XY} = \sum X_i Y_i - \frac{\left(\sum X_i\right)\left(\sum Y_i\right)}{n} = 300 - \frac{(64)(32)}{8} = 44.$$

Dividing the sums of squares SS_X and SS_Y by their degrees of freedom (i.e. by $n - 1$) converts them into the variances s_X^2 and s_Y^2. Similarly, dividing the sum of products by its degrees of freedom gives the **covariance**, commonly denoted by s_{XY}:

$$s_{XY} = \text{covariance}(X, Y) = \frac{SP_{XY}}{df}.$$

The covariance is much like a variance but refers to the common, or joint, variation of the two variables rather than to their dispersion.

The size of SP_{XY} (or the covariance s_{XY}) depends both on the association between X and Y and on their individual variabilities s_X and s_Y. The familiar **correlation coefficient** r_{XY} is a measure that reflects only the association between the two variables. It is found by dividing the covariance by the product of the two standard deviations or by dividing the sum of products by the square root of the product of the two sums of squares:

$$r_{XY} = \frac{s_{XY}}{s_X s_Y} = \frac{SP_{XY}}{\sqrt{SS_X SS_Y}}. \tag{15.3}$$

The correlation coefficient is sensitive to a particular form of relationship between X and Y, one that can be represented by a straight line. It ranges between -1 when there is a perfect negative linear relationship between X and Y and $+1$ when there is a perfect positive linear relationship. Intermediate values indicate imperfect linear relationships between the two variables, and zero implies that no such relationship is present. For the data in Table 15.1, the correlation is

$$r_{XY} = \frac{SP_{XY}}{\sqrt{SS_X SS_Y}} = \frac{44}{\sqrt{(56)(48)}} = \frac{44}{51.846} = 0.849.$$

This value is positive, meaning that high values are associated with high and low with low, and its magnitude is far enough from zero to indicate a substantial relationship between the variables.

The Linear Regression Equation

Quantities like the covariance and the correlation coefficient indicate that X and Y are related, but they do not tell what this relationship looks like. The simplest way to describe a relationship between two variables is by a straight line, that is, by the linear regression equation we introduced in our discussion of trend analysis (Equation 5.1, p. 93):

$$Y = b_0 + b_1 X.$$

The slope b_1 indicates the steepness of the line and the intercept b_0 is its height when it crosses the vertical axis at $X = 0$.

Many straight lines can be drawn through a set of points, and it is important to pick the best one. What line is "best" depends on what it will be used for. In linear regression, the line is thought of as providing the best prediction $\widehat{Y}_i$ of the value of Y_i based on the value of X_i:

$$\widehat{Y}_i = b_0 + b_1 X_i. \tag{15.4}$$

Values of the slope and the intercept are chosen to minimize the total error of prediction, as measured by the sum of the squared deviations:

$$SS_{\text{error}} = \sum (Y_i - \widehat{Y}_i)^2.$$

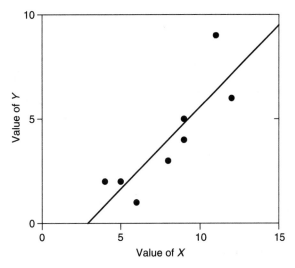

Figure 15.1: The eight observations from Table 15.1 along, with the regression line used to predict Y_i from X_i.

Finding the line this way is an instance of the principle of least squares that we mentioned in Chapter 14 (p. 296), which is why we used the same symbol, $\widehat{Y}_i$, that we used for the estimates in the last chapter. A mathematical analysis of the principle of least squares shows that the regression coefficient and intercept obey two rules:

- The regression coefficient b_1 is the ratio of the covariance of X and Y to the variance of X or, equivalently, the ratio of the sum of products to the sum of squares for the predictor:

$$b_1 = \frac{s_{XY}}{s_X^2} = \frac{SP_{XY}}{SS_X}. \tag{15.5}$$

- The regression intercept b_0 takes the value that makes the regression line pass through the mean of both variables, i.e. when X equals $\overline{X}$, the predicted value of Y is $\overline{Y}$:

$$b_0 = \overline{Y} - b_1\overline{X}. \tag{15.6}$$

We can apply these equations to the eight points in Table 15.1. First, the slope is found from Equation 15.5:

$$b_1 = \frac{SP_{XY}}{SS_X} = \frac{44}{56} = 0.786.$$

Then, using this slope in Equation 15.6, the intercept is calculated:

$$b_0 = \overline{Y} - b_1\overline{X} = 4.0 - (0.786)(8.0) = -2.288.$$

The regression equation that results is

$$\widehat{Y}_i = -2.288 + 0.786X_i.$$

This line is plotted in Figure 15.1, along with the eight points from which it was calculated.

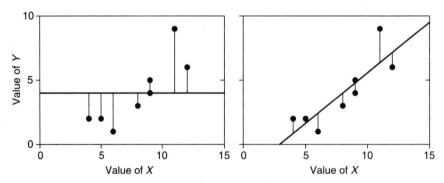

Figure 15.2: Deviation of the Y scores in Table 15.1 about the mean $\overline{Y}$ (left) and the regression line $\widehat{Y}_i = b_0 + b_1 X_i$ (right).

Residual Variation and the Linear Model

We do not expect prediction based on behavioral measures to be perfect, although we do want a good regression line to make relatively small errors. But relative to what alternative? As a point of reference, we can use the prediction we would make if we knew the distribution of Y but not the specific value of X_i. The best that we could do then would be to predict $\overline{Y}$ for all scores. The difference between these two sets of predictions—predicting the mean and predicting from the regression equation—is illustrated for our example in Figure 15.2. The left panel shows a plot of the data along with a horizontal line at $\overline{Y} = 4.0$, which is the predicted value without using the covariate. The vertical lines extending from each point to that prediction are the errors, that is, the amount by which the simple guess of the mean is wrong. The sum of the squares of these deviations measures the total amount of prediction error. Table 15.2 shows this calculation in detail. The first block of two columns contains the original data, copied from Table 15.1. The next block of three columns shows the calculation when the individual X_i's are unknown. The first of these columns gives our prediction, which is $\overline{Y} = 4.0$ for all the scores. Next, this value is subtracted from each score, and in the third column these differences are squared. The sum at the bottom of this column gives the sum of squared errors around the mean:

$$SS_Y = \sum(Y_i - \overline{Y})^2 = 48.0.$$

This is the same value that we found in Table 15.1.

How much is this value reduced when X_i is known and we use the regression line as a prediction? The right panel of Figure 15.2 shows the deviations of Y_i from $\widehat{Y}_i$. Clearly, these deviations are much smaller than those about the mean. The last three columns of Table 15.2 show the calculation of the error of prediction using $\widehat{Y}_i$. In the first column, the prediction $\widehat{Y}_i$ is based on the regression equation we calculated above. For the first subject, the prediction is

$$\widehat{Y}_1 = b_0 + b_1 X_1 = -2.288 + (0.786)(11) = 6.358.$$

The next two columns contain the prediction errors (i.e. $Y_i - \widehat{Y}_i$) and their square, calculated in the same manner as the prediction errors when X_i is unknown. The sum

Table 15.2: The residual errors of the mean and the regression line fitted to the scores in Table 15.1.

Subj.	Data X_i	Data Y_i	$\bar{Y}$	X_i Unknown $Y_i-\bar{Y}$	X_i Unknown $(Y_i-\bar{Y})^2$	X_i Known $\widehat{Y}_i$	X_i Known $Y_i-\widehat{Y}_i$	X_i Known $(Y_i-\widehat{Y}_i)^2$
1	11	9	4.0	5.0	25.0	6.358	2.642	6.980
2	6	1	4.0	−3.0	9.0	2.428	−1.428	2.039
3	5	2	4.0	−2.0	4.0	1.642	0.358	0.128
4	8	3	4.0	−1.0	1.0	4.000	−1.000	1.000
5	9	5	4.0	1.0	1.0	4.786	0.214	0.046
6	4	2	4.0	−2.0	4.0	0.856	1.144	1.309
7	9	4	4.0	0.0	0.0	4.786	−0.786	0.618
8	12	6	4.0	2.0	4.0	7.144	−1.144	1.309
Sum	64	32		0.0	48.0		0.000	13.429

of the squared errors at the bottom of the last column reflects the quality of the fit. We will denote it as $SS_{Y|X}$, with the subscript meaning "Y given that X is known":

$$SS_{Y|X} = \sum(Y_i - \widehat{Y}_i)^2 = 13.429.$$

The error has dropped from $SS_Y = 48.000$ to $SS_{Y|X} = 13.429$ now that X_i is known. This difference represents the amount of the Y variability that can be attributed to the regression equation:

$$SS_{\text{regression}} = SS_Y - SS_{Y|X} = 48.000 - 13.429 = 34.571.$$

This value is more usefully expressed as a proportion of the original SS_Y, a ratio that can be shown to equal the square of the correlation coefficient:

$$r_{XY}^2 = \frac{SS_{\text{regression}}}{SS_Y} = \frac{34.571}{48.000} = 0.720.$$

This quantity is often interpreted by saying that the regression "explains" about 72 percent of the variability of the Y scores.

You may have noticed the similarity between Table 15.2 and the table of deviations we used to apply the general linear model to the one-way analysis of variance (Table 14.1, p. 293). In both tables, the data are described in two ways. In Table 14.1 these two ways were not knowing and knowing the group classification; in Table 15.2 they are not knowing and knowing X_i. The block of three columns in Table 15.2 labeled "X_i Unknown" describe the data with a model that consists of a single constant plus random error:

$$Y_i = \beta_0 + E_i. \tag{15.7}$$

The block labeled "X_i Known" describes them with a model that also includes a term that depends on X_i:

$$Y_i = \beta_0 + \beta_1 X_i + E_i. \tag{15.8}$$

Both of these equations are linear models because they consist of a sum of terms.

The procedures for tests using the general linear model applies to regression. We will describe them briefly because they appear in the analysis of covariance. The two models of Equations 15.7 and 15.8 constitute a pair of null-hypothesis and alternative-hypothesis models, which differ in their dependence on X_i. Equation 15.8 is the alternative-hypothesis model, and Equation 15.7 is the null-hypothesis model. In the terminology of the last chapter, the sum of squared deviations around the single number $\overline{Y}$ is the unexplained variability under the null hypothesis, $SS_{\text{unexp}}^{H_0} = 48.0$, and that around the regression line is the unexplained variability under the alternative hypothesis, $SS_{\text{unexp}}^{H_1} = 13.429$. There are N observations, and Equation 15.7 contains one quantity that must be estimated from the data (the intercept β_0), while Equation 15.8 contains two (the slope β_1 and intercept β_0). The degrees of freedom for each model equals the number of observations less the number of estimated parameters (Equation 14.5, p. 297):

$$df_{\text{unexp}}^{H_0} = N - 1 \quad \text{and} \quad df_{\text{unexp}}^{H_1} = N - 2.$$

In our example, $df_{\text{unexp}}^{H_0} = 8 - 1 = 7$ and $df_{\text{unexp}}^{H_1} = 8 - 2 = 6$. We can now use Equations 14.4 and 14.8 to construct a test of the null hypothesis that $\beta_1 = 0$, as described in Problem 15.2.

Before we leave linear regression, we should mention a further point. In regression, we expect there to be errors in predicting Y_i from X_i, and we represent these errors as deviations of the scores on the dependent variable from the values predicted by the regression line, $Y_i - \widehat{Y}_i$ (the vertical lines in Figure 15.2). By the least-squares principle (p. 296), we pick the coefficients b_0 and b_1 of the regression equation so that the sum of squares of these deviations is as small as possible. This approach is proper because our goal in regression is to predict the value of Y from X, not the other way around. A consequence of attributing any errors in prediction to the dependent variable is to "flatten out" the regression line. If there were no error in prediction (i.e. $r_{XY} = 1.0$) then an observation one standard deviation above the mean of X would be matched by a prediction $\widehat{Y}_i$ that was one standard deviation above the mean of Y, and so forth. When the prediction rule is imperfect, as it always is in psychological research, the predicted scores $\widehat{Y}_i$ are somewhat closer to their mean than the values for X_i from which they are predicted. Specifically, an observation for which X_i is one standard deviation away from $\overline{X}$ leads to a prediction $\widehat{Y}_i$ that is r_{XY} standard deviations away from $\overline{Y}$. Thus, when the correlation is $r_{XY} = 0.5$, an X_i one standard deviation above $\overline{X}$ will produce a predicted $\widehat{Y}_i$ that is only half a standard deviation above $\overline{Y}$. In the worst case, when there is no linear relationship between X and Y and $r_{XY} = 0$, we predict the mean of Y, regardless of the value of X_i. The fact that $\widehat{Y}_i$ is always closer to its mean in standard deviation units than is X_i is known as **regression to the mean**. It is a consequence of the fact that the regression line was chosen to minimize the errors in the Y direction, not in the X direction. Regression to the mean has various confusing and paradoxical implications that are described in books on regression or research design. We mention it here because of its relationship to one of the assumptions of the analysis of covariance we will discuss later.

15.2   The Analysis of Covariance

In the discussion of linear regression in the last section, only one group of scores was involved, and the goal was to relate one of the pair of measures to the other. In contrast, the analysis of covariance involves two or more groups, and its goal is to compare the means of a dependent variable Y. In this respect, it is like the analysis of variance. However, as in regression, a second score X is also available from each subject. The relationship between X and Y is used to reduce the unexplained variability in the design and to improve the power in testing hypotheses about differences among the means. In essence, the analysis of covariance combines an analysis of variance, in the form of the general linear model (Section 14.1), with a regression analysis.

For an illustration, let's return to the experiment we introduced in Section 11.5 as an example of a blocked design. The researcher was studying the effects of instructional material on how well college students learn basic concepts in statistics. To make the example simple, suppose there were just $a = 2$ instructional conditions. Before the introduction of the instructional material, the students completed a test of generalized quantitative ability. In Section 11.5 this information was used to form several blocks of students with similar scores who were randomly assigned to the different treatments. After completing the training, the students were given a test on basic statistical concepts (the dependent variable, Y_{ij}). Now suppose the researcher was unable to score the ability tests until after the assignment to conditions had to be made. Thus, although the ability-test scores X_{ij} were recorded, they were not used in the random assignment of students to groups. Data for $n = 8$ subjects per group, considerably exaggerated to make their pattern obvious, are given at the top of Table 15.3 (we used the eight scores for condition a_1 as our regression example in Table 15.1). If you just consider the dependent variable Y_{ij}, it is clear that the distribution of scores for the two groups overlap considerably, with low and high scores occurring in both conditions. This impression is confirmed by the analysis of variance summarized at the bottom of the table. The F statistic of 1.81 is not significant.

Because we have the covariate available, we can do more. When we plot the pairs of scores for the second group in a scatterplot, we find a relationship between X and Y similar to the one in Figure 15.1 for the first group. Figure 15.3 is a scatterplot for both groups, using solid points for group a_1 and open ones for group a_2. You will notice that for any given value of X, the Y_{ij} scores from group a_2 (the open points) are almost always above those for group a_1 (the solid points). That is, when the X scores are held constant, subjects from group a_2 consistently surpass those from group a_1. This difference is the basis for the analysis of covariance.

We now turn to the details. The analysis of covariance compares two regression analyses of the data, one in which no group differences are allowed, and another in which the vertical separation of the regression lines depends on the group. The dashed line in Figure 15.3 is a regression line using all 16 subjects without regard to which group they come from. It would be the one we would calculate if we did not know how the subjects were grouped. Using the procedures from the last section (Equations 15.5 and 15.6), this line is

$$\widehat{Y}_{ij} = -0.403 + 0.720 X_{ij}. \tag{15.9}$$

For the second regression analysis, we use two lines that have the same slope, but have intercepts b_{01} and b_{02} that depend on groups:

$$\widehat{Y}_{i1} = b_{01} + b_1 X_{i1} \quad \text{and} \quad \widehat{Y}_{i2} = b_{02} + b_1 X_{i2}. \tag{15.10}$$

Thus, unlike the first regression line, they allow the means of the two groups to differ. Because they have the same slope b_1, the relationship between X and Y does not

Table 15.3: *Quantitative ability test scores X and scores on statistical concepts Y after one of two methods of instruction (factor A). An analysis of variance (bottom) does not indicate a difference between the means of Y.*

Observations of X and Y

	Group a_1		Group a_2	
	X	Y	X	Y
	11	9	3	2
	6	1	7	3
	5	2	11	7
	8	3	9	12
	9	5	5	5
	4	2	10	9
	9	4	7	6
	12	6	4	4
Mean:	8.00	4.00	7.00	6.00

Analysis of variance table for Y

Source	SS	df	MS	F
A	16.00	1	16.00	1.81
S/A	124.00	14	8.86	
Total	140.00	15		

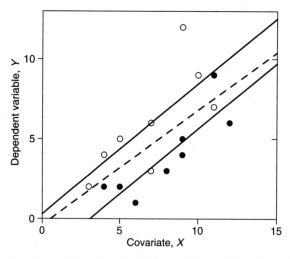

Figure 15.3: *Scatterplot of the data in Table 15.3 (solid points for group a_1 and open points for group a_2). The dashed line is the regression line based on the two groups combined and the solid lines are regression lines with a common slope and separate intercepts.*

depend on the group. To calculate this slope (known as the **pooled within-group regression slope**), we use an extension of Equation 15.5 that combines the sum of cross products and sum of squares from both groups:

$$b_1 = \frac{SP_{XY}(\text{group 1}) + SP_{XY}(\text{group 2})}{SS_X(\text{group 1}) + SS_X(\text{group 2})}. \tag{15.11}$$

We calculated $SS_X = 56$ and $SP_{XY} = 44$ for group 1 in Table 15.1. Corresponding values for group 2 are $SS_X = 58$ and $SP_{XY} = 49$, and the common slope is

$$b_1 = \frac{SP_{XY}(\text{group 1}) + SP_{XY}(\text{group 2})}{SS_X(\text{group 1}) + SS_X(\text{group 2})} = \frac{44 + 49}{56 + 58} = 0.816.$$

Next we calculate the two intercepts using Equation 15.6:

$$b_{01} = \bar{Y}_1 - b_1 \bar{X}_1 = 4.0 - (0.816)(8.0) = -2.528,$$

$$b_{02} = \bar{Y}_2 - b_1 \bar{X}_2 = 6.0 - (0.816)(7.0) = 0.288$$

The result is the pair of solid lines in Figure 15.3:

$$\widehat{Y}_{i1} = -2.528 + 0.816 X_{i1} \quad \text{and} \quad \widehat{Y}_{i2} = 0.288 + 0.816 X_{i2}. \tag{15.12}$$

Consider what Figure 15.3 would look like if the means of both X and Y were the same in both groups. For one thing, there would no longer be a vertical separation between the two solid lines. Both would pass through the same point $(\bar{X}, \bar{Y})$. They would also have the same pooled regression slope b_1. A second characteristic is less obvious. Not only would the slopes of the two solid lines be the same, they would also be the same as that of dashed line fitted to the data of the combined groups. Thus, when the groups did not differ in their means, the three regression lines would be identical and the description of the data based on separate lines for the two groups would be no better in terms of prediction error than one based on a single line from the combined groups.

The difference between a description of the data based on the separate groups and one based on the combined groups is the basis for the analysis of covariance:

> The analysis of covariance tests for differences between groups by comparing a description of the data based on a single regression line to one based on lines with the same slope and different intercepts for each group.

The group difference is measured by the extent to which one of the individual-group regression lines is higher than the other.

The Analysis of Covariance and the General Linear Model

An effective way to understand the analysis of covariance is to express the tests with the general linear model. As applied to the ordinary analysis of variance, this approach tests the hypothesis of equal group means by comparing a model for the scores in which the means could differ to one in which they are the same (Equations 14.1 and 14.2):

Alternative-hypothesis model: $\qquad Y_{ij} = \mu_T + \alpha_j + \mathsf{E}_{ij},$

Null-hypothesis model: $\qquad Y_{ij} = \mu_T + \mathsf{E}_{ij}.$

The null hypothesis that the means are the same (i.e. that $\alpha_j = 0$) is rejected when the alternative-hypothesis model fits substantially better than the null-hypothesis model.

For the analysis of covariance, this pair of models is modified by allowing the scores also to depend on X_{ij}:

Alternative-hypothesis model: $\mathsf{Y}_{ij} = \beta_0 + \beta_1 X_{ij} + \alpha_j + \mathsf{E}_{ij},$ (15.13)

Null-hypothesis model: $\mathsf{Y}_{ij} = \beta_0 + \beta_1 X_{ij} + \mathsf{E}_{ij}.$

Under the null-hypothesis model, the data are described by a single regression line with slope β_1 and intercept β_0 (the dashed line in Figure 15.3), while under the alternative-hypothesis model, they are described by lines with different intercepts for each group, $\beta_0 + \alpha_1$ in group a_1, $\beta_0 + \alpha_2$ in group a_2, and so forth. As in the ordinary analysis of variance, the null hypothesis is rejected when the difference between the fits of the two models implies that $\alpha_j \neq 0$ for some groups.

The general-linear-model procedure translates a comparison of models into a statistical test by looking at the variability that is unexplained under each description. To review, the sums of squares $SS_{\text{unexp}}^{H_0}$ and $SS_{\text{unexp}}^{H_1}$ are based on the discrepancies between the data (Y_{ij}) and the predictions ($\widehat{Y}_{ij}$) under the null-hypothesis and the alternative-hypothesis models, respectively. The difference between these values is the sum of squares for the effect:

$$SS_{\text{effect}} = SS_{\text{unexp}}^{H_0} - SS_{\text{unexp}}^{H_1}.$$

The error sum of squares to which this effect is compared is based on deviations of the scores from the values predicted by the alternative-hypothesis model, i.e. $SS_{\text{unexp}}^{H_1}$.

To complete the test, we need the degrees of freedom. Each model contains the same number of parameters as the standard analysis of variance plus one additional parameter β_1. As a result, the degrees of freedom for the models are one smaller than the standard values (Equations 14.6 and 14.7, p. 297):

$$df_{\text{unexp}}^{H_0} = N - 2 \quad \text{and} \quad df_{\text{unexp}}^{H_1} = N - a - 1. \qquad (15.14)$$

The difference between these values is the familiar $df_A = a - 1$. The error degrees of freedom are $df_{\text{error}} = df_{\text{unexp}}^{H_1}$, one less than the error degrees of freedom in the analysis of variance.

The hypothesis tested by the analysis of covariance, as stated in the principle above, refers to differences in the heights of the regression lines—their intercepts—not to differences in the group means. However, by keeping the regression slopes the same for all groups, differences in the means are matched by differences in height. When the means do not differ (the null hypothesis is true), neither do the regression lines; when the means differ (the null hypothesis is false) the lines have different heights. Thus, the null hypotheses in the analysis of covariance (which concerns heights) has the same meaning as the null hypothesis in the ordinary analysis of variance (which concerns means).[2]

Returning to our example, we can use the regression equation for the null-hypothesis model (Equation 15.9) to obtain a set of estimates for Y_{ij} and the two equations for the alternative-hypothesis model (Equations 15.12) to obtain another set. For each set, we determine the discrepancy between the data and the estimate ($Y_{ij} - \widehat{Y}_{ij}$), square the deviations, and sum them to produce a sum of squares. This procedure

---

[2]As we will discuss in Section 15.7, when random assignment is not used to form the groups, the two null hypotheses can be quite different.

(which we actually let a computer do) gives us the unexplained sums of squares for the two models:
$$SS_{\text{unexp}}^{H_0} = 78.772 \quad \text{and} \quad SS_{\text{unexp}}^{H_1} = 48.132.$$
These have $N - 2 = 14$ and $N - a - 1 = 13$ degrees of freedom, respectively. The effect sum of squares is the difference between these two values:
$$SS_A = SS_{\text{unexp}}^{H_0} - SS_{\text{unexp}}^{H_1} = 78.772 - 48.132 = 30.640.$$
Because there are two groups, the degrees of freedom for this sum of squares is $df_A = a - 1 = 1$. Completing the analysis, the mean squares are
$$MS_A = \frac{SS_A}{df_A} = 30.640, \quad \text{and} \quad MS_{\text{error}} = \frac{SS_{\text{unexp}}^{H_1}}{df_{\text{unexp}}^{H_1}} = \frac{48.132}{13} = 3.702.$$
The test statistic is $F = 30.640/3.702 = 8.28$, which is significant ($F_{.05(1,13)} = 4.67$). This value is substantially greater than the value of $F = 1.81$ from the analysis of variance in Table 15.3 that did not take account of the covariate.

The larger F ratio in this example has two origins. The most important is a smaller error term—$MS_{\text{error}} = 3.702$ versus $MS_{S/A} = 8.86$ from Table 15.3. In the ordinary analysis of variance, the error term is the variability around the group means:
$$SS_{S/A} = \sum (Y_{ij} - \bar{Y}_j)^2$$
(e.g., Equation 2.5, p. 26). In the analysis of covariance, it is the variability around the predicted values from the regression line appropriate to the group:
$$SS_{\text{error}} = \sum (Y_{ij} - \hat{Y}_{ij})^2.$$
Because X_{ij} is used in finding $\hat{Y}_{ij}$, there is less unexplained variability in the analysis of covariance. Almost all analyses of covariance show this improvement.

In this example, F is also increased because the two regression lines are slightly farther apart than the original means. Using the regression lines in Equations 15.12,
$$b_{02} - b_{01} = 0.288 - (-2.528) = 2.816, \quad \text{but} \quad \bar{Y}_2 - \bar{Y}_1 = 6.00 - 4.00 = 2.00.$$
This change increases MS_A from 16.00 in the analysis of variance to 30.64 in the analysis of covariance. However, the direction of this change is a happenstance of the particular sample, and it might go the other way in another study, or even a replication of this one. In short, the analysis of covariance reduces the size of the error term but does not systematically change the size of the effect.

Table 15.4 summarizes these calculations as they might be reported by a computer program (your program may put the rows in a different order, include some different information, or exclude some). It contains two tests. The most important is the test of the difference between the two groups we just described. It appears in the second row. Of secondary interest is the test of the covariate in the first row. That test tells us whether there is a linear association between X and Y, or more specifically whether the solid lines in Figure 15.3 are tilted.[3] The last three rows of the table

---

[3]You can calculate this sum of squares using the principles of the general linear model. For the alternative-hypothesis model, use the standard analysis-of-covariance model (Equation 15.13), with the error sum of squares in Table 15.4. For the null-hypothesis model, use the analysis-of-variance model that allows the means to differ but does not include the covariate (Equation 14.1), with the error sum of squares in Table 15.3. These two models differ in that the former includes the regression term $\beta_1 X_i$ and the latter does not. The difference between these sums of squares is SS_X, and $df_X = 1$ because there is one regression coefficient.

Table 15.4: Analysis of covariance for variable Y in Table 15.3.

Source	SS	df	MS	F
Covariate, X	75.868	1	75.868	20.49*
Groups, A	30.640	1	30.640	8.28*
Model	91.868	2		
Error	48.132	13	3.702	
Total	140.000	15		

* $p < .05$

show the partitioning of the total sum of squares ($SS_Y = 140.000$) into the fit of the alternative-hypothesis model (the portion that is somehow "explained" by the linear model) and an unexplained portion due to error. You may notice that the sums of squares for the covariate and the groups do not exactly add up to the sum of squares for the overall model:

$$SS_X + SS_A = 75.868 + 30.640 = 106.508, \quad \text{but} \quad SS_{\text{model}} = 91.868.$$

This difference is a consequence of nonorthogonality issues that we will discuss later and is a characteristic of the analysis of covariance, even when the group sizes are equal. To correctly accommodate it, you should be sure that your program calculates Type III sums of squares.

Performing an analysis of covariance with most modern computer programs is straightforward. The data entered for each subject include the group designation, the covariate X_{ij}, and the dependent variable Y_{ij}. When you specify the analysis to be run, you have to identify all three variables: the group classification as the independent variable, X_{ij} as the covariate, and Y_{ij} as the dependent variable. Then you proceed as you would for a one-way analysis of variance. For some programs, you may need to tell it to calculate the adjusted treatment means $\overline{Y}_j'$ that we will discuss next.

15.3   Adjusted Means

The primary purpose of the analysis of covariance in an experimental setting is to increase power by removing variability from the error term. A secondary result is to make more precise estimates of the treatment means. As you know, one source of the error in estimating treatment effects comes from assigning subjects randomly to conditions. Random assignment assures that there are no systematic differences among groups, but it also produces treatment groups that are rarely perfectly matched. When covariate scores are available, however, we have some information about the individuals in each group. We can use this information to reduce the effects of accidental variation on the treatment means and to obtain more comparable estimates of the effects.

Figure 15.4 shows graphically how this adjustment is made, using our numerical example (for some other examples, see Huitema, 1980, pp. 31–38). The group regression lines have the same slope and each passes through the point defined by their respective means, $\overline{X}_j$ and $\overline{Y}_j$. These values are $\overline{X}_1 = 8.0$ and $\overline{Y}_1 = 4.0$ for group a_1 and $\overline{X}_2 = 7.0$ and $\overline{Y}_2 = 6.0$ for group a_2; these points are marked by the $+$ signs on the regression lines. There is a difference of two points on the dependent variable ($\overline{Y}_1 - \overline{Y}_2 = 4.0 - 6.0 = -2.0$), but there is also a difference of one point on the covariate

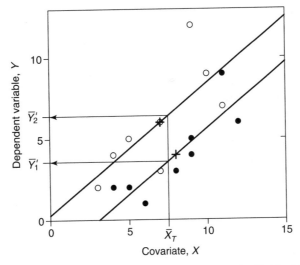

Figure 15.4: The adjustment of the means for the data in Table 15.3. The + signs mark the original, unadjusted, means.

$(\bar{X}_1 - \bar{X}_2 = 8.0 - 7.0 = 1.0)$, presumably brought about by accidents of sampling. This latter difference indicates that the groups are not quite comparable. Because the variables X and Y are positively correlated, the group with an accidentally larger value of $\bar{X}_j$ probably would also have a slightly larger value of $\bar{Y}_j$, even if there was no effect of the treatment factor. We can use the group regression lines to predict what the means $\bar{Y}_j$ would have been had the two groups been equal on the covariate—that is, had $\bar{X}_1 = \bar{X}_2 = \bar{X}_T$. First, we calculate the grand mean $\bar{X}_T = (8.0 + 7.0)/2 = 7.5$ and then find the values of $\hat{Y}$ that are predicted by the two group regression lines at that point on the X axis. These steps are indicated in Figure 15.4 by the vertical line rising from $\bar{X}_T = 7.5$ to intersect the two regression lines and the two horizontal lines extending from the two points of intersection to the ordinate. The values $\bar{Y}'_j$ taken off the vertical axis are known as **adjusted means**—we denote them by a prime. Numerically, using the regression lines from Equations 15.12, their values are

$$\bar{Y}'_1 = b_{01} + b_1\bar{X}_T = -2.528 + (0.816)(7.5) = -2.528 + 6.120 = 3.592,$$
$$\bar{Y}'_2 = b_{02} + b_1\bar{X}_T = 0.288 + (0.816)(7.5) = 0.288 + 6.120 = 6.408.$$

On the graph, you can think of sliding the original means marked by the + signs along the regression lines to bring them to the vertical line at $\bar{X}_T$.

The term *adjusted mean* comes about because we can think of these values as representing an adjustment of the original means $\bar{Y}_j$ to take account of the covariate differences:

$$\bar{Y}'_j = \bar{Y}_j + b_1(\bar{X}_T - \bar{X}_j). \tag{15.15}$$

This equation gives the same result as we found above:

$$\bar{Y}'_1 = \bar{Y}_1 + b_1(\bar{X}_T - \bar{X}_1) = 4.0 + (0.816)(7.5 - 8.0) = 4.0 - 0.408 = 3.592,$$
$$\bar{Y}'_2 = \bar{Y}_2 + b_1(\bar{X}_T - \bar{X}_2) = 6.0 + (0.816)(7.5 - 7.0) = 6.0 + 0.408 = 6.408.$$

The adjustments $b_1(\bar{X}_T - \bar{X}_j)$ always add up to zero, which is why in this case (where $a = 2$) they take symmetrical values, -0.408 and $+0.408$.

The adjustment for group differences can either increase or decrease the differences among the means, and thus increase or decrease the treatment mean square, depending on the direction of the slope of the regression line and on the pattern of the covariate means. In Figure 15.4, when the point representing the observed mean for group a_1 is moved along the regression line to $\bar{X}_T = 7.5$, the adjusted mean $\bar{Y}_1'$ decreases, because $\bar{X}_1 > \bar{X}_T$. For group a_2, the movement is in the opposite direction (to the right and upward), increasing $\bar{Y}_2'$. Because group a_1 already had the smaller of the two means on the dependent variable, these shifts increased the difference between the two groups. Had the covariate means been in the other order (i.e. with $\bar{X}_1 < \bar{X}_2$), the adjustment would have moved the means closer together. In a randomized design, differences in $\bar{X}_j$ are the result of sampling accidents, so half the time they increase the differences in $\bar{Y}_j$ and half they decrease them. The point of making the adjustment, however, is not to make the differences larger or smaller but to make them more accurate estimates of the population values. Whichever the case, any change in the mean square for the effect should be minor in comparison with the reduction in the size of the error term produced by removing the association of Y with X.

Contrasts on the Adjusted Means

You can investigate any comparison on the adjusted means that you would consider with unadjusted data. How these contrasts are chosen remains as we described in Chapters 4 and 5, but the calculation of the test statistics is more complicated. Because the relationships among the groups change when the covariate is taken into account, we recommend that you let the computer do the work. However, because you may sometimes need to conduct a particular test after having completed the computer analysis, we will describe a procedure by which you can obtain approximate tests for contrasts. The values will not be exactly the same as the more accurate values calculated by the computer, but they are sufficient for exploring the data.

Our approximate calculation is based on the t tests for groups with unequal variances we discussed in Section 7.5. To use it, you need to ask your computer program to calculate the adjusted means $\bar{Y}_j'$ with their standard errors $s_{M_j'}$. First, you calculate the observed value of contrast on the adjusted means:

$$\widehat{\psi}' = \sum c_j \bar{Y}_j'. \tag{15.16}$$

The prime on $\widehat{\psi}'$ is to remind us that we are using adjusted means. Next, you approximate the standard error of the contrast using the standard errors of the means (see Equation 7.12):

$$\widehat{\sigma}_{\psi'} \approx \sqrt{\sum c_j^2 s_{M_j'}^2}. \tag{15.17}$$

We have used the approximate equal sign ($\approx$) because these calculations do not take into account some of the complexities introduced by the adjustment. It is more accurate when the covariate means are not very different from each other. When we divide $\widehat{\psi}'$ by its estimated standard error $\widehat{\sigma}_{\psi'}$, we get a t statistic with degrees of freedom equal to those of the error from the overall analysis:

$$t = \widehat{\psi}'/\widehat{\sigma}_{\psi'}. \tag{15.18}$$

Table 15.5: Data and means for the testing of contrasts in the analysis of covariance.

Observations of X and Y

	Group a_1		Group a_2		Group a_3	
	X	Y	X	Y	X	Y
	11	9	3	2	3	2
	6	1	7	3	8	8
	5	2	11	7	7	5
	8	3	9	12	10	8
	9	5	5	5	4	3
	4	2	10	9	5	4
	9	4	7	6	9	6
	12	6	4	4	5	4

Means and standard errors

	a_1	a_2	a_3
Means, $\bar{Y}_j$	4.000	6.000	5.000
Std. Devn., s_j	2.619	3.295	2.204
Adj. Means, $\bar{Y}'_j$	3.285	6.102	5.613
Std. Error of $\bar{Y}'_j$	0.584	0.574	0.581

To illustrate, we will add a third group to our numerical example. The data, summary statistics, adjusted means, and standard errors calculated by the computer are shown in Table 15.5—the omnibus analysis of covariance, not shown, is significant. Consider two contrasts, one comparing group a_1 to the average of groups a_2 and a_3, the other comparing the latter groups to each other. The observed values of these contrasts are

$$\widehat{\psi}'_1 = \bar{Y}'_1 - \tfrac{1}{2}\bar{Y}'_2 - \tfrac{1}{2}\bar{Y}'_3 = 3.285 - \tfrac{1}{2}(6.102) - \tfrac{1}{2}(5.613) = -2.572$$

$$\widehat{\psi}'_2 = \bar{Y}'_2 - \bar{Y}'_3 = 6.102 - 5.613 = 0.489.$$

Using Equation 15.17, the approximate standard errors for these tests are

$$\widehat{\sigma}_{\psi'_1} \approx \sqrt{c_1^2 s_{M'_1}^2 + c_2^2 s_{M'_2}^2 + c_3^2 s_{M'_3}^2}$$
$$= \sqrt{1^2(0.584)^2 + (-\tfrac{1}{2})^2(0.574)^2 + (-\tfrac{1}{2})^2(0.581)^2} = 0.713,$$

$$\widehat{\sigma}_{\psi'_2} \approx \sqrt{1^2(0.574)^2 + (-1)^2(0.581)^2} = 0.817.$$

The first contrast gives $t = -2.572/0.713 = -3.61$, which is significant; the second gives $t = 0.489/0.817 = 0.60$, which is not. The standard errors of these contrasts reported by a computer program are $\widehat{\sigma}_{\psi'_1} = 0.722$ and $\widehat{\sigma}_{\psi'_2} = 0.815$, which are little different from our approximate values.

15.4 Extensions of the Design

The one-way analysis of covariance can be extended to more complex designs in several ways. One possibility is to expand the one-way group structure to a factorial design; a second is to include more than one covariate. Both extensions are natural, in that they arise directly from the linear model. Both are also easy to conduct using standard computer programs—all you do is specify the additional factors or covariates.

Factorial Designs

The most common extension of the one-way analysis of covariance is to a factorial design. The linear model for this design combines the model for the factorial design (Equation 11.14, p. 225) with that for a one-way analysis of covariance (Equation 15.13):

$$Y_{ijk} = \beta_0^{reg} + \beta_1^{reg} X_{ijk} + \alpha_j + \beta_k^{anova} + (\alpha\beta)_{jk} + E_{ijk}. \qquad (15.19)$$

To keep the notation straight while holding to the standard letters, we have used the superscripts *reg* and *anova* to distinguish between the parameters β of the regression model and those of the analysis-of-variance model associated with factor B. In the output of a computer analysis of this design, you will find tests of the two main effects and the interaction, which are the effects of interest. The program should also test the covariate, which simply verifies that the common slope of the group regression lines is significantly different from zero. As was the case for the single-factor analysis of covariance, Type III sums of squares should be used.

Like its one-factor counterpart, the factorial analysis of covariance has two advantages over the standard analysis. First, extracting the variability associated with the covariate reduces the size of the error term and increases the power of the tests. Second, the hypotheses that are tested concern the adjusted group means $\overline{Y}'_{ij}$, from which differences on the covariate have been removed. Thus, the resulting tests are both more powerful and more precise than those of the ordinary factorial analysis of variance. The difference is illustrated by the 2×2 factorial design in Table 15.6. An analysis of variance for the variable Y (not shown), using the scores in the upper panel, reveals two significant main effects ($F_A = 5.44$ and $F_B = 9.42$, with $F_{.05}(1, 12) = 4.75$), but not a significant interaction ($F_{A \times B} = 3.39$). The summary of the analysis of covariance in the middle panel reveals that the F statistics for all three treatment effects are larger than those without the covariate. The interaction is now significant ($F_{.05}(1, 11) = 4.84$). The increase in power results from a reduction in error variance from $MS_{S/A} = 4.416$ in the analysis of variance to $MS_{error} = 3.022$ in the analysis of covariance. The adjusted means are given at the bottom of Table 15.6. They are more accurate estimates of the population values then the unadjusted values.

Given the significant $A \times B$ interaction, you would probably want to follow up with tests of simple effects. One warning here: When we described the analytical analysis of a two-way design in Section 12.4, we suggested that it is possible to simplify the calculations by selecting a subset of the data and calculating the sum of squares as if it were a complete design. For example, the sum of squares for a simple effect can be calculated from a one-way analysis of the relevant row or column. This approach does not work for the analysis of covariance. The adjusted means depend on the pooled regression slope calculated from the complete data, and for consistency, the same adjustment must be used throughout the analysis. Calculations based on part of the data could well yield a somewhat different adjustment. Using the computer to analyze simple effects is often a little tricky, but you can calculate the sums of squares for the simple effects using the adjusted means $\overline{Y}'_{ij}$ and Equations 12.4–12.7. It is tested, of course, using the adjusted MS_{error} from the overall analysis of covariance.

Table 15.6: A two-factor analysis of covariance.

Observations of X and Y

	a_1b_1		a_1b_2		a_2b_1		a_2b_2	
	X	Y	X	Y	X	Y	X	Y
	2	11	5	10	2	12	4	15
	1	8	5	8	3	7	5	12
	5	8	1	10	4	6	3	16
	4	7	3	11	1	11	4	13

Analysis of covariance

Source	SS	df	MS	F
Covariate, X	16.509	1	16.509	5.46*
A	22.563	1	22.563	7.47*
B	53.040	1	53.040	17.55*
$A \times B$	19.707	1	19.707	6.52*
Model	92.196	4		
Error	33.241	11	3.022	
Total	125.438	15		

$^* p < .05$

Unadjusted and adjusted means

	a_1b_1	a_1b_2	a_2b_1	a_2b_2
Means, $\bar{Y}_{ij}$	8.500	9.750	9.000	14.000
Adj. Means, $\bar{Y}'_{ij}$	8.308	9.942	8.424	14.576

If the example experiment had been larger with more levels of the two factors, all the various analytical tests that we discussed in Chapters 12 and 13 could be performed—contrast-by-factor interactions, interaction contrasts, simple contrasts, and main comparisons. Where these analysis reduce to contrasts with one degree of freedom, you can use the approximate methods at the end of the last section (Equations 15.16 and 15.17) or have your computer program test them in a one-way analysis of covariance with ab groups, as described in Section 14.4.

Additional Covariates

In some research situations, two (or more) potential covariates are available. The natural impulse is to use them both, hoping to attain greater precision—more accurate means and a smaller error term. With many computer programs it is easy to add covariates: Simply list the variables in the covariate section of the design specification and proceed as usual. The linear model involved is also straightforward. Denote the two covariates by $X^{(1)}$ and $X^{(2)}$. For the one-way design, the model contains two regression terms and the group effect α_j:

$$Y_{ij} = \beta_0 + \beta_1^{(1)} X_{ij}^{(1)} + \beta_1^{(2)} X_{ij}^{(2)} + \alpha_j + E_{ij}. \tag{15.20}$$

The analysis estimates two slope regression coefficients, $b_1^{(1)}$ and $b_1^{(2)}$, and it creates an analysis of covariance table that looks like that in the single-covariate analysis except that it contains tests of both regression coefficients.

Despite the ease with which you can add covariates, you should not do so without considerable thought. When the two covariates are uncorrelated with each other, each makes independent adjustments to the means and the error sum of squares is reduced by the regression sum of squares associated with each of them. That is not the case when the two covariates are correlated. Large correlations, in particular, cause problems. Both the adjusted means and the power of the tests are affected in complicated ways, and the accuracy of the analysis may be less than when either covariate is used alone. Unfortunately, correlated covariates are more common than uncorrelated ones. Consider our example of a researcher who uses the analysis of covariance to reduce the variability due to differences in quantitative ability in college students learning statistical concepts. It is easy enough to collect data on measures such as quantitative and verbal performance or college GPA and use all of them as covariates. But these variables are certainly correlated, and a researcher who uses all of them may be worse off than one who uses only the single most appropriate covariate.

The issues involved in using multiple covariates are complex, and belong to the domain of multivariate statistics. We will limit ourselves to a few suggestions. First, do not use more than one covariate unless they are logically unrelated quantities and their values are not appreciably correlated (except, as we discuss in the next section, as part of the analysis of the assumptions of a single-covariate design). Second, never use more than two covariates. Finally, look carefully at the results of your analysis to see that they are sensible. The means adjusted with both covariates should not be far from those adjusted with one of them, nor from the unadjusted means. When you find unexpected differences, use a simpler analysis or seek help.

15.5   Assumptions of the Analysis of Covariance

All the assumptions of the analysis of variance (see Chapter 7 and Section 14.5) apply also to the analysis of covariance. In addition, it requires three further assumptions about the covariate and its relationship to the dependent variable.[4] These assumptions are needed to ensure that the linear model (Equation 15.13) holds.

The first two assumptions concern the nature of the relationship between X and Y and the third concerns the way in which the error random variable E_{ij} fits the linear model:

- **Linearity of regression:** The relationship between X and Y in each group is a straight line.
- **Homogeneity of regression:** The slopes of the regression lines in the different groups are the same.
- **Exact measurement of the covariate:** All the uncertainty lies in the measurement of Y; the covariate X is measured without error.

---

[4]Useful discussions are found in Glass et al. (1972), Huitema (1980, Chapter 8), and Maxwell et al. (1993).

Table 15.7: *Two groups of scores in which the slope of the covariate regression differ sizably, with a test for heterogeneous slope.*

Data illustrating heterogeneity of regression slope

	Group a_1		Group a_2	
	X	Y	X	Y
	2	5	3	2
	2	4	5	2
	3	6	5	4
	4	4	6	4
	4	7	6	6
	6	3	8	4
	7	5	9	6
	8	6	9	8
	8	3	10	7
	9	3	11	5
	10	2	12	7
	11	4	13	10
Mean:	6.17	4.33	8.08	5.42

Summary of analysis of covariance testing for differences in slope

Source	SS	df	MS	F
Covariate, X	8.713	1	8.713	4.44*
Groups, A	26.157	1	26.157	13.34*
$A \times X$ interaction	39.788	1	39.788	20.29*
Model	55.413	3		
Error	39.212	20	1.961	
Total	94.625	23		

* $p < .05$

We will examine the first two assumptions in this section, illustrating their effects on the analysis and explaining how to test whether they have been violated. The third assumption is most relevant when the groups actually differ on the covariate, so we will wait to discuss it until Section 15.7.

Homogeneity of Regression

The second of the three assumptions is the most important in practice, so we consider it first. The scores given in Table 15.7 and plotted in Figure 15.5 demonstrate its violation in exaggerated form. The two dashed regression lines in the figure are calculated separately for each group. Clearly, their slopes ($b_1 = -0.229$ for group a_1 and $b_1 = 0.632$ for group a_2) are not the same—even their signs differ. However, they are not the lines used in the analysis of covariance. It is based on two regression lines that have the *same* slope. The two solid lines in Figure 15.5 are drawn through

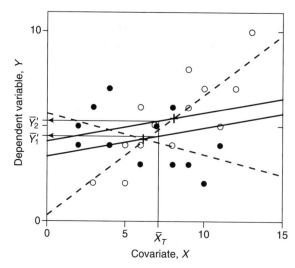

Figure 15.5: *A scatterplot of the scores in Table 15.7. The solid lines are the best fitting regressions as calculated by the analysis of covariance, the dashed lines are regression lines for the individual groups, and the crosses mark the group means.*

the means with the pooled within-group regression slope of $b_1 = 0.200$ (as calculated by Equation 15.11). They do not describe the data accurately. Although a computer program will calculate adjusted means based on these lines (they are 4.525 and 5.225), there is so much disparity between the data and the model that they make no sense as descriptions of the groups. Moreover, the test of whether they differ is useless.

It is a good idea to check for differences among the group regression coefficients before undertaking an analysis of covariance. A check is particularly important when your data come from natural groups or when you suspect that your treatment may affect the slopes. A plot such as Figure 15.5 is a good place to start, but it should be supplemented with the formal test described next. If this test is not significant, then you can turn to the analysis of covariance with renewed confidence, but when it is, you must proceed with care.

A test for differences in slope determines whether the relationship between X and Y depends on the treatment factor, that is, whether factors A and X interact. Many computer programs allow you to include this interaction in the model (but you may need to hunt around in the documentation to discover how to do it). The bottom panel of Table 15.7 shows this computer analysis for our example. It includes three test statistics, one for the covariate X, one for the groups A, and one for the $A{\times}X$ interaction, but only the latter is of interest.[5] The value of $F = 20.29$ (against $F_{.05}(1, 20) = 4.35$) for the interaction indicates that the regression slopes in the two groups are different in the two groups. It throws the entire the analysis of covariance into doubt.

---

[5]The other two tests are not the same as those in an ordinary analysis of covariance and neither they nor the adjusted means are typically reported.

This test for differences in slope—an $A \times X$ interaction—involves the comparison of two linear models:

Null-hypothesis model: $\qquad\qquad Y_{ij} = \beta_0 + \beta_1 X_{ij} + \alpha_j + \mathsf{E}_{ij},$

Alternative-hypothesis model: $\qquad Y_{ij} = \beta_0 + \beta_1^{(1)} X_{ij}^{(1)} + \beta_1^{(2)} X_{ij}^{(2)} + \alpha_j + \mathsf{E}_{ij}.$

The null-hypothesis model is the standard analysis-of-covariance model with a single slope β_1 for all groups. The alternative-hypothesis model has different regression slopes for the two groups. It uses two new variables, which we call $X_{ij}^{(1)}$ and $X_{ij}^{(2)}$, each of which focuses on a different group. The value of $X_{ij}^{(1)}$ is equal to X for subjects in group a_1 and equal to 0 for subjects in group a_2; the value of $X_{ij}^{(2)}$ is exactly the opposite, being equal to 0 in group a_1 and to X in group a_2. When this model is fitted, different regression slopes ($\beta_1^{(1)}$ and $\beta_1^{(2)}$) are obtained for the two groups. A sum of squares for the $A \times X$ interaction is found by subtracting the unexplained variability of the two models (Equation 14.4, p. 297):

$$SS_{A \times X} = SS_{\text{unexp}}^{(H_0)} - SS_{\text{unexp}}^{(H_1)}.$$

You can use this quantity to test for a difference in regression slopes when your program does not have an easy way to specify the interaction.

What should you do when you find a difference in slopes? If you only want to establish differences among the means of the dependent variable, your best alternative is to forget the covariate and revert to an analysis of variance. Alternatively, you might want to determine the values of X for which the groups differ on the dependent variable Y. Consider what happens when we group the data from Table 15.7 by low, medium, and high scores on X and calculate means of Y:

	$X < 6$	$6 \leq X \leq 8$	$X > 8$
a_1	5.20	4.25	3.00
a_2	2.67	4.67	7.17

For subjects with values of X below 6, group a_1 is superior to group a_2; for values between 6 and 8, there is essentially no difference; and for values above 8, group a_2 is superior to group a_1. This is why it didn't make sense to talk about an overall difference the adjusted means.[6] We might, however, want to follow up this classification of the data by determining the values of X for which the groups differ significantly and those for which they do not. A procedure known as the **Johnson-Neyman technique** has been developed to identify these regions (Johnson & Neyman, 1936; Johnson & Fay, 1950; see Chapter 13 of Huitema, 1980 for an example and Hunka (1995) for software). With two groups and one covariate, the ranges of X for which the groups differ are not difficult to calculate, but otherwise, the calculations are quite complex and their interpretation subtle.

Linearity of Regression

The analysis-of-covariance model fits the data with straight regression lines. Nonlinear relationships, although less common than differences in slope, can compromise the

---

[6]The same ambiguity occurs in a blocked design, where an interaction between treatments and blocks implies that the treatment differences varies with the levels of the blocking factor. We have mentioned the difficulty of interpreting a main effect in the presence of an interaction before.

Table 15.8: Two groups of scores in which the relationship between covariate and the dependent variable is curved. The columns labeled $X^{(\text{quad})}$ are quadratic scores used in the test for curvature summarized at the bottom.

Data illustrating curvature of regression.

	Group a_1			Group a_2	
X	$X^{(\text{quad})}$	Y	X	$X^{(\text{quad})}$	Y
1	49	7	3	25	10
3	25	5	4	16	9
3	25	7	4	16	8
4	16	4	6	4	9
5	9	3	7	1	5
5	9	5	8	0	7
7	1	3	9	1	6
9	1	4	10	4	5
10	4	6	11	9	9
11	9	5	13	25	9
12	16	8	14	36	8
13	25	7	14	36	10
Mean: 6.92		5.33	8.58		7.92

Summary of analysis of covariance testing for curvature

Source	SS	df	MS	F
Covariate X	1.061	1	1.061	0.55
Covariate $X^{(\text{quad})}$	26.259	1	26.259	13.58*
Groups, A	38.566	1	38.556	19.94*
Model	66.948	3		
Error	38.677	20	1.934	
Total	105.625	23		

* $p < 0.5$

analysis. The scores in Table 15.8, plotted in Figure 15.6, illustrate the problem. The relationship between X and Y in both groups is distinctly U-shaped. But suppose an ordinary analysis of covariance had been performed using X as the covariate. The figure shows the lines of equal slope fitted to the two groups by this analysis. Clearly, they do not describe the data, being too high in the middle of the range of X and too low at the ends.

Violations of linearity can affect both the adjusted means and the error term. The size of the error term is always affected. In Figure 15.6, the variability of the scores around the two lines is not a good representation of their actual variability. In fact, the sum of squared deviations about these lines is only slightly smaller than $SS_{S/A}$ from a standard analysis of variance (they are $SS_{\text{error}} = 64.936$ and $SS_{S/A} = 65.583$, respectively), and because of the change in degrees of freedom, the mean square in

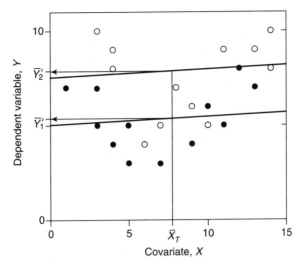

Figure 15.6: *A scatterplot of the scores in Table 15.8. The dashed lines are the best fitting regressions as calculated in the analysis of covariance.*

the analysis of covariance is larger. The analysis of covariance is actually less sensitive than an analysis of variance in this example! The effects on the adjusted means is more complicated and depends on particular slopes and curvature. In Figure 15.6, where the regression lines are essentially flat, the adjusted means (they are 5.37 and 7.88) are not much different from the original means (they are 5.33 and 7.92). In other cases, they could be considerably different, in which case their interpretation as representative values of the observed data is questionable.

To test a set of data for nonlinearity of regression, you can create a new covariate that allows curved lines to be fitted and see if adding it to the model improves the fit. We saw in our discussion of trend analysis (Section 5.2) that adding a quadratic term allowed us to look for curvature. Thus, we can allow curvature of the regression line by including a covariate $X_{ij}^{(\text{quad})}$ that depends on the squares of X_{ij}. It gives us a pair of models to compare:

Null-hypothesis model: $Y_{ij} = \beta_0 + \beta_1 X_{ij} + \alpha_j + \mathsf{E}_{ij},$

Alternative-hypothesis model: $Y_{ij} = \beta_0 + \beta_1 X_{ij} + \beta_1^{(\text{quad})} X_{ij}^{(\text{quad})} + \alpha_j + \mathsf{E}_{ij}.$

The first of these is the standard analysis-of-covariance model with straight regression lines and the second can have curved lines. We could simply use $X_{ij}^{(\text{quad})} = X_{ij}^2$ as the new covariate, but the resulting values can be inconveniently large, and they will be correlated with the original X_{ij}. It is better to subtract the covariate grand mean $\bar{X}_T$ from X_{ij} before squaring:

$$X_{ij}^{(\text{quad})} = (X_{ij} - \bar{X}_T)^2. \tag{15.21}$$

After making this change, the absolute size of the covariate is greatly reduced, as is its correlation with X_{ij}. For numerical convenience, you can use an integer or other round value near $\bar{X}_T$ instead of $\bar{X}_T$ itself and achieve the same result. For our example, $\overline{X}_T = 7.75$ which is close to 8, so we can take $X_{ij}^{(\text{quad})} = (X_{ij} - 8)^2$ for the second covariate. Values of this new variable are given in data panel of Table 15.8, and the summary of the analysis of covariance using both X and $X^{(\text{quad})}$ is given at the bottom. Our primary interest is the test of $X^{(\text{quad})}$, and it is significant, indicating that adding curvature improves the fit of the regression lines. We conclude that linearity of regression is violated.

When a curved relationship between the covariate and the dependent variable is found, you don't need to abandon the analysis of covariance. One possibility is to perform the analysis using both covariates. The group effect in this analysis at the bottom of Table 15.8 tests whether the heights of the curved regression lines are different. In our example, this effect is significant, and the difference between the adjusted means ($\overline{Y}_2' - \overline{Y}_1' = 7.924 - 5.326 = 2.598$) tells us that the line for group a_2 is about $2\frac{1}{2}$ points above that for group a_1. We could describe this finding as the result of an analysis of covariance with a quadratic covariate.

A better way to treat a nonlinear relationship between X and Y is to transform the covariate X so that its relationship with Y becomes a straight line. Most books on regression describe transformations that you can try. Once you have a straight-line relationship between the transformed value of X and Y, you can go ahead and look for group differences in Y with a normal single-covariate analysis of covariance. Problem 15.7 illustrates the analysis using Table 15.8.

15.6   Blocking and the Analysis of Covariance

At the start of this chapter, we mentioned the similarity between the analysis of covariance and the analysis of variance with blocked subjects. Both remove variability from the error term to improve the power and precision of the analysis. We noted that the analysis of covariance is like a post-hoc blocked design, in that neither the variable used to create the blocks nor the covariate is involved in the assignment of subjects to groups. Although their goals are the same, the two methods make their adjustments in different ways. Both procedures begin with the measurement of an ancillary variable, but they differ on how this information is used.

The largest difference between the two approaches arises because the model for the analysis of covariance specifies that the relationship between covariate and dependent variable is a straight line. In contrast, a blocked design allows any form of relationship. This specificity gives the analysis of covariance more power when its assumptions are satisfied. On the other hand, issues such as the linearity of the regression, which is a potential problem in the analysis of covariance, are irrelevant to the blocking design. There is no need for a blocking classification to be quantitative at all; we could block groups of subjects using a classification variable, say, college major or political affiliation, for which an analysis of covariance makes no sense. This difference extends to the measurement of the interaction. In a blocked design, the test for an interaction emerges naturally from the factorial form of the design as a treatment-by-blocks effect and is often a part of the researcher's plan. In the analysis of covariance, the interaction refers specifically to differences in the slope of the individual group regression lines and is often examined only to test the assumption of equal slopes.

There are also some important similarities. Both procedures reduce the size of the error term and increase the power of the tests. Both provide more accurate assessments of the effects. In each procedure, the test statistics do not refer to the ordinary means ($\overline{Y}_j$ for the analysis of covariance or $\overline{Y}_{A_j}$ for a blocked design), but to the means after an adjustment ($\overline{Y}'_j$ and the estimated means, respectively). In the analysis of covariance, the adjustments are taken from the regression lines, as if the covariate in all groups had the common value $\overline{X}_T$. In the blocked design, they are provided by calculating the means for the main effects using equally weighted groups procedure (Section 14.3), as if the blocking factor had been equally distributed over the groups.

Which procedure should you use? Post-hoc blocking is the only possibility when the ancillary variable is not numerical, and it is preferable when nonlinearities or complex interactions with the treatment conditions are expected. However, the analysis of covariance has more power when its assumptions are satisfied. The advantages of the analysis of covariance increase with the correlation between X and Y (as calculated within the groups, not for the data set as a whole). In an early study, Feldt (1958) showed that when this correlation is less than about .2, neither method provides any advantage over a simple one-way analysis of variance, and when it exceeds .6, the analysis of covariance is distinctly preferable. In between, either approach works about equally well. Later investigations (e.g., Maxwell, Delaney, & Dill, 1984) reemphasize the importance of the *form* of the relationship between the two variables. If the regression is not linear, blocking is preferable; otherwise, the analysis of covariance is the method of choice.

15.7 Preexisting Covariate Differences

Throughout this chapter, we have emphasized two uses of the analysis of covariance: reduction of error and adjustment of the means. When the subjects have been randomly assigned to treatment conditions, there is little reason to expect systematic differences in the covariate means, and so the primary effect of the analysis is a reduction in the size of the error term. The adjustment of the means simply takes care of any accidental imbalance in the covariate. When the groups are defined by a classification factor, however, the situation can be quite different. With a preexisting classification, group differences in the covariate X may well arise from systematic differences among the populations.[7]

Suppose you are comparing the performance on a cognitive task of two groups of patients diagnosed with damage in different areas of the brain. It is not unusual in such studies to find that performance is partially related to the age of the patient. Obviously, in a neuropsychological study such as this, it is not possible to assign subjects to groups, randomly or otherwise. You simply form the groups by selecting from a record of patients who fit your criteria. But what can you do when you find that there are differences in the average ages of the two samples? Any differences you find in performance between the two groups may be due to the location of the damage,

---

[7]A third possibility is that random assignment was used, but that the covariate was not measured until after the treatment was given, and its values were affected by the treatment itself. The analysis of covariance is not appropriate here. The dependent variable and the covariate here are better thought of as a single bivariate (two-part) observation. If you have such data you should turn to such techniques as the multivariate analysis of variance in Sections 17.2 and 19.3.

Table 15.9: Ages and error score for two groups with damage in two brain locations. The bottom panels give the analysis of variance and analysis of covariance. Note that order of the means $\bar{Y}_j$ and the adjusted means $\bar{Y}_j'$ are reversed.

Two groups with differences in both covariate and dependent variable

	Group a_1		Group a_2	
	X	Y	X	Y
	62	3	68	5
	63	4	70	7
	63	5	71	6
	64	5	72	8
	64	6	72	9
	65	5	73	7
	66	4	73	8
	66	7	74	9
	67	6	75	11
	67	8	76	10
	68	7	77	9
	69	9	77	11
Mean:	65.33	5.75	73.17	8.33
Adj. Mean:		8.14		5.95

Analysis of variance

Source	SS	df	MS	F
Location, A	40.042	1	40.042	12.08*
Error, S/A	72.917	22	3.314	
Total	112.958	23		

* $p < .05$

Analysis of covariance

Source	SS	df	MS	F
Age, X	51.413	1	51.413	50.21*
Location, A	7.875	1	7.875	7.69*
Model	91.455	2		
Error	21.504	21	1.024	
Total	112.958	23		

* $p < .05$

to difference in age, or to both factors. It is very tempting to use the adjusted means from the analysis of covariance to remove the effects of age.

The top panel of Table 15.9 gives a set of data in which we have exaggerated the covariate effects to make the issues more obvious. In this example, the X scores are ages and the Y scores are the number of errors made on the cognitive task. As you can

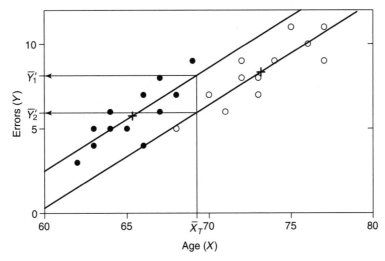

Figure 15.7: Scatterplot of the data in Table 15.9, with patients in a_1 designated with solid circles and those in a_2 with open circles. The solid lines are group regression lines used by the analysis of covariance, the crosses mark the group means $\bar{Y}_j$, and the adjusted means $\bar{Y}'_j$ are indicated on the ordinate.

see from the means of Y, group a_1 made fewer errors than group a_2, a difference that is significant when tested with an analysis of variance in the middle panel. However, group a_1 was also younger than group a_2, also a significant difference ($F = 58.55$). Finally, the scatterplot in Figure 15.7 clearly shows an appreciable correlation between the age and the number of errors.

What happens when the analysis of covariance is applied to these data? There is a significant A effect (Table 15.9, bottom), but what does it mean? In Figure 15.7, the plus signs mark the two pairs of means, $(\bar{X}_1, \bar{Y}_1)$ and $(\bar{X}_2, \bar{Y}_2)$, and the two solid lines are the regression lines that pass through these points. The adjusted means $\bar{Y}'_j$ lie on these lines at the average age of the combined sample ($\bar{X}_T = 69.25$ years). These adjusted means, which may be read off the Y axis of the plot as in Figure 15.4, are given in Table 15.9. You can see that when adjusted for age differences, the outcome is reversed. Group a_1 now has a higher value than group a_2. According to the adjusted means, the researcher could say that whenever there were two patients with the same age, the one with damage of the type in group a_1 would be expected to make more errors than the one with damage of the type in group a_2. The statistical analysis in Table 15.9 supports this conclusion—the difference between the adjusted means is significant with $F = 7.69$.

The two analyses in Table 15.9 test very different things. The standard analysis of variance tests for differences in the mean number of errors between the groups, without regard to any differences in age. The analysis of covariance takes the age into account by projecting how two patients of the same age would differ. In the extreme case illustrated here, the two results are altogether different.

Our example shows both the attractive features and the dangers of the analysis of covariance applied to data with unequal covariate means. On the positive side, it allows the groups to be compared on an equivalent basis, which was impossible with the unadjusted means because of the difference in age. The researcher who has made these calculations knows more about the situation than if only the unadjusted means had been examined. However, the correction is statistical, based on the linear model, and describes how the data *might have been* (if the ages were comparable), but not what they actually were. In short, the analysis of covariance here is not simply a more accurate way to test the hypotheses of the analysis of variance, as it was when there were no systematic group differences in X_{ij}. It now tests an altogether different set of hypotheses. When describing the analysis, it is particularly important to make clear which results depend on the analysis of covariance; specifically, it is essential that you do not simply report "means" without making it clear whether you are referring to unadjusted means or adjusted means.

The use of the analysis of covariance in situations like this has engendered a great deal of discussion among practitioners and methodologists. We only have space to touch on three issues. First, the interpretation of the analysis of covariance here depends very strongly on the validity of the linear model (Equation 15.13). If the slopes of the individual group regression lines were even a little different from each other or the relationship between X and Y was just somewhat nonlinear, then the size and nature of the adjustment would change and with it, perhaps, the outcome of the analysis. The sensitivity of the analysis to these assumptions increases as the distributions of the groups on the covariate diverge. The farther the group means $\bar{X}_j$ lie from $\bar{X}_T$, the more small violations of linearity or homogeneity of regression affect the adjusted means. Whenever working with preexisting groups, it is crucial to go through the checks of the assumptions in Section 15.5.

The second issue is interpretational. The adjusted means, which are what the analysis of covariance compares, are estimated at $\bar{X}_T$, which may not be a representative value for the groups involved. Look back at Table 15.9. We have ordered the data in terms of increasing ages of the patients. The overall average age of the patients ($\bar{X}_T = 69.25$) years falls at the extremes of both groups—the high end of group a_1 and the low end of group a_2. When we think of the adjusted means as the scores of patients of comparable age, we are comparing one of the oldest members of group a_1 to the one of the youngest members of group a_2. Whether such a comparison is sensible depends on the details of the study. In the extreme case, where the groups do not overlap at all, there may be no individuals from either group to which the conclusions apply. Lord (1969) gives a wonderfully concise statement of this problem.

The third issue, which is by far the most subtle, concerns the assumption of no measurement error in X. The linear model for the analysis of covariance (Equation 15.13) expresses Y as a combination of the group effect, the regression, and the error in measuring Y. There is no provision for error in measuring X. In fact, measurement errors are common in psychological data. With a covariate like age, there is no difficulty in determining it accurately. But a quantity like quantitative ability is another matter. Any measurement we have of this construct is imperfect and subject to the same sorts of error as the dependent variable. This inaccuracy contributes additional variability to the data that is not taken into account by the analysis of covariance. The effect of this additional variability is to reduce the slope of the empirical regression line relative to its true value—an instance of the phenomenon of regression to the mean that we mentioned on page 318. The effect is the same as if we made a mistake in determining the slope of the regression lines. Thus, the difference between the adjusted means revealed by the analysis of covariance may be partially an artifact of mismeasurement of the covariate. Lord (1967), has another nice, short illustration of the difficulty.[8]

We cannot make a definitive recommendation about the use of the analysis of covariance to adjust for preexisting differences among the groups on the covariate. Statistical adjustment is one of the most delicate and problematic parts of data analysis. Its vulnerabilities can be so severe as to invalidate any conclusions, yet there are important questions that are hard to approach any other way. Some researchers reject it as too risky; others are more sanguine. They feel that the ability of the analysis to place the groups on a comparable level exceeds its risks. Our feeling is that this analysis, like any other statistical technique, is just one of many tools for looking at a set of data. When the relevant populations differ on important variables, it is better to make the adjustments and compare the results to the unadjusted analysis than to give up studying the problem or to pretend that the differences between the populations do not exist. You will need to judge each such application for yourself. However, if you use the analysis of covariance to remove differences among preexisting groups, you should be prepared to explain, and possibly defend, your results. You should certainly report both the original and adjusted means, along with those of the covariate. You may want to buttress your argument with an analysis of the regression slopes and curvatures, and show that these assumptions are not appreciably violated. If either slope differences or nonlinearities are present, you should look for other ways to approach your problem.

15.8 Effect Sizes, Power, and Sample Size

The analysis of effect sizes and power for the analysis of covariance is very similar to its counterparts for other designs. There are two important differences, however. The first of these concerns the type of effect size to be calculated. The single-factor analysis of covariance gives sums of squares for two systematic effects, one expressing the differences among the treatment groups, the other the slope of the group regression lines (the parameters α_j and β_1, respectively). Either complete or partial measures of association could be defined, but only the partial measures are appropriate for the analysis of covariance.[9] The second difference is that the error term in analysis of covariance does not equal the within group error $\sigma^2_{S/A}$, but to the variablity after the effects of the covariate have been removed.[10]

The partial effect size for factor A is the ratio of the variability of the effect to the sum of that variability and the error variability (Equation 11.21, p. 233):

$$\omega^2_{\langle A \rangle} = \frac{\sigma^2_A}{\sigma^2_A + \sigma^2_{\text{error}}}. \tag{15.22}$$

---

[8]A modern approach to these measurement problems comes from covariance structure analysis (e.g., Bollen, 1989).

[9]A complete measure, which sets the variability among the groups against the total variability in the study, is more comparable to the effect size in an ordinary one-way analysis of variance.

[10]A third difference, applicable only when the covariate differs systematically among the groups, is that hypotheses concern the means adjusted for these systematic differences.

In the analysis of covariance, the effect variability has the same meaning that it did in the one-way design, $\sigma_A^2 = \sum \alpha_j^2/a$, but the error variability refers to the variance of the scores around the group regression lines with common slope, not to that around the means. It is smaller than the within-group variability by a factor equal to one minus the square of the correlation between X and Y within the groups. In population terms, this correlation is denoted by ρ_{XY} (the Greek letter is a lower-case rho, pronounced "row," which corresponds to the Latin letter r), so

$$\sigma_{\text{error}}^2 = \sigma_{S/A}^2 (1 - \rho_{XY}^2). \tag{15.23}$$

If you have population values available, you can use Equations 15.22 and 15.23 to obtain an effect size, as we will illustrate below.

To estimate the partial effect size from the results of an experiment, you start with the F statistic from the analysis of covariance and use the same formula that applies to ordinary one-way and two-way designs (Equation 8.12, p. 164, and Equation 11.22, p. 233):

$$\widehat{\omega}_{\langle A \rangle}^2 = \frac{df_A(F_A - 1)}{df_A(F_A - 1) + N}, \tag{15.24}$$

where N is the total number of subjects in all groups, here an. As an illustration, return to the example in Table 15.3. From Table 15.4, $F_A = 8.28$, and so Equation 15.24 gives

$$\widehat{\omega}_{\langle A \rangle}^2 = \frac{df_A(F_A - 1)}{df_A(F_A - 1) + N} = \frac{(1)(8.28 - 1)}{(1)(8.28 - 1) + 16} = \frac{7.28}{23.28} = 0.313.$$

This is quite a large effect, as is obvious from the scatterplot.

Squared correlation ratios R^2 are also used to measure effect size. As in other designs (e.g., Equation 11.24, p. 234), they are calculated by replacing the variances in the formulas for ω^2 with sums of squares. Thus, replacing σ_A^2 by SS_A and σ_{error}^2 by SS_{error} in Equation 15.22 gives the squared correlation ratio for the analysis of covariance:

$$R_{\langle A \rangle}^2 = \frac{SS_A}{SS_A + SS_{\text{error}}}. \tag{15.25}$$

For example, using the sums of squares from Table 15.4:

$$R_{\langle A \rangle}^2 = \frac{SS_A}{SS_A + SS_{\text{error}}} = \frac{30.640}{30.640 + 48.132} = 0.389.$$

The squared correlation ratio does not compensate for inflation due to sampling variability, so its value is larger than the value of $\widehat{\omega}_{\langle A \rangle}^2 = 0.313$ found above.

Determining Power or Sample Size

Because the analysis of covariance uses a smaller error term than the analysis of variance, it requires smaller samples to attain a given degree of power. These sample sizes can be found with a minor modification of the procedure in Section 8.4.[11] The central idea is to find the partial ω^2 and convert it to power or sample size using the charts in Appendix A.7 or the quick table of sample sizes (Table 8.1). The process is particularly simple when a previous analysis of covariance is used as a model for a new

---

[11] Because of their similarity, most authors subsume these calculations with those for the ordinary analysis of variance. For discussion of the analysis of covariance, see Cohen (1988, pp. 379–380) and Rogers and Hopkins (1988).

study. We first calculate $\widehat{\omega}^2_{\langle A \rangle}$ from Equation 15.24 and then apply the sample-size table or the power charts. The relevant formula for a one-way design is Equation 8.18 (p. 174) and that for a factorial design is Equation 11.25 (p. 236).

The calculation is a little more complicated when we want to use the results of an analysis of variance to estimate sample size for a new study that uses a covariate. We need to convert $\widehat{\omega}^2_A$ from the analysis of variance to the $\omega^2_{\langle A \rangle}$ we expect to find in the new study with an analysis of covariance. This conversion uses the correlation ρ_{XY} between the covariate and the dependent variable in the new study. In Equation 15.23 we saw that using a covariate reduces σ^2_{error} to a proportion $1 - \rho^2_{XY}$ of its value without the covariate. This change increases the size of the partial effect size. The relationship between the effect size ω^2_A in the ordinary one-way analysis of variance and the partial effect size $\omega^2_{\langle A \rangle}$ in the analysis of covariance is

$$\omega^2_{\langle A \rangle}(\text{ancova}) = \frac{\sigma^2_A}{\sigma^2_A + (1 - \rho^2_{XY})\sigma^2_{S/A}} = \frac{\omega^2_A}{\omega^2_A + (1 - \omega^2_A)(1 - \rho^2_{XY})}. \tag{15.26}$$

When $\rho^2_{XY} = 0$, the analysis of covariance has no effect and $\omega^2_{\langle A \rangle}$ is the same as the ordinary ω^2_A, and when $\rho^2_{XY} = 1$, there is no residual error, and $\omega^2_{\langle A \rangle} = 1$. Of course, any real application falls between these extremes. Equation 15.26 also applies to effects in a factorial design, with the effect sizes on the right replaced with the partial effect sizes from the ordinary analysis, $\omega^2_{\langle A \rangle}$, $\omega^2_{\langle B \rangle}$, or $\omega^2_{\langle A \times B \rangle}$, depending on which effect is being used to determine the sample size.

In Chapter 8 (see p. 172), we looked at the power to detect a four-point difference between two groups in a situation in which the within-group standard deviation σ_{error} was about 10. We found that for this effect $\omega^2_A = 0.038$, or about 0.04, and obtained the rather gloomy result that we needed a sample size of $n = 60$ to attain the unimpressive power of .60. Now suppose we have identified a potential covariate that pilot research tell us is correlated with our dependent variable at about $\rho_{XY} = 0.6$. How much will the analysis of covariance reduce the sample-size demands? We calculate the new effect size using the second part of Equations 15.26:

$$\omega^2_{\langle A \rangle}(\text{ancova}) = \frac{\omega^2_A}{\omega^2_A + (1 - \omega^2_A)(1 - \rho^2_{XY})} = \frac{0.04}{0.04 + (1 - 0.04)(1 - 0.6^2)} = 0.061.$$

Turning to Table 8.1 (p. 173), we see that for an effect of this size in a two-group design, we need about 40 subjects for a power of .60. Alternatively, if we use the original sample size of $n = 60$, the power is increased to almost .80 (from Table 8.1, a sample size of $n = 63$ is needed to reach a power of .80). The advantages of the analysis of covariance in this situation are clearly apparent.

For another illustration, suppose the $A \times B$ interaction in a 3×4 factorial design with $n = 12$ subjects per group had fallen just short of significance ($F = 2.05$ with 6 and 132 degrees of freedom). The study is to be replicated using a relatively weak covariate with $\rho_{XY} = 0.35$, and the researcher would like to have a power of at least .80 to detect the interaction, should it be as before. First, Equation 11.22 (p. 233) is used to estimate the partial effect size for the original study:

$$\widehat{\omega}^2_{\langle A \times B \rangle} = \frac{df_{A \times B}(F_{A \times B} - 1)}{df_{A \times B}(F_{A \times B} - 1) + abn} = \frac{(6)(2.05 - 1)}{(6)(2.05 - 1) + (3)(4)(12)} = 0.042.$$

Now, using Equation 15.26, we estimate the size for the new study

$$\omega^2_{\langle A \times B \rangle}(\text{ancova}) = \frac{\omega^2_{\langle A \times B \rangle}}{\omega^2_{\langle A \times B \rangle} + (1 - \omega^2_{\langle A \times B \rangle})(1 - \rho^2_{XY})}$$

$$= \frac{0.042}{0.042 + (1 - 0.042)(1 - 0.35^2)} = 0.048.$$

Finally, we use the power charts in Appendix A.7 to determine the sample size for the replication. From the chart for $df_{\text{num}} = df_{A \times B} = 6$, $df_{\text{denom}} = 100$, and a power of .80, we find $\phi = 1.4$; and with Equation 11.25 (p. 236),

$$N = \phi^2(df_{\text{effect}} + 1)\frac{1 - \omega^2_{\langle \text{effect} \rangle}}{\omega^2_{\langle \text{effect} \rangle}} = (1.4^2)(6 + 1)\frac{1 - 0.048}{0.048} = 272.113.$$

Solving for the sample size per group, $n = N/ab = 272.11/12 = 22.7$, or somewhere around 23 subjects are needed per group, nearly twice that of the original study. As you can determine from Equation 11.25, the sample size for an ordinary analysis of variance under these circumstances is n is about 28, so the proposed introduction of the covariate has only a modest effect, principally because the correlation of the covariate and the dependent variable is small.

The first part of Equation 15.26 can also be used to determine sample sizes from theoretically determined estimates of the population means μ_j, the within group variance $\sigma^2_{S/A}$, and the correlation ρ_{XY}. From the means, find the effects α_j and the effect variance $\sigma_A = \sum \alpha_j / a$. Then substitute into Equation 15.26 to get ω^2_A for the study and use the power charts.

Exercises

15.1. The data in Table 15.7 show two groups with a quite sizable difference in slope. Using the procedures in Section 15.1, verify that the slopes of the regression lines calculated separately for group a_1 is $b_1 = -0.229$ and for group a_2 is $b_1 = 0.632$.

15.2. Use the principles of the general linear model to test whether the slope β_1 of the regression line in Figure 15.1 is different from zero. First use the sums of squares in Table 15.2 to obtain $SS^{H_0}_{\text{unexp}}$ and $SS^{H_1}_{\text{unexp}}$ according to the two models in Equations 15.7 and 15.8. Then use Equations 14.4 and 14.8 to calculate the sum of squares for the regression effect and its degrees of freedom. With this information, complete the table

Source	SS	df	MS	F
Regression				
Error				
Total				

15.3. Suppose an instructor in a statistics class wants to evaluate the effectiveness of three teaching assistants. For one class session, the students are randomly divided into three groups, each of which receives a lecture on power and effect size from one of the assistants. At the next meeting of the class, the students are given a quiz on the material. The results of the quiz (Y_{ij}), together with scores from a statistical aptitude test administered at the beginning of the semester (X_{ij}), are as follows:

	Group a_1		Group a_2		Group a_3	
	X	Y	X	Y	X	Y
	50	48	45	42	47	40
	55	44	40	37	44	36
	53	42	41	34	37	33
	54	37	53	32	45	31
	40	46	54	37	40	30
	25	29	53	28	25	28
	53	39	23	8	53	41
	41	43	32	11	45	35
	45	30	30	11	34	24
	19	13	20	5	23	16
	10	27	13	6	32	25
	20	22	10	1	20	15
Mean	38.75	35.00	34.50	21.00	37.00	29.50
Std. Devn.	16.05	10.80	15.61	15.20	10.62	8.39

Use a computer program to investigate the following questions:

a. Did the random assignment of the students to the three lectures result in reasonably equivalent groups on the statistical aptitude test?

b. Does an analysis of variance reveal any systematic differences on the quiz administered following the lectures given by the teaching assistants?

c. What does an analysis of covariance reveal? How do the adjusted means compare to those from the original analysis? In what ways is this analysis an improvement over the analysis of variance?

15.4. In Section 15.5 (see p. 333), we described a way to test the assumption of equal slopes in the analysis of covariance by setting up variables $X^{(j)}$ specific to each group and comparing the analysis of covariance using these variables to the ordinary analysis of covariance.

a. Use the computer to apply this test to the data in Problem 15.3.

b. If your program has a way to test the $A \times X$ interaction directly, compare your results to those you found in part a.

15.5. The analysis of covariance of the data from two-factor experiment in Table 15.6 revealed a significant $A \times B$ interaction. Use the adjusted means to test the simple effects of factor B.

15.6. Using the data and results from Problem 15.3, determine the following:

a. The size of the effect, as estimated from the analysis of variance and the analysis of covariance.

b. The sample size needed in a replication of the study using the same covariate to have a power of .9 to detect the observed effect.

c. The sample size required with an ordinary analysis of variance and the same power.

d. The power an analysis of variance would have if the sample size equaled the value you estimated in part b and the covariate was not used.

15.7. When the relationship between the covariate X and the dependent variable Y is bowl shaped, it can often be straightened by replacing X by the squared distance to the point where Y is minimum. Figure 15.6 shows that the data in Table 15.8 have this form. The minimum of Y occurs approximately where $X = 8$ (coincidentally, near its mean). Thus, the variable $X_{ij}^{(\mathrm{quad})} = (X_{ij} - 8)^2$ is a candidate transformation.

a. Make of scatterplot of $X_{ij}^{(\mathrm{quad})}$ and Y for the two groups and comment on their form.

b. Use a computer to test for a difference between the groups using $X_{ij}^{(\mathrm{quad})}$ as a covariate.

15.8. On pages 171–172 we illustrated the determination of sample size for three different single-factor designs. How would those sample sizes change if we were able to introduce a covariate with $\rho_{XY} \approx .45$?

Part V

WITHIN-SUBJECT DESIGNS

All the experimental designs in the preceding chapters have shared the characteristic that each subject is exposed to a single treatment condition. Such designs are known as **between-subjects designs** because all sources of variability extracted in the analysis of variance represent differences between (or among) subjects. There are also designs in which each subject serves in some or all the treatment conditions. Naturally enough, such designs are referred to as **within-subject designs**, reflecting the fact that the key effects are now based on differences among the scores of the individual subjects. These designs are also called **repeated-measures designs**, which emphasizes the multiple measures taken from each subject. Either term is satisfactory; however, we will primarily refer to these designs as within-subject designs.

A substantial proportion of the experiments conducted in the behavioral sciences make use of within-subject designs. There are several reasons for this prevalence. For one, they are an obvious choice to study phenomena that are expressed as differences among behavioral measures at different times, such as learning, transfer of training, forgetting, attitude change, and so on. For another, they allow more efficient use of limited subject resources—more information is obtained by collecting several scores from each subject than by collecting only one. Third, two scores obtained from a single subject are usually more similar to each other than they are to the scores of different subjects, a fact that typically gives within-subject comparisons greater power and sensitivity than a between-subjects design with the same number of observations. Against these advantages must be set the additional complexity of the assumptions underlying the analyses, to be described in Sections 17.1 and 17.2.

Although we have spoken of between-subjects and within-subject *designs* above, it also makes sense to speak of between-subjects and within-subject *factors*. In a single-factor design, the factor of interest may either be studied between subjects (leading to a between-subjects design) or within each subject (leading to a within-subject design). With two or more factors, several configurations of factors are possible. Consider a two-factor design with two levels of factor A and three levels of factor B, i.e. with six conditions in all. In the standard between-subjects design, such as those we discussed in Part III, this design with $n = 3$ subjects per group requires $abn = (2)(3)(3) = 18$ subjects:

Both A and B in this $A \times B$ design are between-subjects factors. We could conduct the same experiment as a within-subject design using only three subjects by treating A and B as within-subject factors and collecting six scores from each subject:

This completely within-subject configuration is referred to as an $A \times B \times S$ design. We will discuss the one-factor version of this design (an $A \times S$ design) in Chapters 16 and 17 and the two-factor version in Chapter 18.

Between-subjects and within-subject factors can be combined in a single design. The 2×3 study above can be constructed with factor A varying between subjects and factor B within subjects, using a total of six subjects:

Such a design is referred to as a **mixed design**. We will denote it by $A \times (B \times S)$. For reasons having to do with the original application of the analysis of variance to agricultural studies, it is also known as a **split-plots design**. When used appropriately, a mixed design combines the advantages of both the between-subjects and within-subject factors, which makes it very popular. We will discuss it in Chapters 19 and 20. We will return to both completely within-subject and mixed designs in Part VI, particularly in Chapter 23.

Within-subject designs can be conducted in two essentially different ways. In a **successive-treatment design**, one treatment condition is administered, then another, then a third, and so forth. In an **intermixed-treatment design**, the treatment conditions are mixed together in such a way that their order is not relevent. The difference between the two designs is easy to see in an example. Suppose that a researcher is interested in studying the effects of the amount of reward on learning words, and plans to present subjects with words to learn and to pay them 1 cent, 5 cents, or 25 cents when they correctly remember them at a later test. In a sequential design, the subjects are given a list and told that they will be paid one amount, say 1 cent for remembering the words. They are tested on these words. Later, perhaps even on another day, they are given a second list with a different reward value, say 25 cents. After this list has been tested, a third list with the 5-cent reward value is presented and tested. In an intermixed version of this design, only a single list is studied on which one-third of the words are marked (say by their color) as worth 1 cent, one-third are marked as worth 5 cents, and one-third are marked as worth 25 cents. The different words are presented one after another in some haphazard order, with the three types of words all mixed up. At the end of the study period, all words are tested together, and the experimenter rewards each word appropriately to the color in which it was originally presented. The recalled words are sorted out to determine how many words of each type were remembered. Both these designs yield three scores for each subject, and they are analyzed in the same way. As you will see in Chapter 17, in a successive-treatment design, the order in which the conditions are presented is a matter for concern, while in an intermixed-treatment design it is not.

16

The Single-Factor Within-Subject Design: Basic Calculations

We begin our discussion with the simplest within-subject design, that with a single within-subject factor and no between-subjects factors. In this chapter we describe the basic analysis of variance, tests of contrasts, effect-size calculations, and power determinations. The presence of the within-subject factor introduces some complications that we will discuss in Chapter 17.

16.1 The Analysis of Variance

The hypotheses that are tested in a within-subject design—the overall effects and the contrasts and comparisons that are extracted from them—are like those for a between-subjects design. However, as we discuss in this chapter, there are important differences in other respects, particularly the structure of the scores and the error terms used to construct the tests.

Design and Notation

Table 16.1 shows the basic structure of the scores in a single-factor within-subject design. The notational system here is very like that for the comparable between-subjects design. Specifically, the scores in the data table are denoted by Y_{ij}, where the first subscript i indicates the subject, and the second subscript j indicates the particular level of factor A. There are a levels of factor A and n subjects. In spite of this similarity, the relationship of the subjects to factor A is different from that in the between-subjects design. In that design, each subject served in only one condition. The subjects were *nested* within the groups, which we symbolized by denoting the subject factor by S/A. Now, each subject supplies one score in each condition. We can therefore think of the subjects as constituting a subject factor that is *crossed* with the treatment factor, similar to the way that factors A and B are crossed in the two-factor between-subjects $A \times B$ design. We will denote this factor by S. Often, the easiest way to think of the single-factor within-subject design is as if it were a factorial experiment in which subjects (factor S) are the levels of the second factor. Thus, it is convenient and accurate to refer to it as an $A \times S$ design.

Table 16.1: The notation system for an $A \times S$ design with $a = 4$ conditions and $n = 3$ subjects.

	Levels of factor A				
Subjects	a_1	a_2	a_3	a_4	Sum
s_1	Y_{11}	Y_{12}	Y_{13}	Y_{14}	S_1
s_2	Y_{21}	Y_{22}	Y_{23}	Y_{24}	S_2
s_3	Y_{31}	Y_{32}	Y_{33}	Y_{34}	S_3
Sum	A_1	A_2	A_3	A_4	T

Table 16.1 also shows the marginal totals. Here the notation for the $A \times S$ design differs from that for a between-subjects design. We can calculate (and will use) marginal sums for both the rows and columns. The column sums A_j are the usual treatment sums, and the row sums S_i are the overall totals for each subject at all levels of factor A. The symbol T continues to signify the grand total of all the scores. Each of the marginal sums corresponds to a mean, which is found by dividing the sum by the number of scores that make it up. There are three types of means: the mean for a treatment condition, the mean score for each subject, and the overall grand mean:

$$\bar{Y}_j = A_j/n, \quad \bar{Y}_{S_i} = S_i/a, \quad \text{and} \quad \bar{Y}_T = T/an.$$

Partitioning the Variability

The amount of variability among the scores in a one-way between-subjects design is measured by the total variability, as expressed by the total sum of squares:

$$SS_T = \sum (Y_{ij} - \bar{Y}_T)^2.$$

Just as the between-subjects variablity in the two-factor $A \times B$ design with crossed factors is divided into two effects and an interaction, the total variability in an $A \times S$ design is divided into SS_A, SS_S and $SS_{A \times S}$. Each of these sums of squares represents a different aspect of the data:

- The size of the treatment sum of squares SS_A is determined by the differences among the treatments, just as it was in the between-subjects design. It is zero when the treatment means are all the same.
- The size of the subject sum of squares SS_S is determined by the extent to which the average scores of the subjects differ one from another.
- The interaction sum of squares $SS_{A \times S}$ measures the interaction between subjects and the treatments. It is determined by the extent to which different subjects react differently to the treatment conditions. It is small when the treatments have a consistent effect for every subject and large when each subject shows a different pattern of response.

These three sums of squares completely partition the variability in the within-subject design.

If you compare these three sources of variability to those for the $A \times B$ design (see p. 214), you will notice two differences. First, there is no within-cell term comparable

Table 16.2: Computational formulas for the $A \times S$ design.

Formulas for the analysis of variance

Source	df	SS	MS	F
A	$a - 1$	$[A] - [T]$	$\dfrac{SS_A}{df_A}$	$\dfrac{MS_A}{MS_{A \times S}}$
S	$n - 1$	$[S] - [T]$	$\dfrac{SS_S}{df_S}$	
$A \times S$	$(a - 1)(n - 1)$	$[Y] - [A] - [S] + [T]$	$\dfrac{SS_{A \times S}}{df_{A \times S}}$	
Total	$an - 1$	$[Y] - [T]$		

Formulas for the bracket terms

$$[A] = \frac{\sum A_j^2}{n} = n \sum \bar{Y}_A^2 \qquad\qquad [S] = \frac{\sum S_i^2}{a} = a \sum \bar{Y}_S^2$$

$$[Y] = \sum Y_{ij}^2 \qquad\qquad\qquad [T] = \frac{T^2}{an} = an \bar{Y}_T^2$$

to $SS_{S/AB}$. With only a single observation within each cell, such a measure of variability cannot be calculated. Second, it is now possible to investigate the differences among the responses of the individual subjects to the full range of treatments by looking at $SS_{A \times S}$. Both of these facts have implications for the analysis.

Computational Formulas

The calculations of the sums of squares for the $A \times S$ design are like those for the two-way $A \times B$ design, except that there is no within-groups factor. Following the steps in Table 11.2 (p. 214), we find that the sources of variance are A and S (Step 1) and $A \times S$ (Step 2). Thus, we need to find a total sum of squares SS_T, two main effects, SS_A and SS_S, and an interaction $SS_{A \times S}$. These sources are listed in the first column in the upper portion of Table 16.2.

Table 11.3 (p. 215) gives the steps we follow to find the degrees of freedom. First, the overall degrees of freedom are one less than the total number of observations:

$$df_T = an - 1.$$

The degrees of freedom for the main effects are one less than the number of levels:

$$df_A = a - 1 \quad \text{and} \quad df_S = n - 1,$$

and the degrees of freedom for the interaction are the product of the degrees of freedom of its component effects:

$$df_{A \times S} = df_A \times df_S = (a - 1)(n - 1).$$

You can verify that the three degrees of freedom add up to df_T, indicating that we have not omitted any effect.

The next column of Table 16.2 gives computational formulas for the sums of squares using bracket terms. These are found from the degrees-of-freedom equations, using the rules in Table 11.4 (p. 216). Each equation is expanded and the result converted to bracket terms. The bracket terms are calculated from either sums or means, as shown at the bottom of Table 16.2. Except for a few details (such as S instead of B), the calculations are the same as those for the two-way factorial design.

The final columns of Table 16.2 give the mean squares and the F ratio used to test the A effect. There is nothing surprising in the mean squares—they are constructed as usual by dividing the sums of squares by their degrees of freedom. The error term for the A main effect is a change, however. It is the interaction mean square $MS_{A \times S}$. This term reflects the extent to which the subjects respond differently to the treatments, and it is this variation, not that of the individual scores within the treatment conditions, that is used to assess the significance of the treatment effect. This error term is the key to the advantage of the within-subject design over its between-subjects counterpart.

One way to understand the error term is to look at how it relates to the division of the variability into between-subjects and within-subject parts. Think back to the single-factor between-subjects design (Chapter 2). In this design, the total sum of squares consists entirely of between-subject differences—each observation is obtained from a different subject—and is partitioned into two parts:

$$SS_T = SS_A + SS_{S/A}.$$

The sum of squares SS_A reflects variation among the treatment effects and any accidental differences arising from the random assignment of subjects to the treatment groups. The sum of squares $SS_{S/A}$ reflects the variation associated with subjects treated alike, specifically individual differences and other uncontrolled sources of variation. In the within-subject design, the partitioning is expanded and the variability designated as between-subjects or within-subject in nature. The variability of the subjects, which was $SS_{S/A}$ before, is partitioned into the between-subjects variation expressed by SS_S and the within-subject differences in reaction to the treatments expressed by $SS_{A \times S}$. The subject effect SS_S measures the consistent differences among individuals that affect the means $\overline{Y}_{S_i}$. The interaction $SS_{A \times S}$, on the other hand, is a within-subject effect that depends on the consistency of the treatment effects for each subject. The treatment sum of squares SS_A is also a within-subject effect—each subject supplies a score for each of the a treatment conditions—so it requires a within-subject error term that expresses how much inconsistency there is in the A effect over subjects. This measure is obtained from $SS_{A \times S}$. We will discuss the error term in more detail when we consider the statistical model in Section 17.2.

You may wonder why we have not specified F tests for either the main effect of subjects or the $A \times S$ interaction. For the subject effect, we could construct a test using $MS_{A \times S}$ as an error term:

$$F_S = \frac{MS_S}{MS_{A \times S}}.$$

However, as you will see when we look at the expected mean squares, this test is negatively biased. The problem with the interaction is different. In the $A \times S$ design, there is only one observation for each combination of A and S, and thus, no way to calculate both a sum of squares for the interaction and an error term that expresses its chance variation. As a practical matter, tests of these two effects are unimportant anyway. We don't need to verify the well-known facts that subjects differ from each other and that they react to treatments differently. Indeed, that variation is why we need the analysis of variance to compare the treatment effects to a measure of error.

Numerical Example

Consider an experiment in which college students search for a particular letter in a string of letters on a computer screen. Half of the time the letter occurs in the string, and half the time it does not, and the subject presses one button when it is and another when it is not. On one third of the trials the letter string is a word (condition a_1), on one third it is a pronounceable nonword (a_2), and on one third it is a unpronounceable set of random letters (a_3). The response measure is the average speed with which subjects correctly detect the target letter, measured in milliseconds (1000 msec equals 1 sec.). The experiment is a single-factor $A \times S$ design with $a = 3$ types of letter strings. Table 16.3 shows data from $n = 6$ students (factor S).

Our first step is to obtain a descriptive summary of the conditions, which we will need when we plot or report the data. Below each column of scores in Table 16.3, we have listed the sum of the Y_{ij} scores (i.e. A_j), the sum of the squared scores Y_{ij}^2, the treatment mean $\overline{Y}_j$, the standard deviation s_j, and the standard error of the mean s_{M_j}. For condition a_1, the last two calculations are

$$s_1 = \sqrt{\frac{\sum Y_{i1}^2 - (A_1)^2/n}{n-1}} = \sqrt{\frac{(745^2 + \cdots + 721^2) - 4{,}512^2/6}{6-1}} = 23.26,$$

$$s_{M_1} = \frac{s_1}{\sqrt{n}} = \frac{23.26}{\sqrt{6}} = 9.50.$$

We plot the treatment means in Figure 16.1, including error bars that extend from one standard error of the mean below the treatment mean to one standard error of the mean above it (recall Section 3.1). You can verify that for the first condition the error bar extends from

$$\overline{Y}_1 - s_{M_1} = 752.00 - 9.50 = 742.52 \quad \text{to} \quad \overline{Y}_1 + s_{M_1} = 752.00 + 9.50 = 761.50.$$

Confidence intervals for the population treatment means are calculated in a similar way, but with the standard error of the mean multiplied by a value from the t table. From Equation 3.4,

$$\overline{Y}_{A_j} - t \, s_{M_j} \leq \mu_j \leq \overline{Y}_{A_j} + t \, s_{M_j}, \tag{16.1}$$

where the value of t is obtained from Appendix A.2 with degrees of freedom equal to $df_{M_j} = n - 1$ and α level equal to 100 minus the confidence when expressed in percent. To construct a 95 percent confidence interval for group a_1, we use the $\alpha = .05$ level from the table and $df_{M_j} = 6 - 1 = 5$ to find $t = 2.57$ from Appendix A.2. Substituting into Equation 16.1 gives the lower and upper limits of the confidence interval:

$$\overline{Y}_1 - t \, s_{M_1} = 752.00 - (2.57)(9.50) = 727.59,$$

$$\overline{Y}_1 + t \, s_{M_1} = 752.00 + (2.57)(9.50) = 776.42.$$

Now we turn to the analysis of variance. The calculations are straightforward. In the original table, we find the subject sums S_i for each subject, which appear as marginal row totals. The overall sum, $T = 13{,}761$, can be found either by adding up

Table 16.3: *Numerical calculations for a single-factor within-subject analysis of variance.*

The AS data table

<table>
<tr><th rowspan="2">Subjects</th><th colspan="3">Types of strings</th><th rowspan="2">Sum</th></tr>
<tr><th>a_1</th><th>a_2</th><th>a_3</th></tr>
<tr><td>s_1</td><td>745</td><td>764</td><td>774</td><td>2,283</td></tr>
<tr><td>s_2</td><td>777</td><td>786</td><td>788</td><td>2,351</td></tr>
<tr><td>s_3</td><td>734</td><td>733</td><td>763</td><td>2,230</td></tr>
<tr><td>s_4</td><td>779</td><td>801</td><td>797</td><td>2,377</td></tr>
<tr><td>s_5</td><td>756</td><td>786</td><td>785</td><td>2,327</td></tr>
<tr><td>s_6</td><td>721</td><td>732</td><td>740</td><td>2,193</td></tr>
<tr><td>Sum</td><td>4,512</td><td>4,602</td><td>4,647</td><td>13,761</td></tr>
<tr><td>$\sum_i Y_{ij}^2$</td><td>3,395,728</td><td>3,534,002</td><td>3,601,223</td><td></td></tr>
<tr><td>Mean</td><td>752.00</td><td>767.00</td><td>774.50</td><td></td></tr>
<tr><td>s_j</td><td>23.26</td><td>29.22</td><td>20.60</td><td></td></tr>
<tr><td>s_{M_j}</td><td>9.50</td><td>11.93</td><td>8.41</td><td></td></tr>
</table>

Calculation of the bracket terms

$$[A] = \frac{\sum A_j^2}{n} = \frac{4{,}512^2 + 4{,}602^2 + 4{,}647^2}{6} = 10{,}521{,}859.5$$

$$[S] = \frac{\sum S_i^2}{a} = \frac{2{,}283^2 + \cdots + 2{,}193^2}{3} = 10{,}528{,}832.3$$

$$[Y] = \sum Y_{ij}^2 = 745^2 + 764^2 + \cdots + 732^2 + 740^2 = 10{,}530{,}953.0$$

$$[T] = \frac{T^2}{an} = \frac{13{,}761^2}{(3)(6)} = 10{,}520{,}284.5$$

Summary of the analysis of variance

Source	SS	df	MS	F
A	$[A] - [T] =$ 1,575.0	2	787.50	14.43*
S	$[S] - [T] =$ 8,547.8	5	1,709.56	
$A \times S$	$[Y] - [A] - [S] + [T] =$ 545.7	10	54.57	
Total	$[Y] - [T] =$ 10,668.5	17		

* $p < .05$

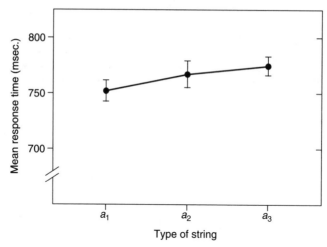

Figure 16.1: A plot of the means from Table 16.3, with error bars showing one standard error of the mean.

the A_j or the S_i—it is a good idea to do both to check your work. In the middle portion of Table 16.3, we find the bracket terms, drawing on numbers obtained from the upper panel. In the bottom panel of the table, these bracket terms are assembled into the analysis of variance. The F statistic for the treatment effects is significant $(F_{.05}(2, 10) = 4.10)$, indicating that the average speed of detection is not the same for the different types of strings.

In most cases, a within-subject design is more sensitive than a between-subjects analysis. We can illustrate the difference by reanalyzing Table 16.3—incorrectly—as if the data had been obtained from a between-subjects design with three independent groups. The resulting analysis, summarized in Table 16.4, no longer finds a significant difference among the means. Comparing the two analyses, you see that the mean square for the main effect of factor A remains the same, but the error term is substantially larger ($MS_{S/A} = 606.23$ instead of $MS_{A \times S} = 54.57$). In the between-subjects analysis, all variation not associated the treatment effect is treated as error, while in the within-subject analysis this variability is partitioned into the S and $A \times S$ parts, and only the latter serves as the error term. Because the variability among subjects is large ($MS_S = 1{,}709.56$ is larger than those of the other effects), the error term in the proper analysis is much smaller than in the incorrect analysis, giving the larger value of the F ratio. This removal of overall subject effects from the error is the key to the advantage of the within-subject design.

16.2   Analytical Comparisons

Tests of specific hypotheses based on contrasts among the treatment means are as important in within-subject designs as they are in between-subjects designs. The various types of comparisons mentioned in Chapters 4 and 5 for the single-factor between-subjects design can be used with within-subject designs. Their construction and interpretation remain as before. There is one important difference, however, and this again lies in the error term.

Table 16.4: An incorrect analysis of the data in Table 16.3 using the formulas for a between-subjects design. The result is no longer significant.

Source	SS	df	MS	F
A	$[A] - [T] = $ 1,575.0	2	787.50	1.30
S/A	$[Y] - [A] = $ 9,093.5	15	606.23	
Total	$[Y] - [T] = $ 10,668.5	17		

Within-Subject Contrasts and Error Variability

A linear contrast is a weighted sum of means, with coefficients that sum to zero:

$$\psi_A = \sum c_j \mu_j \quad \text{where} \quad \sum c_j = 0.$$

We estimate ψ_A by substituting the observed means $\overline{Y}_j$ for the μ_j, giving $\widehat{\psi}_A$. The sum of squares for this contrast is

$$SS_{\psi_A} = \frac{n\widehat{\psi}_A^2}{\sum c_j^2}. \tag{16.2}$$

This sum of squares is associated with one degree of freedom, so $MS_{\psi_A} = SS_{\psi_A}$. Thus far, the analysis is identical to that for a between-subjects design (Chapter 4).

What error term should we use to test this contrast? In the between-subjects designs, the mean square for a contrast was tested against the same error term that was used for the omnibus test, $MS_{S/A}$ (Equation 4.6, p. 70). In within-subject designs, the corresponding error term ($MS_{A \times S}$) is not appropriate. Research has shown that tests of contrasts are severely affected by even minor violations of the circularity assumption that we will discuss in the next chapter (see, for example, Boik, 1981). The safest strategy is to test each contrast against a measure of its own variability, just as we did for the between-subjects designs when the variances were heterogeneous (Section 7.5). This error term should express the extent to which the values of the contrast ψ_A vary over the individual subjects, that is, it should be the interaction of the *contrast* with subjects. The F ratio is

$$F_{\psi_A} = \frac{MS_{\psi_A}}{MS_{\psi_A \times S}}. \tag{16.3}$$

Testing a Within-Subject Contrast

There are many ways to find the error term we need in Equation 16.3. We will use an important and very handy shortcut here. The hypothesis we want to test concerns the average value of the contrast over subjects and the error is based on the variability of that contrast among them. We can find both of these quantities by calculating the value of the contrast for each subject, then finding the mean and standard deviation of these numbers. By calculating the individual contrast values, we simplify the data from a two-factor arrangement of the individual Y_{ij} scores to a single column of contrast values. Tests on these values lead to conclusions that are identical to those provided by Equation 16.3, but reached by a simpler set of procedures.

We will illustrate the analysis by testing the hypothesis that letters are identified more quickly when they appear in words than when they appear in either nonwords

Table 16.5: *Calculation of the contrast variable for $\psi = -\mu_1 + (\frac{1}{2})\mu_2 + (\frac{1}{2})\mu_3$ from the AS table of Table 16.3.*

Subjects	Types of strings a_1	a_2	a_3	Contrast $\widehat{\psi}_i$
s_1	745	764	774	24.0
s_2	777	786	788	10.0
s_3	734	733	763	14.0
s_4	779	801	797	20.0
s_5	756	786	785	29.5
s_6	721	732	740	15.0

Sum　112.5

Mean　18.75

$\sum \widehat{\psi}_i^2$ 2,367.25

or random strings of letters. More formally, we will test the hypothesis that $\psi_A = -\mu_1 + (\frac{1}{2})\mu_2 + (\frac{1}{2})\mu_3 = 0$. Table 16.5 shows how the table of observations is simplified. On the left we have copied the original scores from Table 16.3, and on the right we have calculated the values of the contrast for the individual subjects $(\widehat{\psi}_i)$. We will refer to $\widehat{\psi}_i$ as a **contrast variable**. For the first subject, its value is

$$\widehat{\psi}_1 = (-1)(745) + (\frac{1}{2})(764) + (\frac{1}{2})(774) = 24.0$$

The mean of the individual contrast values gives us the value of the contrast:

$$\widehat{\psi}_A = \sum \widehat{\psi}_i/n = 112.5/6 = 18.75.$$

This value is the same as the value calculated from the means:

$$\widehat{\psi}_A = -\overline{Y}_1 + (\frac{1}{2})\overline{Y}_2 + (\frac{1}{2})\overline{Y}_3$$
$$= -752.0 + (\frac{1}{2})(767.0) + (\frac{1}{2})(774.5) = 18.75.$$

There are two related ways to test the hypothesis that the mean of the contrast is zero, one based on the t test and the other on the analysis of variance and the F test.

Using a Single-Sample t Test. The simplest way to test the hypothesis that the mean value of a contrast variable is zero is to use the t test described in Section 4.4. The logic behind the test remains the same, but the formulas here are a little different. The test statistic is the ratio of the mean of the contrast variable $\widehat{\psi}$ to the standard error of the mean derived from the n observations of the contrast variable:

$$t = \widehat{\psi}/s_{M_\psi}.$$

The standard error of the mean s_{M_ψ} is calculated the same way we calculated the standard error of the scores in Table 16.3:

$$s_{M_\psi} = \sqrt{s_\psi^2/n} \quad \text{where} \quad s_\psi^2 = \frac{\sum \widehat{\psi}_i^2 - (\sum \widehat{\psi}_i)^2/n}{n-1}.$$

Critical values for this statistic are found in Appendix A.2 with $n-1$ degrees of freedom. Applying these equations to the contrast variable in Table 16.5 gives

$$s_{\widehat{\psi}}^2 = \frac{\sum \widehat{\psi}_i^2 - (\sum \widehat{\psi}_i)^2/n}{n-1} = \frac{2{,}367.25 - (112.5)^2/6}{6-1} = \frac{257.875}{5} = 51.58,$$

$$s_{M_\psi} = \sqrt{s_{\widehat{\psi}}^2/n} = \sqrt{51.58/6} = \sqrt{8.597} = 2.93,$$

$$t = \frac{\widehat{\psi}_A}{s_{M_\psi}} = \frac{18.75}{2.93} = 6.40.$$

This statistic has $df = n - 1 = 6 - 1 = 5$ degrees of freedom, and the critical value is $t_{.05}(5) = 2.57$. We can reject the hypothesis that $\psi_A = 0$ and conclude that letters are detected faster in words than in nonwords or random letter strings combined.

Using the Analysis of Variance and the F Test. Another way to test whether the mean of a group of numbers is zero is to use an F test. This procedure uses the test of the grand mean introduced in Chapter 3 (see p. 37). The sum of squares for the grand mean is equal to the bracket term $[T]$, and because there is no group variable involved in the contrast variable, the error is equal to the variability among subjects. Using the subscript ψ to remind us that the calculations pertain to the contrast variable, not the original scores, we produce the sum of squares

$$SS_{\text{G.M.}_\psi} = [T_\psi] = n\widehat{\psi}_A^2 \quad \text{and} \quad SS_{S_\psi} = [Y_\psi] - [T_\psi] = \sum \widehat{\psi}_i^2 - n\widehat{\psi}_A^2. \qquad (16.4)$$

These sums of squares have 1 and $n-1$ degrees of freedom, respectively. They lead directly to mean squares and an F ratio. At the top of Table 16.6 we have summarized the relevant formulas, labeling the two effects by their meaning in this analysis as ψ_A and $\psi_A \times S$. At the bottom of the table, we apply these formulas to the contrast ψ_A we tested with the t statistic. From the information in Table 16.5, we calculate the two bracket terms:

$$[T_\psi] = n\widehat{\psi}_A^2 = (6)(18.75)^2 = 2{,}109.38 \quad \text{and} \quad [Y_\psi] = \sum \widehat{\psi}_i^2 = 2{,}367.25.$$

These values are used to calculate the sums of squares in the bottom half of Table 16.6 and to complete the analysis of variance. The value of $F = 40.90$ clearly exceeds the critical value of $F_{.05}(1,5) = 6.61$, allowing us again to conclude that letters are detected faster when they appear in words than in nonwords and random letter strings combined.

The two methods of the testing the contrast—the t and F tests—are equivalent, as they are for any single degree-of-freedom test. The F is just the square of the t, as we can readily verify:

$$t^2 = 6.40^2 = 40.96 \quad \text{compared to} \quad F = 40.90.$$

The difference is attributable to rounding in the calculations and would diminish had we carried more places.

The size of the sums of squares calculated from Equation 16.4 depends on the magnitude of the coefficients used to define ψ_A. Before we can relate the sums of squares to those from the original analysis (for example, to determine a residual sum of squares as a measure of the failure of a description, as in Equation 4.16, p. 82), we must divide each sum of squares by the sum of the squared coefficients:

$$\text{Adjusted } SS = \frac{SS \text{ based on } \psi}{\sum c_j^2}. \qquad (16.5)$$

Table 16.6: *Using an F test of the contrast variable from Table 16.5 to test the hypothesis that $\psi_A = 0$.*

Formulas for the analysis of variance

Source	Bracket term	SS	df	F
ψ_A	$[T_\psi] = n\widehat{\psi}_A^2$	$[T_\psi]$	1	$\dfrac{MS_{\psi_A}}{MS_{\psi_A \times S}}$
$\psi_A \times S$	$[Y_\psi] = \sum \widehat{\psi}_i^2$	$[Y_\psi] - [T_\psi]$	$n-1$	

Numerical calculations based on Table 16.5

Source	SS	df	MS	F
ψ_A	$[T_\psi] = 2{,}109.38$	1	2,109.38	40.90*
$\psi_A \times S$	$[Y_\psi] - [T_\psi] = 257.87$	5	51.57	

*$p < .05$

This adjustment puts them on the same basis as the original analysis. In our example, $\sum c_j^2 = (-1)^2 + (\frac{1}{2})^2 + (\frac{1}{2})^2 = 1.5$, and the adjusted sums of squares are

$$SS_{\psi_A} = \frac{2{,}109.38}{1.5} = 1{,}406.25 \quad \text{and} \quad SS_{\psi_A \times S} = \frac{257.87}{1.5} = 171.91.$$

These revised sums of squares can be compared directly with the appropriate sums of squares in the overall analysis.[1] We will illustrate this adjustment in our example of a two-factor within-subject analysis in Section 18.2.

Error Control for Within-Subject Contrasts

When several contrasts are investigated, questions of error control arise. There are fewer ways to control the error rate in a within-subject design than there were for the between-subjects designs in Chapter 6. The fact that the scores for the subjects are intercorrelated and the need to use different error terms to test different contrasts complicates the application of many of these correction procedures. For example, there is no commonly used equivalent to the Tukey test or the sequential Fisher-Hayter or Newman-Keuls tests that arise from it, and your statistical package may not offer any procedures for controlling familywise Type I error at all.

When the number of contrasts being tested is not large, the Bonferroni or Šidák-Bonferroni corrections are useful. As we described in Section 6.3, these procedures control familywise error by adopting a more stringent level of significance for the additional tests. In the Bonferroni procedure, the nominal familywise significance level α_{FW} is divided by the number of tests, and all tests are evaluated at the $\alpha = \alpha_{FW}/c$ significance level. The Šidák-Bonferroni test works in a similar way, but uses the significance level calculated according to Equation 6.5. These levels are given in Appendix A.4, which also gives the critical values needed for a t test.

---

[1] This adjustment may seem a little more convincing when you combine it with the first of Equations 16.4 and discover that then $SS_{\psi_A} = n\widehat{\psi}_A^2 / \sum c_j^2$, which is the standard formula for the sum of squares of a contrast that we have been using throughout.

The Bonferroni-based tests work best with small sets. They are conservative when the number of contrasts is large (for example, when a is large and all pairwise comparisons are examined), and there is no way to apply them to the set of all possible contrasts. The Scheffé test in Section 6.5 was designed to control experimentwise error in this type of situation for a between-subjects design. A comparable test that controls the experimentwise error over all possible contrasts in a within-subject design is obtained by comparing the observed F to the critical value[2]

$$F_{\text{crit}} = \frac{df_A \times df_{A \times S}}{df_{A \times S} - df_A + 1} F_{\alpha_{EW}}(df_A, df_{A \times S} - df_A + 1). \tag{16.6}$$

In our example, we had $a = 3$ groups and $n = 6$ subjects, so $df_A = 2$ and $df_{A \times S} = 10$. For a post-hoc test at the $\alpha_{EW} = .10$ level, say, the critical value is

$$F_{\text{crit}} = \frac{(2)(10)}{10 - 2 + 1} F_{.10}(2,\ 10 - 2 + 1) = \frac{20}{9} F_{.10}(2,\ 9) = \frac{20}{9}(3.01) = 6.69.$$

This value is considerably larger than the critical value for an uncorrected test at the same significance level ($F_{.10}(1,\ 10) = 3.29$).

16.3 Effect Size and Power

In our discussions of the between-subjects designs, we stressed the value of estimating treatment effects and of using power calculations when planning an experiment. Naturally, the same arguments apply to within-subject designs. However, the details of the procedure must be modified to accommodate the structure of this design.

Estimating Treatment Effects

Estimates of treatment effects were developed for use with single-factor between-subjects designs. We saw in Section 11.6 that when these measures are extended to factorial designs, two types of effect size are possible, one that expresses the variability of an effect relative to the total variability in the study (the complete measure) and the other to the variability of the effect and the error used to test it (the partial measure):

$$\omega_{\text{effect}}^2 = \frac{\sigma_{\text{effect}}^2}{\sigma_{\text{total}}^2} \quad \text{and} \quad \omega_{\langle \text{effect} \rangle}^2 = \frac{\sigma_{\text{effect}}^2}{\sigma_{\text{effect}}^2 + \sigma_{\text{error}}^2}.$$

The same distinction applies in the one-factor within-subject design. The complete measure of the size of an effect is expressed relative to the total variability in the study, while the partial measure is expressed only relative to the variability that affects the $A \times S$ interaction that is used as an error term of MS_A:

$$\omega_A^2 = \frac{\sigma_A^2}{\text{total variability}} \quad \text{and} \quad \omega_{\langle A \rangle}^2 = \frac{\sigma_A^2}{\sigma_A^2 + \text{variability affecting } A \times S}. \tag{16.7}$$

Of these, the partial measure is by far the most useful, primarily because the variability affecting $A \times S$ does not include the differences among subjects, and one of the reasons to adopt a within-subject design is specifically to exclude this variability. We have

---

[2]The value is developed from the multivariate approach to a within-subject design, which we will discuss on page 375. See Section 4.2 of Harris (1985, 2001) where post-hoc testing in the multivariate analysis of variance is specifically presented.

written Equations 16.7 partly in words. We will replace these words with symbols after we have developed the model for the within-subject design in Section 17.2.[3]

The best way to obtain a value for partial omega squared from the results of an experiment is to work with the F ratio. For the partial measure, this estimate is quite straightforward and is identical to the corresponding equation for the between-subjects design (Equation 8.12):

$$\widehat{\omega}_{\langle A \rangle} = \frac{(a-1)(F_A - 1)}{(a-1)(F_A - 1) + an}. \tag{16.8}$$

As a numerical illustration, consider our example of the speed of searching for letters in words, nonwords, and random strings (see Table 16.3). Using values from the summary analysis of variance table, we find

$$\widehat{\omega}^2_{\langle A \rangle} = \frac{(a-1)(F_A - 1)}{(a-1)(F_A - 1) + an} = \frac{(3-1)(14.43 - 1)}{(3-1)(14.43 - 1) + (3)(6)} = \frac{26.86}{44.86} = 0.599.$$

The estimate of partial ω^2 applies to the population from which the scores were obtained. There are also a variety of purely descriptive effect measures that do not include any correction for sampling variability. One of these, the squared correlation ratio, denoted either R^2 or η^2, is calculated by several computer packages. The partial version of this statistic for the one-way within-subject design is

$$R^2_{\langle A \rangle} \text{ or } \eta^2_{\langle A \rangle} = \frac{SS_A}{SS_A + SS_{A \times S}} \tag{16.9}$$

(compare to Equation 11.24, p. 234). For our example, it takes the value

$$R^2_{\langle A \rangle} = \frac{SS_A}{SS_A + SS_{A \times S}} = \frac{1,575.0}{1,575.0 + 545.7} = \frac{1,575.0}{2,120.7} = 0.743.$$

As you can see, this value is larger than $\widehat{\omega}^2_{\langle A \rangle}$, a feature that can mislead a researcher into thinking that an effect is larger than it really is.

Obtaining estimates for the complete effect size in this design is considerably more complicated than it is for the partial effect size. We will see in Section 17.2 that there are more sources of variability that affect σ^2_{total} than it is possible to estimate from the results of a single experiment. A consequence of this ambiguity is that only a range for the complete effect size can be given—and sometimes quite a wide range at that (if you want to see the details, look at Section 8.5.2 of Myers & Well, 1991). Partly for this reason, but primarily because it is much more useful, we will concentrate on the partial effect sizes.

Power and Sample Size

As with the other designs we have discussed, power and sample-size calculations in the within-subject design are based on the measures of effect size. Because the effects in question should be expressed relative to the error term that will be used to test them—the $A \times S$ interaction, in this case—the partial measure is the appropriate effect size to use. Either the power of a new study to find an effect of a particular size or the sample-size needed to detect it can be found.

---

[3]Because the variability is different, a measure of effect size from a within-subject design is not directly comparable to one from a between-subjects design. See Morris and DeShon (2002) for a discussion of the differences and how they may be reconciled.

When basing the plans for a within-subject design on the results of an earlier one, you can obtain a value for $\widehat{\omega}^2_{\langle A \rangle}$ by applying Equation 16.8 to the previous results. You can also determine the partial effect size from hypothesized population values using the second part of Equations 16.7:

$$\omega^2_{\langle A \rangle} = \frac{\sigma^2_A}{\sigma^2_A + \text{variability affecting } A \times S}.$$

The numerator in this equation, σ^2_A, is the average of the individual squared effects (Equation 8.9, p. 163). The variability term in the denominator is harder to specify, depending as it does on sources of information that are not easy to determine. It is most conveniently estimated by taking $MS_{A \times S}$ from some roughly comparable experiment or by using estimates of subject variability within the treatment conditions (σ^2) and the correlation between the measures (ρ) to estimate

$$\text{variability affecting } A \times S = \sigma^2(1 - \rho^2).$$

To use this formula, we have to assume that all the treatments scores have approximately the same correlation ρ with each other. As we will see, this is one of the assumptions of the model.

Once you have an estimate of the anticipated partial effect size, you can follow the procedures described in Section 8.4 for the single-factor between-subjects design. When its effect sizes and power levels meet your needs, you can use Table 8.1. For other levels of power and values of effect size, you will need to use the power charts in Appendix A.7. The following example illustrates both procedures.

Suppose a graduate student in an enology program is planning an experiment to determine whether allowing a wine to "breathe" improves its taste. He conducts a pilot study in which he asks subjects to judge the wine from three bottles that they believe contained different wines. The bottles actually contain the same wine, but differ in how long they have been open. One bottle is poured immediately after opening (a_1), the others 30 or 60 minutes after opening (a_2 and a_3, respectively). Each subject rates each of the three wines using a 10-point scale, where 1 is poor and 10 is excellent. Table 16.7 gives the results for $n = 5$ subjects. As you can see from the mean ratings, the longer the wine was opened, the more poorly it was rated. Unfortunately, the F statistic is not significant. Given this intriguing outcome, the student plans to repeat the experiment and wants a power of .90 to detect this particular outcome.

The first step in determining the appropriate sample size is to estimate the partial effect size. Substituting the F ratio from Table 16.7 into Equation 16.8 gives

$$\widehat{\omega}^2_{\langle A \rangle} = \frac{(a-1)(F_A - 1)}{(a-1)(F_A - 1) + an} = \frac{(3-1)(1.46 - 1)}{(3-1)(1.46 - 1) + (3)(5)} = \frac{0.92}{15.92} = 0.058.$$

We can look up the sample size in Table 8.1 (p. 173), using the closest entry, $\omega^2 = .06$. In the section of the table for power = .90, we find the value $n = 68$ at the interasection of the row labeled $\omega^2 = .06$ and the column labeled $a = 3$. This large sample size and consequent cost of the wine might force the student to reevaluate the feasibility of the project. Again, we are reminded about the realities of power and the sample size needed to replicate a particular finding.

For values of power or sample size outside those provided by Table 8.1, you use the power charts in Appendix A.7. The procedures are identical to those in Section 8.4.

Table 16.7: Data and analysis of a wine-tasting experiment.

The AS data table

	a_1 0 min	a_2 30 min	a_3 60 min	Sum
Subjects				
s_1	3	4	2	9
s_2	7	5	7	19
s_3	4	3	4	11
s_4	6	4	4	14
s_5	6	6	3	15
Sum	26	22	20	68
Mean	5.20	4.40	4.00	

Summary of the analysis of variance

Source	SS	df	MS	F
A	3.733	2	1.867	1.46
S	19.733	4	4.933	
$A{\times}S$	10.267	8	1.283	
Total	33.733	14		

First, you locate an appropriate value of the noncentrality parameter from the charts. For the enology study, we use the chart for $df_A = 2$, the line for an initial guess of $df_{\text{error}} = 50$, and the desired power of .9 on the ordinate to find $\phi \approx 2.1$ on the abscissa. This value is combined with the estimate of the partial effect size obtained from the original experiment using Equation 8.18 (p. 174):

$$n = \phi^2 \frac{1 - \omega^2_{\langle A \rangle}}{\omega^2_{\langle A \rangle}} \tag{16.10}$$

$$= (2.1^2)\frac{1 - 0.058}{0.058} = (4.41)(16.241) = 71.62,$$

or $n = 72$. This value is a little inflated because the initial guess of $df_{\text{error}} = 50$ was too small. As we described on page 175, the calculations could be amended by using $df_{\text{error}} = (3-1)(72-1) = 142$. The result is a sample size of about 68 or 69 subjects. Thus, either the sample-size table or the power calculations tell the student that he needs about 70 subjects to achieve his stated goals in this proposed research.

You may be wondering why such a large sample size is needed to replicate the earlier finding. The problem (if it is a problem) arises from the modest size of the effect and the desire for a power as high as .9. You may also wonder whether a between-subjects design would be any better. It would not. In a between-subjects design, all variability other than the effect itself is part of the error term, so sample-size calculations must be based on the complete ω^2_A, not the partial $\omega^2_{\langle A \rangle}$. Following the procedures of Myers and Well (1991), which we don't show, we determined a range for $\widehat{\omega}_A^2$ between 0.026 to 0.057, the smaller value being more plausible than the larger. Using Table 8.1 and $\widehat{\omega}_A^2 = 0.03$, we find that this value implies a sample size of $n = 138$ subjects *for each group*, i.e. a total of 414 subjects. For this example, the between-subjects design needs nearly six times the number of subjects as the within-subject design.

16.4 Computer Analysis

All the major computer packages contain procedures for the analysis of within-subject designs. For the most part, the data are entered in the programs in a subject-by-score table of the sort that we have shown at the top of Table 16.3. The rows of this array correspond to the n subjects and the columns to the a scores for each subject. You then identify which score applies to the first treatment condition, which to the second, and so forth. Finally, you invoke the within-subject (or repeated-measures) module of the program.

After running the program, there are a few things that you need to watch out for when interpreting the resulting output. First, you will probably find that the output contains various subsidiary tests, some of which you will recognize, and some of which you will not. We will mention some (but not all) of these later in the book. Do not be unduly disturbed by them. Look for the things you need in the output, not for those you don't. You should be able to find the quantities we have described somewhere in the output. We strongly recommend that you try out your program on one of our examples so you can be sure you are extracting the appropriate numbers from the output.

One thing that you are likely to find is several different test statistics. As we will discuss when we consider the mixed design, the multivariate form of the analysis of variance can be tested in several ways—you may encounter names like Wilk's lambda, Roy's largest root, or various trace statistics. For the purely within-subject designs, these statistics all lead to the same F value. You can ignore these tests at this point.

The analysis-of-variance table produced by the program may be organized somewhat differently from the ones we have presented. As you have seen for the analysis of contrasts (and will see for the factorial designs we consider later), each effect is tested against a different error term, specifically its interaction with subjects. Rather than labeling these terms as subject interactions, they may be labeled simply "Error." In some programs, they are reported on the same line as the effect being tested or on an adjacent line. The subject effect S is a between-subjects effect, and you may find it relegated to a different part of the output, along with a test of the hypothesis that the grand mean equals zero. As we mentioned above (p. 359), this test may be useful when testing a contrast variable, but it is rarely needed otherwise.

Finally, the situation with regard to contrasts can be complicated. Some programs test sets of contrasts by default. For example, you may find that your program has conducted a trend analysis or compared the first group to every other group, regardless of whether the tests make sense or not. Although you may be able to change the default contrasts, the options offered may or may not be applicable to your design. If they are not, you will need to find a way to specify the contrast you really want to test. Most programs provide ways to include specific contrasts into the analysis, but many users find these procedures confusing or difficult to implement. You will have to refer to whatever documentation came with the software or to a manual prepared by others. We have often found it easier to construct a contrast variable and test it, than to try to figure out the program. All programs have ways to define new variables based on old ones and automatically add them to the subject-by-score data table. For example, you can have the computer apply the formula $-Y_{i1} + (1/2)Y_{i2} + (1/2)Y_{i3}$ to calculate individual values for the contrast $\psi = -1\mu_1 + (1/2)\mu_2 + (1/2)\mu_3$, just as we did in Table 16.5. You then have the program analyze the new values using either a single-group t test or the analysis of variance for a between-subjects design without any group factors. If you plan to combine the tests of several contrasts or subtract them from the omnibus analysis to obtain a residual, you will need to adjust the sums of squares for the size of the coefficients, as we did with Equation 16.5.[4]

Exercises

16.1. Desert iguanas are thought to use their tongues to obtain information about their environment by sampling odors that may be important for their reproduction and survival. Pedersen (1988) studied the rates of tongue extrusions in desert iguanas who were exposed to sands collected from $a = 5$ different environments.[5] These consisted of clean sand (a_1), sand from an iguana's home cage (a_2), sand from cages housing other iguanas (a_3), sand from cages housing western whiptail lizards (a_4), and sand from cages housing desert kangaroo rats (a_5). The latter two species are frequently seen in close contact with desert iguanas in their natural habitat. A total of $n = 10$ iguanas served in the experiment. Each was tested in each condition on successive days; the order of testing was randomly determined for each animal. The iguanas were videotaped during each 30-minute test session; the response measure was the number of tongue extrusions observed during each test session. The data were:

Source of sand in testing cage

Subject	Clean sand a_1	Home cage a_2	Iguanas a_3	Lizards a_4	K. Rats a_5
1	24	15	41	30	50
2	6	6	0	6	13
3	4	0	5	4	9
4	11	9	10	14	18
5	0	0	0	0	0
6	8	15	10	15	38
7	8	5	2	6	15
8	0	0	0	11	54
9	0	3	2	1	11
10	7	7	4	7	23

---

[4]When you enter coefficients of a contrast directly into a program for testing, be aware that most programs do not make this adjustment, and the sums of squares that they report for the contrasts may not be on the same scale as those of the omnibus effects. Before you start combining them, experiment with the program to determine what it does—you might check that the sums of squares for a set of orthogonal contrasts adds up to the omnibus sum of squares and that multiplying all the coefficients by a constant (say doubling them) does not change the reported sum of squares. You can always fall back on contrast variables and making the adjustment yourself.

[5]These data were generously provided by Dr. Joanne Pedersen.

a. Perform an analysis of variance. Are there differences among the group means?

b. A rich variety of meaningful questions can be examined with this experiment. For example, condition a_1 (clean sand) provides information about the rate at which each iguana extrudes its tongue in the absence of any special odors; thus, it is of interest to compare each of the other four conditions with this reference condition. Of perhaps greater interest are comparisons between conditions representing different odors—for example, home cage versus other iguanas, other iguanas versus lizards and kangaroo rats, lizards versus kangaroo rats, and so on. Certain complex comparisons may also be interesting: clean sand versus all other conditions combined, home cage and other iguanas combined versus lizard and kangaroo rat combined, and so on. From among this large set of meaningful questions, conduct the following single-df comparisons:
   i. Clean sand versus home cage. (Use the t procedure.)
   ii. Other iguanas versus home cage. (Use the F procedure.)
   iii. Kangaroo rats versus lizards and other iguanas combined.

c. The contrasts above were planned and may require no control for Type I error. However, a researcher with these data will certainly want examine the means for any unanticipated differences. For such a post-hoc analysis, error control is appropriate. What is the critical value of F using the Scheffé-like correction in Equation 16.6 at the 10 percent level?

d. Use the partial measure of effect size to estimate how many iguanas would be necessary to replicate these findings with a power of .9. How many would be needed if a between-subjects design were used? (Hint: The simplest way to proceed is to reanalyze the data as a between-subjects design and use the resulting F to estimate n.)

16.2. Keppel, Postman, and Zavortink (1968) had subjects learn a list of 10 pairs of words on one day and recall the pairs two days later. Following recall, the subjects learned a second list of pairs, and these were also recalled after a delay of two days. This cycle of learning-recall-learning-recall was continued for six lists. The independent variable was the ordinal position of a particular list; that is, whether the list was learned and recalled first, second, through sixth in the sequence. There were $n = 8$ subjects in the experiment. Their recall data for the $a = 6$ lists were:

Ordinal list position (A)

Subject	a_1	a_2	a_3	a_4	a_5	a_6
1	7	3	2	2	1	1
2	4	8	3	8	1	2
3	7	6	3	1	5	4
4	8	6	1	0	2	0
5	7	2	3	0	1	3
6	6	3	3	1	1	1
7	4	2	0	0	0	0
8	6	7	5	1	3	2

a. Perform an analysis of variance on these data.
b. Plot the means bounded by error bars on a graph.

c. You will note that the resulting function has a general downward slope (a linear trend). Is there any statistical support for this observation?

d. The plot of the means also suggests the presence of nonlinear trend. Is there any statistical support for this possibility?

16.3. Consider the experiment we described on page 348 that examined the effects of monetary reward on the recall of words. A study of this effect could be conducted as a intermixed-treatment design. The researcher prepares 60 slides, each containing one word. Twenty of the words are printed in red, 20 in green, and 20 in blue. The subjects are told that red words are worth 1 cent, green words are worth 5 cents, and blue words are worth 10 cents (treatments a_1, a_2, and a_3, respectively). The words are presented to each subject in a different random order. The experimenter counts the number of recalled words sorted according to their monetary value to produce three scores for that subject. Recall data for a miniature version of this experiment with $n = 6$ subject are given below.

	Word value		
Subject	a_1	a_2	a_3
s_1	3	8	23
s_2	3	13	19
s_3	4	5	23
s_4	5	11	20
s_5	7	17	18
s_6	6	5	17

a. Is there an effect of the word's value on recall?

b. Is the relationship between the amount of reward and word recall linear? You will need to construct special coefficients for this analysis (see pp. 80–81).

c. How well does the linear function describe the outcome of this experiment?

We will return to these data in Problem 17.3.

17

The Single-Factor Within-Subject Design: Further Topics

In the last chapter, we presented the techniques you need to conduct and interpret a single-factor within-subject analysis of variance. As we indicated, this design offers a substantial gain in power and convenience. However, these advantages, like all such benefits, come with certain costs. A within-subject design requires changes in the assumptions that underlie the tests, making it more likely that they will be violated. We discuss these issues and their correction in this chapter.

17.1 Advantages and Limitations

We start with a comparison of the between-subjects and within-subject designs. In brief, a study conducted with a within-subject design obtains more data from each subject than one conducted with a between-subjects design, and the analysis has a smaller error term. Set against these gains are the facts that repeated observations of a subject cannot be collected under constant conditions, and that any earlier observation has the potential to influence later ones. Moreover, the assumptions that underlie the analysis are more complex than those of the between-subjects designs.

Advantages of the Within-Subject Design

The three principal advantages of a within-subject design over a between-subjects design are more efficient use of subject resources, greater comparability of the conditions, and reduced error variance. The most obvious of these is the economy of the design. By taking several observations from each subject, much more data can be collected in a short period of time. The advantage is particularly great when each subject is "expensive," either because only a few are available or because a considerable amount of preparation or instruction is necessary before the study can begin. The efficiency of the within-subject designs certainly accounts for their wide use in behavioral research.

From a statistical point of view, a great advantage of the within-subject designs is its increased control of subject variability. The subjects that come into an experiment are not equivalent in ability, or on any other factor, for that matter. In a between-subjects design, they are randomly assigned to independent groups. Although random assignment eliminates the chance of *systematic* differences among the groups (other than those that arise from the treatments), *accidental* differences among groups will arise because different subject are assigned to each group. These chance differences are superimposed on whatever treatment effects are produced by the experimental manipulations. In the within-subject design, we select a single group of subjects and have them serve in every treatment condition, thus ensuring that comparable subject differences are present in each condition.

The third advantage of the within-subject design goes along with the second. By making the conditions more similar, the size of the error term used to test for differences among the treatments is reduced. Any study involves two types of random variability, one reflecting consistent differences among the subjects, the other reflecting variation from one observation to another. Among the second set are momentary changes in attention and motivation, and variation in the physical environment or the testing apparatus. Both types of variability affect the accidental differences among treatments in a between-subjects design, but only the second affects differences among treatments in a within-subject design. As you saw in the last chapter, the appropriate error term to compare with the within-subject treatment effect is the treatment-by-subject interaction. This variability is almost always less than the pooled within-group variability used to test the effect in a between-subjects design, which increases the test's power.

Limitations of Within-Subject Designs

The within-subject design has both statistical and nonstatistical limitations. The statistical problems mostly concern the sensitivity of the assumptions of the analysis. The scores produced by a single subject are more alike than are the scores produced by different subjects. In a statistical sense, this similarity means that the observations are not independent. The model on which the analysis is based must say something about this dependence, and these extra assumptions make the model more complex and more vulnerable to violation. In contrast, in a between-subjects design, the experimental procedure assures that the observations from different subjects are independent. Thus, there is a simplicity to a between-subjects design that is absent from its within-subject counterpart. We will discuss these issues in Sections 17.2 and 17.3.

The nonstatistical problems arise from the fact that the repeated observations must necessarily take place under somewhat different conditions, and some aspect of this difference, other than the treatment being investigated, can affect the scores. These differences do not affect between-subjects designs, because only a single score is recorded. We will refer to these differences as **incidental effects**—systematic differences that are incidental to the actual treatment manipulation. We will review them here and then discuss methods for controlling them in Sections 17.4 and 17.5.

Incidental differences among the treatments can arise for a variety of reasons. One general class concerns nonspecific changes in the subject, such as practice and fatigue. If a subject becomes tired or bored, performance will drop for the later observations, regardless of the treatment involved. Similarly, if a subject becomes better at the task or at following instructions, performance will improve. In an inter-mixed-treatment design, changes like these affect all treatments equally. They may increase the variability of the data, but they do not bias the results. In a successive-treatment design, however, the conditions are affected unequally. Practice effects help the conditions administered late in testing, while fatigue effects hurt them. Effects of this type should be considered whenever a successive-treatment study is planned.

A second form of incidental differences arises when different treatments must use different material. In an experiment on memory, for example, subjects must be given a different set of material to learn with each new treatment—they cannot relearn the same material over and over again. If one set of material is easier to remember than another, it will give an advantage to the treatment condition in which it is used. Effects of this type influence both successive-treatment and intermixed-treatment designs.

The other types of nonstatistical problems relate to the specific nature of the treatments. These can roughly be divided into three groups, each with different causes and cures: carryover effects, contrast effects, and context effects. A **carryover effect** occurs when a treatment has a transient effect that carries over to affect whatever condition is administered immediately after it. Consider a study that evaluates the effect of a drug by looking at behavior following doses of different sizes. A large dose may depress behavior, both immediately and for some period of time thereafter. If the tests are not spaced by a sufficiently long interval, the next test will be affected not only by the currently administered drug, but by the continued effect of the earlier drug. In contrast, a small dose (or particularly a placebo control) has little or no continuing effect. Carryover effects can be both physical and psychological. For example, Sheehe and Bross (1961) remark that the effectiveness of an analgesic agent in reducing the perception of pain is substantially reduced when it follows an ineffective agent, even when sufficient time has elapsed that no possibility of chemical mediation exists. In this case, the carryover is psychological, with the patients perhaps temporarily losing confidence in painkillers.

A **contrast effect** is a carryover effect that occurs when two treatments interact in a way that depends on both conditions. Suppose a researcher is studying the effects of giving praise, reproof, or no feedback during a learning task with second-grade children. The effect of no feedback, say, may be quite different when it follows the praise condition than when it follows the reproof condition. Another example is the reward study mentioned in the introduction to Part V (p. 348). The 5-cent reward for a successful outcome might be valued more if it is preceeded by a 1-cent reward than if it is preceeded by a 50-cent reward. Carryover effects of these sorts are possible only in a within-subject design, and where they are severe, the best approach may be to use a between-subjects design. Where they are more mild, it may be sufficient simply to ensure that the conditions are not always presented in the same order.

The very act of being measured in one treatment condition can change the subject, so that later observations are contaminated. With learned material, for example, it is impossible to test a subject on the same material twice, because the first test functions as an additional learning trial, and influences the later test. A subject who has been tested 10 minutes after learning, for example, is likely to remember more at 30 minutes than one who was not tested. There are more extreme forms of this phenomenon, generally known as **context effects**, in which a subject's behavior is influenced by the context provided by exposure to other conditions in an experiment. A surprise test can only be given once; after that subjects will expect additional tests and alter their behavior accordingly. Studies of incidental learning, in which subjects are tested for what they can remember of material presented without formal instructions to learn, have this problem. Once they have been tested the first time, subjects will expect additional tests and later learning will not be incidental. The most extreme form of these effects come from the physiological manipulations such as an operation, which obviously cannot be undone.

Consider a few other examples of potential context effects. If subjects are told that performance on a given task is a measure of intelligence (as a way of increasing their motivation), how will they view any future tasks where the set is changed? If subjects are told to employ one strategy when learning a set of material, will they be able to adopt a new one when the conditions are switched? If subjects are misled about what will happen in one treatment condition—a technique used in so-called deception experiments—will they believe what the researcher says about later treatments? If some of the experimental conditions are frightening or distasteful, how will subjects react when they are told that other conditions will be milder? For example, if they have been punished for an error with an electric shock, will they be unaffected by this experience when they are told they will not be shocked in another condition? These are all examples of situations that probably should not be studied in within-subject designs. Greenwald (1976) provides a useful discussion of these sorts of problems.

The discovery that an otherwise well-designed within-subject study is subject to serious carryover or context effects does not completely render the study useless. When each treatment has appeared first for some of the subjects, it is possible to analyze just the data from the first testing session. Performance at this point is completely uncontaminated by the effects of prior testing. Although this retreat to a between-subjects design loses the increased power and comparability of the groups associated with a within-subject design, it restores the interpretability of the results, which is obviously the most important consideration.

17.2   The Statistical Model

Like all statistical procedures, the analysis of the within-subject design is based on a set of assumptions about how the data are produced—the statistical model for a score Y_{ij}. Although the configuration of the data looks superficially like that of a between-subjects design, there are critical differences in the way the scores are represented. Here we develop the statistical model, and in the next section we discuss the effect of violating one of the key assumptions.

The difference between the models for the between-subjects and within-subject designs lies in the assumption of independence of the scores. The fact that several scores come from the same subject causes the scores in different conditions to be correlated—for example, a subject that produces a high score under one treatment is likely to have a high score under another. We can observe this dependence by calculating the correlation coefficients among the three conditions in the numerical example from the last chapter (Table 16.3). When we take the six scores for a_1 and correlate them with the matching six scores for a_2, we find $r_{12} = 0.938$. The correlations between the other two pairs of scores are also substantially greater than zero,

$r_{13} = 0.947$ and $r_{23} = 0.937$. The within-subject observations are not independent of each other, and the statistical model needs to accommodate these dependences.

Two different models have been applied to within-subject data. They differ in whether scores from a subject are treated as separate entities or are treated together. In the **univariate approach**, each score Y_{ij} is viewed as a separate random variable made up of systematic and random components, including a component specific to the subject. In the **multivariate approach**, all the scores from a single subject are treated as a single statistical entity. In Table 16.3, for example, the univariate approach treats the first subject's scores as $Y_{11} = 745$, $Y_{12} = 764$, and $Y_{13} = 774$, but the multivariate approach treats them as $\mathbf{Y}_1 = (745, 764, 774)$; we use the boldface letter to indicate that the observation is multivariate. The two representations have different sets of assumptions and lead to two different forms of the analysis of variance. The univariate approach leads to the analysis described in Chapter 16, and the multivariate approach leads to the **multivariate analysis of variance** or **MANOVA**. The multivariate analysis is the more flexible of the two, and it requires fewer assumptions about the data. However, as a result, when this flexibility is not required, it is less powerful than the univariate approach. We will emphasize the univariate approach for several reasons. First, its assumptions are often satisfied, or nearly so, with experimental data. Second, it lends itself to the type of multifactor experiments that are common in behavioral research. Both of these properties have made it popular with researchers. Finally, it is computationally easier than the multivariate model, making it a good place to develop one's understanding of the techniques.

Both models require the usual cluster of random-sampling assumptions. In particular, each subject's data must be independent of the data from every other subject, and the same distribution must apply to every subject. Note that the assumption of independence applies to the subjects, not to the individual scores, which will be correlated because of the consistency of subjects. As always, these assumptions are critical to the analysis. Without them, the population to which the inferences apply is unclear, and the results of the analysis are potentially biased or irrelevant. The two models also specify, in somewhat different forms, the assumption of a normal distribution, as we will amplify below.

The Univariate Model

One way to think of the univariate model for the within-subject analysis of variance is as a specialized form of the randomized-blocks design from Section 11.5. In that design, blocks of subjects were formed whose scores were expected to be relatively similar. Subjects within these blocks were then randomly assigned to the conditions, and the blocks were treated as a factor in the design. Because the variability associated with differences among blocks was systematically removed, the treatment effects were both better balanced and less variable than they would have been in a simple between-subjects design. In applying this model to a within-subject design, we treat each subject as a block. Like a block in the randomized-blocks design, the scores for a single subject in a within-subject design are more similar to each other than they are to the scores of the other subjects.

The parallel to a randomized-blocks design correctly suggests that a linear model similar to the two-factor model for that design can be used (Equation 11.14, p. 225).

There are some important differences, however, in the nature of any uncontrolled error. In a randomized-blocks design, the blocks are chosen systematically, while in a within-subject design, the subjects are chosen randomly. Moreover, although there are often several subjects in each condition within a block, subjects in the within-subject design provide only one score per condition. With these modifications, a score Y_{ij} is expressed by the equation

$$Y_{ij} = \mu_T + \alpha_j + S_i + (S\alpha)_{ij} + E_{ij}. \tag{17.1}$$

The grand mean μ_T and the treatment effect α_j are familiar. The remaining terms define the different sources of unsystematic variability:

1. *The overall ability of the subject,* S_i. Some subjects produce, on average, high scores and others low. The random variable S_i represents the deviation of these mean scores from the grand mean. It has a normal distribution with a mean of 0 and a variance of σ_S^2.

2. *The idiosyncratic response of the subject in a particular condition,*[1] $(S\alpha)_{ij}$. Differences in skill, ability, or predilection make some subjects perform better in one condition, others in another. These effects constitute a treatment-by-subject interaction. Because the subjects are randomly selected, it is represented by a random variable. It has a normal distribution, with a mean of 0 and a variance of $\sigma_{A\times S}^2$.

3. *The variability of the individual observations,* E_{ij}. Even in the same condition, a particular subject would not produce the identical score each time the same treatment was administered. The uncertainty about this aspect of performance is represented by the random variable E_{ij}, which has a normal distribution with a mean of 0 and a variance of σ_{error}^2.

You can compare this model to the linear model for a one-way between-subjects design, $Y_{ij} = \mu_T + \alpha_j + E_{ij}$. Although the three sources of variability S_i, $(S\alpha)_{ij}$, and E_{ij} are present there (see the discussion of experimental error in Chapter 2 on pp. 19–20), they are indistinguishable. As a result, the variabilities σ_S^2, $\sigma_{A\times S}^2$, and σ_{error}^2 of the within-subject design are lumped together as the single error variance σ_{error}^2 of the between-subjects design.

The effect of the three sources of unsystematic variability is to make the mean squares more complicated than they were in the between-subjects designs. Calculations (which we will not go through) show that

$$\left. \begin{aligned} \text{E}(MS_A) &= \frac{n}{a-1}\sum \alpha_j^2 + \sigma_{A\times S}^2 + \sigma_{\text{error}}^2, \\ \text{E}(MS_S) &= a\sigma_S^2 + \sigma_{\text{error}}^2, \\ \text{E}(MS_{A\times S}) &= \sigma_{A\times S}^2 + \sigma_{\text{error}}^2. \end{aligned} \right\} \tag{17.2}$$

Let's look at the terms that make up these mean squares. The mean square for the treatment effect A, which is the term we want to test, is influenced by two of the three sources of error: the interaction of the treatment factor with subjects and the

---

[1]We have reversed the order of the two letters in this effect from that used in earlier editions of this book. This change keeps their order and that of the subscripts in alignment, with the first (S or i) referring to subjects and the second (α or j) to the treatment conditions.

variability of the individual observations. Under the null hypothesis, when all the treatment effects α_j are zero, $\text{E}(MS_A)$ reduces to $\sigma^2_{A \times S} + \sigma^2_{\text{error}}$. The denominator of the F ratio must match this sum, and the $A \times S$ interaction does. It should be clear now why the error term for the A effect is the $A \times S$ interaction. The expected mean squares also show why there is no pure test of the S effect, as we mentioned on pages 353–354. The error variance σ^2_{error}, which would be the necessary term, never appears in isolation, so it cannot be independently estimated. An F test that used $MS_{A \times S}$ as an error term would be biased.[2]

The univariate model constrains the possibilities for the variances of the scores and the correlations among them. Calculations based on Equation 17.1 show that when it holds, two things happen. First, the variances of all the treatment conditions are identical. Second, the same thing happens to correlations between the scores; they too are identical. These conditions are often referred to as **homogeneity of variance** and **homogeneity of correlation**, respectively. When these restrictions hold, the data are said to show **compound symmetry**. We will talk more about the implications of these restrictions in Section 17.3.

The Multivariate Model

The alternative to the univariate representation is the multivariate model. This model treats all the scores from a subject as a single multipart random variable that contains the individual scores within it. The complete set of observations for subject s_i is the multivariate random variable

$$\mathbf{Y}_i = (\mathsf{Y}_{i1}, \mathsf{Y}_{i2}, \ldots, \mathsf{Y}_{ia}). \tag{17.3}$$

The model itself simply says that this random variable has what is known as a **multivariate normal distribution**, which is a generalization of the normal distribution that allows for the correlations among several variables. The parameters of this model, corresponding to the μ, α_j, etc. of the univariate model, are the parameters of the multivariate distribution. They are of three types: the means μ_j of the individual scores, the variances σ^2_j of these scores, and the correlations between the pairs of scores. The null hypothesis tested by the multivariate analysis of variance is the same as that tested by the univariate form, namely, that the μ_j are all identical.

The way the two models differ is in how the variability among the scores is expressed. We saw above that the univariate model imposes compound symmetry on the data. All the scores must have the same variance, and the correlations between any pair of scores must be the same. The multivariate model completely relaxes this requirement. It can accommodate any pattern of variances and correlations. Because of this flexibility, it applies to situations for which the univariate model is inappropriate. This robustness comes at a cost, however. The multivariate analysis, in effect, must estimate all those variances and correlations from the data, and this process reduces the amount of information that can be brought to bear on the differences among the means. As a result, when the assumptions of the univariate model hold, the multivariate tests have less power. Without going into the details, this reduction

---

[2]These quantities allow us to complete the equations for the effect size that we expressed by words in Equation 16.7. The total variability is $\sigma^2_A + \sigma^2_S + \sigma^2_{A \times S} + \sigma^2_{\text{error}}$, and the variability that affects $A \times S$ is just $\sigma^2_{A \times S} + \sigma^2_{\text{error}}$.

in power is reflected by the denominator degrees of freedom under the two models. For the example in Table 16.3, $df = 10$ for the univariate model and $df = 4$ for the multivariate model, leading to critical values for the respective F tests of $F_{.05}(2, 10) = 4.10$ and $F_{.05}(2, 4) = 6.94$.

The multivariate analysis of variance gives rise to several different test statistics, and the programs (which you will surely use to conduct this procedure) usually give several of them. They all give the same result for completely within-subject designs— those that have only within-subject factors. We will return to the different test statistics when we consider the mixed design.

There is one place where the two approach are the same. The test of a contrast under the multivariate model uses the procedure described in Section 16.2. The calculation of the contrast-by-subjects interaction as an error term for each contrast has the effect of matching the error to the observed variability of that contrast, which is exactly what the multivariate model does. We will discuss below some situations where the univariate approach can be used and some where the multivariate approach is better. You can disregard these distinctions when you are testing contrasts.

17.3   The Sphericity Assumption

We mentioned that the univariate model implies the twin conditions of homogeneity of variance and homogeneity of correlation, that is, of compound symmetry. These assumptions ensure that tests based on the univariate model are valid. Actually, because the hypothesis of no treatment effect concerns only *differences* between scores, a slightly weaker assumption is all that is needed. Compound symmetry need not hold for the scores themselves, but only for the differences between pairs of scores. This condition is referred to as **circularity** or **sphericity** (the difference between these terms need not concern us, and we will use the latter term). We will emphasize the somewhat more stringent assumption of compound symmetry, because it is expressed directly in terms of the data and easier to relate to an actual study.

To avoid violations of compound symmetry, the various observations should be of the same type and measured in a similar way. Of course, measures of completely different quantities, such a response time and the proportion of errors, should never be treated as a within-subject "factor," even when they are collected on the same subjects. However, even measures that seem superficially similar may create a problem. Consider a memory researcher who asks subjects to recall a story. The facts are divided into several categories (for example, those describing the characters, those describing the action, those that are incidental to the story, etc.), and the researcher wants to compare the proportion of each type that each subject recalls. The problem here is that these proportions, being based on different numbers of original facts and having different rates of recall, are also likely to have systematically different variances. The correlations among them may also vary. To take another example, suppose a researcher has measured the skills of a group of children using tests of verbal skills, arithmetic skills, and motor skills. Although all of these tests capture the idea of *skill*, they measure different concepts. The school-related measures of verbal and arithmetic skills are likely to be more highly correlated with each other than either is to the motor task. In both cases, a test based on the multivariate model should be used.

Time-series data are another source of violations of compound symmetry. Suppose the same measure is taken from the subjects at different times, such as on different trials in a learning experiment. With these data, adjacent scores are likely to be more highly correlated than are scores observed at widely spaced intervals. Even when the variances are the same, compound symmetry may fail because the correlations are heterogeneous. A similar situation arises in a study that measures changes during the course of therapy. Suppose a standardized measure of pathology is administered before treatment is started, at the midpoint of treatment, and after the treatment is finished, and these values are to be compared. The correlation between the scores measured before and after therapy is likely to be lower than the correlation between either of them and the middle scores. The danger of temporal heterogeneity is particularly high when many measurements have been taken.

There are tests for violations of sphericity or compound symmetry. The most widely used of these, a likelihood-ratio test statistic W developed by Mauchly (1940), is included in a number of computer programs. This statistic should *not* be significant for the analysis to proceed. For example, a computer analysis of the data in Table 16.3 gave $W = 0.758$, with a descriptive level of $p = 0.575$. Because this value is far from significant, we can proceed with the within-subject analysis of variance without concern. There are some important limitations to Mauchly's test, however. It has been criticized both for a lack of sensitivity to small violations (which can nevertheless affect the F test) and for positive biases when the data contain a disproportionate number of extreme scores. A test due to John (1971) is superior (see Cornell, Young, Seaman, & Kirk, 1992, for a comparison of several tests and references to earlier work, and Kirk, 1995, pp. 277–278, for examples of its use). It has not been widely implemented in the computer packages.

The tests of sphericity, like those of heterogeneity of variance in between-subjects designs, have their own assumptions. Their vulnerability to violations of these assumptions is not well understood, particularly those relating to failure of normality, but they are certainly different from those of the analysis of variance. Just as with homogeneity of variance in the between-subjects designs, you should be cautious about making decisions regarding the analysis procedure based only on apparent heterogeneity of the variances and correlations. Substantial violations force one to use the multivariate procedure, but in more ambiguous cases, the choice between approaches should be supported by a consideration of the measures themselves and an assessment of the plausibility of homogeneity and potential sources of heterogeneity. It is particularly confusing for readers of one's research to switch back and forth between different types of test statistic within the analysis of a single study or group of studies.

Dealing with Violations of Sphericity

When sphericity is violated, the omnibus tests based on the randomized-blocks model are biased positively. Tests using the critical value of F at, say, $\alpha = .05$ from Appendix A.1, may actually have a real, but unknown, significance level greater than .05. If we do not make some sort of adjustment, then we will be too likely to falsely reject the null hypothesis. There are four approaches we can take. Three of these attempt to salvage the omnibus test: measure the magnitude of violation of sphericity and adjust the critical value of F upward to accommodate it, use a conservative critical value based on the largest possible violation of heterogeneity, or turn to the multivariate approach. The fourth possibility is to forget about the omnibus test and emphasize tests of contrasts, which are immune to violations of sphericity.

The first way to eliminate the bias of the F test is to evaluate it against a larger critical value, obtained by reducing the degrees of freedom when entering Appendix A.1. Box (1954a) suggested using the values

$$df_{num} = \varepsilon(a-1) \quad \text{and} \quad df_{denom} = \varepsilon(a-1)(n-1), \tag{17.4}$$

where ε measures the extent to which sphericity is violated. When sphericity holds, $\varepsilon = 1$ and the degrees of freedom are those of the uncorrected test. When sphericity is violated, $\varepsilon < 1$, which reduces both df_{num} and df_{denom} and gives a larger critical value for F.

The problem now is to find a value for ε. Its true value depends on the actual variances and correlations in the population, which we do not know. There is no unambiguous way to estimate it. Among the possibilities are methods suggested by Geisser and Greenhouse (1958) and by Huynh and Feldt (1976), of which the latter has the greater power. Both values are calculated by many of the packaged programs.[3] Either method gives a larger critical value than the uncorrected test, which protects against an inflated Type I error rate.

Another approach is to pick the smallest value that ε can attain, whatever the variances and correlations may be, which happens to be $\varepsilon = 1/(a-1)$. Using this worst-case value, the observed F ratio is evaluated against the critical value obtained from Appendix A.1 with

$$df_{num} = \frac{a-1}{a-1} = 1 \quad \text{and} \quad df_{denom} = \frac{(a-1)(n-1)}{a-1} = n-1. \tag{17.5}$$

These values are those that would have been used had the study involved but two conditions, a fact that makes them easier to remember. Because this **conservative F test** was suggested by Geisser and Greenhouse (1958), it is often associated with their names, but you should distinguish it from the correction that uses their estimate of ε mentioned in the previous paragraph. The big advantages of the conservative test is that it is easy to use, requires no special tables, and can be applied even when access to the original data is no longer possible. Applied to the example of Table 16.3, the conservative degrees of freedom are

$$df_{num} = 1 \quad \text{and} \quad df_{denom} = n - 1 = 6 - 1 = 5.$$

Looking in the F tables, we find that $F_{.05}(1,5) = 6.61$, which is larger than the unadjusted value of $F_{.05}(2,10) = 4.10$. Because the observed value of $F = 14.43$ exceeded the conservative criterion, we can reject the null hypothesis without worrying about violations of sphericity.

The difficulty with the conservative criterion is that it can give an ambiguous result. When the observed F falls between the unadjusted critical value and the conservative value—between 4.10 and 6.61 in our example—we can't tell whether to retain or reject the null hypothesis. The uncorrected criterion says "reject," and the conservative one says "retain." The researcher then has several alternatives, all of which require a computer. One possibility is to use one or the other of the specific values of ε to adjust

---

[3]Kirk (1995) and Myers and Well (1991) give examples of the calculations.

the degrees of freedom for the standard F ratio. Another possibility is to use a test based on the multivariate approach. It does not require the assumption of sphericity, so its results apply regardless of the pattern of variances and correlations in the data. A researcher should choose one of these approaches, not switch between them on an ad-hoc basis. On the whole, we favor the multivariate approach. It cleanly avoids the need to assume anything about sphericity, and it is based on a straightforward model for the data. It is currently more frequently used than the other possibilities. Any of these alternatives are less powerful than the ordinary F test when sphericity holds, so they should not be used unless necessary.[4]

In summary, we suggest that you start by looking at whatever indications of sphericity failures you have—a consideration of the design and the type of measures you are using and any statistics such as Mauchly's test. If you do not see difficulties, continue with the univariate test. If you do find cause to worry, try the conservative test. If the null hypothesis cannot be rejected using the standard criterion or can be rejected using the conservative criterion, you have your conclusion. If it falls in between, either use the multivariate test or focus on single-df hypotheses.

17.4 Incidental Effects

A subject's scores in any within-subject design are necessarily obtained under different conditions. Although, these differences are what distinguish the conditions that are being studied, they are affected by aspects of the experimental context that are incidental to the question under investigation. In a study using a successive-treatment design, the order in which the conditions are administered is the most obvious of these differences. One observation is made first, another second, and so forth. Unless the point of the study *is* the sequence of observations, as it would be if they were successive learning trials or patient status before, during, and after therapy, the order in which the treatments are given is incidental to the purposes of the study. Without taking this incidental factor into consideration, the experimenter would have to worry about whether performance on the later tests was improved because the early tests let the subject practice the task or was reduced because the subject became tired or bored with the study.

Other incidental aspects of the study apply to both successive-treatment and intermixed-treatment designs. The particular materials used in the task often must be varied in order to accommodate the repeated measurements. Consider a study in which subjects try to learn as much as possible about a briefly seen picture while performing some unrelated task, such as copying down the lyrics of a song or taking dictation over a telephone. Each subject serves in all conditions. The primary point of the study is to see which interfering activities makes the picture harder to remember. However, each time the subject is tested, a different picture must be used, and some of these pictures will be intrinsically easier to remember than the others. Always assigning the same picture to a given treatment condition confounds picture differences

---

[4]Their actual power depends on how sphericity is violated, which is unknown. There is some evidence that the various approaches have similar power under many natural ways that sphericity is violated with real data (Rasmussen, Heumann, Heumann, & Botzum, 1989).

with treatment effects. Like the order in which the conditions are administered, the differences among the pictures constitute an incidental aspect of the study.[5]

Factors such as the position in the testing sequence or the type of material are examples of the nuisance variables described in Chapter 1. When such a variable becomes an explicit factor in the design, we will refer to it as either a **nuisance factor** or an **incidental factor**. In a well-designed study the experimental conditions are not systematically affected by, or confounded with, such factors. If condition a_1 were always administered first, a_2 second, and so forth, we could never tell whether any differences in performance between them were due to the treatment or to practice or fatigue effects. Similarly, if a particular picture were always used for condition a_1, another always for condition a_2, and so on, we could never tell whether better performance in one condition was due to the treatment being studied or the use of an easier picture.

The biases that arise when the treatments are confounded with incidental aspects of the study, such as the order of testing or the materials, can be avoided by breaking up any consistent relationship between them. There are two ways to do this. In **randomization**, the relationship between the treatments and the incidental aspects of the study is chosen randomly; in **counterbalancing**, it is constructed in a way that systematically balances the incidental effects across the study. Each approach has advantages and disadvantages.[6]

Randomization

The randomization procedures are the easiest to apply. Little advanced planning is necessary. When each subject comes into the experiment, the order in which the conditions are administered is chosen randomly from among all possible orders, and any different types of material are randomly assigned to the conditions. The random orders break up any systematic relationship between the incidental aspects of the procedure and the treatment conditions. Randomization is particularly effective when several incidental factors must be accommodated, and the type of systematic counterbalancing that we will discuss next is prohibitively complex. Another advantage is that randomization does not require any special analysis procedures—the analysis we described in the last chapter applies without alteration.

Convenient as it is, randomization has two disadvantages. First, it cannot assure that the incidental factor is completely balanced across treatments. Just as it is unlikely that the random assignment of subjects in a between-subjects design results in perfectly equated groups, so the random assignment of materials or orders is unlikely to perfectly balance them over the treatment conditions. Second, the random variability of the incidental factors is absorbed in the error term $MS_{A \times S}$. Because the size of this term determines the power of the test, any procedure that can reduce it is helpful.

---

[5]We will discuss other ways in which the selection of material affects the statistical analysis in Chapter 24.

[6]The assignment of subjects to conditions in a between-subjects design may also be random or systematic. In a completely randomized design, subjects are assigned randomly; in a randomized-blocks design (Section 11.5), they are systematically grouped into blocks to create more homogeneous groups and to reduce the error term. Counterbalancing does the equivalent thing with nuisance variables.

Counterbalancing and the Latin Square

The alternative to randomization is counterbalancing: assigning an incidental factor systematically so each level occurs equally often with each treatment condition. In this way, any effects of the incidental factor apply equally to every condition. A counterbalanced design also allows the variablity of the incidental effect to be extracted as a sum of squares and eliminated from the error term. The result is to increase both the accuracy and the power of the tests. The downside of counterbalancing is the additional complexity introduced into the design—in the planning, in conducting the study itself, and in the analysis of the data.

The different methods of counterbalancing, particularly in the larger designs, can become very complicated. We will discuss only the simplest designs. Our discussion, we hope, will make the issues clear and help you deal with many practical situations. In more complex studies, particularly those with several nuisance factors, you will need to find a more comprehensive treatment or seek expert advice.

Suppose we are planning a study with four conditions that will be administered one after another in a successive-treatment design. The possibility of practice effects makes it unsatisfactory to administer the treatment conditions in the same order to all subjects—for example, condition a_1 first, a_2 second, and so forth. If we did, condition a_1 would have fresh but unpracticed subjects, and the later conditions would be affected by increasing amounts of fatigue and practice. To avoid this confounding, we can adopt the counterbalanced experimental plan in Table 17.1. The table on the left displays an idealized pattern of scores from four subjects tested on the four conditions. The columns represent the testing order, beginning with the first test, which we will denote p_1, through the fourth (p_4). Subject s_1 receives the treatments in the order a_1, a_2, a_3, a_4. For subject s_2, the order is changed to a_2, a_4, a_1, and a_3, and the other two subjects receive still different orders, as indicated in the table. Look at what this arrangement has done to the relationship between the treatments and the positions in which they were given. Treatment a_1 appears once in the first position, once in the second, once in the third, and once in the fourth. The same holds for the other three levels of factor A. No condition receives any advantage or disadvantage by appearing more often towards the beginning or the end of the testing sequence. Any practice or fatigue effects are spread evenly over the four treatment conditions.

The arrangement of the conditions in Table 17.1 is known as a **Latin square**. The name is derived from the fact that the pattern of conditions within the square is traditionally denoted by Latin letters—if we replace conditions a_1 to a_4 by the letters A, B, C, and D, respectively, the arrangement is

$$\begin{array}{llll} A & B & C & D \\ B & D & A & C \\ C & A & D & B \\ D & C & B & A \end{array}$$

The key feature of the Latin square arrangement is that every letter appears exactly once in each row and each column. It is the basic tool that an experimenter uses to set up a design in which an incidental factor is systematically counterbalanced over the treatment conditions.

Table 17.1: *An idealized pattern of scores from four subjects tested in a Latin square design. The left panel shows the data arranged by the order of testing; the right panel shows it arranged by condition.*

Subject		Testing position (P)				Treatment condition (A)			
	p_1	p_2	p_3	p_4	a_1	a_2	a_3	a_4
s_1	a_1	a_2	a_3	a_4	p_1	p_2	p_3	p_4
	4	11	8	14	4	11	8	14
s_2	a_2	a_4	a_1	a_3	p_3	p_1	p_4	p_2
	7	10	11	9	11	7	9	10
s_3	a_3	a_1	a_4	a_2	p_2	p_4	p_1	p_3
	1	8	13	15	8	15	1	13
s_4	a_4	a_3	a_2	a_1	p_4	p_3	p_2	p_1
	6	5	14	12	12	14	5	6
Mean	4.50	8.50	11.50	12.50	8.75	11.75	5.75	10.75

On the right-hand side of Table 17.1, the data are rearranged so that the columns correspond to the treatment conditions, and each cell is labeled by the position in which that treatment was given. Each position appears once for each treatment, so the design is still a Latin square. At the bottom of both tables we have calculated the means—on the left, the means for each position; on the right those for each treatment condition. Main effects of both factors appear to be present. There is a practice effect with the means increasing with testing position from $\bar{Y}_{P_1} = 4.50$ to $\bar{Y}_{P_4} = 12.50$ and a treatment effect with means ranging from $\bar{Y}_{A_3} = 5.75$ to $\bar{Y}_{A_2} = 11.75$. Using the Latin square design allows each effect to be measured independently of the other.

We have plotted the scores from Table 17.1 as a function of condition and of testing position in Figure 17.1. We constructed the figure by extracting the four scores for each treatment condition (the columns in the right-hand part of the table), plotting each set according to testing position, and finally connecting each set of four points. This graph emphasizes the treatments and the testing positions but ignores the fact that the points on any of the lines were obtained from different subjects. Inspection of the figure reveals a marked practice effect, but one that is exactly the same for each treatment condition (this is why we referred to the pattern as "idealized" above); in addition, the clear separation of the curves suggests the presence of a treatment effect that is the same at each testing position. We know from the marginal means in Table 17.1 that there is a steady improvement in performance with successive testing positions and that condition a_3 is the worst and a_2 is the best, with the other two conditions in the middle.

This example shows how the failure to counterbalance would have corrupted the results. Look at the difference between the two extreme conditions, as revealed by the treatment column means in Table 17.1, $\bar{Y}_{A_2} - \bar{Y}_{A_3} = 11.75 - 5.75 = 6.00$. Suppose all the conditions had been tested in the order a_3, a_1, a_4, a_2, the same as the order given to subject s_3. The difference between these two conditions for this particular subject is the largest of all four subjects ($15 - 1 = 14$). With this testing order, then, the practice

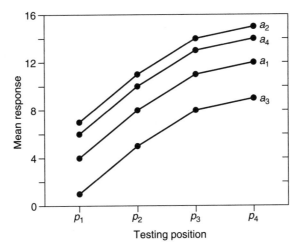

Figure 17.1: The scores in Table 17.1 plotted to show the treatment and practice effects.

effect mixes with the treatment effect in a way that exaggerates this difference. On the other hand, suppose the reverse order a_2, a_4, a_1, a_3 had been used, as it was for subject s_2. With this order, the practice effects work against the treatment effects—the difference between a_2 and a_3 is actually in the opposite direction ($7-9 = -2$). No single testing order gives an uncontaminated measure of the treatment effect. Only by averaging over all the testing orders do we get a faithful picture of the effect.

Constructing a Counterbalanced Design

The example in Table 17.1 is too small and the results are too regular to be more than an illustration. We would rarely conduct a four-treatment study with only four subjects. Instead, we would increase the sample size by including additional counterbalanced sets of four subjects. The same Latin square could be used over and over, or each set could use a different Latin square.

The first task in setting up such a design is to choose the Latin square that will be used to match the conditions and the incidental factor for a block of subjects. Other things being equal, the best strategy is to pick this square haphazardly. We do this by first writing the letters A, B, C, and so forth across the first row and down the first column, then filling in the remainder of the square, so that each letter appears once in each row and column. The resulting configuration is said to be a **standard Latin square**. For $a = 2$ and $a = 3$, there is only one standard square:

$$
\begin{array}{|cc|}
\hline
A & B \\
B & A \\
\hline
\end{array}
\quad \text{and} \quad
\begin{array}{|ccc|}
\hline
A & B & C \\
B & C & A \\
C & A & B \\
\hline
\end{array}
$$

When $a = 4$, there are four possibilities:

$$
\begin{array}{|c|}
\hline
\text{A B C D} \\
\text{B A D C} \\
\text{C D A B} \\
\text{D C B A} \\
\hline
\end{array}
\quad
\begin{array}{|c|}
\hline
\text{A B C D} \\
\text{B A D C} \\
\text{C D B A} \\
\text{D C A B} \\
\hline
\end{array}
\quad
\begin{array}{|c|}
\hline
\text{A B C D} \\
\text{B C D A} \\
\text{C D A B} \\
\text{D A B C} \\
\hline
\end{array}
\quad \text{and} \quad
\begin{array}{|c|}
\hline
\text{A B C D} \\
\text{B D A C} \\
\text{C A D B} \\
\text{D C B A} \\
\hline
\end{array}
$$

After this, the number of standard Latin squares increases rapidly.[7]

Once a standard Latin square is chosen, the columns are assigned to the incidental factor and the letters to the treatments. For example, Table 17.1 was derived from the fourth square. As the incidental factor in our example is the order of testing, the assignment of the columns is taken as the position in the testing sequence. If the incidental factor had been different types of materials and the Latin square was being used to counterbalance the materials, then they should be assigned to the columns randomly. In both situations, the assignment of the treatments to the letters within the square should also be made randomly. This procedure should be repeated for each block of a subjects in the study. We suggest that you use a new Latin square for each block of subjects to minimize the influence of any accidental effects that may arise from the particular choice of the square or the sequences of conditions that it contains.

Set against the advantages of systematic counterbalancing, are two limitations. One is that counterbalanced designs require more planning than randomized designs. You need to work out the Latin squares before you start. The second is that the study must be conducted in complete squares. The number of subjects must be a multiple of the number of treatments, which can be impractical when the number of treatments is large. Subjects who fail to complete the sequence of treatments will need to be replaced in order to maintain the balance, and if the pool of subjects is limited, you may be left with a partial design. Incomplete Latin square blocks are difficult to analyze using the procedures we will describe in this chapter. If nothing else, you can ignore the counterbalancing and analyze the design as if the nuisance factor had been randomized, although by doing so you will lose some of the benefits of counterbalancing.

Carryover Effects and Digram-Balanced Squares

Designs that use a successive-treatment design deserve special attention. The example in Table 17.1 illustrated the importance of balancing practice or fatigue effects in these designs. The Latin square provides this balance by assuring that each treatment appears once in each position. However, these designs do have the risk of the carryover and context effects discussed on page 371. One treatment can influence the next, either because of its direct effects or because the subject compares them. It is important to construct the design in a way that minimizes the influence of these effects.

---

[7]When $a = 5$ and $a = 6$, there are 56 and 9,408 standard squares, respectively, and the number grows to 7,580,721,483,160,132,811,489,280 when $a = 10$ (McKay & Rogoyski, 1995). Finding a Latin square of a higher order can be a matter of tedious trial and error unless one of the cyclic or digram-balanced squares we mention below is used. Table XV of Fisher and Yates (1953) gives some standard Latin squares ranging in size from 4×4 to 12×12, and programs to generate them are available.

To see why carryover effects require some additional attention, consider two studies counterbalanced according to the two standard Latin squares

$$
\begin{array}{|cccc|}
\hline
A & B & C & D \\
B & C & D & A \\
C & D & A & B \\
D & A & B & C \\
\hline
\end{array}
\quad \text{and} \quad
\begin{array}{|cccc|}
\hline
A & B & C & D \\
B & D & A & C \\
C & A & D & B \\
D & C & B & A \\
\hline
\end{array}
$$

Both designs are Latin squares, so each treatment appears equally often in each position. There is no problem at this point. However, the left-hand square does not treat the possibility of carryover effects very well. It is an instance of what is known as a **cyclic Latin square** in which each row is created from the one above it by moving one letter from the beginning of the sequence to its end. Thus, the sequence A B C D in the first row becomes B C D A in the second when the A is moved from the left to the right. Repeating this operation generates the remaining rows of the square. Although it is easy to construct this square, it has the serious disadvantage that it maximizes carryover effects. Treatment B always follows A, treatment C always follows B, and so on.

Contrast the cyclic Latin square on the left with the Latin square on the right. In this square, each condition follows each of the others exactly once. For example, A appears once after B, once after C, and once after D. The same holds for the other conditions. In this way, the differential effects of carryover are made more comparable over the conditions. Latin squares such as this are said to be **digram-balanced** or **row-balanced**. The use of a digram-balanced Latin square is greatly to be preferred for successive-treatment designs, especially when carryover effects are likely or when the number of subjects (hence the number of different Latin square blocks) is small.

There is a simple way to turn a cyclic Latin square into a digram-balanced square (Sheehe & Bross, 1961), which we will illustrate with the 4 × 4 cyclic square above. Start by taking each row of the square and writing it in reverse order. Then interleaving the original and reversed sequences, first a letter from the original sequence, then one from the reversed, and so on. From the first row of the cyclic square, we get

Original sequence:	A		B		C		D	
Reversed sequence:		D		C		B		A
Interleaved sequence:	A	D	B	C	C	B	D	A

Repeating this procedure for each line of the square gives a rectangular array twice as wide as the original square. Split this array down the middle to produce two squares:

$$
\begin{array}{|cccccccc|}
\hline
A & D & B & C & C & B & D & A \\
B & A & C & D & D & C & A & B \\
C & B & D & A & A & D & B & C \\
D & C & A & B & B & A & C & D \\
\hline
\end{array}
\quad \text{gives the squares} \quad
\begin{array}{|cccc|}
\hline
A & D & B & C \\
B & A & C & D \\
C & B & D & A \\
D & C & A & B \\
\hline
\end{array}
\begin{array}{|cccc|}
\hline
C & B & D & A \\
D & C & A & B \\
A & D & B & C \\
B & A & C & D \\
\hline
\end{array}
$$

The rows of the second square are just the reverse of those of the first. Each of these arrays is a Latin Square and each is digram balanced. You could use either one.

This procedure only gives two digram-balanced squares when the number of conditions is even. When it is odd, balance is attained only when *both* of the squares are used. For $a = 3$ and $a = 5$, for example, these squares are

<table>
<tr><td>A C B
B A C
C B A</td><td>B C A
C A B
A B C</td><td>and</td><td>A E B D C
B A C E D
C B D A E
D C E B A
E D A C B</td><td>C D B E A
D E C A B
E A D B C
A B E C D
B C A D E</td></tr>
</table>

In each case, neither square alone achieves digram balancing, but together each pair of squares does. For $a = 3$, the left-hand square has two occurrences of the sequences A C, C B, and B A and no occurrence of the other three possibilities; the right-hand square corrects this imbalance with two occurrences of the missing sequences B C, C A, and A B. Over both squares, every possible pair occurs twice. When all six orders are used, the study is digram balanced. The two squares for $a = 5$ have the same double representation of pairs of letters. In an experiment, you would use the same random assignment of treatment conditions to the letters for a pair of squares. When several replications of the digram-balanced square (or squares) are needed, different random assignments of the treatments to the letters should be used for each replication.

17.5   Analyzing a Counterbalanced Design

In the last section, we described how counterbalancing can spread the effects of a nuisance factor—either position or materials—equally over the treatment conditions, making them more comparable. The analysis described in Chapter 16 is often used for these studies. Although that approach is correct as far as it goes, it is not the optimal way to analyze studies with counterbalancing. Because it does not explicitly take account of the incidental factor, its error term is larger (on average) than necessary, and power is lost.

The Omnibus Analysis

We will illustrate the analysis using the numerical example in Table 17.2. These data are for a successive-treatment study with $a = 3$ treatments in which digram balancing was used, both to take care of position effects and to balance any carryover effects. Each of the $n = 6$ subjects received a different order of the three conditions, as indicated on the left side of the data table. These sequences form the two Latin squares required to achieve digram balancing when the number of conditions is odd. As in Table 17.1, we have listed the data twice, once organized by the order in which the conditions were administered (factor P), and once by the treatment conditions (factor A). Below the data are two analyses of variance, one calculated on the left (position) table, the other on the right (treatment) table. Because the same scores are used in each, the bracket terms $[Y] = 2{,}771$, $[S] = 2{,}450.333$, and $[T] = 2{,}380.500$ are the same for both analyses, as are SS_S, and SS_{total}. For the position analysis, $[P] = 2{,}491.500$, and for the treatment analysis, $[A] = 2{,}514.833$. As you can see, in neither of these analyses does the test statistic exceed its critical value of $F_{.05}(2, 10) = 4.10$.

Table 17.2: The analysis of a within-subject design with a counterbalanced factor (here, practice effects).

AS data matrices for practice and treatment effects

Order of Treatments		Position			Treatments			Sum
		p_1	p_2	p_3	a_1	a_2	a_3	
s_1	(a_1, a_2, a_3)	8	12	9	8	12	9	29
s_2	(a_2, a_3, a_1)	13	14	8	8	13	14	35
s_3	(a_3, a_1, a_2)	6	9	15	9	15	6	30
s_4	(a_1, a_3, a_2)	0	12	18	0	18	12	30
s_5	(a_2, a_1, a_3)	14	13	19	13	14	19	46
s_6	(a_3, a_2, a_1)	7	18	12	12	18	7	37
	Sum	48	78	81	50	90	67	207
	Mean	8.00	13.00	13.50	8.33	15.00	11.17	

Summaries of the standard analysis of variance for the two tables

Source	SS	df	MS	F
P	$[P] - [T] = 111.000$	2	55.500	2.65
S	$[S] - [T] = 69.833$	5	13.967	
$A \times P$	$[Y] - [P] - [S] + [T] = 209.667$	10	20.967	
Total	$[Y] - [T] = 390.500$	17		

Source	SS	df	MS	F
A	$[A] - [T] = 134.333$	2	67.167	3.60
S	$[S] - [T] = 69.833$	5	13.967	
$A \times S$	$[Y] - [A] - [S] + [T] = 186.334$	10	18.633	
Total	$[Y] - [T] = 390.500$	17		

Summary of the analysis of variance, including counterbalancing

Source	SS	df	MS	F
A	$[A] - [T] = 134.333$	2	67.167	7.13*
P	$[P] - [T] = 111.000$	2	55.500	5.89*
S	$[S] - [T] = 69.833$	5	13.967	
Residual	$SS_T - SS_A - SS_P - SS_S = 75.334$	8	9.417	
Total	$[Y] - [T] = 390.500$	17		

* $p < .05$

Although neither effect is significant in a separate analysis, the means for both position and treatment do seem to differ appreciably among themselves. In particular, the treatments administered second or third (p_2 or p_3) appear to have a considerable advantage over the those administered first (p_1). Instead of examining the two effects separately, we can combine the two analyses to substantially increase the power. A very important characteristic of a Latin square design is that the three main effects (position, treatment, and subjects) are mutually orthogonal. As we have seen before, orthogonal effects express distinct and separable portions of the variability. This fact makes it possible to reduce the error term. We simply subtract the sums of squares for all three main effects (not just two of them) from the total sum of squares to obtain the error term:

$$SS_{\text{residual}} = SS_{\text{total}} - SS_A - SS_P - SS_S. \tag{17.6}$$

A similar relationship applies to the degrees of freedom:

$$df_{\text{residual}} = df_{\text{total}} - df_A - df_P - df_S. \tag{17.7}$$

When the counterbalanced factor has any appreciable effect, even if not significant, the mean square for the residual error term is smaller than it is in the standard analysis. The tests are more powerful. This is what happens in Table 17.2. In the complete analysis-of-variance table in the bottom panel, the sums of squares for the three main effects are listed, just as they were calculated in the simpler analyses (you can still use the same computational formulas). The error sum of squares, calculated from Equation 17.6, is equal to

$$SS_{\text{residual}} = 390.500 - 134.333 - 111.000 - 69.833 = 75.334,$$

with $17 - 2 - 2 - 5 = 8$ degrees of freedom. The mean square is 9.417, considerably smaller than in either separate analysis, and now both treatment and practice effects are significant.[8]

How a computer package treats a Latin square design (if at all) varies considerably from program to program. The three factors A, S and P are not completely crossed (not all three-factor combinations are present), so you can't instruct the program to conduct a standard within-subject analysis with factors A and P. You will probably want to seek advice. Fortunately, if your program does not handle it (or if the instructions are incomprehensible), you can let the computer do the worst of the calculations, then piece the analysis together by hand. First, you would have a program calculate two one-way within-subject analyses, one using the treatments as a factor and the other using the incidental variable (position, in our example). Depending on your program, you may have to enter the data twice, once arranged according to the levels of the treatment factor and once according to the incidental factor. Now combine the relevant parts of the two analyses by hand, exactly as in Table 17.2.

The Importance of Interactions in a Latin Square

You will have noticed that although the analysis of the Latin square in Table 17.2 contains three main effects (factors A, P, and S), it has no interactions. This fact is

---

[8] We mentioned above the design in which a single Latin square is replicated several times (although we prefer the use of different squares). Data from this design can either be analyzed in the way that we describe in Section 17.5 or by a more complicated analysis that is described, for example, by Winer et al. (1991, p. 702, Plan 5) or by Myers and Well (1991, Section 11.5.1).

an important characteristic of the analysis of a Latin square design. The particular configuration of conditions in a Latin square makes it impossible to extract information about any interaction that may be present.[9]

The impossibility of testing interactions in a Latin square makes the design inappropriate in situations where interactions are likely to be present or where they are important to the researcher. If we felt that the treatments factor A interacted with the incidental factor P, then we should consider a design in which we could obtain specific information about this interaction. For example, if practice is the incidental factor, we might consider a design in which subjects receive the same treatment several times in a row, with a different group assigned to each treatment. The result is a two-factor experiment in which the number of repetitions constitutes the within-subject factor and the treatments are the between-subjects factor. We will discuss this mixed design in Chapters 19 and 20. Where similar effects of the incidental factor are expected in all of the treatment conditions, however, the Latin square is an excellent choice.

Another consequence of the lack of information about interactions is more subtle. Interactions may be present, whether or not we measure them. Suppose you have reason to believe that an interaction between subjects and position is possible. For example, some subjects might show little effect of practice and others a large one. Let's assume that subject s_1 in Table 17.1, who received the treatments in the order a_1, a_2, a_3, and a_4, gained more by practice than any other subject. This large practice effect would benefit the treatments that were tested late in the sequence—in this case, increasing the average for treatment a_4, which appeared at the end of the sequence, relative to a_1, which appeared at the beginning. Or, suppose subject s_4 became bored and stopped trying. Because of the particular order that this subject received (a_4 first and a_1 last), condition a_4 would again benefit relative to a_1. All of these differences would increase the variability among the treatment means. In this example, the problem is exaggerated because only four subjects and one Latin square were used. With more realistic sample sizes, these effects would become less acute, although they would never be eliminated.

In general, each main effect in a simple Latin square design is confounded with the interaction of the other two factors. The example above showed that when subjects and positions interact (a $P \times S$ interaction), there is an increase in the variability of the A effect.[10] Such an occurrence complicates the interpretation of the main effect of treatments. When large differences in the extent to which individual subjects are affected by the incidental factor are expected, it may be better to use a design that allows the $P \times S$ interaction to be explicitly measured (perhaps by repeating the orders for several subjects).

Analytical Effects in Counterbalanced Designs

We would like the gain in sensitivity that we obtain by removing the effects of a nuisance factor from the omnibus analysis to apply to any analytical analyses we might

---

[9]By making repeated observations of a square, it is possible to obtain partial information about certain interactions. However, this approach to interaction is not widely used by experimenters.

[10]This phenomenon is known as **aliasing**, because two ostensibly different effects, here A and $P \times S$, are, in effect, different names for the same sum of squares. Aliasing in some form affects any design that does not have a complete factorial structure.

Table 17.3: Steps to test an effect after removing the influence of an incidental factor from the individual scores.

1. Organize the data by the levels of the nuisance factor P, and calculate the individual means $\bar{Y}_{P_k}$ and the grand mean $\bar{Y}_T$. Use these values to determine the effects $\bar{Y}_{P_k} - \bar{Y}_T$.
2. Subtract the appropriate incidental effect from each of the original scores to equate the levels of the nuisance factor. Verify that the P means are identical and that the means (or sums) for the other factors have not changed.
3. Reorganize the adjusted data by the treatment factor (or factors).
4. Calculate the sums of square for any effects to be tested and for their error terms using the standard formulas.
5. Adjust the degrees of freedom for each error term by subtracting the degrees of freedom for the effect from its original value.
6. Using the adjusted degrees of freedom, calculate means squares and F ratios as usual.

consider testing. It is possible to adjust the error terms for these tests to remove the nuisance effects, adapting the analysis we described for the omnibus test. However, another approach is usually somewhat easier, particularly when several analytical effects will be tested. Instead of adjusting the error term by subtracting sums of squares from SS_T (see Equation 17.6), we remove the effects of the nuisance factor directly from the data themselves. We can then analyze the data in the usual way, except for an adjustment to the degrees of freedom for the error term.

Table 17.3 summarizes the steps involved. In Steps 1 and 2, the effects of the nuisance factor (practice, fatigue, materials, etc.) are calculated, and subtracted from the scores Y_{ij} to create a new data table. As a result, the nuisance factor has no effect in this table of adjusted data. The next two steps—reorganizing the data into a conventional table and calculating sums of squares—are similar to those we follow in the ordinary analysis. However, because we subtracted the nuisance effects in Step 2, they do not affect these values. Step 5 is important. We must adjust the degrees of freedom for the error term of whatever test we are running to take account of the variability that we have removed from the data. The size of this adjustment is the same as the effect we are testing:

$$df_{\text{error}}(\text{adjusted}) = df_{\text{error}}(\text{uncorrected}) - df_{\text{effect}}. \qquad (17.8)$$

Finally, the analysis is completed as usual.

We will illustrate the procedure using the data from Table 17.2. In the upper left of this table, we have already organized the data by the three levels of factor P and calculated the means $\bar{Y}_{P_k}$. The three practice effects are the differences of these means from the grand mean $\bar{Y}_T = 11.5$:

$$\bar{Y}_{P_1} - \bar{Y}_T = 8.0 - 11.5 = -3.5,$$

$$\bar{Y}_{P_2} - \bar{Y}_T = 13.0 - 11.5 = 1.5,$$

$$\bar{Y}_{P_3} - \bar{Y}_T = 13.5 - 11.5 = 2.0.$$

In Step 2, we subtract these practice effects from the individual scores. Thus, we subtract -3.5 from every score in the first column (i.e. add 3.5 to them), 1.5 from every score in the second column, and 2.0 from every score in the third column. The upper left panel of Table 17.4 shows the results of this subtraction. By raising the scores in p_1 by 3.5, we have compensated for the relative disadvantage of having been observed on the first test. The scores in the other columns, which benefited from the effects of practice, have been lowered appropriately. You can see that these adjustments have removed the practice effects by calculating the means of each column. They are all equal to 11.5, showing that the adjustment has, in effect, created a set of data that is uncontaminated by practice. These scores are reorganized by the treatment factor A (Step 3) in the upper center of Table 17.4. The means of these columns are the same as those in Table 17.2, which verifies that adjusting for practice has not changed the treatment effects.

With the practice effect removed from the Y_{ij} scores, we can analyze the data by almost the same procedures that we use for a within-subject design without counterbalancing. First consider a comparison between condition a_1 and the other two conditions, using the coefficients $\{-1, \frac{1}{2}, \frac{1}{2}\}$. We first calculate contrast values $\widehat{\psi}_i$ on the adjusted scores. These values are given in the right-hand column at the top of Table 17.4—for example, $\widehat{\psi}_1 = (-1)(11.5) + (\frac{1}{2})(10.5) + (\frac{1}{2})(7.0) = -2.75$. The value of the contrast $\widehat{\psi}_A$ equals the average of the $\widehat{\psi}_i$ or the contrast applied to the treatment means:

$$\widehat{\psi}_A = \sum c_j \bar{Y}_j = (-1)(8.33) + (\frac{1}{2})(15.00) + (\frac{1}{2})(11.17) = 4.755$$

(the difference between the two is due to rounding, and $\widehat{\psi}_A = 4.75$ is more accurate). The bracket terms for the analysis (using the formulas in Table 16.6) are

$$[T_\psi] = n\widehat{\psi}_A^2 = (6)(4.75)^2 = 135.375,$$

$$[Y_\psi] = \sum \widehat{\psi}_i^2 = (-2.75)^2 + \cdots + (3.50)^2 = 234.250,$$

and from these bracket terms, the sums of squares are

$$SS_{\psi_A} = [T_\psi] = 135.375 \quad \text{and} \quad SS_{\psi_A \times S} = [Y_\psi] - [T_\psi] = 98.875.$$

Now Step 5 comes into play. We must adjust the degrees of freedom for the error term by subtracting the degrees of freedom for the effect (Equation 17.8):

$$df_{\text{error}}(\text{adjusted}) = df_{\text{error}}(\text{uncorrected}) - df_{\text{effect}}$$

$$= df_{\psi_A} \times S - df_{\psi_A} = (n-1) - 1 = 5 - 1 = 4.$$

The remainder of the analysis is summarized in the center panel of Table 17.4. The observed F of 5.48 is not significant ($F_{.05}(1, 4) = 7.71$).[11]

Having adjusted the individual scores, we can go on and perform other analyses without repeating Steps 1–3. We will illustrate the procedure by redoing the overall analysis. At the bottom of Table 17.4, we show the sums of squares calculated according to the formulas in Table 16.2 (p. 352). Before calculating the F ratio, we adjust

---

[11]We could obtain the same results using a t test (pages 358–359) on the adjusted scores, but we would need to use the adjusted degrees of freedom when calculating the denominator.

Table 17.4: The direct removal of a counterbalanced variable (practice effects) from the data in Table 17.2. The upper panel contain the scores with the practice effects removed and a contrast variable $\hat{\psi}_i$. The lower panels summarize the analysis of the contrast and the overall effects.

Adjusted AS data matrices

	Position			**Treatments**			**Contrast**
	p_1	p_2	p_3	a_1	a_2	a_3	$\hat{\psi}_i$
s_1	11.5	10.5	7.0	11.5	10.5	7.0	-2.75
s_2	16.5	12.5	6.0	6.0	16.5	12.5	8.50
s_3	9.5	7.5	13.0	7.5	13.0	9.5	3.75
s_4	3.5	10.5	16.0	3.5	16.0	10.5	9.75
s_5	17.5	11.5	17.0	11.5	17.5	17.0	5.75
s_6	10.5	16.5	10.0	10.0	16.5	10.5	3.50
Sum	69.0	69.0	69.0	50.0	90.0	67.0	28.50
Mean	11.50	11.50	11.50	8.33	15.00	11.17	4.75

Analysis of the contrast $\psi = -\mu_1 + \frac{1}{2}(\mu_2 + \mu_3)$

Source	SS	df	MS	F
ψ_A	$[T_\psi] = 135.375$	1	135.375	5.48
Error	$[Y_\psi] - [T_\psi] = 98.875$	4	24.719	

Overall analysis of variance

Source	SS	df	MS	F
A	$[A] - [T] = 134.333$	2	67.167	7.13*
S	$[S] - [T] = 69.833$	5	13.967	
Error	$[Y] - [A] - [S] + [T] = 75.334$	8	9.417	
Total	$[Y] - [T] = 279.500$	17		

* $p < .05$

the degrees of freedom according to Step 5 (Equation 17.8):

$$df_{\text{error}}(\text{adjusted}) = df_{\text{error}}(\text{uncorrected}) - df_{\text{effect}}$$

$$= df_{A \times S} - df_A = (a-1)(n-1) - (a-1) = (2)(5) - 2 = 8.$$

Notice two things about this value. First, it is equal to the residual degrees of freedom in Table 17.2. We have simply calculated the same quantity in two ways. Second, the adjustment of the degrees of freedom is different from the one needed to test the contrast—we subtracted $df_A = 2$ for the omnibus test and $df_\psi = 1$ for the contrast. The adjustment depends on the effect being tested. Once we have the degrees of freedom, the calculations proceed as before. The final F ratio is the same as the one we obtained by adjusting the sums of squares (Table 17.2). Incidentally, comparing the two results is a handy way to verify that no errors were made in subtracting the position effect, particularly when you have a computer to do the calculations.

17.6 Missing Data in Within-Subject Designs

In Section 7.2, we discussed the problems that arise when observations are missing or otherwise lost in a between-subjects design. We distinguished between random (or ignorable) loss, in which the chance that an observation is lost does not depend on what that score would have been, and nonrandom (or nonignorable) loss, in which it does. In the latter case, particularly, our inferences may be compromised. Concern about the loss of observations transcends questions about equal or unequal sample sizes—a nonignorable loss of subjects is a problem even if we are able to obtain new subjects to replace the missing ones. The same issues apply to the loss of data in within-subject designs. When the data from some subjects are completely unobtainable, we should ask why it happened and how it affects our inferences.

With a within-subject design, another problem arises. It is possible for some, but not all, of the observations from a subject to be missing. The problem that confronts an investigator with incomplete data from a subject is what to do with the remainder of that subject's data.

Three Approaches to Partially Missing Data

The analysis of data with missing scores can be quite complicated when the proportion of data that has been lost is great—you will need the assistance of a statistician. However, the occasional loss of a few observations is common, and any researcher who uses within-subject designs needs to have a way to deal with it. At the present time, the statistical treatment of this problem is actively being researched, and we expect that new approaches will appear in the next few years (for a current review, see Schafer & Graham, 2002).

Three general approaches have been suggested: to abandon the subject altogether, to base the calculations for each part of the analysis on whatever data apply to that part, and to find a way to use all the data to fit the overall model for the analysis of variance. When only a few observations are missing, the differences among these approaches, as far as the conclusions are concerned, are minor. As the proportion of damaged scores increases, however, they can differ substantially.

One warning at the outset. The current versions of the standard computer packages do not handle incomplete observations in a very sophisticated manner; in some cases, the approach taken by default is the least appropriate one. So, when your data contain incomplete observations, it is particularly important to determine what your program is doing. Only then can you be sure that a reasonable strategy is being used.

Complete-Case Analysis. The simplest approach to incomplete data is to work only with the subjects that gave complete information. This procedure, known as **complete-case analysis** or **casewise deletion**, abandons all the data from every subject that lacks any observations. In certain respects, this is the safest solution because no statistical assumptions need be made about the missing data (although inferential concerns may still remain if the losses are nonignorable). Moreover, because only subjects with complete sets of scores are used, the same subjects figure in every calculation, and the analysis is consistent across the different treatment conditions. Complete-case analysis is also very easy to use. Perhaps because it requires so few direct assumptions, it is the default taken by many computer programs. When subjects are inexpensive or plentiful, and the amount of lost data is small, it is the most convenient approach.

Eliminating subjects is not benign, however. It does not remove any sampling bias created by the loss of data. If a subject who would have received high scores under all the treatments is deleted, the treatment means will be smaller than they would have been had the subject been included. Another difficulty is that casewise deletion can eliminate a considerable amount of data. If the chance of lost or damaged data is moderately high, deleting all subjects who lack any observation eliminates much of the original sample. The cost to the power and efficiency of the design can be substantial. Finally, deleting subjects upsets any counterbalancing scheme that has been adopted. When a Latin square has been used to balance the effects of some incidental factor, deleting one subject from the square destroys the balance. It can only be restored by dropping all subjects in that square, clearly an unpleasant course of action.

Available-Case Analysis.   Another approach to missing observations is known as **available-case analysis**. In it, each test or quantity is calculated using as much of the data as possible. Thus, the mean $\overline{Y}_1$ is based on all subjects giving a score for condition a_1, the mean $\overline{Y}_2$ is based on all those giving a score for condition a_2, and so on. When a correlation between two scores or the difference between them must be calculated, it is based on all subjects that have scores in both conditions. This approach salvages the greatest amount of information from the data. It works acceptably when the amount of missing information is not great.

The available-case analysis is widely used in survey research. In a large survey, almost every respondent is missing some response, which means that a complete-case analysis would exclude most of the data. Instead, researchers simply summarize all the available data for every question in the survey. This approach makes much less sense for the analysis of data from experimental research, where the goal is to compare the different treatments. An available-case analysis of the contrast $\psi = \mu_2 - \mu_1$ would use only those subjects having valid scores for *both* condition a_1 and a_2 because both are needed to calculate the value of the contrast variable ψ_i. The test of another contrast, say $\psi = \mu_3 + \mu_4 - 2\mu_5$, would be based a different set of subjects. When the amount of missing data is small, the sets of subjects entering into each of the calculations are roughly the same, but when the amount of missing data is large, appreciably different sets of subjects are used for each contrast, and the results can be inconsistent.

Model Fitting.   The big defect with available-case analysis is its piecemeal nature. There is no overall principle that binds the different parts of the analysis together and makes them coherent. The way to overcome this problem is to use the linear model for the scores described in Section 17.2 (see Equation 17.1). The parameters of this model are fitted using all available data at once, both those from the complete subjects and those from the incomplete ones. In this way, all the information is used and all the results are coherent. The trick is to find a way to fit the model without the process becoming computationally impossible.

Several approaches to fitting the linear model to partial data have been developed, most of which are beyond the scope of this book.[12] We will describe only one, known as **imputation**. In imputation, values are assigned to the missing scores that are consistent with the rest of the data, then the expanded data are analyzed *as if* they had been complete. Data imputation has been used informally for over a century, and recent statistical research has put it on a structured and consistent basis. It is a practical way for a researcher to handle a small-to-moderate amount of missing data.

Imputing Missing Scores

If you want to impute values for missing scores to complete your data, you can't just substitute any arbitrary values for them. The values must be consistent with both the data that were observed and the linear model for the design. Imputing the scores so that they satisfy these criteria is the hard part of the process. Once the data table is complete, only a minor modification of the procedure we described in the last chapter is necessary to analyze it.

There are two basic ways that imputation is applied, differing in how the error part of the model is treated. One approach, which we will explain below, involves picking the missing scores without concern about error, and adjusting the degrees of freedom for the error term. The other approach includes a random quantity in the imputed value that is selected to be consistent with the variability of the observed data. This form of imputation is more complicated than the other and is only starting to be used, so we will not describe it further.

The imputation of a score can be based directly on the linear model or can use various shortcut formulas. We will describe the linear-model approach briefly because it applies to any design, then use shortcuts for numerical calculation. The linear model for a one-way within-subject design (Equation 17.1) is

$$Y_{ij} = \mu_T + \alpha_j + S_i + (S\alpha)_{ij} + E_{ij}.$$

In this model, the terms $(S\alpha)_{ij}$ and E_{ij} are unique to the particular observation. When an observation is missing, we have no way to tell what values they would have had. However, the data that are not missing give information about μ_T, α_j, and S_i. Suppose we ignore the unique terms $(S\alpha)_{ij}$ and E_{ij} and concentrate on the rest of the model. A missing score Y_{ij} would then be estimated by adding up estimates of the three quantities we know something about:

$$\widehat{Y}_{ij} = (\text{estimate of } \mu_T) + (\text{estimate of } \alpha_j) + (\text{estimate of } S_i).$$

The process of finding these three estimates is a little tricky. If we had a complete table of data, then we could estimate them by the quantities $\bar{Y}_T$, $\bar{Y}_{A_j} - \bar{Y}_T$, and $\bar{Y}_{S_i} - \bar{Y}_T$, respectively. We would get

$$\widehat{Y}_{ij} = \bar{Y}_T + (\bar{Y}_{A_j} - \bar{Y}_T) + (\bar{Y}_{S_i} - \bar{Y}_T) = \bar{Y}_{A_j} + \bar{Y}_{S_i} - \bar{Y}_T. \tag{17.9}$$

---

[12]Research in this area is very active. Many methods are based on an important technique known as **maximum-likelihood estimation**, which we mention because you will see the name in other treatments of the missing-data problem. Both the standard analysis of variance and the imputation procedure we describe below are instances of maximum-likelihood estimation.

Although we don't have a complete data table, we can still use this equation to get imputed values. First we provisionally replace the missing data with reasonable guesses—say the mean of all valid data—then we calculate one missing score after another until we get stable values.[13] We illustrate this repetitive process, known as **iteration**, below.

When only one score is missing, we can impute a value to it without iteration. First, we calculate the column sums, the row sums, and the grand total for the data *without* the score that is to be imputed; call them A_j^-, S_i^-, and T^-, using the minus superscript to distinguish these sums from those based on complete data. Then we assign a value to the missing score by substituting these sums into the equation[14]

$$\widehat{Y}_{ij} = \frac{aA_j^- + nS_i^- - T^-}{(a-1)(n-1)}. \tag{17.10}$$

Problem 17.4 illustrates the use of this equation to impute a single missing score.

When several scores are missing, Equation 17.10 must be used repeatedly to impute values. We start by assigning rough values to the missing scores—say, the average of the available scores in the row or column, or the grand mean of all the available scores. The actual data and the guesses constitute a complete data table. Now we delete one of the guesses and apply Equation 17.10 to replace it. Then we do the same thing for the next missing score. We continue the process until all the missing scores have been replaced with values from Equation 17.10. We are not done yet because the calculations for the first scores have not benefited from the values assigned to the later ones. So, we repeat the entire process of deleting and replacing again, starting with the first missing score and ending with the last. Then we go on to a third round. The process does not continue forever, however. After the first couple of rounds, the changes in the missing values become smaller and smaller. Eventually, to whatever accuracy we wish, the values cease to change, giving us our final imputed scores.

As an example, consider the small set of scores at the upper-left of Table 17.5. Five subjects serve in each of $a = 4$ conditions. Two scores are missing: Y_{43} from subject s_4 in treatment a_3 and Y_{24} from subject s_2 in treatment a_4 (marked by • in the table), say because of equipment failure. Because the loss is at random and the sample size is small, it makes sense to recover the information in the remaining three scores from the two subjects. For convenience in later calculations, we have also included the incomplete marginal sums. To impute values for the two missing scores, we proceed as follows:

1. For our initial, reasonable-guess estimates, we use the means of the available scores in that treatment condition:

$$\widehat{Y}_{43}^{(1)} = \text{mean for } a_3 = (6 + 4 + 9 + 12)/4 = 7.75,$$

$$\widehat{Y}_{24}^{(1)} = \text{mean for } a_4 = (8 + 12 + 9 + 14)/4 = 10.75.$$

---

[13]This procedure (and Equation 17.10, below, for that matter) is an instance of a general approach that gives maximum-likelihood estimates when data are missing, known as the **EM algorithm** (Dempster, Laird, & Rubin, 1977; see Little & Rubin, 1987).

[14]You may wonder where we got Equation 17.10. For the completed data, the marginal total A_j is equal to $A_j^- + \widehat{Y}_{ij}$, so $\bar{Y}_{A_j} = A_j/n = (A_j^- + \bar{Y}_{ij})/n$. Similar equations apply to $\bar{Y}_{S_j}$ and $\bar{Y}_T$. Now substitute these values into Equation 17.9 and solve algebraically for the imputed score to produce Equation 17.10.

Table 17.5: A within-subject design with two missing observations (marked by •) and the analysis after imputing the missing values.

Data with missing scores (left) and with their final imputed values (right)

	a_1	a_2	a_3	a_4	Sum		a_1	a_2	a_3	a_4	Sum
s_1	4	6	6	8	24		4	6	6	8	24
s_2	2	3	4	•	9		2	3	4	6.07	15.07
s_3	8	10	9	12	39		8	10	9	12	39
s_4	5	7	•	9	21		5	7	7.16	9	28.16
s_5	9	9	12	14	44		9	9	12	14	44
Sum	28	35	31	43	137		28	35	38.16	49.07	150.23

Summary of the analysis of variance

Source	SS	df	MS	F
A	46.157	3	15.386	27.09*
S	134.820	4	33.705	
A×S	5.681	10	0.568	
Total	186.658	17		

* $p < .05$

The superscript, which we have put in parentheses to distinguish it from an exponent, indicates that these are our first round of estimates. The data with these values inserted are shown in the top of Table 17.6.

2. The second-round estimates make use of Equation 17.10 to revise the guesses from the initial round. First, we apply the equation to Y_{43}. As shown on the left in the lower panel of Table 17.6, we mark this score as missing and calculate the relevant marginal sums, A_3^- and S_4^-, and the total T^-, which we have entered in the table. We now use Equation 17.10 to produce a new estimate:

$$\widehat{Y}_{43}^{(2)} = \frac{aA_3^- + nS_4^- - T^-}{(a-1)(n-1)} = \frac{(4)(31) + (5)(21) - 147.75}{12} = 6.771.$$

The superscript indicates that this is our second round. We now turn to the other missing value, $\widehat{Y}_{24}$. We create the table on the right in Table 17.6 by replacing $Y_{43}^{(1)}$ by $\widehat{Y}_{43}^{(2)}$, marking Y_{24} as missing, and recalculating the marginal information. Then, using Equation 17.10 again,

$$\widehat{Y}_{24}^{(2)} = \frac{aA_4^- + nS_2^- - T^-}{(a-1)(n-1)} = \frac{(4)(43) + (5)(9) - 143.771}{12} = 6.102.$$

3. When we insert $\widehat{Y}_{24}^{(2)} = 6.102$ into the table, we change the quantities we used to calculate $\widehat{Y}_{43}$, so that value is no longer correct. We need to begin the process again, by declaring Y_{43} missing, recalculating the marginal information, and reapplying Equation 17.10. The result is $\widehat{Y}_{43}^{(3)} = 7.158$. Similarly, this new estimate of $\widehat{Y}_{43}$ forces us to recalculate the other missing score, which becomes

Table 17.6: Two steps involved in imputing the missing scores in Table 17.5.

First-round assignment $\widehat{Y}^{(1)}$ (based on column means)

4	6	6	8
2	3	4	10.75
8	10	9	12
5	7	7.75	9
9	9	12	14

Second-round assignments $\widehat{Y}^{(2)}$

Score Y_{43}

4	6	6	8	24
2	3	4	10.75	19.75
8	10	9	12	39
5	7	•	9	21
9	9	12	14	44
28	35	31	53.75	147.75

Score Y_{24}

4	6	6	8	24
2	3	4	•	9
8	10	9	12	39
5	7	6.771	9	27.771
9	9	12	14	44
28	35	37.771	43	143.771

$\widehat{Y}_{24}^{(3)} = 6.070$. These two new estimates are much closer to $\widehat{Y}_{43}^{(2)}$ and $\widehat{Y}_{24}^{(2)}$ than those values were to our starting values $\widehat{Y}_{43}^{(1)}$ and $\widehat{Y}_{24}^{(1)}$. The smaller differences show that we are converging on the final values.

4. The next pair of estimates are $\widehat{Y}_{43}^{(4)} = 7.161$ and $Y_{24}^{(4)} = 6.070$. The changes now are very small. In fact, because the last estimate, $Y_{24}^{(4)}$, has not changed to three decimal places from the previous round, the results from a fifth round of estimates would be the same as the fourth. Convergence is complete and we have our imputed values. The end result is shown in the upper right portion of Table 17.5.[15]

Values calculated by iterating with Equation 17.10 do not depend on the starting values; we will arrive at the same final values whether we start with the incomplete column means, as we did, or the incomplete row means (which are $9/3 = 3.00$ and $21/3 = 7.00$ for subjects s_2 and s_4, respectively), or even the grand mean ($137/18 = 7.611$).

With the imputed values in place, the data are analyzed normally, except that the degrees of freedom for the interaction must be reduced by the number of imputed scores. Thus, both $df_{A \times S}$ and df_{total} are 2 less than they would normally be (i.e. 10 and 17 instead of $(a - 1)(n - 1) = 12$ and $an - 1 = 19$ respectively). The complete analysis is given at the bottom of Table 17.5. With 3 and 10 degrees of freedom, the F is significant.

After imputing the scores, you may want to use a computer program to calculate the actual analysis of variance. Of course, the program has no way to tell that some of your data are real observations and some have been imputed. You use the computer for the analysis on the completed data, but you will need to go back and correct

---

[15]You may have wondered why we labeled this procedure a "short-cut" process. We assure you that approaches that do not use Equation 17.10 require considerably more calculation.

the degrees of freedom for the error term to account for the imputed scores, then recalculate the mean square $MS_{A \times S}$ and the F ratio.

The shortcut imputation equation can be expanded to include a counterbalancing factor. The estimation equation analogous to Equation 17.10 is

$$\widehat{Y}_{ij} = \frac{aA_j^- + nS_i^- + pP_k^- - 2T^-}{(a-1)(n-1)-(a-1)}, \tag{17.11}$$

where P_k^- is the marginal sum without the score that is to be imputed for the data at level p_k with the missing score excluded. When only one score is missing, this equation is used directly (see Problem 17.5 for an example). When several scores are missing, iteration is required. The steps involved in imputing the scores are like those for the design without counterbalancing:

- For the first-round estimates, $\widehat{Y}_{ij}^{(1)}$, set the missing scores to the mean of the complete scores for the relevant treatment, subject, or position, or even to the grand mean.
- For the second-round estimates, $\widehat{Y}_{ij}^{(2)}$, take each missing score in turn, strike it from the table, calculate the marginal sums, estimate $\widehat{Y}_{ij}^{(2)}$ from Equation 17.11, and replace the first-round estimate with it.
- Repeat this procedure for as many rounds needed—that is, until the estimated scores stop changing.

At this point, you have a complete set of data, which you can analyze as directed in Table 17.3. To summarize,

- Calculate the practice effects based on the complete data set and subtract them from the individual Y_{ij} scores. Reorganized the data by the treatments.
- Conduct the analysis of variance as before. Remember to reduce the error degrees of freedom for *both* the removal of practice effects and the imputation of the missing scores.

Exercises

17.1. An experiment is conducted in which four different drugs (a_2, a_3, a_4, and a_5) and a placebo (a_1) are administered to each of $n = 5$ different animals. The response measure consists of the number of discrimination problems solved within a given time limit. The data follow. As in Table 17.1, each score is given with a position number p_k that identifies the order in which the observations were made (for example, the first subject received the conditions in the order a_3, a_2, a_1, a_4, a_5).

	a_1		a_2		a_3		a_4		a_5	
s_1	p_3	11	p_2	11	p_1	9	p_4	6	p_5	7
s_2	p_4	8	p_1	13	p_5	2	p_2	10	p_3	5
s_3	p_1	13	p_3	9	p_4	3	p_5	4	p_2	6
s_4	p_2	12	p_5	3	p_3	6	p_1	13	p_4	6
s_5	p_5	7	p_4	8	p_2	8	p_3	9	p_1	13

a. Conduct a standard analysis of variance on these data.
b. Follow the procedures in Table 17.2 to remove practice effects from the analysis.

17.2. Suppose the researcher in Problem 17.1 is interested in testing two additional hypotheses: (1) a comparison between the placebo control (a_1) and an average of the other drug groups and (2) a comparison among the four different drugs (conditions a_2–a_5). This latter comparison tests an "omnibus" hypothesis ($H_0: \mu_2 = \mu_3 = \mu_4 = \mu_5$), of the sort we considered for a single-factor between-subjects design in Section 4.7.

a. Conduct both tests using the uncorrected data.

b. Adjust the data to remove the practice effects from the individual scores and test the two hypotheses (see pp. 389–393). For the omnibus hypothesis, you will need to subtract from the error as many degrees of freedom as there are in that hypothesis.

17.3. As described, the experiment in Problem 16.3 contains a serious flaw. The same words are always assigned the same monetary value. A good researcher would eliminate this confounding by counterbalancing the assignment of the colors (i.e. the sets of words) to the values. Let factor A stand for the monetary values as before (1 cent, 5 cents, and 10 cents), and let c_1, c_2, and c_3 stand for the colors (red, green, and blue, respectively). The table below shows how the colors and conditions were matched up for each subject. For example, the assignment (a_2, a_3, a_1) for subject s_2 indicates that the red words (c_1) were valued at 5 cents, the green words (c_2) at 10 cents, and the blue words (c_3) at 1 cent.

	Word set		
Subject	c_1	c_2	c_3
s_1	a_1	a_2	a_3
s_2	a_2	a_3	a_1
s_3	a_3	a_1	a_2
s_4	a_1	a_3	a_2
s_5	a_2	a_1	a_3
s_6	a_3	a_2	a_1

Use this information to answer the questions in Problem 16.3, taking account of the counterbalancing and the unequal intervals.

17.4. In Table 16.3 (p. 355), we presented the results of a within-subject study in which subjects attempted to determine as quickly as possible whether a particular letter appeared in a string of letters. Suppose a recording error was made and the sixth subject's score for the random string was unusable.

a. Impute a value to the missing score using Equation 17.10.

b. Insert the imputed score into the data set and conduct an analysis of variance.

c. Suppose the first score of s_3 is also missing. Use Equation 17.10 to impute the two missing scores.

17.5. Suppose in the counterbalanced study illustrated in Table 17.2, subject s_4 was missing the score for condition a_3 (it appeared in position p_2; the actual value in the table is 12). Use Equation 17.11 to impute a value for this score, then complete the analysis.

18

The Two-Factor
Within-Subject Design

In the last two chapters, we considered the single-factor within-subject $A{\times}S$ design, in which every subject receives all levels of a single independent variable. The natural extension of this design is to a pure two-factor within-subject $A{\times}B{\times}S$ design, in which every subject receives all the ab treatment combinations that arise by crossing two factors, A and B. This design is the topic of the present chapter. Another form of two-factor design mixes between-subjects and within-subject effects, with one factor of each type. We will discuss these designs in Chapters 19 and 20. Designs of all types with more than two experimental factors will be treated in Part VI.

A factorial design with two within-subject factors has all the advantages and disadvantages of the single-factor within-subject design. On the one hand, the error variance is usually less than in the between-subjects design, giving these designs greater power. They are also more efficient, in that they collect several observations from each subject. On the other hand, the number of measures that are obtained from each subject is larger than in most single-factor designs, raising difficulties with fatigue or practice effects, selection of appropriate sets of material, and violation of assumptions. The analysis of these designs is similar to that discussed in Chapter 16, being primarily a matter of partitioning the within-subject variability into appropriate main effects and interactions and selecting the correct error terms.

18.1 The Overall Analysis

The overall analysis of the $A{\times}B{\times}S$ design combines elements of both the between-subjects $A{\times}B$ design and the within-subject $A{\times}S$ design. The factorial treatment effects—the main effects of factor A and factor B and the $A{\times}B$ interaction—are calculated with the same computational formulas used for the $A{\times}B$ design. The three error terms required in this design, one for each effect, are calculated in ways similar to those used with the $A{\times}S$ design.

Design and Notation

The design and notational system are described in Table 18.1. Each letter or combination of letters refers to a unique quantity calculated from the data. The ABS table

Table 18.1: Notation for the $A \times B \times S$ design.

ABS table

| | a_1 | | | a_2 | | |
	b_1	b_2	b_3	b_1	b_2	b_3
s_1	Y_{111}	Y_{112}	Y_{113}	Y_{121}	Y_{122}	Y_{123}
s_2	Y_{211}	Y_{212}	Y_{213}	Y_{221}	Y_{222}	Y_{223}
s_3	Y_{311}	Y_{312}	Y_{313}	Y_{321}	Y_{322}	Y_{223}

AB table

	b_1	b_2	b_3	Sum
a_1	AB_{11}	AB_{12}	AB_{13}	A_1
a_2	AB_{21}	AB_{22}	AB_{23}	A_2
Sum	B_1	B_2	B_3	T

AS table

	a_1	a_2	Sum
s_1	SA_{11}	SA_{12}	S_1
s_2	SA_{21}	SA_{22}	S_2
s_3	SA_{31}	SA_{32}	S_3
Sum	A_1	A_2	T

BS table

	b_1	b_2	b_3	Sum
s_1	SB_{11}	SB_{12}	SB_{13}	S_1
s_2	SB_{21}	SB_{22}	SB_{23}	S_2
s_3	SB_{31}	SB_{32}	SB_{33}	S_3
Sum	B_1	B_2	B_3	T

is the data table in which the individual Y_{ijk} scores are recorded. The subscript i here refers to the individual subjects, j to the levels of factor A, and k to the levels of factor B. As diagrammed, each of $n = 3$ subjects contributes a total of $ab = (2)(3) = 6$ scores, one for each treatment condition.

Three two-way tables, shown in the lower parts of Table 18.1, are obtained by summing the ABS table over one of its three factors. The AB table is formed by summing the Y_{ijk} scores in each treatment combination. The sums in this table provide the information needed to calculate the means for the treatment conditions $\overline{Y}_{jk}$ and the sums of squares for the treatment effects. The other two tables are used to calculate sums of squares involving factor S, which are the error terms. The AS table contains sums obtained by collapsing over the b treatments. For example, SA_{11} equals the sum of the three Y_{ijk} scores for s_1 obtained at level a_1, and SA_{32} equals the sum of the three Y_{ijk} scores for s_3 obtained at level a_2.[1] The AS table is identical to the data table for an $A \times S$ design, except that it contains sums of b observations. Similarly, the BS table contains sums obtained by collapsing over factor A and is like the table from a single-factor design in which factor B the a within-subject factor.

---

[1] We have reversed the order of the two letters representing the sums in the AS and BS tables from that used in earlier editions of this book so that the order of the two letters and the subscripts correspond. We have not changed the order of the letters designating the tables themselves, as the original order emphasizes the fact that the AS and BS tables provide the information for $A \times S$ and $B \times S$ interactions, respectively.

Each of the two-way tables has marginal sums, formed by summing over the rows or the columns. For example, the two one-dimensional arrays containing the A and B sums are found by summing the AB table over the rows and columns, respectively. Similarly, the AS table gives the A and S sums. Adding up any of these one-dimensional arrays gives the grand sum T.

Sources of Variance and Sums of Squares

The overall analysis of the $A \times B \times S$ design is summarized in Table 18.2. The first column lists the sources of variability. We can determine these using the procedure in Table 11.2 (p. 214). First we put down the three factors, A, B, and S. In Step 2, we note that every pair of factors is crossed, giving the interactions $A \times B$, $A \times S$, and $B \times S$. Moreover, all three-way combinations are present—each subject gives a score for each combination of a_j and b_k—so the table includes a three-factor $A \times B \times S$ interaction. We will have more to say about three-way interactions in Part VI; here it is enough to realize that it expresses the way that the $A \times B$ interaction varies over subjects. The design contains no nesting, so Step 3 does not apply, and we are done.

The rest of the table gives formulas for calculating the sums of squares associated with these sources of variability. They were obtained with the rules we gave in Table 11.3 (p. 215) and Table 11.4 (p. 216). The degrees of freedom for the various effects are determined from the names of the sources. For each main effect, the degrees of freedom equal the number of levels less one:

$$df_A = a - 1, \quad df_B = b - 1, \quad \text{and} \quad df_S = n - 1.$$

The other effects in this design are interactions, and each is the product of the degrees of freedom of its component effects:

$$df_{A \times B} = df_A \times df_B = (a - 1)(b - 1),$$
$$df_{A \times S} = df_A \times df_S = (a - 1)(n - 1),$$
$$df_{B \times S} = df_B \times df_S = (b - 1)(n - 1),$$
$$df_{A \times B \times S} = df_A \times df_B \times df_S = (a - 1)(b - 1)(n - 1).$$

Each formula for the degrees of freedom forms the basis for a computational formula for a sum of squares. Following the steps in Table 11.4, we expand the formula into a series of simple products, then replace each product by the corresponding bracket term. For example, the degrees of freedom for the $A \times S$ effect are

$$df_{A \times S} = (a - 1)(n - 1) = an - a - n + 1,$$

which becomes the formula for the sum of squares:

$$SS_{A \times S} = [AS] - [A] - [S] + [T].$$

These computational formulas appear in the third column of Table 18.2. The bracket terms are calculated from the tables of sums or means. To illustrate with the bracket term $[BS]$, we square the entries of the BS table, sum the squares, and divide by a, which is the number of scores entering into each of the SB_{ik} sums:

$$[BS] = \frac{\sum (SB_{ik})^2}{a}.$$

Table 18.2: Computational formulas for the sums of squares in an $A \times B \times S$ design.

Source	df	SS	Bracket term
A	$a - 1$	$[A] - [T]$	$[A] = \dfrac{\sum A_j^2}{bn}$
B	$b - 1$	$[B] - [T]$	$[B] = \dfrac{\sum B_k^2}{an}$
$A \times B$	$(a-1)(b-1)$	$[AB] - [A] - [B] + [T]$	$[AB] = \dfrac{\sum AB_{jk}^2}{n}$
S	$n - 1$	$[S] - [T]$	$[S] = \dfrac{\sum S_i^2}{ab}$
$A \times S$	$(a-1)(n-1)$	$[AS] - [A] - [S] + [T]$	$[AS] = \dfrac{\sum SA_{ij}^2}{b}$
$B \times S$	$(b-1)(n-1)$	$[BS] - [B] - [S] + [T]$	$[BS] = \dfrac{\sum SB_{ik}^2}{a}$
$A \times B \times S$	$(a-1)(b-1)$ $\times (n-1)$	$[Y] - [AB] - [AS] - [BS]$ $+[A] + [B] + [S] - [T]$	$[Y] = \sum Y^2$
Total	$abn - 1$	$[Y] - [T]$	$[T] = \dfrac{T^2}{abn}$

Formulas for all the bracket terms appear in the last column of Table 18.2. We can find the same values using means instead of sums and multiplying by the number of scores rather than dividing. For example, using the AB table,

$$[AB] = n \sum \overline{Y}_{AB_{jk}}^2.$$

We need a bracket term for every table or set of marginal sums in Table 18.1. These terms correspond to the list of effects in Table 18.2—a discrepancy tells us we made a mistake in working out the design.

Selecting the Error Term

The mean squares for the analysis are calculated as usual by dividing each sum of squares by its corresponding number of degrees of freedom. To create the F statistics, each testable mean square is divided by the mean square of an error term. We must pick these error terms appropriately. You will recall from our discussion of the $A \times S$ design (p. 353 and pp. 373–375) that, in addition to any treatment effects, MS_A was influenced by both the treatment-by-subject interaction $A \times S$ and the variability of an individual observation (the different sources are especially evident in the expected mean squares, Equations 17.2, p. 374). The two sources of error posed no problem for the evaluation of the significance of factor A, however, because the interaction mean square $MS_{A \times S}$ provided a measure of those same two sources of variability.

An analogous argument (which could be made rigorous by considering the expected mean squares) applies in the present design. Consider the A effect. Its sum of squares is calculated from the AS table in Table 18.1. Ignoring factor B, we could view this table as the results of a single-factor within-subject $A \times S$ experiment. The influences on MS_A here are identical to those in an actual one-factor design, namely the effect itself, the interaction of factor A with subjects, and the variability of the individual observations. Thus, the error term is the same as in the simpler design:

$$F_A = \frac{MS_A}{MS_{A \times S}}.$$

In the same way, the B main effect is derived from the BS table, which can be thought of as a single-factor $B \times S$ design. So the MS_B is influenced by any treatment effects, the variation of the B effect over subjects, and the variability of the individual observations. The appropriate error term to test it is the $MS_{B \times S}$ interaction:

$$F_B = \frac{MS_B}{MS_{B \times S}}.$$

The third systematic effect is the $A \times B$ interaction. Its mean square is affected by any $A \times B$ interaction that is present, by the way the $A \times B$ interaction varies from subject to subject, and by the variability of the observations. The variation of an interaction over a third factor is a three-factor interaction—here the variation of the $A \times B$ intraction with subjects makes a three-way $A \times B \times S$ interaction. The F ratio needed to test the $MS_{A \times B}$ uses this three-way interaction:

$$F_{A \times B} = \frac{MS_{A \times B}}{MS_{A \times B \times S}}.$$

You can see that there is a pattern to these error terms:

> *The error term for any within-subject effect is the interaction of that effect with subjects.*

Applying the rule here, we have as error terms,

$$A \times S \text{ for } A, \quad B \times S \text{ for } B, \quad \text{and} \quad A \times B \times S \text{ for } A \times B.$$

We will make considerable use of this principle throughout our treatment of within-subject and mixed designs.

We have not given error terms to test either the subject effect S or its interactions. These mean squares can be tested using the three-way interaction $A \times B \times S$ as an error term, but the resulting test is negatively biased, as we discussed for the $A \times S$ design in Section 17.2 (see pp. 353–354). In practice, these tests do not contain any useful information, and typically they are neither performed nor reported.

A Numerical Example

Suppose a researcher is interested in comparing the speed with which words differing in emotional value are learned. An $A \times B \times S$ design is used. Each of $n = 8$ college-student subjects studies a list of 60 different words. Twenty words are judged to be of negative emotional value (a_1), 20 positive (a_2), and 20 neutral (a_3). Within each of these categories, 5 words are presented once (b_1), 5 are presented twice (b_2), 5 three times (b_3), and 5 four times (b_4). The assignment of specific words to the different presentation conditions is determined randomly for each subject. The list of words, which is randomly ordered for each subject, is presented at the rate of two seconds per word, and after the study period, the subjects are given 5 minutes to recall the words in any order. Each subject receives each type of word under every condition of

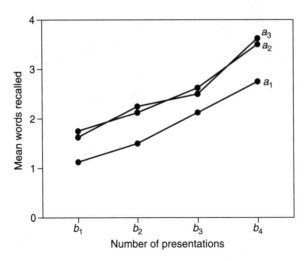

Figure 18.1: A plot of the means from Table 18.3.

repetition, so both independent variables are within-subject factors. They are crossed to make a 3×4 within-subject design. Because the presentation order is randomized for each subject, the design uses intermixed treatments. The Y_{ijk} scores, which give the number of words from each of the 12 treatment combinations that were recalled on the test, are shown at the top of Table 18.3.

To complete the calculations, we need three tables of sums (or means), each formed by combining the scores over one of the three factors. The middle part of Table 18.3 gives an AB table of sums, constructed by summing the Y_{ijk} scores over the $n = 8$ subjects of factor S, and a similar table of means $\overline{Y}_{AB_{ij}}$. These means are plotted in Figure 18.1, with the quantitative factor B on the axis, as we suggested in Chapter 12 (see p. 248). At the bottom of Table 18.3 are the AS and BS tables of sums, formed by summing over the $b = 4$ levels of factor B and the $a = 3$ levels of factor A, respectively. By now, you certainly know how to use the ABS data table to obtain $[Y]$ and the AB table to obtain the bracket terms $[AB]$, $[A]$, $[B]$, and $[T]$. From the last two tables, we also calculate $[AS]$ and $[BS]$, and, from their row marginal sums, $[S]$. To illustrate one of these calculations,

$$[AS] = \frac{\sum SA_{ij}^2}{b} = \frac{6^2 + 8^2 + 8^2 + \cdots + 7^2 + 8^2 + 11^2}{4} = 557.000.$$

Values for the full set of bracket terms are summarized in Table 18.4.

The remainder of the analysis is quite straightforward. The only thing to remember is that each F ratio is constructed using a different error mean square: the A effect is tested with $MS_{A \times S}$, the B effect is tested with $MS_{B \times S}$, and the interaction is tested with $MS_{A \times B \times S}$, in accordance with the principle stated above. Both main effects are significant, but the interaction is not. A look at the marginal means in the center of Table 18.3 (or the plot in Figure 18.1) shows clearly that the A effect is primarily the result of the difference of the negative words (condition a_1) from the other two types of words. Not surprisingly, the B means reveal an increase in performance with the

Table 18.3: *The data for recall of three types of words (factor A) after 1, 2, 3, or 4 trials of study (factor B). Below the data table are the marginal sums and the means of the conditions.*

ABS table of scores Y_{ijk}

	a_1				a_2				a_3			
	b_1	b_2	b_3	b_4	b_1	b_2	b_3	b_4	b_1	b_2	b_3	b_4
s_1	1	1	2	2	1	2	2	3	1	2	2	3
s_2	2	2	3	4	2	3	4	5	3	3	3	5
s_3	2	3	3	3	3	4	3	4	2	3	3	4
s_4	0	1	0	2	1	2	2	3	2	2	2	3
s_5	1	1	2	2	1	1	2	3	1	1	2	2
s_6	1	2	3	3	2	3	3	5	2	3	4	4
s_7	1	1	2	3	2	1	2	3	1	1	2	3
s_8	1	1	2	3	1	2	2	3	2	2	3	4

Marginal sums and means for $A \times B$ conditions

AB sums

	b_1	b_2	b_3	b_4	Sum
a_1	9	12	17	22	60
a_2	13	18	20	29	80
a_3	14	17	21	28	80
Sum	36	47	58	79	220

AB table of means

	b_1	b_2	b_3	b_4	Mean
a_1	1.125	1.500	2.125	2.750	1.875
a_2	1.625	2.250	2.500	3.625	2.500
a_3	1.750	2.125	2.625	3.500	2.500
Mean	1.500	1.958	2.417	3.292	2.292

Marginal $A \times S$ and $B \times S$ tables of sums

AS table

	a_1	a_2	a_3	Sum
s_1	6	8	8	22
s_2	11	14	14	39
s_3	11	14	12	37
s_4	3	8	9	20
s_5	6	7	6	19
s_6	9	13	13	35
s_7	7	8	7	22
s_8	7	8	11	26
Sum	60	80	80	220

BS table

	b_1	b_2	b_3	b_4	Sum
s_1	3	5	6	8	22
s_2	7	8	10	14	39
s_3	7	10	9	11	37
s_4	3	5	4	8	20
s_5	3	3	6	7	19
s_6	5	8	10	12	35
s_7	4	3	6	9	22
s_8	4	5	7	10	26
Sum	36	47	58	79	220

Table 18.4: Summary of the analysis of variance of the data in Table 18.3.

Source	Bracket terms	SS	df	MS	F
A	$[A] = 512.500$	8.333	2	4.167	10.94*
B	$[B] = 546.250$	42.083	3	14.028	44.68*
$A{\times}B$	$[AB] = 555.250$	0.667	6	0.111	0.82
S	$[S] = 543.333$	39.166	7	5.595	
$A{\times}S$	$[AS] = 557.000$	5.334	14	0.381	
$B{\times}S$	$[BS] = 592.000$	6.584	21	0.314	
$A{\times}B{\times}S$	$[Y] = 612$	5.666	42	0.135	
Total	$[T] = 504.167$	107.833	95		

*$p < .05$

number of study opportunities. The lack of an interaction suggests that this increase is approximately the same for the three types of words. It appears, then, that the emotional value of the words has an effect after one presentation that neither increases nor diminishes with the additional presentations in this experiment.

18.2   Contrasts and Other Analytical Analyses

When an independent variable has more than two levels, we turn to analytical comparisons to examine detailed hypotheses. In factorial designs, we have available additional analytical procedures that dissect the interaction effects—the analysis of simple effects, simple contrasts, and interaction components. In Chapters 12 and 13, we discussed their use in the context of a two-factor between-subjects design. The overall strategy for selecting the analytical effects to test is the same in the two-factor within-subject design as it was in its between-subjects counterpart. When a study is in the planning stage, we may identify one or more contrasts or special analyses that are specifically implied by our theory and should be investigated as planned tests. Later on, various post-hoc analyses help to follow up the results. If an interaction were found, then we would look at simple effects or at interaction components. If no interaction were present or if the interaction was dominated by the main effects, then we would concentrate on a detailed analysis of the main effects. We will examine these types of analyses in this section.

The principal way in which the analytical analysis of between-subjects and within-subject designs differ is in the choice of error term. Following the principle on page 405, each effect—simple effect, contrast, interaction contrast, and so forth—is tested against its interaction with subjects. In Table 18.5, we have stated two applications of this principle, one for contrasts and one for analyses such as simple effects. The approaches work with most designs with within-subject factors, and both are relatively easy to implement with most computer programs.

Analyzing a Contrast

We begin with the analysis of a contrast based on one of the independent variables. Our interest may be in the contrast itself (e.g., ψ_A) or in its interaction with the other

Table 18.5: Principles for calculating analytical effects with within-subject factors.

1. Any effect involving a contrast on a within-subject factor is tested against an error term that includes the interaction of that contrast with subjects. To calculate this error term, create a contrast variable by applying the contrast to each subject's data, then analyze these values as if they come from a simpler design.
2. Any within-subject effect involving a portion of the data (e.g., a simple effect) is tested against an error term derived exclusively from those data. To calculate this error term, simply extract these data and analyze them as if they come from a simpler design.

factor (e.g., $\psi_A \times B$). You saw in Section 16.2 that the error term needed to test a contrast could be found by creating a contrast variable and analyzing it. To create the variable, we calculate the contrast value for each subject. Either a t test or an F test can be used to test whether its mean differed from zero. The first rule in Table 18.5 expresses this idea.

As an example, let's investigate the shape of the function relating recall to the number of presentations (factor B) for the data in Table 18.3. Factor B is quantitative and has equally spaced levels, so, as Chapter 5 explains, a natural approach is to look for linear trend and nonlinear effects. The coefficients of the contrast variable for linear trend are obtained from Appendix A.3:

$$\psi_{B_{\text{linear}}} = -3\mu_1 - \mu_2 + \mu_3 + 3\mu_4.$$

Because the means increase over factor B, the values of this contrast will generally be positive. Applying these coefficients to the individual Y_{ijk} scores gives us three values of the contrast variable for each subject, one for each level of factor A, which we will denote simply by $\widehat{\psi}_{ij}$. Thus, the 12 individual Y_{ijk} scores for the first subject in Table 18.3 become three values of the linear contrast variables:

$$\text{negative words } (a_1): \widehat{\psi}_{11} = (-3)(1) + (-1)(1) + (1)(2) + (3)(2) = 4,$$

$$\text{positive words } (a_2): \widehat{\psi}_{12} = (-3)(1) + (-1)(2) + (1)(2) + (3)(3) = 6,$$

$$\text{neutral words } (a_3): \widehat{\psi}_{13} = (-3)(1) + (-1)(2) + (1)(2) + (3)(3) = 6.$$

The upper portion of Table 18.6 contains the results of these calculations. They transform the original ABS data table into the functional equivalent of an AS table from a single-factor within-subject design. We can analyze the linear trend component by treating the $\widehat{\psi}_{ij}$ as if they were scores from an actual $A \times S$ design. Afterward, we will translate the results back to the context of the original $A \times B \times S$ design. Each effect in the reduced design becomes one that applies to the contrast.

At the bottom of the table of contrast values in Table 18.6, we have given the mean value of the contrast for each level of factor A and their grand mean. The analysis of these numbers as an $A \times S$ design lets us conduct two tests:

- We can test whether the grand mean of the contrast values (G.M.$_\psi$ = 5.83) differs from zero. If it does, then we can conclude that $\psi_{B_{\text{linear}}}$ is nonzero in the original design.

Table 18.6: Linear trend contrasts calculated for each subject and word type for the data in Table 18.3 (upper panel). The lower panel gives the analysis of variance of the contrast variable.

Linear contrasts calculated on individual subject data

Word type (factor A)

	Negative $\widehat{\psi}_{i1}$	Positive $\widehat{\psi}_{i2}$	Neutral $\widehat{\psi}_{i3}$	Sum
s_1	4	6	6	16
s_2	7	10	6	23
s_3	3	2	6	11
s_4	5	6	3	14
s_5	4	7	4	15
s_6	7	9	7	23
s_7	7	4	7	18
s_8	7	6	7	20
Sum	44	50	46	140
Mean	5.50	6.25	5.75	5.83

Summary of the analysis of variance of the contrast values

Source of variation					
For $\widehat{\psi}_{ij}$	For Y_{ijk}	SS	df	MS	F
G.M.$_\psi$	$\psi_{B_{\text{linear}}}$	816.667	1	816.667	131.93*
A_ψ	$A \times \psi_{B_{\text{linear}}}$	2.333	2	1.167	0.43
S_ψ	$\psi_{B_{\text{linear}}} \times S$	43.333	7	6.190	
$A \times S_\psi$	$A \times \psi_{B_{\text{linear}}} \times S$	37.667	14	2.691	
*$p < .05$					

- We can test whether the group means (with observed values of 5.50, 6.25, and 5.75) differ from each other. If they do, then we can conclude that $\psi_{B_{\text{linear}}}$ interacts with factor A, that is, that the slopes of the linear relationship depend on the treatment.

According to the principle on page 405, the error for any within-subject effect is the interaction of that effect with subjects. Applying this principle to within-subject contrast effects, the F statistics we need to test these hypotheses in the full two-factor design are

$$F_{B_{\text{linear}}} = \frac{MS_{B_{\text{linear}}}}{MS_{B_{\text{linear}} \times S}} \quad \text{and} \quad F_{A \times B_{\text{linear}}} = \frac{MS_{A \times B_{\text{linear}}}}{MS_{A \times B_{\text{linear}} \times S}}.$$

In the single-factor reduced design, the same hypotheses are tested by the ratios

$$F_{\text{G.M.}_\psi} = \frac{MS_{\text{G.M.}_\psi}}{MS_{S_\psi}} \quad \text{and} \quad F_{A_\psi} = \frac{MS_{A_\psi}}{MS_{A \times S_\psi}}.$$

We have informally put the subscript ψ on the various terms to remind ourselves that we are dealing with the contrast variable.

We find the sums of squares for the analysis from a standard one-way within-subject $A \times S$ analysis applied to the contrast values $\widehat{\psi}_{ij}$ in Table 18.6. We need four sums of squares. Three of these are the conventional A, S, and $A \times S$ effects from that design, and the fourth is the effect associated with the grand mean, which has a sum of squares equal to the bracket term $[T]$ (Equation 16.4, p. 359). All the parts come together in the analysis summary at the bottom of Table 18.6. The first of the two columns under "Sources of variation" lists the sources from the single-factor analysis of $\widehat{\psi}_{ij}$, using the labels appropriate for an $A \times S$ design, again flagged with the subscript ψ. The second column describes those sources in terms of their meaning in the analysis of the two-factor within-subject design. The first source, the grand mean, is equivalent to $\psi_{B_{\text{linear}}}$, and each of the remaining sources becomes an interaction of that source with the contrast. The remainder of the summary table gives the numerical analysis. Using the linear contrast values as data, the bracket terms are calculated from the formulas in Table 16.2 (p. 352), giving

$$[A_\psi] = 819.000, \quad [S_\psi] = 860.000, \quad [Y_\psi] = 900.000, \quad \text{and} \quad [T_\psi] = 816.667.$$

Table 16.2 also indicates how to combine the bracket terms into sums of squares. These are reported at the bottom of Table 18.6. The test of the main linear comparison in the first row is significant, allowing us to conclude that recall increases steadily with the number of presentations. The test of the $A \times \psi_{B_{\text{linear}}}$ interaction in the second row is not significant, indicating that the size of the linear contrast does not vary over the different types of words.

As we explained in Chapter 5 (see p. 94), although this analysis demonstrates that recall improves with the number of presentations, it does not tell us whether the underlying function is a straight line. To find out, we need to test for nonlinear trend, which we can do in two different ways. One possibility is to assess the quadratic trend using the coefficients 1, -1, -1, and 1 from Appendix A.3. Without showing the details, a one-way within-subject analysis of variance based on the quadratic contrast values resulted in $F = 3.72$ for the overall quadratic term and $F = 0.30$ for the interaction with factor A, neither of which is significant.

The other procedure uses a less-focused test of the residual variability that is expressed by the sum of squares not accounted for by the linear component. In Chapter 5, we calculated SS_{residual} by subtracting SS_{linear} from the omnibus sum of squares. Before we can do that here, we have to put both sums of squares on the same basis by adjusting for the particular contrast coefficients that we used to calculate ψ_B. This adjustment is made by dividing each contrast sum of squares by the sum of the squared coefficients, $\sum c_k^2$ (see Equation 16.5, p. 359). The adjustment factor here is

$$\sum c_k^2 = (-3)^2 + (-1)^2 + 1^2 + 3^2 = 20.$$

Thus, the two adjusted sums of squares from Table 18.6 for the main comparison are

$$SS_{\psi_B} = \frac{816.667}{20} = 40.833 \quad \text{and} \quad SS_{\psi_B \times S} = \frac{43.333}{20} = 2.167.$$

Table 18.7 shows the analysis of variance table for the analysis of linear and nonlinear trend. The table is a little complicated, so we will go through it carefully. It is divided

Table 18.7: Analysis of the linear and nonlinear effects of trials (factor B) and its interaction with word type (factor A).

Source	SS	df	MS	F
B	42.083	3		
$\psi_{B_{\text{linear}}}$	40.833	1	40.883	131.88*
$B_{\text{nonlinear}}$	1.250	2	0.625	1.98
$A \times B$	0.667	6		
$A \times \psi_{B_{\text{linear}}}$	0.117	2	0.059	0.44
$A \times B_{\text{nonlinear}}$	0.550	4	0.138	1.02
$B \times S$	6.584	21		
$\psi_{B_{\text{linear}}} \times S$	2.167	7	0.310	
$B_{\text{nonlinear}} \times S$	4.417	14	0.316	
$A \times B \times S$	5.666	42		
$A \times \psi_{B_{\text{linear}}} \times S$	1.883	14	0.135	
$A \times B_{\text{nonlinear}} \times S$	3.783	28	0.135	

*$p < .05$

into four parts, each associated with one of the effects involving factor B in the original analysis of Table 18.4. The top part refers to the main effects of B, that is, to main contrasts, and the second part to the interaction of the contrast with factor A. The other two parts refer to the corresponding error terms, which are the interactions of the effects with S. Within each part, the top line contains the sum of squares and degrees of freedom from the original analysis, copied from Table 18.4, and the second line contains the sum of squares and degrees of freedom from the analysis of the linear contrast in Table 18.6, after adjustment for $\sum c_k^2$. The third line contains the difference between the two. For example, in the first part,

$$SS_{B_{\text{nonlinear}}} = SS_B - SS_{\psi_{B_{\text{linear}}}} = 42.083 - 40.833 = 1.250,$$

with degrees of freedom equal to $3 - 1 = 2$. The F tests are then conducted normally, using the appropriate error terms from the lower part of the table. Notice that because both the numerator and denominator sums of squares have been adjusted by the same factor, the F ratios for the tests involving $\psi_{B_{\text{linear}}}$ are unchanged from their counterparts in Table 18.6. Neither of the two nonlinear effects is significant.

Simple Effects and Contrasts

The analysis of a simple effect makes use of the second principle in Table 18.5: When we have an effect involving a portion of the within-subject data, we isolate those data and analyze them separately. As an example, consider the simple effect of number of presentations for the positive words, factor B at treatment condition a_2 (although the nonsignificant $A \times B$ interaction suggests that a more appropriate analysis would focus on the main effects). We begin by isolating in the upper portion of Table 18.8 the portion of the data that we wish to analyze (ignoring for the moment the contrast variable in the box on the right). The values within the body of this table are the four recall scores for each subject for the positive words. Because only one level of factor

Table 18.8: The analysis of the simple effects of the trials factor B for words with positive emotional value (level a_2). The scores Y_{i2k} are extracted from Table 18.3. The final column shows values of the simple contrast variable ψ_i at a_2 $= Y_{i24} - Y_{i21}$.

The portion of the ABS table at a_2 and a contrast variable $\widehat{\psi}_i$ at a_2

	b_1	b_2	b_3	b_4	Sum	$\widehat{\psi}_i$ at a_2
s_1	1	2	2	3	8	2
s_2	2	3	4	5	14	3
s_3	3	4	3	4	14	1
s_4	1	2	2	3	8	2
s_5	1	1	2	3	7	2
s_6	2	3	3	5	13	3
s_7	2	1	2	3	8	1
s_8	1	2	2	3	8	2
Sum	13	18	20	29	80	16
Mean	1.625	2.250	2.500	3.625	10.000	2.00

Summary of the analysis of variance

Source	SS	df	MS	F
B at a_2	16.75	3	5.583	24.70*
S at a_2	16.50	7	2.357	
$B \times S$ at a_2	4.75	21	0.226	
Total	38.00	31		

*$p < .05$

A is involved, the table has the form of a single-factor within-subject design with the number of presentations as the independent variable. Thus, we analyze these data exactly like an actual one-factor within-subject design, using the formulas in Table 16.2 (p. 352). The effect of the number of presentations is significant.

Usually a significant simple effect should be followed up by tests of one or more simple comparisons or contrasts. Because factor B is quantitative, we could look at the trend components here, but instead, we will examine the related contrast $\psi_B = \mu_4 - \mu_1$ that compares recall of the words receiving one presentation with those receiving four. To keep most of the contrast values positive, we will use the coefficients -1, 0, 0, and 1. Again, the analysis follows the steps described for the one-way within-subject design in Section 16.2. In the single-column block to the right in Table 18.8, we have calculated the 8 values of the contrast variable $\widehat{\psi}_i$ at a_2 that express the observed values of this contrast—we have elaborated the notation slightly to make explicit the source of the contrast variable. Then, following the one-way procedure that leads to an F test (pp. 359–360), we calculate the two bracket terms,

$$[S_\psi] = \sum \widehat{\psi}^2_{i \text{ at } a_2} = 2^2 + 3^2 + \cdots + 1^2 + 2^2 = 36,$$

$$[T_\psi] = \frac{(\sum \widehat{\psi}_{i \text{ at } a_2})^2}{n} = \frac{16^2}{8} = 32.00.$$

From these bracket terms, we find the sums of squares for the contrast ψ_B at a_2 and its error term:

$$SS_{\psi_B \text{ at } a_2} = [T_\psi] = 32.00$$

$$SS_{\psi_B \times S \text{ at } a_2} = [S_\psi] - [T_\psi] = 36 - 32.00 = 4.00.$$

The error has $n - 1 = 7$ degrees of freedom, and the F statistic is

$$F = \frac{MS_{\psi_B \text{ at } a_2}}{MS_{\psi_B \times S \text{ at } a_2}} = \frac{32/1}{4.00/7} = \frac{32}{0.571} = 56.04.$$

The result, which is significant, indicates that recall for the positive words is greater after four presentations than after only one.

Interaction Contrasts

Chapter 13 showed how interaction contrasts (also called interacting contrasts or contrast interactions) are used to follow up interactions and understand their meaning. First a little review of Section 13.2. Two contrasts, $\psi_A = \sum c_{A_j} \mu_j$ and $\psi_B = \sum c_{B_k} \mu_k$ (each with coefficients that sum to zero), interact when the value of one varies according to the pattern of the other. This interaction is measured by an interaction contrast, which is either calculated by applying one contrast to the other,

$$\psi_{AB} = \sum c_{B_k} \psi_{A \text{ at } b_k} = \sum c_{A_j} \psi_{B \text{ at } a_j}, \tag{18.1}$$

or by a single contrast over all the groups,

$$\psi_{AB} = \sum c_{jk} \mu_{jk} \quad \text{with} \quad c_{jk} = c_{A_j} c_{B_k}. \tag{18.2}$$

As with other contrasts, we test the hypothesis that the interaction contrast ψ_{AB} is zero by comparing its value $\widehat{\psi}_{AB}$ to a measure of its variability, which in this case is the interaction of the contrast with subjects, $\psi_A \times \psi_B \times S$.

Our strategy for testing an interaction contrast in a two-factor within-subject design is the one we have used for the other within-subject contrasts: Create a contrast variable, calculate its value $\widehat{\psi}_i$ for each subject, and test whether their mean is zero. We can use either Equations 18.1 and 18.2, whichever is the most convenient:

$$\widehat{\psi}_i = \sum c_{A_j} \widehat{\psi}_{B_i \text{ at } a_j} = \sum c_{B_k} \widehat{\psi}_{A_i \text{ at } b_k} \tag{18.3}$$

$$= \sum c_{jk} Y_{ijk} \quad \text{with} \quad c_{jk} = c_{A_j} c_{B_k}. \tag{18.4}$$

We did not find a significant overall interaction in our numerical example and ordinarily would not follow it up by testing an interaction contrast, but we can still use the data for an illustration. Suppose we wanted to see whether the slope of the line for factor B for the negative words differed from that of the other two types combined (condition a_1 compared to an average of a_2 and a_3). The interacting contrasts are

$$\psi_A = 2\mu_{A_1} - \mu_{A_2} - \mu_{A_3} \quad \text{and} \quad \psi_{B_{\text{linear}}} = -3\mu_{B_1} - \mu_{B_2} + \mu_{B_3} + 3\mu_{B_4}.$$

We already created three contrast variables for $\psi_{B_{\text{linear}}}$ (one for each level of factor A) in Table 18.6, so we can calculate the values of the interaction contrast $\widehat{\psi}_i$ by applying ψ_A to them (Equation 18.3). We have copied the values of $\widehat{\psi}_{B_{\text{linear}}}$ from Table 18.6 on the left side of Table 18.9. Now, applying the contrast ψ_A to the first row,

$$\widehat{\psi}_1 = \sum c_{A_j} \widehat{\psi}_{B_1 \text{ at } a_j} = (2)(4) + (-1)(6) + (-1)(6) = -4.$$

Table 18.9: *The linear contrast variable* $\widehat{\psi}_{B_i \text{ at } a_j}$ *for each subject and word type (from Table 18.6) and the interaction contrast variable* $\widehat{\psi}_i$ *calculated from them.*

	a_1	a_2	a_3	$\widehat{\psi}_i$
s_1	4	6	6	−4
s_2	7	10	6	−2
s_3	3	2	6	−2
s_4	5	6	3	1
s_5	4	7	4	−3
s_6	7	9	7	−2
s_7	7	4	7	3
s_8	7	6	7	1

Sum −8
Mean −1.0

This value is entered at the top of the single-column table on the right. The remaining values in this column are calculated the same way. This approach—calculating an interaction contrast as a contrast of simple contrasts—is handy when working with a computer, for the simple contrast variables have usually been obtained as part of an earlier analysis.

The other way to create the contrast variable is to combine the coefficients of the individual contrasts using Equation 18.4 and apply the result to the full set of scores. Following the procedure illustrated in Table 13.4 (p. 273), we find the interaction coefficients c_{jk} to be

— a_1 —				— a_2 —				— a_3 —			
b_1	b_2	b_3	b_4	b_1	b_2	b_3	b_4	b_1	b_2	b_3	b_4
−6	−2	2	6	3	1	−1	−3	3	1	−1	−3

We now calculate an interaction contrast variable $\widehat{\psi}_i$ by applying these coefficients to each subject's Y_{ijk} scores from the *ABS* table in Table 18.3. Again using the first subject as an example:

$$\widehat{\psi}_1 = (-6)(1) + (-2)(1) + \cdots + (-1)(2) + (-3)(3) = -4.$$

This value is the same as the one we obtained from Equation 18.3.

We will complete the analysis using the F test procedure. The data for each subject have been reduced to a single value—the value of the interaction contrast. We are left with a single set of n scores, the mean of which is the interaction contrast $\widehat{\psi}_{AB}$. We use their variability for the error term to test the hypothesis that ψ_{AB} is zero. Again following the one-way procedure of Chapter 16 (pp. 359–360), we find the two bracket terms:

$$[S_\psi] = \sum \widehat{\psi}_i^2 = (-4)^2 + (-2)^2 + \cdots + 3^2 + 1^2 = 48,$$

$$[T_\psi] = n\widehat{\psi}_{AB}^2 = (8)(-1.0)^2 = 8.0.$$

From these bracket terms we obtain the sums of squares:

$$SS_{\psi_A \times \psi_B} = [T_\psi] = 8.0$$

$$SS_{\psi_A \times \psi_B \times S} = [S_\psi] - [T_\psi] = 48 - 8.0 = 40.0.$$

With 1 and 7 degrees of freedom, the F ratio for the interaction contrast is

$$F = \frac{MS_{\psi_A \times \psi_B}}{MS_{\psi_A \times \psi_B \times S}} = \frac{8.0/1}{40.0/7} = \frac{8.0}{5.714} = 1.40.$$

As we would expect from the lack of a significant overall interaction, the interaction contrast is not significant.

   If we want to combine the sums of squares for an interaction contrast with those from the overall analysis or with those based on other contrasts, we need to adjust them for their particular coefficients. Once again, the adjustment consists of dividing each sum of squares by the sum of the squared coefficients (Equation 16.5, p. 359), as was done in Table 18.7. The sum of the squared coefficients for an interaction contrast can be calculated from either the coefficients of the individual contrasts or from the combined coefficients:

$$\text{sum of squared coefficients} = \left(\sum c_{A_j}^2 \right) \left(\sum c_{B_k}^2 \right) = \sum c_{jk}^2.$$

In the example we have been considering, $\sum c_{A_j}^2 = 6$ and $\sum c_{B_k}^2 = 20$, so the adjustment factor is $(6)(20) = 120$. You will obtain the same value by summing the squared interaction coefficients c_{ij}. The adjusted sums of squares are

$$\frac{SS_{\psi_A \times \psi_B}}{\sum c_{jk}^2} = \frac{8.0}{120} = 0.067 \quad \text{and} \quad \frac{SS_{\psi_A \times \psi_B \times S}}{\sum c_{jk}^2} = \frac{40.0}{120} = 0.333.$$

In this form, they can be subtracted from the sums of squares from the omnibus analysis in Table 18.4 to obtain residual sums of squares.

Use of the Computer Packages

The computer packages can analyze a two-way within-subject design almost as easily as they can a one-way design. The data are organized in essentially the same way. Instead of a table with n rows, one for each subject, and a columns, one for each score, the table now contains ab columns, like that at the top of Table 18.3. These ab columns are assigned (however the program may do it) to the ab combinations of the two within-subject factors. Then you run the appropriate module of the program to produce the overall analysis.

   Where complications arise is in the analytical analyses. As you have seen, both here and in Chapters 12 and 13, a factorial design opens the way to a wealth of analytical tests—main contrasts, simple effects, simple contrasts, interaction components, and others. It is not surprising, then, that the computer packages do not provide an automatic analysis that applies to any design (which is not to say that they could not do better than they do). There is simply no substitute for taking a hand in directing the analysis yourself. Let the goals of the study and its results guide you in selecting the effects you test.

   Our approach to analytical analyses is compatible with computer use:

- For analyses involving contrasts, have the computer calculate the contrast values you need and add them to the original data set. For example, the four new columns in Table 18.6 (three sets of contrast values and, if needed, their sum) would be added to the 12 columns in Table 18.3.
- For analyses involving the simple effects, isolate the relevant portion of the data by selecting only those columns of the data table when you specify the analysis. For example, the simple effect Table 18.8 required only four out of the 12 columns of Table 18.3.

In either case, you conduct these analyses using the standard methods appropriate to a single-factor design.

Because most complex designs involve several distinct analyses, it is rarely possible to combine them all in a single computer run. Expect that you will have to run the programs several times, that you will go back and forth between the data and the programs, and that you may end up having to put certain sections together by hand. This complexity is no more than a reflection of the complexity of the research process.

18.3 Assumptions and the Statistical Model

The data for a two-factor design can be thought of as if they had come from a single-factor design with ab treatment levels. This equivalence makes our discussion of the assumptions of the $A \times S$ design in Section 17.2 apply more or less directly to the $A \times B \times S$ design. In particular, two approaches to the analysis are possible—a univariate approach, which we described above, and a multivariate approach. The former is simpler and more powerful, but entails the important assumption of sphericity, which may not be satisfied. The multivariate is more general and can accommodate data for which this assumption is violated. We have emphasized the former approach because of its greater simplicity and its frequent use for the type of experimental data most relevant our readers. We will not reiterate our earlier discussion here, but will limit ourselves to some comments that specifically relate to the two-way design.

The Linear Model

The univariate linear model for the two-factor design can be constructed from the model for a one-way design. That model (Equation 17.1, p. 374) is

$$Y_{ij} = \mu + \alpha_j + S_i + (S\alpha)_{ij} + E_{ij}.$$

In the two-way design, the treatments term α_j is replaced by terms for the two main effects and their interaction, $\alpha_j + \beta_k + (\alpha\beta)_{jk}$. A similar expansion is made for the interaction term $(S\alpha)_{ij}$. With the expanded terms marked by braces, the resulting linear model is

$$Y_{ijk} = \mu + \overbrace{\alpha_j + \beta_k + (\alpha\beta)_{jk}}^{\alpha_j} + S_i + \overbrace{(S\alpha)_{ij} + (S\beta)_{ik} + (S\alpha\beta)_{ijk}}^{(S\alpha)_{ij}} + E_{ijk}. \qquad (18.5)$$

In the same manner as Equations 17.2, each of these terms is captured, along with random differences, by one of the mean squares. In Table 18.10, we have listed the expected mean squares for the different effects of the analysis.

Table 18.10 shows how the terms of the linear model affect the mean squares of the analysis. In the first column, we have listed the mean squares, and in the second their

Table 18.10: Expected mean squares and error terms for the univariate model for the two-way within-subject design.

Source	Expected mean square	Error term
MS_A	$\dfrac{bn}{a-1}\sum \alpha_j^2 + b\sigma_{A\times S}^2 + \sigma_{\text{error}}^2$	$A\times S$
MS_B	$\dfrac{an}{b-1}\sum \beta_k^2 + a\sigma_{B\times S}^2 + \sigma_{\text{error}}^2$	$B\times S$
$MS_{A\times B}$	$\dfrac{n}{(a-1)(b-1)}\sum (\alpha\beta)_{jk}^2 + \sigma_{A\times B\times S}^2 + \sigma_{\text{error}}^2$	$A\times B\times S$
MS_S	$ab\sigma_S^2 + \sigma_{\text{error}}^2$	
$MS_{A\times S}$	$b\sigma_{A\times S}^2 + \sigma_{\text{error}}^2$	
$MS_{B\times S}$	$a\sigma_{B\times S}^2 + \sigma_{\text{error}}^2$	
$MS_{A\times B\times S}$	$\sigma_{A\times B\times S}^2 + \sigma_{\text{error}}^2$	

expected values (whose derivation we will skip). Each mean square contains, first, a component involving the parameters of that particular effect, and second, one or more error components. These expected mean squares support our assertion on page 405 that each effect is tested against its interaction with subjects. Compare the expected mean square for any of the principal effects (A, B, and $A\times B$) with other expected mean squares in the table. In each case, the mean square that matches the error part of the expected mean square is the interaction with subjects (the terms $A\times S$, $B\times S$, and $A\times B\times S$, respectively). You can also see why the sources involving the subject factor have no error terms. They contain the error variance σ_{error}^2, but there is no term to estimate it.

The Assumption of Sphericity

The assumption of sphericity (or the more restrictive, but easier to understand, assumption of compound symmetry) applies to the full set of ab treatments in the two-factor design. We would, of course, like these assumptions to be satisfied, as they allow us to use the more powerful univariate procedures. So, we should consider each factor to see whether it is consistent with this assumption—the sort of analysis we described at the start of Section 17.3. It would be possible, for example, for there to be differences in the variability of variances or correlations associated with factor A but not factor B. The Mauchly (1940) test is available here, although it suffers from the insensitivity and biases we mentioned in connection with the one-way design. Many packaged programs provide it, often separately for each factor and for the interaction. You should interpret these tests cautiously and to couple them with consideration of how the data were generated.

Where sphericity is violated, we have the same three options we had for the one-way design. One possibility is to fall back on the multivariate approach. We briefly described the basis for this approach on page 375. Many analysis-of-variance programs provide the multivariate tests. As in the one-way design, they typically report as many as four different test statistics, all of which are equivalent for this design. The cost of this approach is reduced power when sphericity holds. The second possibility is to conduct the analysis mainly through the use of single-df contrasts using the methods of Section 18.2. As in the one-way design, the assumptions for a test of a contrast are equivalent to those for the multivariate procedure. We can use these focused tests without concern either for sphericity or loss of power.

The third possibility is to adjust the univariate analysis to compensate for any violations of sphericity. As with the one-way design (Equations 17.4, p. 378), these corrections are made by reducing the degrees of freedom to a fraction ε of their former size. The adjustments apply to both the numerator and the denominator, and they can differ for the different treatment effects. For example, the degrees of freedom used to determine the critical value for factor B are

$$df_{\text{num}} = \varepsilon_B(b-1) \quad \text{and} \quad df_{\text{denom}} = \varepsilon_B(b-1)(n-1).$$

Analogous adjustments, with constants ε_A and $\varepsilon_{A \times B}$, apply to the A and $A \times B$ effects, respectively. There are two versions of these tests associated with Geisser and Greenhouse (1958) and with Huynh and Feldt (1976).

The most extreme form of these corrections is the Geisser-Greenhouse conservative test, in which all ratios are tested against the values that would have been used had there been just two levels of each factor,

$$df_{\text{num}} = 1 \quad \text{and} \quad df_{\text{denom}} = n - 1. \tag{18.6}$$

This simple correction is conservative, however. It gives an unambiguous result only when the null hypothesis is rejected. In our numerical example, Equations 18.6 tell us that all three effects should be compared to a critical value from Appendix A.1 with $df_{\text{num}} = 1$ and $df_{\text{denom}} = n - 1 = 8 - 1 = 7$, namely $F_{.05}(1, 7) = 5.59$. Both main effects remain significant, so these results stand without regard to any violations of sphericity. The interaction is not significant, but, because it also was not significant by the original test, that conclusion also stands.

What to report among this welter of tests is confusing. Remember our suggestions for the $A \times S$ design. First, consider whether the nature of the variables being measured (and perhaps the Mauchly tests) indicates that sphericity is satisfied. If so, continue with the univariate test. If concerns remain, then look at the Geisser-Greenhouse conservative test to see if it still indicates the presence of an effect. When the standard and conservative tests disagree, you can use either the multivariate procedure or test the important single-df contrasts. We strongly recommend that you use the same analysis procedure for all three effects in the analysis of variance. It will confuse a reader of your research report if you use one type of test for the A effect, another for the B effect, and perhaps a third for the $A \times B$ interaction.

18.4 Counterbalancing of Nuisance Variables

The need to eliminate the effects of incidental or nuisance factors is just as great for a two-factor within-subject design as it is for a single-factor design. A researcher's goal is to be sure that the levels of this factor are not systematically related to any of the treatment conditions. Any confounding is avoided in the ways we discussed in Chapter 17, adjusted to accommodate the factorial design. As in the one-way design, it is always possible to use randomization. All that is required is to assign the levels of the nuisance factor randomly to the treatments, using a new order for each subject. The resulting data are analyzed as described in Section 18.1. However, the precision and the power of the design are increased by systematic counterbalancing.

In some studies, only one of the two factors needs counterbalancing. Consider a design in which the levels of one factor are intermixed, while those of the other are tested successively. The researcher here wants to counterbalance the order of presentation of the successive factor to minimize the influence of practice or fatigue effects. Presentation order is essentially irrelevant for the intermixed factor. To be specific, suppose a researcher is interested in how accurately subjects perceive simulated three-dimensional displays as a function of their overall level of brightness (factor A: very dim, dim, or moderate) and the degree of stereoscopic disparity between the eyes (factor B: small, medium, or large). Factor B can be examined with an intermixed-treatment design. Each subject receives a block of 45 trials, containing 15 trials at each disparity level, presented in a different random order for each subject. A subject's score for each level of disparity is the number of correct responses in these 15 trials. However, the brightness factor A cannot be varied this way. Adaptation and contrast effects make trial-to-trial variation of the brightness factor undesirable, so it must remain the same throughout a session. Each subject is tested successively in three blocks of 45 trials, one at each level of brightness. Naturally, the researcher is concerned about the possibility of practice effects and wants to counterbalance the orders of the three brightness sessions. Because only factor A is varied between these sessions, only it needs to be counterbalanced. The top panel in Table 18.11 shows example scores from six subjects. The order of the brightness conditions (factor A), given on the left, is counterbalanced using two Latin squares that together are digram-balanced to minimize carryover effects (Section 17.4). Each subject's scores are given on the right, arranged by the order in which the levels of factor A were administered (first, second, or third; factor P) and the levels of disparity (factor B).

In other circumstances, both factors need to be counterbalanced. In such designs, there are ab treatment conditions, and there must be this many levels of the nuisance factor for complete balancing. To illustrate, suppose a researcher is studying how much readers remember from advertisements in a magazine. Each subject is asked to spend half an hour reading stories in a made-up magazine that includes 12 full-page advertisements, two advertising each of six products. Sometime later, the subjects are given a test about the contents of the magazine, which includes questions about each advertisement and the advertisers. For each advertisement, they receive a score between 0 (remember nothing) and 30 (remember everything). Each tested advertisement appears twice in the magazine. The experimental factors concern the way these two presentations occur. Sometimes the two advertisements are placed on adjacent pages, sometimes they are separated by two pages, and sometimes they are separated by six. These three conditions constitute factor A. Factor B varies the relationship between each pair of repeated advertisements; in one case, the two advertisments are identical (level b_1), and in the other, they are different advertisements for the same product (level b_2). Each subject, then, provides the $3 \times 2 = 6$ Y_{ijk} scores of an $A \times B \times S$ design. The experimenter is concerned that the scores may be affected by the particular products and the way the advertisements are written, some of which are inevitably more interesting, compelling, or memorable than others. To

Table 18.11: *Two examples of counterbalanced data in a two-factor design. In the upper panel, factor A is counterbalanced for order; in the bottom panel, both factors are balanced for material (products in the example).*

Only factor A counterbalanced

		— p_1 —			— p_2 —			— p_3 —		
	Order	b_1	b_2	b_3	b_1	b_2	b_3	b_1	b_2	b_3
s_1	a_1, a_2, a_3	7	3	5	11	6	9	10	8	10
s_2	a_2, a_3, a_1	13	8	9	12	10	12	12	8	10
s_3	a_3, a_1, a_2	4	5	5	9	6	6	12	9	12
s_4	a_1, a_3, a_2	6	2	6	12	4	10	8	6	7
s_5	a_2, a_1, a_3	4	3	3	5	4	4	6	6	5
s_6	a_3, a_2, a_1	4	1	2	10	6	8	10	6	8

Both factors counterbalanced

					Products		
	Treatments	p_1	p_2	p_3	p_4	p_5	p_6
s_1	0S 0D 2S 2D 6S 6D	16	6	15	15	19	14
s_2	0D 0S 2D 2S 6D 6S	8	15	14	16	14	22
s_3	2S 2D 6S 6D 0S 0D	22	17	25	16	14	8
s_4	2D 2S 6D 6S 0D 0S	18	16	14	21	7	17
s_5	6S 6D 0S 0D 2S 2D	22	11	12	4	12	14
s_6	6D 6S 0D 0S 2D 2S	18	23	9	17	15	20
s_7	6D 6S 2D 2S 0D 0S	14	21	15	17	4	15
s_8	6S 6D 2S 2D 0S 0D	21	8	15	9	8	4
s_9	0D 0S 6D 6S 2D 2S	11	15	15	25	14	21
s_{10}	0S 0D 6S 6D 2S 2D	17	5	21	13	16	16
s_{11}	2D 2S 0D 0S 6D 6S	14	12	6	12	13	22
s_{12}	2S 2D 0S 0D 6S 6D	23	19	19	9	26	19
	Mean	17.0	14.0	15.0	14.5	13.5	16.0
	Effect	2.0	−1.0	0.0	−0.5	−1.5	1.0

counterbalance these effects, each of the six treatment conditions is tested the same number of times with each product and its associated advertisements. To implement this plan, the researcher counterbalances the products with 6×6 Latin squares.[2] The bottom panel of Table 18.11 shows example data for two sets of six subjects in this experimental plan. We have designated the conditions with a mnemonic code—the digit 0, 2, or 6 for the number of intervening pages and the letter S or D for same and different. The shorter descriptions are usually easier to use and help to avoid errors

---

[2]You may notice that there are other incidental aspects of the design that the researcher might also worry about, such as the order in which the different types of advertisement appeared in the magazine. The researcher here, we will assume, deems these aspects to be less influential than the products, and so decides to control them either by randomization or by some expansion of the design. Such complexities or compromises are inevitable: There is always something else that *could* be counterbalanced.

in constructing the squares and assigning the products to the conditions. Factor P is the counterbalancing factor, which here refers to products, not positions.

Analysis of a Single Counterbalanced Factor

There are several more or less equivalent ways to analyze a counterbalanced $A \times B \times S$ design. We will describe an approach here that follows conceptually from our discussion of the one-way design in Section 17.4. You may, however, encounter others, particularly in computer applications.

When the counterbalancing applies to one of the two factors only, it is easiest to adjust the sums of squares and degrees of freedom, as we did for the one-factor design in Table 17.2. Suppose factor P has been used to counterbalance any effects of the order in which the levels of factor A are presented, as in the upper panel of Table 18.11. Four steps are required to analyze this design.

1. Organize the data by the two design factors A and B, and conduct the analysis using the standard within-subject analysis of variance.
2. Organize the data by the counterbalancing factor P and factor B, as we have done in Table 18.11, and calculate the sum of squares SS_P for this factor, again using the standard formula; you will not need the other sums of squares from this analysis. With a computer, you can analyze the complete $P \times B \times S$ design and use only SS_P.
3. Adjust the sum of squares and degrees of freedom for the $A \times S$ interaction from the first analysis by subtracting comparable quantities for factor P from the second analysis.
4. Recalculate the mean square for the $A \times S$ interaction and the F ratio for factor A using the adjusted values. The other sources and the other F tests are unaffected by this adjustment.

Table 18.12 illustrates this analysis, using the data from the top panel of Table 18.11. First, we use the sequences on the left to reorganize the data by the treatment conditions; the results are given in the upper panel of Table 18.12. The lower panel shows the analysis of this table (ignore, for the moment, the two lines in italics). We won't show the calculations here, as they follow the standard procedure described in Section 18.1. In the second step, we use the table of data at the top of Table 18.11 to calculate SS_P. The position sums are $P_1 = 90$, $P_2 = 144$, and $P_3 = 153$; the grand sum is $T = 387$; and

$$[P] = \frac{90^2 + 144^2 + 153^2}{18} = 2{,}902.500,$$

$$[T] = \frac{387^2}{54} = 2{,}773.500,$$

$$SS_P = [P] - [T] = 2{,}902.500 - 2{,}773.500 = 129.000.$$

This sum of squares has $df_P = p - 1 = 3 - 1 = 2$. We then adjust the sum of squares and degrees of freedom for the $A \times S$ interaction by subtracting these values from corresponding terms in the first analysis:

$$SS_{A \times S}(\text{residual}) = SS_{A \times S} - SS_P = 173.444 - 129.000 = 44.444,$$

$$df_{A \times S}(\text{residual}) = df_{A \times S} - df_P = 10 - 2 = 8.$$

Table 18.12: Analysis of the data in the top panel of Table 18.11. The lines in italics for the A and A×S effects include adjustment for the nuisance factor P.

Data organized by experimental condition

| | — a_1 — | | | — a_2 — | | | — a_3 — | | |
	b_1	b_2	b_3	b_1	b_2	b_3	b_1	b_2	b_3
s_1	7	3	5	11	6	9	10	8	10
s_2	12	8	10	13	8	9	12	10	12
s_3	9	6	6	12	9	12	4	5	5
s_4	6	2	6	8	6	7	12	4	10
s_5	5	4	4	4	3	3	6	6	5
s_6	10	6	8	10	6	8	4	1	2

Analysis of variance for the above table

Source	SS	df	MS	F
A	21.000	2	10.500	0.61
$A\,(corrected)$	*21.000*	*2*	*10.500*	*1.89*
B	81.333	2	40.667	18.67*
$A \times B$	2.667	4	0.667	0.54
S	178.389	5	35.678	
$A \times S$	173.444	10	17.344	
$A \times S\,(residual)$	*44.444*	*8*	*5.556*	
$B \times S$	21.778	10	2.178	
$A \times B \times S$	24.889	20	1.244	

*$p < .05$

Finally, we recalculate the mean square for the error term and use it to test the significance of the main effect of factor A:

$$MS_{A \times S}(\text{residual}) = \frac{SS_{A \times S}(\text{residual})}{df_{A \times S}(\text{residual})} = \frac{44.444}{8} = 5.556,$$

$$F_A = \frac{MS_A}{MS_{A \times S}(\text{residual})} = \frac{10.500}{5.556} = 1.89.$$

We have included these calculations as the italic lines in the summary of the analysis in Table 18.12. With 2 and 8 degrees of freedom, this test still does not reach significance, but it is much closer than it was without the correction. Note that factor B, which was not involved in the counterbalancing, does not require a correction, nor does the $A \times B$ interaction.

When you only want to look at the overall effects, you are now done. But when you also want to examine contrasts or simple effects, you need to remove the incidental effects counterbalancing from these analyses as well. This is most easily accomplished by adjusting the individual scores before conducting these analyses, using the procedure we described for the single-factor design in Section 17.5 (see pp. 389–393). Following the steps in Table 17.3, we arrange the data by the three levels of factor

P, calculate the effects of the nuisance factor, and subtract these effects from the individual scores (Steps 1 and 2). For example, the effect at p_1 in Table 18.11 is $\bar{Y}_{P_1} - \bar{Y}_T = 5.000 - 7.167 = -2.167$, which is subtracted from all the scores from counterbalance condition p_1. In Step 3, we reorganize these adjusted scores according to the two treatment factors A and B. Now we test any effects we wish in the same way they are tested in a standard two-factor within-subject analysis, except that we adjust the degrees of freedom by subtracting the degrees of freedom of the effect (Step 5 and Equation 17.8). Because only factor A was counterbalanced, these adjustments only apply to effects associated with that factor. To illustrate with some of these effects:

$$df_{\psi_A \times S}(\text{adjusted}) = df_{\psi_A \times S} - df_{\psi_A} = (n-1) - 1,$$

$$df_{A \times S \text{ at } b_k}(\text{adjusted}) = df_{A \times S \text{ at } b_k} - df_{A \text{ at } b_k} = (a-1)(n-1) - (a-1),$$

$$df_{\psi_A \times S \text{ at } b_k}(\text{adjusted}) = df_{\psi_A \times S \text{ at } b_k} - df_{\psi_A \text{ at } b_k} = (n-1) - 1.$$

Problem 18.4 provides an example of this analysis.

Analysis of Two Counterbalanced Factors

When one of the two factors is counterbalanced, only the tests involving that factor are affected. With two counterbalanced factors, all the tests must be adjusted. Again among the several equivalent ways to do the analysis, the one in which the effects of the nuisance variable are subtracted from the scores is easiest.

To apply the steps in Table 17.3 (p. 390) to the numerical example at the bottom of Table 18.11, we first calculate the mean for each product (i.e. each of the ab levels of factor P) and subtract the grand mean $\bar{Y}_T = 15.00$ to obtain the effects of the counterbalancing factor. Both the means and the effects are given at the bottom of the original table of data. In Step 2, we subtract these effects from the scores in their respective columns to give the adjusted scores at the top of Table 18.13. As you can verify, the columns now have the same mean, indicating that the differences among the different products have been successfully removed.

The third step involves reorganizing the scores according to the spacing conditions and advertisement types, as shown at the bottom of Table 18.13. For example, the assignment of treatments to products on the left of the upper table tells us that the first score of s_1 is from condition 0S, so its value of 14.0 has been put into the first column in the lower table, and the fourth score of s_{12} is from condition 0D, so 9.5 is placed in the second column. We have labeled the columns both with the mnemonic code for the conditions and with the conventional $a_j b_k$ notation. It is easy to make a mistake when reorganizing the data, so be sure to check that the row totals and the treatment means are the same before and after the reorganization.

We can now conduct any analysis we want on these adjusted scores. Table 18.14 shows the summary of the overall analysis of variance. The calculation of the sums of squares is the same as in any $A \times B \times S$ design. As in all these analyses, we have to adjust the degrees of freedom for the error terms before testing (Step 5 and Equation 17.8). To take one example,

$$df_{A \times S}(\text{adjusted}) = df_{A \times S} - df_A = (a-1)(n-1) - (a-1)$$
$$= (2 \times 11) - 2 = 22 - 2 = 20.$$

Table 18.13: *Adjustment of the scores for the nuisance factor in a 3×2 counterbalanced design.*

Data with the material effects subtracted

	Treatments	p_1	p_2	p_3	p_4	p_5	p_6
s_1	0S 0D 2S 2D 6S 6D	14.0	7.0	15.0	15.5	20.5	13.0
s_2	0D 0S 2D 2S 6D 6S	6.0	16.0	14.0	16.5	15.5	21.0
s_3	2S 2D 6S 6D 0S 0D	20.0	18.0	25.0	16.5	15.5	7.0
s_4	2D 2S 6D 6S 0D 0S	16.0	17.0	14.0	21.5	8.5	16.0
s_5	6S 6D 0S 0D 2S 2D	20.0	12.0	12.0	4.5	13.5	13.0
s_6	6D 6S 0D 0S 2D 2S	16.0	24.0	⁊ 9.0	17.5	16.5	19.0
s_7	6D 6S 2D 2S 0D 0S	12.0	22.0	15.0	17.5	5.5	14.0
s_8	6S 6D 2S 2D 0S 0D	19.0	9.0	15.0	9.5	9.5	3.0
s_9	0D 0S 6D 6S 2D 2S	9.0	16.0	15.0	25.5	15.5	20.0
s_{10}	0S 0D 6S 6D 2S 2D	15.0	6.0	21.0	13.5	17.5	15.0
s_{11}	2D 2S 0D 0S 6D 6S	12.0	13.0	6.0	12.5	14.5	21.0
s_{12}	2S 2D 0S 0D 6S 6D	21.0	20.0	19.0	9.5	27.5	18.0
	Mean	15.0	15.0	15.0	15.0	15.0	15.0

Adjusted data arranged by treatment condition

	0S	0D	2S	2D	6S	6D
	a_1b_1	a_1b_2	a_2b_1	a_2b_2	a_3b_1	a_3b_2
s_1	14.0	7.0	15.0	15.5	20.5	13.0
s_2	16.0	6.0	16.5	14.0	21.0	15.5
s_3	15.5	7.0	20.0	18.0	25.0	16.5
s_4	16.0	8.5	17.0	16.0	21.5	14.0
s_5	12.0	4.5	13.5	13.0	20.0	12.0
s_6	17.5	9.0	19.0	16.5	24.0	16.0
s_7	14.0	5.5	17.5	15.0	22.0	12.0
s_8	9.5	3.0	15.0	9.5	19.0	9.0
s_9	16.0	9.0	20.0	15.5	25.5	15.0
s_{10}	15.0	6.0	17.5	15.0	21.0	13.5
s_{11}	12.5	6.0	13.0	12.0	21.0	14.5
s_{12}	19.0	9.5	21.0	20.0	27.5	18.0
Mean	14.75	6.75	17.08	15.00	22.33	14.08

Table 18.14: Summary analysis of variance for Table 18.13.

Source	SS	df	MS	F
A	706.583	2	353.292	234.90*
B	672.222	1	672.222	465.53*
$A \times B$	146.194	2	73.097	69.155*
S	343.333	11	31.212	
$A \times S$	30.083	$22 - 2 = 20$	1.504	
$B \times S$	14.444	$11 - 1 = 10$	1.444	
$A \times B \times S$	21.139	$22 - 2 = 20$	1.057	
Total	1,933.998	$71 - 5 = 66$		

*$p < .05$

The calculation of the mean squares and the F ratios now proceeds normally. In this example, all the effects are significant. To test contrasts and simple effects on the adjusted data, we follow the procedures in Section 18.2. The only change required is the adjustment of the degrees of freedom for the error terms. The calculations are like those for the design with one counterbalanced factor described above. For example, the adjusted degrees of freedom for the error term of an interaction contrast are

$$df_{\psi_A \times \psi_B \times S}(\text{adjusted}) = df_{\psi_A \times \psi_B \times S} - df_{\psi_A \times \psi_B} = (n - 1) - 1.$$

18.5   Effect Size and Sample Sizes

In this section, we will consider how the concepts of effect size and power apply to the two-factor within-subject design. However, our discussion here cannot be completely satisfactory. First, the situation *is* complicated. When a design contains two within-subject factors, the same problems of estimation that affect the complete ω^2 for the single factor within-subject design arise (see p. 362), and we can only determine a range for the effect size. Second, the appropriate principles and conventions, particularly for the analysis of effect size, have not been established by the research community. We will offer some suggestions on how to proceed, but with substantial caveats.

Measuring the Effect Size

The easiest way to obtain a measure of effect size, in this design as in others, is to calculate the squared correlation ratio (R^2 or η^2) in its complete or partial form, using sums of squares from the analysis of variance summary table:

$$R^2_{\text{effect}} = \frac{SS_{\text{effect}}}{SS_{\text{total}}} \quad \text{or} \quad R^2_{\langle \text{effect} \rangle} = \frac{SS_{\text{effect}}}{SS_{\text{effect}} + SS_{\text{error}}}. \tag{18.7}$$

The partial measure is more appropriate in most situations and is calculated by many computer packages. Using the summary analysis of variance in Table 18.4 for our example, the partial effect size for factor A is

$$R^2_{\langle A \rangle} = \frac{SS_A}{SS_A + SS_{A \times S}} = \frac{8.333}{8.333 + 5.334} = 0.610,$$

and values for the other effects are $R^2_{\langle B \rangle} = 0.865$, and $R^2_{\langle A \times B \rangle} = 0.105$.

The squared correlation ratios are inflated by random error because they treat any accidental differences among the means as if they had been systematic. This makes them look larger than they should, and calculations based on them underestimate the sample size needed to replicate an effect. The quantity ω^2, being expressed in terms of population values, is a more desirable measure. For within-subject designs, the partial effect size (again, the most useful measure) is the variability of the effect over the sum of that variability and the error variability that affects it. For example, the variability of the main-effect parameters for factor A is expressed by the ratio $\sigma_A^2 = \sum \alpha_j^2 / a$ (Equation 8.9, p. 163). To find $\omega_{\langle A \rangle}^2$, the effect variability σ_A^2 is divided by the sum of σ_A^2 itself and the random variability that affects A (Equation 16.7, p. 361). This random variability is composed of the $A \times S$ interaction and the error of an individual observation, $\sigma_{A \times S}^2$ and σ_{error}^2, respectively. Putting these parts together, the partial effect size is

$$\omega_{\langle A \rangle}^2 = \frac{\sigma_A^2}{\sigma_A^2 + \sigma_{A \times S}^2 + \sigma_{\text{error}}^2}. \tag{18.8}$$

The same logic leads to partial effect sizes for the other two effects:

$$\omega_{\langle B \rangle}^2 = \frac{\sigma_B^2}{\sigma_B^2 + \sigma_{B \times S}^2 + \sigma_{\text{error}}^2} \quad \text{and} \quad \omega_{\langle A \times B \rangle}^2 = \frac{\sigma_{A \times B}^2}{\sigma_{A \times B}^2 + \sigma_{A \times B \times S}^2 + \sigma_{\text{error}}^2}.$$

Although the partial ω^2 statistics are straightforward to define theoretically, they are difficult to use practically. We almost never know enough about the sources of random error to specify values for these various terms in these equations, particularly those expressing interactions with subjects. Estimating them from data also runs into problems. There are four different types of random error involved in these equations, with variances $\sigma_{A \times S}^2$, $\sigma_{B \times S}^2$, $\sigma_{A \times B \times S}^2$, and σ_{error}^2, but there are only three mean squares available to estimate them, $MS_{A \times S}$, $MS_{B \times S}$, and $MS_{A \times B \times S}$. We cannot determine four numbers starting with only three. As a result, only ranges for the sizes of the main effects can be determined, not single values (Dodd & Schultz, 1973). Depending on the relative sizes of the variability of the individual observations (expressed by σ_{error}^2) and the interaction of the effect with subjects ($\sigma_{A \times S}^2$), the partial effect size for the main effect of A falls between

$$\frac{df_A(F_A - 1)}{df_A(F_A - 1) + abn} \quad \text{and} \quad \frac{df_A(F_A - 1)}{df_A(F_A - 1) + an}. \tag{18.9}$$

The ranges that result can be too broad to be useful—for example, they indicate that the size of the main effect of word type (factor A) in our example falls between 0.172 and 0.453. An analogous pair of formulas can be written for the main effect of B by substituting df_B and F_B for df_A and F_A and bn for an in the denominator of the formula on the right. A single estmate can be obtained for the $A \times B$ interaction by using Equation 11.22 (p. 233). However, it has little practical value because the estimates of partial omega squared for the main effects are so uncertain.

The problems we have in estimating partial ω^2 for main effects affect how we interpret the squared correlation ratio R^2. Its value (which was $R_{\langle A \rangle}^2 = 0.610$ in the example) is always larger than the upper end of the range of $\omega_{\langle A \rangle}^2$ (which was 0.453). It is inflated for two reasons, first because it ignores the effect of sampling on the means and second because it treats the ambiguity in the error variances in a way that gives it the largest possible value.

Sample-Size Calculations

The situation is more satisfactory when we want to transfer the effect size from one study to another. When both factors in the new experiment have the same number of levels as they did in the original experiment and we are willing to assume that the relationships among the types of random variability ($\sigma^2_{A \times S}$, $\sigma^2_{B \times S}$, $\sigma^2_{A \times B \times S}$, and σ^2_{error}) do not change, we can apply Equation 11.22 (p. 233) and Equation 11.25 (p. 236) to the analysis. When we put these two equations together and simplify them algebraically, we get

$$n_{\text{new}} = \left[\frac{\phi^2 (df_{\text{effect}} + 1)}{df_{\text{effect}} (F_{\text{effect}} - 1)} \right] n_{\text{old}}, \tag{18.10}$$

where n_{new} = the sample size in the new study,
    ϕ = the noncentrality parameter from Appendix A.7,
    df_{effect} = the degrees of freedom for the effect (here A, B, or $A \times B$),
    F_{effect} = the observed F ratio,
    n_{old} = the sample size in the original study.

The calculations are like those in Section 11.7, except we do not have to estimate the partial effect size as an intermediate step. Equation 18.10 is very general. We can use it here for either of the main effects or for the interaction. It also applies to both between-subjects and within-subject designs, and to studies with any number of factors.

To illustrate Equation 18.10, we will estimate the sample size necessary to detect the A main effect in our numerical example at a power of .90:

$$n_{\text{new}} = \left[\frac{\phi^2 (df_A + 1)}{df_A (F_A - 1)} \right] n_{\text{old}} = \left[\frac{(2.15)^2 (2 + 1)}{(2)(10.94 - 1)} \right] (8) = \frac{(13.87)(8)}{19.88} = 5.6,$$

where we found the value of $\phi \approx 2.15$ from the power function at $df_{\text{denom}} = 30$ in the chart for $df_{\text{num}} = 2$. The new study needs a sample size of about 6 students to detect the earlier A effect. The F statistic for the $A \times B$ interaction was 0.82. This value is less that one, and Equation 18.10 simply does not apply. There is no meaningful way to determine a replication sample size for this effect.

There are two things you should remember when you use Equation 18.10. First, the value of these estimated sample sizes depends on characteristics of the original study that are not immediately apparent from the calculation itself. For a within-subject design, these include the number of levels of any other factors and the nature of the random variability in the design. For example, you should not apply it to a new $A \times B \times S$ study in which levels of B have been added or deleted or in which its conditions are substantially different from those in the original study. Second, each effect in the design leads to a different sample size. In our numerical example, the B effect is largest and requires the smallest sample of subjects, the A effect is next, and the interaction is not large enough to determine a specific size for a replication. The sample size to use is the value from the smallest effect that you wanted to detect, in this case factor A.

Exercises

18.1. A researcher tests the hypothesis that vowels are more poorly detected than consonants in the presence of white noise. A laboratory computer was programmed to "speak" a selection of 80 vowels and 80 consonants (factor A) and to present 20 of each under four equally spaced intensities of white noise, chosen to make their detection difficult but not impossible (factor B). The computer selected a different set of vowels and consonants for each of $n = 5$ subjects, randomized their order and randomly assigned the noise level to each letter. Subjects were warned two seconds before each letter was presented and responded by typing the letter they believed they had heard on a keyboard. Below are the number of errors made by each subject under the $ab = (2)(4) = 8$ conditions.

	a_1				a_2			
	b_1	b_2	b_3	b_4	b_1	b_2	b_3	b_4
s_1	3	5	6	9	4	5	8	12
s_2	7	11	11	12	11	12	14	18
s_3	9	13	12	14	10	16	13	14
s_4	4	8	7	11	6	9	9	13
s_5	1	3	4	5	3	5	7	9

a. Conduct an analysis of variance on these data.

b. The analysis reveals significant main effects, but a not an $A \times B$ interaction, indicating that we should focus our attention on the marginal means. Since factor A has two levels, only factor B requires further analysis. Plot the $\bar{Y}_{B_j}$ marginal means to see that the number of errors increases with the noise.

   i. Is there a linear relationship between noise level and the mean number of errors.

   ii. Is the linear function sufficient to describe the data, or are nonlinear effects needed?

18.2. An instructor in a course on social psychology decides to conduct a demonstration experiment on stereotyping. She divides a small class into one group that will design and administer the experiment and another that will serve as subjects. The first group prepares three short biographical sketches of women engaged in three different lines of work—a university professor at the University of California (b_1), a California state politician (b_2), and a chief executive of a corporation operating in California (b_3)—and three sketches of men engaged in the same lines of work. They present the descriptions one at a time in different random orders to the $n = 5$ subjects, who indicate on a 13-point scale how much they admired each individual (13 = definitely admire, 1 = definitely do not admire, and 7 = halfway between). The design is a two-factor within-subject experiment in which factor A specifies the gender of the rated individual, and factor B the types of work. Ficticious rating data are as follows:

—Women—			—Men—		
$a_1 b_1$	$a_1 b_2$	$a_1 b_3$	$a_2 b_1$	$a_2 b_2$	$a_2 b_3$
10	7	9	9	5	6
9	8	9	9	4	5
7	9	7	8	4	5
7	10	7	7	3	4
7	10	6	6	2	3

a. Conduct a standard analysis of variance on these data and describe the outcome.

b. The interaction is significant, so determine if the ratings of the three types of employment differ for the women described and if they differ for the men.

c. It appears in the last part that only the differences among the ratings of the men are significant. Follow up this finding by testing the simple comparison between the mean rating for the university professor and the combined rating for the politician and the executive.

d. Is the significant simple comparison found for the men in the last part significantly different from the corresponding simple comparison for the women?

18.3. An experimenter asks subjects to read a story of an incident and to rate how much the major character in the story is to blame for the events described. Four stories are constructed by modifying the same basic plot. In two of the four stories the events are intentional, and in two they are accidental (factor A); for one of each set of two, the consequences are minor, and for one serious (factor B). Each of 8 subjects reads the four stories and rates them, giving a final score between 0 (completely blameless) and 20 (completely to blame). Because the order in which the stories are read may have an effect, they are presented in a counterbalanced order. The first two subjects receive the stories in one order, the next two in a different order, and so on. Each story appears first for two subjects, second for two subjects, etc. The orders (factor O) that were used and the observed data are given below.

		Accidental (a_1)		Purposeful (a_2)	
		Mild (b_1)	Serious (b_2)	Mild (b_1)	Serious (b_2)
		1st	3rd	2nd	4th
Order 1	s_1	9	10	17	9
	s_2	9	7	16	8
		4th	2nd	3rd	1st
Order 2	s_1	1	9	14	12
	s_2	4	11	18	16
		3rd	1st	4th	2nd
Order 3	s_1	3	13	12	13
	s_2	4	14	13	13
		2nd	4th	1st	3rd
Order 4	s_1	5	5	17	11
	s_2	5	5	16	9

Analyze these data, taking into consideration the different orders in which the stories were presented.

18.4. This problem is based on the data in the upper portion of Table 18.11—an $A \times B \times S$ design in which only factor A (brightness conditions) is counterbalanced.

a. Conduct a $P \times B \times S$ analysis to determine whether there is a significant effect of the order in which subjects are tested under the different brightness conditions.

b. Remove the practice effects from each of the Y_{ijk} scores. Verify that the practice effects have been removed from the modified data. Perform an analysis of variance on the corrected data organized by the experimental conditions. Remember to recalculate the degrees of freedom for the $A \times S$ interaction before calculating the mean square for the error term and the resulting value of F.

c. Although the A main effect is not significant, test the hypothesis that the difference in accuracy under the very dim condition (a_1) and the other two conditions combined is zero.

18.5. Suppose you were interested in replicating the findings of the numerical example summarized in Table 18.4, using an entirely different set of words. What minimum sample size would you need to have a power of 0.8 to detect an effect of the observed size?

19

The Two-Factor Mixed Design: Overall Analysis

Within-subject factorial designs are extremely popular, and for good reason: They examine the effects of several independent variables simultaneously and offer greater sensitivity than a between-subjects counterpart. As we indicated in the introduction to this part (see p. 348), two types of within-subject designs are possible when two independent variables are manipulated factorially: the $A \times B \times S$ design, in which every subject receives all the treatment combinations, and the $A \times (B \times S)$ design, in which each subject receives only the treatments of one factor. In this latter design, each subject receives all levels of factor B in conjunction with a single level of factor A. This **mixed design** has one between-subjects factor and one within-subject factor.

Mixed factorial designs are more common than pure within-subject factorial designs. They are particularly useful when it is impossible or inadvisable to manipulate a factor within a subject. Obviously, classification factors cannot be varied within a subject. For example, individuals who are suffering from damage to different areas of the brain or who are diagnosed with certain medical or mental conditions must be part of different groups, as must groups of subjects with different characteristics, such as gender, educational background, or political beliefs. Repeated observations also cannot be used when the treatment alters the subject in some way, as with instructions that influence a person's attitude or set—see the examples on page 371. In any of these cases, however, a second factor can still be included as a within-subject variable to form a mixed design. Finally, there are experiments in which the full factorial combination of treatments results in so many combinations that they would overwhelm, exhaust, or confuse the subjects. Here it may be feasible to vary one factor between subjects and one within subjects—a mixed design—providing some of the advantages of a within-subject design (more efficient use of the subjects, increased sensitivity, and greater power).

19.1 The Overall Analysis of Variance

The mixed design combines aspects of the designs we have already considered. Its substantive factors are crossed, so the hypotheses tested are the same as those of the

Table 19.1: Notational system for the $A \times (B \times S)$ design.

Original ABS table containing the scores Y_{ijk} and subject sums SA_{ij}

		b_1	b_2	b_3	Sum
	s_{11}	Y_{111}	Y_{112}	Y_{113}	SA_{11}
a_1	s_{21}	Y_{211}	Y_{212}	Y_{213}	SA_{21}
	s_{31}	Y_{311}	Y_{312}	Y_{313}	SA_{31}
	s_{12}	Y_{121}	Y_{122}	Y_{123}	SA_{12}
a_2	s_{22}	Y_{221}	Y_{222}	Y_{223}	SA_{22}
	s_{32}	Y_{321}	Y_{322}	Y_{323}	SA_{32}

Summary tables of sums

		AB table					Subject sums	
	b_1	b_2	b_3	Sum			a_1	a_2
a_1	AB_{11}	AB_{12}	AB_{13}	A_1			SA_{11}	SA_{12}
a_2	AB_{21}	AB_{22}	AB_{23}	A_2			SA_{21}	SA_{22}
Sum	B_1	B_2	B_3	T			SA_{31}	SA_{32}
							A_1	A_2

other factorial designs, be they between-subjects or within-subject. The definition and calculation of the three systematic effects (the A and B main effects and the $A{\times}B$ interaction) come directly from the $A{\times}B$ factorial. In the selection of error terms, the individual factors take on their between-subjects or within-subject character. The between-subjects factor (which we will prototypically indicate as factor A) acts like the factor in a one-way design with independent groups, while the within-subject factor (prototypically, factor B) acts like the factor in a within-subject design.

Design and Notation

Table 19.1 shows the notational system for the mixed design. The subjects here are indicated by s_{ij}, with the double subscript indicating the number of a subject (the subscript i) in a particular group (the subscript j). For example, s_{32} is the third subject in group a_2. The individual scores Y_{ijk} form an ABS data table. We have arranged this table with the individual subjects as rows, and the several measures from each subject as columns. This format keeps the between-subjects aspect of the design (the blocks of rows) separate from the within-subject aspect (the columns). It is also the format used by most computer packages. The ABS table here contains within it two BS tables separated by a line, one at level a_1 of factor A and the other at level a_2.

The first step in working with these data is to extract the summary AB table by summing over the n subjects within each group and treatment combination. We also need the subjects' marginal row sums SA_{ij}, formed by summing over the b scores in the ABS table.[1] It is also convenient to arrange these values in a table, as if they

---

[1] For changes in notion from the previous edition, see footnote 1 (p. 402).

were the scores in a single-factor design. There is no overall BS summary table. The AB table contains the ab sums AB_{jk} corresponding to the experimental conditions. As such, it is comparable to the AB table from any other two-factor design. We can use it to calculate the marginal sums A_j and B_k and the grand total T. The marginal sums A_j table can also be found from the table of subject sums. From each of these sums we can find a corresponding mean:

$$\bar{Y}_{AB_{jk}} = \frac{AB_{jk}}{n}, \quad \bar{Y}_{A_j} = \frac{A_j}{bn}, \quad \bar{Y}_{B_k} = \frac{B_k}{an}, \quad \text{and} \quad \bar{Y}_T = \frac{T}{abn}.$$

Sums of Squares and Degrees of Freedom

In Table 11.2 (p. 214) we introduced the steps that determine which sources of variance are relevant to a particular design. We start with the basic factors A, B, and S. Next, we form all legitimate interactions of these three factors. For factor A, we have an $A \times B$ interaction because every level of factor A combines with every level of factor B. There is no interaction of factors A and S, because each subject receives only one level of factor A. Turning to factor B, we already know that it is crossed with factor A to give an $A \times B$ interaction. Because it is a within-subject factor, it is also crossed with S (every subject receives every level of factor B), giving a $B \times S$ interaction. There is no three-factor $A \times B \times S$ interaction, because each combination of factors B and S appears at only one level of factor A. In Step 3 we determine whether we have to add slashes to indicate nesting. In the case of S, different subjects appear at each level of factor A, so we must write it as S/A, just as we did in the one-way between-subjects design. The $B \times S$ interaction is a little more complex. In Table 19.1, the ABS data table contains two BS subtables, each involving different subjects. Thus, we measure the $B \times S$ interaction twice, once for each level of factor A, and we must write it as $B \times S/A$ to reflect this nesting. In summary, the total sum of squares has the five components listed in the first column of Table 19.2:

$$A, \quad B, \quad A \times B, \quad S/A, \quad \text{and} \quad B \times S/A.$$

With the sources of variability in hand, we can turn to the degrees of freedom. Here we follow the rules in Table 11.3 (p. 215). There are abn scores, so $df_T = abn - 1$ degrees of freedom overall. You will recognize most of the sources in Table 19.2 from designs we have treated before, and their degrees of freedom are the same. The source we have not seen before is $B \times S/A$, and it makes a good illustration of the rules. Because B and S interact, we multiply their respective degrees of freedom, $b - 1$ and $n - 1$. Because different subjects are involved in the $B \times S$ interaction in each of the groups, we also need to add the number of levels to the right of the slash, namely a, giving the product

$$df_{B \times S/A} = (b - 1) \times (n - 1) \times a = a(b - 1)(n - 1).$$

Each degrees-of-freedom statement, when expanded, tells us how to calculate the corresponding sum of squares. We use the rules in Table 11.4 (p. 216), and the results are given in the third column of Table 19.2. The formulas for the main effects, the $A \times B$ interaction, and total are identical to those in other two-way designs. Again the new $B \times S/A$ source provides an example. Expanding the degrees of freedom gives

$$df_{B \times S/A} = a(b - 1)(n - 1) = abn - ab - an + a,$$

Table 19.2: Computational formulas for the sums of squares in an $A \times (B \times S)$ design.

Source	df	SS	Bracket term
A	$a - 1$	$[A] - [T]$	$[A] = \dfrac{\sum A_j^2}{bn}$
S/A	$a(n - 1)$	$[AS] - [A]$	$[AS] = \dfrac{\sum SA_{ij}^2}{b}$
B	$b - 1$	$[B] - [T]$	$[B] = \dfrac{\sum B_k^2}{an}$
$A \times B$	$(a - 1)(b - 1)$	$[AB] - [A] - [B] + [T]$	$[AB] = \dfrac{\sum AB_{jk}^2}{n}$
$B \times S/A$	$a(b - 1)(n - 1)$	$[Y] - [AB] - [AS] + [A]$	$[Y] = \sum Y_{ijk}^2$
Total	$abn - 1$	$[Y] - [T]$	$[T] = \dfrac{T^2}{abn}$

and so the formula for the sum of squares is

$$SS_{B \times S/A} = [Y] - [AB] - [AS] + [A].$$

We have listed the formulas for the bracket terms (using sums) in the last column.

The sums of squares for the five effects can be classified into those that relate purely to the between-subjects aspect of the experiment and those that also (or only) involve the within-subject aspect. This classification is a useful way to organize the effects, particularly for mixed designs with more than two factors. Look back at the diagram of the design in Table 19.1. The table of sums SA_{ij} is constructed by reducing each subject's data set to a single number by summing over the levels of factor B. Thus, any effects that are calculated from these sums depend only on differences among the subjects, not on any aspect of the scores that involves within-subject differences. The between-subjects effects, A and S/A, are calculated from this table, and the between-subjects sum of squares is the sum of those individual sums of squares:

$$SS_{\text{between}} = SS_A + SS_{S/A}.$$

The between-subjects sum of squares can also be calculated by treating the SA_{ij} table as if it were data in a one-way design and finding their total variability:

$$SS_{\text{between}} = [AS] - [T]$$

(see Equation 2.13, p. 30; here $[AS]$ plays the role of $[Y]$ in the one-way analysis). You can verify that the two equations for SS_{between} are equivalent by substituting bracket terms (Table 19.2) for SS_A and $SS_{S/A}$ in the first equation and simplifying the result.

The sums of squares that are not between-subjects effects all involve the within-subject factor B. They are classified as within-subject effects. Their sums of squares add up to the within-subject sum of squares:

$$SS_{\text{within}} = SS_{\text{total}} - SS_{\text{between}}$$
$$= SS_B + SS_{A \times B} + SS_{B \times S/A}.$$

Table 19.3: Principles for choosing error terms in designs. See Table 24.3 for the extension of these principles to designs with random factors.

> 1. Each completely between-subjects effect is tested against the variability among the subjects within the groups.
> 2. Each effect involving within-subject factors is tested against the interaction of the within-subject portion of that effect with the subject factor.

The distinction between the between-subjects and within-subject effects also applies to the degrees of freedom. For the between-subjects variation, there are an subjects in all (n subjects in each group and a groups), so that

$$df_{\text{between}} = \text{number of subjects} - 1 = an - 1.$$

There are b scores from each subject, each set associated with $b-1$ degrees of freedom, and an subjects, so the degrees of freedom for the within-subject effects are

$$df_{\text{within}} = (\text{number of subjects})(\text{scores from each subject} -1) = an(b - 1).$$

Using the values in Table 19.2, we can show that the degrees of freedom for both the between-subjects and within-subject effects sum to their appropriate totals:

$$df_{\text{between}} = df_A + df_{S/A} = (a - 1) + a(n - 1) = an - 1,$$

$$df_{\text{within}} = df_B + df_{A \times B} + df_{B \times S/A}$$
$$= (b - 1) + (a - 1)(b - 1) + a(b - 1)(n - 1) = an(b - 1).$$

These sums provide a check that all the effects are listed and are classified correctly.

Mean Squares and F Ratios

As usual, the mean squares are calculated by dividing each sum of squares by the appropriate number of degrees of freedom. Table 19.3 states the principles by which the error terms are chosen. We have set them out in a table because they apply to all the designs in this book except those in Chapters 24 and 25.

How do these principles apply to the mixed design? Because the main effect of factor A is based solely on the between-subjects factor, the first principle is relevant, and the error term is the within-groups mean square:

$$F_A = \frac{MS_A}{MS_{S/A}}.$$

This ratio is identical to the F for the omnibus effect in an actual single-factor between-subjects design. The other two effects involve the within-subject factor B, and, according to the second principle, the error term in each case is the interaction of factor B with factor S, which here is nested in factor A:

$$F_B = \frac{MS_B}{MS_{B \times S/A}} \quad \text{and} \quad F_{A \times B} = \frac{MS_{A \times B}}{MS_{B \times S/A}}.$$

Consider these three ratios more closely. The use of $MS_{S/A}$ to evaluate the significance of the between-subjects main effect is easy to understand. We could calculate the mean score $\overline{Y}_{SA_{ij}}$ for each subject (or the corresponding sums SA_{ij}) and analyze them as if they had been obtained from a single-factor between-subjects experiment. The F ratios in the two analyses are identical.

The justification for the within-subject error term is more subtle, and many people have difficulty with it at first. Consider the data in the ABS table at one of the levels of factor A, say, a_1. This portion of the ABS table can be thought of as a single-factor within-subject design involving factor B and n subjects. The error term for evaluating the differences among the treatment means in this subtable is the $B \times S$ interaction. The same argument holds for the $B \times S$ table at the other levels of factor A. When these data are brought together in the factorial design, the variation among the b means at each level of factor A is reflected in the B main effect and the $A \times B$ interaction. The error term for these two factorial treatment effects, $MS_{B \times S/A}$, is a combination—actually an average—of the separate $B \times S$ interactions at each level of A, each of which is the appropriate error term for its portion of the data. We can justify the use of $MS_{B \times S/A}$ as the error term for the B main effect by noting that both it and the error term are based on averages taken over the levels of the between-subjects factor A. What about the $A \times B$ interaction? It involves both within-subject and between-subjects differences, so which error term should be used? You can think of its error term, $MS_{B \times S/A}$, as a combination of both aspects of the design. For the within-subject factor B, the error is based on the variation of this factor over subjects, i.e. $B \times S$, and for the between-subjects factor A, the error is based on the variation of subjects within groups, i.e. S/A. Both influences are represented when we put these two parts together to form $B \times S/A$.

A Numerical Example

Our example is based on an experiment described by a student in one of our classes. The study investigated the effects of certain brain lesions on how well kangaroo rats could recover seeds they had previously placed in various hiding places or caches. One of the independent variables (factor B) was the number of "landmarks" available in the testing area for the animals to orient their caches—rocks, clusters of brush, small trees, and various man-made objects such as pipes, trash cans, etc. These objects could be easily moved around or removed by the researcher to create environments with 0, 4, 8, or 16 landmarks. Every animal was tested in each of these $b = 4$ conditions. The other independent variable (factor A) was a physiological manipulation. For two groups, the same amount of brain tissue was removed either from the hippocampus, an area known to be important for spatial memory (a_1), or from an area that is not (a_2). Group a_3 was a control group in which an operation was performed but no brain tissue removed. There were $n = 4$ animals in each of the $a = 3$ groups. Each animal was given a fixed period to hide their caches of seeds, then tested one day later to see the proportion of the hidden seeds that was recovered. The researcher expected that successful recovery would increase with the number of landmarks and that the animals with lesions of the hippocampus would show poorer recovery of seeds than the other two groups and be less affected by the number of landmarks. In summary, the design is a mixed factorial with $n = 4$ subjects assigned to each of $a = 3$ operation groups of the between-subjects factor A, and each subject tested once under each of the $b = 4$ landmark conditions of the within-subject factor B. The 48 percentage

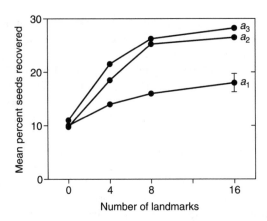

Figure 19.1: The mean percentage of recovered seeds given in Table 19.4. The error bar indicates a typical standard error of the mean based on the pooled data.

scores obtained from the $an = 12$ kangaroo rats are given in the ABS data array in the upper left of Table 19.4.

The top portion of Table 19.4 also contains two summary tables. The cell and marginal means are given in the middle portion of the table and plotted in Figure 19.1. To avoid cluttering up the figure, and because standard errors based on such small samples are deceptively variable, the plot shows only one typical standard error of the mean on the plot calculated from the pooled data.[2] The researcher's hypotheses were generally supported: Successful recovery increases with the number of landmarks, and group a_1 with the hippocampus removed was less successful than the other two groups, which appear to differ only slightly. An interaction may be present, as the hippocampal group is less affected by the number of landmarks than are the other groups, which again appear to be similar. Another way to state the interaction is that the three operation groups do not differ appreciably when no landmarks are present (condition b_1), and that the hippocampal group diverges from the other two as the number of landmarks increases from 4 (condition b_2) to 16 (condition b_4).

The bracket terms and the way that they are combined into sums of squares are given in Table 19.2. They are readily calculated from the sums in Table 19.4. We have entered them in an additional column in the summary of the analysis of variance at the bottom of that table. All the treatment effects are significant. The next step in the analysis would be to determine exactly what these omnibus effects show, as we will describe in the next chapter.

The Composite Nature of the Error Terms

We mentioned above that it is helpful to think of the $A \times (B \times S)$ design as a collection of separate $B \times S$ designs, one at each level of A. This conception is useful when trying to understand the error terms. These terms simply aggregate the corresponding effects over the smaller designs. Table 19.5 shows this process numerically. Here the data

---

[2]We could obtain this value by averaging the individual standard errors, or from the within-cell mean squares, as described in footnote 3 on page 452.

Table 19.4: Numerical example of an $A \times (B \times S)$ design. Three groups of kangaroo rats (factor A) were tested in environments with different numbers of landmarks (factor B). The scores are the percentage of cached seeds recovered one day later.

Tables of scores and sums needed for the analysis of variance

ABS data table

		b_1	b_2	b_3	b_4
	s_{11}	13	14	17	20
	s_{21}	10	11	15	14
a_1	s_{31}	13	19	18	22
	s_{41}	4	12	14	16
	s_{12}	5	13	21	24
	s_{22}	8	18	25	27
a_2	s_{32}	14	19	26	26
	s_{42}	12	24	29	29
	s_{13}	13	24	28	32
	s_{23}	9	22	22	24
a_3	s_{33}	14	22	28	28
	s_{43}	8	18	27	29

AB table

	b_1	b_2	b_3	b_4	Sum
a_1	40	56	64	72	232
a_2	39	74	101	106	320
a_3	44	86	105	113	348
Sum	123	216	270	291	900

Subject sums SA_{ij}

	a_1	a_2	a_3
	64	63	97
	50	78	77
	72	85	92
	46	94	82
Sum	232	320	348

Treatment and marginal means

	b_1	b_2	b_3	b_4	Mean
a_1	10.00	14.00	16.00	18.00	14.50
a_2	9.75	18.50	25.25	26.50	20.00
a_3	11.00	21.50	26.25	28.25	21.75
Mean	10.25	18.00	22.50	24.25	18.75

Summary of the analysis of variance

Source	Bracket terms	SS	df	MS	F
A	$[A] = 17{,}333.00$	458.00	2	229.000	6.85*
S/A	$[AS] = 17{,}634.00$	301.00	9	33.444	
Between S		759.00	11		
B	$[B] = 18{,}280.50$	1,405.50	3	468.500	127.76*
$A \times B$	$[AB] = 18{,}894.00$	155.50	6	25.917	7.07*
$B \times S/A$	$[Y] = 19{,}294$	99.00	27	3.667	
Within S		1,660.00	36		
Total	$[T] = 16{,}875.00$	2,419.00	47		

*$p < .05$

Table 19.5: Separate analyses of variance for the three groups in Table 19.4.

$B \times S$ design at a_1

	b_1	b_2	b_3	b_4	Source	SS	df	MS	F
s_{11}	13	14	17	20	B	140.0	3	46.67	13.11*
s_{21}	10	11	15	14	S	110.0	3	36.67	
s_{31}	13	19	18	22	$B \times S$	32.0	9	3.56	
s_{41}	4	12	14	16	Total	282.0	15		

$B \times S$ design at a_2

	b_1	b_2	b_3	b_4	Source	SS	df	MS	F
s_{12}	5	13	21	24	B	708.5	3	236.17	78.72*
s_{22}	8	18	25	27	S	128.5	3	42.83	
s_{32}	14	19	26	26	$B \times S$	27.0	9	3.00	
s_{42}	12	24	29	29	Total	864.0	15		

$B \times S$ design at a_3

	b_1	b_2	b_3	b_4	Source	SS	df	MS	F
s_{13}	13	24	28	32	B	712.5	3	237.50	53.49*
s_{23}	9	22	22	24	S	62.5	3	20.83	
s_{33}	14	22	28	28	$B \times S$	40.0	9	4.44	
s_{43}	8	18	27	29	Total	815.0	15		

from Table 19.4 have been broken into three blocks, one for each group, and analyzed as separate $B \times S$ designs using the formulas from Chapter 16. Now we combine the sums of squares for the subject-related factors over the three blocks:

$$SS_{S \text{ at } a_1} + SS_{S \text{ at } a_2} + SS_{S \text{ at } a_3} = 110.0 + 128.5 + 62.5 = 301.0$$

$$SS_{B \times S \text{ at } a_1} + SS_{B \times S \text{ at } a_2} + SS_{B \times S \text{ at } a_3} = 32.0 + 27.0 + 40.0 = 99.0$$

These sums are identical to $SS_{S/A}$ and $SS_{B \times S/A}$, respectively, in the standard analysis of variance (Table 19.4). The same relationships hold for the degrees of freedom:

$$df_{S/A} = \sum df_{S \text{ at } a_j} \quad \text{and} \quad df_{B \times S/A} = \sum df_{B \times S \text{ at } a_j}.$$

Two points about these calculations are noteworthy. First, they show that the two error terms are truly "within A." All the information embodied in the individual sums of squares is obtained from inside the groups at levels of A. These within-group calculations are simply combined across the groups. Second, they demonstrate again how measures of variability are combined over groups by separately pooling their numerators and denominators. In Chapter 3, we saw that the mean square $MS_{S/A}$ was such a composite (Equation 3.15, p. 58). Here the same thing holds:

$$MS_{S/A} = \frac{\sum SS_{S \text{ at } a_j}}{\sum df_{S \text{ at } a_j}} \quad \text{and} \quad MS_{B \times S/A} = \frac{\sum SS_{B \times S \text{ at } a_j}}{\sum df_{B \times S \text{ at } a_j}}.$$

When the group sizes are equal, the mean squares themselves can be averaged, as you can verify using the numbers in Tables 19.4 and 19.5 (see Equation 3.9, p. 54).

Pooling the terms in the numerator and denominator separately is the more general approach, however.

Removing Incidental Effects

In any design where multiple measures are taken from each subject, incidental differences between the conditions are important. For example, practice effects are of concern when different conditions are administered sequentially. In our example with the kangaroo rats, the researcher would wisely have counterbalanced the order in which the four landmark conditions were tested. Doing so spreads the effects of practice or familiarity equally over the within-subject conditions. However, as we explained in Section 17.5, any effects associated with the order in which the conditions are presented contribute to the within-subject error term, in this case, $MS_{B \times S/A}$. The sensitivity of the design is increased by removing them.

The ways of removing the effects of an incidental variable in a mixed design are like those for other within-subject designs. One possibility is to subtract the effects of the nuisance factor from each score, as we summarized in Table 17.3 (p. 390). After the effects of the nuisance factor are removed, a standard analysis applies, except that $b - 1$ is subtracted the degrees of freedom for the error term (Equation 17.8):[3]

$$df_{B \times S/A}(\text{adjusted}) = df_{B \times S/A} - df_B = a(b-1)(n-1) - (b-1).$$

If the incidental factor had an appreciable effect, the new F ratios will be larger than the unadjusted ratios.

19.2 Statistical Model and Assumptions

The analysis of the mixed two-factor within-subject design is based on a particular statistical model and several assumptions. Both the model and the assumptions combine the between-subjects and within-subject aspects of the design.

The Statistical Model

In our discussion of the single-factor within-subject design in Section 17.2, we distinguished between two models for the scores, the univariate model that treated each observation as a single random variable and the multivariate model that treated each subject's observations as a single multivariate random variable. The same distinction applies to the model for the mixed design. It is important to be aware of the two representations, because they lead to different test statistics, both of which are calculated by many computer programs.

The Univariate Model. The univariate model has the same form as the models for the other designs. The score of subject s_{ij} in group a_j when given treatment b_k is represented by a random variable Y_{ijk}. This random variable is a sum of terms, one for the grand mean, one for each of the measurable effects, and one for random error:

$$Y_{ijk} = \mu_T + \alpha_j + \beta_k + (\alpha\beta)_{jk} + S_{ij} + (S\beta)_{ijk} + E_{ijk}.$$

---

[3]Where the nuisance factor may interact with the between-subjects factor, it is better to remove its incidental effects separately from each group. In this case, $a(b-1)$ degrees of freedom should be subtracted from $df_{B \times S/A}$.

The interpretation of the terms of this model is best understood by comparing them to those from the other linear models we have described. The parameters μ_T, α_j, β_k, and $(\alpha\beta)_{jk}$ are identical to those representing the grand mean, the main effects, and the interaction in the other two-factor designs (the between-subjects design in Equation 17.1, p. 374, and the within-subject design in Equation 18.5, p. 417). The three terms, S_{ij}, $(S\beta)_{ijk}$, and E_{ijk}, express the three sorts of error specified for the single-factor within-subject design (again Equation 17.1). They correspond, respectively, to the variation among subjects, to the way that the within-subject factor B interacts with subjects, and to the uncontrolled sources of variability.

You are unlikely to make much direct use of this linear model. We present it here to show how the structure of the scores in the mixed design is built up from that in its component designs and to contrast it with the multivariate model.

The Multivariate Model.   The use of the univariate model for the scores in a mixed design implies a willingness to accept the same set of sphericity assumptions about the variability of the within-subject factor B that applies to the other within-subject designs. One way to avoid them is to treat the b scores from a subject as a single multivariate observation. For each subject s_{ij} from group j, the b scores of the within-subject factor are collectively represented by a multivariate random variable with b components:

$$\mathbf{Y}_{ij} = (Y_{ij1}, Y_{ij2}, \ldots, Y_{ijb}).$$

The linear model describes the distribution of these multivariate random variables. For each of the between-subjects groups, $\mathbf{Y}_{ij}$ has a multivariate normal distribution, like that in the single-factor design (p. 375). In the mixed design, the model goes on to describe how this distribution depends on the group classification. For the most part, the details of these assumptions need not concern us, but we will refer to the multivariate structure as we discuss the assumptions and the testing alternatives.

Assumptions

The assumptions of the mixed design combine those for its between-subjects and within-subject parts. The between-subjects assumptions are almost the same as those for the one-way design (see pp. 134–135). At the core are the two fundamental assumptions concerning the subject population: The observations from any subject must be independent of those from every other subject, and the distribution of observations is the same for every subject within a group. These assumptions are critical. When they fail, the analysis cannot be trusted. The remaining assumptions concern the form of the distribution. As in all the analysis-of-variance models, a normal distribution is assumed. The more critical assumption concerns the variability of this distribution. Because each subject provides b scores (factor B), their variability is summarized by b variances (one for each score) and by the set of correlations among them (one for each pair of scores). The between-subjects assumption regarding these variances and correlations is that they do not depend on the group. It is the counterpart of the assumption of homogeneity of variance we made for the pure between-subjects designs. In the mixed design, because both variances and correlations are involved, it is known as **homogeneity of covariance**. These assumptions apply to both the univariate and the multivariate versions of the analysis.

The within-subject assumption applies only to the univariate model. Recall that in the single-factor within-subject design (Section 17.3), it was necessary to assume sphericity. This assumption implied that the variances of the different treatment scores were all the same and that the correlations among them were identical. The same holds for the variances and covariances within the groups in the mixed design. It is important to distinguish this sphericity assumption from the assumption of homogeneity of covariance. The first refers to the within-subject aspect of the study, the second to the between-subjects aspect. Their violations have different implications for the analysis. Taken together, they imply that the covariance matrices are spherical and that they are the same across the groups. These combined assumptions are sometimes referred to as **multisample sphericity**.

Violation of the Assumptions

Violating the assumptions changes the properties of the test by altering the probability of committing a Type I error (rejecting the null hypothesis when it actually holds). Three issues are important here: violations of sphericity (for the within-subject factor), violations of homogeneity of covariance (for the between-subjects factor), and the equality of the sample sizes. Sample size, of course, is not an assumption of the tests, but the effect of violating the other assumptions is greater when the sizes of the groups are different.[4]

First consider violations of the sphericity assumption, such as differences in the variances of the scores or differences among the correlations between them. The situation here is fairly simple. There is no appreciable effect on tests of the between-subjects factor A (remember that it averages over the within-subject factor). However, there is an increase in the probability of falsely rejecting the null hypotheses for the within-subject effects, as much as doubling the nominal α level. This problem can be addressed by any of the approaches we discussed in Section 17.3. The first of these is to evaluate the F statistics against a critical value with reduced degrees of freedom. In the $A \times (B \times S)$ design, the two within-subject effects are tested with

$$df_{\text{num}} = \varepsilon(b-1) \quad \text{and} \quad df_{\text{denom}} = \varepsilon\, a(b-1)(n-1),$$

$$df_{\text{num}} = \varepsilon(a-1)(b-1) \quad \text{and} \quad df_{\text{denom}} = \varepsilon\, a(b-1)(n-1),$$

where ε measures the extent to which sphericity is violated (Equation 17.4). Two methods of estimating ε may appear in computer output, one associated with Geisser and Greenhouse and the other associated with Huynh and Feldt. The second approach is to turn to the multivariate analysis, which we describe below. These approaches are only feasible by computer.

The third approach is to use the conservative form of the degrees-of-freedom correction. Here $\varepsilon = 1/(b-1)$, and the F's are compared to tabled values with

$$df_{\text{num}} = 1 \quad \text{and} \quad df_{\text{denom}} = a(n-1) \qquad \text{for } B,$$
$$df_{\text{num}} = a-1 \quad \text{and} \quad df_{\text{denom}} = a(n-1) \qquad \text{for } A \times B.$$

---

[4]If you want to probe these issues more deeply, you can start with the recent reviews by Keselman, Algina, Kowalchuk, and Wolfinger (1999) and Keselman, Algina, and Kowalchuk (2001, 2002).

For our numerical example, we would use $F_{.05}(1, 9) = 5.12$ for B and $F_{.05}(2, 9) = 4.26$ for $A \times B$, instead of $F_{.05}(3, 27) = 2.98$ and $F_{.05}(6, 27) = 2.47$, respectively. Because our corresponding test statistics were $F = 127.76$, and $F = 7.07$, we would also reject both null hypotheses. The conservative form of the Geisser-Greenhouse test is accurate only when maximum heterogeneity is present; for less severe violations, the test overcorrects and is too conservative.

Now consider violations of between-group homogeneity of covariance. As in the between-subjects design (Section 7.3), unequal sample sizes make a difference. It appears that the different corrected significance levels and the multivariate tests are reasonably satisfactory whenever the groups sizes are equal. When the group sizes are unequal, the proportion of Type I errors deviates from α. It is greater than α when the smaller groups are more variable than the others, and it is less than α when the smaller groups are less variable. In the first case, we are too likely to find spurious results; in the second we lack power. These effects can be appreciable. There are ways to treat these problems, several of which are discussed in the articles we cited in footnote 4 above. A multivariate version of the Welch-James approach we mentioned for between-subjects designs (see pp. 155–156) is promising, but unfortunately, this is another area where the ways of testing have moved ahead of the readily available computer applications. Perhaps the situation will change soon, but for now, you will either have to turn to special-purpose programs or get help. As a practical solution, the best alternative is to strive for equal groups, and, when that is not possible, to be aware of the biases and compensate for them in interpreting the results.

19.3   The Multivariate Alternative

The multivariate approach to the analysis of variance of the mixed design relaxes the assumption of sphericity allowing any correlations among the treatment scores as long as they are consistent across the groups. Thus, it can safely be applied whenever sphericity is in doubt.[5] It is unrealistic to try to conduct a multivariate analysis by hand, but many computer programs include the tests in their analysis-of-variance module. A researcher should be prepared to recognize these tests and interpret them correctly.

The multivariate analysis, as implemented in the standard computer packages, tests the same set of hypotheses as does the univariate analysis. Table 19.6 shows the tests as they are applied to our numerical example data in Table 19.4. The test involving the between-subjects factor (factor A) is identical to the test in the univariate analysis—the mean square for the effect and for its error are the same as those for A and S/A in Table 19.4. The tests involving the within-subject factor (factor B) are different. The most striking thing about them is that the program provides four different test statistics. Each of these can be converted, at least approximately, to an F statistic. For the main effect of B, these statistics all give the same value of F, but in this example the values for the $A \times B$ interaction are different. The differences among these values are an indication of the fact that in a design with several groups and several measures per subject, there are many forms of interaction, and each test

---

[5]The multivariate test is also applicable when a researcher wants to use several distinct dependent variables to show a difference among groups. The univariate analysis of variance would be completely inappropriate in such a situation.

Table 19.6: Tests from the multivariate analysis of Table 19.4.

Analysis of between-subjects effects

Source	SS	df	MS	F
A	458.000	2	229.000	6.847*
Error	301.000	9	33.444	

$* p < .05$

Analysis of within-subject effects

Effect	Statistic	Value	Degrees of freedom Effect	Degrees of freedom Error	F
B	Pillai's Trace	.968	3	7	70.767*
	Wilks' Lambda	.032	3	7	70.767*
	Hotelling's Trace	30.329	3	7	70.767*
	Roy's Largest Root	30.329	3	7	70.767*
$A \times B$	Pillai's Trace	.926	6	16	2.299
	Wilks' Lambda	.173	6	14	3.280*
	Hotelling's Trace	4.216	6	12	4.216*
	Roy's Largest Root	4.076	3	8	10.869*

$* p < .05$

statistic is sensitive to them in its own way. These statistics are described in any book on multivariate statistics. It is not necessary to understand how they work in detail, but a researcher needs to have some idea of why they differ.

The four tests divide into two types. The statistic labeled **Roy's largest root** is based on the contrasts that could be formed among the four B means. In essence, its value is determined by the contrast that shows the largest effect. The significance level for this test takes account of the fact that this contrast is determined from the observed means and variability. As we have seen, however, when more than two groups are involved in a comparison, more than one contrast is necessary to completely express the omnibus effect. The other three statistics, **Pillai's Trace**, **Wilks' Lambda**, and **Hotelling's Trace**, are compound tests involving all the contrasts. In some cases, such as the main effect here, they give the same value; in other cases, such as the $A \times B$ interaction here, they vary in the emphasis they place on different aspects of the difference. When this happens, they usually lead to different values of F.

Tables of the significance levels for the various statistics have been compiled, and critical values can be looked up in them (Timm, 1975, gives a good selection). Most computer programs use a formula that converts the values of these test statistics to an F statistic. In some cases this conversion is exact; in others it is only approximate. In either case, the result can be referred to the usual F tables. You can deduce some properties of the multivariate tests by looking at these values and comparing them with the results of the univariate tests in Table 19.4. First, the multivariate statistics vary among themselves in their power and the degree to which they are likely to find a particular result significant. In our example, one of the tests, Pillai's trace, does not find the interaction to be significant. This reduced power, we hasten to add, is not a property of the Pillai statistic in general, but results from the particular pattern of data in this example. Second, the F values are generally lower than their counterparts in the univariate analysis—Roy's root looks like an exception, but it has fewer degrees of freedom, and its exact p value is actually larger. This reduction reflects the lower power of the multivariate tests. They circumvent the need to assume sphericity, but their increased robustness has a cost when sphericity holds.

Which of these statistics should a researcher use? We cannot make a single recommendation, because which one is most robust or powerful depends on many factors that differ from one experiment to another in complex ways (Krzanovski & Marriott, 1994, Appendix A.9). Our suggestion is to look at Roy's root statistic when the situation is one in which a single contrast among the treatments is the best way to interpret them. Otherwise, there is some evidence that, among the omnibus statistics, Pillai's trace has slightly better properties than the others (Olson, 1976), and so we would choose to report it. The situation is far from obvious, however.

19.4   Missing Data and Unequal Sample Sizes

The issues raised by unequal samples and missing data in mixed designs are similar to those we discussed before. They can be divided into those that arise from the loss of complete subjects and those that arise from the loss of part of a subject's data. Loss of complete subjects is only a problem when it creates a bias in the sample (see Section 7.2). Unequal subject sizes pose no insurmountable problems when (1) they do not arise from nonignorable loss, and (2) all the data from each defective subject are missing. Procedures based on the general linear model are used here, with Type III sums of squares. You will certainly use a computer to conduct the analysis.

The loss of part of a subject's data raises the issues we discussed in Section 17.6. When only a few subjects are affected, you can employ the complete-case analysis. The subjects with missing data are simply dropped from the analysis. If practical, they may be replaced with new and complete subjects, an option that is particularly relevant when the design also involves counterbalancing. When more than a few observations are missing, when the number of scores per subject is large, or when the number of complete subjects is small, the costs of restricting the analysis to complete cases is uncomfortably large. It may be better to impute values to the missing scores so that a complete analysis can be conducted. You can use the procedures on pages 395–399, applied separately for each between-subjects group. For example, if one subject in group a_2 were missing the score for treatment b_3, then the method would be applied to the $B \times S$ table of scores for group a_2 without regard to what happened in the other groups. The $df_{B \times S/A}$ is reduced by one for each imputed score.

19.5   Effect Sizes and Sample-Size Calculations

The joint presence of between-subjects and within-subject factors in the mixed design complicates the measurement of effect sizes. The two types of factors must be treated differently, and, for the within-subject factor, the same ambiguities we saw in the two-factor within-subject design (Section 18.5) arise. When all you need is a descriptive measure of effect size, however, you can use the sample-based estimates of the squared partial correlation ratio R^2 that many computer programs provide:

$$R^2_{\langle\text{effect}\rangle} = \frac{SS_{\text{effect}}}{SS_{\text{effect}} + SS_{\text{error}}}.$$

To illustrate for the three systematic effects, using the information in Table 19.4,

$$R^2_{\langle A \rangle} = \frac{SS_A}{SS_A + SS_{S/A}} = \frac{458.00}{458.00 + 301.00} = 0.603,$$

$$R^2_{\langle B \rangle} = \frac{SS_B}{SS_B + SS_{B \times S/A}} = \frac{1{,}405.50}{1{,}405.50 + 99.00} = 0.934,$$

$$R^2_{\langle A \times B \rangle} = \frac{SS_{A \times B}}{SS_{A \times B} + SS_{B \times S/A}} = \frac{155.50}{155.50 + 99.00} = 0.611.$$

Note that the error sum of squares in the denominator of $R^2_{\langle A \rangle}$ is different from that in $R^2_{\langle B \rangle}$ and $R^2_{\langle A \times B \rangle}$.

When you want to do power calculations based on another study, R^2 is not appropriate. You need to use a measure that takes into account the effects of sampling. For the between-subjects factor A, the situation is simple. It is measured with respect to its between-subjects variability, and can be treated like a factor in the equivalent completely between-subjects design. For the $A \times (B \times S)$ design, then, factor A is treated like the factor in the single-factor between-subjects design, and the equations we presented in Chapter 8 apply. Specifically, in our example we could ask what is the sample size needed for a replication of the kangaroo-rat study to have a 95 percent chance of detecting the between-subjects lesion effect. First we obtain an effect-size estimate from Equation 8.12 (p. 164), using the F values from Table 19.4 (p. 439). Because we have ignored factor B altogether, the value we get is the partial effect size:

$$\widehat{\omega}^2_{\langle A \rangle} = \frac{df_A(F_A - 1)}{df_A(F_A - 1) + an} = \frac{(2)(6.85 - 1)}{(2)(6.85 - 1) + (3)(4)} = 0.494.$$

This value is somewhat smaller than the value of $R^2_{\langle A \rangle}$ we calculated above. The effects in our miniature example are large, so we will use as a starting value the power function for $df_{\text{denom}} = 20$ (instead of our more usual 50), and from the power charts we obtain $\phi \approx 2.45$. We calculated $\omega^2_{\langle A \rangle}$ as a one-way design, and so we use the formula appropriate to that equation (Equation 8.18, p. 174) to obtain the new sample size

$$n = \phi^2 \frac{1 - \omega^2_{\langle A \rangle}}{\omega^2_{\langle A \rangle}} = (2.45^2)\frac{1 - 0.494}{0.494} = 6.15,$$

or about 7 animals per condition.

For the effects based on the within-subject factors, we encounter the complications we found in assessing effect size for the other within-subject designs. For sample-size determination, however, we can treat the properties of the initial experiment as given and work from them. The general expression of Equation 18.10 (p. 428) applies. For example, suppose we wanted the same power (.95) to detect the interaction effect in a replication of this study. Applying this equation to the interaction,

$$n_{\text{new}} = \left[\frac{\phi^2(df_{A \times B} + 1)}{df_{A \times B}(F_{A \times B} - 1)} \right] n_{\text{old}}$$

$$= \left[\frac{(1.9)^2(6 + 1)}{(6)(7.07 - 1)} \right] (4) = \frac{(25.27)(4)}{36.42} = 2.78,$$

where we chose the value of $\phi \approx 1.9$ from the $df_{\text{denom}} = 30$ in the chart for $df_{\text{num}} = 6$. The new sample size is estimated to be about $n = 3$ subjects per group. This value is atypically small because the effect in this artificial example is so large. Moreover, if we wanted to detect both effects at a power of .95 or higher, we would need to choose the largest estimate of sample size, which in this example, would be $n = 7$ from our calculations for replicating the A main effect.

Exercises

19.1. A child psychologist is interested in determining whether third-grade children would improve over a series of recall tests administered after a single study trial. A total of 12 children in a class individually studied a list of 36 common words for 5 seconds each and then attempted to remember them on a 2-minute recall test. After five minutes, they were asked to recall the same words again with no intervening study. In total, they were given $b = 4$ recall tests administered after the initial first study. The children were divided equally into three groups that received different words to study. One group (a_1) studied a list of unrelated words, while the other two groups studied lists consisting of words from 12 different categories—for example, colors, foods, domestic pets, etc.—with three examples from each category. For one group (a_2) the words were strongly associated with the category, while for the other (a_3) they were less strongly associated. The data below were obtained. Perform a standard analysis of variance with these data. Save your calculations for the exercises in Chapter 20.

	a_1 (Unrelated)					a_2 (Strongly Related)					a_3 (Weakly Related)			
	b_1	b_2	b_3	b_4		b_1	b_2	b_3	b_4		b_1	b_2	b_3	b_4
s_{11}	2	5	5	6	s_{12}	9	11	12	15	s_{13}	6	9	10	10
s_{21}	5	7	9	12	s_{22}	12	15	14	19	s_{23}	10	10	13	13
s_{31}	11	13	14	15	s_{32}	16	20	15	20	s_{33}	10	13	14	15
s_{41}	8	12	2	14	s_{42}	15	19	17	22	s_{43}	10	6	11	14

19.2. Subjects are given a vigilance task in which they detect targets on a simulated radar screen during a 40-minute test session. Factor A consists of three types of displays: black targets on a white background (a_1), white targets on a black background (a_2), and amber targets on a black background (a_3). Each subject is given three 40-minute test sessions, one per day (factor B). The response measure consists of the number of targets detected during the test session. The data for $n = 4$ subjects per condition are given below. Perform a standard analysis of variance with these data. Save your calculations for the exercises in Chapter 20.

	a_1 (black on white)				a_2 (white on black)				a_3 (amber on black)		
	b_1	b_2	b_3		b_1	b_2	b_3		b_1	b_2	b_3
s_{11}	23	24	27	s_{12}	15	20	27	s_{13}	23	34	38
s_{21}	20	21	25	s_{22}	18	25	32	s_{23}	19	32	32
s_{31}	23	29	28	s_{32}	24	26	33	s_{33}	24	32	38
s_{41}	14	22	24	s_{42}	22	31	36	s_{43}	18	28	37

20

The Two-Factor Mixed Design: Analytical Analyses

As we saw for the other two-factor designs, an overall analysis can be followed up by a variety of analytical comparisons. All these analyses are available for the $A \times (B \times S)$ mixed factorial. The nature of the independent variables and the logic of the study determine which questions are important, not whether they concern the between-subjects factor, the within-subject factor, or both. Thus, in this chapter, we will not discuss *why* you would choose to investigate a particular contrast, but will concentrate on *how* the questions are tested.

The analytical analyses in this chapter include simple effects, main contrasts, simple contrasts, and interaction components. Each of these effects is tested by the ratio of a measure of the effect to a measure of the error that influences it. For contrasts, we can conduct the test using either a t statistic or an F statistic. In general, the numerator of these ratios—the observed contrast $\widehat{\psi}$ in the t test or the sum of squares SS_ψ in the F test—are calculated in the same way as in any other factorial design.

The error terms are another matter. Think back to how we tested analytical comparisons in between-subjects and within-subject designs. For the between-subjects $A \times B$ design (with homogeneous variances), all the effects were tested against the same error measure $MS_{S/AB}$. The selection of the correct error term was more complicated for the $A \times S$ and $A \times B \times S$ within-subject designs. Here it was necessary to construct a different error term for each test by crossing the tested effect with the subject factor. Because a mixed design contains between-subjects and within-subject factors, however, no single testing strategy can apply to all analyses. The appropriate error term depends on how the effect relates to the between-subjects and within-subject variability. We will organized our discussion this way.

To anticipate the distinctions we will make and summarize them when we are done, Table 20.1 lists the types of hypotheses and the error terms used to test them. We have divided the effects into three categories based on their relationship to the within-subject factor: those involving only the between-subjects factor, those involving only the within-subject factor, and those involving the interaction of both types of factor.

Table 20.1: *Error terms for the different types of analytical analyses of an* $A \times (B \times S)$ *design. The error terms in the column labeled Restricted are based only on the scores of that simple effect; those in the column labeled Pooled are combined over the other levels of that factor and are appropriate when the variation in that factor is homogeneous.*

	Error term	
Source	Restricted	Pooled
Between-subjects effects		
ψ_A	S/A	
A at b_k	S/A at b_k	Within cell
ψ_A at b_k	S/A at b_k	Within cell
Within-subject effects		
ψ_B	$\psi_B \times S/A$	
B at a_j	$B \times S$ at a_j	$B \times S/A$
ψ_B at a_j	$\psi_B \times S$ at a_j	$\psi_B \times S/A$
Interaction effects		
$\psi_A \times B$	$B \times S/A$	
$A \times \psi_B$	$\psi_B \times S/A$	
$\psi_A \times \psi_B$	$\psi_B \times S/A$	

20.1 Analysis of the Between-Subjects Factor

This section describes analyses conducted purely on the between-subjects factor A, as main comparisons, simple effects, or simple contrasts. In these analyses, each subject contributes a single piece of information—a mean over the levels of factor B for a main comparison, and a score at one level of B for the simple effect or contrast. Thus, these analyses are the equivalent to those of an actual single-factor between-subjects design. The error terms are consistent with this interpretation.

Consider the three effects in the first section of Table 20.1. The main contrast is constructed from the means $\overline{Y}_{A_j}$. Like a contrast ψ_A among the means of a single-factor between-subjects design, it is tested against the same error term used to test the omnibus A effect, which for both designs is S/A. When concern is with the simple effects (the second two lines of Table 20.1), the same principle applies, except that attention is restricted to the scores for the specific simple effect. To test the simple effect of A at b_k, the scores at b_k are treated like observations from a one-way between-subjects design. The error term for an actual one-way design is S/A; the analysis here simply appends "at b_k" for both the effects and the error terms.[1]

Testing the simple effects and contrasts at level b_k against the error term $MS_{S/A \text{ at } b_k}$ is safe because it involves only the scores from the treatment level b_k that is actually being examined. When the variances of the ab treatment conditions in the entire experiment are homogeneous, greater power is obtained by using an error

---

[1]In Section 7.5, we described how the tests are modified when the group variances are unequal. You can use the same procedure here, calculating the variance of the contrast using Equation 7.12 and testing it with Equations 7.11 and 7.13.

Table 20.2: Mean percentage of seeds recovered by each animal, obtained by averaging over the within-subject factor in Table 19.4.

	a_1	a_2	a_3
	16.00	15.75	24.25
	12.50	19.50	19.25
	18.00	21.25	23.00
	11.50	23.50	20.50
Mean	14.50	20.00	21.75

term that pools the within-group variablity from all the levels of factor B:

$$SS_{\text{within cell}} = \sum SS_{S/A \text{ at } b_k} \quad \text{with} \quad df_{\text{within cell}} = \sum df_{S/A \text{ at } b_k}.$$

The relationship of the simple effects to the marginal effects (Equation 12.8, p. 253) allows these sums to be obtained by combining the S/A and $B \times S/A$ effects. The **within-cell mean square**, therefore, is more conveniently calculated by the ratio

$$MS_{\text{within cell}} = \frac{SS_{S/A} + SS_{B \times S/A}}{df_{S/A} + df_{B \times S/A}}. \tag{20.1}$$

Because $MS_{\text{within cell}}$ involves all the treatments, it may be either larger or smaller than $MS_{S/A \text{ at } b_k}$. It will have more degrees of freedom. When the number of subjects per group is small and the treatments have comparable variability, the $MS_{\text{within cell}}$ is an improvement over the less powerful error term based on the scores at a single level of factor B. We have listed two alternatives for the error term in Table 20.1, the more conservative alternative in the middle column and the more powerful alternative on the right.

Examples of Between-Subjects Tests

Our examples in this chapter use the data from the study on kangaroo rats recovering caches of seeds in the last chapter (Table 19.4).

Main-Effect Contrasts. Tests of contrasts involving the between-subjects factor A are conducted by ignoring the within-subject factor. There are two ways to approach the tests. One possibility is to work from the mean score for each subject. In Table 20.2 we have calculated these values by dividing each sum in the AS table (given in Table 19.4) by $b = 4$. We could use these means either to test the main effect of A or to calculate and test any contrasts that concern the main effect. This approach is particularly useful in helping to conceptualize how the hypotheses are tested.[2]

The second approach is to work directly with quantities available from the overall analysis. Consider a comparison of the group receiving a hippocampal lesion (a_1) with the combined groups receiving either a lesion from another area or no lesion at all (a_2 and a_3). The coefficient set for this contrast is $\{-1, \frac{1}{2}, \frac{1}{2}\}$. The contrast value and

---

[2]If you actually analyzed Table 20.2 (see Problem 20.3), you would find that because four scores were averaged, both SS_A and $SS_{S/A}$ are a quarter their size in the original analysis (Table 19.4, bottom). However, because the two values change by the same proportion, the F ratio (and the conclusion) is the same.

its sum of squares are calculated just as we did in the one-way analysis (Equation 4.4, p. 68, and Equation 4.5, p. 69), except that we must remember that bn scores contribute to each mean, not simply n. Substituting the marginal means $\overline{Y}_{A_j}$ from Table 19.4 or Table 20.2 into these equations, we find that

$$\widehat{\psi}_A = \sum c_j \overline{Y}_{A_j} = (-1)(14.50) + (\tfrac{1}{2})(20.00) + (\tfrac{1}{2})(21.75) = 6.375,$$

$$SS_{\psi_A} = \frac{bn\widehat{\psi}_A^2}{\sum c_j^2} = \frac{(4)(4)(6.375)^2}{(-1)^2 + (\tfrac{1}{2})^2 + (\tfrac{1}{2})^2} = \frac{650.250}{1.5} = 433.500.$$

As indicated in Table 20.1, the error term for this analysis is the within-groups mean square $MS_{S/A}$ from the between-subjects portion of the overall analysis. With one degree of freedom, $MS_{\psi_A} = SS_{\psi_A}$, and

$$F = \frac{MS_{\psi_A}}{MS_{S/A}} = \frac{433.500}{33.444} = 12.96.$$

This value is significant ($F_{.05}(1,9) = 5.12$), implying that the kangaroo rats with the hippocampal lesions recovered a significantly smaller percentage of their caches of seeds than the average of the other two groups.

Simple Effects.   The simple effects of factor A at b_k are based on what we can view as a single-factor between-subjects experiment at one level of the repeated factor. As we have indicated in Table 20.1, the error term reflects the pooled variability of the subjects within the groups at the appropriate level of factor B, i.e. S/A at b_k. Consider the kangaroo rats in the condition in which 16 landmarks were available (level b_4). The relevant portion of the original ABS data table from Table 19.4 is shown at the top of Table 20.3. These data correspond to a between-subjects single-factor design with three independent groups of $n = 4$ subjects. To test for a simple effect, we analyze them as if they were from an ordinary one-way design, producing the result at the bottom portion of the table. The F is significant, indicating that the groups differ in recovering seeds with 16 landmarks present.

If we assume that the within-group variances are the same for the different landmark conditions, we can construct a test with a greater number of degrees of freedom using the within-cell error term (Equation 20.1). Taking values from the original omnibus analysis-of-variance table (Table 19.4, bottom), the new error term is

$$MS_{\text{within cell}} = \frac{SS_{S/A} + SS_{B \times S/A}}{df_{S/A} + df_{B \times S/A}} = \frac{301.00 + 99.00}{9 + 27} = \frac{400.00}{36} = 11.111.$$

Here $MS_{\text{within cell}}$ is somewhat larger than the error term for the simple effect, so the test statistic $F = 120.250/11.111 = 10.82$ is a little smaller. However, it is a more accurate estimate of the error variability, and with more degrees of freedom it reduces the critical value from $F_{.05}(2,9) = 4.26$ to $F_{.05}(2,36) = 3.26$ (we estimated this value from Appendix A.1). The test, therefore, has greater power.[3]

---

[3]The composite standard error of the mean illustrated in Figure 19.1 is based on this within-cell mean square. We divided it by the sample size ($n = 4$) and took the square root to obtain the standard error of the mean: $s_M = \sqrt{MS_{\text{within cell}}/n} = \sqrt{11.111/4} = 1.67$.

Table 20.3: *The simple effect of lesion type (factor A) for the 16-landmark condition (level b_4), using the data in Table 19.4.*

Data table for level b_4

	a_1	a_2	a_3
	20	24	32
	14	27	24
	22	26	28
	16	29	29
Mean	18.00	26.50	28.25

Summary of the analysis of variance

Source	Bracket terms	SS	df	MS	F
A at b_4	$[A] = 7,297.25$	240.50	2	120.250	12.62*
S/A at b_4	$[Y] = 7,383.00$	85.75	9	9.528	
Total	$[T] = 7,056.75$	326.25			

*$p < .05$

Simple Comparisons. A simple comparison is examined in the same way as a comparison in an actual single-factor between-subjects experiment. The analysis is applied to the means in Table 20.3, and it uses the same error term as the test for a simple effect. Again, Equations 4.4 and 4.5 give the sum of squares. Continuing with the comparison between group a_1 to the average of the other two groups, we obtain

$$\widehat{\psi}_{A \text{ at } b_4} = \sum c_j \bar{Y}_{j4} = (-1)(18.00) + (\tfrac{1}{2})(26.50) + (\tfrac{1}{2})(28.25) = 9.375,$$

$$SS_{\psi_A \text{ at } b_4} = \frac{n\widehat{\psi}_{A \text{ at } b_4}^2}{\sum c_j^2} = \frac{(4)(9.375)^2}{1.5} = 234.375.$$

There are now n subjects contributing to each mean. Using the conservative error term calculated from the restricted data (we could also use $MS_{\text{within cell}}$),

$$F = \frac{MS_{\psi_A \text{ at } b_4}}{MS_{S/A \text{ at } b_4}} = \frac{234.375}{9.528} = 24.60.$$

Again the effect is significant ($F_{.05}(1,9) = 5.12$), indicating that when 16 landmarks were provided, the animals in the hippocampal group recovered fewer seeds than those in the other two groups combined.

20.2 Analysis of the Within-Subject Factor

The three purely within-subject effects—main contrasts, simple effects, and simple contrasts—are exact counterparts to the three between-subjects effects, but their relationship to the subject factor S/A requires them to be treated differently. An effect involving a within-subject factor needs an error term that is an interaction of that effect with the subject factor. In Table 18.5 (p. 409), we gave two rules that allowed us to analyze both contrasts and simple effects in the two-factor within-subject design. Both rules apply to the mixed design, and together they determine how to analyze the within-subject factor

Contrasts

As the first rule in Table 18.5 states, the simplest way to approach the analysis of a within-subject contrast is to define a contrast variable. The variable is created by calculating the value of the contrast from each subject's scores. This calculation reduces the complexity of the design by eliminating the within-subject factor and replacing it with a single value. Hypotheses about those values then are tested in the context of the simpler design. Thus, hypotheses about contrasts in the original design become hypotheses about mean values in the reduced design.

In our example, consider whether the average percentage of seed recovery increases with the number of landmarks. This question is investigated by looking at the linear trend. Because the levels of factor B are not evenly spaced (they are 0, 4, 8, and 16 landmarks), we need a specialized set of linear trend coefficients. Following the procedure on pages 105–106, we find this set to be $\{-7, -3, 1, 9\}$. These coefficients sum to zero and lie on a straight line when plotted against the number of landmarks. Now we use $\psi_{B_{\text{linear}}}$ to create a contrast variable $\widehat{\psi}_{ij}$. The process is summarized at the top of Table 20.4. On the left, we calculate the values of $\widehat{\psi}_{ij}$ using the original ABS data taken from Table 19.4. For example, using the first subject in group a_2,

$$\widehat{\psi}_{12} = \sum c_k Y_{12k} = (-7)(5) + (-3)(13) + (1)(21) + (9)(24) = 163.$$

The contrast variable reduces the within-subject factor B to a set of single scores. At the far right, we have rearranged these numbers in a 3-by-4 table, as if they were data from an actual single-factor between-subjects design.

The main contrast here assesses whether success in retrieving seeds increases with the number of landmarks. The null hypothesis that $\psi_B = 0$ is evaluated by testing whether the grand mean of the an individual contrast values differs from zero. We can perform the test as part of an analysis of variance. This approach is the same one we used for the two-factor within-subject design (see Table 18.6, p. 410), except that here we use a between-subjects analysis instead of a within-subject analysis. The relevant formulas are those in Chapters 2 and 3, including the test for the grand mean on page 37. The analysis of variance (including bracket terms) is summarized at the bottom of Table 20.4. Note that we have included a row for the test of the grand mean (labeled G.M.$_\psi$ in the first column; it might be called the test for the intercept by some computer programs). We also gave two names for each source of variability, the first as it would be labeled in a single-factor between-subjects analysis (flagged with the subscript ψ), and the other as it is interpreted in the mixed design. The hypothesis of no linear trend ($\psi_{B_{\text{linear}}} = 0$) corresponds to the test that the grand mean is zero. The error term for this test is the pooled within-groups source of the one-way design (S/A_ψ), which here is equivalent to the $\psi_{B_{\text{linear}}} \times S/A$ interaction, the error term for this test in Table 20.1. The result is significant, and the value of $\widehat{\psi}_{B_{\text{linear}}}$ is positive, implying that recovery of the seeds increases with the number of landmarks.

The contrast-variable approach is quite straightforward when performed by computer. First have the program calculate the values of the contrast variable, then use

Table 20.4: The analysis of the linear trend of the number of landmarks (factor B) for the data in Table 19.4.

Individual contrast values $\widehat{\psi}_{ij}$ calculated and arranged as a single-factor design

		b_1	b_2	b_3	b_4	$\widehat{\psi}_{ij}$
	s_{11}	13	14	17	20	64
	s_{21}	10	11	15	14	38
a_1	s_{31}	13	19	18	22	68
	s_{41}	4	12	14	16	94
	s_{12}	5	13	21	24	163
	s_{22}	8	18	25	27	158
a_2	s_{32}	14	19	26	26	105
	s_{42}	12	24	29	29	134
	s_{13}	13	24	28	32	153
	s_{23}	9	22	22	24	109
a_3	s_{33}	14	22	28	28	116
	s_{43}	8	18	27	29	178

	a_1	a_2	a_3
	64	163	153
	38	158	109
	68	105	116
	94	134	178
Sum	264	560	556
Mean	66.0	140.0	139.0

Summary of the analysis of variance

Source of variation						
For $\widehat{\psi}_{ij}$	For Y_{ijk}	Bracket	SS	df	MS	F
G.M.$_\psi$	$\psi_{B_{\text{linear}}}$	$[T_\psi] = 158{,}700$	158,700	1	158,700.0	208.94*
A_ψ	$A{\times}\psi_{B_{\text{linear}}}$	$[A_\psi] = 173{,}108$	14,408	2	7,204.0	9.48*
S/A_ψ	$\psi_{B_{\text{linear}}}{\times}S/A$	$[Y_\psi] = 179{,}944$	6,836	9	759.56	
Total$_\psi$			21,244	11		

*$p < .05$

its between-subjects module to perform the one-way analysis and compute the tests. One advantage of conducting the complete analysis in Table 20.4 (as a computer would do), is that it also tests for the $A{\times}\psi_{B_{\text{linear}}}$ interaction. We get two results for the price of one here. We will discuss this test when we consider interactions in the next section.

As we noted in Chapter 5, researchers usually have two concerns in a trend analysis: Is there evidence for linear trend and are any other trend components present? The plot of the means in Figure 19.1 (p. 438) showed (in addition to the obvious increase in performance captured by the linear trend) that the lines appear to bend over, suggesting a quadratic component. We could test for this component directly using coefficients calculated specially for the unequally-spaced groups (they are the set {7, $-4, -8, 5$}). An easier approach is to look for nonlinear effects generally by calculating the residual portion of the treatment effect:

$$SS_{B_{\text{nonlinear}}} = SS_B - SS_{B_{\text{linear}}}.$$

Before subtracting, we have to adjust the sum of squares calculated from the contrast variable to take account of the coefficients of $\psi_{B_{\text{linear}}}$ (see Equation 16.5, p. 359 and the application on p. 411). The adjustment is made by dividing the original sums of squares by the sum of squared coefficients, $\sum c_k^2 = (-7)^2 + (-3)^2 + 1^2 + 9^2 = 140$:

$$SS_{B_{\text{linear}}} = \frac{158{,}700.0}{140} = 1{,}133.571 \quad \text{and} \quad SS_{B_{\text{linear}} \times S/A} = \frac{6{,}836.0}{140} = 48.829.$$

Subtracting these sums of squares from the relevant sums of squares from the overall analysis (Table 19.4), we find

$$SS_{B_{\text{nonlinear}}} = SS_B - SS_{B_{\text{linear}}} = 1{,}405.50 - 1{,}133.571 = 271.929,$$

$$SS_{B_{\text{nonlinear}} \times S/A} = SS_{B \times S/A} - SS_{B_{\text{linear}} \times S/A} = 99.00 - 48.829 = 50.171.$$

The degrees of freedom are also obtained by subtraction: $df_{B_{\text{nonlinear}}} = 3 - 1 = 2$ and $df_{B_{\text{nonlinear}} \times S/A} = 27 - 9 = 18$. The resulting F is

$$F_{B_{\text{nonlinear}}} = \frac{MS_{B_{\text{nonlinear}}}}{MS_{B_{\text{nonlinear}} \times S/A}} = \frac{271.929/2}{50.171/18} = \frac{135.965}{2.787} = 48.785.$$

It is significant ($F_{.05}(2, 18) = 3.55$), implying that success in finding seeds is not exclusively linear.

Simple Effects

The most straightforward way to analyze the simple effects of the within-subject factor at one level of the between-subjects factor is to extract the scores from the relevant group and analyze them exactly as if they had been produced by an actual $B \times S$ within-subject design—the second principle in Table 18.5. We reported this analysis in Table 19.5 (p. 440) when discussing composite error terms. Here, our interest is in simple effects. Suppose we want to determine whether the effect of the number of landmarks for the group of kangaroo rats in the hippocampal condition is significant (factor B at level a_1 of factor A). We copied the portion of the data table from the first block of Table 19.4 into the upper portion of Table 20.5 (ignore for the moment the contrast variable to the right). The structure of the data is identical to that for an actual single-factor within-subject design, so we can conduct this analysis as described in Table 16.2 (p. 352). The analysis is summarized in the lower portion of Table 20.5. As you can see, the simple effect is significant.

This analysis uses the error term $B \times S$ at a_1 from the restricted data, the term listed in the middle column of Table 20.1. However, sometimes we can pool the error terms over the levels of the between-subjects factor to attain greater power. This logic led us to test the simple effects in a two-way between-subjects design against the overall S/AB error term (e.g., Table 12.2, p. 251). The situation is more subtle in the mixed design because we have to assume homogeneity of covariance (see p. 443), rather than just homogeneity of variance. When we can make this assumption, we can use the error term $MS_{B \times S/A}$ from the overall analysis, giving a more stable estimate of unsystematic variability, a gain in denominator degrees of freedom, and an increase in power. In the present example, $MS_{B \times S/A} = 3.667$ and $F = 46.667/3.667 = 12.73$. Although the F is actually slightly smaller here (it might as likely have been larger), the real gain is in the critical value of the statistic. For the original error term, $df_{B \times S}$ at $a_1 = (b-1)(n-1) = 9$ and $F_{.05}(3, 9) = 3.86$, while for the pooled error term, $df_{B \times S/A} = a(b-1)(n-1) = 27$ and $F_{.05}(3, 27) = 2.97$ (estimated from Appendix A.1). The gain in power is appreciable.

Table 20.5: *Analysis of the simple effects of the number of landmarks (factor B) for the kangaroo rats with hippocampal lesions (group a_1). The contrast variable $\widehat{\psi}_{i\ at\ a_1}$ is based on the contrast $\psi_B = \mu_4 - \mu_1$.*

ABS data table for level a_1 with values of a contrast variable $\widehat{\psi}_{i\ at\ a_1}$

	b_1	b_2	b_3	b_4	Sum	$\widehat{\psi}_{i\ at\ a_1}$
s_{11}	13	14	17	20	64	7
s_{21}	10	11	15	14	50	4
s_{31}	13	19	18	22	72	9
s_{41}	4	12	14	16	46	12
Sum	40	56	64	72	232	32
Mean	10.0	14.0	16.0	18.0		8.0

Summary of the analysis of variance

Source	Bracket terms	SS	df	MS	F
B at a_1	$[B] = 3{,}504$	140	3	46.667	13.12*
S at a_1	$[S] = 3{,}474$	110	3	36.667	
$B{\times}S$ at a_1	$[Y] = 3{,}646$	32	9	3.556	
Total	$[T] = 3{,}364$	282	15		

* $p < .05$

Simple Comparisons

Simple comparisons are important, both as planned tests for specific effects and to follow up significant simple effects. So, the significant simple effect of the number of landmarks for the hippocampal group identified above might be followed by a trend analysis, as we did with the main comparison earlier. However, we will illustrate the procedure by comparing the mean for 16 landmarks with that for 0 landmarks, using the coefficient set $\{-1, 0, 0, 1\}$. The observed value of this contrast is positive ($\widehat{\psi}_{B\ at\ a_1} = \bar{Y}_{14} - \bar{Y}_{11} = 18.0 - 10.0 = 8.0$). To test its significance, the contrast value is converted to a sum of squares and compared to an appropriate error term.

The analysis is equivalent to the analysis of a single-df comparison in a single-factor within-subject design. Specifically, it uses the formulas we presented in Table 16.6 (p. 360), adapted to the present analysis. Starting with the data from the simple effect, a contrast value $\widehat{\psi}_{i\ at\ a_1}$ based on ψ_B is calculated for each subject. For example, the contrast value for the first subject is $\widehat{\psi}_{1\ at\ a_1} = (-1)(13) + \cdots + (1)(20) = 7$. These values are shown on the right in the upper portion of Table 20.5. From these values,

$$[T_\psi] = n\widehat{\psi}_{B\ at\ a_1}^2 = (4)(8.0)^2 = 256 \quad \text{and} \quad [Y_\psi] = \sum \widehat{\psi}_{i\ at\ a_1}^2 = 7^2 + \cdots + 12^2 = 290.$$

The sums of squares for the two effects are

$$SS_{\psi_B} = [T_\psi] = 256 \quad \text{and} \quad SS_{\psi_B \times S} = [Y_\psi] - [T_\psi] = 34,$$

with 1 and $n - 1 = 3$ degrees of freedom. The test statistic is

$$F = \frac{MS_{\psi_B}}{MS_{\psi_B \times S}} = \frac{256.0}{34.0/3} = 22.59.$$

The result is significant, indicating that the hippocampal group is more successful at retrieving seeds in a environment with 16 landmarks than with none.

As was the case for the simple effect, when homogeneity of covariance across the groups can be assumed, a more powerful test can be made by using $MS_{\psi_B \times S/A}$ as the error term instead of $MS_{\psi_B \times S}$ at a_1. This error term is found by calculating the contrast variable $\widehat{\psi}_{i \text{ at } a_j}$ for every subject in the full study, then analyzing these values in a complete between-subjects analysis of variance as we did in Table 20.4. In our example, analyzing $\widehat{\psi}_{i \text{ at } a_j}$ in the full design gives $MS_{\psi_B \times S} = 11.06$ with 9 degrees of freedom, and $F = 23.15$.

20.3 Analyses Involving the Interaction

The last two sections discussed analytical analyses that concern the effect of one of the factors, either as a main effect or a simple effect. This section covers analyses that focus on interaction components, that is, on portions of the omnibus $A \times B$ interaction. We will consider three types of effect. Two are interaction components constructed by crossing a contrast (either between-subjects or within-subject) with the other factor ($\psi_A \times B$ and $A \times \psi_B$, respectively). The third is the interaction between two contrasts ($\psi_A \times \psi_B$ or, more compactly, ψ_{AB}). The bottom lines of Table 20.1 list the error terms for each of these interaction components. A general principle applies to these error terms: when a contrast involves the between-subjects factor, the full within-subject factor appears in the error, but when a contrast involves the within-subject factor, only its interaction with subjects appears.

Analysis of the $\psi_A \times B$ Interaction Component

To examine the interaction of a between-subjects contrast ψ_A with a within-subject factor B, we need an effect sum of squares that expresses the variation of ψ_A among the different B treatments ($\psi_A \times B$) and an error sum of squares that expresses how the within-subject B factor varies with S, which is $B \times S/A$. The first sum of squares can be found using Equation 13.10 (p. 279):

$$SS_{\psi_A \times B} = \frac{n \sum_k (\widehat{\psi}_{A \text{ at } b_k} - \widehat{\psi}_A)^2}{\sum c_j^2},$$
(20.2)

where $\widehat{\psi}_{A \text{ at } b_k}$ = the contrasts at levels b_k of factor B,
  $\widehat{\psi}_A$ = the contrast on the marginal means.

The degrees of freedom for this contrast are

$$df_{\psi_A \times B} = df_{\psi_A} \times df_B = (1)(b-1) = b-1.$$

The error term, $MS_{B \times S/A}$, is taken from the omnibus analysis.

As an example, consider the contrast comparing the hippocampal group a_1 with the average of the other groups, $\psi_A = (-1)\mu_{A_1} + (\frac{1}{2})\mu_{A_2} + (\frac{1}{2})\mu_{A_3}$, which we analyzed as a main contrast in Section 20.1. We found there that $\widehat{\psi}_A = 6.375$. We calculate the values of the simple contrasts with the means from Table 19.4 (p. 439); for b_1,

$$\widehat{\psi}_{A \text{ at } b_1} = c_1 \overline{Y}_{11} + c_2 \overline{Y}_{21} + c_3 \overline{Y}_{31}$$
$$= (-1)(10.00) + (\frac{1}{2})(9.75) + (\frac{1}{2})(11.00) = 0.375.$$

The simple contrasts at levels b_2, b_3, and b_4 are 6.000, 9.750, and 9.375, respectively. Although all four simple contrasts are positive, implying that the hippocampal group retrieved fewer seeds than the others, the effect is smallest when no landmarks are provided and largest when 8 or 16 landmarks are present. Now we substitute these values in Equation 20.2 to find the sum of squares:

$$SS_{\psi_A \times B} = \frac{n \sum_k (\widehat{\psi}_{A \text{ at } b_k} - \widehat{\psi}_A)^2}{\sum c_j^2}$$

$$= \frac{(4)[(0.375 - 6.375)^2 + \cdots + (9.375 - 6.375)^2]}{(-1)^2 + (\frac{1}{2})^2 + (\frac{1}{2})^2} = \frac{(4)(56.531)}{1.5} = 150.749.$$

This sum of squares has $b - 1 = 3$ degrees of freedom. The error mean square, which we obtain from Table 19.4, is $MS_{B \times S/A} = 3.667$, and

$$F = \frac{MS_{\psi_A \times B}}{MS_{B \times S/A}} = \frac{150.749/3}{3.667} = 13.70.$$

The result is significant ($F_{.05}(3, 27) = 2.97$), showing that the difference between the hippocampal group and the others depends on the number of landmarks.

Analysis of the $A \times \psi_B$ Interaction Component

Although an $A \times \psi_B$ interaction is conceptually equivalent to a $\psi_A \times B$ interaction, the two are evaluated differently in the mixed design because their relationship to the repeated factor is different. Effects calculated from within-subject factors require an error term based on a subject interaction—in this case, $\psi_B \times S/A$, as indicated in Table 20.1. The simplest way to investigate an $A \times \psi_B$ interaction is to calculate a contrast value for every subject and reduce the data to a one-way between-subjects design. Both the main contrast and its interaction can be tested from this table. Because most researchers are interested in both effects, they are usually tested together.

Specifically, let's consider again the analysis of linear trend for factor B. We began this analysis in Table 20.4 when we constructed the contrast variable $\widehat{\psi}_{ij}$ and tested the main contrast $\psi_{B_{\text{linear}}}$. We commented then that the contrast variable could also be used to test for an $A \times \psi_{B_{\text{linear}}}$ interaction. The mean values of $\widehat{\psi}_{ij}$ for the three levels of factor A (given in the small table on the upper right of Table 20.4) are 66.0, 140.0, and 139.0. These values are positive, indicating that performance increased with the number of landmarks for all groups. However, the mean for the hippocampal group (a_1) is less than half the means for the other two groups, which do not appear to differ. These observations suggest that $\psi_{B_{\text{linear}}}$ interacts with factor A. To verify this observation, we turn to the second test in the analysis of the contrast variable at the bottom of Table 20.4. The A effect here is significant ($F = 9.48$, compared to $F_{.05}(2, 9) = 4.26$), and, as we noted in the second column of sources, it corresponds to the $A \times \psi_B$ interaction.

Analysis of the $\psi_A \times \psi_B$ Interaction Contrast

The interaction of two contrasts offers the most detailed assessment of an interaction. The factor-by-contrast interactions we just considered are more focused than the overall $A \times B$ interaction, but they are not as precise as an interaction contrast. The degree of specificity of these different interactions is expressed by their degrees of freedom. In our numerical example, the omnibus $A{\times}B$ interaction had $df_{A{\times}B} = (a-1)(b-1) = (2)(3) = 6$, while the contrast-by-factor interactions had $df_{\psi_A{\times}B} = b - 1 = 3$ and $df_{A{\times}\psi_B} = a - 1 = 2$. The contrast-by-contrast interaction has only a single degree of freedom.

As a contrast of a contrast, the interaction contrast can also be written as a single contrast ψ_{AB} applied to all the conditions with the coefficient c_{jk} equal to the product $c_{A_j}c_{B_k}$ (Equation 13.5, p. 272). As such, its value is calculated either by applying these joint coefficients to the means of the treatment conditions or by applying one of the contrasts to the values of the other:

$$\widehat{\psi}_{AB} = \sum c_{jk}\overline{Y}_{jk} = \sum c_{A_j}\widehat{\psi}_B \text{ at } a_j = \sum c_{B_k}\widehat{\psi}_A \text{ at } b_k. \tag{20.3}$$

The sum of squares can then be then calculated following the general approach of Equation 12.1 (p. 245) (i.e. $n\widehat{\psi}_{AB}^2 / \sum c_{jk}^2$). Because an interaction contrast in a mixed design involves a within-subject contrast, it requires its own error term. Following the principles in Table 19.3, this term is created by crossing the within-subject contrast with subjects and pooling the result over the levels of the between-subjects factor. The error term is the $\psi_B{\times}S/A$ interaction listed in Table 20.1. It is the same error term used to evaluate the $A{\times}\psi_B$ interaction we just discussed.

An interaction contrast can be interpreted as a contrast applied to a contrast variable (the last two terms of Equation 20.3), and testing it this way is usually easier for a computer. Instead of finding an overall value for $\widehat{\psi}_{AB}$, define a contrast variable based on ψ_B, calculate its value for each subject, and analyze these values as a between-subjects design. Suppose we bring together the between-subjects comparison of the hippocampal group to the other two groups and the within-subject contrast for the linear effect of the number of landmarks:

$$\psi_A = (-1)\mu_{A_1} + (\tfrac{1}{2})\mu_{A_2} + (\tfrac{1}{2})\mu_{A_3},$$
$$\psi_{B_{\text{linear}}} = (-7)\mu_{B_1} + (-3)\mu_{B_2} + 1\mu_{B_3} + 9\mu_{B_4}.$$

We have already calculated the contrast variable $\widehat{\psi}_{ij}$ for $\psi_{B_{\text{linear}}}$ in Table 20.4. All we must do is to apply the one-way procedures from Chapter 4 to the group means and complete the analysis. The mean values of the contrast variable for the three lesion groups are 66.0, 140.0, and 139.0. Using Equation 4.4 (p. 68) and Equation 4.5 (p. 69),

$$\widehat{\psi}_{AB} = (-1)(66.0) + (\tfrac{1}{2})(140.0) + (\tfrac{1}{2})(139.0) = 73.5,$$

$$SS_{\psi_{AB}} = \frac{n\widehat{\psi}_{AB}^2}{\sum c_j^2} = \frac{(4)(73.5)^2}{1.5} = 14{,}406.0.$$

The contrast sum of squares has one degree of freedom, and the error term is S/A_ψ (interpreted here as $\psi_{B_{\text{linear}}}{\times}S/A$):

$$F = \frac{MS_{\psi_A{\times}\psi_B}}{MS_{B_{\text{linear}}{\times}S/A}} = \frac{14{,}406.0}{759.56} = 18.97.$$

It is significant ($F_{.05}(1,9) = 5.12$).

To interpret this interaction, we start with the three mean values of the linear contrast values $\psi_{B_{\text{linear}}}$. All three groups have a positive mean, indicating the more landmarks there were, the more seeds were recovered. The interaction contrast ψ_{AB} expresses a particular comparison of this effect, namely, one that contrasts groups a_2

and a_3 with the hippocampal group a_1. The fact that the interaction contrast was positive implies that the nonhippocampal groups exhibited a stronger relationship between the number of landmarks and seed recovery than the hippocampal group. Turning the interpretation the other way around, the effect of the hippocampal lesions was to reduce the extent to which the number of landmarks was able to aid in the recovery of the seeds.

Exercises

20.1. The $A \times B$ interaction in Problem 19.2 was significant. One useful way to study a significant interaction is by examining the simple effects.

a. Analyze the simple effect of the three radar displays for each of the test sessions.

b. As a follow-up analysis, use the data from the third session (level b_3) to test the pairwise comparison between a_1 and a_2.

20.2. Another approach to the interaction in Problem 19.2 is to analyze the simple effects of the three test sessions (factor B) for the individual radar displays (factor A).

a. Analyze the simple effect of sessions for each of the $a = 3$ radar displays.

b. As follow-up analyses, test the following simple comparisons, using the data from the group detecting targets on the amber radar screen (level a_3):

    i. A pairwise comparison between the first and third test sessions.

    ii. A complex comparison between the first test session and the last two.

20.3. Analyze the data in Table 20.2, and test the contrast with the coefficient set $\{-1, \frac{1}{2}, \frac{1}{2}\}$, treating it as a one-way design and using the formulas appropriate to such a design. Observe how the sums of squares are reduced, but the conclusions given in the text do not change.

20.4. Factor A in Problem 19.1 suggests a number of single-df comparisons that may be used to examine corresponding contrast-by-factor components.

a. Assess the significance of the $\psi_A \times B$ interaction involving the comparison between the groups that learned strongly related and weakly related words ($\psi_A = \mu_2 - \mu_3$).

b. Describe this interaction in words.

c. A natural next step is to determine which of the tests show a difference between the two groups. Test the significance of the difference on the fourth test (level b_4).

20.5. Now look at a factor-by-contrast interaction based on the repeated factor (factor B) in the data in Problem 19.1. Examine the change in recall between the first and the fourth tests, $\psi_B = \mu_4 - \mu_1$.

a. Assess the significance of this $A \times \psi_B$ interaction.

b. Describe this interaction in words.

c. Test this contrast as a simple comparison in the group that learned the unrelated words (a_1).

20.6. Suppose the researcher in Problem 19.1 had theoretical reasons to compare recall on the last two tests (b_3 and b_4). An interaction contrast is created by combining this comparison with a comparison for factor A. Test the significance of the interaction contrast created by crossing the comparison between the last two tests with the comparison in Problem 20.4 that contrasted highly related and weakly related words. Describe what you can conclude.

20.7. When analyzing the radar displays in Problem 19.2, many researchers would examine trend components. Let's concentrate on the linear trend component.

a. Test the significance of the factor-by-contrast interaction formed by crossing the linear component of factor B with all three levels of factor A.

b. Test the significance of the interaction contrasts formed by crossing the linear component with each of the following comparisons.

    i. A comparison between the two groups detecting targets on a black background (a_2 and a_3).

    ii. A comparison between the group detecting targets on a white background (a_1) with the average of the two groups detecting targets on a black background.

Part VI

HIGHER FACTORIAL DESIGNS AND OTHER EXTENSIONS

In previous chapters we introduced the concepts needed to analyze one-way and two-way factorial designs. Now we will look at how those principles are extended to studies with three or more factors. When finished, we will have the building blocks to analyze most varieties of the analysis of variance.

Higher-order designs are used for at least three distinct reasons. First, a multifactor design allows us to look at complex interactions involving several factors at once. Some studies are conducted specifically to look at these interactions (we will give an example in Section 21.2). Second, researchers frequently use a three-way design, say, as a way to combine several two-way designs without substantial cost. In such studies, the higher-order interactions are incidental to the original point. We noted in Part III that a two-factor design provides information on two main effects without increasing the number of subjects that are required; the same holds for higher designs. The third reason to add factors to an experiment is to control error. As we emphasized in our discussion of blocking (Section 11.5), including a factor that accounts for a portion of the subject variability makes the groups more homogeneous, decreases the size of the error term, and increases the power of the tests. If you look through the research literature for complex studies, you will find factors employed for all of these purposes. Not uncommonly, all three appear in a single experiment.

We begin our discussion in Chapters 21 and 22 with the three-way factorial design. In both chapters we emphasize the analysis of the between-subjects factorial, as it allows us to describe, with the fewest additional complications, the basic analysis of variance and how the analysis of simple effects and of interaction components gives a detailed picture of the results. In Chapter 23 we extend this discussion to three-way designs with one or more within-subject factors. Although this extension does not alter the type of questions that we might ask, it changes the way that error terms are selected for the various tests, as you saw for the two-factor designs in Chapters 16–20.

Chapters 24 and 25 introduce some conceptually new material. Throughout our earlier treatment, we have assumed that the levels of the factors were chosen in a systematic and meaningful way and that the design was a complete factorial, with measurements recorded for every combination of the factor levels. Each of these characteristics can be modified. In some experiments, the levels of a factor are not chosen systematically and are meaningful only as representatives of a much larger population. In a word-learning experiment, for example, a researcher might include several different lists of words to give an idea of the generality of the phenomenon— that is, to determine whether the same pattern of results is observed with the different lists. The list factor in this study is not interesting for what it tells the researcher about the specific lists, but for the information it gives about the extent to which other results may depend on the choice of list. As you will see, the proper analysis of a study involving this type of **random factor** requires a change in the error term for some of the F ratios. We consider the analysis of experiments with random factors in Chapter 24. Up to this point, we have assumed that all the substantive factors in a multifactor design are crossed—every level of one factor appears at every level of the others. In Chapter 25 we describe designs that include a **nested factor**, which is one for which *different* levels appear at each level of another factor. We had to wait until here to discuss these designs because nested factors are almost always also random. Our discussion in these two chapters refers to the two- and three-factor designs. However, the same issues apply to designs with more than three factors.

For the most part, you will use a computer when you analyze data from these designs. Hand calculation with larger designs is possible, but it is incredibly time consuming and a fertile ground for computational errors. Accordingly, we will place less emphasis on calculational formulas and more on the conceptual basis of the techniques and the approaches you will use with a computer.

You will find some of the material in these chapters, especially that involving the analytical analyses, to be complex and difficult. We do not expect that everything we write will be clear in a single reading. Facility with the techniques will really emerge only as you begin applying them to your own data. We expect that at that time, you will return to these chapters, both as a reference and as a guide.

21

The Three-Factor Design: The Overall Analysis of Variance

In our discussion of the one- and two-way designs, we separated the description of the overall analysis of variance from that of the analytical follow-up needed to interpret the results. We keep to this organization in our treatment of the three-factor design. This chapter describes the overall analysis; the next describes the subsidiary tests.

21.1 Components of the Three-Way Design

It is helpful to start by picturing the configuration of groups in a three-way factorial design. As you will recall, the groups in a one-factor design form a one-dimensional array, and those in a two-factor design form a rectangular array. Continuing with this geometrical representation, we view the three-way factorial as a rectangular solid in which each dimension corresponds to a factor and each cell to a group. Figure 21.1 illustrates this three-dimensional configuration for a design in which factor A has 3 levels, factor B has 4 levels, and factor C has 2 levels. The total design, then, has $abc = (3)(4)(2) = 24$ groups, each of which contains a separate sample of subjects. This particular design would be referred to as a $3 \times 4 \times 2$ factorial.

To be concrete, consider an extension of the two-factor experiment we described at the start of Section 13.1 (see Table 13.1, p. 268). That study concerned the effects of verbal feedback given during the acquisition of different types of learning material on memory tested one week later. Factor A was a feedback manipulation during the learning portion of the experiment: a control condition that received no verbal feedback (a_1) and two treatment conditions that received either positive or negative feedback (a_2 and a_3, respectively). Factor B was the types of learning material: low-frequency words with low emotional content (b_1), high-frequency words with low emotional content (b_2), and high-frequency words with high emotional content (b_3). The dependent variable was the number words that subjects recalled one week after learning. Now suppose a developmental factor is added to determine whether the

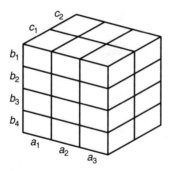

Figure 21.1: Geometrical representation of the data table in a three-way factorial design.

earlier results, obtained for fifth-grade students, extend to older subjects. Factor C is the age of the subjects: a fifth-grade group (c_1) and a group of high-school seniors (c_2). The researcher is interested in whether the effects that appear for the fifth-grade students also apply to the older students.

We can easily expand the notational system for the two-way design from Table 11.1 (p. 212) to accommodate the third factor by adding a fourth subscript l to designate the levels of factor C. Thus, we refer to the individual scores as Y_{ijkl}, where the subscript i represents the subjects within any given group, and the three subscripts j, k, and l represent the levels of factors A, B, and C, respectively. Table 21.1 gives a set of data such as might be obtained from this design.

Table 21.1: Number of words recalled for two age groups studying one of three different types of words and receiving one of three types of feedback.

	Fifth grade (c_1)			Seniors (c_2)		
	None	Pos.	Neg.	None	Pos.	Neg.
	(a_1)	(a_2)	(a_3)	(a_1)	(a_2)	(a_3)
	7	6	10	10	6	9
	7	8	8	8	9	10
Low F, Low E (b_1)	9	7	8	9	8	7
	10	9	6	7	7	7
	9	9	8	8	10	9
	7	6	7	7	6	8
	8	8	7	8	7	8
High F, Low E (b_2)	9	8	6	9	9	6
	10	9	9	9	9	9
	10	9	9	11	10	9
	7	3	2	6	6	6
	7	5	3	7	8	5
High F, High E (b_3)	10	3	4	8	6	7
	7	6	5	9	9	8
	9	5	5	9	8	9

Group Means and Marginal Means

The primary summary of a set of data such as Table 21.1 are the group means,

$$\bar{Y}_{jkl} = \frac{ABC_{jkl}}{n_{jkl}}, \text{ where } ABC_{jkl} = \sum_i Y_{ijkl}.$$

When the groups are the same size, as in the example, n_{jkl} in this formula is simply n. These means are given in the ABC **table of group means** in the upper part of Table 21.2. The interpretation of any set of data begins with these means. Figure 21.2 plots the cell means and provides an overall view of the results.

The three-way ABC table of group means can be reduced to simpler tables by averaging them over one or more of its factors. You are already familiar with this procedure in the two-factor design, where the two-way AB table of group means is averaged over the rows and columns to produce the marginal means for the two factors. Applying this notion to the three-factor design, we create the **two-way marginal means** by averaging the group means over one of the factors:

$$\bar{Y}_{AB_{jk}} = \frac{\sum_l \bar{Y}_{ABC_{jkl}}}{c}, \quad \bar{Y}_{AC_{jl}} = \frac{\sum_k \bar{Y}_{ABC_{jkl}}}{b}, \quad \text{and} \quad \bar{Y}_{BC_{kl}} = \frac{\sum_j \bar{Y}_{ABC_{jkl}}}{a}.$$

We give the results in the middle part of Table 21.2. There are three two-way tables, each corresponding to a face (i.e. a margin) of the cubic array of Figure 21.1. To take one example, the topmost mean on the left in the two-way marginal AB table is

$$\bar{Y}_{AB_{11}} = \frac{\bar{Y}_{ABC_{111}} + \bar{Y}_{ABC_{112}}}{c} = \frac{8.4 + 8.4}{2} = 8.4.$$

We find the **one-way marginal means** by averaging the group means $\bar{Y}_{ABC_{jkl}}$ across two factors:

$$\bar{Y}_{A_j} = \frac{\sum_{k,l} \bar{Y}_{ABC_{jkl}}}{bc}, \quad \bar{Y}_{B_k} = \frac{\sum_{j,l} \bar{Y}_{ABC_{jkl}}}{ac}, \quad \text{and} \quad \bar{Y}_{C_l} = \frac{\sum_{j,k} \bar{Y}_{ABC_{jkl}}}{ab}.$$

For example, the mean for all the control conditions (a_1), as shown in the one-way configuration on the left of Table 21.2, is

$$\bar{Y}_{A_1} = \frac{\bar{Y}_{ABC_{111}} + \bar{Y}_{ABC_{121}} + \bar{Y}_{ABC_{131}} + \bar{Y}_{ABC_{112}} + \bar{Y}_{ABC_{122}} + \bar{Y}_{ABC_{132}}}{bc}$$

$$= \frac{8.4 + 8.8 + 8.0 + 8.4 + 8.8 + 7.8}{(3)(2)} = 8.367.$$

We can also calculate these means by averaging either of the relevant two-way marginal means; for the example we just calculated,

$$\bar{Y}_{A_1} = \frac{\sum \bar{Y}_{AB_{1k}}}{b} = \frac{8.4 + 8.8 + 7.9}{3} = 8.367,$$

$$\bar{Y}_{A_1} = \frac{\sum \bar{Y}_{AC_{1l}}}{c} = \frac{8.400 + 8.333}{2} = 8.367.$$

When calculating by hand, it's a good idea to check your work by calculating the one-way marginal means with both formulas. You should verify a few other means from Table 21.2 if you are uncertain as to how they are calculated. Finally, the grand mean, $\bar{Y}_T = 7.600$, is calculated as the average of the group means in the three-way table or in any of the two-way and one-way tables—for example,

$$\bar{Y}_T = \frac{\sum \bar{Y}_{ABC_{jkl}}}{abc} = \frac{\sum \bar{Y}_{AB_{jk}}}{ab} = \frac{\sum \bar{Y}_{A_j}}{a}.$$

Table 21.2: Group means (upper) and marginal means (lower) for the recall scores in Table 21.1.

Group means $(\overline{Y}_{ABC_{jkl}})$

	Fifth grade (c_1)			Seniors (c_2)		
	None	Pos.	Neg.	None	Pos.	Neg.
	a_1	a_2	a_3	a_1	a_2	a_3
Low F, Low E (b_1)	8.4	7.8	8.0	8.4	8.0	8.4
High F, Low E (b_2)	8.8	8.0	7.6	8.8	8.2	8.0
High F, High E (b_3)	8.0	4.4	3.8	7.8	7.4	7.0

Two-way marginal means $(\overline{Y}_{AB_{jk}}, \overline{Y}_{AC_{jl}}, \text{and } \overline{Y}_{BC_{kl}})$

	b_1	b_2	b_3			c_1	c_2			c_1	c_2
a_1	8.4	8.8	7.9		a_1	8.400	8.333		b_1	8.067	8.267
a_2	7.9	8.1	5.9		a_2	6.733	7.867		b_2	8.133	8.333
a_3	8.2	7.8	5.4		a_3	6.467	7.800		b_3	5.400	7.400

One-way marginal means $(\overline{Y}_{A_j}, \overline{Y}_{B_k}, \text{and } \overline{Y}_{C_l})$

a_1	a_2	a_3		b_1	b_2	b_3		c_1	c_2
8.367	7.300	7.133		8.167	8.233	6.400		7.200	8.000

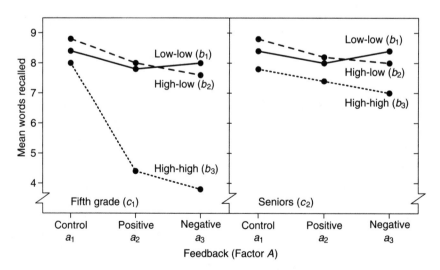

Figure 21.2: Plots of the cell means at the top of Table 21.2.

Effects and Hypothesis Tests

Consider again the two-way configurations of marginal means in Table 21.2. There are three such configurations, one for each pair of factors. From your knowledge of two-factor designs, you would expect to obtain information about the interaction of each pair of factors, $A{\times}B$, $A{\times}C$, and $B{\times}C$. You would also get information about the A, B, and C main effects from the one-way configurations at the bottom of Table 21.2. Each of the effects based on these marginal means may or may not be present, and each of them is tested in the analysis of variance. Thus, in a three-way design, each one-way set of marginal means determines a main effect, and each two-way set determines an interaction. In addition, there is a three-way interaction, which comes from the three-way table of group means. In all, the analysis of variance of a three-way factorial design with factors A, B, and C gives tests of seven terms:

$$A, \quad B, \quad C, \quad A{\times}B, \quad A{\times}C, \quad B{\times}C, \quad \text{and} \quad A{\times}B{\times}C$$

(or eight if you count the grand mean). Each of these effects is associated with a sum of squares and, ultimately, with an F ratio.

The Statistical Model and its Assumptions

The analysis of the three-way design is based on a linear model like the models for the one- and two-way designs (Equation 7.3, p. 133, and Equation 11.14, p. 225, respectively). In the three-way design, the linear model separates the score Y_{ijkl} into a mean for the group, μ_{jkl}, and an individual random error E_{ijkl}, and then replaces the group mean by the grand mean μ_T and an effect parameter for every term listed above. It differs from the simpler models only in the number of systematic terms it contains. Using the third Greek letter gamma to refer to the third factor C, the model is

$$Y_{ijkl} = \mu_{jkl} + E_{ijkl}$$
$$= \mu_T + \alpha_j + \beta_k + \gamma_l + (\alpha\beta)_{jk} + (\alpha\gamma)_{jl} + (\beta\gamma)_{kl} + (\alpha\beta\gamma)_{jkl} + E_{ijkl}. \quad (21.1)$$

The single-letter parameters α_j, β_k and γ_l express the treatment main effects of the three factors, the double-letter parameters $(\alpha\beta)_{jk}$, $(\alpha\gamma)_{jl}$, and $(\beta\gamma)_{kl}$ express the two-way interactions, and the triple-letter parameter $(\alpha\beta\gamma)_{jkl}$ expresses the three-way $A{\times}B{\times}C$ interaction. Each of these parameters derives from the underlying population mean or from lower-order effects. To take a few examples,

$$\alpha_j = \mu_j - \mu_T \quad \text{where} \quad \mu_j = \frac{1}{bc}\sum_{k,l}\mu_{jkl} \quad \text{and} \quad \mu_T = \frac{1}{abc}\sum\mu_{jkl}, \quad (21.2)$$

$$(\alpha\beta)_{jk} = (\mu_{jk} - \mu_T) - \alpha_j - \beta_k \quad \text{where} \quad \mu_{jk} = \frac{1}{c}\sum_l\mu_{jkl}, \quad (21.3)$$

$$(\alpha\beta\gamma)_{jkl} = (\mu_{jkl} - \mu_T) - \alpha_j - \beta_k - \gamma_l - (\alpha\beta)_{jk} - (\alpha\gamma)_{jl} - (\beta\gamma)_{kl}. \quad (21.4)$$

These interaction parameters are defined as the deviation of the marginal or cell mean from μ_T, with any lower-level effects subtracted (as we did for the two-factor model in Equation 11.13, p. 225). Each of the tests in the three-way analysis of variance refers to the null hypothesis that one type of parameter is zero.

Because the fundamental structure of the model is like that of the simpler designs, the assumptions that underlie it are the same. You still have to worry about the independence of the observations and about homogeneity of variance, but you do not need to be too concerned about other details of the specific distributional form, at least not if the sample size is large. You can apply our discussions in Chapter 7 and Sections 11.4 and 14.5 to the three-way between-subjects design or, for that matter, to larger factorial designs.

21.2 The Three-Way Interaction

The main effects and two-way interactions in a three-way design are interpreted in the ways we have discussed in earlier chapters. For example, the presence of a B main effect implies that the three means $\overline{Y}_{B_k}$ (in the lower part of Table 21.2) are not the same. Similarly, the presence of an $A \times B$ interaction indicates that the simple effects of one factor in the marginal tables of the $\overline{Y}_{AB}$ means change with the levels of the other factor. The most important new concept is the **three-way interaction**, also sometimes known as a **triple interaction** or a **second-order interaction**. It is distinctly more difficult to understand than the two-way interactions, so we will describe it and give an example before we turn to the analysis itself.

Simple Interactions

Although it is natural to think of the three-factor design as forming the three-dimensional configuration of groups in Figure 21.1, it is also useful to think of it as a series of two-factor experiments. You will recall from Chapter 10 that we could think of a two-way factorial as a series of one-way designs, one for each level of the other factor. We can do a similar thing with the three-way design. The three-factor design is treated as a series of two-factor designs, one for each level the third factor. For example, we can think of the design in Figure 21.1 as a pair of $A \times B$ studies, one at level c_1 and the other at level c_2, as shown in the top of Table 21.3. Taken together, these two studies contain the original data from the three-way table in Figure 21.1. We could equally well treat this design as a series of $A \times C$ experiments or a series of $B \times C$ experiments, as illustrated in the lower parts of Table 21.3. Each of these ways of viewing the ABC table places a different emphasis on particular factors of the design. Of course, however they are interpreted, the contents of the individual cells still come from the original ABC table of means.

Using the analysis principles for a two-way table, we could look at any one of the separate two-way tables in Table 21.3 to determine if it shows an interaction. We will refer to these as **simple interactions** (some authors call them **conditional interactions**). The two designs at the top of Table 21.3 give the simple $A \times B$ interaction at level c_1 and the simple $A \times B$ interaction at level c_2; the four designs in the middle give the simple $A \times C$ interactions at levels b_1, b_2, b_3, and b_4; and the three designs at the bottom give the simple $B \times C$ interactions at the three levels of a_j. These simple interactions are the building blocks from which the triple interaction is constructed.

The Three-Way Interaction

You will recall that a two-way interaction is present when the simple effects of one factor are not the same at all levels of the other factor. The three-way interaction is defined similarly, using the set of simple interactions in a three-way table. Suppose we represent the three-dimensional figure in Figure 21.1 as the pair of two-way AB

Table 21.3: Three ways to interpret the three-way $2 \times 4 \times 3$ factorial design in Figure 21.1.

Two $A \times B$ experiments at the different levels of factor C.

Four $A \times C$ experiments at the different levels of factor B.

Three $B \times C$ at the different levels of factor A.

tables at the top of Table 21.3. Each of these tables may or may not show a simple two-way interaction. The three-way interaction compares their particular magnitude and form:

> A three-way interaction is present when the simple interactions of two variables differ with the levels of the third variable.

When no interaction is present, the simple interactions are the same, and they also agree with two-way interaction in the two-way configuration of marginal means. When an interaction is present, at least two of the simple interaction effects are different, and they cannot all duplicate the interaction based on the two-way marginal means.

It is important to realize several things about this definition. First, when we talk about the size of a simple interaction, we are not speaking about some overall measure of effect size, such as omega squared. Instead, we are speaking about both its form *and* its magnitude—both aspects are important. The separate importance of these two aspects is illustrated by the fact that a three-way interaction can occur (1) when the simple interactions have the same size, say as measured by omega squared, but differ in their shape or form and (2) when they have the same form, but differ in their size. Second, the definition says nothing about whether the simple interactions are statistically significant. It is quite possible for a triple interaction to be present when both simple interactions are significant, when one is significant and one is not, or even when neither is significant. Third, the definition does not depend on which of the three representations in Table 21.3 we use. It doesn't matter whether we compare the simple $A \times B$ interaction at different levels of C, the simple $A \times C$ interaction at the levels of B, or the simple $B \times C$ interaction at the levels of A. If any one set reflects a three-way interaction, so do all the others.

An Example of a Three-Way Interaction

Three-way interactions are subtle. One way to acquire a feeling for them is to look at a concrete example. This illustration comes from an experiment reported by Petty, Cacioppo, and Heesacker (1981), who proposed that making a person actively think about an argument for or against a particular topic would lead to a corresponding change in attitude. The subjects were undergraduate students, and the issue in question was whether a comprehensive examination should be given to all undergraduates at the end of their senior year. The students read an editorial presenting eight arguments in favor of the exam and later filled out a questionnaire measuring their attitudes to the proposal. The study used a $2 \times 2 \times 2$ factorial design with three independent variables:

- Factor A was the *strength* of the arguments offered in favor of the exam, either *strong* or *weak* (a_1 and a_2, respectively).
- Factor B was the *involvement* of the students with the proposed examination, either *low* involvement (level b_1) when the students were told that the proposal was being offered by the president of a geographically distant university and that it would not take place for 10 years, or *high* involvement (level b_2) when they were told that their university president was considering the introduction of the examination in the next academic year.
- Factor C was the *style* in which each argument was summarized. In the *regular* style (level c_1) it ended with a simple summary (for example, "Thus, instituting a comprehensive exam would be an aid to those who seek admission to graduate and professional schools"), and in the *rhetorical* style (level c_2) it ended with a question to the reader (for example, "Don't you agree that ... ").

There were $n = 20$ students randomly assigned to the $abc = 8$ treatment groups. Among several response measures, all of which supported the same conclusion, was an 11-point rating scale (slightly modified for this example) on which +5 indicated that a student "agreed completely" with the proposed comprehensive exam, −5 indicated that a student "did not agree at all," and 0 was the point of ambivalence toward the proposal. Table 21.4 shows the group means, and they are plotted in Figure 21.3.

The main goal of this study was the triple interaction. To understand why this was the case, consider the independent variables strength and involvement for the regular condition (factors A and B at c_1). The authors predicted an $A \times B$ interaction: Strong arguments (a_1) were expected to produce attitudes more favorable to the proposal than the weak ones (a_2), but only for students who received the editorial that involved them with the issue (b_1). The authors reasoned that these students would pay closer attention to the arguments and be more influenced by them than the students who were less involved (b_2). Those students would show little difference in attitude. The means in the 2×2 table for c_1 on the left of Table 21.4 and Figure 21.3 show this pattern. The strength of the arguments had little effect for low-involvement students (0.04

Table 21.4: Agreement with a proposal for a comprehensive examination, as a function of the strength and style of the argument and the involvement of the raters (after Petty et al., 1981). From R. E. Petty, J. T. Cacioppo, and M. Heesacker, Effects of rhetorical questions on persuasion: A cognitive response analysis, Journal of Personality and Social Psychology, *1981, 40, 432–440. Copyright 1981 by the American Psychological Association. Adapted by permission.*

	Regular form (c_1)		Rhetorical form (c_2)	
	Low (b_1)	High (b_2)	Low (b_1)	High (b_2)
Strong (a_1)	0.04	0.75	0.61	0.05
Weak (a_2)	−0.10	−0.66	−0.46	−0.24

and −0.10 for strong and weak arguments, respectively), but the high-involvement students showed a much more substantial difference (0.75 and −0.66, respectively).

Now consider the interaction of argument strength and involvement at level c_2 of the style factor. Here the arguments were summarized with a rhetorical question. Petty et al. argued that the rhetorical style would influence the low- and high-involvement students differently. Students in the low-involvement condition would pay more attention to the arguments when the rhetorical questions forced them to consider their attitudes directly, but students in the high-involvement condition would be distracted by them. By this reasoning, the form of the $A \times B$ interaction at c_2 would be quite different from that at c_1. The low-involvement students would be *more* affected by the strength of the arguments than high-involvement students. The means in Table 21.4 and Figure 21.3 agree with this prediction: There is a larger difference in attitude for the low-involvement students (0.61 and −0.46) than for the high-involvement students (0.05 and −0.24).

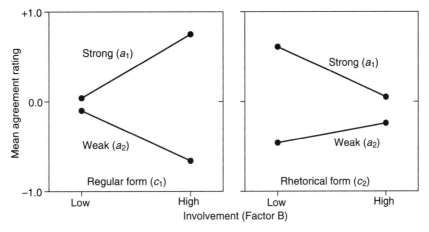

Figure 21.3: Plot of the data in Table 21.4. From R. E. Petty, J. T. Cacioppo, and M. Heesacker, Effects of rhetorical questions on persuasion: A cognitive response analysis, Journal of Personality and Social Psychology, *1981, 40, 432–440. Copyright 1981 by the American Psychological Association. Adapted by permission.*

Each the two $2{\times}2$ designs in Figure 21.3 displays an interaction of strength and involvement. In the full three-way design, these interactions are simple $A{\times}B$ interactions at c_k. They are in opposite direction—the high-involvement students show a larger difference between strong and weak arguments than the low-involvement students with the regular summaries, and the reverse with the rhetorical summaries. This difference implies a three-way interaction. We can find numerical support for this observation by calculating the value of an interaction contrast in each table. Recall from our discussion of the $2{\times}2$ design that the size of an interaction is measured by the contrast

$$\psi_{A{\times}B} = \mu_{11} - \mu_{21} - \mu_{12} + \mu_{22}$$

(Equations 11.15, p. 227). For the simple interaction in a $2{\times}2{\times}2$ design, this equation is

$$\psi_{A{\times}B \text{ at } c_l} = \mu_{11l} - \mu_{21l} - \mu_{12l} + \mu_{22l}. \tag{21.5}$$

Let's apply it to the simple $A{\times}B$ interactions for the means in Table 21.4:

$$\widehat{\psi}_{A{\times}B \text{ at } c_1} = \overline{Y}_{111} - \overline{Y}_{211} - \overline{Y}_{121} + \overline{Y}_{221}$$
$$= 0.04 - (-0.10) - 0.75 + (-0.66) = -1.27,$$

$$\widehat{\psi}_{A{\times}B \text{ at } c_2} = \overline{Y}_{112} - \overline{Y}_{212} - \overline{Y}_{122} + \overline{Y}_{222}$$
$$= 0.61 - (-0.46) - 0.05 + (-0.24) = 0.78.$$

The two values are substantial, suggesting the presence of a simple $A{\times}B$ interaction in both cases, and they are *opposite* in sign. Their difference implies that a three-way interaction is present. Just as with an interaction in a two-way design, a plot of the results helps to visualize the three-way interaction. The two displays in Figure 21.3 each reveal the presence of a simple interaction of strength and involvement and a comparison of them shows that they are reversed. This interaction can be plotted three ways, using the three types of simple interaction ($A{\times}B$ at c_l, $A{\times}C$ at b_k, and $B{\times}C$ at a_j; see Problem 21.5). You may find that one plot reveals the three-way interaction more effectively than the others.

Interpreting the Three-Way Interaction

When we considered the meaning of the interaction in a two-way design in Chapter 12, we pointed out that the *mathematical* definition of an interaction is not necessarily the best way to interpret its *substantive* meaning (see Section 12.3 and pages 253–255, especially Figure 12.3). The discussion of simple effects is often more understandable, even though they mix variability that mathematically belongs to one of the main effects with that of the interaction. In short, the interaction is the route to determining that the simple effects differ, but we have to look at the simple effects themselves to understand what the interaction means. The same thing holds for the three-way design: The three-way interaction tells us that the two simple interactions differ, but we have to look at them separately (and perhaps at the simple main effects that make them up) when we determine what the interaction means. Our goal is never to "interpret the three-way interaction," but to understand the entirety of the study in which the three-way interaction appears.

The experiment by Petty et al. shows this difference very clearly. Our discussion earlier centered around the two simple $A{\times}B$ interactions and the observation that

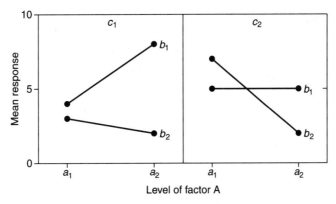

Figure 21.4: Means in a 2×2×2 study for which all three-factor interactions are present but there is no three-way interaction.

the simple interaction of argument strength (factor A) and issue involvement (factor B) was substantially different for the two types of argument summary (factor C). The comparison of these simple interactions made theoretical sense even though these effects combine variability from the $A{\times}B{\times}C$ interaction with that from the overall $A{\times}B$ interaction.

A complementary problem can arise when a three-way interaction is *not* present. Although the simple interactions then are mathematically identical, their substantive interpretations need not be the same. The situation is particularly confusing when all the two-way interactions are present. Under these circumstances, any of the two-way configurations cannot be understood without reference to the third factor, and you must interpret the pattern of means in the same way that you would were a three-factor interaction present. Figure 21.4 illustrates this point. There is no three-factor interaction in this figure, as we can verify by calculating the interaction contrast (Equation 21.5) for each simple interaction and observing that they are the same:

$$\widehat{\psi}_{A{\times}B \text{ at } c_1} = \overline{Y}_{111} - \overline{Y}_{211} - \overline{Y}_{121} + \overline{Y}_{221} = 4 - 8 - 3 + 2 = -5,$$

$$\widehat{\psi}_{A{\times}B \text{ at } c_2} = \overline{Y}_{112} - \overline{Y}_{212} - \overline{Y}_{122} + \overline{Y}_{222} = 5 - 5 - 7 + 2 = -5.$$

The values are the same, implying no three-way interaction. However, all two-way interactions are present. The immediate impression is that the two simple $A{\times}B$ interactions at c_l are different. At c_1, performance at level a_2 is substantially greater than at a_1 for b_1, but it is slightly lower for b_2; at c_2, factor A has no effect for b_1, but a_2 is much worse than a_1 for b_2. In most research settings, you would say that different processes are operating in the two panels. It would be a mistake to interpret the data using the marginal AB means, without considering the two simple AB tables at the levels of factor C. The upshot is that when you find that all the factors of a three-way (or higher) design are mutually involved in interactions, be it as three two-way interactions or a three-way interaction, you must turn to the analysis of analysis of simple interactions and simple effects to understand what is going on.

As these examples show, higher-order effects are not easy to understand. Anyone—the present authors emphatically included!—who has attempted to understand a three-way interaction (or three two-way interactions) has had to struggle to find a satisfactory way to think about it. There is no single set of rules that ensures a clear explanation. The overall significance tests help you to decide when you can simplify the picture, but they are limited guides. You should begin by looking at the two-way tables created by holding one factor fixed and treating them as if they were actual two-factor designs. What you do next depends on what these tables (and the tests of their effects) show. You may need to look at simple effects, simple interactions, or some combination of them. To get at the great richness of information in a three-factor study, you will need the type of analytical analysis we discuss in Chapter 22.

21.3   Computational Procedures

You will almost certainly use a computer to perform the brute numerical work when you analyze a three-factor design, and it is essential when the samples have different sizes and you need to use the general-linear-model approach (see Chapter 14). Nevertheless, it is instructive to look at the computational procedure. It shows the logic of the analysis, helps when examining summary data, and provides a set of checks that help you recognize errors in specifying your design to the program. Because many of the principles remain the same as in the one- and two-way designs, our presentation will be brief. We will start with the general characteristics of the design, describe some specifically computational matters, then return to our numerical example. Because our intent is to show the conceptual basis of the analysis, we will assume equal samples of n subjects in each group.

Sources of Variability and Degrees of Freedom

The first step in working through any analysis is to determine the structure of the design—the sources of variability, how the sums of squares are partitioned, and the degrees of freedom associated with each source.

We listed the steps used to determine the effects in a two-factor design in Table 11.2 (p. 214). We can apply them here:

1. *List the factors.* They are A, B, C, S.

2. *Add the interactions corresponding to any combination of crossed factors to the list.* In this design, all the experimental factors are crossed (each level of one appears at all levels of the others), but S is not crossed with any other factor. Our augmented list is

$$A, \quad B, \quad C, \quad A{\times}B, \quad A{\times}C, \quad B{\times}C, \quad A{\times}B{\times}C, \quad S.$$

3. *Include the nesting.* In this design, only factor S is nested. There are different subjects at each combination of the three design factor, so we write the last effect in the list as S/ABC.

Each of these effects has its associated degrees of freedom. These are obtained from the rules in Table 11.3 (p. 215). The derivations are exactly like those for the two-factor design we presented when we introduced these rules (Table 11.5), except that this design includes one more factor (A, B, and C, instead of A and B). We give the results in Table 21.5. You can check that the degrees of freedom for the sources we

Table 21.5: Degrees of freedom and computational formulas for the three-factor between-subjects design.

Source	df	Sum of squares
A	$a-1$	$[A]-[T]$
B	$b-1$	$[B]-[T]$
C	$c-1$	$[C]-[T]$
$A{\times}B$	$(a-1)(b-1)$	$[AB]-[A]-[B]+[T]$
$A{\times}C$	$(a-1)(c-1)$	$[AC]-[A]-[C]+[T]$
$B{\times}C$	$(b-1)(c-1)$	$[BC]-[B]-[C]+[T]$
$A{\times}B{\times}C$	$(a-1)(b-1)(c-1)$	$[ABC]-[AB]-[AC]-[BC]$ $+[A]+[B]+[C]-[T]$
S/ABC	$abc(n-1)$	$[Y]-[ABC]$
Total	$abcn-1$	$[Y]-[T]$

derived in the two-factor design are the same, and that those involving factor C are determined by the same rules. As is appropriate, the individual degrees of freedom add up to df_T, so we have not omitted anything in this listing of the sources.

The Computational Details

The computational aspects of the three-factor between-subjects design are also similar to those of the two-factor design. Table 21.5 also shows the formulas obtained from the degrees-of-freedom statements using the rules in Table 11.4 (p. 216). If you compare them to those in Table 11.5, you will see that the principal difference is the addition of factors involving factor C. You will notice that, very conveniently, the formulas for the main effects and two-way interactions are identical to their forms in the one-way and two-way designs. For example, the equation $SS_A = [A]-[T]$ is the same regardless of whether it applies to a one-way, a two-way, or a higher design.[1]

The bracket terms are determined by the rules in Table 11.4. When working with the means, you first locate the table of means with the same letters as in the bracket term you wish to calculate, square all its entries and add them up, then multiply the sum by the number of scores that contributed to each of the means. We illustrate these calculations in our numerical example below. When working with the sums, you perform the same operations on the tables of sums, except that you divide the sum of the squared quantities by the number of scores that contribute to each of them.

The rest of the analysis follows procedures we have described repeatedly for the other designs. Mean squares are obtained by dividing each sum of squares by its corresponding degrees of freedom. All the tests in this design are of between-subjects effects, so they all use the same error term, $MS_{S/ABC}$.

---

[1]With many computer programs, you can calculate the sums of squares by entering the means as if they were data, analyzing this "$n = 1$" experiment, and multiplying the resulting sums of squares by the actual value of n. This trick is handy when you have the means, perhaps from a summary of an analysis, but lack the original scores.

A Numerical Example

Our numerical example is based on the experiment in Tables 21.1 and 21.2. The fifth graders (on the left in Figure 21.2) show the interaction between the feedback variable (factor A) and the types of words (factor B) that we examined in Chapter 13. Both positive and negative verbal feedback administered during learning have a negative effect on the memory for words of high emotional content (b_3) and little if any effect on the memory for words of low emotional content (b_1 and b_2). When we look at the high-school seniors in the right-hand panel, we find that feedback has at most a small effect on memory. The interaction that appeared for the younger subjects is absent here. Because the interaction of factors A and B is not the same at both levels of the factor C, we might expect to find a three-way interaction.

The Analysis of Variance. Our first step in the analysis of variance would be to calculate the group and marginal means from the data in Table 21.1 (already given in Table 21.2). We then square the entries in each table of means, sum them, convert them to bracket terms. To take one example, starting with the table of the factor A means $\bar{Y}_{A_j}$,

$$\sum \bar{Y}_{A_j}^2 = 8.367^2 + 7.300^2 + 7.133^2 = 174.176,$$

$$[A] = bcn \sum \bar{Y}_{A_j}^2 = (3)(2)(5)(174.176) = 5{,}225.280.$$

The other bracket terms are calculated similarly:

$$\sum \bar{Y}_{B_k}^2 = 175.442, \qquad [B] = acn \sum \bar{Y}_{B_k}^2 = 5{,}263.260,$$

$$\sum \bar{Y}_{C_l}^2 = 115.840, \qquad [C] = abn \sum \bar{Y}_{C_l}^2 = 5{,}212.800,$$

$$\sum \bar{Y}_{AB_{jk}}^2 = 530.480, \qquad [AB] = cn \sum \bar{Y}_{AB_{jk}}^2 = 5{,}304.800,$$

$$\sum \bar{Y}_{AC_{jl}}^2 = 349.884, \qquad [AC] = bn \sum \bar{Y}_{AC_{jl}}^2 = 5{,}248.260,$$

$$\sum \bar{Y}_{BC_{kl}}^2 = 352.924, \qquad [BC] = an \sum \bar{Y}_{BC_{kl}}^2 = 5{,}293.860,$$

$$\sum \bar{Y}_{ABC_{jkl}}^2 = 1{,}070.800, \qquad [ABC] = n \sum \bar{Y}_{ABC_{jkl}}^2 = 5{,}354.000.$$

The last two bracket terms are based on the grand mean and the raw scores:

$$[T] = abcn\bar{Y}_T^2 = (3)(3)(2)(5)(7.600^2) = 5{,}198.400 \quad \text{and} \quad [Y] = \sum Y^2 = 5{,}490.$$

With the bracket terms in hand, we use the computational formulas in Table 21.5 to find the sums of squares. These values, with the mean squares and F ratios, are in Table 21.6. The three main effects and the $B \times C$ interaction are significant; the other interactions are not.

Interpreting the Results

The fact that only one of the interactions is significant makes our the results easier to interpret. First, we notice that although the feedback factor (factor A) has a substantial main effect, it does not participate in any interactions. Its effects are reasonably consistent over the other factors, so the marginal means are representative of its effects. You can see in Figure 21.2 that the ordering of the three feedback conditions is the same for each combination of the other two factors. Word type (factor B) and age

Table 21.6: Analysis of variance table for the data in Table 21.1.

Source	SS	df	MS	F
Feedback (A)	26.880	2	13.440	7.11*
Word type (B)	64.860	2	32.430	17.17*
Grade (C)	14.400	1	14.400	7.62*
$A \times B$	14.660	4	3.665	1.94
$A \times C$	8.580	2	4.290	2.27
$B \times C$	16.200	2	8.100	4.29*
$A \times B \times C$	10.020	4	2.505	1.33
S/ABC	136.000	72	1.889	
Total	291.600	89		

* $p < .05$

group (factor C) both have significant main effects, but the significant interaction indicates we must be cautious about interpreting these main effects. A look at the $\overline{Y}_{BC}$ marginal means in Table 21.2 tells us that the negative effect of the emotional words on memory is much greater for the younger children than for the older ones. Figure 21.5 summarizes the significant effects from the study. We have drawn this figure with the ordinate extending all the way to zero (compare it with Figure 21.2), which is a useful way to give a feeling for the absolute size of the effects.

The lack of a significant three-way interaction is a little disappointing, as we had expected the fifth graders and the seniors to differ. We should not conclude that the same simple $A \times B$ interaction is present at each level of C, however. For one thing, that would be to accept a null hypothesis; for another, the test of the interaction is an omnibus test and is less specific than the question that generated the study. In Section 13.2, we found an interaction for the fifth graders in which the difference between the control and combined feedback conditions was larger for the words of high emotional content than for the words of low emotional content. We will address this specific effect as part of the three-way interaction with the analytical procedures in the next chapter.

21.4 Effect Size, Sample Size, and Power

Most of the material on effect size and power described for the two-factor design in Sections 11.6 and 11.7 applies directly to the three-factor design. This section, therefore, is largely review. Only in our discussion of effect sizes will we encounter anything new.

Effect Sizes

To construct a measure of effect size in a factorial design, we must decide what variation should be used as the background for the effect. In the two-factor designs, we distinguished between *complete* statistics, which used all the variability, and *partial* statistics, which used only the effect and error variability. Standards as to what to report are not well established. We would argue that the partial statistics are most appropriate when the *other* factors in the design are experimental—i.e. included in

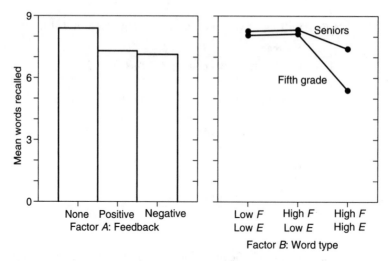

Figure 21.5: Plots of the A and B×C effects for the scores in Table 21.1.

the design to look at new effects—and complete measures are appropriate when the other factors are created as blocking factors used to reduce the variability. However, you won't find full consistency here.

Partial Effect Size.   Suppose we are trying to find the effect size for factor A. When factors B and C are experimental factors, as in our numerical example, their magnitudes (or that of their interactions) should not affect the effect size for factor A. Here, a partial statistic is appropriate. Based on population values, the partial ω^2 statistic is given by Equation 11.21:

$$\omega^2_{\langle\text{effect}\rangle} = \frac{\sigma^2_{\text{effect}}}{\sigma^2_{\text{effect}} + \sigma^2_{\text{error}}}, \tag{21.6}$$

where σ^2_{effect} = average sum of squared parameters from the linear model,
σ^2_{error} = error variance for this effect.

When estimates from another study are needed, we use Equation 11.22:

$$\widehat{\omega}^2_{\langle\text{effect}\rangle} = \frac{df_{\text{effect}}(F_{\text{effect}} - 1)}{df_{\text{effect}}(F_{\text{effect}} - 1) + N}, \tag{21.7}$$

where N is the total number of subjects in the study (here $abcn$). As in Equations 11.23 and 11.24, you can also calculate the correlation ratio R^2 by replacing σ^2 with a sum of squares in Equation 21.6 or $(F - 1)$ with F and N by df_{error} in Equation 21.7. Many computer programs report partial R^2 as their measure of effect size.

Because our example does not include any blocking factors, the partial measures are the appropriate way to summarize the effects. The size of the main effect of feedback, estimated from Equation 21.7, is

$$\widehat{\omega}^2_{\langle A\rangle} = \frac{(a - 1)(F_A - 1)}{(a - 1)(F_A - 1) + N} = \frac{(3 - 1)(7.11 - 1)}{(3 - 1)(7.11 - 1) + 90} = \frac{12.22}{102.22} = 0.120.$$

The presence of the substantial $B \times C$ interaction makes the size of the other two main effects, word type or grade level, difficult to interpret in isolation. The effect of word type, for example, is much larger for the younger subjects than for the older ones, so an average effect size based on the main effect is misleading. It makes more sense to treat these outcomes as simple effects, as we will do in the next chapter. We would certainly want to measure the size of the significant $B \times C$ interaction of emotionality and grade:

$$\widehat{\omega}^2_{\langle B \times C \rangle} = \frac{(b-1)(c-1)(F_{B \times C} - 1)}{(b-1)(c-1)(F_{B \times C} - 1) + N}$$

$$= \frac{(3-1)(2-1)(4.29 - 1)}{(3-1)(2-1)(4.29 - 1) + 90} = \frac{6.58}{96.58} = 0.068.$$

We could also calculate the size of the three-way interaction:

$$\widehat{\omega}^2_{\langle A \times B \times C \rangle} = \frac{(a-1)(b-1)(c-1)(F_{A \times B \times C} - 1)}{(a-1)(b-1)(c-1)(F_{A \times B \times C} - 1) + N}$$

$$= \frac{(3-1)(3-1)(2-1)(1.33 - 1)}{(3-1)(3-1)(2-1)(1.33 - 1) + 90} = \frac{1.32}{91.32} = 0.014.$$

Although not significant, it appears to be a small effect. We will use this information when we consider sample sizes in the next section.

Complete Effect Size. The complete effect size is appropriate when the other two factors in the design are both blocking factors, so that they are part of the intrinsic variation of the factor. Equation 11.18 gives the population values:

$$\omega^2_{\text{effect}} = \frac{\sigma^2_{\text{effect}}}{\sigma^2_{\text{total}}} = \frac{\sigma^2_{\text{effect}}}{\sum \sigma^2 + \sigma^2_{\text{error}}}, \tag{21.8}$$

where the sum $\sum \sigma^2$ includes all the effects and interactions in the design (i.e. σ^2_A through $\sigma^2_{A \times B \times C}$). The estimate follows Equation 11.20:

$$\widehat{\omega}^2_{\text{effect}} = \frac{df_{\text{effect}}(F_{\text{effect}} - 1)}{\sum [(df)(F - 1)] + N}, \tag{21.9}$$

where again the sum is over the seven systematic effects. Although the complete statistics are not meaningful for our current example (all three independent variables are research factors), it is interesting to compare $\widehat{\omega}_A$ with the partial value $\widehat{\omega}^2_{\langle A \rangle} = 0.120$. From Equation 21.9,

$$\widehat{\omega}^2_A = \frac{df_A(F_A - 1)}{df_A(F_A - 1) + df_B(F_B - 1) + \cdots + df_{A \times B \times C}(F_{A \times B \times C} - 1) + N}$$

$$= \frac{(2)(7.11 - 1)}{(2)(7.11 - 1) + (2)(17.17 - 1) + \cdots + (2)(4.29 - 1) + (4)(1.33 - 1) + 90}$$

$$= \frac{12.22}{65.38 + 90} = 0.079.$$

Including all the effects as part of the background variability substantially reduces the magnitude of the effect.

Semipartial Effect Size. The partial and complete effect sizes are used when the other two factors in the design are either both experimental or both blocking, respectively. What if your design contains one of each? If you follow our guidelines to include sources of variation associated with the effect and the blocking factor, but not those associated with the experimental factors, then you need a mixed or **semipartial** ω^2. This measure is constructed by excluding from the sums in Equations 21.8 and 21.9 any terms that involve the experimental factor. For example, when factor B is a blocking factor and factor C is experimental, you would exclude the terms containing factor C, namely C, $A \times C$, $B \times C$, and $A \times B \times C$. Without worrying about establishing a formal notation, the result is

$$\text{semipartial } \omega_A^2 = \frac{\sigma_A^2}{\sigma_A^2 + \sigma_B^2 + \sigma_{A \times B}^2 + \sigma_{S/ABC}^2},$$

in population terms, and as an estimate from the data of an experiment, it is

$$\text{semipartial } \widehat{\omega}_A^2 = \frac{df_A(F_A - 1)}{df_A(F_A - 1) + df_B(F_B - 1) + df_{A \times B}(F_{A \times B} - 1) + N}.$$

Note that factor C does not appear in either equation.

Sample-Size Calculations

In Section 11.7 we described two ways to determine sample size, one based on population values, the other on estimates (Equations 11.25, p. 236). These approaches are completely general, and they apply to the three-way design without change. When reasonable guesses at prospective population parameters are available, the total number of subjects needed for a study is:

$$N = \frac{\phi_{\text{effect}}^2 (df_{\text{effect}} + 1)\sigma_{\text{error}}^2}{\sigma_{\text{effect}}^2}. \tag{21.10}$$

To find the individual group sizes n, divide N by the number of groups (here abc). If the result is fractional, use the next largest integer. When working from a target experiment, the estimates are based on the partial effect size regardless of whether the other factors in the study are experimental or blocking:

$$N = \phi_{\text{effect}}^2 (df_{\text{effect}} + 1)\frac{1 - \omega_{\langle\text{effect}\rangle}^2}{\omega_{\langle\text{effect}\rangle}^2}. \tag{21.11}$$

There are actually seven different values for N (and, consequently, n) that could be found using either of these equations, one for each systematic effect in the design. Ideally, you would use the largest of these to plan your experiment. All the other effects would then have at least your desired power. However, planning is rarely, if ever, so complete. Typically, only a few effects are well enough established to be used. Moreover, the significance of certain effects are not of particular interest, even though they are part of the analysis. For example, a researcher may decide to include gender as a factor out of curiosity as to whether it interacts with some other factor, but without any presupposition as to whether any effects are present. The outcome of these tests is incidental to the success or failure of the study, so they do not figure into the planning of sample size. The explicit tests of blocking factors, and especially their interactions, are also irrelevant.

Our numerical example provides an illustration that uses the three-way interaction. When we discussed the analysis of variance at the end of Section 21.3, we noted the importance of the three-factor interaction, even though it was not significant. We might want to replicate the study with more subjects and greater power. Because this interaction would be the primary motivation for the replication, we would use it, not the other effects, to determine the sample size. We estimated the size of the interaction earlier in this section to be $\widehat{\omega}^2_{\langle A \times B \times C \rangle} = 0.014$. Going into the power table for $df_{A \times B \times C} = 4$ in Appendix A.7 (and knowing that we will need well more than 90 subjects overall), we find that a power of 80 percent implies a noncentrality parameter of $\phi_{A \times B \times C} \approx 1.6$. Then, using Equation 21.11, we obtain

$$N = \phi^2_{A \times B \times C}(df_{A \times B \times C} + 1) \frac{1 - \omega^2_{\langle A \times B \times C \rangle}}{\omega^2_{\langle A \times B \times C \rangle}}$$

$$= (1.6^2)(4 + 1) \frac{1 - 0.014}{0.014} = (12.80) \frac{0.986}{0.014} = 901.49.$$

This projected sample size is quite large and may exceed the researcher's resources. There are several ways to reduce its demands. One is to strengthen the manipulation so that the effect is larger. For example, using a longer list of words might increase the difference between groups. Another is to reduce the uncontrolled variability of the scores, perhaps by introducing a blocking factor or a covariate, or perhaps by using a more homogeneous sample of subjects. Conducting the study as a within-subject or mixed design (if feasible) would also decrease the unexplained variability. A third approach is to focus the study on the most critical aspects of the results. As we will see in the next chapter, most of the effect involves two reinforcement conditions (feedback—either positive or negative—and no feedback) and two types of words (low and high emotional content). If the study were reformulated with just these levels, it would be a 2×2×2 design and require fewer than half as many subjects as the original 3×3×2 design.

Power

The power of a three-factor design to detect a particular effect is calculated in the same way as in the two-way design. Equations 11.26 (p. 238) are used to translate a variability estimate σ^2_{effect} or a partial effect size $\omega^2_{\langle \text{effect} \rangle}$ into a value of ϕ that can be referred to the power charts:

$$\phi^2_{\text{effect}} = \frac{N \sigma^2_{\text{effect}}}{(df_{\text{effect}} + 1)\sigma^2_{\text{error}}} = \frac{N \omega^2_{\langle \text{effect} \rangle}}{(df_{\text{effect}} + 1)(1 - \omega^2_{\langle \text{effect} \rangle})}. \tag{21.12}$$

When you have data from an actual experiment, simply estimate $\widehat{\omega}_{\langle \text{effect} \rangle}$ with Equation 21.7 and use the second part of Equations 21.12. When you have means, you use them to calculate σ^2_{effect}. First, find values for the parameters of the linear model using Equations 21.2, 21.3, 21.4, or their equivalents for the other factors, as illustrated on page 237. Then combine the parameters into a variance; for example

$$\sigma^2_A = \frac{1}{a}\sum \alpha^2_i \quad \text{and} \quad \sigma^2_{A \times B} = \frac{1}{ab}\sum (\alpha\beta)^2_{ij}.$$

Finally, insert this variance, along with an estimate of σ^2_{error}, into the first part of Equations 21.12 to obtain the noncentrality ϕ. We illustrated these calculations on page 239.

Exercises

21.1. This exercise provides practice identifying three-way interactions. The table below gives means from 10 three-way $2 \times 2 \times 2$ factorial experiments (assume that they are without error). For each set of means, indicate which effects—main effects, two-way interactions, and three-way interactions are present. When can the main effects be interpreted unambiguously?

	a_1 b_1 c_1	a_1 b_1 c_2	a_1 b_2 c_1	a_1 b_2 c_2	a_2 b_1 c_1	a_2 b_1 c_2	a_2 b_2 c_1	a_2 b_2 c_2
Examples								
1	1	1	1	1	3	3	3	3
2	2	2	1	1	3	3	2	2
3	3	2	2	1	4	3	3	2
4	1	1	3	3	3	3	1	1
5	1	2	2	3	2	3	1	2
6	2	0	1	1	4	2	3	3
7	2	4	1	3	0	3	1	4
8	2	3	1	4	0	4	1	3
9	2	2	1	1	4	4	3	4
10	1	0	2	3	2	3	1	0

21.2. If you have access to a computer program for the analysis of variance, apply it to the scores in Table 21.1 to duplicate the analysis in Table 21.6.

21.3. A school system is considering adopting one of three supplementary workbooks designed to improve the spelling ability of third-grade children (factor A). Over a four-week period, children completed the lessons in the workbooks as homework that was collected and graded daily. At the end of the four weeks, they were given one of three 60-word spelling tests—words from the fourth-grade level (b_1), third-grade level (b_2), or second-grade level (b_3). A total of 36 girls (c_1) and 36 boys (c_2) were randomly assigned in equal numbers to the $ab = (3)(3) = 9$ conditions. The number of errors each child made on the spelling test is given below:

	a_1 b_1	a_1 b_2	a_1 b_3	a_2 b_1	a_2 b_2	a_2 b_3	a_3 b_1	a_3 b_2	a_3 b_3
c_1	7	2	4	10	4	7	13	9	8
	4	4	3	7	6	4	10	8	5
	5	3	0	6	3	5	13	9	6
	6	3	3	8	5	5	8	10	6
c_2	7	2	1	6	1	1	12	7	7
	5	3	3	5	3	3	13	6	7
	5	4	2	5	4	3	11	7	4
	6	1	2	6	5	0	12	6	6

a. Find and plot the means in an appropriate way.

b. Conduct an analysis of variance. Save your calculations for Problem 22.3.

c. Given the outcome of the analysis, to what sources of variance would you now pay close attention?

d. Estimate partial omega squared for the significant effects. Save this information for Problem 22.3.

21.4. The educational psychologist conducting the research in Problem 21.3 is concerned about the fact that the three-way interaction was not significant. What new sample size would he need to detect this interaction (if it is present) at a power of .80?

21.5. We presented the experiment by Petty et al. as an example of a three-way interaction (see pages 472–474).

a. The plot the group means in Figure 21.3 shows the AB configurations at the two levels of C. This plot emphasizes the simple interactions of strength (A) and involvement (B) and how they change at the different levels of factor C. The three-way interaction is visible whichever set of simple interactions you may plot. Plot the means as AC configurations at the levels of B and as BC configurations at the levels of A.

b. In all three plots (the two here and the one in Figure 21.3), you have a choice as to which variable to place on the abscissa. Although these plots contain the same means, one arrangement is often more effective and informative than other. Replot each of these graphs with the other variable on the abscissa and consider their relative effectiveness. (Petty et al. plotted the BC configurations with factor C on the abscissa.)

c. Calculate the sums of squares for the analysis of variance using the group means from Table 21.4, which are based on $n = 20$ subjects each.

d. You need an error term to complete the analysis of variance. Although Petty et al. did not report an error term for this analysis, they did report that $F = 29.83$ for the main effect of factor A (strength of argument). You can calculate the value of $MS_{S/ABC}$ from this statistic by solving the equation $F_{effect} = MS_{effect}/MS_{error}$ to give

$$MS_{error} = MS_{effect}/F_{effect}.$$

Calculate the value of $MS_{S/ABC}$, and complete the analysis of variance.

22

The Three-Factor Design: Analytical Analysis

When only the main effects in a three-factor design are significant, we can approach the analysis more or less as we did with a one-way design, looking separately at each of the main effects. However, when several interaction effects are present—and especially the three-way interaction—then the task of relating the various patterns of means to interpretable phenomena can be quite difficult. Even more than for the two-way design, there can be no blueprint for a successful interpretation. We will describe several approaches and suggest when they are applicable. You will often need more than one of them, but rarely all, in a single study.

Designs with three or more factors are typically analyzed by computer. Nevertheless, you may sometimes find that the analytical effect you want to test is difficult or confusing to specify to the program. You may need to supplement its work with some hand calculation. Because you will be starting out from a computer analysis, our discussion below is based on the cell means, which are most direct for secondary calculation.

22.1 Overview of the Analytical Analysis

There are very many analytical effects that might be tested in a three-way design. In any particular study, only some of these will provide useful information. To avoid confusion (or perhaps in spite of it), we will survey the types of effects and how they come about before we turn to the technical matters of how they are tested.

Figure 22.1 illustrates some of the analytical effects involving factor A in a three-factor design. At the upper-left is a $4 \times 4 \times 3$ ABC table of group means $\overline{Y}_{ABC_{jkl}}$, drawn as a rectangular solid with factor A along the vertical axis. This three-way table can be reduced to a two-way AB table in two ways. One possibility is to *average over factor C*, producing the marginal AB table of means $\overline{Y}_{AB_{jk}}$ shown at the lower left; each cell in this table contains cn observations, and it is functionally equivalent to a two-factor design. The other possibility is to *select one level of factor C* (say, c_2) and to form the AB table of group means $\overline{Y}_{ABC_{jk2}}$ shown at the right; each cell in this table contains n observations, and it is also equivalent to a two-factor design.

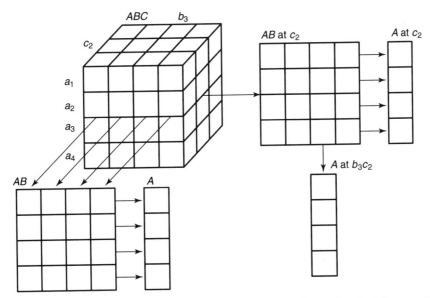

Figure 22.1: The variety of analytical effects that can be extracted from a three-way design. Not shown are the contrasts and contrast interactions that are part of any effect with more than one degree of freedom.

In the figure, selecting (or extracting) is indicated by a single arrow and combining (or averaging) by multiple arrows. Both AB tables of means provide the data for an $A \times B$ interaction, but they differ in their meaning. More specifically, the marginal AB table provides the information for a test of the overall $A \times B$ interaction in the standard analysis described in Chapter 21. The AB table at c_2, on the other hand, yields the test for a simple interaction—the $A \times B$ interaction based on the means at this particular level of factor C. Which of these AB tables is the most useful depends on the outcome of the standard analysis.

We can extract one-way effects from each of these two-way tables, just as we extract them from the two-way table of an actual two-factor design. For example, both tables produce information about *marginal effects*, obtained by combining the means over one of the factors; these are represented for factor A in the figure by the multiple arrows to the right of each AB table. For the marginal AB table, averaging over factor B produces a one-way table containing the marginal means $\overline{Y}_{A_j}$, while for the simple AB table at c_2, it produces a one-way table containing the marginal means $\overline{Y}_{AC_{j2}}$. The first marginal table expresses the A main effect, and the second expresses the simple effect of factor A at a particular level of factor C (here c_2). Both AB tables can be sliced horizontally or vertically to create additional one-way tables. With reference to factor A, the marginal AB table yields a one-way table for each level of factor B; these one-way tables express the simple effects of factor A at b_k—the same type of simple effects we obtained from an actual two-factor design in Chapter 12. The simple AB table at c_2 yields a set of one-way tables that also express the simple effects of factor A, but in this case at a particular combination of the levels for

Table 22.1: *Types of A effect and contrasts that are testable in a three-factor design. Numbers in parentheses indicate the page on which the test is discussed.*

Effect	Contrasts	
A	ψ_A (p. 496)	
A at c_l (p. 497)	ψ_A at c_l (p. 497)	
A at $b_k c_l$ (p. 493)	ψ_A at $b_k c_l$ (p. 493)	
$A \times B$	$\psi_A \times B$ (p. 498)	$\psi_A \times \psi_B$ (p. 499)
$A \times B$ at c_l (p. 491)	$\psi_A \times B$ at c_l (p. 494)	$\psi_A \times \psi_B$ at c_l (p. 495)
$A \times B \times C$	$\psi_A \times B \times C$ (p. 504)	$\psi_A \times \psi_B \times C$ (p. 504)
	$\psi_A \times \psi_B \times \psi_C$ (p. 502)	

the other two factors—the simple effect of A at $b_3 c_2$. Some authors (e.g., Winer et al., 1991) refer to this effect as a **simple simple effect**; but, to avoid excess terminology, we will just call it a simple effect and make clear that it is conditioned on the specified values of two factors. A sketch like Figure 22.1 is an excellent way to work out the effects in a complex design, and to decide which of them should be tested.

Figure 22.1 does not show the full array of effects that are possible in a three-way design. We have omitted many testable effects that are functionally equivalent to those we do show. Still concentrating on factor A, there are the simple effects of A at b_k (equivalent to A at c_l), the $A \times C$ interaction (equivalent to $A \times B$), and the simple $A \times C$ interaction at b_k (equivalent to $A \times B$ at c_l). Moreover, similar diagrams apply to the B and C effects. We have also emphasized the overall effects. For any single-factor effect with more than one degree of freedom, contrasts could be constructed; for any two-factor effect, interaction components. Each of these tests a more precise hypothesis than the overall effect.

Table 22.1 summarizes the types of contrasts and interaction components that are available in a three-way design. On the left, we list in separate rows the different effects that pertain to factor A and on the right, the contrast effects obtained from them. The first three rows contain effects based on the means involving factor A alone. The contrasts that form part of these effects are a main contrast (ψ_A), a simple contrast in the marginal AC means at a level of factor C (ψ_A at c_l), and a simple contrast for a particular combination of the other two factors (ψ_A at $b_k c_l$). Although all three contrasts involve factor A alone, they differ in the source of the means—the marginal means $\overline{Y}_{A_j}$, the two-way marginal means $\overline{Y}_{AC_{jl}}$, and the individual group means $\overline{Y}_{ABC_{jkl}}$, respectively.

The next two rows are analyses that involve means based jointly on factors A and B. The first of these is the $A \times B$ interaction in the marginal AB table of means $\overline{Y}_{AB_{jk}}$. Applying a contrast ψ_A to these means results in either a contrast-by-factor interaction $\psi_A \times B$ or a two-factor interaction contrast $\psi_A \times \psi_B$. The second is the simple two-way interaction $A \times B$ at c_l in the AB table of group means $\overline{Y}_{ABC_{jkl}}$ at c_l. A detailed analysis of this simple interaction might involve testing the interaction of ψ_A with factor B at c_l or the interaction contrast $\psi_A \times \psi_B$ at c_l.

Finally, there is the three-way interaction $A \times B \times C$, which uses the full three-way table of group means $\overline{Y}_{jkl}$. Analytical analyses of this interaction are three-way interactions in their own right, differing only in the number of factors converted to contrasts. These effects include the interaction of a contrast with two intact factors (e.g., $\psi_A \times B \times C$), an interaction of two contrasts with one intact factor (e.g., $\psi_A \times \psi_B \times C$), and a three-way interaction of contrasts ($\psi_A \times \psi_B \times \psi_C$).

With this many effects that could apply to a three-factor design, some strategy to select the ones to examine is essential. First, recall that an analytical analysis can be planned or post hoc. In the former case, the tests are constructed before the data are seen and involve specific questions; in the latter, the overall effects are examined first, and the analytical analysis is undertaken to interpret any significant effects. The way that we identify the effects to test in the two cases are somewhat different. A planned analysis is usually developed from the lower-level effects: An important single-factor effect or contrast is identified, that effect is hypothesized to vary over another factor producing an interaction, and that interaction is posited to vary with a third factor. In contrast, an unplanned analysis tends to starts with higher-level effects and work down to the lower-order effects.

Frequently, but not inevitably, these two approaches are mirrored in the analytical instruments they use. The post-hoc approach often involves an *analysis of simple effects*, in which the sources of an interaction are isolated by looking at simple effects. A planned analysis is more likely to focus on the *analysis of interaction components*, in which the contribution of specific single-*df* comparisons to the interaction is assessed. We saw the same distinction in the two-way design between the simple-effect approach (Chapter 12) and the interaction-component approach (Chapter 13).

We will organize our discussion of the three-factor tests around the structure in Figure 22.1. First, we look at the many types of simple effects available to interpret an interaction. There are two levels of interaction in the three-factor design—the three-way interaction based on the individual group means and the two-way interactions based on two-way marginal means. For the former, we focus on the simple two-way tables selected from the full table, such as AB table at c_l to the right in Figure 22.1; for the later, on the two-way tables of marginal means formed by collapsing over one of the factors, such as the marginal AB table at the bottom of Figure 22.1. We discuss the analyses based on the cell means in Section 22.2 and those based on the marginal means in Section 22.3. Also in Section 22.3, we discuss contrasts formed from tables of marginal means—main contrasts and two-way interaction components. Both analyses draw on our understanding of an actual two-factor design. We then turn to the components that directly involve the three-factor structure of the design— the three-way interaction contrasts in Section 22.4 and the interaction of contrasts with the other intact factors in Section 22.5. To help you locate these tests, we have indicated in Table 22.1 the page numbers where we begin to describe them.

Throughout this chapter we will use the numerical example of word learning from the last chapter. The dependent variable was the number of words recalled, factor A was defined by three feedback conditions (none, positive, and negative), factor B by three types of learning materials (low frequency–low emotionality, high frequency–low emotionality, and high frequency–high emotionality), and factor C by two subject populations (fifth-grade children and high-school seniors). Keeping to a single example allows us to illustrate all the calculations with a single set of data (the scores in Table 21.1 and the means in Table 21.2), but you should recognize that because the overall analysis showed only one significant interaction, many of these tests would never be assessed on a post-hoc basis because they were not justified statistically.

22.2   Analyses Involving the Cell Means

We now turn to the analysis of the simple effects and simple interactions based on the means of the individual groups (the cell means as opposed to the marginal means). As we noted, this approach is likely to be used when investigating a significant $A \times B \times C$ interaction or a combination of two-way interactions in the overall analysis. It represents a generalization of the related procedures we described for a two-factor design (Chapter 12). You may want to review that chapter as you read this one.

Simple Effects As an Analysis Strategy

You will recall that the presence of an $A \times B$ interaction in a two-factor study implies that the simple effects of one independent variable depend on the levels of the other independent variable. That difference leads us to look at the simple effects themselves, to identify which of them are significant and which are not, and to interpret what this pattern of statistical outcomes might mean. The same logic applies to the three-factor design. As we discussed in Section 21.2, the presence of an $A \times B \times C$ interaction implies that the two-factor simple interactions vary with the third factor. Look back at Table 21.3, where we interpreted a three-way design as sets of two-factor experiments. A three-way interaction implies that the two-way interactions in these tables are not the same across the levels of the third variable. This fact suggests we should look at the separate simple interactions—in whichever direction is most comprehensible— whenever a three-way interaction is present. We could analyze them in much the same way we analyzed an $A \times B$ interaction in an actual two-way design.

Actually, things are not quite this simple. As our discussion on pages 474–476 indicates (see especially Figure 21.4), it is usually necessary to look at the simple effects whenever all three factors are involved in mutual interactions, be they the three-factor interaction or the three two-way interactions. Our strategy is

- When an $A \times B \times C$ interaction or all three two-way interactions are present, then look at the simple two-way effects at each level of the third factor.
- When the three-way interaction is absent and no more than two two-way interactions are present, then examine the effects in one or more of the two-way marginal tables.

When the first principle applies, the analysis focuses on the individual treatment means $\overline{Y}_{ABC}$. When the second principle applies, the results of the three-way study collapse into less complex one-way or two-way tables of marginal means. Our discussion of the example in the last chapter, where one significant two-way interaction was present, illustrates this approach (see pages 478–479).

You should not take the strategy implied by these principles as an obligatory plan. We urge you to be flexible and allow the dictates of your study determine the analysis. Statistical analysis, after all, is the servant of the researcher, not the master. No fixed rules apply to every case. Particular hypotheses that are relevant to the research questions are developed in the initial planning stages of an experiment, and these sometimes create the need for tests that fall outside our suggestions (we will see an example below). We also urge you to be flexible when you begin to divide a three-way analysis into simple effects. On page 248, we offered some suggestions for choosing a useful set of simple effects in a two-way design. You should consider these when you are working with a three-way design. We have been surprised at how often a change in the orientation of the analysis—picking a different set of simple interactions—highlights a different aspect of the study and leads to new insights.

The analyses we consider in this section all involve effects that refer directly to differences among the means of the individual groups in the three-way classification. We begin with the simple two-way interactions, such as $A \times B$ at c_l. From there we turn to the simple effects conditioned on the levels of the other two factors (e.g, A at $b_k c_l$). Within each of these effects, we consider simple interactions involving contrasts (e.g., $\psi_A \times B$ at c_l and $\psi_A \times \psi_B$ at c_l) and simple contrasts (e.g., ψ_A at $b_k c_l$).

Simple Interactions

Suppose we have some data with a significant three-way interaction or three significant two-way interactions. Our strategy above tells us to look at the simple interactions. We start by picking one of the three ways to organize the analysis: $A \times B$ at c_l, $A \times C$ at b_k, or $B \times C$ at a_j (Table 21.3, p. 471). Let's say we pick the simple $A \times B$ interactions at the levels of factor C. The strategy now is the treat the two-way AB tables at each c_l exactly as we do in the two-way design.

To conduct these analyses on a computer, you want to restrict its operation to the appropriate portion of the data, say to the set of ab groups at level c_1 of factor C. You could actually edit your data file so it contains only the relevant scores (after saving a copy of the original file, of course), but many programs have shortcuts that split the entire data set according to the levels of one of the variables. Once that is done, you use the program to conduct a two-way analysis for each level of the factor C. When you have the mean squares for the effects, you test them against the error term from the overall analysis.[1] You may need to calculate the final F ratios by hand.

When the data are available only as means, some hand calculation is necessary. The formulas for a two-way analysis can be adapted in the same way that we adapted the one-way formulas to calculate the simple effects in the two-way design (see Equation 12.5, p. 250). You will recall that in terms of the means, the sum of squares for the $A \times B$ interaction is

$$SS_{A \times B} = [AB] - [A] - [B] + [T]$$
$$= n \sum \bar{Y}_{AB_{jk}}^2 - bn \sum \bar{Y}_{A_j}^2 - an \sum \bar{Y}_{B_k}^2 + abn\bar{Y}_T^2$$

(see Table 11.5, p. 217). To adapt these formulas to simple interactions, we need only restrict the means to the appropriate level of factor C:

$$SS_{A \times B \text{ at } c_l} = [AB \text{ at } c_l] - [A \text{ at } c_l] - [B \text{ at } c_l] + [T \text{ at } c_l]$$
$$= n \sum_{j,k} \bar{Y}_{ABC_{jkl}}^2 - bn \sum_j \bar{Y}_{AC_{jl}}^2 - an \sum_k \bar{Y}_{BC_{kl}}^2 + abn\bar{Y}_{C_l}^2. \tag{22.1}$$

---

[1] Unless heterogeneity of variance is present. Then separate error terms should be found for each set of simple interactions, as we discussed in Section 11.4 (see page 228). These analyses are conducted exactly like a two-way analysis, including its error term.

Table 22.2: Means from the two AB subtables for c_1 and c_2 for the analysis of simple interactions (from Table 21.1).

Fifth graders $(\bar{Y}_{jk1})$	Low F Low E	High F Low E	High F High E	
	b_1	b_2	b_3	Mean
None (a_1)	8.4	8.8	8.0	8.400
Positive (a_2)	7.8	8.0	4.4	6.733
Negative (a_3)	8.0	7.6	3.8	6.467
Mean	8.067	8.133	5.400	7.200

Seniors $(\bar{Y}_{jk2})$	Low F Low E	High F Low E	High F High E	
	b_1	b_2	b_3	Mean
None (a_1)	8.4	8.8	7.8	8.333
Positive (a_2)	8.0	8.2	7.4	7.867
Negative (a_3)	8.4	8.0	7.0	7.800
Mean	8.267	8.333	7.400	8.000

The degrees of freedom for this sum of squares are the same as they would be in an actual two-factor design, namely $df_{A \times B \text{ at } c_l} = (a-1)(b-1)$. The resulting mean square is normally tested against the error mean square from the overall analysis.

Numerical Example.   The overall analysis of our numerical example (Table 21.6, p. 479) did not reveal a significant $A \times B \times C$ interaction, and because only one two-way interaction was significant, an exploration of the simple interactions would not be done as a post-hoc analysis. We will illustrate the calculation, however. Table 22.2 reproduces the means $\bar{Y}_{ABC_{jkl}}$ from Table 21.1 divided into two AB subtables, one for the fifth graders (c_1) and one for the seniors (c_2). Each mean is based on $n = 5$ subjects.

For the simple $A \times B$ interaction at c_1, we calculate the bracket terms

$$[AB \text{ at } c_1] = n \sum \bar{Y}_{jk1}^2 = (5)(8.4^2 + 7.8^2 + \cdots + 4.4^2 + 3.8^2) = 2{,}462.000$$

$$[A \text{ at } c_1] = bn \sum \bar{Y}_{AC_{j1}}^2 = (3)(5)(8.400^2 + 6.733^2 + 6.467^2) = 2{,}365.731$$

$$[B \text{ at } c_1] = an \sum \bar{Y}_{BC_{k1}}^2 = (3)(5)(8.067^2 + 8.133^2 + 5.400^2) = 2{,}405.733$$

$$[T \text{ at } c_1] = abn\bar{Y}_{C_1}^2 = (3)(3)(5)(7.200^2) = 2{,}332.800.$$

Putting these values together in Equation 22.1 gives

$$SS_{A \times B \text{ at } c_1} = 2{,}462.000 - 2{,}365.731 - 2{,}405.733 + 2{,}332.800 = 23.336.$$

This effect has $(3-1)(3-1) = 4$ degrees of freedom, so $MS_{A \times B \text{ at } c_1} = 23.336/4 = 5.834$. The error term $MS_{S/ABC} = 1.889$ is taken from Table 21.6, and the F ratio is

$$F = \frac{MS_{A \times B \text{ at } c_1}}{MS_{S/ABC}} = \frac{5.834}{1.889} = 3.09.$$

The test has $df_{\text{num}} = 4$ and $df_{\text{denom}} = 72$ and is tested against the closest lower value in Appendix A.1, $F_{.05}(4, 70) = 2.50$. The effect is significant. If you want to check your understanding of these calculations, you can verify that the second table gives a sum of squares of

$$SS_{A \times B \text{ at } c_2} = 2{,}892.000 - 2{,}882.529 - 2{,}888.133 + 2{,}880.000 = 1.338.$$

The simple effect of $A \times B$ at c_2 is decidedly not significant.

Simple Effects and Simple Contrasts

The presence of a simple interaction suggests the same sort of analysis that follows an interaction in an actual two-factor design: either simple effects or interaction components (contrast-by-factor interactions or interaction contrasts). We will discuss simple effects here and simple interaction components later. For either of these approaches, we are on familiar ground. It does not matter that the data come from a three-factor design; as we have seen with the simple $A \times B$ interaction, the formulas correspond to those appropriate for an actual two-factor design. The difference here is that the simple effects are conditionalized on the levels of *two* factors (e.g., A at $b_k c_l$ or ψ_A at $b_k c_l$) instead of one (A at b_k or ψ_A at b_k).

We begin with the analysis of the simple effects of a factor at a particular combination of the levels of the other two factors. As illustrated in Figure 22.1, this analysis is based on the column of means labeled A at $b_3 c_2$, which extends below the two-way table on the right. To illustrate, let's look at the effect of feedback (factor A) for the list of high-frequency words with high emotional content (b_3) and the fifth-grade students (c_1). The treatment means for this analysis are equivalent to those in a single-factor design. Isolating the third column in the upper portion of Table 22.2, we obtain

$$SS_{A \text{ at } b_3 c_1} = [A \text{ at } b_3 c_1] - [T \text{ at } b_3 c_1] = n \sum \bar{Y}_{j31}^2 - an\bar{Y}_{B_3 C_1}^2$$

$$= (5)(8.0^2 + 4.4^2 + 3.8^2) - (3)(5)(5.400^2)$$

$$= 489.00 - 437.40 = 51.60.$$

This sum of squares has $a - 1 = 2$ degrees of freedom, so the mean square is $MS_{A \text{ at } b_3 c_1} = 51.60/2 = 25.80$. Using the overall error term, the test statistic is $F = 25.80/1.889 = 13.66$, which is significant ($F_{.05}(2, 70) = 3.13$). You can verify that the corresponding analyses for the other two word lists are not significant—for b_1, $F = 0.427/1.889 = 0.23$, and for b_2, $F = 1.908/1.889 = 1.01$.

As you saw for a two-factor design, the presence of a simple effect with more than one degree of freedom often initiates a search for meaningful comparisons within it. It is an easy matter to extend this analysis to a three-factor design. Several single-*df* comparisons suggest themselves here, most of which we discussed when we introduced this example in Section 13.1. Let's look at the comparison between the control and the combined feedback conditions, which is expressed by the coefficient set $\{1, -\frac{1}{2}, -\frac{1}{2}\}$. Using the means from the third column of Table 22.2, the contrast value is

$$\hat{\psi}_{A \text{ at } b_3 c_1} = (1)(8.0) + (-\frac{1}{2})(4.4) + (-\frac{1}{2})(3.8) = 3.9.$$

The sum of squares for this contrast follows the general formula given by Equation 12.1 (p. 245):

$$SS_\psi = \frac{N_{\text{mean}}\widehat{\psi}^2}{\sum c^2}, \tag{22.2}$$

where N_{mean} = the number of scores that contribute to each mean,
  $\widehat{\psi}$ = the value of the contrast being tested,
  $\sum c^2$ = the sum of the squared coefficients defining ψ.
We will use this equation many times throughout this chapter. Adapting it to this simple comparison, the sum of squares is

$$SS_{\psi_A \text{ at } b_3c_1} = \frac{n\widehat{\psi}^2_{A \text{ at } b_3c_1}}{\sum c_j^2} = \frac{(5)(3.9)^2}{1^2 + (-\frac{1}{2})^2 + (-\frac{1}{2})^2} = \frac{76.05}{1.5} = 50.700.$$

This contrast, like any other, has 1 df. The resulting test statistic, $F = 50.700/1.889 = 26.84$, is significant $(F_{.05}(1, 70) = 3.98)$.

Simple Interaction Components

Whenever a simple interaction has more than one degrees of freedom, we may need to look at simple interaction components—simple contrast-by-factor interactions (e.g., $\psi_A \times B$ at c_l) or simple interaction contrasts (e.g., ψ_{AB} at c_l). Each is calculated exactly as if it were taken from an actual two-way design. Consider the simple contrast-by-factor interaction first. In Chapter 13 we presented two ways to calculate its sum of squares. One of these used the contrast values directly (Equation 13.10, p. 279). Adapted to the present situation, it is

$$SS_{\psi_A \times B \text{ at } c_l} = \frac{n\sum_k(\widehat{\psi}_{A \text{ at } b_kc_l} - \widehat{\psi}_{A \text{ at } c_l})^2}{\sum c_j^2}. \tag{22.3}$$

The other (Equation 13.11) uses the sums of squares of the separate effects. It becomes

$$SS_{\psi_A \times B \text{ at } c_l} = \sum_k SS_{\psi_A \text{ at } b_kc_l} - SS_{\psi_A \text{ at } c_l}. \tag{22.4}$$

Of course, either formula gives the same result.

As our example, we will take the contrast ψ_A that compares the positive and the negative groups. The coefficient set is $\{0, 1, -1\}$. Applied to the means in the upper part of Table 22.2, it gives

$$\widehat{\psi}_{A \text{ at } b_1c_1} = \bar{Y}_{211} - \bar{Y}_{311} = 7.8 - 8.0 = -0.2,$$
$$\widehat{\psi}_{A \text{ at } b_2c_1} = \bar{Y}_{221} - \bar{Y}_{321} = 8.0 - 7.6 = 0.4,$$
$$\widehat{\psi}_{A \text{ at } b_3c_1} = \bar{Y}_{231} - \bar{Y}_{331} = 4.4 - 3.8 = 0.6,$$
$$\widehat{\psi}_{A \text{ at } c_1} = \bar{Y}_{AC_{21}} - \bar{Y}_{AC_{31}} = 6.733 - 6.467 = 0.266.$$

Then using Equation 22.3 to get the sum of squares,

$$SS_{\psi_A \times B \text{ at } c_1} = \frac{n\sum_k(\widehat{\psi}_{A \text{ at } b_kc_1} - \widehat{\psi}_{A \text{ at } c_1})^2}{\sum c_j^2}$$

$$= \frac{(5)[(-0.2 - 0.266)^2 + (0.4 - 0.266)^2 + (0.6 - 0.266)^2]}{1^2 + (-1)^2}$$

$$= \frac{(5)(0.347)}{2} = 0.868.$$

With $df_{\psi_A \times B \text{ at } c_1} = b - 1 = 2$, we get $MS_{\psi_A \times B \text{ at } c_1} = 0.868/2 = 0.434$ and $F = 0.434/1.889 = 0.23$, which is not significant. We will illustrate a calculation similar to Equation 22.4 when we discuss contrast-by-factor interactions below.

For a simple interaction contrast, the general formula of Equation 22.2 applies. As an example, let's cross the same ψ_A with a comparison between the high-frequency words of low and high emotionality, a contrast expressed by the coefficient set $\{0, 1, -1\}$. Combining the two contrasts into the interaction contrast ψ_{AB}, the coefficients $c_{jk} = c_{A_j} c_{B_k}$ are

$$
\begin{array}{c|ccc}
 & \multicolumn{3}{c}{c_{B_k}} \\
c_{A_j} & 0 & 1 & -1 \\
\hline
0 & 0 & 0 & 0 \\
1 & 0 & 1 & -1 \\
-1 & 0 & -1 & 1 \\
\end{array}
$$

Using the means in the top half of Table 22.2 and disregarding the cells with a coefficient of zero, the contrast is

$$\widehat{\psi}_{AB} = 8.0 - 7.6 - 4.4 + 3.8 = -0.2.$$

Then using the general formula of Equation 22.2,

$$SS_{\psi_{AB}} = \frac{n\widehat{\psi}_{AB}^2}{\sum c_{jk}^2} = \frac{(5)(-0.2)^2}{4} = 0.05.$$

The resulting $F = 0.05/1.889 = 0.03$ is not significant.

Summary

Although the tests we have just illustrated are not justified on a purely post-hoc basis (the $A \times B \times C$ interaction was not significant), you should appreciate the systematic nature of the analysis strategy. When the three-way interaction is significant, we conclude that the simple two-way interactions are not the same, and we look at these simple interactions systematically. Once significant simple interactions are identified, we continue the analysis by examining simple effects and contrasts. In the numerical example, we found a significant, simple two-way interaction between feedback and types of words for the fifth-graders ($A \times B$ at level c_1), implying that the effects of feedback are not the same for the different types of words. Further analysis of the simple effects of the feedback variable in this subset of the data helps to identify the conditions responsible for the interaction. As we noted in Chapter 13, however, we cannot automatically assume that contrasts that are significant at one level of the other variable and not in another are actually different from each other. We need help from the type of interaction contrast we discussed there, which we will develop further in Section 22.4.

22.3   Effects Based on Marginal Means

The last section focused on simple effects based on the cell means $\overline{Y}_{jkl}$; in the present section we will examine effects based on marginal means. To sort out when each approach is useful, think back to our discussion of an interaction in a two-way design

(Section 10.2). You saw there that the main-effect means, say $\overline{Y}_{A_j}$, are averages of the means $\overline{Y}_{jk}$ that make up the simple effects at b_k. When an $A{\times}B$ interaction is present, the main effects (differences among the $\overline{Y}_{A_j}$) do not describe the simple effects (differences among the $\overline{Y}_{jk}$ at the different levels of B). The same holds for the main effects and two-factor interactions in a three-factor design. They are averages of the corresponding simple effects and interactions. For example, the $A{\times}B$ interaction is an average of the simple $A{\times}B$ interactions at c_l. When all the factors participate in simultaneous two-way interactions or in a three-way interaction, the two-way interactions do not describe the comparable simple interactions. In that case, the procedures in the last section are needed. However, when there is no three-way interaction and at most one or two two-factor interactions, the remaining interactions stand by themselves, and we can interpret them directly, knowing that they are representative of the effects at each level of the third factor.

These analyses are conducted on the marginal means, either single factor or two factor. For interpretation purposes, these configurations can be treated as three one-way designs or as three two-factor designs. Either way, we are back to familiar procedures. The overall effects are those tested by the standard analysis of variance (for example, the A, B, and $A{\times}B$ effects), and the analytical analyses are conducted exactly as they would be in an actual single-factor or two-factor design. This process shows how an overall analysis at one level is translated to a simpler analysis at another, a procedure that is equally relevant to analyzing designs with more than three factors. We will look first at main-effect contrasts and then contrasts that are components of the two-way interaction.

Main-Effect Contrasts

Main-effect contrasts are important when a factor with more than two levels does not participate in any interactions. For example, in the original analysis of our numerical example, we found an A effect, but no $A{\times}B$, $A{\times}C$, or $A{\times}B{\times}C$ interactions. The A main effect, therefore, can be examined in isolation. Looking at the marginal means $\overline{Y}_{A_j}$ in the left panel of Figure 21.5 (p. 480) suggests a comparison between the no-feedback condition and the combined feedback conditions. Using the $\overline{Y}_{A_j}$ means from the one-way configuration for factor A in Table 21.2 (p. 468), the contrast is

$$\widehat{\psi}_A = \overline{Y}_{A_1} + (-\tfrac{1}{2})\overline{Y}_{A_2} + (-\tfrac{1}{2})\overline{Y}_{A_3} = 8.367 + (-\tfrac{1}{2})(7.300) + (-\tfrac{1}{2})(7.133) = 1.151.$$

Each mean is based on bcn scores, so Equation 22.2 gives

$$SS_{\psi_A} = \frac{bcn\widehat{\psi}_A^2}{\sum c_{A_j}^2} = \frac{(3)(2)(5)(1.151^2)}{1^2 + (-\tfrac{1}{2})^2 + (-\tfrac{1}{2})^2} = \frac{39.744}{1.5} = 26.496.$$

The contrast is significant ($F = 26.496/1.889 = 14.03$; $F_{.05}(1, 70) = 3.98$).

Before leaving this type of analysis, we should point out again that analyzing a main effect is only relevant when it does not participate in appreciable interactions. When it does, any attempt to "interpret the main effect" is unnecessary and frequently misleading. Generally, the most fruitful analyses is at the levels of the simple effects. Nevertheless, we have seen too many researchers waste effort trying to make sense of a main effect before considering its interactions.

Simple Effects Based on Marginal Two-Way Tables

In the original analysis of our example, we found the significant $B{\times}C$ interaction plotted in Figure 21.5 (p. 480). The additional presence of the significant B and C main effects implies that we will obtain the clearest understanding of this interaction by looking at the simple effects and simple contrasts based on the BC table of marginal means.

Simple Effects. Consider the simple effects of word type (factor B) for the different subject populations (levels of factor C). The relevant means from Table 21.2 are

	c_1	c_2
b_1	8.067	8.267
b_2	8.133	8.333
b_3	5.400	7.400
Mean	7.200	8.000

To obtain a computational formula for these simple effects, look back at the simple effects for the two-way designs in Section 12.4. The relevant equation, adapted here for factors B and C from Equations 12.5–12.7, is

$$SS_{B \text{ at } c_l} = [B \text{ at } c_l] - [T \text{ at } c_l] = n \sum_k \overline{Y}^2_{BC_{kl}} - bn\overline{Y}^2_{C_l}.$$

Before using this formula here, we need to change the multipliers to reflect the fact that the BC marginal means are averaged over factor A, by replacing n and bn with an and abn, respectively:

$$SS_{B \text{ at } c_l} = [B \text{ at } c_l] - [T \text{ at } c_l] = an \sum_k \overline{Y}^2_{BC_{kl}} - abn\overline{Y}^2_{C_l}. \tag{22.5}$$

Substituting the means from the first column in the table above, we obtain

$$SS_{B \text{ at } c_1} = an \sum \overline{Y}^2_{BC_{k1}} - abn\overline{Y}^2_{C_1}$$
$$= (3)(5)(8.067^2 + 8.133^2 + 5.400^2) - (3)(3)(5)(7.200^2)$$
$$= 2{,}405.733 - 2{,}332.800 = 72.933.$$

This sum of squares has $b - 1 = 2$ degrees of freedom, $MS_{B \text{ at } c_1} = 72.933/2 = 36.467$, and the test statistic is $F = 36.467/1.889 = 19.30$. It is significant $(F_{.05}(2, 70) = 3.13)$. You can check that the other simple effect is smaller than this one $(SS_{B \text{ at } c_2} = 8.133)$ (which is why we have an interaction) and that it is not significant $(F = 2.15)$.

We mentioned previously that to analyze a simple effect using a computer, the easiest approach is to isolate the relevant part of the data and to calculate the appropriate main effects. In the example above, we would separate the data by the levels of factor C. We could then perform one-way analyses of the B factor, ignoring factor A altogether. The resulting sums of squares are tested against the error sum of squares from the full analysis to produce the results above.

Simple Contrasts. We could follow up a significant simple effect based on a factor with more than two levels with an examination of simple comparisons. Specifically, a contrast $\psi_{B \text{ at } c_l} = \sum c_{B_k}\mu_k$ in the BC two-way configuration is estimated by

$\widehat{\psi}_B$ at $c_l = \sum_k c_{B_k} \overline{Y}_{BC_{kl}}$. The sum of squares for this comparison (in which each mean is based on an scores) is calculated by adapting Equation 22.2:

$$SS_{\psi_B \text{ at } c_l} = \frac{an \widehat{\psi}_B^2 \text{ at } c_l}{\sum c_{B_k}^2}.$$

This equation differs only in the multiplier an from its counterpart for the two-way design (Equation 12.12, p. 256). We will illustrate the calculations with the contrast ψ_B at $c_1 = \mu_{BC_{11}} + \mu_{BC_{21}} + (-2)\mu_{BC_{31}}$:

$$\widehat{\psi}_B \text{ at } c_1 = \overline{Y}_{BC_{11}} + \overline{Y}_{BC_{21}} + (-2)(\overline{Y}_{BC_{31}})$$
$$= 8.067 + 8.133 + (-2)(5.400) = 5.400,$$

$$SS_{B \text{ at } c_1} = \frac{an \widehat{\psi}_B^2 \text{ at } c_1}{\sum c_{B_k}^2} = \frac{(3)(5)(5.400)^2}{6} = 72.900.$$

With one degree of freedom, $MS_{B \text{ at } c_1} = 72.900$, the error term is $MS_{S/ABC} = 1.889$, and $F = 72.900/1.889 = 38.59$. The contrast is significant ($F_{.05}(1, 70) = 3.98$). We conclude that the fifth-grade students recalled fewer words of high emotional content (b_3) than students receiving words of low emotional context (b_1 and b_2 combined).

Interaction Components Based on Marginal Means

Suppose now that we have examined a simple contrast ψ_B at c_l for several different values of l. A natural step is to check whether their values are different. To do so, we must test for a contrast-by-factor interaction, in this case, the $\psi_B \times C$ interaction of contrast ψ_B with factor C. This test helps us interpret the significant two-way marginal interaction $B \times C$. These interaction components are tested in the same way as the similar simple contrast-by-factor interactions in Section 22.2 (Equations 22.3 and 22.4), except that marginal means are used, and the multipliers n in the earlier equations now are the number of scores contributing to these means.

We will illustrate the calculations using Equation 22.4, the formula we did not use earlier. With this approach, we need to calculate the sums of squares of the c simple contrasts, sum them, and then subtract the sum of squares for the main contrast ψ_B:

$$SS_{\psi_B \times C} = \sum SS_{\psi_B \text{ at } c_l} - SS_{\psi_B}.$$

Suppose we wish to determine whether the recall for the high-frequency words differed with their emotional content. This question focuses on levels b_2 and b_3 of factor B and leads to the coefficient set $\{0, 1, -1\}$. We start by calculating this contrast for the two age groups:

$$\widehat{\psi}_B \text{ at } c_1 = 8.133 - 5.400 = 2.733 \quad \text{and} \quad \widehat{\psi}_B \text{ at } c_2 = 8.333 - 7.400 = 0.933.$$

Next, we calculate the corresponding sums of squares using the general formula (Equation 22.2, appropriately modified):

$$SS_{B \text{ at } c_1} = \frac{an \widehat{\psi}_B^2 \text{ at } c_1}{\sum c_{B_k}^2} = \frac{(3)(5)(2.733^2)}{2} = 56.020$$

$$SS_{B \text{ at } c_2} = \frac{an \widehat{\psi}_B^2 \text{ at } c_2}{\sum c_{B_k}^2} = \frac{(3)(5)(0.933^2)}{2} = 6.529.$$

We also need the main contrast and its sum of squares. The main contrast is based on the marginal means $\bar{Y}_{B_k}$ from Table 21.2 (p. 468):

$$\hat{\psi}_B = \bar{Y}_{B_2} - \bar{Y}_{B_3} = 8.233 - 6.400 = 1.833.$$

The general sum of squares formula is modified to reflect the number of scores contributing to the $\bar{Y}_B$ means:

$$SS_{\psi_B} = \frac{acn\hat{\psi}_B^2}{\sum c_k^2} = \frac{(3)(2)(5)(1.833^2)}{2} = 50.398.$$

We now use Equation 22.4 to calculate

$$SS_{\psi_B \times C} = \sum SS_{\psi_B \text{ at } c_l} - SS_{\psi_B} = (56.020 + 6.529) - 50.398 = 12.151.$$

This sum of squares has $c - 1 = 1$ degree of freedom and $F = 12.151/1.889 = 6.43$. It is significant ($F_{.05}(1, 70) = 3.98$). Thus, for the high-frequency words, the effect of emotional content on recall depends on the age of the children. We will test this hypothesis another way in Table 22.6.

When a contrast-by-factor interaction is associated with more than one degree of freedom, it can be refined by looking at the interaction contrasts that contribute to it. The $A \times B$ interaction in our example has sufficient degrees of freedom to provide a realistic example of the calculations. We saw in Chapter 13 that an interaction contrast ψ_{AB} corresponds to an ordinary contrast over the entire set of means with coefficients that are products of the coefficients of the individual contrasts (Equation 13.5, p. 272). We can form such a contrast here, then use Equation 22.2 to calculate its sum of squares. Consider the contrasts $\psi_A = \mu_1 + (-\frac{1}{2})\mu_2 + (-\frac{1}{2})\mu_3$ and $\psi_B = \mu_2 - \mu_3$. The coefficients c_{jk} of the interaction contrast are the products

		c_{B_k}		
		0	1	-1
c_{A_j}	1	0	1	-1
	$-\frac{1}{2}$	0	$-\frac{1}{2}$	$\frac{1}{2}$
	$-\frac{1}{2}$	0	$-\frac{1}{2}$	$\frac{1}{2}$

With these coefficients and the marginal means $\bar{Y}_{AB_{jk}}$ in Table 21.2, we obtain $\hat{\psi}_{AB} = -1.40$. Then applying Equation 22.2 and using Equation 13.7 (p. 273) to calculate the sum of squared coefficients,

$$SS_{\psi_{AB}} = \frac{cn\hat{\psi}_{AB}^2}{(\sum c_{A_j}^2)(\sum c_{B_k}^2)} = \frac{(2)(5)(-1.40)^2}{(1.5)(2)} = \frac{19.600}{3} = 6.533.$$

With one degree of freedom and the usual error term, $F = 6.533/1.889 = 3.46$, which is not significant ($F_{.05}(1, 70) = 3.98$).

22.4 Three-Factor Interaction Components

Before a study is conducted, researchers sometimes pick one or more three-way interaction components to be investigated in a planned analysis. The decision to look at a particular interaction is typically motivated by considering the simple effects and comparing them as interactions—the opposite of the post-hoc analysis strategy that starts with the discovery of a significant interaction. First an important simple effect is identified, for example A at $b_k c_l$, and a simple contrast ψ_A at $b_k c_l$ within it. Next, the researcher asks whether the simple contrast is likely to be modulated by one of the other factors. If the simple contrast is expected to vary with, say, factor C, then the simple interaction component $\psi_A \times C$ at b_k is implicated, and within it the more precise $\psi_A \times \psi_C$ at b_k effect. When the possibility that this latter effect, in turn, may change over the levels of factor B is considered, the three-way interaction component $\psi_A \times B \times \psi_C$ is obtained, and it finally leads to the ψ_{ABC} interaction contrast. Frequently, one or two such interaction components embody the central theoretical ideas of a study.

The interaction components focus entirely on variablity expressed by the interaction term $A \times B \times C$ in the overall analysis. These tests differ from those involving simple effects, which combine variablity from lower and higher-order terms, a point we discussed for the two-factor design in Sections 12.3 and 12.4. It is this aspect of interaction components that makes them such a powerful way to express specific hypotheses about the interaction.

Interaction Components As Precise Effects

You can get a feeling for the way an interaction component focuses on a particular part of an interaction effect by considering the different types of interaction components created with pairwise contrasts and counting the number of means involved. Consider the $3 \times 3 \times 3$ factorial design depicted in Table 22.3. At the top of the table is the original configuration of cell means. We have placed an X in all the cells of the ABC matrix to emphasize the fact that all treatment conditions contribute to the overall three-way interaction. With all 27 cells involved in this interaction, the effect inevitably has a somewhat undifferentiated character, which is reflected in the fact that the $A \times B \times C$ interaction is associated with 8 degrees of freedom.

Now suppose we introduce the pairwise contrast $\psi_A = \mu_1 - \mu_2$ on factor A and look at the $\psi_A \times B \times C$ interaction component. By doing so we stop looking at the groups with an a_3 classification. The cells involved in this contrast-by-factors interaction are those indicated by an X in the second panel of Table 22.3. In the reduced $2 \times 3 \times 3$ table, a three-way interaction corresponds to the interaction of ψ_A with the other two independent variables—a more focused picture of the interaction of the three factors than that provided by the overall $A \times B \times C$ interaction. It has 4 degrees of freedom.

We obtain a further level of analytical precision by introducing the pairwise contrast $\psi_B = \mu_2 - \mu_3$ on factor B. It leads to a $\psi_A \times \psi_B \times C$ interaction, which involves the 12 marked cells in the third panel of Table 22.3 and has only 2 degrees of freedom.

The greatest precision occurs when all three factors are expressed as contrasts, forming an $\psi_A \times \psi_B \times \psi_C$ interaction. The last panel of the table introduces the pairwise contrast $\psi_C = \mu_1 - \mu_2$ on factor C. The resulting interaction is maximally precise, having only one degree of freedom. This three-way interaction is expressed by the eight X's, which form a $2 \times 2 \times 2$ factorial design. This component of the three-way interaction is the **interaction contrast**. With one degree of freedom, it can be refined no further. As in a two-way table, the interaction contrast can be written as a contrast $\widehat{\psi}_{ABC}$ applied to the means of the full three-way table.

Table 22.3: Cells involved in interaction components of increasing specificity.

		c_1			c_2			c_3		
		b_1	b_2	b_3	b_1	b_2	b_3	b_1	b_2	b_3
$A \times B \times C$	a_1	X	X	X	X	X	X	X	X	X
	a_2	X	X	X	X	X	X	X	X	X
	a_3	X	X	X	X	X	X	X	X	X

		b_1	b_2	b_3	b_1	b_2	b_3	b_1	b_2	b_3
$\psi_A \times B \times C$	1	X	X	X	X	X	X	X	X	X
	-1	X	X	X	X	X	X	X	X	X
	0									

		0	1	-1	0	1	-1	0	1	-1
$\psi_A \times \psi_B \times C$	1		X	X		X	X		X	X
	-1		X	X		X	X		X	X
	0									

		0	1	-1	0	1	-1	0	1	-1
$\psi_A \times \psi_B \times \psi_C$	1		X	X		X	X			
	-1		X	X		X	X			
	0									

A different way to view Table 22.3 is as the successive application of contrasts to the simple effects. This conceptualization is particularly valuable when constructing the interaction contrast theoretically. Suppose we start with a readily comprehensible contrast ψ_A and apply it to the simple effects of factor A for the different combinations of factors B and C:

$$\psi_{A \text{ at } b_k c_l} = \sum_j c_{A_j} \mu_{jkl}. \tag{22.6}$$

In the second panel of Table 22.3, there are nine of these pairwise simple contrasts, one per column. Next, we cross this set of simple contrasts with contrast ψ_B to produce a simple interaction contrast ψ_{AB} at each level of factor C:

$$\psi_{AB \text{ at } c_l} = \sum_k c_{B_k} \psi_{A \text{ at } b_k c_l} = \sum_{j,k} c_{A_j} c_{B_k} \mu_{jkl}. \tag{22.7}$$

These interaction contrasts are expressed in the three subtables of the third panel of Table 22.3. You can think of them either as a comparison of contrast values (the center part of Equation 22.7) or as a contrast on the cell means (the right-hand part). Finally, we apply contrast ψ_C to compare the simple $A \times B$ interaction contrasts over the third factor:

$$\psi_{ABC} = \sum_l c_{C_l} \psi_{AB \text{ at } c_l} = \sum_{k,l} c_{B_k} c_{C_l} \psi_{A \text{ at } b_k c_l} = \sum_{j,k,l} c_{A_j} c_{B_k} c_{C_l} \mu_{jkl}. \tag{22.8}$$

This equation provides three ways to calculate ψ_{ABC} and three ways to think about its meaning: as a comparison of the simple $A \times B$ interaction contrasts (the left-hand part), as an interaction contrast of the simple contrasts $\psi_{A \text{ at } b_k c_l}$ conditioned on the specified value of two factors (the middle part), and as a contrast on the cell means (the right-hand part). We can write the third form of the interaction contrast as

$$\psi_{ABC} = \sum c_{jkl}\mu_{jkl} \quad \text{where} \quad c_{jkl} = c_{A_j} c_{B_k} c_{C_l}. \tag{22.9}$$

There is nothing about Equations 22.6–22.9 that requires the pairwise contrasts of Table 22.3 to be used. They apply to complex contrasts—trend components, comparisons of pooled conditions, etc.—as easily as to pairwise ones.

Evaluating the Three-Way Interaction Contrast

An interaction contrast is simply another single-df contrast involving group means, and as such, it is tested by applying the same general strategy used for all such contrasts. First, we calculate the observed value of the contrast $\widehat{\psi}_{ABC}$. Next, we find the sum of squares using Equation 22.2. Finally, we evaluate that sum of squares using the overall $MS_{S/ABC}$ as the error term. The first step, calculating $\widehat{\psi}_{ABC}$, can be accomplished either by working with the individual contrasts or directly with the group means. We illustrate both approaches below.

An important aspect of the example in Chapter 13 was the way in which the no-feedback and the combined feedback conditions interacted with the emotional content of the words. A *planned* question for the three-factor design is whether this outcome interacts with the age levels. This question implies a three-way interaction contrast based on three contrasts:

No feedback vs. feedback:	$\psi_A = \mu_1 + (-\tfrac{1}{2})\mu_2 + (-\tfrac{1}{2})\mu_3$
Low vs. high emotional value:	$\psi_B = \mu_2 - \mu_3$
Fifth graders vs. seniors:	$\psi_C = \mu_1 - \mu_2$

Table 22.4 illustrates how to calculate this interaction contrast as a contrast of contrasts. We start by calculating ψ_A for each combination of factors B and C. It is helpful to do this in two steps. First, we average the group means of Table 22.2 for the two feedback groups, $(\bar{Y}_{2kl} + \bar{Y}_{3kl})/2$, and place them in the table along with the means for the no-feedback groups $(\bar{Y}_{1kl})$. Next, we subtract the combined feedback mean from the no-feedback mean for each combination of the other two factors to obtain values of $\psi_{A \text{ at } b_k c_l}$, given in the columns to the right. You may notice what looks like an interaction for the fifth graders. In the left-hand table, the difference between no-feedback and combined feedback is appreciably smaller for words of low emotional content than for words of high emotional content ($\widehat{\psi}_{A \text{ at } b_1 c_1} = 1.0$ compared to $\widehat{\psi}_{A \text{ at } b_2 c_1} = 3.9$). This interaction effect is $\widehat{\psi}_{AB \text{ at } c_1} = 1.0 - 3.9 = -2.9$. The same interaction for the high-school seniors is much smaller and in the opposite direction: $\widehat{\psi}_{AB \text{ at } c_2} = 0.7 - 0.6 = 0.1$. The difference between the values of these two contrasts, calculated at the bottom of the table, is the value of the three-factor interaction contrast ($\widehat{\psi}_{ABC} = -3.0$).

To see whether this three-way interaction contrast is significantly different from zero, we calculate its sum of squares. As part of the calculation, we need the sum of the squared coefficients, which we calculate by multiplying the sums of the squared coefficients for the component contrasts, as we did in the two-way case (Equation 13.7, p. 273):

$$\sum c_{jkl}^2 = (\sum c_{A_j}^2)(\sum c_{B_k}^2)(\sum c_{C_l}^2).$$

Table 22.4: Calculating the value of a three-way interaction contrast $\widehat{\psi}_{ABC}$ with simple contrasts.

	Fifth grade No Fdbk	Fdbk	$\widehat{\psi}_{A \text{ at } b_k c_1}$	Seniors No Fdbk	Fdbk	$\widehat{\psi}_{A \text{ at } b_k c_2}$
Low Emot.	8.8	7.8	1.0	8.8	8.1	0.7
High Emot.	8.0	4.1	3.9	7.8	7.2	0.6

$$\widehat{\psi}_{A \times B \text{ at } c_1} = -2.9 \qquad \widehat{\psi}_{A \times B \text{ at } c_2} = 0.1$$

$$\widehat{\psi}_{A \times B \times C} = \widehat{\psi}_{A \times B \text{ at } c_1} - \widehat{\psi}_{A \times B \text{ at } c_2} = -2.9 - 0.1 = -3.0$$

Now we apply the general formula for the sum of squares (Equation 22.2) to give:

$$SS_{\psi_{ABC}} = \frac{n\widehat{\psi}_{ABC}^2}{(\sum c_{A_j}^2)(\sum c_{B_k}^2)(\sum c_{C_l}^2)} = \frac{(5)(-3.0)^2}{(1.5)(2)(2)} = \frac{45.00}{6} = 7.500.$$

As usual, the error term is $MS_{S/ABC} = 1.889$. The resulting $F = 7.500/1.889 = 3.97$ falls just short of significance ($F_{.05}(1, 70) = 3.98$).

The other way to calculate the contrast value $\widehat{\psi}_{ABC}$ is to work directly with the individual group means using Equations 22.9. In Table 22.5, the coefficients of the three contrasts are arrayed around the perimeter of a three-way table and their product is formed in the center. For example,

$$c_{231} = c_{A_2} c_{B_3} c_{C_1} = (-\tfrac{1}{2})(-1)(1) = \tfrac{1}{2}.$$

It is a good idea to verify that the entries in this table sum to zero in every direction. Direct calculation of $\widehat{\psi}_{A \times B \times C}$ and $\sum c_{jkl}^2$ from these coefficients gives the same value we obtained earlier. When working by hand, we prefer to calculate contrast values from the simple contrasts as in Table 22.4. The simple contrasts we find on the way are useful in understanding just what the interaction means, and the calculations are somewhat less prone to mistakes. We need the simple contrast values anyway to interpret the three-factor interaction contrast. On the other hand, writing the interaction contrast as a single contrast over all groups is usually necessary to get a computer to run the analysis, so you should be prepared to use either approach.

Before we leave this example, notice that this interaction contrast nearly reaches the 5 percent significance level, whereas the overall three-way interaction in the standard analysis of variance was not even close (Table 21.6, p. 479). This difference illustrates again the importance of planned interaction contrasts. A significant interaction contrast may be masked by the averaging that takes place when we test an omnibus

Table 22.5: Calculating the coefficients for an interaction contrast

		$c_{C_1} = 1$			$c_{C_2} = -1$		
		c_{B_1}	c_{B_2}	c_{B_3}	c_{B_1}	c_{B_2}	c_{B_3}
		0	1	−1	0	1	−1
$c_{A_1} =$	1	0	1	−1	0	−1	1
$c_{A_2} = -\tfrac{1}{2}$		0	$-\tfrac{1}{2}$	$\tfrac{1}{2}$	0	$\tfrac{1}{2}$	$-\tfrac{1}{2}$
$c_{A_3} = -\tfrac{1}{2}$		0	$-\tfrac{1}{2}$	$\tfrac{1}{2}$	0	$\tfrac{1}{2}$	$-\tfrac{1}{2}$

effect with several degrees of freedom. Of course, concern for Type I error would stop you from testing an *unplanned* interaction contrast in this way, but when the logic underlying the study leads to the specific interaction contrast, the test focuses the full power of the design on the research question.

Simple Contrasts

The presence of a three-way interaction implies differences among the simple two-way interactions. When a significant three-way interaction contrast has been found, we will usually want to go back and look at the simple interactions and simple contrasts that make it up. In effect, we will be proceeding from the three-way interaction of Equation 22.8 back to the two-way simple interaction contrasts of Equation 22.7 and the simple contrasts of Equation 22.6.

Although we calculated these effects earlier (page 495), we will give one more example. Table 22.4 contains specific values for the contrast $\widehat{\psi}_A$ at $b_k c_l$. These values suggest that the interaction of feedback and emotional content is present for the fifth graders, but not for the seniors. To investigate this possibility, we look at the interaction of ψ_A with the contrast $\psi_B = \mu_2 - \mu_3$. Our general formula for the sum of squares now gives us

$$SS_{\psi_{AB} \text{ at } c_1} = \frac{n\widehat{\psi}^2_{A \times B \text{ at } c_1}}{(\sum c^2_{A_j})(\sum c^2_{B_k})} = \frac{(5)(-2.9^2)}{(1.5)(2)} = \frac{42.05}{3} = 14.017.$$

This interaction is significant, $F = 14.017/1.889 = 7.42$ ($F_{.05}(1, 70) = 3.98$). The corresponding simple interaction contrast for the seniors gives $SS_{\psi_{AB} \text{ at } c_2} = 0.017$, which is not significant.

22.5   Contrast-by-Factor Interactions

There are times when some of your independent variables will not lend themselves to single-*df* comparisons and will not form an interaction contrast. An alternative approach is to see whether a contrast changes with another factor. For example, in our schematic Table 22.3, you may want to know whether the value ψ_A varies with factors B and C (the second panel of the table) or whether the ψ_{AB} interaction varies with C (the third panel). Because both B and C have more than two levels, these interactions are compound effects, with more than one degree of freedom.

There are two approaches to calculating the sums of squares for contrast-by-factor interactions. When the contrast is a comparison between two groups, the analysis can be conducted by extracting the relevant portion of the data and analyzing it by an ordinary three-way analysis of variance. When the contrast involves more than two groups, then a procedure adapted particularly to contrasts is needed. We can, however, make use of the formulas used for an ordinary two-factor design.

Suppose the contrast ψ_A compares two means. All you need do is extract the relevant portions of the data—the cells marked by X in Table 22.3—and conduct the analysis as an ordinary factorial. The sums of squares produced by this analysis express the contrast and its interaction. For example, in the second panel of Table 22.3, a 2×3×3 analysis would be performed. In this analysis, the new factor A has $a = 2$ levels, corresponding to the two levels of ψ_A, and the resulting factor is equivalent to a contrast. The $A \times B$, $A \times C$, and $A \times B \times C$ interactions calculated from this reduced table of means would give the sums of squares, respectively, for the $\psi_A \times B$, $\psi_A \times C$, and $\psi_A \times B \times C$ interactions, the three contrast-by-factor interactions possible for this analysis. In the third panel, where both A and B are reduced to pairwise contrasts, the analysis corresponds to a $2 \times 2 \times 3$ design and the resulting sources of interaction, $A \times C$, $B \times C$, and $A \times B \times C$, correspond to the $\psi_A \times C$, $\psi_B \times C$, and $\psi_{A \times B} \times C$ contrast-by-factor interactions. The effort involved in conducting these analyses, either by hand or with a computer, is no greater than that required for an ordinary three-factor analysis of variance. As always, however, unless heterogeneity of variance is present, $MS_{S/ABC}$ from the omnibus analysis is used for the error term.

Because this strategy uses the actual cell means from the overall design, it will not work when contrasts involving three or more means are used. We calculated the sums of squares for the contrast-by-factor interactions in Section 13.4 by applying the formulas for a one-way analysis of variance to the contrast values and adjusting them for the particular coefficients in the contrasts (see Equation 13.10, p. 279). The same strategy works with the three-factor design. We begin by calculating the value of the contrast in question (say, $\widehat{\psi}_A$) for all levels of the other two variables. This step creates a $B \times C$ factorial. Next, we calculate sums of squares based on these values as if they had been means from an analysis with n subjects per cell. Finally, we divide the resulting sums of squares by $\sum c_j^2$ for the contrast. The mean squares we get are tested against the mean square error from the overall design.[2] Each effect produced by this special analysis is interpreted as the corresponding interaction of the contrast with the effect; so $B \times C$ in the analysis actually expresses $\psi_A \times B \times C$, B and C express $\psi_A \times B$ and $\psi_A \times C$, respectively, and the grand mean expresses ψ_A. An attractive feature of this approach is that it makes all of these effects available at once. They may all be needed to interpret the outcome.[3]

Let's apply this procedure to the contrast $\psi_A = \mu_1 + (-\frac{1}{2})\mu_2 + (-\frac{1}{2})\mu_3$. First, we calculate the value of this contrast for all combinations of factors B and C. We calculated these values for levels b_2 and b_3 and gave them in the columns to the right of the subtables in Table 22.4. The values for level b_1 are calculated similarly. The bc contrast values are assembled in Table 22.6, which we treat as if they were the means in a $B \times C$ design by calculating their row and column marginal means. From this point on, we apply the ordinary formulas for a two-factor design (with $n = 5$) to find the bracket terms:

$$[BC_{\psi_A}] = (5)(0.5^2 + 0.2^2 + 1.0^2 + 0.7^2 + 3.9^2 + 0.6^2) = (5)(17.35) = 86.750,$$
$$[B_{\psi_A}] = (2)(5)(0.35^2 + 0.85^2 + 2.25^2) = (10)(5.908) = 59.080,$$
$$[C_{\psi_A}] = (3)(5)(1.80^2 + 0.50^2) = (15)(3.490) = 52.350,$$
$$[T_{\psi_A}] = (3)(2)(5)(1.15^2) = (30)(1.323) = 39.690.$$

---

[2]Do not confuse this use of this derived contrast factor, which is just used to obtain the sums of squares for the different effects, with its use in the within-subject designs (for example, Table 18.6, p. 410), where it also gives the error term.

[3]For an analysis in which two of the factors are represented by contrasts—a contrast-by-factor analysis ($\psi_A \times \psi_B \times C$)—the group means are first transformed into the contrast values $\widehat{\psi}_{AB_{jk}}$ and then subjected to a one-way analysis of variance. The resulting sums of squares are divided by $(\sum c_{A_j})(\sum c_{B_k})$ and tested against $MS_{S/ABC}$. In this case, the C effect will be $\psi_A \times \psi_B \times C$ interaction and the grand mean $\psi_A \times \psi_B$.

Table 22.6: Analysis of the $\psi_A \times B \times C$ interaction component based on the contrast values ($\widehat{\psi}_A$) from Table 22.4.

Contrast values from Table 22.4 arranged as means for an analysis of variance

	c_1	c_2	Mean
b_1	0.5	0.2	0.35
b_2	1.0	0.7	0.85
b_3	3.9	0.6	2.25
Mean	1.80	0.50	1.15

Summary of the analysis of variance

Source					
Calculated	Interpreted	SS	df	MS	F
G.M.	ψ_A	26.460	1	26.460	14.01*
B	$\psi_A \times B$	12.927	2	6.464	3.42*
C	$\psi_A \times C$	8.440	1	8.440	4.47*
$B \times C$	$\psi_A \times B \times C$	10.007	2	5.004	2.65
	S/ABC	136.000	72	1.889	

*$p < .05$

The sum of squares for the three-way contrast-by-factor interaction $\psi_A \times B \times C$ is equal to the sum of squares for an ordinary $B \times C$ two-factor interaction divided by $\sum c_j^2$:

$$SS_{\psi_A \times B \times C} = \frac{[BC_{\psi_A}] - [B_{\psi_A}] - [C_{\psi_A}] + [T_{\psi_A}]}{\sum c_j^2}$$

$$= \frac{86.750 - 59.080 - 52.350 + 39.690}{1.5} = \frac{15.010}{1.5} = 10.007.$$

The other terms give the marginal and the main contrasts:

$$SS_{\psi_A \times B} = \frac{[B_{\psi_A}] - [T_{\psi_A}]}{\sum c_j^2} = \frac{59.080 - 39.690}{1.5} = 12.927,$$

$$SS_{\psi_A \times C} = \frac{[C_{\psi_A}] - [T_{\psi_A}]}{\sum c_j^2} = \frac{52.350 - 39.690}{1.5} = 8.440,$$

$$SS_{\psi_A} = \frac{[T_{\psi_A}]}{\sum c_j^2} = \frac{39.690}{1.5} = 26.460.$$

(The last sum of squares was calculated as a main comparison in Section 22.3.) The entire analysis is summarized at the bottom of Table 22.6. We have listed the sources from the special analysis of variance on the left side of the first column and the equivalent sources for the three-factor design on the right.

22.6 Extension to Higher-Order Designs

Clearly, a three-factor design contains a great deal of information, and its analysis is quite complicated. Considerable experience will be needed before you can take full advantage of this valuable research tool. Manipulating several independent variables simultaneously and discovering how they jointly influence behavior greatly expands our ability to examine phenomena realistically and comprehensively, but once any sort of complex interaction appears, sorting out the effects is hard. There is no single approach that applies to every three-factor design. You will have to take the time to study the group means and the different sets of marginal means carefully. Drawing graphs of the different sets of means is always valuable, and, when you begin to interpret the various interactions, the actual process of making a table of contrast values like Table 22.4 can be very illuminating.

We have emphasized the way that the analysis of a three-factor design is built on analytical techniques from the two-factor designs. The higher-order analyses are for the most part outgrowths or expansions of simpler tests, and most analyses in this chapter depend on a mastery and understanding of the two-factor analyses. You may need to move back and forth between this chapter and Chapters 12 and 13 to appreciate how the simpler tests apply to the complex design, and we encourage you to do so.

This general approach extends to designs with four or more factors with few changes. Of course, the variety and complexity of the hypotheses increase, but the testing strategies do not. You can generalize the simple effects and interactions here to designs with more factors, and test them in essentially the ways we have described.

The analysis of a multifactor design involves an interplay between the planned investigation of specific questions and the exploratory analysis that follows up a significant interaction. Both approaches are needed in most studies. When the single-*df* contrasts are not planned or obvious, an analyses of simple effects usually dominates the data analysis. But when the interaction components—the contrast-by-factor interactions and interaction contrasts—express clear research questions, their analysis will receive more emphasis. Your ability of use these approaches creatively and productively will improve as you apply them to your own research.

The approach you take to the analysis does not depend on whether you conduct the analysis by hand, computer, or some of both. Do not expect to be able to run a computer program once and find that the output contains everything you need. As your first results suggest new analyses, you will need to return to the computer to calculate different contrasts or to test new hypotheses. The interpretation of a complex design is an iterative process in which plotting, calculating, testing, and, above all, thinking all play a part.

Exercises

22.1. If you have access to a computer program for the analysis of variance, apply it to the scores in Table 21.1 to duplicate the analyses in this chapter.

22.2. An experimenter is interested in the effects on pilot error of three new cockpit designs, each based on a different application of human-factors principles (factor B). A simulated cockpit of each type is built (at considerable cost), and the researcher plans to look at the magnitude of error accumulated by experienced pilots "flying" in each. The researcher is also interested in the way that the pilot's training in the cockpit interacts with the cockpit design, so proposes to use three training conditions (factor A): no training, training by written instruction only (desk training), and actual simulator training. There are three types of pilots available for the study (factor C): civilian, commercial, and military. As a dependent variable the number of errors made during a one hour simulation flight is measured. The experimenter uses $n = 10$ pilots in each condition and obtains the following means:

	Civilian (c_1)			Commercial (c_2)			Military (c_3)		
Training	b_1	b_2	b_3	b_1	b_2	b_3	b_1	b_2	b_3
None (a_1)	13.4	16.2	15.8	9.1	10.2	11.8	8.2	15.1	14.3
Desk (a_2)	6.5	10.9	8.7	3.8	16.6	13.2	7.0	9.8	6.4
Simulator (a_3)	9.1	11.4	11.1	4.8	9.2	6.8	4.6	8.8	7.3

For each of the following questions, identify the nature of the test and then calculate the appropriate sum of squares.

a. The type of pilot has no effect on the outcome.
b. Some types of cockpit designs are better for pilots who have had no specific training on that design (the *none* condition) while others are better for pilots who have been specifically trained on that simulator (the *simulator* condition).
c. Desk training is as good as simulator training.
d. Cockpit design b_1 produces the same number of errors as the average of designs b_2 and b_3.
e. The difference between desk and simulator training is the same for commercial pilots as for military pilots.

22.3. The analysis in Problem 21.3 revealed that the three-way interaction was not significant. Consequently, we would look next at the two-way interactions instead of the simple interaction effects. The interaction of the three workbooks (factor A) and gender (C) was the only significant two-way interaction in the analysis.

a. In Section 12.1, we discussed different strategies for interpreting a significant two-way interaction depending on the relative dominance of the interaction and the main effects. One way to decide which situation applies is to study a plot of the marginal means. What do the $\overline{Y}_{AC}$ means tell you here?
b. Another way is to compare partial effect sizes (calculated in Problem 21.5) for the $A{\times}C$ interaction and the two main effects. What does this comparison show?
c. Do the three workbooks differ from one another? Control your tests for Type I error using the Fisher-Hayter procedure.
d. How are these pairwise differences modulated by the gender factor?

22.4. Let's assume the following contrasts lie behind the design summarized in Table 21.2 (p. 468):

$$\psi_{A_1} = \mu_2 - \mu_3, \quad \psi_{A_2} = \mu_1 - \tfrac{1}{2}(\mu_2 + \mu_3), \quad \psi_{A_3} = \mu_1 - \mu_2, \quad \text{and} \quad \psi_{A_4} = \mu_1 - \mu_3;$$
$$\psi_{B_1} = \mu_1 - \mu_2 \quad \text{and} \quad \psi_{B_2} = \mu_2 - \mu_3;$$
$$\psi_{C_1} = \mu_1 - \mu_2.$$

a. There are eight three-way interaction contrasts that may be constructed by combining these planned contrasts. We illustrated one of these in Section 22.4. What are the remaining seven and what aspect of the $A \times B \times C$ interaction does each capture?

b. Test the interaction contrast formed by crossing ψ_{A_4}, ψ_{B_2}, and ψ_{C_1}.

22.5. A set of means in which three two-way interactions are present is easy to confuse with a three-way interaction (for example, see Figure 21.4, p. 475). The following set of means, which have no three-way interaction, illustrate the point:

	c_1		c_2	
	b_1	b_2	b_1	b_2
a_1	3.25	3.75	5.75	6.25
a_2	7.25	2.75	5.75	1.25

a. Plot the data following the format used for Figure 21.4. Is the absence of a three-way interaction more obvious under these circumstances? Explain.

b. Use Equation 22.7 to calculate the value of the $A \times B$ simple interaction at both levels of factor C. Demonstrate that a three-way interaction is absent.

22.6. The analysis of the study by Petty et al. (1981) in Problem 21.5 found a significant the three-way interaction. Because the authors predicted a particular form of this interaction, they conducted additional analyses to seek support for their theoretical predictions.

a. They predicted a significant simple interaction of argument strength (factor A) and involvement (factor B) for both the regular and the rhetorical stylistic forms (factor C). Verify that both of these predicted simple interactions are significant (use $MS_{S/ABC} = 0.710$ as the error term).

b. They also predicted different *forms* for these two simple interactions:

- When the arguments were presented in the regular style (level c_1), strong arguments (a_1) would result in a more favorable attitude than weak arguments (a_2) for the highly involved students (b_1), but have little effect for the less involved students (b_2).

- When the arguments were presented in the rhetorical style (level c_2), the results would reverse: strong arguments would result in a more favorable attitude than weak arguments only for the less involved students.

Were these predictions supported?

23

Within-Subject
and Mixed Designs

The last two chapters concerned the completely between-subjects three-factor design. There are also three-factor designs in which one or more factors is varied within subjects. As far as the effects and their interpretation go, these designs are identical to their between-subjects counterpart. Specifically, their interpretation uses the same collection of analytical analyses that we discussed in Chapter 22. Where they differ is in the error terms needed to perform the tests. This chapter examines the differences between the between-subjects design and its within-subject variants. You need to understand this material even when you will use a computer to do the calculations. As you will see, the relationship between the types of analytical effects and their error terms is complex enough that you must have control of the analysis process.

23.1 Varieties of Three-Factor Designs

Because any independent variable can be either a between-subjects factor or a within-subject factor, there are four basic types of three-way designs:

- When all factors are varied between subjects, we have the $A \times B \times C$ design of Chapters 21 and 22.
- When one factor, say factor C, is varied within subject and the others between subjects, we have an $A \times B \times (C \times S)$ design. It is one counterpart of the two-factor mixed design of Chapters 19 and 20.
- When two factors, B and C, are varied within subject and factor A between subjects, we have an $A \times (B \times C \times S)$ design. It is another mixed design.
- When all factors are varied within subject, we have a completely within-subject $A \times B \times C \times S$ design. It is the counterpart of the two-factor within-subject design in Chapter 18.

Table 23.1 shows the data layouts for the three designs involving within-subject factors for a 2×2×2 factorial experiment, with $n = 2$ observations in each of the $abc = (2)(2)(2) = 8$ treatment conditions. As with the between-subjects three-factor design, the individual scores are designated by Y_{ijkl}, where subscript i identifies a subject

Table 23.1: The $ABCS$ data layouts for the three-way factorial designs that include a within-subject factor.

The $A \times B \times (C \times S)$ design

			c_1	c_2
a_1	b_1	s_{111}	Y_{1111}	Y_{1112}
		s_{211}	Y_{2111}	Y_{2112}
	b_2	s_{112}	Y_{1121}	Y_{1122}
		s_{212}	Y_{2121}	Y_{2122}
a_2	b_1	s_{121}	Y_{1211}	Y_{1212}
		s_{221}	Y_{2211}	Y_{2212}
	b_2	s_{122}	Y_{1221}	Y_{1222}
		s_{222}	Y_{2221}	Y_{2222}

The $A \times (B \times C \times S)$ design

		b_1c_1	b_1c_2	b_2c_1	b_2c_2
a_1	s_{11}	Y_{1111}	Y_{1112}	Y_{1121}	Y_{1122}
	s_{21}	Y_{2111}	Y_{2112}	Y_{2121}	Y_{2122}
a_2	s_{12}	Y_{1211}	Y_{1212}	Y_{1221}	Y_{1222}
	s_{22}	Y_{2211}	Y_{2212}	Y_{2221}	Y_{2222}

The $A \times B \times C \times S$ design

	$a_1b_1c_1$	$a_1b_1c_2$	$a_1b_2c_1$	$a_1b_2c_2$	$a_2b_1c_1$	$a_2b_1c_2$	$a_2b_2c_1$	$a_2b_2c_2$
s_1	Y_{1111}	Y_{1112}	Y_{1121}	Y_{1122}	Y_{1211}	Y_{1212}	Y_{1221}	Y_{1222}
s_2	Y_{2111}	Y_{2112}	Y_{2121}	Y_{2122}	Y_{2211}	Y_{2212}	Y_{2221}	Y_{2222}

in a particular condition and the remaining subscripts the levels of the three factors: subscript j the levels of factor A, subscript k the levels of factor B, and subscript l the levels of factor C. In the table, each subject corresponds to a row, and the observations in a particular within-subject condition to a column. Note that we have used a compound index for the subjects in the mixed designs, just as we did for the two-factor mixed design (Table 19.1, p. 433). For each mixed design, the first part (the subscript i) designates the subject within a group and the other parts the group to which that subject belongs.

All the designs in Table 23.1 involve the same number of observations, $abcn$, which here equals 16. There is a trade-off between the number of scores per subject and the number of subjects. As the number of scores per subject increases, the number of subjects decreases. This, of course, is a signal benefit of a within-subject design.

23.2 The Overall Analysis

The analysis of both the completely within-subject and the mixed designs follows principles that are essentially the same as those that we discussed for the two-factor designs of the same type. We will begin by reviewing them.

Effects and Sources of Variability

The three independent variables in these designs have a factorial structure. Every level of factor A appears with every level of factors B and C, and with every $B \times C$ combination. The same holds for every other way of viewing the design. Thus, as in the three-factor between-subjects design, in addition to the test of the grand mean (the null hypothesis that $\mu_T = 0$), there are seven testable effects—three main effects (A, B, and C), three two-way interactions ($A \times B$, $A \times C$, and $B \times C$), and one three-way interaction ($A \times B \times C$).

The three designs differ in the structure of the subject source of variability. We saw that in the $A \times B \times C$ design the subjects are nested within the different combinations of the three factors, and so the subject source is denoted S/ABC. In the $A \times B \times (C \times S)$ design at the top of Table 23.1, subjects are nested in combinations of factors A and B, so that the subject factor is denoted S/AB, just as it was in the two-factor $A \times B$ design. In the $A \times (B \times C \times S)$ design, they are nested only within factor A, and the subject factor is denoted S/A. Finally, in the $A \times B \times C \times S$ design, there is no nesting of subjectsand the subject factor is just denoted by S.

The within-subject factors in these designs are crossed with subjects, which gives rise to interactions. In the $A \times B \times (C \times S)$ design, factor C is crossed with subjects. Four $C \times S$ components appear in Table 23.1, one within each of the ab separate blocks. The interaction, with its nesting included, is denoted $C \times S/AB$. The other mixed design, $A \times (B \times C \times S)$, has more subject interactions. Specifically, the subjects are crossed with factor B, factor C, and with their combination, all within the a levels of factor A. This design, then, includes $B \times S/A$, $C \times S/A$, $B \times C \times S/A$ interactions. Finally, in the completely within-subject design, the subjects are crossed with all the other factors, giving rise to seven interactions, from $A \times S$ to $A \times B \times C \times S$.

Selection of the Error Terms

Particularly when we are working with the mixed designs, it is helpful to begin by sorting the effects into those that are entirely measured between subjects and those that include one or more within-subject factors. In Table 23.2 we have made this division for the three within-subject designs and also segregated the measurable sources into effects and error. First consider the classification of the substantive effects— three main effects, three two-way interactions, and the three-way interaction. For the $A \times B \times (C \times S)$ design on the left, there are four between-subjects effects (the grand mean, A, B, and $A \times B$); for the $A \times (B \times C \times S)$ design in the middle, there are two (the grand mean and A); and in the $A \times B \times C \times S$ design on the right, only the grand mean is a between-subjects effect. We have included the test of the grand mean among these effects because you will find it in the output of many computer programs, often labeled as the *intercept*. The remaining effects are classified as within-subject effects.

Now turn to the error terms. They are determined by the two principles we introduced when we discussed the two-factor mixed design (Table 19.3, p. 436):

Table 23.2: Substantive effects and error terms for the three-way factorial designs with one or more within-subject factor.

$A \times B \times (C \times S)$		$A \times (B \times C \times S)$		$A \times B \times C \times S$	
Effect	Error	Effect	Error	Effect	Error
Between-subjects effects					
G.M.	S/AB	G.M.	S/A	G.M.	S
A	S/AB	A	S/A		
B	S/AB				
$A \times B$	S/AB				
Within-subject effects					
				A	$A \times S$
		B	$B \times S/A$	B	$B \times S$
C	$C \times S/AB$	C	$C \times S/A$	C	$C \times S$
		$A \times B$	$B \times S/A$	$A \times B$	$A \times B \times S$
$A \times C$	$C \times S/AB$	$A \times C$	$C \times S/A$	$A \times C$	$A \times C \times S$
$B \times C$	$C \times S/AB$	$B \times C$	$B \times C \times S/A$	$B \times C$	$B \times C \times S$
$A \times B \times C$	$C \times S/AB$	$A \times B \times C$	$B \times C \times S/A$	$A \times B \times C$	$A \times B \times C \times S$

1. Each completely between-subjects effect is tested against the variability among the subjects within the groups.

2. Each effect involving within-subject factors is tested against the interaction of the within-subject portion of that effect with the subject factor.

The first principle indicates that we test the pure between-subjects effects with exactly the same error term that would be used had the within-subject factors been ignored and one observation been recorded from each subject. Thus in the $A \times B \times (C \times S)$ design, the four between-subjects effects are tested as they would be in an actual two-factor $A \times B$ design, using the error term S/AB. Similarly, in the $A \times (B \times C \times S)$ design, the tests of the two between-subjects effects are equivalent to those in an actual single-factor design and use the error term S/A. These error terms are listed next to the effects in Table 23.2.

The second principle determines the error terms for the within-subject effects. In the $A \times B \times (C \times S)$ design, all the within-subject effects involve factor C. Hence the error term for every effect is the interaction of C with the subject effect S/AB, that is, $C \times S/AB$. In the $A \times (B \times C \times S)$ design, there are three different error terms. For the B and $A \times B$ effects, the error is the interaction of the within-subject factor B with subjects, namely $B \times S/A$. Similarly, for the C and $A \times C$ effects, the error term is $C \times S/A$, and for the $B \times C$ and $A \times B \times C$ effects, it is $B \times C \times S/A$. In the completely within-subject design, the error term for each effect is that effect's interaction with subjects, $A \times S$ through $A \times B \times C \times S$, as listed in Table 23.2. Incidentally, these principles are completely general and apply without change to designs with any number of factors.

Degrees of Freedom and Calculations

The degrees of freedom for these designs are determined by a direct application of the rules for the two-factor between-subjects design in Table 11.3 (p. 215). The middle three steps concern us here:

1. The main effect of a factor has degrees of freedom equal to the number of levels of that factor less one.
2. An interaction has degrees of freedom equal to the product of the degrees of freedom of its separate parts.
3. When a source has a slash in its name, multiply the degrees of freedom for the effect or interaction by the number of levels of the factors listed to the right of the slash (or the leftmost slash, if there is more than one).

Take as an example one of the more complicated sources of variability, $B{\times}C{\times}S/A$. Its degrees of freedom are the product of terms for each of the four factors. The value for each of the three interacting terms (B, C, and S) is one less than the corresponding number of levels, and the value for the nesting factor A is its number of levels:

$$df_{B{\times}C{\times}S/A} = (b{-}1)(c{-}1)(n{-}1)a.$$

In the unlikely event that you must calculate by hand, you can use the rules we described in Table 11.4 (p. 216) to expand the degrees-of-freedom formulas and to convert them to sums of squares. We will not review these familiar steps again.

When using the computer, you need to organize your data properly and to specify the design correctly. The basic organization for each design is typically the one in Table 23.1: There is a column for each score, plus as many columns as are needed to indicate each subject's group assignment. For the $A{\times}B{\times}(C{\times}S)$ design, say with $c = 2$, each subject would be represented by four numbers, two to indicate the levels of j and k (factors A and B, respectively) and two for the observations Y_{ijk1} and Y_{ijk2} at the two levels of factor C. For the $A{\times}(B{\times}C{\times}S)$ design, there is one grouping variable and bc columns of data, and for the $A{\times}B{\times}C{\times}S$ design, there are no grouping variables, simply abc columns of data. The way that design itself is specified varies from program to program.

After running a computer analysis, be sure to check the output to see that the groups have the proper layout, that the means are correct (verify a few—you don't need to check them all), and that the degrees of freedom are what they should be. A common error in using a program is to specify the design incorrectly. Usually when that happens, either the structure of the analysis will be wrong or one or another of these quantities will be incorrect.

23.3   Two Examples of Mixed Designs

We will illustrate each of the two mixed designs with an example. The examples show the effects and error terms we described above and, in Section 23.5, how analytical analyses are applied. You can also use them as test data to verify that you using a computer program correctly.[1] To keep the examples simple, we use an unrealisti-

---

[1] If you do so, note that our numerical calculations use intermediate values that have been rounded. Because a computer carries many more places in its internal arithmetic, the answers the program provides will differ slightly from those we give.

Table 23.3: *Numerical example of a mixed three-way factorial design with two between-subjects factors (A and B) and one within-subject factor (C).*

		Data			**Analysis of variance**				
		c_1	c_2	c_3	Source	SS	df	MS	F
a_1b_1	s_{111}	11	5	3	A (drugs)	176.167	2	88.084	3.44
	s_{211}	12	10	5	B (drive)	0.694	1	0.694	0.03
a_1b_2	s_{112}	17	11	11	$A{\times}B$	309.722	2	154.861	6.05*
	s_{212}	18	16	13	S/AB	153.500	6	25.583	
a_2b_1	s_{121}	20	14	13	Between	640.083	11		
	s_{221}	12	10	9	C (days)	191.167	2	95.584	37.01*
a_2b_2	s_{122}	16	10	10	$A{\times}C$	7.667	4	1.917	0.74
	s_{222}	20	18	14	$B{\times}C$	1.722	2	0.861	0.33
a_3b_1	s_{131}	23	17	18	$A{\times}B{\times}C$	11.111	4	2.778	1.08
	s_{231}	22	19	22	$C{\times}S/AB$	31.000	12	2.583	
a_3b_2	s_{132}	14	8	8	Within	242.667	24		
	s_{232}	18	16	12	Total	882.750	35		

$*p < .05$

cally small amount of data—only two or three subjects per condition—so we will not emphasize the significance or nonsignificance of the "results."

The $A{\times}B{\times}(C{\times}S)$ Design

For this example, let's return to the two-factor between-subjects experiment in Section 11.3. In that study, the ability of monkeys to solve discrimination problems was studied as a function of certain drug conditions (control, drug X, and drug Y) and drive levels (one hour and 24 hours of food deprivation). Suppose the experiment is expanded by testing the monkeys over three days under the same conditions, but with different sets of discrimination problems. The design includes the original independent variables as between-subjects factors—drug conditions (factor A) and food deprivation (factor B)—and adds the three testing days (factor C) as a within-subject factor. Data for $n = 2$ subjects are given on the left of Table 23.3.

The analysis of variance for these data is summarized on the right of Table 23.3. We have divided the output into the between-subjects and within-subject effects, as they are in the output of many computer programs. Each set of effects involves a different error term, S/AB for the between-subjects effects and $C{\times}S/AB$ for the within-subject effects. Two effects are significant: an interaction of the drug conditions and food deprivation and a main effect of days. The means responsible for these two effects are

	1 hr	24 hr		Day 1	Day 2	Day 3
Control	7.67	14.33		16.92	12.83	11.50
Drug X	13.00	14.67				
Drug Y	20.17	12.67				

With only one significant two-way interaction and a nonsignificant $A \times B \times C$ inter-action, a follow-up analysis would focus on the two-way marginal AB table and the one-way marginal C table. Moreover, the fact that these two effects involve different factors (A and B for the interaction and C for the main effect) indicates that we can interpret them independently. The pattern of the AB marginal means on the left essentially duplicates the $A \times B$ interaction in Table 11.8 (p. 221)—a sizeable effect of the drug conditions (factor A) for the subjects under one hour of food deprivation (b_1) and little or no effect under 24 hours (b_2). The means for the main effect of factor C on the right exhibit a steady decrease in errors over the three days of testing.

The $A \times (B \times C \times S)$ Design

We will base our example of this type of mixed design on the numerical example in Table 18.3 (p. 407). College students were given a list of 60 words to study and recalled them at the end of the study period. The original list contained equal numbers of words of different emotional value (negative, positive, and neutral), and equal numbers of each type of word were presented either 1, 2, 3, or 4 times—we only use three levels in this example. Suppose we include the gender of the subjects as a third factor. The resulting design is a mixed three-factor experiment, $A \times (B \times C \times S)$, in which factor A (gender) is a between-subjects factor and factor B (emotional value) and C (presentations) are the within-subject factors. Data from this study are presented at the top of Table 23.4.

The results of the analysis of variance are given in the bottom of Table 23.4. Again we have separated the two types of effects, but this time the within-subject portion of the design requires a different error term for each combination of within-subject factors. One of the two-way interactions ($A \times B$) and two of the main effects (B and C) are significant. The means responsible for these effects are

	Neg.	Pos.	Neut.		1 time	2 times	3 times
Female	1.89	3.33	3.33		1.89	2.83	3.33
Male	2.44	2.78	2.33				

The follow-up analyses would concentrate on the interaction of word type and gender and on the main effect of the number of presentations.

23.4   Analytical Analyses in the $A \times B \times C \times S$ Design

The analytical procedures for the three-factor between-subjects design also apply to the within-subject designs. We can use any of the many effects and contrasts in Table 22.1 (p. 488). Their sums of squares are calculated as we described there, and their interpretation is unchanged by the within-subject nature of the factors. What makes the situation more complicated is the error terms. We consider the analytical analysis of the pure within-subject design in this section and that of the mixed designs in the next.

Error-term selection in the three-factor within-subject design follows the principles we introduced in Table 18.5 (p. 409) for the two-factor $A \times B \times S$ design:

Table 23.4: Numerical example of a mixed three-way factorial design with one between-subjects factor (A) and two within-subject factors (B and C).

		— c_1 —			— c_2 —			— c_3 —		
		b_1	b_2	b_3	b_1	b_2	b_3	b_1	b_2	b_3
	s_{11}	1	1	2	1	3	2	2	4	2
Female a_1	s_{21}	2	3	3	2	4	4	3	5	4
	s_{31}	1	2	3	3	3	5	2	5	5
	s_{12}	2	1	1	2	2	2	3	3	2
Male a_2	s_{22}	3	2	3	3	4	3	5	5	4
	s_{32}	1	2	1	2	3	3	1	3	2

Analysis of variance

Source	SS	df	MS	F
A (gender)	1.500	1	1.500	0.25
S/A	24.370	4	6.093	
Between	25.870	5		
B (word type)	7.704	2	3.852	5.47*
$A \times B$	5.778	2	2.889	4.10*
$B \times S/A$	5.630	8	0.704	
C (presentations)	19.370	2	9.685	18.04*
$A \times C$	0.111	2	0.056	0.10
$C \times S/A$	4.296	8	0.537	
$B \times C$	4.074	4	1.019	3.73
$A \times B \times C$	0.444	4	0.111	0.41
$B \times C \times S/A$	4.370	16	0.273	
Within	51.777	48		
Total	77.647	53		

$*p < .05$

1. Any effect involving a contrast on a within-subject factor is tested against an error term that includes the interaction of that contrast with subjects. To calculate this error term, create a contrast variable by applying the contrast to each subject's data, then analyze these values as if they come from a simpler design.

2. Any within-subject effect involving a portion of the data (e.g., a simple effect) is tested against an error term derived exclusively from those data. To calculate this error term, simply extract these data and analyze them as if they come from a simpler design.

The calculations are very similar to those in the two-factor case in Section 18.2, so we will only describe the application of the rules briefly.

Two types of simple effects arise in three-factor designs: those that are defined by the levels of one factor, for example, A at c_1 or $A \times B$ at c_1, and those that are defined by the levels of two factors, for example A at $b_1 c_2$. The direct way to analyze any of these simple effects is to restrict attention to the relevant levels of the conditioning factor (c_1 or $b_1 c_2$ in these examples), and analyze the design as a simpler one. We illustrated this procedure for the two-factor within-subject design in Table 18.8 (p. 413), and it applies here unchanged.

When you are interested in looking at a contrast, you can analyze it by replacing the relevant factor or factors by a contrast variable, then analyzing the resulting design. The test of the grand mean in the reduced analysis is equivalent to the test of the main contrast, and the other tests are equivalent to those of the interaction of this contrast with the corresponding factor or contrasts in the reduced design. We illustrated this process for the two-factor design in Table 18.6 (p. 410). When the single-df effect in question is actually an interaction contrast—e.g., ψ_{AB} or ψ_{ABC}—we reduce the two or three factors involved to a single contrast variable and test the hypothesis that the mean of the resulting single column of scores is zero, using either an analysis of variance or a t test. We illustrated this procedure on pages 414–416.

Each type of analysis—restriction to a single level of a factor or construction of a contrast variable—reduces the design to one with fewer factors, and any effects that it involves are obtained, along with their correct error terms, by the analysis of this simpler arrangement of the data.

23.5   Analytical Analysis in Mixed Designs

We now turn to the two mixed designs, $A \times B \times (C \times S)$ and $A \times (B \times C \times S)$. These are by far the most complicated designs we have covered, and we know that it will be difficult to appreciate the details until you analyze your own experiment. Our treatment here is, therefore, more of a reference than a set of facts to be learned. However, once you can apply an analytical analysis to these designs, you will be well on your way to analyzing any sort of design.

The complexity of the three-factor mixed designs does not arise from the effects that are tested—these are the same as in the pure between-subjects or within-subject designs—but from the way that they are tested. Our discussion will concentrate on how to select the appropriate error term for a given effect. We will describe the possibilities in general first, then illustrate them numerically.

Contrasts in the Entire Design

We begin with the analytical effects that involve the entire design. These effects, which are listed in the first column of Table 23.5, are grouped into three categories—main contrasts, two-way interaction components, and three-way interaction components. We discussed the meaning of these effects in Section 22.1 (and throughout that chapter) in the context of the between-subjects design. The other two columns specify the error terms for the $A \times B \times (C \times S)$ and $A \times (B \times C \times S)$ designs. This listing of effects and error terms is complicated, partly because we are covering two designs, partly because we have listed all types of effects in the table, but primarily because the error terms depend on whether the factors involved are manipulated between subjects or within subjects.

Table 23.5: *Error terms in the two three-factor mixed designs for contrast effects and interaction contrasts over the full set of data.*

	Error Terms	
Effect	$A \times B \times (C \times S)$	$A \times (B \times C \times S)$
ψ_A	S/AB	S/A
ψ_B	S/AB	$\psi_B \times S/A$
ψ_C	$\psi_C \times S/AB$	$\psi_C \times S/A$
$\psi_A \times B$	S/AB	$B \times S/A$
$A \times \psi_B$	S/AB	$\psi_B \times S/A$
$\psi_A \times \psi_B$	S/AB	$\psi_B \times S/A$
$\psi_A \times C$	$C \times S/AB$	$C \times S/A$
$A \times \psi_C$	$\psi_C \times S/AB$	$\psi_C \times S/A$
$\psi_A \times \psi_C$	$\psi_C \times S/AB$	$\psi_C \times S/A$
$\psi_B \times C$	$C \times S/AB$	$\psi_B \times C \times S/A$
$B \times \psi_C$	$\psi_C \times S/AB$	$B \times \psi_C \times S/A$
$\psi_B \times \psi_C$	$\psi_C \times S/AB$	$\psi_B \times \psi_C \times S/A$
$\psi_A \times B \times C$	$C \times S/AB$	$B \times C \times S/A$
$A \times \psi_B \times C$	$C \times S/AB$	$\psi_B \times C \times S/A$
$A \times B \times \psi_C$	$\psi_C \times S/AB$	$B \times \psi_C \times S/A$
$\psi_A \times \psi_B \times C$	$C \times S/AB$	$\psi_B \times C \times S/A$
$\psi_A \times B \times \psi_C$	$\psi_C \times S/AB$	$B \times \psi_C \times S/A$
$A \times \psi_B \times \psi_C$	$\psi_C \times S/AB$	$\psi_B \times \psi_C \times S/A$
$\psi_A \times \psi_B \times \psi_C$	$\psi_C \times S/AB$	$\psi_B \times \psi_C \times S/A$

The error terms for these effects are derived from the pair of principles in Table 23.6, a version of those we presented in Table 19.3 (p. 436). They indicate that the completely between-subjects effects are tested against the between-subjects error terms in the two designs—S/AB or S/A, respectively—and that effects involving within-subject factors are tested against interactions with subjects.

Let's apply these principles to some of the effects in Table 23.5. The between-subjects effects are the easiest. In the $A \times B \times (C \times S)$ design, these effects are the

Table 23.6: *Principles for finding contrast-effect error terms in mixed designs.*

1. Any effect involving only between-subjects factors is tested against the variability among the subjects within the groups.
2. Any effect involving a contrast on a within-subject factor is tested against an error term that includes the interaction of that contrast with subjects. To calculate this error term, create a contrast variable by applying the contrast to each subject's data, then analyze these values as if they come from a simpler design.

contrasts ψ_A and ψ_B and the interactions $\psi_A \times B$, $A \times \psi_B$ and $\psi_A \times \psi_B$. They are all tested against the nested subject factor S/AB. In the $A \times (B \times C \times S)$ design, the only pure between-subjects effect is ψ_A, and it is tested against S/A.

The remaining effects in Table 23.5 involve some within-subject information and the second principle applies. For these effects, the error terms are the interaction of the within-subject portion of the effects with subjects, that is, with S/AB or S/A, depending on the design. As a simple example, the main contrast ψ_C, which is a within-subject factor in both designs, is tested against $\psi_C \times S/AB$ in the $A \times B \times (C \times S)$ design and $\psi_C \times S/A$ in the $A \times (B \times C \times S)$ design. As a more complex example, consider the two-way contrast-by-factor interaction $B \times \psi_C$. In the $A \times B \times (C \times S)$ design, only C is a within-subject factor, and the effect is tested against the interaction of ψ_C and the subject factor S/AB, i.e. $\psi_C \times S/AB$. In the $A \times (B \times C \times S)$ design, the effect is tested against the interaction of the two within-subject factors $(B \times \psi_C)$ with the subject factor S/A, i.e. $B \times \psi_C \times S/A$.

To obtain the sums of squares for effects and error terms involving within-subject contrasts, the second principle in Table 23.6 tells us to construct a contrast variable. For example, to investigate the $A \times \psi_C$ interaction in either of the two designs, we create the contrast variable $\widehat{\psi}_{ijk}$ by calculating ψ_C for each subject. We then analyze the resulting numbers as a two-factor design involving factors A and B—a completely between-subjects factorial for the $A \times B \times (C \times S)$ design and a mixed factorial for the $A \times (B \times C \times S)$ design. This approach automatically produces the error terms in Table 23.5. We will give several numerical examples below.

Simple Effects

The questions addressed by simple effects are richly diverse, particularly when contrasts are added to the analysis. The selection of error terms to test these effects is much more complicated in mixed designs than in either completely between-subjects or within-subject designs. One approach is to analyze the simple effects directly by isolating the observations relevant to the question and analyzing the data as if they come from a simpler design. This direct analysis leads to a **restricted error term**. If within-subject contrasts are involved, we can use contrast variables to simplify the design further.

When the between-groups homogeneity assumptions are met, the restricted error terms can be averaged over the groups to form a **pooled error term**, also sometimes known as the **within-cell error**. This error term has more degrees of freedom than the restricted error term, and hence gives tests with greater power. Instead of actually averaging the restricted error terms, the pooled error term can be calculated by combining two or more sums of squares from the overall analysis. The principles for selecting error terms are summarized in Table 23.7. The first pair of principles distinguishes between restricted and pooled error terms, and the second pair indicates how pooled error terms are obtained from the summary of the overall analysis.

Table 23.8 lists the many types of simple effects for these designs, along with their error terms. We will go through this table slowly. It is divided into three sections. The first contains the different types of simple effects involving a between-subjects factor (factor A in both designs). Here we have both simple effects and contrasts based on two-way marginal means (A at b_k and at c_l) and those based on cell means

Table 23.7: Principles required to determine error terms for simple effects in mixed designs.

Restricted and pooled error terms for simple effects

> 1. A restricted error term is derived exclusively from that portion of the data defining a given simple effect. To calculate this error term, simply extract these observations and analyze the data as if they come from a simpler design.
> 2. A pooled error term averages an entire set of restricted error terms. When appropriate, tests using pooled error terms are more powerful than those using restricted error terms.

Calculating pooled error terms from the overall analysis

> 1. When simple effects are restricted exclusively to the levels of a between-subjects factor (or factors), the pooled error term is the one used to test the corresponding effect in the overall analysis. This type of pooling is relatively common.
> 2. When simple effects are restricted to the levels of a within-subject factor (or factors), the pooled error term combines the corresponding error for the tested factor from the overall analysis and its interaction with the restricted factor. This type of pooling is less common and more problematic.

(A at $b_k c_l$). The second section lists the corresponding simple effects and contrasts involving a within-subject factor (factor C in both designs).[2] The final section includes the simple interactions involving all three pairs of factors—$A \times B$ at c_l, $A \times C$ at b_k, $B \times C$ at a_j, and their related simple interaction components. The four right-hand columns contain the error terms for these effects.

The first member of the first pair of principles in Table 23.7 tells us that we can test simple effects by restricting our attention to the observations actually involved in the effect and leads to the error terms in the columns of Table 23.8 labeled *Restricted.* As an example of restricted error terms, consider the simple effect of A at c_l. Restricting the analysis to the scores at c_l creates a simpler design. For the $A \times B \times (C \times S)$ design, this subset of data corresponds to a two-factor between-subjects design, $A \times B$. The A effect in this reduced design has the error term S/AB (see Table 11.6, p. 218), and so in the three-factor design the error is S/AB at c_l. Similarly, in the $A \times (B \times C \times S)$ design, the restricted data set forms a two-factor mixed design, $A \times (B \times S)$. The error term for the A effect in this restricted design is S/A (see pages 436–437), and in the full design it is S/A at c_l. You may find it helpful to illustrate these restricted data subsets in the numerical examples of Tables 23.3 and 23.4 by blocking out all but the scores at c_1 and noting the subdesign that results. Another example is the simple effect of

---

[2]The table does not include simple effects for factor B. In the $A \times B \times (C \times S)$ design, where both A and B are between-subjects factors, they look like the effects for factor A, and for the $A \times (B \times C \times S)$ design, where both B and C are within-subject factors they look like those for factor C.

Table 23.8: *The varieties of simple effects in the two three-factor mixed designs, with their error terms. Sums of squares that are combined in the pooled error term are indicate by a sum of effects.*

Effect	$A{\times}B{\times}(C{\times}S)$ Restricted	Pooled	$A{\times}(B{\times}C{\times}S)$ Restricted	Pooled
A at b_k		S/AB	S/A at b_k	$S/A + B{\times}S/A$
ψ_A at b_k		S/AB	S/A at b_k	$S/A + B{\times}S/A$
A at c_l	S/AB at c_l	$S/AB + C{\times}S/AB$	S/A at c_l	$S/A + C{\times}S/A$
ψ_A at c_l	S/AB at c_l	$S/AB + C{\times}S/AB$	S/A at c_l	$S/A + C{\times}S/A$
A at $b_k c_l$	S/AB at c_l	$S/AB + C{\times}S/AB$	S/A at $b_k c_l$	$\star$
ψ_A at $b_k c_l$	S/AB at c_l	$S/AB + C{\times}S/AB$	S/A at $b_k c_l$	$\star$
C at b_k	$C{\times}S/A$ at b_k	$C{\times}S/AB$	$C{\times}S/A$ at b_k	$C{\times}S/A + B{\times}C{\times}S/A$
ψ_C at b_k	$\psi_C{\times}S/A$ at b_k	$\psi_C{\times}S/AB$	$\psi_C{\times}S/A$ at b_k	$\psi_C{\times}S/A + B{\times}\psi_C{\times}S/A$
C at a_j	$C{\times}S/B$ at a_j	$C{\times}S/AB$	$C{\times}S$ at a_j	$C{\times}S/A$
ψ_C at a_j	$\psi_C{\times}S/B$ at a_j	$\psi_C{\times}S/AB$	$\psi_C{\times}S$ at a_j	$\psi_C{\times}S/A$
C at $a_j b_k$	$C{\times}S$ at $a_j b_k$	$C{\times}S/AB$	$C{\times}S$ at $a_j b_k$	$C{\times}S/A + B{\times}C{\times}S/A$
ψ_C at $a_j b_k$	$\psi_C{\times}S$ at $a_j b_k$	$\psi_C{\times}S/AB$	$\psi_C{\times}S$ at $a_j b_k$	$\psi_C{\times}S/A + B{\times}\psi_C{\times}S/A$
$A{\times}B$ at c_l	S/AB at c_l	$S/AB + C{\times}S/AB$	$B{\times}S/A$ at c_l	$B{\times}S/A + B{\times}C{\times}S/A$
$\psi_A{\times}B$ at c_l	S/AB at c_l	$S/AB + C{\times}S/AB$	$B{\times}S/A$ at c_l	$B{\times}S/A + B{\times}C{\times}S/A$
$A{\times}\psi_B$ at c_l	S/AB at c_l	$S/AB + C{\times}S/AB$	$\psi_B{\times}S/A$ at c_l	$\psi_B{\times}S/A + \psi_B{\times}C{\times}S/A$
$\psi_A{\times}\psi_B$ at c_l	S/AB at c_l	$S/AB + C{\times}S/AB$	$\psi_B{\times}S/A$ at c_l	$\psi_B{\times}S/A + \psi_B{\times}C{\times}S/A$
$A{\times}C$ at b_k	$C{\times}S/A$ at b_k	$C{\times}S/AB$	$C{\times}S/A$ at b_k	$C{\times}S/A + B{\times}C{\times}S/A$
$\psi_A{\times}C$ at b_k	$C{\times}S/A$ at b_k	$C{\times}S/AB$	$C{\times}S/A$ at b_k	$C{\times}S/A + B{\times}C{\times}S/A$
$A{\times}\psi_C$ at b_k	$\psi_C{\times}S/A$ at b_k	$\psi_C{\times}S/AB$	$\psi_C{\times}S/A$ at b_k	$\psi_C{\times}S/A + B{\times}\psi_C{\times}S/A$
$\psi_A{\times}\psi_C$ at b_k	$\psi_C{\times}S/A$ at b_k	$\psi_C{\times}S/AB$	$\psi_C{\times}S/A$ at b_k	$\psi_C{\times}S/A + B{\times}\psi_C{\times}S/A$
$B{\times}C$ at a_j	$C{\times}S/B$ at a_j	$C{\times}S/AB$	$B{\times}C{\times}S$ at a_j	$B{\times}C{\times}S/A$
$\psi_B{\times}C$ at a_j	$C{\times}S/B$ at a_j	$C{\times}S/AB$	$\psi_B{\times}C{\times}S$ at a_j	$\psi_B{\times}C{\times}S/A$
$B{\times}\psi_C$ at a_j	$\psi_C{\times}S/B$ at a_j	$\psi_C{\times}S/AB$	$B{\times}\psi_C{\times}S$ at a_j	$B{\times}\psi_C{\times}S/A$
$\psi_B{\times}\psi_C$ at a_j	$\psi_C{\times}S/B$ at a_j	$\psi_C{\times}S/AB$	$B{\times}\psi_C{\times}S$ at a_j	$B{\times}\psi_C{\times}S/A$

$\star$: $S/A + B{\times}S/A + C{\times}S/A + B{\times}C{\times}S/A$

the within-subject factor C at b_k. Restricting the data to b_k turns both three-factor designs into an $A{\times}(C{\times}S)$ mixed design. The error term for the C effect in this design is $C{\times}S/A$, which in the full design is $C{\times}S/A$ at b_k. The other error terms in Table 23.8 are determined similarly. We have not listed restricted tests for the A at b_k effects in the $A{\times}B{\times}(C{\times}S)$ design because they are completely between-subjects effects, so they are tested against the pooled term, as in Chapter 12.

The second pair of principles in Table 23.7 concern the pooling of error terms to increase power. The tests that use the restricted error terms are safe because they do not require homogeneity assumptions, but when these assumptions can be made, a better estimate of the error—one based on more data and with more degrees of freedom—gives greater power. The first of the two principles concerns simple effects at a level of a between-subjects factor, and the second concerns simple effects at a level of a within-subject factor. Earlier we indicated that instead of averaging corresponding error terms from all levels of the conditioning factor, we can use either an error source from the overall analysis or an average of several of them. These error terms are given in the two columns of Table 23.8 labeled *Pooled*.

Pooling over a between-subjects factor in this way is a fairly common procedure. Consider the simple effect of C at a_j. By the first principle, it can be tested against an error term that combines the restricted error terms over all levels of the between-subjects conditioning factor A. In the $A \times B \times (C \times S)$ design, the error terms $C \times S/B$ at a_j are aggregated over all levels of factor A, which gives $C \times S/AB$; in the $A \times (B \times C \times S)$ design, $C \times S$ at a_j is aggregated similarly to produce $C \times S/A$. We encountered this type of pooling with the two-factor mixed design on page 456.

Pooling over a within-subject factor is somewhat rarer. Consider the simple effect of A at c_l. The second principle applies here. It says that the test is against an error term that combines the restricted error terms over the levels of factor C. This pooling produces the type of *within-cell mean square* that appeared for the two-factor mixed design (see Equation 20.1, p. 451). The result is a sum of terms from the standard analysis, one being the error term for the effect that is being tested (here the A effect), the other being the interaction of that error term with the conditioning factor (here factor C). For the $A \times B \times (C \times S)$ design, the error term for the A at c_l effect combines the S/AB effect (the error term for the A effect) and the $C \times S/AB$ effect (the interaction of that error term with C):

$$MS_{\text{within cell}} = \frac{SS_{S/AB} + SS_{C \times S/AB}}{df_{S/AB} + df_{C \times S/AB}}. \tag{23.1}$$

In Table 23.8, we have abbreviated this combination as $S/AB + C \times S/AB$ to save space. For the A at c_l effect in the $A \times (B \times C \times S)$ design, a similar pooling gives $S/A + C \times S/A$. Pooling over the within-subject factor is considered more risky than pooling over a between-subjects factor because heterogeneity of variance is more likely among different measures than among different groups.

Numerical Examples

There are too many effects in Tables 23.5 and 23.8 to give worked examples for every one, but we will illustrate most common types. As you will see, the analysis is considerably less formidable than the number of possibilities suggests. Moreover, the number of separate analyses can often be reduced by testing several hypotheses within a single analysis.

Analyses Involving Only Between-Subjects Effects. The effects that involve only the between-subjects factors are the simpler to test. When a hypothesis involves exclusively between-subjects factors, the within-subject factors play no role in the analysis. For the $A \times B \times (C \times S)$ design, these are the various effects involving A, B, or $A \times B$; and for the $A \times (B \times C \times S)$ design, they involve only the effects of factor A. The most direct and interpretable way to conduct the analyses is to remove the within-subject factor completely, either by combining the within-subject information or by restricting the data to an appropriate level of the within-subject factor, depending on the hypothesis being tested. We illustrated both approaches in the two-factor mixed design in Section 20.1 (see Tables 20.2 and 20.3) and will apply them here to the data for the $A \times B \times (C \times S)$ design in Table 23.3. The between-subjects factors A and B in this design are the drug given and the amount of food deprivation, respectively, and the within-subject factor C is the day of testing.

We consider first the analysis of a contrast, both as a main comparison and as an interaction with the other between-subjects factor. For a between-subjects contrast, consider ψ_A with coefficient set $\{-1, \frac{1}{2}, \frac{1}{2}\}$ that compares the control condition (a_1) to the two drug groups (a_2 and a_3 combined). The significant $A \times B$ interaction implies we should examine both the main contrast and the contrast-by-factor interaction $\psi_A \times B$. We can conduct these tests as a single analysis. We start by averaging over the unused within-subject factor C (testing days) and subjects to form the AB table of means in Table 23.9. Each cell mean $\overline{Y}_{jk}$ here is based on $cn = 6$ of the original scores and the means $\overline{Y}_{A_j}$ are based on $bcn = 12$ scores. Next we calculate SS_{ψ_A} and $SS_{\psi_A \times B}$ as if these means came from an actual $A \times B$ design (Section 13.4; see Table 13.7). To the right of the means in Table 23.9 we enter the values of $\widehat{\psi}_A$ for both levels of factor B and the marginal means. At this point we might notice that there is a considerable difference between $\widehat{\psi}_A$ for the 1-hour and 24-hour deprivation groups, which suggests that the interaction will be important. We then calculate the three sums of squares using our standard formula (given most recently in Equation 22.2):

$$SS_{\psi_A} = \frac{N_{\text{mean}}\widehat{\psi}_A^2}{\sum c_j^2}.$$

Here $N_{\text{mean}} = cn = 6$ for $\overline{Y}_{jk}$ and $bcn = 12$ for the marginal means $\overline{Y}_{A_j}$. Thus, for the main contrast, we get

$$SS_{\psi_A} = \frac{bcn\widehat{\psi}_A^2}{\sum c_j^2} = \frac{(12)(4.126^2)}{1.5} = 136.191.$$

As the first row of Table 23.5 tells us, the resulting mean square is evaluated against $MS_{S/AB} = 25.583$, obtained from the overall analysis in Table 23.3, giving $F = 136.191/25.583 = 5.32$. It is not significant ($F_{.05}(1,6) = 5.99$). We now turn to the $\psi_A \times B$ interaction, for which we need the sums of squares for the simple contrasts. For the simple contrast at level b_1,

$$SS_{\psi_A \text{ at } b_1} = \frac{cn\widehat{\psi}_A^2{}_{\text{ at } b_1}}{\sum c_j^2} = \frac{(6)(8.917^2)}{1.5} = 318.052.$$

You can verify that $SS_{\psi_A \text{ at } b_2} = 1.774$. The sum of squares for the $\psi_A \times B$ interaction is obtained using Equation 13.11 (p. 280):

$$SS_{\psi_A \times B} = \sum SS_{\psi_A \text{ at } b_k} - SS_{\psi_A} = (318.052 + 1.774) - 136.191 = 183.635.$$

This contrast-by-factor interaction has $df_{\psi_A \times B} = b - 1 = 1$ (Equation 13.12) and is also tested against $MS_{S/AB}$. It is significant ($F = 7.18$), showing that ψ_A varies with the deprivation time.

This analyses duplicates the procedures used to analyze an actual $A \times B$ design. In fact, any of the analyses we discussed in Chapters 12 and 13 for an actual $A \times B$ design

Table 23.9: Marginal means and the analysis of a between-subjects contrast and its interaction with another between-subjects factor in a mixed design, using data from Table 23.3.

	Control	Drug X	Drug Y	$\widehat{\psi}_A$	SS_{ψ_A}
1 hr.	7.667	13.000	20.167	8.917	318.052
24 hr.	14.333	14.667	12.667	-0.666	1.774
$\overline{Y}_{A_j}$	11.000	13.834	16.417	4.126	136.191

can be applied to the two-factor table created by averaging over the within-subject factor.

The other type of between-subjects hypotheses are the simple effects at a given level of a within-subject factor. As an example, consider what happened on the last testing day (level c_3). The data for this level, extracted from Table 23.3, are at the top of Table 23.10. We analyze these numbers exactly like an ordinary two-factor between-subjects design, obtaining the results in the lower panels. In the summary table, we have indicating the conditioning on C by writing A at c_3, B at c_3, etc. The error term here ($MS_{S/AB}$ at c_3) is the restricted error term identified in Table 23.8. If we can assume the error terms at the other levels of factor C are homogeneous, we can increase the power of the test by pooling them. Table 23.8 tells us to combine S/AB and $C \times S/AB$ effects according to Equation 23.1:

$$MS_{\text{within cell}} = \frac{SS_{S/AB} + SS_{C \times S/AB}}{df_{S/AB} + df_{C \times S/AB}} = \frac{153.500 + 31.000}{6 + 12} = \frac{184.5}{18} = 10.25.$$

The increase in power comes because this mean squares has more degrees of freedom than the unpooled values (not from differences in the size of the error mean square). For the tests of the simple effect of A and the simple $A \times B$ interaction, the critical values is $F_{.05}(2, 18) = 3.55$ instead of $F_{.05}(2, 6) = 5.14$ for the restricted error term.

Analyses Involving Within-Subject Effects.   Analyses involving within-subject variability are more complicated than those of pure between-subjects effects because each effect needs a different error term. This error term is found by crossing the tested effect with subjects. In practice, the use of contrast variables and restricted data sets frequently makes the work relatively straightforward. Either constructing a contrast variable or restricting the data reduces the size of the data table, and this smaller table can be treated as if it came from a simpler design. This approach stays close to the results and is easy to use with a computer. We will illustrate this approach with the data for the $A \times (B \times C \times S)$ design in Table 23.4.

The number of presentations (factor C) in the example is a quantitative variable, to which a linear trend contrast applies. Using the linear trend coefficients $\{-1, 0, +1\}$, we calculate three contrast values for each subject, one for each level of factor B, taking the data from Table 23.4. For subject s_{11} the contrast scores are

$$\widehat{\psi}_{111} = -1 + 0 + 2 = 1, \quad \widehat{\psi}_{112} = -1 + 0 + 4 = 3, \quad \text{and} \quad \widehat{\psi}_{113} = -2 + 0 + 2 = 0.$$

Table 23.10: Analysis of the between-subjects simple interaction $A \times B$ at level c_3 of the within-subject factor from Table 23.3.

Observations on the third day c_3

	a_1		a_2		a_3	
	b_1	b_2	b_1	b_2	b_1	b_2
	3	11	13	10	18	8
	5	13	9	14	22	12

AB table of means

	b_1	b_2	Mean
a_1	4.0	12.0	8.00
a_2	11.0	12.0	11.50
a_3	20.0	10.0	15.00
Mean	11.67	11.33	11.50

Analysis of simple effects at level c_3

Source	SS	df	MS	F
A at c_3	98.000	2	49.000	8.17*
B at c_3	0.333	1	0.333	0.06
$A \times B$ at c_3	164.667	2	82.334	13.72*
S/AB at c_3	36.000	6	6.000	
Total	299.000	11		

*$p < .05$

The top panel of Table 23.11 gives values of the contrast variable for all the subjects. This table looks like the data from a mixed design with between-subjects factor A and within-subject factor B. It is analyzed using the formulas for an actual two-factor mixed design, giving the summary table (including the test of the grand mean) in the bottom panel. We have given two descriptions of each source of variability, one appropriate to an $A \times (B \times S)$ mixed design, labeled with a subscript ψ to indicate that the analysis was conducted with contrast scores, the other interpreting them in terms of the linear contrast ψ_C in the $A \times (B \times C \times S)$ mixed design. The two between-subjects effects (G.M.$_\psi$ and A_ψ) are tested against S/A_ψ, and the two within-subject effects (B_ψ and $A \times B_\psi$) against $B \times S/A_\psi$. Expressed as sources in the $A \times (B \times C \times S)$ design, these two error terms are $\psi_C \times S/A$ and $B \times \psi_C \times S/A$, as specified in Table 23.5.

This approach enabled us to test both a contrast (ψ_C) and three contrast-by-factor interactions ($A \times \psi_C$, $B \times \psi_C$, and $A \times B \times \psi_C$) in the same analysis. We could test any effect that is appropriate for an actual two-factor mixed design (Chapter 20) in the same way. To assess a $\psi_B \times \psi_C$ interaction contrast, for example, we would apply a contrast to factor B to produce a single score for each subject, as in Table 20.4 (p. 455), and test the grand mean. Similarly, we could test a contrast ψ_A in

Table 23.11: Analysis of a linear trend contrast for the within-subject factor C using the data in Table 23.4. The between-subjects and total sums of squares includes the grand mean.

Linear contrast variable $\widehat{\psi}_{ijk}$ created from factor C

	a_1				a_2		
	b_1	b_2	b_3		b_1	b_2	b_3
s_{11}	1	3	0	s_{12}	1	2	1
s_{21}	1	2	1	s_{22}	2	3	1
s_{31}	1	3	2	s_{32}	0	1	1

Analysis of variance of the linear contrasts

Source of variation					
For $\widehat{\psi}_{ijk}$	For Y_{ijkl}	SS	df	MS	F
G.M.$_\psi$	$\psi_{C_{\text{linear}}}$	37.556	1	37.556	42.25*
A_ψ	$A \times \psi_{C_{\text{linear}}}$	0.222	1	0.222	0.25
S/A_ψ	$\psi_{C_{\text{linear}}} \times S/A$	3.556	4	0.889	
Between		3.778	6		
B_ψ	$B \times \psi_{C_{\text{linear}}}$	7.111	2	3.556	9.14*
$A \times B_\psi$	$A \times B \times \psi_{C_{\text{linear}}}$	0.444	2	0.222	0.57
$B \times S/A_\psi$	$B \times \psi_{C_{\text{linear}}} \times S/A$	3.111	8	0.389	
Within		10.666	12		
Total		14.444	18		

*$p < .05$

the between-subjects factor to examine a $\psi_A \times \psi_C$ interaction contrast, following the procedure on pages 451–452. Combining both the calculation of the $\psi_B \times \psi_C$ contrast variable and the application of ψ_A, we could test the three-way interaction contrast $\psi_A \times \psi_B \times \psi_C$. Analyzing the contrast variable always gives us the correct error term.

What about simple effects? Suppose we wanted to analyze the female subjects (level a_1 of factor A). The easiest approach is to separate out the data for these subjects and analyze them directly as a $B \times C \times S$ two-factor within-subject design, following the procedures for an actual two-factor within-subject design in Chapter 18. The top panel of Table 23.12 shows the result.[3] Only the two simple main effects, B at a_1 and C at a_1 are significant. When the error variability for the female and male subjects are comparable, more powerful tests are obtained by pooling the error terms for the female and male subjects. These pooled error terms are taken from the original analysis—that is, $B \times S/A$ and $C \times S/A$, for the two simple effects, and $B \times C \times S/A$ for

---

[3]The error terms in this table are those specified in Table 23.8. Although that table lists only tests for factor C, you can determine the appropriate error terms for the other within-subject factor B by substituting B for C.

Table 23.12: Simple effects of factor B and C for the female subjects in Table 23.4 using restricted and pooled error terms.

Analysis using the restricted error terms

Source	SS	df	MS	F
B at a_1	12.519	2	6.260	8.25*
$B \times S$ at a_1	3.037	4	0.759	
C at a_1	11.185	2	5.593	21.59*
$C \times S$ at a_1	1.037	4	0.259	
$B \times C$ at a_1	3.037	4	0.759	2.21
$B \times C \times S$ at a_1	2.741	8	0.343	
Total	33.556	24		

*$p < .05$

Analysis using pooled error terms from Table 23.4

Source	SS	df	MS	F
B at a_1	12.519	2	6.260	8.89*
$B \times S/A$	5.630	8	0.704	
C at a_1	11.185	2	5.593	10.42*
$C \times S/A$	4.296	8	0.537	
$B \times C$ at a_1	3.037	4	0.759	2.78
$B \times C \times S/A$	4.370	16	0.273	

*$p < .05$

the simple interaction, as indicated in Table 23.8. The summary of this alternative analysis is found at the bottom of Table 23.12. The conclusions remain unchanged.

Exercises

Note: If you have access to a computer program, use it to perform the calculations for the following problems.

23.1. In the analysis of the $A \times B \times (C \times S)$ design in Table 23.3, the $A \times B$ interaction and C main effect were significant. Examine the interaction more closely.
a. Test the simple effects of the drug manipulation (factor A) at the two levels of food deprivation (b_1 and b_2).
b. If either of these simple effects is significant, test the following simple contrasts:
  i. One drug versus the other.
  ii. The control versus the combined drug conditions.
c. Examine the interaction of the level of food deprivation and a contrast expressing the difference between the two drug conditions.

23.2. The other significant effect in Table 23.3 was the main effect of factor C (days of testing). Examine it more closely.
a. Do the number of errors decrease steadily over the $c = 3$ days?
b. How well does a straight line describe this decrease?

23.3. The analysis of Table 23.4 revealed a significant main effect of word type (factor B) and an interaction with the gender of the subjects (factor A). Inspection of the means shows that females recalled fewer negative words than the other word types (positive and neutral), while males were relatively unaffected by word type. Analyze these observations systematically.

a. Test the simple effects of word type for the female and male subjects.

b. The simple effect of word type is significant only for the females. Probe this effect further by testing for a difference between the negative words and a combination of the positive and neutral words for the female subjects.

c. To conclude the contrast in the last part is actually different for male and female subjects, you need to examine the interaction of this contrast with gender. Test this marginal $A \times \psi_B$ interaction.

24

Random Factors and Generalizing Results

The focus of this chapter is the generalization of the results of an experiment. We have extensively discussed generalization over subjects—that our results should apply to subjects other than the ones we specifically test. Here we consider ways to generalize over other aspects of the design. Central to this process is the concept of a random factor. We will begin by discussing the generalization process and defining the notions of fixed and random factors. Then we will describe how the decision to treat certain factors as random changes the statistical analysis, and in particular the way F tests are constructed. Finally, we will illustrate the analysis by working out several specific designs. Our treatment of random factors continues in Chapter 25.

24.1 Statistical Generalization over Design Factors

The goal of the investigator in all psychological research is to make statements that apply to a larger collection of individuals and instances than it is possible to explicitly study. We collect data from groups of subjects, but as we discussed in Chapter 1, we intend these observations to apply to other, unstudied subjects.

Statistical and Extrastatistical Generalization

There are two approaches to generalization in research—statistical and extrastatistical—and most studies use both. The F test is an example of **statistical generalization**. We assume that our data constitute a random sample from some larger population and use our knowledge of sampling to test hypotheses and make estimates about this population. However, some aspects of every study cannot use statistical generalization. We cannot sample everything, so some form of **extrastatistical generalization** is always necessary. For instance, much research draws on samples of subjects taken from university classes. Because these samples are obtained by some haphazard process, it is quite reasonable to treat them as random samples (even if strictly they are not). However, the results are usually generalized to other individuals who had no possibility of being included in the sample. The students at one university are usually treated as equivalent to those at another. This assertion is not based on any form of statistical inference. It is simply that we feel, and can convince others, that to treat them as equivalent is reasonable. How plausible these generalizations are depends on how much we want to generalize. As generalizations get broader, their reasonableness becomes more problematic. Are we justified in treating our English-speaking subjects as equivalent to, say, Spanish-speaking ones? Are we justified in applying what we found with our college-age students to 40-year-old or 70-year-old adults? Our F tests have nothing to say about whether these extrastatistical generalizations are reasonable or not.

The same kind of issues of generalization pertain to aspects of the study other than the selection of subjects. Suppose you are interested in the way the organization of a story affects how well people remember it. To investigate this question, you have your subjects—undergraduate students—read a passage that tells a story, then write a summary of it a week later. Some students see an organized version of the story and some a disorganized version. To be efficient, you decide to conduct the experiment in the laboratory sections of an introductory psychology class. One week you hand each student a sheet containing a one-page story and, on the back of the sheet, a series of questions about it—these are to ensure that the students read the story. They read the passage, answer the questions, and return the sheet to you. When the section meets the next week, you hand out a blank sheet, and ask everyone to summarize what they remember about last week's story. You score each person's response by the number of "key facts" that they recall. The story that a subject receives is one of two basic types: organized and disorganized. You create these two types by writing the story in its organized form, then altering it to put its parts out of order. You are concerned about the possibility that a given story may be more or less affected by the disorganization, so you use three different stories, each of which has an organized and a disorganized form. Let's say that the sections in which you will conduct the study each contains 12 students, and you give two students from each section one form of each story. There are five sections available to you, and you administer the experiment in each of them.

The independent variable of primary interest in this example is the organizational factor (A). When combined with story version (factor B) and sections (C), you have a three-factor design, with data such as those at the top of Table 24.1. We studied this design in Chapter 21 and gave the formulas needed to analyze it in Section 21.3. We will not go through the details again, but go directly to the analysis summary at the bottom of Table 24.1. This is the analysis you would obtain by default if you entered these data into one of the standard statistical programs.

Several types of generalization are important to the interpretation of this experiment. The most fundamental is to the subject population, which is what the analysis of variance in Table 24.1 provides. However, your study was designed to look at the effects of organization of stories on recall, and the statements that you want to make concern the effects of organization in general. You do not want to confine them to the three stories you used, nor to the five sections that happened to be available. You certainly want your results to apply to other stories like them and, more broadly, to other types of written material. Similarly, you are not interested in the particular sections that you happened to use, but want to generalize your results both to other sections like them, and to other groups of subjects. In fact, you probably hope that

Table 24.1: Data for a story-recall experiment, with their analysis as a standard, completely randomized, three-factor design.

Original data

	Organized (a_1)			Disorganized (a_2)		
	Story b_1	Story b_2	Story b_3	Story b_1	Story b_2	Story b_3
Section c_1	16	11	10	12	10	10
	14	9	12	11	12	11
Section c_2	15	10	12	7	9	9
	11	8	10	9	7	7
Section c_3	13	10	11	8	7	8
	11	8	9	6	8	6
Section c_4	11	6	9	10	11	11
	9	8	11	8	9	11
Section c_5	9	7	8	9	11	10
	11	5	8	10	8	8

Standard analysis of variance (all factors fixed)

Source	SS	df	MS	F
Organization (A)	14.017	1	14.017	7.19*
Stories (B)	32.433	2	16.217	8.32*
Sections (C)	62.667	4	15.667	8.03*
$A \times B$	40.033	2	20.017	10.27*
$A \times C$	54.400	4	13.600	6.97*
$B \times C$	13.733	8	1.717	0.88
$A \times B \times C$	0.800	8	0.100	0.05
S/ABC	58.500	30	1.950	
Total	276.583	59		

* $p < .05$

the section factor is irrelevant, for if it did make a difference, that would considerably complicate the interpretation of your results.

What we have said here about the stories and the sections is just like what we said about subjects in Chapter 1. We study a particular group of subjects and treat them in the analysis as if they were a random sample from a large population. We use statistical generalization (the F test) to draw conclusions that apply to this population, and we use extrastatistical generalization to extend the results to other groups for which the random-sampling argument is less plausible. We also want to extend these ideas to other features of the experiment such as the stories or sections. In the analysis presented in Table 24.1, these extensions are only accomplished extrastatistically.

Fixed and Random Factors

Before discussing how to extend the statistical inferences to aspects of the study other than subjects, we need to draw a distinction between two idealized types of factors, which provide the models for the analysis. When we speak of a **fixed factor**, we refer to one whose levels have been chosen rationally. In the experiment above, the organization factor A is fixed—the two forms of the story were not chosen haphazardly, but are the point of the study. Similarly, the levels of a quantitative factor are also chosen thoughtfully. For example, in a study involving amounts of reinforcement on learning, a researcher might choose groups with 2, 4, 6, and 8 units of reward, and interpolate the results for amounts falling between these points. These levels are not chosen haphazardly, but are selected as the best way to probe the continuum.

In contrast, a **random factor** is one in which the levels are chosen unsystematically—strictly speaking, by random sampling from a large population. The random-sampling assumption links the sample to the population and allows us to make statistical generalizations. The quintessential example of a random factor is the subject factor. The individual levels of a random factor have no particular meaning in themselves; they are merely representatives of a much larger collection.

Fixed and random factors are idealized models, and real data never conform exactly to either one. How a researcher chooses to interpret a particular factor depends on how the levels of the factor were chosen and whether the intended inferences will be based on statistical or extrastatistical considerations. The organization factor in the story example can only be described as fixed, but the other factors could be either fixed or random. The sections factor is the easiest to classify. Almost certainly the specific sections (levels) chosen were not of systematic interest. Moreover, each one could be replaced with a new section without changing the nature of the study. The factor would best be described as random. That choice would be inappropriate, however, if the sections differed in some systematic way—for example, if one was a section of honors students, another a section for nonmajors, and so forth. The story factor is more problematic. If the stories were originally chosen to span a range of types—say, with three levels of difficulty—then that factor would be fixed. If they were just a haphazard collection of stories, then the random description is better. Our point here is that fixed and random factors do not exist in the world, but are interpretations we impose when designing and analyzing a study. There is some latitude in which model we assign to a particular factor, although the choice should be made in a way that is consistent with the goals of the research and will be accepted by those to whom it is to be presented.[1] The example illustrates the two types of factors that are often described as random: The stories are instances of *experimental material*, and the sections are *groups of subjects*.

---

[1] The contentiousness of the issue is illustrated by a series of articles some years ago in the *Journal of Verbal Learning and Verbal Behavior* concerning the appropriateness of treating linguistic stimuli, such as the stories in the example above, as random—see Clark (1973, 1976), Forster and Dickinson (1976), Wike and Church (1976), Wickens and Keppel (1983), and other articles cited therein. Clark argues that because asymmetries in publication policy make it easy to publish significant results and hard to publish their refutation, the systematic inflation of Type I error probability produced by the incorrect use of the fixed-effect model has a pernicious influence on the progress of science.

Table 24.2: *The effect of a random factor: The three stories in the actual experiment (lower) were chosen randomly from a population of 10 (upper).*

Mean recall from the full population of stories

Organization	b_1	b_2	b_3	b_4	b_5	b_6	b_7	b_8	b_9	b_{10}	Mean
				Potential levels of story factor B							
a_1	12	5	9	11	5	11	8	6	9	4	8.00
a_2	10	9	9	9	3	5	6	14	5	10	8.00
Mean	11	7	9	10	4	8	7	10	7	7	

Mean recall in the actual experiment

Organization	b_4	b_2	b_6	Mean
	Actual stories chosen			
a_1	11	5	11	9.00
a_2	9	9	5	7.67
Mean	10	7	8	8.34

    Almost every study has at least one fixed factor. The primary manipulation(s) of the study are always fixed factors. Control or blocking factors are also fixed, even if incidental to the purposes of the study—gender, for example, is a fixed factor. The subject factor is always random, and optionally, a study may include one or (less often) two random factors. Studies with more than two random factors (other than subjects) are intractable and rarely seen.

24.2   Random Factors and the F Ratio

The decision to treat a factor as random introduces a new source of random variability, which must be accommodated in the analysis. To understand where this variability comes from and how it affects the study, consider a simplified version of the story experiment. Ignore the section factor, and suppose there were only 10 stories that could possibly have been written and that the organization manipulation was ineffective. The top panel of Table 24.2 shows the number of key facts that would be recalled if each of the 10 stories were tested. There are differences among the stories, both in their average level of recall and in the particular effect of the organization manipulation, but the two population means are identical, each equal to 8.00 facts.

    The actual experiment uses three stories, not all 10. Suppose the researcher chooses these randomly. The second part of Table 24.2 shows the means for a study with three randomly selected stories—as it happened, stories b_4, b_2, and b_6. In this sample, means of the two organization conditions are not equal—they are 9.00 and 7.67 facts. Because only part of the original population has been sampled, a difference between the conditions has appeared. Moreover, had another set of stories been chosen, this difference would not be the same. For example, had the sample consisted of stories b_2, b_7 and b_{10}, the means would have been 5.67 and 8.33. A third selection would give yet another pair of values. The process of sampling has introduced variability into the study's results.

Table 24.3: Steps for assigning error terms in designs with random factors.

1. List the usual sources of variability in the design.
2. List the influences affecting each source. These include (a) the source itself, (b) any sources that arise by crossing the original source with a random factor (or combination of factors), and (c) any source in which random effects (and only random effects) are nested within the original source.
3. Identify the denominator for each *F* ratio by selecting another source (or constructing one, if necessary) that includes all the influences except the effect that is to be tested.

Over all the samples that *might* have been taken, sometimes the a_1 mean is greater than the a_2 mean and sometimes the reverse. The situation is reminiscent of the sampling demonstration in Table 3.4 (p. 49), in which a set of scores was randomly divided into two groups 45 times. The different samples of scores had different means, and the appraisal of any systematic effect had to be set against the random variation produced by sampling. For samples of subjects, we have to evaluate the size of the observed effect against a measure of subject variability. We only say that there is an effect when the difference between the conditions is too large to be likely to be due to sampling alone. We saw in Chapter 2 (see pp. 21–22) how this logic was the basis for the *F* statistic:

$$F = \frac{\text{effect} + \text{error}}{\text{error}}. \tag{24.1}$$

The analysis with random factors other than subjects is similar. We still compute an *F* statistic, but its denominator is different from the one we would have used had no random factors been present.

The principle by which we select the error term for this ratio is simple:

> *The error term for a treatment effect includes the variability of every random effect that influences the treatment mean square.*

This principle is easy to state, but applying it to an actual study is more work. It is best accomplished by following the three steps we give in Table 24.3.

Table 24.4 shows how these three steps are applied to the simplified story experiment in Table 24.2. The design is a 2×3 between-subjects factorial with several subjects tested in each cell. There is an organization factor *A*, a story factor *B*, and a subject factor *S/AB*. Factor *A* is fixed, and factors *B* and *S/AB* are random. In the first step, we list in the first column of Table 24.4 the sources of variability, which for this design are *A*, *B*, *A×B* and *S/AB*. The middle column contains the list of sources that influence the mean squares.[2] Consider the treatment effect *A*. Step 2a

---

[2]In mathematical terms, these "influences" are the terms that contribute to the expected value of the mean square. We could work out these expectations in mathematical detail (for example, as in Equation 7.5), but the demonstration would add little. However, some other texts present the mean squares in mathematical form. Strictly speaking, these calculations show that the finite population in Table 24.2 requires a slightly different error term than the one we give here, but, in practice, you will not need it.

Table 24.4: Error terms for a two-factor between-subjects design with fixed factor A and random factor B.

Source	Influences on Mean Square	Error Term
A	A, $A{\times}B$, S/AB	$A{\times}B$
B	B, S/AB	S/AB
$A{\times}B$	$A{\times}B$, S/AB	S/AB
S/AB	S/AB	—

tells to include the source itself. Step 2b indicates that any source formed by crossing factor A with a random factor has a potential influence; the one possibility here is the $A{\times}B$ interaction, so it is listed. Step 2c refers to sources consisting of random effects nested within the original source. Only one source meets this specification, namely, the random effects of subjects within the ab groups, so S/AB is added to the list. Thus, there are three influences on MS_A: any real difference among the conditions, the variability of subjects, and, as the example in Table 24.2 demonstrated, the extent to which the treatment effect varies from one story to the next, which is to say, the $A{\times}B$ treatment-by-story interaction. The influences of random sampling on the other treatment sources are simpler. Because the levels of factor A are not sampled, it does not contribute additional variability to either B or $A{\times}B$. Moreover, neither of these effects is crossed with the random source S/AB, which means that step 2b does not apply. Thus, both B and $A{\times}B$ are influenced only by themselves (step 2a) and by S/AB (step 2c). The final source, S/AB, has no influences other than itself.

In the third step, we use the lists of influences to select the error term for an F ratio. For the organization factor A, we put MS_A in the numerator of this ratio and choose an error term to divide it by. As our principle above states, the error term is a mean square that has the same influences as the effect, except for the effect itself. From Table 24.4, we see that

$$\text{influences on } A \approx (A) + (A{\times}B) + (S/AB).$$

We have used the wavy sign $\approx$ instead of an equals sign in this "equation" to indicate that it is schematic, not exact. We group these influences into a systematic part (the *effect*) and a random part (the *error*):

$$\text{effect} \approx (A) \quad \text{and} \quad \text{error} \approx (A{\times}B) + (S/AB).$$

Thus, we must find a mean square for the error that is influenced by $A{\times}B$ and S/AB. Looking at the second column of Table 24.4, we find that the $A{\times}B$ interaction has exactly these two terms. It is the error term we need. We have listed this choice in the third column. When constructing these F ratios, we find it helpful to write them qualitatively, in the form of Equation 24.1:

$$F = \frac{MS_A}{MS_{A{\times}B}} \approx \frac{\overbrace{(A)}^{\text{effect}} + \overbrace{(A{\times}B) + (S/AB)}^{\text{error}}}{\underbrace{(A{\times}B) + (S/AB)}_{\text{error}}}.$$

Obviously, this F ratio is different from that in the conventional analysis in which B is treated as a fixed factor. With B fixed, the error term is the within-groups mean square $MS_{S/AB}$. You can see that this F ratio is inappropriate for this design by writing it in schematic form using the influences from Table 24.4:

$$F = \frac{MS_A}{MS_{S/AB}} \approx \frac{(A) + (A \times B) + (S/AB)}{(S/AB)}.$$

The numerator contains an extra term $(A \times B)$ that is not part of the denominator, and because the term refers to variability—always a positive value—the test is biased toward rejecting the null hypothesis.

We can figure out how to test the remaining effects by looking at the other rows of Table 24.4. The mean squares of both the B and $A \times B$ effects are influenced only by their own variability and that of subjects. Thus, each is tested against the within-groups error term, S/AB, as given in the final column. In most experiments of this sort, these tests are of little interest. Just as the observation that subjects differ is not very profound, the observation that the stories vary in memorability, or are differently affected by the organization manipulation, is not particularly revealing (if they were, they would probably be construed as a systematic—that is, fixed—factor). Finally, the subject source, S/AB, has no other influences. Within the confines of this design, there is no way of testing it, as we have indicated by replacing the error term by a dash.

24.3 Error Terms in Random-Factor Designs

The last section showed, for a two-factor between-subjects design, how a decision to treat a factor other than subjects as random changes the error term used to test the main effect of the factor of primary interest. In this section, we will examine other designs, first the other between-subjects design, then the within-subject designs, and finally the mixed designs. The basic principles involved remain as we described them in Table 24.3, but their manifestation can be different. You need to be aware of these principles if you are going to use these analyses. The packaged computer programs usually do not perform them correctly without some intervention and possibly some hand calculation (we give an example in Problem 24.1).

Completely Between-Subjects Designs

We start with the three-factor between-subjects design. Suppose factor C in an $A \times B \times C$ design is random. Applying our three steps, we begin by listing the sources of variability for this design in the first column of Table 24.5. Next, we list in the second column of Table 24.5 the effects that influence the mean squares of these sources: the source itself, any interaction of the source with the random factor C, and the nested S/ABC effect. Because A, B, and $A \times B$ are crossed with C, their mean squares are affected by all three types of influences. The mean squares for the other four treatment sources, which all involve the random factor C, are influenced only by the source itself and subjects. In the third step, we identify as an error term a source that has every influence as the target source except the source itself. For the first three target sources, the error term is the interaction of the source with the random factor C. For example, the $A \times B$ interaction has

$$\text{influences on } A \times B \approx (A \times B) + (A \times B \times C) + (S/ABC),$$

Table 24.5: Error terms for an $A{\times}B{\times}C$ design with fixed factors A and B and random factor C.

Source	Influences on Mean Square	Error Term
A	A, $A{\times}C$, S/ABC	$A{\times}C$
B	B, $B{\times}C$, S/ABC	$B{\times}C$
$A{\times}B$	$A{\times}B$, $A{\times}B{\times}C$, S/ABC	$A{\times}B{\times}C$
C	C, S/ABC	S/ABC
$A{\times}C$	$A{\times}C$, S/ABC	S/ABC
$B{\times}C$	$B{\times}C$, S/ABC	S/ABC
$A{\times}B{\times}C$	$A{\times}B{\times}C$, S/ABC	S/ABC
S/ABC	S/ABC	—

which divides up into

$$\text{effect} \approx (A{\times}B) \quad \text{and} \quad \text{error} \approx (A{\times}B{\times}C) + (S/ABC).$$

The proper error for this source is the $A{\times}B{\times}C$ interaction. The error term for the next four sources is $MS_{S/ABC}$, and there is no error term for S/ABC.

When two of the three factors in a between-subjects design are random, the analysis is more complicated. The story-recall study in Table 24.1 is an example. The organization factor A clearly should be treated as fixed, but the researcher could treat both the story factor B and the section factor C as random. In Table 24.6, we again start by listing the sources of variability, then determine the influences. The result for the fixed factor A is somewhat surprising. The influences include the A effect, the within-groups source S/ABC, and *three* interactions of factor A with the random factors—$A{\times}B$, $A{\times}C$, and $A{\times}B{\times}C$. These additional influences appear because factor A is crossed with each of the two random factors and with their interaction, which is also random. The next four sources (B, C, $A{\times}B$, and $A{\times}C$) each includes one random factor, and according to step 2b in Table 24.3, each will gain an influence consisting of an interaction between that source and the other random factor: both B and C gain $B{\times}C$ and both $A{\times}B$ and $A{\times}C$ gain $A{\times}B{\times}C$. The final three sources are like those of an ordinary analysis—the first two mean squares are influenced by themselves and S/ABC, and the subject source is only influenced by itself.

The final step is to identify the error terms. For all but the A effect, we can find the error term by separating the influences into effect and error parts and locating another source the table that has only the error part as its influences. For example, the influences for the $A{\times}B$ interaction divide into

$$\text{effect} \approx (A{\times}B) \quad \text{and} \quad \text{error} \approx (A{\times}B{\times}C) + (S/ABC).$$

An error term with these influences is provided by $MS_{A{\times}B{\times}C}$. The A effect is a problem, however. When we divide its influences into effect and error parts, we find that it requires the F ratio

$$F = \frac{MS_A}{MS_{\text{error-}A}} \approx \frac{(A) + (A{\times}B) + (A{\times}C) + (A{\times}B{\times}C) + (S/ABC)}{(A{\times}B) + (A{\times}C) + (A{\times}B{\times}C) + (S/ABC)}.$$

Table 24.6: Error terms for an $A \times B \times C$ design with fixed factor A and random factors B and C (Table 24.1).

Source	Influences on Mean Square	Error Term
A	A, $A \times B$, $A \times C$, $A \times B \times C$, S/ABC	see below
B	B, $B \times C$, S/ABC	$B \times C$
C	C, $B \times C$, S/ABC	$B \times C$
$A \times B$	$A \times B$, $A \times B \times C$, S/ABC	$A \times B \times C$
$A \times C$	$A \times C$, $A \times B \times C$, S/ABC	$A \times B \times C$
$B \times C$	$B \times C$, S/ABC	S/ABC
$A \times B \times C$	$A \times B \times C$, S/ABC	S/ABC
S/ABC	S/ABC	—

There is no mean square in the table that has the set of influences needed for the error term. The crux of the difficulty is that the error term must include both the $(A \times B)$ and $(A \times C)$ influences, but no mean square, except the one we want to test, contains them both. The only way to find the correct term is to combine several mean squares. If we add $MS_{A \times B}$ and $MS_{A \times C}$ together, the result is closer to what we want:

$$MS_{A \times B} + MS_{A \times C}$$
$$\approx [(A \times B) + (A \times B \times C) + (S/ABC)] + [(A \times C) + (A \times B \times C) + (S/ABC)].$$

It is not quite the error term we need, however, because it contains $(A \times B \times C)$ and (S/ABC) twice. The $MS_{A \times B \times C}$ contains both of these duplicated terms, and when we subtract it, we get the correct error term:

$$MS_{\text{error-}A} = MS_{A \times B} + MS_{A \times C} - MS_{A \times B \times C}$$
$$\approx (A \times B) + (A \times C) + (A \times B \times C) + (S/ABC). \qquad (24.2)$$

The resulting ratio of MS_A to $MS_{\text{error-}A}$ is

$$F' = \frac{MS_A}{MS_{\text{error-}A}} = \frac{MS_A}{MS_{A \times B} + MS_{A \times C} - MS_{A \times B \times C}}.$$

This ratio is known as a **quasi-F statistic** and is usually denoted by F' to indicate that it is not the usual F ratio.[3] The quasi-F statistic has a distribution that is close to (although not exactly the same as) an F distribution, so that critical values can be looked up in the standard tables following the procedure we describe in the next paragraph.[4]

One thing remains to complete the test. We need the degrees of freedom associated with the combined mean squares. A result due to Satterthwaite (1946) gives an

---

[3]Do not confuse the quasi-F statistic with the noncentral F distribution, for which F' is also often used.

[4]Another way to test the A effect is to construct a quasi-F statistic with $MS_A + MS_{A \times B \times C}$ in the numerator and $MS_{A \times B} + MS_{A \times C}$ in the denominator. If you work out the influences for these two sums, you will see that they differ only by the term (A) in the numerator and thus satisfy the criterion for an appropriate ratio. Similar ratios are formed for other quasi-F statistics by moving the terms with negative signs from the denominator of the ratio and adding them to the numerator. Our impression is that this quasi-F ratio is slightly inferior to the one we present in the text.

Table 24.7: *Analysis of variance for the data in Table 24.1, treating factor A as fixed and factors B and C as random. The sums of squares, degrees of freedom, and mean squares from Table 24.1 appear on the left, and the proper error terms and revised F ratios appear on the right. The quasi-F statistic is printed in italics.*

| | —Effect— | | | —Error term and F test— | | | |
Source	SS	df	MS	Error	MS	df	F
A	14.017	1	14.017	$MS_{\text{error-}A}$	33.517	4.6	*0.42*
B	32.433	2	16.217	$MS_{B\times C}$	1.717	8	9.44*
C	62.667	4	15.667	$MS_{B\times C}$	1.717	8	9.12*
$A\times B$	40.033	2	20.017	$MS_{A\times B\times C}$	0.100	8	200.17*
$A\times C$	54.400	4	13.600	$MS_{A\times B\times C}$	0.100	8	136.00*
$B\times C$	13.733	8	1.717	$MS_{S/ABC}$	1.950	30	0.88
$A\times B\times C$	0.800	8	0.100	$MS_{S/ABC}$	1.950	30	0.05
S/ABC	58.500	30	1.950				
Total	276.583	59					

$p^* < .05$

approximate value for the degrees of freedom of any composite mean square. Suppose $MS_{\text{comb}} = MS_U \pm MS_V \pm MS_W \pm$ etc., where U, V, W are any effects or interactions and the signs denoted by $\pm$ can be either plus or minus. The number of degrees of freedom for this mean square is approximately equal to

$$df_{\text{comb}} = \frac{MS^2_{\text{comb}}}{\dfrac{MS^2_U}{df_U} + \dfrac{MS^2_V}{df_V} + \dfrac{MS^2_W}{df_W} + \text{etc.}}. \tag{24.3}$$

Note that the signs in the denominator here are all plus, regardless of whether they were plus or minus when MS_{comb} was calculated. This value is unlikely to be an integer, and it is conventionally rounded down to the next smallest integer to use the F tables. Applied to the quasi-F statistic for A constructed above, Equation 24.3 is

$$df_{\text{error-}A} = \frac{MS^2_{\text{error-}A}}{\dfrac{MS^2_{A\times B}}{df_{A\times B}} + \dfrac{MS^2_{A\times C}}{df_{A\times C}} + \dfrac{MS^2_{A\times B\times C}}{df_{A\times B\times C}}}. \tag{24.4}$$

We can now complete the analysis of the data in Table 24.1. The calculation of the sums of squares and mean squares is the same as for the fixed-effect design, and they are duplicated on the left side of Table 24.7. The changed part of the analysis involves the F tests. The appropriate error term for each effect, as specified in Table 24.6, is listed on the right side of the table along with its degrees of freedom. For the A effect, the error term is calculated according to Equation 24.2:

$$MS_{\text{error-}A} = MS_{A\times B} + MS_{A\times C} - MS_{A\times B\times C} = 20.017 + 13.600 - 0.100 = 33.517.$$

With this error term, the value of the quasi-F is

$$F' = \frac{MS_A}{MS_{\text{error-}A}} = \frac{14.017}{33.517} = 0.418.$$

We have entered it in Table 24.7 using italic type to remind us that it is not a standard F. The degrees of freedom for the test, from Equation 24.4, are

$$df_{\text{error-}A} = \frac{MS^2_{\text{error-}A}}{\dfrac{MS^2_{A \times B}}{df_{A \times B}} + \dfrac{MS^2_{A \times C}}{df_{A \times C}} + \dfrac{MS^2_{A \times B \times C}}{df_{A \times B \times C}}}$$

$$= \frac{33.517^2}{\dfrac{20.017^2}{2} + \dfrac{13.600^2}{4} + \dfrac{0.100^2}{8}} = \frac{1{,}123.4}{200.340 + 46.240 + 0.001} = 4.6.$$

From the F table we find $F_{.05}(1, 4) = 7.71$, and so the observed F' is not significant. The outcome of the test has changed substantially—the organization effect is significant when the stories and sections are treated as fixed factors (Table 24.1), but not when their variabilities are taken into consideration. Viewed against the three sampled variables—stories, sections, and subjects—the superior recall of the organized stories could plausibly be a sampling accident.

The issues that apply to error terms for main effects and interactions when random factors are involved extend to any analytical analyses. Generally, such analyses— main comparisons, simple effects, simple contrasts, and interaction components—are confined to the sources based on fixed effects. By their nature as members of a random sample, the individual levels of the random factor are rarely of interest. For example, in the experiment presented Table 24.1, the main effect of the organization factor (A) is of primary interest whereas effects involving stories (B) and sections (C) are not. If factor A had more than two levels, any main comparisons ψ_A would be tested against the overall error term $MS_{\text{error-}A}$. In general, the error term for testing any analytical effect based exclusively on fixed factors in a between-subjects factorial is the one appropriate for the intact factor. Consider a three-way factorial with two fixed factors, A and B and one random factor C (Table 24.5). Any effect involving the fixed factor A (i.e. ψ_A, A at b_k, and ψ_A at b_k) is tested against the error term used for the A main effect ($MS_{A \times C}$). Similarly, any effect involving both fixed factors, such as $\psi_A \times B$, $A \times \psi_B$, and $\psi_A \times \psi_B$, is tested against the error term $MS_{A \times B \times C}$ for the $A \times B$ effect. In the somewhat unusual event that we wanted to look at a simple effect at one level of the random factor (e.g., A at c_l), we would simply isolate the portion of the data at that level and analyze it as a single-factor fixed-effect design.

Completely Within-Subject Designs

The same principles that apply to the between-subjects factorial designs let us select error terms for within-subject factorial designs with random factors. These designs are less common than are between-subjects factorials, but are sometimes necessary.

The simplest of these designs is the $A \times B \times S$ design in which each subject is tested under every one of the ab treatment conditions. We discussed the analysis of this design when both factors are fixed in Chapter 18. Consider an example in which one of the factors is random. Suppose a clinical psychologist is studying the changes during therapy of prosocial statements of clients trying to overcome antisocial tendencies. Three sessions are videotaped (factor A), one at the beginning of therapy, a second in the middle, and a third at the end. The levels of this factor are specifically chosen, and the factor is fixed. Each tape is rated by four therapists who are selected from a pool of

Table 24.8: Error terms for a two-factor within-subject with fixed factor A and random factor B.

Source	Influences on MS_{source}	Error term
A	A, $A{\times}B$, $A{\times}S$, $A{\times}B{\times}S$	quasi-F
B	B, $B{\times}S$	$B{\times}S$
$A{\times}B$	$A{\times}B$, $A{\times}B{\times}S$	$A{\times}B{\times}S$
S	S, $B{\times}S$	$B{\times}S$
$A{\times}S$	$A{\times}S$, $A{\times}B{\times}S$	$A{\times}B{\times}S$
$B{\times}S$	$B{\times}S$	—
$A{\times}B{\times}S$	$A{\times}B{\times}S$	—

experienced clinicians. They view each videotape and give the session an overall rating from strongly antisocial to strongly prosocial. The four ratings constitute factor B in the analysis. The $a = 3$ tapes from $n = 5$ clients are evaluated by all $b = 4$ therapists; thus, the design is an $A{\times}B{\times}S$ factorial, with tapes, raters, and clients as the three factors. Because the particular therapists are not of interest per se and were not chosen systematically, factor B can be treated as a random factor.

The analysis of this design follows the fixed-factor analysis in Chapter 18 through the calculation of the mean squares. To determine the error terms, we apply the three steps in Table 24.3, as shown in Table 24.8. The first column lists the standard sources of variability in the $A{\times}B{\times}S$ design. The session factor A is fixed and factors B (raters) and S (clients) are random. In the second column, we apply the second step of the procedure to determine the influences affecting each source. The mean square for the main effect of session (factor A) is influenced by itself and by its interaction with any random effects crossed with it. There are three random effects, B, S, and $B{\times}S$, and their interactions with A are all influences. The influences for the other sources are less complex. For the next four sources they consist of the effect itself and its interaction with the other random factor; for the last two the only influence is the effect itself. The list of influences tells us that to test the A effect we need an error term that includes three interactions, $A{\times}B$, $A{\times}S$, and $A{\times}B{\times}S$. There is no single source that contains all of these, so we must use the quasi-F approach. A composite error term $MS_{\text{error-}A}$ is formed by adding the mean squares $MS_{A{\times}B}$ and $MS_{A{\times}S}$, then removing the duplicated effect $(A{\times}B{\times}S)$ by subtracting $MS_{A{\times}B{\times}S}$:

$$MS_{A{\times}B} + MS_{A{\times}S} - MS_{A{\times}B{\times}S}$$
$$\approx [(A{\times}B) + (A{\times}B{\times}S)] + [(A{\times}S) + (A{\times}B{\times}S)] - (A{\times}B{\times}S)$$
$$= (A{\times}B) + (A{\times}S) + (A{\times}B{\times}S).$$

The resulting quasi-F statistic is

$$F' = \frac{MS_A}{MS_{A{\times}B} + MS_{A{\times}S} - MS_{A{\times}B{\times}S}}. \tag{24.5}$$

The numerator degrees of freedom are those of MS_A; those in the denominator are found from the approximation in Equation 24.3.

To test contrasts involving the fixed factor in this design, we use a quasi-F ratio identical to the one for the A main effect (Equation 24.5) except that the relevant mean squares involve the contrast ψ_A instead of A:

$$F' = \frac{MS_{\psi_A}}{MS_{\psi_A \times B} + MS_{\psi_A \times S} - MS_{\psi_A \times B \times S}}.$$

A contrast variable can be used to calculate the mean squares in this equation, as we described in Section 18.2 (see Table 18.6, p. 410). Suppose we wished to compare the ratings of the last session with those of the first two—the contrast $\psi_A = \mu_3 - \frac{1}{2}(\mu_1 + \mu_2)$. We create the contrast variable $\widehat{\psi}_{ik}$ by calculating this contrast b times for each subject, once at each level of factor B. These values form a $B \times S$ design in which the sources of variability, including the grand mean, all represent effects that involve ψ_A in the actual design. In terms of the contrast-variable design, the quasi-F is

$$F' = \frac{MS_{\text{G.M.} \cdot \psi}}{MS_{B_\psi} + MS_{S_\psi} - MS_{B \times S_\psi}}.$$

The degrees of freedom are obtained from Equation 24.3.

We must raise a caution here. The purpose of introducing a random factor into a design is to allow generalization over both its variability and that of subjects (factors B and S, respectively). Because the quasi-F statistic can be awkward to use, some researchers have adopted the strategy of calculating two F statistics, one based on each of the random factors:

$$F_S = \frac{MS_A}{MS_{A \times S}} \quad \text{and} \quad F_B = \frac{MS_A}{MS_{A \times B}} \tag{24.6}$$

(or F_1 and F_2, as they are sometimes designated). An effect of the fixed factor A is deemed present if *both* of these F statistics are significant. In our example, the first analysis would treat the subject factor S as random and ignore the differences among raters (factor B), and the second analysis would treat the rater factor B as random and ignore the differences among subjects (factor S). This strategy is incorrect. Leaving aside questions of multiple testing, it does not eliminate the problem of bias that was the original reason for introducing the random effect into the design. The test given by F_S is valid only if factor B is fixed, and the test given by F_B is valid only if subjects are fixed. Neither assumption is correct, and, worse, they are inconsistent with each other. As you can see from the list of influences in Table 24.8, the error term for A must include *both* the $A \times S$ and $A \times B$ effects. Each of the two separate tests omits one part of the correct error term, so each is biased in favor of rejecting the null hypothesis. If you wish to generalize statistically over both subjects and materials, you need to use the quasi-F statistic of Equation 24.5.[5]

Within-subject designs with three factors are treated in essentially the same way as a two-factor design. Recall that in this design there are seven major effects—three main effects and four interactions—and that each is tested against its interaction with

---

[5]You may encounter studies in which only F_S and F_B are reported. When only these are available, a lower bound for the quasi-F statistic due to Clark (1973) is obtained by calculating $\min F' = F_B F_S / (F_B + F_S)$, with $df_{\text{num}} = a - 1$ and $df_{\text{denom}} = (F_B + F_S)^2 / (F_B^2 / df_{A \times B} + F_S^2 / df_{A \times S})$. Although this statistic is biased against rejecting the null hypothesis, that bias is usually small. It is much preferable to the separate tests (see Raaijmakers, Schrijnemakers, & Gremmen, 1999, for a discussion of this recommendation).

subjects (Table 23.2, p. 513). Now suppose factor C is random. Of the seven effects, the ones most likely to interest the researcher are those involving the fixed factors (the A and B main effects and the $A \times B$ interaction). The mean square for each of these effects is influenced by its own variability and by any variability produced by crossing it with the three random components S, C, and $C \times S$:

- MS_A is influenced by A, $A \times S$, $A \times C$, and $A \times C \times S$,
- MS_B is influenced by B, $B \times S$, $B \times C$, and $B \times C \times S$,
- $MS_{A \times B}$ is influenced by $A \times B$, $A \times B \times S$, $A \times B \times C$, and $A \times B \times C \times S$.

Each error term must contain the last three influences. The situation is essentially the same as in the two-factor $A \times B \times S$ design (Table 24.8) for the A main effect, and the quasi-F statistic is like the one found there. The remainder of the design is worked out in Problem 24.2. It would be possible to make similar calculations for a design with one fixed factor and two random factors, but, as we will discuss in Section 24.4, the power of this design is low, and it would be useful only when a huge amount of data is available.

Mixed Designs

A mixed $A \times (B \times S)$ design has both a between-subjects factor A and a within-subject factor B. One of these factors will be fixed, but the other may be random. The effects of the random factor are like those of the comparable two-factor design, either between-subjects or within-subject, as the case may be. Both designs occur fairly often in research.

A between-subjects random factor arises when all levels of the primary manipulation of the study are given to each subject (factor B) and the subjects are differentiated in groups (factor A), either because of some natural grouping (like the class sections in the example at the start of this chapter) or because they have been assigned different sets of material. Consider a modification of the within-subject study in which raters examined videotapes from early, middle, and late in therapy for prosocial statements. Suppose the therapist raters do not have the time to rate all three sessions from every client. To reduce their workload, each rater is given only some of the subjects to rate. These groups of clients create a between-subjects factor (A) and the sessions are a within-subject factor (B). The upper panel of Table 24.9 shows a schematic picture of the data.

The other form of mixed design has a within-subject random factor and a between-subjects fixed factor. This design arises when the primary manipulation is between-subjects, and several observations are obtained for each subject using different sets of material. The study described in Table 2.1 (p. 16) has this form. In it, subjects learned obscure facts, either without specific learning instructions or with instructions to use a particular mnemonic technique. The type of instruction (factor A) is a fixed factor. There were 20 different facts to learn, and these can be treated as a random factor B. The upper portion of Table 24.10 shows a simplified data structure for this design, to which Table 2.1 conforms. The structure of the data in Tables 24.9 and 24.10 is the same. Each design has two levels of the between-subjects factor, three levels of the within-subject factor, and three subjects. What differentiates these two designs is which factor is fixed and which random.

Table 24.9: Data table and error terms for a mixed design with random between-subjects factor A and fixed within-subject factor B.

Simplified configuration of the data

		b_1	b_2	b_3
		Early	Middle	Late
Rater 1 (a_1)	s_{11}	Y_{111}	Y_{112}	Y_{113}
	s_{21}	Y_{211}	Y_{212}	Y_{213}
	s_{31}	Y_{311}	Y_{312}	Y_{313}
Rater 2 (a_2)	s_{12}	Y_{121}	Y_{122}	Y_{123}
	s_{22}	Y_{221}	Y_{222}	Y_{223}
	s_{32}	Y_{321}	Y_{322}	Y_{323}

Influences and error terms for the analysis

Source	Influences on MS	Error term
A (Raters)	$A, S/A$	S/A
S/A	S/A	—
B (Session)	$B, A{\times}B, B{\times}S/A$	$A{\times}B$
$A{\times}B$	$A{\times}B, B{\times}S/A$	$B{\times}S/A$
$B{\times}S/A$	$B{\times}S/A$	—

Table 24.10: Data table and error terms for a mixed design with fixed between-subjects factor A and random within-subject factor B.

Simplified configuration of the data

		b_1	b_2	b_3
		Fact 1	Fact 2	Fact 3
Control (a_1)	s_{11}	Y_{111}	Y_{112}	Y_{113}
	s_{21}	Y_{211}	Y_{212}	Y_{213}
	s_{31}	Y_{311}	Y_{312}	Y_{313}
Mnemonic (a_2)	s_{12}	Y_{121}	Y_{122}	Y_{123}
	s_{22}	Y_{221}	Y_{222}	Y_{223}
	s_{32}	Y_{321}	Y_{322}	Y_{323}

Influences and error terms for the analysis

Source	Influences on MS	Error term
A (Condition)	$A, A{\times}B, S/A, B{\times}S/A$	quasi-F
S/A	$S/A, B{\times}S/A$	—
B (Facts)	$B, B{\times}S/A$	$B{\times}S/A$
$A{\times}B$	$A{\times}B, B{\times}S/A$	$B{\times}S/A$
$B{\times}S/A$	$B{\times}S/A$	—

The test statistics are worked out in the bottom portions of the two tables, in the same format we have used for other designs. The sources of variability (column one) and their mean squares are the same as those in a fixed-effect $A \times (B{\times}S)$ design (Table 19.2, p. 435), but the list of influences and error terms (column two) depends on the pattern of fixed and random factors. A random factor influences the mean square for a fixed factor through its interaction with that factor (step 2b in Table 24.3). When the between-subjects factor A is viewed as random (the raters in Table 24.9), its interaction with the fixed factor B is an influence on MS_B. A comparison of the influences for the other mean squares listed in this column reveals that the $A{\times}B$ interaction is the appropriate error term to test this effect.

When the within-subject factor B is viewed as random (the facts in Table 24.10), the influences of the random factor are more complicated. There are four influences on the fixed effect A: the A effect itself (step 2a in Table 24.3), the interaction $A{\times}B$ with the random effect (step 2b), and the random sources S/A and $B{\times}S/A$ nested within A (step 2c). The appropriate error term cannot be found within the table, so a quasi-F statistic must be constructed. The list of influences in Table 24.10 makes it clear that both $MS_{A\times B}$ and $MS_{S/A}$ are part of the error term. Their overlap (the $B{\times}S/A$ effect) is removed by subtracting $MS_{B\times S/A}$:

$$F' = \frac{MS_A}{MS_{A\times B} + MS_{S/A} - MS_{B\times S/A}}. \tag{24.7}$$

We can apply this analysis to the data from Table 2.1 in Table 24.11. The sums of squares, degrees of freedom, and mean squares are calculated as for any two-factor mixed design (Table 19.2, p. 435). Now we use Equation 24.7 to test for a difference between the two groups:

$$F' = \frac{MS_A}{MS_{A\times B} + MS_{S/A} - MS_{B\times S/A}} = \frac{2.025}{0.206 + 0.362 - 0.223} = \frac{2.025}{0.345} = 5.87.$$

There is one degree of freedom in the numerator, and the number of degrees of freedom in the denominator (Equation 24.3) is

$$df_{\text{error-}A} = \frac{(MS_{A\times B} + MS_{S/A} - MS_{B\times S/A})^2}{\dfrac{MS_{A\times B}^2}{df_{A\times B}} + \dfrac{MS_{S/A}^2}{df_{S/A}} + \dfrac{MS_{B\times S/A}^2}{df_{B\times S/A}}}$$

$$= \frac{(0.345)^2}{(0.206)^2/19 + (0.362)^2/30 + (0.223)^2/570} = \frac{0.119}{.00669} = 17.8.$$

The result is significant ($F_{.05}(1, 17) = 4.45$).

24.4   Design Considerations with Random Factors

As you have seen, a random factor is accommodated by changing the error term used to calculate the F ratio. This change has two effects. First, the error term is generally larger than the one that would have been used without the random factor. This increase occurs because new sources of variability come into play. Second, the denominator of the ratio has fewer degrees of freedom than it would have if the random factor were treated as fixed. As these differences suggest, we pay a price when we decide to generalize statistically: The power of the tests is reduced. The numerical

Table 24.11: Analysis of the data in Table 2.1 (p. 16) with the facts (B) treated as a random factor. The quasi-F statistic is printed in italics.

Source	SS	df	MS	F
A	2.025	1	2.025	*5.87**
S/A	10.869	30	0.362	
B	5.681	19	0.299	1.34
A×B	3.913	19	0.206	0.92
B×S/A	127.006	570	0.223	
Total	141.494	639		

$* \ p < .05$

example in Tables 24.1 and 24.7 illustrate both effects. The denominator of the F ratio for the A main effect is 1.950 when both stories and class sections are treated as fixed factors (Table 24.1), but it is 33.517 when they are treated as random factors (Table 24.7); and the critical value of F increases from $F_{.05}(1, 30) = 4.17$ to $F_{.05}(1, 4) = 7.71$. The loss of power should not be unexpected—as we attempt to make stronger statistical statements, we demand more of our data.

You should take this loss of power into consideration when you design a study that includes a random factor. There is not much you can do about the size of the error term—its increase is the mechanism by which the wider generalization is accomplished. However, you do have some control over the degrees of freedom, which depend, in part, on the number of levels of the factors. To have powerful tests, the random factors need as many levels as possible. The principle here is the same that applies to subjects. You would not expect a study with only two subjects per group to clearly differentiate among the treatments. The sets of material and subject groupings that form random factors are no different. In the story-organization study, we would have a difficult time generalizing statistically had we used only two stories or administered the study in only two sections. The word-recall example from Chapter 2 had 20 levels of the random factor and is a more appropriate use of a random factor than the oversimplified example with the stories.

In planning a study, you should think carefully about the random aspects of the design. A decision to allow the statistical generalization over a random factor involves more than a change in the statistical analysis. Both the subjects and the new random factor jointly determine the size of the error term, and a powerful test requires adequate samples of both. The power of an analysis with several sources of error is largely limited by the most variable or most poorly sampled factor. Increasing the number of subjects per cell is of little value if the power of the design is limited by another random factor. Your energy is better invested in obtaining more levels of the random factor. Consider a between-subjects design with a two-level factor of interest A, a crossed random factor B, and a pool of 96 subjects. One possibility is to use $b = 3$ levels of the random factor with $n = 16$ subjects in each of the $ab = (2)(3) = 6$ cells; another is to use $b = 6$ levels with $n = 8$ subjects in each of the $ab = (2)(6) = 12$ cells. Although the number of subjects assigned to each level of A is the same, the two designs do not have the same power. The error term for the A main effect is the $A \times B$ interaction (Table 24.4). In the design with $b = 3$, factor A is tested with $a - 1 = 1$ and $(a - 1)(b - 1) = 2$ degrees of freedom. The critical value of F at the 5 percent level is 18.51. In the design with $b = 6$, the test is on 1 and 5 degrees of freedom, giving a critical value of 6.61. Unless the random factor were extremely stable or the subjects extremely variable, the second design is much more powerful.

To understand what is gained and lost by including a random factor in a design, it is helpful to compare how the generalization over stories is made in three versions of the story experiment (ignoring the sections factor):

1. One story is given to every subject, this story being presented in organized form to half the subjects and in disorganized form to the other half. The result is a single-factor between-subjects design with two groups.

2. A large pool of stories is collected. For each subject, a story is taken randomly from the pool, without regard to group assignment. This story is used only once, either in its organized or disorganized form. Again, the result is a single-factor between-subjects design with two groups, but this time each subject is tested with a different story.

3. A set of b stories is sampled from a large pool of stories. A group of $2n$ subjects is assigned to each story. For half of these subjects the story is presented in organized form, for the other half in disorganized form. The result is a $2 \times b$ design with n subjects per group.

Each design has advantages and difficulties, and there are circumstances under which each is best. In Design 1, there is no variation attributable to the story, so it gives the most stable results and the greatest power. However, there is also no way to evaluate how much the results depend on the choice of the particular story. To use this design, one must believe that all stories are affected by organization in the same way—an assumption that is certainly somewhat incorrect. Several different stories must be used if a feeling about the generality of the effects is to be obtained. In Design 2, many stories are used, and because their differences are incorporated in the within-group variability, one can generalize over them. The conclusions that can be drawn from this study have a generality that is lacking the single-story design. The downside of this design is that different stories are used in each group, so part of the observed difference between groups may be due to these differences, not to organization. Design 3 combines the advantages of both one-factor designs, although at some cost in complexity. As in Design 2, the use of several stories allows more general conclusions. When stories are treated as a random factor, the generalization is statistical. As in Design 1, comparisons between both forms of the same story are possible, thus removing from the error the variability due to the overall differences in the memorability of the stories. We have seen this argument in a couple of places before, most notably in our discussion of the randomized blocks design in Section 11.5 (although there the blocking was systematic, not random) and in our treatment of incidental factors in within-subject designs in Section 17.4.

These three experimental designs illustrate three ways to accommodate a source of variablity that is not central to the research question under study: hold it constant (Design 1), randomize over it (Design 2), or block across its levels (Design 3). A

Table 24.12: The analysis of variance reported by a computer program for the data in Table 24.1, treating factors A and B as fixed and factor C as random.

Source	—Effect— SS	df	MS	—Error term and F test— Error	MS	df	F
A	14.017	1	14.017	$MS_{A \times C}$	13.600	4	1.03
B	32.433	2	16.217	$MS_{B \times C}$	1.717	8	9.44*
C	62.667	4	15.667	$MS_{\text{error-}C}$	15.217	5	1.03
$A \times B$	40.033	2	20.017	$MS_{A \times B \times C}$	0.100	8	200.17*
$A \times C$	54.400	4	13.600	$MS_{A \times B \times C}$	0.100	8	136.00*
$B \times C$	13.733	8	1.717	$MS_{A \times B \times C}$	0.100	8	17.167
$A \times B \times C$	0.800	8	0.100	$MS_{S/ABC}$	1.950	30	0.05
S/ABC	58.500	30	1.950				
Total	276.583	59					

$p^* < .05$

$MS_{\text{error-}C} = MS_{A \times C} + MS_{B \times C} - MS_{A \times B \times C}; \ df_{\text{error-}C} = 4.968$

fourth possibility, nesting, is discussed in the next chapter. As you examine research in psychology, you will find numerous instances of each of these approaches, as researchers strive to balance power, simplicity, and generalizability within a single study.

Exercises

24.1. We discussed but did not illustrate the analysis of a three-factor between-subjects design in which one of the factors is treated as random (see Table 24.5).

a. Perform this analysis using the information in Table 24.1.

b. The output in Table 24.12 was obtained from a popular software program. Compare your analysis with it and note where the two analyses do not agree. Try to figure out what the program did. This demonstration illustrates why we urge you to try out your statistical program with some data you understand before using it.

24.2. At the end of our discussion of the within-subject designs (pages 543–544), we mentioned the three-factor within-subject design with fixed factors A and B and random factor C. Work out the error terms for this design in a table like Table 24.8.

24.3. The three-factor within-subject design with one fixed factor and two random factors is not commonly used, but it provides practice in working out an analysis with random factors present. Construct a table specifying the usual sources of variability, the effects influencing them, and the appropriate F tests.

25

Nested Factors

Factorial designs are usually employed in multifactor experiments. These designs include all possible combinations of the levels of the independent variables—the factors are said to be *crossed*—and they allow researchers to examine the interactions among factors. To know how the effect of factor A varies with the levels of factor B, every level of A is combined with every level of B. However, some factors cannot be crossed because each level of one factor can appear only at a single level of the other. Such factors are said to be **nested**, and we discuss them here.

25.1   Nested Factors

The difference between crossing and nesting can be shown diagrammatically with a pair of $A \times B$ tables:

Crossed   Nested

	b_1	b_2	b_3
a_1	X	X	X
a_2	X	X	X
a_3	X	X	X

and

	b_1	b_2	b_3	b_4	b_5	b_6	b_7	b_8	b_9
a_1	X	X	X						
a_2				X	X	X			
a_3							X	X	X

The combinations of A and B that are included in the design are marked with an X. In the crossed design (left), every combination of levels is included; in the nested design (right), each level of one factor contains a unique set of levels of the other factor. We will refer to factor A here as the **outer** or **nesting factor** and factor B as the **inner** or **nested factor**. Nested factors are also called **hierarchical factors**.[1]

    Nested Material.   One situation in which nested factors occur is when the material used for one experimental condition differs from that used for another. Consider another story-memory study. Subjects read a story, perform some incidental task,

---

[1]The name derives from the fact that the sources of variablity arise at several levels in the statistical description of the design. Recent increases in computer power have allowed similar **hierarchical linear models** to be used more widely in other domains of data analysis, particularly with regression (e.g., Raudenbush & Bryk, 2001).

and are tested for their retention of the story. The stories differ in the familiarity of their content. Some have familiar settings and are easily integrated into the subjects' existing knowledge; others are exotic and difficult to integrate. The researcher wants to determine whether familiar stories are better remembered than exotic ones (factor A). Because some individual stories are easy to remember and others are hard, the researcher cannot use just one story of each type. Otherwise, story familiarity (the independent variable) and story memorability (differences among stories) are confounded. To increase the generality of the results, the researcher includes several stories of each type (factor B). The researcher decides it is not possible to make familiar and exotic versions of the same story (as was possible with the organized and disorganized stories in the last chapter). A story with a familiar setting cannot be made exotic without making it sound artificial and vice versa. Therefore, different stories must be used in the two conditions. Because the b familiar stories are unrelated to the b exotic ones, this factor is nested within the two levels of the familiarity factor.

Exactly what the data look like in this study depends on how many stories each subject sees. In Table 25.1 we have illustrated three possibilities. All three designs involve six stories, of which $b = 3$ are the familiar stories at a_1 (labeled b_{11}, b_{12}, and b_{13}) and three are the exotic stories at a_2 (labeled b_{21}, b_{22} and b_{23}). The first design is completely between-subjects: There are 30 subjects, each of whom reads and recalls one story. The second design is completely within subject: Five subjects read every story. Although this design needs far fewer subjects than the first, many researchers would be concerned because it allows subjects to contrast the familiar settings with the exotic settings. The third design is a mixed design that avoids this problem. Each subject in this design sees only the three stories of a single type. Each of the three designs produces the same number of observations for each story (that is, $n = 5$), but this is accomplished with different overall numbers of subjects.

The three designs in Table 25.1 have two common characteristics. First, the story factor B is not crossed with the familiarity factor A, but is nested within it. If it were crossed, it would be possible to match each story in level a_1 with a particular story in level a_2 and vice versa. We could do that in the example in the last chapter, where the two conditions were created by forming a disorganized version of each organized story. Here no such matching is possible, because each story is unique to its particular type. Second, the nested factor is one that would normally be characterized as a random factor—that is, the stories of each type are best viewed as a sample drawn from a population of such stories. To analyze the data in Table 25.1, we need to take into account both the different configurations of the factors and the random nature of the materials factor. We will describe this analyses in Section 25.2.

Nested Groups of Subjects. Another common situation in which nesting arises is when the subjects are formed into smaller groups or blocks. For example, suppose that in a two-group between-subjects design, it proved convenient to run the study with groups of five subjects at a time—we saw a similar situation in Table 24.1 (p. 532) where, in a study conducted in a classroom setting, every treatment condition was tested in each classroom. However, sometimes all the subjects in each group must be assigned to the same condition. For example, it might be necessary to read the

Table 25.1: Three two-factor nested designs for the story-recall experiment, differing in the number of observations from each subject.

Completely between-subjects design

	Familiar (a_1)			Exotic (a_2)		
	b_{11}	b_{12}	b_{13}	b_{21}	b_{22}	b_{23}
	14	13	15	7	8	13
	15	12	17	8	6	10
	12	15	15	7	11	11
	13	16	16	7	11	11
	13	12	15	8	11	10

Completely within-subject design

	Familiar (a_1)			Exotic (a_2)		
	b_{11}	b_{12}	b_{13}	b_{21}	b_{22}	b_{23}
s_1	13	12	12	7	12	12
s_2	16	13	18	10	12	11
s_3	15	13	14	5	8	8
s_4	12	13	15	7	11	13
s_5	15	13	14	5	8	12

Mixed design: familiarity between-subjects, stories within-subject

	Familiar (a_1)				Exotic (a_2)		
	b_{11}	b_{12}	b_{13}		b_{21}	b_{22}	b_{23}
s_{11}	13	11	15	s_{12}	7	9	13
s_{21}	16	11	16	s_{22}	9	6	11
s_{31}	13	16	17	s_{32}	7	10	10
s_{41}	13	14	16	s_{42}	9	13	16
s_{51}	13	12	16	s_{52}	8	11	11

instructions aloud or present material on slides to everyone together. Table 25.2 shows a set of data in which six groups of $n = 5$ subjects are formed and $b = 3$ of them are randomly assigned to each of the two levels of factor A. Notice the similarity of this design to the first of the designs in Table 25.1. The group factor B here has the same relationship to factor A as the story factor had there. The particular instances (groups) appear within the levels of factor A, but are not crossed with it. Although they differ in whether the subgroups of subjects are distinguished by treatment (the particular stories the subjects receive) or are incidental to the point of the study (the subgroups), from a formal standpoint, the two designs are alike. They are analyzed in the same way. We will give another example in Problem 25.5.

Table 25.2: *Data from a two-condition between-subjects study conducted with* $b = 3$ *subgroups of* $n = 5$ *subjects assigned to each condition.*

	Condition a_1			Condition a_2	
b_{11}	b_{12}	b_{13}	b_{21}	b_{22}	b_{23}
6	12	9	12	24	16
8	15	10	15	27	15
9	15	11	18	26	18
5	14	8	16	27	14
5	11	9	17	25	14

Notation. We need to extend our notation to describe the nested factors. To denote the nesting relationship, we follow the symbol for the nested factor by a slash, then give the nesting factor—the factor within which the nesting occurs. In each of the designs we illustrated, factor B (stories or groups) is nested within factor A (the treatments). It is designated by B/A rather than simply by B. We have already seen one form of nesting: that of subjects in ordinary between-subjects designs. In those designs, unique subjects serve in each condition. Thus, we denote the subject factor in the single-factor between-subjects design by S/A instead of just S.

The subject factor in the design at the top of Table 25.1 and in Table 25.2 involves a double level of nesting. In the latter case, for example, subjects are nested within the subgroups (each subject is uniquely a member of a subgroup), and these groups are nested within the treatments (each subgroup is uniquely a member of a treatment condition). We denote this double nesting by writing $S/B/A$.[2]

The nested factor B is random in all our examples, as it is in practically every case in which a nested factor is used in psychological research. Nested factors are used when we want to increase the generality of an inference by including several instances, such as types of material or subgroups of subjects. These instances are typically not chosen systematically. The fact that different instances appear at the levels of the factor of primary interest (factor A in our examples) affects the variability in the design. Any sampling accidents associated with the nested factor directly influence the treatment effect. For example, if we happened to choose some particularly memorable stories in the exotic condition, we would have increased its mean. The fact that such sampling accidents can occur, just as they can in assigning subjects to conditions, argues for treating the nested factor as random, so that the basis for generalization is statistical.

25.2 Analysis of the Nested Designs

Three steps are involved in working out the analysis of variance for any experimental design: determining the sources of variability; finding the sums of squares, degrees of freedom, and mean squares associated with these effects; and determining the proper

---

[2]Our notation for nesting, although common, is not universal. Some writers use $B(A)$ where we used B/A. Also, it is not necessary to keep track of the double nesting in order to analyze the design, so some writers use only the leftmost slash, writing S/AB where we have $S/B/A$. However, we prefer the notation to reflect the structure of the design, not just the calculations, so we use the double-slashed representation.

error term for the F tests. We described these steps for factorial designs, and here we extend them to designs with nested factors. In doing so, we will give our most general application of the principles that underlie any analysis of variance.

Before we start, a note about the computer packages. We expect that you will use a computer to do the calculations here (although the rules we give are sufficient for hand calculation). However, as of this writing, the analyses we describe in this chapter cannot be done by SPSS and SAS using their graphical interfaces. To use the programs, therefore, you will need to understand the analysis sufficiently well to guide the program's interpretation of the design and its choice of error term. This degree of control will require you to use some of the more advanced features of the program.

The analysis of a design that contains a nested factor differs in two ways from that of the designs we encountered in the preceding chapters. First, when a factor is nested, certain interactions that we would otherwise expect to find are not defined and cannot be measured. Thus, there are fewer sources of variability in a nested design than in a comparable crossed design, and there are associated changes in the degrees of freedom and the way that the sums of squares are calculated. Second, because nested factors are almost always random, their variability must be accounted for in selecting the denominators of the F ratio used to test the principal effects.

The Sources of Variability

We start the analysis by determining the measurable sources of variability—those for which a sum of squares can be calculated. One principle determines them:

> *Each main effect and each combination of crossed factors creates a measurable source of variability.*

Thus, we saw in Section 21.1 that a completely crossed three-factor design has a source of variability for every main effect and for every possible interaction among the factors. The number of sources involving the subject factor depends on which factors are crossed with subjects—whether the design is completely between-subjects, completely within-subject, or mixed. The same principle applies to nested designs. As it implies, only crossed factors create an interaction effect; nested factors do not.

To apply this principle, we use the three steps in Table 11.2 (p. 214). First we list each factor as a source of variability. Each of the three designs in Table 25.1 has three factors: the story type (factor A), the stories themselves (factor B), and the subjects (factor S). Thus, each design contains these three main effects. Second, we list any interactions among the factors. Because different stories are used at each level of factor A, factors A and B do not cross, and these designs lack the $A \times B$ interaction that would be present in a complete factorial. Because stories are nested within story type, we denote it by B/A, as specified in the third step of Table 11.2. Thus far, the same analysis applies to all three designs:

$$A, \quad B/A, \quad \text{and} \quad S.$$

The designs differ in how the subject factor is represented—that is, whether factor S crosses with either of the other two factors or is nested in one or both of them.

First, consider the completely between-subjects design, in which each subject receives only one of the stories (Table 25.1, top). The subjects are nested within a particular story and that story is nested within a particular type of story (familiar or exotic), creating a double level of nesting. As we noted earlier, we write this subject factor as $S/B/A$ to reflect this specific structure. Because none of these factors cross in this design, there are no interactions. Thus, the only sources of variability are the three main effects:

$$A, \quad B/A, \quad \text{and} \quad S/B/A.$$

The design in Table 25.2 has the same structure (although the subgroups are defined differently), so has the same sources of variability.

In the second design in Table 25.1, the observations are completely within subject. As a result, each subject receives both story types and all the stories of each type, making possible interactions between factor S and both of these factors. Because A and B do not cross, there is no three-factor interaction. The interaction between story type (A) and subjects (S) does not involve any nesting (each subject receives both types of stories) and is denoted $A \times S$. The interaction between the stories (B/A) and subjects does involve nesting, and we need to apply the third step in Table 11.2 to specify the source appropriately. Because B is nested within A, its interaction with factor S is also nested. In the layout of the design, you can see this nested interaction by the separate tables at each level of factor A—although the same subjects are involved, they receive entirely unrelated sets of familiar and exotic stories. We write this interaction as $B \times S/A$. The complete list of effects is

$$A, \quad B/A, \quad S, \quad A \times S, \quad \text{and} \quad B \times S/A.$$

The mixed design (Table 25.1, bottom) falls in between the other two. Because each subject receives only the stories of one type (familiar or exotic), they are nested within factor A, and this factor is designated S/A. The subjects are crossed with the stories (factor B)—each subject receives every story of a particular type—creating a $B \times S$ interaction. This interaction is also nested within A (you can see a distinct $B \times S$ table at each level of A in Table 25.1), so the effect is written $B \times S/A$. The final list of effects is

$$A, \quad B/A, \quad S/A, \quad \text{and} \quad B \times S/A.$$

Degrees of Freedom and Sums of Squares

The next step in the analysis is to work out the details. We have seen in earlier chapters that the place to start is with the degrees of freedom. These values can be used to generate the formulas for the sums of squares, and they let you check whether your design has been correctly specified to a computer program (see Problem 25.4). We gave the relevant rules in Table 11.3 (p. 215). The first of these rules tells us that in all three designs (as in other two-factor designs we have seen) there are $df_T = abn - 1$ degrees of freedom in all.

For the most part, the individual effects have designations we have seen in other designs before, hence the same degrees of freedom—factor A, for example, always has $a - 1$ degrees of freedom. There are two new sources: B/A which occurs in all three designs and $S/B/A$ which occurs in the between-subjects design. The degrees of freedom for either of these effects are obtained from the second and fourth rules. For the B/A source, the second rule indicates that the B effect has $b - 1$ degrees of freedom and the fourth rule states that the degrees of freedom for the nested effect

B/A equals the product of the degrees of freedom for the B effect and the a levels of factor A (which appears to the right of the slash):

$$df_{B/A} = a(b-1).$$

For the $S/B/A$ source, there are two layers of nesting, but as the fourth rule states, only the leftmost slash is important. Thus, the degrees of freedom for the $S/B/A$ source equals the product of degrees of freedom for any given group (i.e. $n-1$) and the number of levels of both factor B and factor A:

$$df_{S/B/A} = ab(n-1).$$

You can check your knowledge of the rules by finding all the degrees of freedom for the three designs (checking back to earlier designs with the same sources when you have questions) and verifying that they sum up to df_T, as prescribed by the fifth rule.

The computational formula for the sum of squares of any source of variability is found from the formulas for the degrees of freedom using the rules in Table 11.4 (p. 216). We will review them here, not because we expect that you will need to perform these calculations, but to put all the parts of the analysis together in one place. First, you expand the degrees-of-freedom formula to a sum of simple products. Then, you replace each product by the corresponding bracket term, remembering that n corresponds to factor S, that the highest-order combination of letters is simply $[Y]$, and that the number 1 turns into $[T]$. For the two new sources,

$$df_{B/A} = a(b-1) = ab - a \qquad \text{leads to} \qquad SS_{B/A} = [AB] - [A],$$
$$df_{S/B/A} = ab(n-1) = abn - ab \qquad \text{leads to} \qquad SS_{S/B/A} = [Y] - [AB].$$

We will illustrate these calculations with the mixed design (the third example in Table 25.1). The relevant bracket terms are

$$[T] = \frac{T^2}{abn} = \frac{362^2}{(2)(3)(5)} = \frac{131{,}044}{30} = 4{,}368.133,$$

$$[A] = \frac{\sum A^2}{bn} = \frac{212^2 + 150^2}{(3)(5)} = \frac{67{,}444}{15} = 4{,}496.267,$$

$$[AB] = \frac{\sum (AB)^2}{n} = \frac{68^2 + \cdots + 61^2}{5} = \frac{22{,}842}{5} = 4{,}568.400,$$

$$[AS] = \frac{\sum (AS)^2}{b} = \frac{39^2 + \cdots + 30^2}{3} = \frac{13{,}606}{3} = 4{,}535.333,$$

$$[Y] = \sum Y^2 = 13^2 + \cdots + 11^2 = 4{,}650.$$

These values are combined to obtain the sums of squares:

$$SS_A = [A] - [T] = 4{,}496.267 - 4{,}368.133 = 128.134,$$

$$SS_{B/A} = [AB] - [A] = 4{,}568.400 - 4{,}496.267 = 72.133,$$

$$SS_{S/A} = [AS] - [A] = 4{,}535.333 - 4{,}496.267 = 39.066,$$

$$SS_{B \times S/A} = [Y] - [AB] - [AS] + [A]$$
$$= 4{,}650 - 4{,}568.400 - 4{,}535.333 + 4{,}496.267 = 42.534,$$

$$SS_T = [Y] - [T] = 4{,}650 - 4{,}368.133 = 281.867.$$

Table 25.3: Analyses of variance for the data in Table 25.1. The quasi-F statistics are printed in italics.

Completely between subjects

Source	SS	df	MS	F
A	182.533	1	182.533	15.42*
B/A	47.334	4	11.834	5.68*
S/B/A	50.000	24	2.083	
Total	279.867	29		

* $p < .05$

Completely within subject

Source	SS	df	MS	F
A	149.633	1	149.633	7.54*
B/A	62.134	4	15.534	8.92*
S	27.133	4	6.783	
A×S	24.200	4	6.050	
B×S/A	27.867	16	1.742	
Total	290.967	29		

* $p < .05$

Mixed: one between-subjects and one within-subject factor

Source	SS	df	MS	F
A	128.134	1	128.134	6.33
B/A	72.133	4	18.033	6.78*
S/A	39.066	8	4.883	
B×S/A	42.534	16	2.658	
Total	281.867	29		

* $p < .05$

We have entered these values in Table 25.3, along with the numerical values for the other examples in Table 25.1. We will discuss the remainder of the analysis below. You will find these numerical examples useful when you are verifying that you are using a computer program correctly.

Relationship to a Completely Crossed Design. The scores Y_{ijk} in any set of data lead to the total sum of squares $SS_{\text{total}} = [Y] - [T]$. This value is partitioned (that is, divided up) into components for the analysis of variance according to the design. As we have seen, a nested arrangement of factors leads to a different partitioning from a crossed arrangement. It is instructive to see how these decompositions are related.

Table 25.4: *Sources of variability for the nested designs in Table 25.1 as constructed from the sources in corresponding completely crossed designs. The sources in the first column treat factors A and B as crossed; those in the second column treat factor B as nested within factor A.*

Between-subjects		Within-subject		Mixed	
Crossed	Nested	Crossed	Nested	Crossed	Nested
A	A	A	A	A	A
B $A{\times}B$ } B/A		B $A{\times}B$ } B/A		B $A{\times}B$ } B/A	
S/AB	$S/B/A$	S	S	S/A	S/A
		$A{\times}S$	$A{\times}S$	$B{\times}S/A$	$B{\times}S/A$
		$B{\times}S$ $A{\times}B{\times}S$ } $B{\times}S/A$			

Consider the B/A effect in any of the three designs. Because the levels of factor B are unique to each level of factor A, the total B/A effect is the sum of the individual effects of B within each level of A, that is, it is the sum of a set of simple effects:

$$SS_{B/A} = \sum SS_{B \text{ at } a_j}.$$

Suppose that we had analyzed the data as if factors A and B were crossed. We pointed out in Chapter 12 that the simple effects combine the effect of one of the main effects with that of the interaction (Equation 12.8, p. 253):

$$\sum SS_{B \text{ at } a_j} = SS_B + SS_{A \times B}.$$

Combining these results gives us the relationship between the sums of squares in the two designs:

$$SS_{B/A}(\text{nested}) = SS_B(\text{factorial}) + SS_{A \times B}(\text{factorial}). \tag{25.1}$$

This relationship also holds for the degrees of freedom:

$$df_{B/A} = df_B + df_{A \times B}.$$

We have summarized these relationships in Table 25.4 for the three designs. For each design, the first column lists the sources of variance when the two factors are crossed, and the second column lists the sources when factor B is nested in A. The braces show which terms of the factorial design are combined to make up those in the nested design.

The relationships in Table 25.4 are useful when you have a computer program that does not let you specify a nested factor. You can analyze the design as a fully crossed factorial design—$A{\times}B$, $A{\times}B{\times}S$, or $A \times (B{\times}S)$, as the case may be—then combine the sums of squares after the fact, as indicated in Table 25.4. For example, if you put the data for the mixed design in Table 25.1 into a program for a factorial $A \times (B{\times}S)$ design, you would discover that $SS_B = 63.267$ and $SS_{A \times B} = 8.867$. Equation 25.1 give the result that we calculated above:

$$SS_{B/A} = SS_B + SS_{A \times B} = 63.267 + 8.866 = 72.133.$$

Table 25.5: The effect of a random nested factor. The three stories in the two actual experiments (lower) were chosen randomly from a population of 10 (upper) at each level of the nesting factor.

Mean recall from the full population of stories

Potential instances of familiar stories (a_1)

b_{11}	b_{12}	b_{13}	b_{14}	b_{15}	b_{16}	b_{17}	b_{18}	b_{19}	$b_{1,10}$	Mean
16	9	13	15	9	15	12	10	13	8	12.00

Potential instances of exotic stories (a_2)

b_{21}	b_{22}	b_{23}	b_{24}	b_{25}	b_{26}	b_{27}	b_{28}	b_{29}	$b_{2,10}$	Mean
10	9	9	9	3	5	6	14	5	10	8.00

Mean recall in two actual experiments

First Sample

	b_{13}	b_{19}	b_{12}	Mean
a_1	13	13	9	11.67

	b_{22}	b_{28}	b_{27}	Mean
a_2	9	14	6	9.67

Second Sample

	b_{11}	b_{13}	b_{12}	Mean
a_1	16	13	9	12.67

	b_{22}	b_{27}	$b_{2,10}$	Mean
a_2	9	6	10	8.33

You can verify, either numerically or by writing the sums of squares using the bracket terms, that the other relationships in Table 25.4 hold.

Error Terms and F Ratios

Before discussing the error terms and F ratios for designs with nesting, we will review the way random factors in the design affect the error term. Our demonstration is like the one that motivated the last chapter (Table 24.2). In that example, no treatment effect was present in the population; here we'll assume that there *is* a treatment effect and show how a random factor increases the variability of the means. Consider the study with familiar and exotic stories at the start of this chapter. Suppose that the stories were drawn from a population of only 10 possibilities of each type, and that there was really a four-item effect of the story manipulation. Table 25.5 shows the scores, were they tested, for all ten stories. Over these populations, the means differ by 4.00 items. In fact, only random samples of three stories of each type are used. Two typical samples—what we might actually have tested—are shown at the bottom of the table. In the first sample, the mean recall differs by 2.00 items (somewhat less than the population), and in the second, it differs by 4.34 items (somewhat more than the population). With other samples, we would obtain other values. The means vary from one sample to another, which they would not do had the entire population been sampled. This variation in the size of the difference is entirely a result of the sampling operation, and it adds to whatever variability arises from the sampling of subjects. To determine whether an observed difference between the conditions is large enough to be deemed significant, we need to account for this increased variability.

To find the error terms for the three nested designs, we apply the steps we introduced for designs with random factors (Table 24.3, p. 535). Table 25.6 shows the results. In each design, factor A (the types of story) is fixed and factors B and S (stories and subjects, respectively) are random. The first column in each table lists the sources of variability that we determined above (Step 1 of Table 24.3). In Step 2, the sources of variability that influence each mean square are listed:

a. the source itself,

b. any sources that arise by crossing the original source with a random factor (or combination of factors), and

c. any source in which random effects (and only random effects) are nested within the original source.

We will discuss Step 3, the finding of the F ratio, below.

As in all the random-effects designs, the influences on the fixed-effect source A (which the researcher cares most about) are the most complicated. Rule a tells us to list it. Rule b says we should list any sources in which a random effect is crossed with A. The two random effects in these designs are the nested factor B/A and factor S. Scanning the list of sources in the three designs, the only time we find one of these factors crossed with A is the $A{\times}S$ interaction in the within-subject design, so we list it as an influence on the A effect for this design. Finally, Rule c tells us to look for random effects nested within factor A. This part of the rule implicates B/A in all three designs, $S/B/A$ in the between-subjects design, $B{\times}S/A$ in the within-subject design, and both S/A and $B{\times}S/A$ in the mixed design. Check over the influences for A in the center column of our tables and see how each entry meets one of the criteria.

The influences for the other sources listed in the table are more straightforward. For the B/A effect we start with the B/A effect itself (Rule a). For the first design, Rule c adds the influence $S/B/A$ (factor S is random), and for the second and third designs, Rule b adds the influence $B{\times}S/A$. Similar logic tells us that the $A{\times}S$ effect in the within-subject design and the S/A effect in the mixed design also include the influence of the $B{\times}S/A$ interaction.

Now we can choose the error term to test A (Step 3 of Table 24.3). For the between-subjects design, we need a source that contains the influences B/A and $S/B/A$, so that

$$F = \frac{MS_A}{MS_{\text{error-}A}} \approx \frac{(A) + (B/A) + (S/B/A)}{(B/A) + (S/B/A)}.$$

This term is provided by $MS_{B/A}$. The other two designs both lack a single source that contains all the influences needed for the error term. For the within-subject design, no single mean square contains the three influences B/A, $A{\times}S$, and $B{\times}S/A$, and for the mixed design, none contains the influences B/A, S/A, and $B{\times}S/A$. They require a quasi-F statistic, which we construct using the procedures in Section 24.3. For example, the within-subject design requires an error term containing B/A, $A{\times}S$, and $B{\times}S/A$, which we obtain by summing $MS_{B/A}$ and $MS_{A{\times}S}$ and subtracting $MS_{B{\times}S/A}$:

$$MS_{B/A} + MS_{A{\times}S} - MS_{B{\times}S/A}$$
$$\approx [(B/A) + (B{\times}S/A)] + [(A{\times}S) + (B{\times}S/A)] - (B{\times}S/A)$$
$$= (B/A) + (A{\times}S) + (B{\times}S/A).$$

Table 25.6: Error terms for the three nested designs in Table 25.1.

Completely between-subjects design

Source	Influence on Mean Square	Error Term
A	A, B/A, $S/B/A$	B/A
B/A	B/A, $S/B/A$	$S/B/A$
$S/B/A$	$S/B/A$	—

Completely within-subject design

Source	Influence on Mean Square	Error Term
A	A, B/A, $A{\times}S$, $B{\times}S/A$	quasi-F
B/A	B/A, $B{\times}S/A$	$B{\times}S/A$
S	S, $B{\times}S/A$	$B{\times}S/A$
$A{\times}S$	$A{\times}S$, $B{\times}S/A$	$B{\times}S/A$
$B{\times}S/A$	$B{\times}S/A$	—

Mixed design

Source	Influence on Mean Square	Error Term
A	A, B/A, S/A, $B{\times}S/A$	quasi-F
B/A	B/A, $B{\times}S/A$	$B{\times}S/A$
S/A	S/A, $B{\times}S/A$	$B{\times}S/A$
$B{\times}S/A$	$B{\times}S/A$	—

Numerically, using the mean squares in Table 25.3, this quasi-F statistic is

$$F' = \frac{MS_A}{MS_{B/A} + MS_{A{\times}S} - MS_{B{\times}S/A}} = \frac{149.633}{15.534 + 6.050 - 1.742} = 7.54.$$

The degrees of freedom in the denominator, found from Equation 24.3 (p. 540), are

$$df_{\text{error-}A} = \frac{(MS_{B/A} + MS_{A{\times}S} - MS_{B{\times}S/A})^2}{\dfrac{MS_{B/A}^2}{df_{B/A}} + \dfrac{MS_{A{\times}S}^2}{df_{A{\times}S}} + \dfrac{MS_{B{\times}S/A}^2}{df_{B{\times}S/A}}}$$

$$= \frac{(19.842)^2}{(15.534)^2/4 + (6.050)^2/4 + (1.742)^2/16} = \frac{393.705}{69.667} = 5.7.$$

We use the next lower integer to access the F table, obtaining $F_{.05}(1,5) = 6.61$. The superior recall of the familiar stories is significant.

The fixed effect in the mixed design also requires a quasi-F statistic, which is described in Problem 25.2. Several of the other effects have error terms and can be tested, although usually these tests are of little or no practical interest. They are given in the final column of Table 25.3.

25.3 Crossing a Nested Factor with Another Factor

The three designs we introduced at the start of this chapter (see Table 25.1) involved a single fixed factor (familiar versus exotic settings) combined with a nested random factor (several stories of each type). Of course, nested factors can be included in designs with two (or more) crossed fixed factors. We will describe one example here, which will give us a chance to work out a complete design with a random nested factor. Consider an experiment in which the effectiveness of two therapies (factor A) is to be compared with male and female clients (factor B). At this point, the design is an $A \times B$ factorial, with interest centering on differences in the effectiveness of the two therapies and it relationship to gender. Both factors are fixed. Because therapists often specialize in a particular form of therapy and differ in their effectiveness, the researcher uses three therapists who specialize in therapy a_1 and three who specialize in therapy a_2. Thus, therapists are a random factor C that is nested within factor A:

Assume that n clients of each gender are available from each of the six therapists.

Our analysis here is like the one for the two-factor design (pp. 554–555). The first step is to identify the measurable sources of variability. To begin, we list the factors, A, B, C, and S. Next we identify the interactions. It helps to be systematic here, so that we don't miss anything. Start with factor A. It is crossed with factor B (the therapies are given to both females and males), forming an $A \times B$ interaction, but it does not cross with either C or S. Now take factor B. It crosses with factor C (each therapist sees both female and male clients), but not with S, giving a $B \times C$ interaction. Finally, factors C and S do not cross with each other (each client sees only one therapist), so there are no other interactions. The last step is to add in the nesting. We indicate that the therapists are nested within the types of therapy by denoting the relevant sources as C/A and $B \times C/A$. For the subject factor, there are separate groups of subjects within each of the abc cells of the design. If this were a factorial design, the subject factor would be nested within each cell of the little table above, and we would write the source as S/ABC. Instead, there is an additional level of nesting in which subjects are nested within a particular combination of gender and therapist (S/BC), which in turn is nested within a type of therapy (factor A). So we write the source as $S/BC/A$. The final list of measurable sources appears in the first column of Table 25.7.

The second column of Table 25.7 contains degrees of freedom for these sources, again found by the rules in Table 11.3 (p. 215). Each is the product of the number of degrees of freedom for the source before the leftmost slash and the number of levels of any nesting factors after that slash. From these listings you could construct the

Table 25.7: Degrees of freedom and error term for a three-factor between-subjects design with crossed fixed factors A and B, and a random factor C nested in A.

Source	df	Influence on Mean Square	Error Term
A	$a-1$	A, C/A, $S/BC/A$	C/A
B	$b-1$	B, $B \times C/A$, $S/BC/A$	$B \times C/A$
$A \times B$	$(a-1)(b-1)$	$A \times B$, $B \times C/A$, $S/BC/A$	$B \times C/A$
C/A	$a(c-1)$	C/A, $S/BC/A$	$S/BC/A$
$B \times C/A$	$a(b-1)(c-1)$	$B \times C/A$, $S/BC/A$	$S/BC/A$
$S/BC/A$	$abc(n-1)$	$S/B \; C/A$	—

computational formulas, as we have illustrated most recently on pages 555–556. The next step is to list, in the third column, the sources that influence these mean squares, using the rules on page 560. For example, factor A is influenced by itself, by any interactions with a random factor (there aren't any), and by any random sources that are nested within A. Both C and S are nested within A, so C/A and $S/BC/A$ appear in the list. The influences on MS_B show a different pattern: the influence of itself, an interaction with the random factor C/A (i.e. $B \times C/A$), and the random subject source that is nested within B (i.e. $S/BC/A$). You can check that the influences for the other effects follow from our rules. In the final column, we select error terms that include all the influences except the effect to be tested. Note that in this design the A effect is tested with a different error term than the B and $A \times B$ effects.

25.4 Planning a Study with Random Factors

Throughout this book, we have recommended beginning the planning process with a consideration of effect sizes and power. When the design includes random nested factors, we are currently on less solid statistical ground. Measures of effect size, such as ω^2, that apply to the population were developed for single-factor designs and extended to factorial designs, but they do not easily apply to designs with several sources of random variability.[3] We have to make do with less formal methods.

There are steps you can take to create a nested design that stands a good chance of detecting critical effects. The most important point is apparent from the error terms in Table 25.6. The error terms by which the research factor is judged (factor A, in our examples) all involve the variability of the nested random factor (factor B/A in the between-subjects design and as part of the quasi-F in the other designs). Hence, to obtain a powerful test, the nested effect needs to have as many degrees of freedom as possible. Without adequate sampling of the nested factor, the F statistic has a small number of degrees of freedom in the denominator and a large critical value. Obtaining more subjects is not much help, unless more levels of the random factor are included. You can see what is happening by looking back at our demonstration

---

[3]The exception is the partial correlation ratio, R^2 (or η^2), which can be calculated from the F ratio and can be used if you need a figure for the effect size. Such measures are inflated by sampling error, both of subjects and of the other random factors in the design.

of sampling error in Table 25.5. Much of the variability comes from the sampling of stories, and obtaining a better estimate of the means in the three stories we used by adding more subjects would not reduce it. Using, say, five or six stories, however, will bring each sample mean closer to the population value and greatly increase the quality of the study. Similar concerns about power make it unwise to include more than one random factor (other than subjects) in a design.

So, what steps can you take if you want to use a random nested factor? First, you should look at design decisions that others have made in your research field—the types of favored (or successful) designs and the sample sizes commonly reported. This information gives you a starting point. Second, you may find that a preliminary study is necessary to check on the procedures and to obtain a feeling for where the largest sources of uncertainty arise. Third, you should strive to obtain an adequate sampling of the random factor. And fourth, just as using a homogeneous population of subjects increases the power of a design, you should minimize the variability of the nested factor to whatever extent is concordant with your goals to generalizing the results statistically.

Exercises

25.1. Complete the analysis of Table 25.2 two ways: ignoring the class factor and including it in the analysis. In the first case, the design is a single-factor between-subjects design with $n = 15$ subjects in each treatment condition; in the second, the design includes the nested factor. How do you explain the difference in the outcome of the F tests of the treatment effect?

25.2. Complete the quasi-F test for the mixed design in Table 25.3.

25.3. Table 25.1 gave data for three designs with random nested factors.
a. If you are using a computer program, duplicate the analyses summarized in Table 25.3.
b. If you need practice with hand calculation, duplicate the analyses for the between-subjects and within-subject designs summarized in Table 25.3.

25.4. Suppose someone conducted the study described in Section 25.3 in which three factors were manipulated in a between-subjects design: type of therapy (A), gender of clients (B), and therapists (C). The data were given to an assistant to analyze who produced the following analysis:

Source	MS	df	F
A	9.0	1	6.0*
B	6.0	1	4.0
C	3.0	2	2.0
$A \times B$	7.5	1	5.0*
$A \times C$	3.6	2	2.4
$B \times C$	3.9	2	2.6
$A \times B \times C$	3.0	2	2.0
S/ABC	1.5	48	

$*p < .05$

a. What's wrong with this analysis?

b. How do the conclusions change when you take the correct structure into account?

c. How would you modify this study to increase the power of the design to detect the effects of therapy and gender?

25.5. Postman and Keppel (1967) reported an experiment in which college students were given training on a list of unrelated words, followed by 0, 2, 4, or 6 trials on a different set of words; then they were asked to recall all the words they had learned in the experiment. The response measure of interest was the number of first-list words recalled. Rather than test the students separately, they were run in small groups of $n = 5$ students each that were randomly assigned to the $a = 4$ different treatment conditions. The groups consisted of volunteers who had agreed to serve in the experiment at the same time and date. Twenty-four groups so formed were randomly assigned in equal numbers to each of the four experimental conditions, $b = 6$ groups per condition.

a. On the basis of this information, list the sources of variability available from this experiment, the effects influencing the resulting mean squares, and the error terms for testing these effects.

b. Suppose you only have available the following mean numbers of words recalled by each subgroup:

	a_1		a_2		a_3		a_4
b_{11}	17.0	b_{12}	11.4	b_{13}	9.0	b_{14}	5.6
b_{21}	13.2	b_{22}	11.2	b_{23}	8.2	b_{24}	9.8
b_{31}	11.6	b_{32}	11.6	b_{33}	9.0	b_{34}	8.0
b_{41}	16.0	b_{42}	9.6	b_{43}	6.4	b_{44}	6.0
b_{51}	14.8	b_{52}	9.6	b_{53}	9.8	b_{54}	8.4
b_{61}	15.4	b_{62}	10.8	b_{63}	6.6	b_{64}	10.6

What sources of variability can you measure from these data and what statistical tests are possible?

c. Determine whether the number of trials on the second list affected the recall of the first list.

26

Higher-Order Designs

The analysis of variance, with all its variants and related techniques, provides you with an enormously powerful set of tools. We have tried to give you some idea of their breadth. As you have seen, they are not just procedures for statistical testing but a whole structure in which research is conducted, from designing experiments and through interpreting them. It is this broader view that has given us our title, *Design and Analysis*. Both parts are interconnected, and together they provide the researcher with the means to look quite carefully at behavior and its causes.

At this point we have discussed the designs with three or fewer factors and illustrated most of the major types. You will sometimes encounter designs that involve more than three factors. The analysis of these designs does not involve any new principles. If you know your way around the three-factor designs, then you will also be able to manage the higher-order designs with some facility. In this chapter, we will very briefly review these principles and comment on their use.

26.1 Multifactor Experiments in the Behavioral Sciences

You might ask why anyone would use an experiment that requires more than three factors. Are three-factor designs not complex enough? To understand, let's look back at the simpler factorial designs. When we introduced the two-factor designs in Chapter 10, we pointed out that they had four advantages over the single-factor design. First, they allowed two single-factor designs to be combined with at most a small increase in the number of subjects required. Second, they let these effects be studied under the same conditions—exactly the same sample of subjects, experimental procedures, and so forth. Third, they allowed an assessment of the interaction, that is, the extent to which the simple effect of one factor changed with the levels of the other. Fourth, when the second factor was a blocking factor, the design allowed variability to be removed that would otherwise have contributed to the error term. The three-factor designs have much the same advantages: They combine three two-factor experiments under comparable conditions without a cost in subjects, and they introduce the three-way interaction that assesses variation in the simple two-factor interactions. When a blocking factor is used, they reduce the error variability over that in the two-factor design.

In Section 21.2, we saw that a three-way interaction is considerably more complicated to interpret than a two-way interaction. Four-factor interactions are still more complex, and their interpretation generally requires us to look at the lower-order effects, of which there are a multitude (marginal and simple main effects, two-way interactions, and three-way interactions). You will rarely, if ever, see a study with four or more factors conducted simply to access a four-factor interaction. Psychological theory is almost never strong enough to make their complex patterns interpretable. On the other hand, the three other advantages of the multifactor designs remain. A researcher may use a design with four factors so that the main effects, two-way, and even three-way, interactions can be examined within a single experiment. By combining several comparisons into the same study, it allows them to be measured at the same time and on the same sample of subjects, greatly increasing the ease with which they can be related and compared. Blocking to reduce the error term is also common.

Often, the focus of a multifactor design is on one or two factors. The other factors are included for secondary (but important) reasons. Sometimes a researcher adds a factor simply to check if it has a main effect or interacts with the primary factors. For example, a gender factor may be added to a study, not because sex differences are the point of the study or are expected to be involved in a four-way interaction, but simply because the investigator wants to know whether it interacts with any of the primary factors. Including an extra factor can also increase the generality of the conclusions. Thus, a study conducted with both men and women gives a more general result than one that uses only men or only women. A different approach to generality is used when a random factor is introduced to allow statistical generalization over such things as materials or groups of subjects—this factor too is usually not included for its substantive contribution. Finally, the importance of blocking factors lies in their ability to increase the power of the design, not for the tests of their effects.

The higher-order factorial designs are limited by the large number of individual cells they contain. A $3 \times 3 \times 3 \times 3$ design has 81 cells, and if a rather minimal $n = 5$ subjects were assigned to each cell, a between-subjects design would require 405 subjects, quite possibly more than are available. This proliferation limits the use of the higher-order completely between-subjects designs.[1] The number of conditions also often makes designs with many factors impractical as completely within-subject designs, by leaving them vulnerable to scheduling or fatigue problems. The most common large studies use a mixed design, that combines between-subjects and within-subject factors. For example, a four-factor mixed design with two three-level between-subjects factors and two three-level within-subject factors, would require $3 \times 3 = 9$ groups with each subject receiving $3 \times 3 = 9$ conditions, both achievable values.

26.2 Analyzing Higher-Order Designs

You will surely use a computer to analyze any design with more than three factors, so we will not discuss computational methods. Nevertheless, it is helpful to be able to work out certain aspects of any design. The principles you need have been presented earlier; we will review and bring them together here.

---

[1]Where the interest is only in the main effects and lower-order interactions, it is possible to construct designs in which tests of the higher-order effects are sacrificed and many of the groups are eliminated. These **confounded factorial designs**, of which the Latin squares in Section 17.4 are an instance, go beyond what we can cover here. For a treatment of these designs, see Kirk (1995, Chapters 13–14) or Winer et al. (1991, Chapters 8–9).

- *The list of effects.* You need to know what effects will be present in the analysis to recognize whether the design has been specified correctly and to plan any analytical analyses that are to follow the overall analysis. The effects are determined by the pattern of crossed and nested factors in the study, and they can be determined using the rules we gave in Table 11.2 (p. 214). We suggest that you sketch out a schematic table of the data, such as those in Table 23.1 (p. 511), to help you visualize the design.

- *The error terms.* The first step in determining the error terms is to decide whether any of the factors are to be treated as random. As we noted in Section 24.1, a given factor may be treated either way, depending on the nature of the study and the generalizations that the researcher wants to support. When all the factors (except subjects) are fixed and the design is properly specified, the computer will assign the error terms correctly. When some factors are random or when the design includes nesting, you may need to intervene. The rules in Table 24.3 (p. 535) (or the simpler set in Table 19.3, p. 436) tell you how to proceed. You should be particularly careful when your design includes crossed random factors that make quasi-F statistics necessary.

- *The degrees of freedom.* Knowing what to expect for the degrees of freedom can be useful as a means of determining that the design has been interpreted properly by the computer. These are directly obtainable from the sources of variability following the rules in Table 11.3 (p. 215).

What about the analytical effects? At first glance, the number of possibilities in a higher-order factorial design appears daunting. However, the same approaches we took for the three-way factorial in Chapters 20 and 23 work here. It is important to remember that, just as a four-factor design is almost never directed at the four-way interaction, it is also rare that analytical questions will be directed at the interpretation of this interaction. In practice, the interpretation of these experiments is almost always be made using simple or marginal main effects and two-factor interactions, with the higher-order analyses being used primarily as a way to determine whether these effects change over the levels of another factor.

You will need to be concerned with analytical effects at two stages of the analysis: when planning the study and in post-hoc analysis after the study is complete. In designing the study, certain simple effects, contrasts, and interaction components will express particular questions that you want to test. Our discussion in Chapters 12 and 13 described how these analytical effects are constructed. Because most larger designs involve only a few substantive factors, these planned analyses will usually involve only one- and two-factors, and you can rely on our discussion of those designs.

Unanticipated effects that are discovered after a study is complete tend to be more complicated because they often involve interactions of three (or more!) factors. They are best approached by reducing higher-order effects to simpler ones. Our discussion of the analytical analysis has emphasized the way that complex effects are interpreted using structures that are less complicated than the design in which they originate. Thus, a three-factor effect can usually be investigated with simple two-factor interactions, and two-factor effects are investigated with simple main effects (Figure 22.1, p. 487). Simple effects and interactions can be analyzed by isolating the relevant portion of the data and treating them as a simpler design. Expressing questions by contrasts also simplify the picture, because a contrast reduces the pattern of effects among the levels of a factor to a single value. For example, the interaction of a contrast with a factor simply expresses the way the contrast varies with that factor, and turns a two-dimensional table of means into a one-dimensional array of contrast values. This simplification is most apparent for within-subject factors, where the factor can replaced by a contrast variable, creating a design with one fewer factor. We illustrated these approaches in our several chapters on analytical effects. As we have said before, all this is much less formidable when you are working with your own data and have a good feeling for of your variables.[2]

Finally, we encourage you to take a hand in the analysis yourself. Do not simply follow the default suggestions of whatever computer program you use. Often it will be simpler to put a few of the results together with your calculator than to try to get the computer to do it. For example, it is usually possible to manipulate a program to conduct the analyses involving special error terms—those associated with random effects and quasi-F ratios, or those needed for pooled error terms in the tests of contrasts (as in Table 23.8, p. 522), but these are often faster to do by hand. As you explore your data, you will discover particular contrasts or analytical effects that you want to examine, and a quick calculation yourself will give you an idea of what they are, even if you will return to the computer later to conduct a comprehensive analysis. In our experience, it is this interplay between the computer, the calculator, and, of course, graph paper that characterizes the most skillful users of the analysis of variance.

Exercises

26.1. Johnson (1986) reported an experiment in which he studied the speed with which subjects could determine whether a predetermined target letter appeared as the first letter in either a word or a string of consonants. The design was an $A \times B \times C \times D \times S$ pure within-subjects factorial, in which each subject received all combinations of four independent variables. Subjects saw a series of displays, half of which were words and half of which were strings of consonants (factor A). On half of the trials, the target letter appeared in the display and on the other half it did not (factor B). The number of letters in the display was either three or six letters (factor C). The final independent variable (factor D) was the delay between the announcement of the target letter and the presentation of the display; this delay was either .5 seconds or 2 seconds. The order of these treatment conditions was counterbalanced over the $n = 32$ subjects. Identify the treatment sources of variance and the error terms with which to evaluate their significance.

26.2. Consider the following experiment reported by Slobin (1966). Subjects were shown pictures depicting some sort of activity together with a sentence describing the objects in the pictures. The subjects' task was to indicate whether or not the sentence accurately described the picture. The design was an $A \times (B \times C \times D \times S)$ mixed factorial

---

[2]Admittedly, finding the correct error term can be tricky, particularly in a mixed design. Once you decide what effects you want to test, turn to Tables 23.6 and 23.7 to figure out the error terms. We illustrated most situations in Section 23.5, which you can use as a guide.

with three within-subject independent variables and one between-subjects variable. The within-subject independent variables were four types of sentences (factor B), the truth or falsity of the descriptive sentences (factor C), and the reversibility or nonreversibility of the subject and object depicted in the picture (factor D; *reversibility* refers to situations in which the "object of action could also serve as the subject" and *nonreversibility* to situations in which "the object could not normally serve as the subject," p. 219). The subjects were drawn from five different age groups (factor A), 6, 8, 10, 12, and 20 years. The design contains a total of $abcd = 5 \times 4 \times 2 \times 2 = 80$ treatment combinations. There were $n = 16$ subjects of each of the four age groups. Identify the treatment sources of variance, and determine the degrees of freedom and the error terms.

26.3. Consider a developmental study in which children from three age groups (factor A) are given three different types of problems (factor B) to solve. Each type of problem is represented by three versions (factor D). Each subject attempts to solve all of the $bd = (3)(3) = 9$ problems and receives a score on each problem indicating the completeness and accuracy of the solution. Because there are not enough children from one location to complete the design, the subjects are drawn from four different schools, creating a fourth factor (C). Each school contributed the same number of children to each age group.

  a. Sketch out a schematic diagram for this study in the form that you would organize the data for a computer analysis.
  b. For each of the main effects, indicate which factors are nested and which cross.
  c. Which of these factors would you view as fixed and which as random?
  d. Identify the measurable sources of variability that make up to total sum of squares.
  e. List the effects that may have an influence of the mean square of each source.
  f. Specify the error term for each effect. Indicate how to construct any quasi-F statistics.

A

Statistical Tables

A.1 Critical Values of the F distribution

df_{den}	α	1	2	3	4	5	6	8	9	10	12	15
2	.100	8.53	9.00	9.16	9.24	9.29	9.33	9.37	9.38	9.39	9.41	9.42
	.050	18.51	19.00	19.16	19.25	19.30	19.33	19.37	19.38	19.40	19.41	19.43
	.025	38.51	39.00	39.17	39.25	39.30	39.33	39.37	39.39	39.40	39.41	39.43
	.010	98.50	99.00	99.17	99.25	99.30	99.33	99.37	99.39	99.40	99.42	99.43
	.001	998.5	999.0	999.2	999.2	999.3	999.3	999.4	999.4	999.4	999.4	999.4
3	.100	5.54	5.46	5.39	5.34	5.31	5.28	5.25	5.24	5.23	5.22	5.20
	.050	10.13	9.55	9.28	9.12	9.01	8.94	8.85	8.81	8.79	8.74	8.70
	.025	17.44	16.04	15.44	15.10	14.88	14.73	14.54	14.47	14.42	14.34	14.25
	.010	34.12	30.82	29.46	28.71	28.24	27.91	27.49	27.35	27.23	27.05	26.87
	.001	167.0	148.5	141.1	137.1	134.6	132.8	130.6	129.9	129.2	128.3	127.4
4	.100	4.54	4.32	4.19	4.11	4.05	4.01	3.95	3.94	3.92	3.90	3.87
	.050	7.71	6.94	6.59	6.39	6.26	6.16	6.04	6.00	5.96	5.91	5.86
	.025	12.22	10.65	9.98	9.60	9.36	9.20	8.98	8.90	8.84	8.75	8.66
	.010	21.20	18.00	16.69	15.98	15.52	15.21	14.80	14.66	14.55	14.37	14.20
	.001	74.14	61.25	56.18	53.44	51.71	50.53	49.00	48.47	48.05	47.41	46.76
5	.100	4.06	3.78	3.62	3.52	3.45	3.40	3.34	3.32	3.30	3.27	3.24
	.050	6.61	5.79	5.41	5.19	5.05	4.95	4.82	4.77	4.74	4.68	4.62
	.025	10.01	8.43	7.76	7.39	7.15	6.98	6.76	6.68	6.62	6.52	6.43
	.010	16.26	13.27	12.06	11.39	10.97	10.67	10.29	10.16	10.05	9.89	9.72
	.001	47.18	37.12	33.20	31.09	29.75	28.83	27.65	27.24	26.92	26.42	25.91
6	.100	3.78	3.46	3.29	3.18	3.11	3.05	2.98	2.96	2.94	2.90	2.87
	.050	5.99	5.14	4.76	4.53	4.39	4.28	4.15	4.10	4.06	4.00	3.94
	.025	8.81	7.26	6.60	6.23	5.99	5.82	5.60	5.52	5.46	5.37	5.27
	.010	13.75	10.92	9.78	9.15	8.75	8.47	8.10	7.98	7.87	7.72	7.56
	.001	35.51	27.00	23.70	21.92	20.80	20.03	19.03	18.69	18.41	17.99	17.56

Numerator degrees of freedom, df_{num}

Numerator degrees of freedom, df_{num}

df_{den}	α	1	2	3	4	5	6	8	9	10	12	15
7	.100	3.59	3.26	3.07	2.96	2.88	2.83	2.75	2.72	2.70	2.67	2.63
	.050	5.59	4.74	4.35	4.12	3.97	3.87	3.73	3.68	3.64	3.57	3.51
	.025	8.07	6.54	5.89	5.52	5.29	5.12	4.90	4.82	4.76	4.67	4.57
	.010	12.25	9.55	8.45	7.85	7.46	7.19	6.84	6.72	6.62	6.47	6.31
	.001	29.25	21.69	18.77	17.20	16.21	15.52	14.63	14.33	14.08	13.71	13.32
8	.100	3.46	3.11	2.92	2.81	2.73	2.67	2.59	2.56	2.54	2.50	2.46
	.050	5.32	4.46	4.07	3.84	3.69	3.58	3.44	3.39	3.35	3.28	3.22
	.025	7.57	6.06	5.42	5.05	4.82	4.65	4.43	4.36	4.30	4.20	4.10
	.010	11.26	8.65	7.59	7.01	6.63	6.37	6.03	5.91	5.81	5.67	5.52
	.001	25.41	18.49	15.83	14.39	13.48	12.86	12.05	11.77	11.54	11.19	10.84
9	.100	3.36	3.01	2.81	2.69	2.61	2.55	2.47	2.44	2.42	2.38	2.34
	.050	5.12	4.26	3.86	3.63	3.48	3.37	3.23	3.18	3.14	3.07	3.01
	.025	7.21	5.71	5.08	4.72	4.48	4.32	4.10	4.03	3.96	3.87	3.77
	.010	10.56	8.02	6.99	6.42	6.06	5.80	5.47	5.35	5.26	5.11	4.96
	.001	22.86	16.39	13.90	12.56	11.71	11.13	10.37	10.11	9.89	9.57	9.24
10	.100	3.29	2.92	2.73	2.61	2.52	2.46	2.38	2.35	2.32	2.28	2.24
	.050	4.96	4.10	3.71	3.48	3.33	3.22	3.07	3.02	2.98	2.91	2.85
	.025	6.94	5.46	4.83	4.47	4.24	4.07	3.85	3.78	3.72	3.62	3.52
	.010	10.04	7.56	6.55	5.99	5.64	5.39	5.06	4.94	4.85	4.71	4.56
	.001	21.04	14.91	12.55	11.28	10.48	9.93	9.20	8.96	8.75	8.45	8.13
11	.100	3.23	2.86	2.66	2.54	2.45	2.39	2.30	2.27	2.25	2.21	2.17
	.050	4.84	3.98	3.59	3.36	3.20	3.09	2.95	2.90	2.85	2.79	2.72
	.025	6.72	5.26	4.63	4.28	4.04	3.88	3.66	3.59	3.53	3.43	3.33
	.010	9.65	7.21	6.22	5.67	5.32	5.07	4.74	4.63	4.54	4.40	4.25
	.001	19.69	13.81	11.56	10.35	9.58	9.05	8.35	8.12	7.92	7.63	7.32
12	.100	3.18	2.81	2.61	2.48	2.39	2.33	2.24	2.21	2.19	2.15	2.10
	.050	4.75	3.89	3.49	3.26	3.11	3.00	2.85	2.80	2.75	2.69	2.62
	.025	6.55	5.10	4.47	4.12	3.89	3.73	3.51	3.44	3.37	3.28	3.18
	.010	9.33	6.93	5.95	5.41	5.06	4.82	4.50	4.39	4.30	4.16	4.01
	.001	18.64	12.97	10.80	9.63	8.89	8.38	7.71	7.48	7.29	7.00	6.71
13	.100	3.14	2.76	2.56	2.43	2.35	2.28	2.20	2.16	2.14	2.10	2.05
	.050	4.67	3.81	3.41	3.18	3.03	2.92	2.77	2.71	2.67	2.60	2.53
	.025	6.41	4.97	4.35	4.00	3.77	3.60	3.39	3.31	3.25	3.15	3.05
	.010	9.07	6.70	5.74	5.21	4.86	4.62	4.30	4.19	4.10	3.96	3.82
	.001	17.82	12.31	10.21	9.07	8.35	7.86	7.21	6.98	6.80	6.52	6.23
14	.100	3.10	2.73	2.52	2.39	2.31	2.24	2.15	2.12	2.10	2.05	2.01
	.050	4.60	3.74	3.34	3.11	2.96	2.85	2.70	2.65	2.60	2.53	2.46
	.025	6.30	4.86	4.24	3.89	3.66	3.50	3.29	3.21	3.15	3.05	2.95
	.010	8.86	6.51	5.56	5.04	4.69	4.46	4.14	4.03	3.94	3.80	3.66
	.001	17.14	11.78	9.73	8.62	7.92	7.44	6.80	6.58	6.40	6.13	5.85

Numerator degrees of freedom, df_{num}

df_{den}	α	1	2	3	4	5	6	8	9	10	12	15
15	.100	3.07	2.70	2.49	2.36	2.27	2.21	2.12	2.09	2.06	2.02	1.97
	.050	4.54	3.68	3.29	3.06	2.90	2.79	2.64	2.59	2.54	2.48	2.40
	.025	6.20	4.77	4.15	3.80	3.58	3.41	3.20	3.12	3.06	2.96	2.86
	.010	8.68	6.36	5.42	4.89	4.56	4.32	4.00	3.89	3.80	3.67	3.52
	.001	16.59	11.34	9.34	8.25	7.57	7.09	6.47	6.26	6.08	5.81	5.54
16	.100	3.05	2.67	2.46	2.33	2.24	2.18	2.09	2.06	2.03	1.99	1.94
	.050	4.49	3.63	3.24	3.01	2.85	2.74	2.59	2.54	2.49	2.42	2.35
	.025	6.12	4.69	4.08	3.73	3.50	3.34	3.12	3.05	2.99	2.89	2.79
	.010	8.53	6.23	5.29	4.77	4.44	4.20	3.89	3.78	3.69	3.55	3.41
	.001	16.12	10.97	9.01	7.94	7.27	6.80	6.19	5.98	5.81	5.55	5.27
17	.100	3.03	2.64	2.44	2.31	2.22	2.15	2.06	2.03	2.00	1.96	1.91
	.050	4.45	3.59	3.20	2.96	2.81	2.70	2.55	2.49	2.45	2.38	2.31
	.025	6.04	4.62	4.01	3.66	3.44	3.28	3.06	2.98	2.92	2.82	2.72
	.010	8.40	6.11	5.18	4.67	4.34	4.10	3.79	3.68	3.59	3.46	3.31
	.001	15.72	10.66	8.73	7.68	7.02	6.56	5.96	5.75	5.58	5.32	5.05
18	.100	3.01	2.62	2.42	2.29	2.20	2.13	2.04	2.00	1.98	1.93	1.89
	.050	4.41	3.55	3.16	2.93	2.77	2.66	2.51	2.46	2.41	2.34	2.27
	.025	5.98	4.56	3.95	3.61	3.38	3.22	3.01	2.93	2.87	2.77	2.67
	.010	8.29	6.01	5.09	4.58	4.25	4.01	3.71	3.60	3.51	3.37	3.23
	.001	15.38	10.39	8.49	7.46	6.81	6.35	5.76	5.56	5.39	5.13	4.87
19	.100	2.99	2.61	2.40	2.27	2.18	2.11	2.02	1.98	1.96	1.91	1.86
	.050	4.38	3.52	3.13	2.90	2.74	2.63	2.48	2.42	2.38	2.31	2.23
	.025	5.92	4.51	3.90	3.56	3.33	3.17	2.96	2.88	2.82	2.72	2.62
	.010	8.18	5.93	5.01	4.50	4.17	3.94	3.63	3.52	3.43	3.30	3.15
	.001	15.08	10.16	8.28	7.27	6.62	6.18	5.59	5.39	5.22	4.97	4.70
20	.100	2.97	2.59	2.38	2.25	2.16	2.09	2.00	1.96	1.94	1.89	1.84
	.050	4.35	3.49	3.10	2.87	2.71	2.60	2.45	2.39	2.35	2.28	2.20
	.025	5.87	4.46	3.86	3.51	3.29	3.13	2.91	2.84	2.77	2.68	2.57
	.010	8.10	5.85	4.94	4.43	4.10	3.87	3.56	3.46	3.37	3.23	3.09
	.001	14.82	9.95	8.10	7.10	6.46	6.02	5.44	5.24	5.08	4.82	4.56
22	.100	2.95	2.56	2.35	2.22	2.13	2.06	1.97	1.93	1.90	1.86	1.81
	.050	4.30	3.44	3.05	2.82	2.66	2.55	2.40	2.34	2.30	2.23	2.15
	.025	5.79	4.38	3.78	3.44	3.22	3.05	2.84	2.76	2.70	2.60	2.50
	.010	7.95	5.72	4.82	4.31	3.99	3.76	3.45	3.35	3.26	3.12	2.98
	.001	14.38	9.61	7.80	6.81	6.19	5.76	5.19	4.99	4.83	4.58	4.33
24	.100	2.93	2.54	2.33	2.19	2.10	2.04	1.94	1.91	1.88	1.83	1.78
	.050	4.26	3.40	3.01	2.78	2.62	2.51	2.36	2.30	2.25	2.18	2.11
	.025	5.72	4.32	3.72	3.38	3.15	2.99	2.78	2.70	2.64	2.54	2.44
	.010	7.82	5.61	4.72	4.22	3.90	3.67	3.36	3.26	3.17	3.03	2.89
	.001	14.03	9.34	7.55	6.59	5.98	5.55	4.99	4.80	4.64	4.39	4.14

Numerator degrees of freedom, df_{num}

df_{den}	α	1	2	3	4	5	6	8	9	10	12	15
26	.100	2.91	2.52	2.31	2.17	2.08	2.01	1.92	1.88	1.86	1.81	1.76
	.050	4.23	3.37	2.98	2.74	2.59	2.47	2.32	2.27	2.22	2.15	2.07
	.025	5.66	4.27	3.67	3.33	3.10	2.94	2.73	2.65	2.59	2.49	2.39
	.010	7.72	5.53	4.64	4.14	3.82	3.59	3.29	3.18	3.09	2.96	2.81
	.001	13.74	9.12	7.36	6.41	5.80	5.38	4.83	4.64	4.48	4.24	3.99
28	.100	2.89	2.50	2.29	2.16	2.06	2.00	1.90	1.87	1.84	1.79	1.74
	.050	4.20	3.34	2.95	2.71	2.56	2.45	2.29	2.24	2.19	2.12	2.04
	.025	5.61	4.22	3.63	3.29	3.06	2.90	2.69	2.61	2.55	2.45	2.34
	.010	7.64	5.45	4.57	4.07	3.75	3.53	3.23	3.12	3.03	2.90	2.75
	.001	13.50	8.93	7.19	6.25	5.66	5.24	4.69	4.50	4.35	4.11	3.86
30	.100	2.88	2.49	2.28	2.14	2.05	1.98	1.88	1.85	1.82	1.77	1.72
	.050	4.17	3.32	2.92	2.69	2.53	2.42	2.27	2.21	2.16	2.09	2.01
	.025	5.57	4.18	3.59	3.25	3.03	2.87	2.65	2.57	2.51	2.41	2.31
	.010	7.56	5.39	4.51	4.02	3.70	3.47	3.17	3.07	2.98	2.84	2.70
	.001	13.29	8.77	7.05	6.12	5.53	5.12	4.58	4.39	4.24	4.00	3.75
35	.100	2.85	2.46	2.25	2.11	2.02	1.95	1.85	1.82	1.79	1.74	1.69
	.050	4.12	3.27	2.87	2.64	2.49	2.37	2.22	2.16	2.11	2.04	1.96
	.025	5.48	4.11	3.52	3.18	2.96	2.80	2.58	2.50	2.44	2.34	2.23
	.010	7.42	5.27	4.40	3.91	3.59	3.37	3.07	2.96	2.88	2.74	2.60
	.001	12.90	8.47	6.79	5.88	5.30	4.89	4.36	4.18	4.03	3.79	3.55
40	.100	2.84	2.44	2.23	2.09	2.00	1.93	1.83	1.79	1.76	1.71	1.66
	.050	4.08	3.23	2.84	2.61	2.45	2.34	2.18	2.12	2.08	2.00	1.92
	.025	5.42	4.05	3.46	3.13	2.90	2.74	2.53	2.45	2.39	2.29	2.18
	.010	7.31	5.18	4.31	3.83	3.51	3.29	2.99	2.89	2.80	2.66	2.52
	.001	12.61	8.25	6.59	5.70	5.13	4.73	4.21	4.02	3.87	3.64	3.40
45	.100	2.82	2.42	2.21	2.07	1.98	1.91	1.81	1.77	1.74	1.70	1.64
	.050	4.06	3.20	2.81	2.58	2.42	2.31	2.15	2.10	2.05	1.97	1.89
	.025	5.38	4.01	3.42	3.09	2.86	2.70	2.49	2.41	2.35	2.25	2.14
	.010	7.23	5.11	4.25	3.77	3.45	3.23	2.94	2.83	2.74	2.61	2.46
	.001	12.39	8.09	6.45	5.56	5.00	4.61	4.09	3.91	3.76	3.53	3.29
50	.100	2.81	2.41	2.20	2.06	1.97	1.90	1.80	1.76	1.73	1.68	1.63
	.050	4.03	3.18	2.79	2.56	2.40	2.29	2.13	2.07	2.03	1.95	1.87
	.025	5.34	3.97	3.39	3.05	2.83	2.67	2.46	2.38	2.32	2.22	2.11
	.010	7.17	5.06	4.20	3.72	3.41	3.19	2.89	2.78	2.70	2.56	2.42
	.001	12.22	7.96	6.34	5.46	4.90	4.51	4.00	3.82	3.67	3.44	3.20
60	.100	2.79	2.39	2.18	2.04	1.95	1.87	1.77	1.74	1.71	1.66	1.60
	.050	4.00	3.15	2.76	2.53	2.37	2.25	2.10	2.04	1.99	1.92	1.84
	.025	5.29	3.93	3.34	3.01	2.79	2.63	2.41	2.33	2.27	2.17	2.06
	.010	7.08	4.98	4.13	3.65	3.34	3.12	2.82	2.72	2.63	2.50	2.35
	.001	11.97	7.77	6.17	5.31	4.76	4.37	3.86	3.69	3.54	3.32	3.08

Numerator degrees of freedom, df_{num}

df_{den}	α	1	2	3	4	5	6	8	9	10	12	15
70	.100	2.78	2.38	2.16	2.03	1.93	1.86	1.76	1.72	1.69	1.64	1.59
	.050	3.98	3.13	2.74	2.50	2.35	2.23	2.07	2.02	1.97	1.89	1.81
	.025	5.25	3.89	3.31	2.97	2.75	2.59	2.38	2.30	2.24	2.14	2.03
	.010	7.01	4.92	4.07	3.60	3.29	3.07	2.78	2.67	2.59	2.45	2.31
	.001	11.80	7.64	6.06	5.20	4.66	4.28	3.77	3.60	3.45	3.23	2.99
80	.100	2.77	2.37	2.15	2.02	1.92	1.85	1.75	1.71	1.68	1.63	1.57
	.050	3.96	3.11	2.72	2.49	2.33	2.21	2.06	2.00	1.95	1.88	1.79
	.025	5.22	3.86	3.28	2.95	2.73	2.57	2.35	2.28	2.21	2.11	2.00
	.010	6.96	4.88	4.04	3.56	3.26	3.04	2.74	2.64	2.55	2.42	2.27
	.001	11.67	7.54	5.97	5.12	4.58	4.20	3.70	3.53	3.39	3.16	2.93
90	.100	2.76	2.36	2.15	2.01	1.91	1.84	1.74	1.70	1.67	1.62	1.56
	.050	3.95	3.10	2.71	2.47	2.32	2.20	2.04	1.99	1.94	1.86	1.78
	.025	5.20	3.84	3.26	2.93	2.71	2.55	2.34	2.26	2.19	2.09	1.98
	.010	6.93	4.85	4.01	3.53	3.23	3.01	2.72	2.61	2.52	2.39	2.24
	.001	11.57	7.47	5.91	5.06	4.53	4.15	3.65	3.48	3.34	3.11	2.88
100	.100	2.76	2.36	2.14	2.00	1.91	1.83	1.73	1.69	1.66	1.61	1.56
	.050	3.94	3.09	2.70	2.46	2.31	2.19	2.03	1.97	1.93	1.85	1.77
	.025	5.18	3.83	3.25	2.92	2.70	2.54	2.32	2.24	2.18	2.08	1.97
	.010	6.90	4.82	3.98	3.51	3.21	2.99	2.69	2.59	2.50	2.37	2.22
	.001	11.50	7.41	5.86	5.02	4.48	4.11	3.61	3.44	3.30	3.07	2.84
110	.100	2.75	2.35	2.13	2.00	1.90	1.83	1.73	1.69	1.66	1.61	1.55
	.050	3.93	3.08	2.69	2.45	2.30	2.18	2.02	1.97	1.92	1.84	1.76
	.025	5.16	3.82	3.24	2.90	2.68	2.53	2.31	2.23	2.17	2.07	1.96
	.010	6.87	4.80	3.96	3.49	3.19	2.97	2.68	2.57	2.49	2.35	2.21
	.001	11.43	7.36	5.82	4.98	4.45	4.07	3.58	3.41	3.26	3.04	2.81
120	.100	2.75	2.35	2.13	1.99	1.90	1.82	1.72	1.68	1.65	1.60	1.55
	.050	3.92	3.07	2.68	2.45	2.29	2.18	2.02	1.96	1.91	1.83	1.75
	.025	5.15	3.80	3.23	2.89	2.67	2.52	2.30	2.22	2.16	2.05	1.94
	.010	6.85	4.79	3.95	3.48	3.17	2.96	2.66	2.56	2.47	2.34	2.19
	.001	11.38	7.32	5.78	4.95	4.42	4.04	3.55	3.38	3.24	3.02	2.78
∞	.100	2.71	2.30	2.08	1.95	1.85	1.77	1.67	1.63	1.60	1.55	1.49
	.050	3.84	3.00	2.61	2.37	2.21	2.10	1.94	1.88	1.83	1.75	1.67
	.025	5.03	3.69	3.12	2.79	2.57	2.41	2.19	2.11	2.05	1.95	1.83
	.010	6.64	4.61	3.78	3.32	3.02	2.80	2.51	2.41	2.32	2.19	2.04
	.001	10.83	6.91	5.43	4.62	4.11	3.75	3.27	3.10	2.96	2.75	2.52

Note: These tables were computed using an adaptation of the algorithm for the integral of the beta function given in Press, Flannery, Teukolsky, and Vetterling (1986).

A.2   Critical Values of the t Distribution

Two-sided α level

df	.200	.100	.050	.020	.010	.005	.002	.001
2	1.89	2.92	4.30	6.96	9.92	14.09	22.33	31.60
3	1.64	2.35	3.18	4.54	5.84	7.45	10.21	12.92
4	1.53	2.13	2.78	3.75	4.60	5.60	7.17	8.61
5	1.48	2.02	2.57	3.36	4.03	4.77	5.89	6.87
6	1.44	1.94	2.45	3.14	3.71	4.32	5.21	5.96
7	1.41	1.89	2.36	3.00	3.50	4.03	4.79	5.41
8	1.40	1.86	2.31	2.90	3.36	3.83	4.50	5.04
9	1.38	1.83	2.26	2.82	3.25	3.69	4.30	4.78
10	1.37	1.81	2.23	2.76	3.17	3.58	4.14	4.59
12	1.36	1.78	2.18	2.68	3.05	3.43	3.93	4.32
14	1.35	1.76	2.14	2.62	2.98	3.33	3.79	4.14
16	1.34	1.75	2.12	2.58	2.92	3.25	3.69	4.01
18	1.33	1.73	2.10	2.55	2.88	3.20	3.61	3.92
20	1.33	1.72	2.09	2.53	2.85	3.15	3.55	3.85
22	1.32	1.72	2.07	2.51	2.82	3.12	3.50	3.79
24	1.32	1.71	2.06	2.49	2.80	3.09	3.47	3.75
26	1.31	1.71	2.06	2.48	2.78	3.07	3.43	3.71
28	1.31	1.70	2.05	2.47	2.76	3.05	3.41	3.67
30	1.31	1.70	2.04	2.46	2.75	3.03	3.39	3.65
35	1.31	1.69	2.03	2.44	2.72	3.00	3.34	3.59
40	1.30	1.68	2.02	2.42	2.70	2.97	3.31	3.55
45	1.30	1.68	2.01	2.41	2.69	2.95	3.28	3.52
50	1.30	1.68	2.01	2.40	2.68	2.94	3.26	3.50
60	1.30	1.67	2.00	2.39	2.66	2.91	3.23	3.46
70	1.29	1.67	1.99	2.38	2.65	2.90	3.21	3.44
80	1.29	1.66	1.99	2.37	2.64	2.89	3.20	3.42
90	1.29	1.66	1.99	2.37	2.63	2.88	3.18	3.40
100	1.29	1.66	1.98	2.36	2.63	2.87	3.17	3.39
110	1.29	1.66	1.98	2.36	2.62	2.86	3.17	3.38
120	1.29	1.66	1.98	2.36	2.62	2.86	3.16	3.37
∞	1.28	1.65	1.96	2.33	2.58	2.81	3.09	3.29

Note: These tables were computed using an adaptation of the algorithm for the integral of the beta function given in Press et al. (1986).

A.3 Coefficients of Orthogonal Polynomials

Coefficients for the orthogonal polynomials for designs with equally spaced intervals.

a	Degree	c_1	c_2	c_3	c_4	c_5	c_6	c_7	c_8	c_9	c_{10}	$\sum c_j^2$
3	Linear	-1	0	1								2
	Quadratic	1	-2	1								6
4	Linear	-3	-1	1	3							20
	Quadratic	1	-1	-1	1							4
	Cubic	-1	3	-3	1							20
5	Linear	-2	-1	0	1	2						10
	Quadratic	2	-1	-2	-1	2						14
	Cubic	-1	2	0	-2	1						10
	Quartic	1	-4	6	-4	1						70
6	Linear	-5	-3	-1	1	3	5					70
	Quadratic	5	-1	-4	-4	-1	5					84
	Cubic	-5	7	4	-4	-7	5					180
	Quartic	1	-3	2	2	-3	1					28
7	Linear	-3	-2	-1	0	1	2	3				28
	Quadratic	5	0	-3	-4	-3	0	5				84
	Cubic	-1	1	1	0	-1	-1	1				6
	Quartic	3	-7	1	6	1	-7	3				154
8	Linear	-7	-5	-3	-1	1	3	5	7			168
	Quadratic	7	1	-3	-5	-5	-3	1	7			168
	Cubic	-7	5	7	3	-3	-7	-5	7			264
	Quartic	7	-13	-3	9	9	-3	-13	7			616
9	Linear	-4	-3	-2	-1	0	1	2	3	4		60
	Quadratic	28	7	-8	-17	-20	-17	-8	7	28		2,772
	Cubic	-14	7	13	9	0	-9	-13	-7	14		990
	Quartic	14	-21	-11	9	18	18	9	-11	-21	14	2,002
10	Linear	-9	-7	-5	-3	-1	1	3	5	7	9	330
	Quadratic	6	2	-1	-3	-4	-4	-3	-1	2	6	132
	Cubic	-42	14	35	31	12	-12	-31	-35	-14	42	8,580
	Quartic	18	-22	-17	3	18	18	3	-17	-22	18	2,860

A.4   Critical Values of the Šidák-Bonferroni t Statistic

Critical values of the Šidák-Bonferroni t at $\alpha_{FW} = .20$

Note: The line of numbers immediately above the table gives the percentages for the tests.

Number of tests

df	2	3	4	5	6	7	8	9	10	11	12
	10.557	7.168	5.426	4.365	3.651	3.137	2.751	2.449	2.207	2.008	1.842
2	2.83	3.53	4.12	4.63	5.09	5.51	5.90	6.27	6.62	6.95	7.27
3	2.29	2.73	3.08	3.36	3.61	3.83	4.03	4.21	4.38	4.53	4.68
4	2.08	2.43	2.70	2.91	3.09	3.25	3.39	3.52	3.63	3.74	3.84
5	1.97	2.28	2.50	2.68	2.83	2.96	3.08	3.18	3.28	3.36	3.44
6	1.90	2.18	2.39	2.55	2.68	2.79	2.90	2.98	3.07	3.14	3.21
7	1.86	2.12	2.31	2.46	2.58	2.68	2.77	2.86	2.93	3.00	3.06
8	1.82	2.07	2.25	2.39	2.51	2.60	2.69	2.76	2.83	2.89	2.95
9	1.80	2.04	2.21	2.35	2.45	2.55	2.63	2.70	2.76	2.82	2.87
10	1.78	2.01	2.18	2.31	2.41	2.50	2.58	2.65	2.71	2.76	2.81
12	1.75	1.98	2.13	2.25	2.35	2.44	2.51	2.57	2.63	2.68	2.73
14	1.73	1.95	2.10	2.22	2.31	2.39	2.46	2.52	2.57	2.62	2.67
16	1.72	1.93	2.08	2.19	2.28	2.36	2.43	2.48	2.53	2.58	2.62
18	1.70	1.91	2.06	2.17	2.26	2.33	2.40	2.46	2.51	2.55	2.59
20	1.70	1.90	2.04	2.15	2.24	2.31	2.38	2.43	2.48	2.53	2.57
22	1.69	1.89	2.03	2.14	2.23	2.30	2.36	2.42	2.46	2.51	2.55
24	1.68	1.88	2.02	2.13	2.21	2.29	2.35	2.40	2.45	2.49	2.53
26	1.68	1.88	2.02	2.12	2.20	2.28	2.34	2.39	2.43	2.48	2.51
28	1.67	1.87	2.01	2.11	2.20	2.27	2.33	2.38	2.42	2.47	2.50
30	1.67	1.87	2.00	2.11	2.19	2.26	2.32	2.37	2.41	2.46	2.49
35	1.66	1.86	1.99	2.09	2.17	2.24	2.30	2.35	2.40	2.44	2.47
40	1.66	1.85	1.98	2.08	2.16	2.23	2.29	2.34	2.38	2.42	2.46
45	1.65	1.84	1.98	2.08	2.16	2.22	2.28	2.33	2.37	2.41	2.45
50	1.65	1.84	1.97	2.07	2.15	2.21	2.27	2.32	2.36	2.40	2.44
60	1.64	1.83	1.96	2.06	2.14	2.20	2.26	2.31	2.35	2.39	2.42
70	1.64	1.83	1.96	2.05	2.13	2.20	2.25	2.30	2.34	2.38	2.41
80	1.64	1.83	1.95	2.05	2.13	2.19	2.25	2.29	2.33	2.37	2.41
90	1.63	1.82	1.95	2.05	2.12	2.19	2.24	2.29	2.33	2.37	2.40
100	1.63	1.82	1.95	2.04	2.12	2.18	2.24	2.28	2.33	2.36	2.40
110	1.63	1.82	1.95	2.04	2.12	2.18	2.23	2.28	2.32	2.36	2.39
120	1.63	1.82	1.94	2.04	2.11	2.18	2.23	2.28	2.32	2.36	2.39
∞	1.62	1.80	1.92	2.02	2.09	2.15	2.20	2.25	2.29	2.33	2.36

Critical values of the Šidák-Bonferroni t at $\alpha_{FW} = .10$

Note: The line of numbers immediately above the table gives the percentages for the tests.

Number of tests

df	2	3	4	5	6	7	8	9	10	11	12
	5.132	3.451	2.600	2.085	1.741	1.494	1.308	1.164	1.048	0.953	0.874
2	4.24	5.24	6.08	6.82	7.48	8.09	8.66	9.19	9.69	10.17	10.63
3	3.15	3.69	4.12	4.47	4.78	5.05	5.30	5.53	5.74	5.94	6.13
4	2.75	3.15	3.45	3.70	3.91	4.09	4.26	4.41	4.54	4.67	4.79
5	2.55	2.88	3.13	3.33	3.49	3.64	3.77	3.88	3.98	4.08	4.17
6	2.43	2.72	2.94	3.11	3.25	3.38	3.48	3.58	3.67	3.75	3.82
7	2.35	2.62	2.81	2.97	3.10	3.21	3.30	3.39	3.46	3.54	3.60
8	2.29	2.54	2.73	2.87	2.99	3.09	3.18	3.25	3.32	3.39	3.45
9	2.25	2.49	2.66	2.80	2.91	3.00	3.08	3.16	3.22	3.28	3.33
10	2.21	2.45	2.61	2.74	2.84	2.93	3.01	3.08	3.14	3.20	3.25
12	2.16	2.38	2.54	2.66	2.76	2.84	2.91	2.97	3.03	3.08	3.13
14	2.13	2.34	2.49	2.60	2.70	2.77	2.84	2.90	2.95	3.00	3.04
16	2.11	2.31	2.45	2.56	2.65	2.73	2.79	2.85	2.90	2.94	2.99
18	2.09	2.29	2.43	2.53	2.62	2.69	2.75	2.81	2.86	2.90	2.94
20	2.07	2.27	2.40	2.51	2.59	2.66	2.72	2.78	2.82	2.87	2.91
22	2.06	2.25	2.39	2.49	2.57	2.64	2.70	2.75	2.80	2.84	2.88
24	2.05	2.24	2.37	2.47	2.55	2.62	2.68	2.73	2.78	2.82	2.85
26	2.04	2.23	2.36	2.46	2.54	2.61	2.66	2.71	2.76	2.80	2.84
28	2.04	2.22	2.35	2.45	2.53	2.59	2.65	2.70	2.74	2.78	2.82
30	2.03	2.21	2.34	2.44	2.52	2.58	2.64	2.69	2.73	2.77	2.81
35	2.02	2.20	2.32	2.42	2.50	2.56	2.61	2.66	2.70	2.74	2.78
40	2.01	2.19	2.31	2.41	2.48	2.54	2.60	2.64	2.69	2.72	2.76
45	2.00	2.18	2.30	2.39	2.47	2.53	2.58	2.63	2.67	2.71	2.74
50	2.00	2.17	2.29	2.39	2.46	2.52	2.57	2.62	2.66	2.70	2.73
60	1.99	2.16	2.28	2.37	2.45	2.51	2.56	2.60	2.64	2.68	2.71
70	1.98	2.16	2.27	2.36	2.44	2.50	2.55	2.59	2.63	2.67	2.70
80	1.98	2.15	2.27	2.36	2.43	2.49	2.54	2.58	2.62	2.66	2.69
90	1.98	2.15	2.26	2.35	2.42	2.48	2.53	2.58	2.61	2.65	2.68
100	1.97	2.14	2.26	2.35	2.42	2.48	2.53	2.57	2.61	2.64	2.67
110	1.97	2.14	2.26	2.34	2.41	2.47	2.52	2.57	2.60	2.64	2.67
120	1.97	2.14	2.25	2.34	2.41	2.47	2.52	2.56	2.60	2.63	2.67
∞	1.95	2.11	2.23	2.31	2.38	2.43	2.48	2.52	2.56	2.59	2.62

Critical values of the Šidák-Bonferroni t at $\alpha_{FW} = .05$

Note: The line of numbers immediately above the table gives the percentages for the tests.

Number of tests

df	2	3	4	5	6	7	8	9	10	11	12
	2.532	1.695	1.274	1.021	0.851	0.730	0.639	0.568	0.512	0.465	0.427
2	6.16	7.58	8.77	9.82	10.77	11.64	12.45	13.21	13.93	14.61	15.26
3	4.16	4.83	5.35	5.80	6.18	6.53	6.84	7.13	7.39	7.64	7.88
4	3.48	3.94	4.29	4.58	4.82	5.04	5.23	5.40	5.56	5.71	5.85
5	3.15	3.52	3.79	4.01	4.20	4.36	4.50	4.63	4.75	4.86	4.96
6	2.96	3.27	3.51	3.69	3.84	3.98	4.10	4.20	4.30	4.38	4.46
7	2.83	3.12	3.32	3.48	3.62	3.74	3.84	3.93	4.01	4.09	4.16
8	2.74	3.00	3.19	3.34	3.46	3.57	3.66	3.74	3.82	3.88	3.95
9	2.68	2.92	3.10	3.24	3.35	3.45	3.53	3.61	3.67	3.74	3.79
10	2.63	2.86	3.03	3.16	3.26	3.36	3.43	3.50	3.57	3.62	3.68
12	2.55	2.77	2.92	3.04	3.14	3.22	3.30	3.36	3.42	3.47	3.51
14	2.50	2.71	2.85	2.97	3.06	3.14	3.20	3.26	3.31	3.36	3.41
16	2.47	2.66	2.80	2.91	3.00	3.07	3.14	3.19	3.24	3.29	3.33
18	2.44	2.63	2.77	2.87	2.95	3.02	3.08	3.14	3.19	3.23	3.27
20	2.42	2.60	2.74	2.84	2.92	2.99	3.05	3.10	3.14	3.19	3.22
22	2.40	2.58	2.71	2.81	2.89	2.96	3.01	3.06	3.11	3.15	3.19
24	2.39	2.57	2.69	2.79	2.87	2.93	2.99	3.04	3.08	3.12	3.16
26	2.37	2.55	2.68	2.77	2.85	2.91	2.97	3.01	3.06	3.10	3.13
28	2.36	2.54	2.66	2.75	2.83	2.89	2.95	3.00	3.04	3.08	3.11
30	2.35	2.53	2.65	2.74	2.82	2.88	2.93	2.98	3.02	3.06	3.09
35	2.34	2.51	2.63	2.72	2.79	2.85	2.90	2.95	2.99	3.02	3.06
40	2.32	2.49	2.61	2.70	2.77	2.83	2.88	2.92	2.96	3.00	3.03
45	2.31	2.48	2.59	2.68	2.75	2.81	2.86	2.90	2.94	2.98	3.01
50	2.31	2.47	2.58	2.67	2.74	2.80	2.85	2.89	2.93	2.96	2.99
60	2.29	2.46	2.57	2.65	2.72	2.78	2.83	2.87	2.91	2.94	2.97
70	2.29	2.45	2.56	2.64	2.71	2.76	2.81	2.85	2.89	2.92	2.95
80	2.28	2.44	2.55	2.63	2.70	2.75	2.80	2.84	2.88	2.91	2.94
90	2.27	2.43	2.54	2.62	2.69	2.75	2.79	2.83	2.87	2.90	2.93
100	2.27	2.43	2.54	2.62	2.68	2.74	2.79	2.83	2.86	2.90	2.92
110	2.27	2.42	2.53	2.61	2.68	2.73	2.78	2.82	2.86	2.89	2.92
120	2.26	2.42	2.53	2.61	2.68	2.73	2.78	2.82	2.85	2.88	2.91
∞	2.24	2.39	2.49	2.57	2.63	2.68	2.73	2.77	2.80	2.83	2.86

Critical values of the Šidák-Bonferroni t at $\alpha_{FW} = .01$

Note: The line of numbers immediately above the table gives the percentages for the tests.

Number of tests

df	2	3	4	5	6	7	8	9	10	11	12
	0.501	0.334	0.251	0.201	0.167	0.143	0.126	0.112	0.100	0.091	0.084
2	14.07	17.25	19.92	22.28	24.41	26.37	28.20	29.91	31.53	33.07	34.54
3	7.45	8.57	9.45	10.20	10.85	11.44	11.97	12.45	12.90	13.33	13.72
4	5.59	6.25	6.75	7.17	7.52	7.83	8.11	8.37	8.60	8.82	9.02
5	4.77	5.24	5.60	5.89	6.13	6.35	6.54	6.71	6.86	7.01	7.14
6	4.31	4.69	4.98	5.20	5.39	5.56	5.70	5.83	5.95	6.06	6.16
7	4.03	4.35	4.59	4.78	4.94	5.08	5.20	5.31	5.40	5.49	5.58
8	3.83	4.12	4.33	4.50	4.64	4.76	4.86	4.95	5.04	5.11	5.19
9	3.69	3.95	4.14	4.29	4.42	4.53	4.62	4.70	4.78	4.85	4.91
10	3.58	3.83	4.00	4.14	4.26	4.35	4.44	4.52	4.58	4.65	4.70
12	3.43	3.65	3.80	3.93	4.03	4.11	4.19	4.26	4.32	4.37	4.42
14	3.32	3.53	3.67	3.79	3.88	3.96	4.02	4.08	4.14	4.19	4.23
16	3.25	3.44	3.58	3.68	3.77	3.84	3.91	3.96	4.01	4.06	4.10
18	3.20	3.38	3.51	3.61	3.69	3.76	3.82	3.87	3.92	3.96	4.00
20	3.15	3.33	3.45	3.55	3.63	3.69	3.75	3.80	3.85	3.89	3.93
22	3.12	3.29	3.41	3.50	3.58	3.64	3.70	3.75	3.79	3.83	3.87
24	3.09	3.26	3.37	3.47	3.54	3.60	3.65	3.70	3.74	3.78	3.82
26	3.07	3.23	3.34	3.43	3.51	3.57	3.62	3.66	3.70	3.74	3.78
28	3.05	3.21	3.32	3.41	3.48	3.54	3.59	3.63	3.67	3.71	3.74
30	3.03	3.19	3.30	3.38	3.45	3.51	3.56	3.61	3.64	3.68	3.71
35	3.00	3.15	3.26	3.34	3.41	3.46	3.51	3.55	3.59	3.62	3.65
40	2.97	3.12	3.23	3.31	3.37	3.42	3.47	3.51	3.55	3.58	3.61
45	2.95	3.10	3.20	3.28	3.34	3.40	3.44	3.48	3.52	3.55	3.58
50	2.94	3.08	3.18	3.26	3.32	3.37	3.42	3.46	3.49	3.53	3.55
60	2.91	3.06	3.15	3.23	3.29	3.34	3.39	3.42	3.46	3.49	3.52
70	2.90	3.04	3.14	3.21	3.27	3.32	3.36	3.40	3.43	3.46	3.49
80	2.89	3.02	3.12	3.19	3.25	3.30	3.34	3.38	3.41	3.44	3.47
90	2.88	3.01	3.11	3.18	3.24	3.29	3.33	3.37	3.40	3.43	3.46
100	2.87	3.01	3.10	3.17	3.23	3.28	3.32	3.36	3.39	3.42	3.44
110	2.86	3.00	3.09	3.16	3.22	3.27	3.31	3.35	3.38	3.41	3.43
120	2.86	2.99	3.09	3.16	3.22	3.26	3.30	3.34	3.37	3.40	3.43
∞	2.81	2.93	3.02	3.09	3.14	3.19	3.23	3.26	3.29	3.32	3.34

Note: These tables were computed using an adaptation of the algorithm for the integral of the beta function given in Press et al. (1986).

A.5   Critical Values for Dunnett's Test

Critical values for Dunnett's test at $\alpha_{FW} = .20$

Number of groups *including control*

df	3	4	5	6	7	8	9	10	11	12
2	2.47	2.80	3.03	3.20	3.33	3.44	3.54	3.62	3.70	3.76
3	2.10	2.36	2.54	2.68	2.78	2.87	2.95	3.01	3.07	3.12
4	1.95	2.18	2.34	2.45	2.55	2.63	2.69	2.75	2.80	2.85
5	1.86	2.08	2.22	2.33	2.42	2.49	2.56	2.61	2.66	2.70
6	1.81	2.01	2.15	2.26	2.34	2.41	2.47	2.52	2.56	2.60
7	1.77	1.97	2.10	2.20	2.28	2.35	2.41	2.46	2.50	2.54
8	1.75	1.94	2.07	2.16	2.24	2.31	2.36	2.41	2.45	2.49
9	1.73	1.91	2.04	2.14	2.21	2.27	2.33	2.37	2.41	2.45
10	1.71	1.89	2.02	2.11	2.19	2.25	2.30	2.35	2.39	2.42
12	1.69	1.87	1.99	2.08	2.15	2.21	2.26	2.30	2.34	2.38
14	1.67	1.85	1.96	2.05	2.12	2.18	2.23	2.28	2.31	2.35
16	1.66	1.83	1.95	2.04	2.11	2.16	2.21	2.25	2.29	2.32
18	1.65	1.82	1.94	2.02	2.09	2.15	2.20	2.24	2.27	2.31
20	1.64	1.81	1.93	2.01	2.08	2.13	2.18	2.22	2.26	2.29
22	1.63	1.80	1.92	2.00	2.07	2.13	2.17	2.21	2.25	2.28
24	1.63	1.80	1.91	1.99	2.06	2.12	2.16	2.20	2.24	2.27
26	1.63	1.79	1.90	1.99	2.05	2.11	2.16	2.20	2.23	2.26
28	1.62	1.79	1.90	1.98	2.05	2.10	2.15	2.19	2.23	2.26
30	1.62	1.78	1.90	1.98	2.04	2.10	2.15	2.19	2.22	2.25
35	1.61	1.78	1.89	1.97	2.03	2.09	2.13	2.17	2.21	2.24
40	1.61	1.77	1.88	1.96	2.03	2.08	2.13	2.17	2.20	2.23
45	1.60	1.77	1.88	1.96	2.02	2.08	2.12	2.16	2.19	2.22
50	1.60	1.76	1.87	1.95	2.02	2.07	2.12	2.15	2.19	2.22
60	1.60	1.76	1.87	1.95	2.01	2.06	2.11	2.15	2.18	2.21
70	1.59	1.75	1.86	1.94	2.01	2.06	2.10	2.14	2.18	2.21
80	1.59	1.75	1.86	1.94	2.00	2.05	2.10	2.14	2.17	2.20
90	1.59	1.75	1.86	1.94	2.00	2.05	2.10	2.13	2.17	2.20
100	1.59	1.75	1.85	1.93	2.00	2.05	2.09	2.13	2.17	2.20
110	1.59	1.75	1.85	1.93	2.00	2.05	2.09	2.13	2.16	2.19
120	1.59	1.75	1.85	1.93	1.99	2.05	2.09	2.13	2.16	2.19
∞	1.58	1.73	1.84	1.92	1.98	2.03	2.07	2.11	2.14	2.17

Critical values for Dunnett's test at $\alpha_{FW} = .10$

Number of groups *including control*

df	3	4	5	6	7	8	9	10	11	12
2	3.72	4.18	4.50	4.74	4.93	5.09	5.23	5.34	5.45	5.54
3	2.91	3.23	3.45	3.62	3.75	3.87	3.96	4.04	4.12	4.18
4	2.60	2.86	3.05	3.18	3.30	3.39	3.47	3.54	3.60	3.65
5	2.43	2.67	2.83	2.96	3.05	3.14	3.21	3.27	3.32	3.37
6	2.33	2.55	2.70	2.81	2.91	2.98	3.05	3.10	3.15	3.20
7	2.26	2.47	2.61	2.72	2.81	2.88	2.94	2.99	3.04	3.08
8	2.22	2.41	2.55	2.65	2.73	2.80	2.86	2.91	2.96	3.00
9	2.18	2.37	2.50	2.60	2.68	2.74	2.80	2.85	2.89	2.93
10	2.15	2.34	2.46	2.56	2.64	2.70	2.75	2.80	2.84	2.88
12	2.11	2.29	2.41	2.50	2.57	2.63	2.69	2.73	2.77	2.81
14	2.08	2.25	2.37	2.46	2.53	2.59	2.64	2.68	2.72	2.76
16	2.06	2.23	2.34	2.43	2.50	2.56	2.61	2.65	2.69	2.72
18	2.04	2.21	2.32	2.41	2.47	2.53	2.58	2.62	2.66	2.69
20	2.03	2.19	2.30	2.39	2.46	2.51	2.56	2.60	2.64	2.67
22	2.02	2.18	2.29	2.37	2.44	2.63	2.54	2.58	2.62	2.65
24	2.01	2.17	2.28	2.36	2.43	2.48	2.53	2.57	2.60	2.64
26	2.00	2.16	2.27	2.35	2.42	2.47	2.52	2.56	2.59	2.62
28	1.99	2.15	2.26	2.34	2.41	2.46	2.51	2.55	2.58	2.61
30	1.99	2.15	2.25	2.33	2.40	2.45	2.50	2.54	2.57	2.60
35	1.98	2.13	2.24	2.32	2.38	2.44	2.48	2.52	2.55	2.58
40	1.97	2.13	2.23	2.31	2.37	2.42	2.47	2.51	2.54	2.57
45	1.96	2.12	2.22	2.30	2.36	2.41	2.46	2.50	2.53	2.56
50	1.96	2.11	2.22	2.29	2.36	2.41	2.45	2.49	2.52	2.55
60	1.95	2.10	2.21	2.28	2.34	2.40	2.44	2.48	2.51	2.54
70	1.95	2.10	2.20	2.28	2.34	2.39	2.43	2.47	2.50	2.53
80	1.94	2.09	2.19	2.27	2.33	2.38	2.42	2.46	2.49	2.52
90	1.94	2.09	2.19	2.27	2.33	2.38	2.42	2.46	2.49	2.52
100	1.94	2.09	2.19	2.26	2.32	2.37	2.42	2.45	2.48	2.51
110	1.94	2.08	2.19	2.26	2.32	2.37	2.41	2.45	2.48	2.51
120	1.93	2.08	2.18	2.26	2.32	2.37	2.41	2.45	2.48	2.51
∞	1.92	2.06	2.16	2.23	2.29	2.34	2.38	2.42	2.45	2.48

Critical values for Dunnett's test at $\alpha_{FW} = .05$

Number of groups *including control*

df	3	4	5	6	7	8	9	10	11	12
2	5.42	6.07	6.51	6.85	7.12	7.35	7.54	7.71	7.85	7.99
3	3.87	4.26	4.54	4.75	4.92	5.06	5.18	5.28	5.37	5.45
4	3.31	3.62	3.83	3.99	4.13	4.24	4.33	4.41	4.48	4.55
5	3.03	3.29	3.48	3.62	3.73	3.82	3.90	3.97	4.03	4.09
6	2.86	3.10	3.26	3.39	3.49	3.57	3.64	3.71	3.76	3.81
7	2.75	2.97	3.12	3.24	3.33	3.41	3.47	3.53	3.58	3.63
8	2.67	2.88	3.02	3.13	3.22	3.29	3.35	3.41	3.46	3.50
9	2.61	2.81	2.95	3.05	3.14	3.20	3.26	3.32	3.36	3.40
10	2.57	2.76	2.89	2.99	3.07	3.14	3.19	3.24	3.29	3.33
12	2.50	2.68	2.81	2.90	2.98	3.04	3.09	3.14	3.18	3.22
14	2.46	2.63	2.75	2.84	2.91	2.97	3.02	3.07	3.11	3.14
16	2.42	2.59	2.71	2.80	2.87	2.92	2.97	3.02	3.06	3.09
18	2.40	2.56	2.68	2.76	2.83	2.89	2.94	2.98	3.02	3.05
20	2.38	2.54	2.65	2.73	2.80	2.86	2.90	2.95	2.98	3.02
22	2.36	2.52	2.63	2.71	2.78	2.83	2.88	2.92	2.96	2.99
24	2.35	2.51	2.61	2.70	2.76	2.81	2.86	2.90	2.94	3.38
26	2.34	2.49	2.60	2.68	2.74	2.80	2.84	2.88	2.92	2.95
28	2.33	2.48	2.59	2.67	2.73	2.78	2.83	2.87	2.90	2.93
30	2.32	2.47	2.58	2.66	2.72	2.77	2.82	2.86	2.89	2.92
35	2.30	2.46	2.56	2.64	2.70	2.75	2.79	2.83	2.86	2.89
40	2.29	2.44	2.54	2.62	2.68	2.73	2.77	2.81	2.84	2.87
45	2.28	2.43	2.53	2.61	2.67	2.72	2.76	2.80	2.83	2.86
50	2.28	2.42	2.52	2.60	2.66	2.71	2.75	2.79	2.82	2.85
60	2.27	2.41	2.51	2.58	2.64	2.69	2.73	2.77	2.80	2.83
70	2.26	2.40	2.50	2.57	2.63	2.68	2.72	2.76	2.79	2.82
80	2.25	2.39	2.49	2.56	2.62	2.67	2.71	2.75	2.78	2.81
90	2.25	2.39	2.49	2.56	2.62	2.66	2.71	2.74	2.77	2.80
100	2.24	2.39	2.48	2.55	2.61	2.66	2.70	2.74	2.77	2.79
110	2.24	2.38	2.48	2.55	2.61	2.65	2.70	2.73	2.76	2.79
120	2.24	2.38	2.47	2.55	2.60	2.65	2.69	2.73	2.76	2.79
∞	2.21	2.35	2.44	2.51	2.57	2.61	2.65	2.69	2.72	2.74

Critical values for Dunnett's test at $\alpha_{FW} = .01$

Number of groups *including control*

df	3	4	5	6	7	8	9	10	11	12
2	12.39	13.83	14.83	15.59	16.20	16.70	17.13	17.50	17.83	18.13
3	6.97	7.64	8.10	8.46	8.75	8.98	9.19	9.37	9.52	9.67
4	5.37	5.81	6.12	6.36	6.56	6.72	6.86	6.98	7.08	7.18
5	4.63	4.98	5.22	5.41	5.56	5.68	5.79	5.89	5.97	6.05
6	4.21	4.51	4.71	4.87	5.00	5.10	5.20	5.28	5.35	5.41
7	3.95	4.21	4.39	4.53	4.64	4.74	4.82	4.89	4.95	5.01
8	3.77	4.00	4.17	4.30	4.40	4.48	4.56	4.62	4.68	4.73
9	3.63	3.85	4.01	4.12	4.22	4.30	4.37	4.43	4.48	4.53
10	3.53	3.74	3.88	3.99	4.08	4.16	4.22	4.28	4.33	4.37
12	3.39	3.58	3.71	3.81	3.89	3.96	4.02	4.07	4.12	4.16
14	3.29	3.47	3.59	3.69	3.76	3.83	3.88	3.93	3.97	4.01
16	3.22	3.39	3.51	3.60	3.67	3.73	3.78	3.83	3.87	3.91
18	3.17	3.33	3.45	3.53	3.60	3.66	3.71	3.75	3.79	3.83
20	3.13	3.29	3.40	3.48	3.55	3.60	3.65	3.69	3.73	3.77
22	3.09	3.25	3.36	3.44	3.50	3.56	3.61	3.65	3.68	3.72
24	3.07	3.22	3.32	3.40	3.47	3.52	3.57	3.61	3.64	3.67
26	3.04	3.19	3.30	3.38	3.44	3.49	3.54	3.58	3.61	3.64
28	3.03	3.17	3.27	3.35	3.41	3.47	3.51	3.55	3.58	3.61
30	3.01	3.15	3.25	3.33	3.39	3.44	3.49	3.52	3.56	3.59
35	2.98	3.12	3.22	3.29	3.35	3.40	3.44	3.48	3.51	3.54
40	2.95	3.09	3.19	3.26	3.32	3.37	3.41	3.44	3.48	3.51
45	2.93	3.07	3.16	3.24	3.29	3.34	3.38	3.42	3.45	3.48
50	2.92	3.05	3.15	3.22	3.27	3.32	3.36	3.40	3.43	3.46
60	2.90	3.03	3.12	3.19	3.25	3.29	3.33	3.37	3.40	3.42
70	2.88	3.01	3.10	3.17	3.23	3.27	3.31	3.34	3.37	3.40
80	2.87	3.00	3.09	3.16	3.21	3.26	3.30	3.33	3.36	3.39
90	2.86	2.99	3.08	3.15	3.20	3.24	3.28	3.32	3.35	3.37
100	2.86	2.98	3.07	3.14	3.19	3.24	3.27	3.31	3.34	3.36
110	2.85	2.98	3.06	3.13	3.18	3.23	3.27	3.30	3.33	3.35
120	2.85	2.97	3.06	3.12	3.18	3.22	3.26	3.29	3.32	3.35
∞	2.80	2.92	3.00	3.06	3.11	3.15	3.19	3.22	3.25	3.27

Note: These tables were calculated using the algorithm in Dunnett (1989), with additions and corrections posted in statlib (lib.stat.cmu.edu).

A.6 Critical Values of the Studentized Range Statistic

Critical values of the Studentized range statistic at $\alpha_{FW} = .20$

df	Number of means										
	2	3	4	5	6	7	8	9	10	12	15
2	2.67	3.82	4.56	5.10	5.52	5.87	6.16	6.41	6.63	7.00	7.44
3	2.32	3.25	3.83	4.26	4.60	4.87	5.10	5.30	5.48	5.78	6.13
4	2.17	3.00	3.53	3.91	4.21	4.45	4.66	4.83	4.99	5.25	5.57
5	2.09	2.87	3.36	3.71	3.99	4.21	4.41	4.57	4.72	4.96	5.25
6	2.04	2.79	3.25	3.59	3.85	4.07	4.25	4.40	4.54	4.77	5.05
7	2.00	2.73	3.18	3.50	3.76	3.96	4.14	4.29	4.42	4.64	4.91
8	1.98	2.69	3.13	3.44	3.69	3.89	4.06	4.20	4.33	4.55	4.80
9	1.96	2.66	3.09	3.39	3.63	3.83	3.99	4.14	4.26	4.47	4.72
10	1.94	2.63	3.05	3.36	3.59	3.78	3.94	4.08	4.21	4.41	4.66
12	1.92	2.60	3.01	3.30	3.53	3.72	3.87	4.01	4.13	4.33	4.57
14	1.90	2.57	2.97	3.26	3.48	3.67	3.82	3.95	4.07	4.26	4.50
16	1.89	2.55	2.95	3.23	3.45	3.63	3.78	3.91	4.03	4.22	4.45
18	1.88	2.54	2.93	3.21	3.43	3.60	3.75	3.88	3.99	4.18	4.41
20	1.87	2.52	2.91	3.19	3.41	3.58	3.73	3.86	3.97	4.15	4.38
22	1.87	2.52	2.90	3.18	3.39	3.56	3.71	3.84	3.95	4.13	4.35
24	1.86	2.51	2.89	3.17	3.38	3.55	3.69	3.82	3.93	4.11	4.33
26	1.86	2.50	2.88	3.16	3.37	3.54	3.68	3.80	3.91	4.09	4.31
28	1.86	2.50	2.88	3.15	3.36	3.53	3.67	3.79	3.90	4.08	4.30
30	1.85	2.49	2.87	3.14	3.35	3.52	3.66	3.78	3.89	4.07	4.28
35	1.85	2.48	2.86	3.13	3.33	3.50	3.64	3.76	3.87	4.04	4.25
40	1.84	2.47	2.85	3.11	3.32	3.48	3.62	3.74	3.85	4.02	4.23
45	1.84	2.47	2.84	3.11	3.31	3.47	3.61	3.73	3.84	4.01	4.22
50	1.84	2.46	2.84	3.10	3.30	3.47	3.60	3.72	3.82	4.00	4.21
60	1.83	2.46	2.83	3.09	3.29	3.45	3.59	3.71	3.81	3.98	4.19
70	1.83	2.45	2.82	3.08	3.28	3.44	3.58	3.70	3.80	3.97	4.17
80	1.83	2.45	2.82	3.08	3.28	3.44	3.57	3.69	3.79	3.96	4.16
90	1.83	2.45	2.81	3.07	3.27	3.43	3.57	3.68	3.78	3.95	4.15
100	1.82	2.44	2.81	3.07	3.27	3.43	3.56	3.68	3.78	3.95	4.15
110	1.82	2.44	2.81	3.07	3.26	3.42	3.56	3.67	3.77	3.94	4.14
120	1.82	2.44	2.81	3.06	3.26	3.42	3.55	3.67	3.77	3.94	4.14
∞	1.81	2.42	2.78	3.04	3.23	3.39	3.52	3.63	3.73	3.90	4.09

Critical values of the Studentized range statistic at $\alpha_{FW} = .10$

Number of means

df	2	3	4	5	6	7	8	9	10	12	15
2	4.14	5.74	6.78	7.54	8.14	8.63	9.05	9.41	9.73	10.26	10.89
3	3.33	4.47	5.20	5.74	6.16	6.51	6.81	7.06	7.29	7.67	8.12
4	3.02	3.98	4.59	5.04	5.39	5.68	5.93	6.14	6.33	6.65	7.03
5	2.85	3.72	4.26	4.67	4.98	5.24	5.46	5.65	5.82	6.10	6.44
6	2.75	3.56	4.07	4.44	4.73	4.97	5.17	5.34	5.50	5.76	6.08
7	2.68	3.45	3.93	4.28	4.56	4.78	4.97	5.14	5.28	5.53	5.83
8	2.63	3.38	3.83	4.17	4.43	4.65	4.83	4.99	5.13	5.36	5.64
9	2.59	3.32	3.76	4.08	4.34	4.55	4.72	4.87	5.01	5.24	5.51
10	2.56	3.27	3.70	4.02	4.26	4.47	4.64	4.78	4.91	5.13	5.40
12	2.52	3.20	3.62	3.92	4.16	4.35	4.51	4.65	4.78	4.99	5.24
14	2.49	3.16	3.56	3.85	4.08	4.27	4.42	4.56	4.68	4.88	5.12
16	2.47	3.12	3.52	3.81	4.03	4.21	4.36	4.49	4.61	4.81	5.04
18	2.45	3.10	3.49	3.77	3.98	4.16	4.31	4.44	4.55	4.75	4.98
20	2.44	3.08	3.46	3.74	3.95	4.12	4.27	4.40	4.51	4.70	4.92
22	2.43	3.06	3.44	3.71	3.92	4.10	4.24	4.36	4.47	4.66	4.88
24	2.42	3.05	3.42	3.69	3.90	4.07	4.21	4.34	4.45	4.63	4.85
26	2.41	3.04	3.41	3.68	3.88	4.05	4.19	4.31	4.42	4.60	4.82
28	2.41	3.03	3.40	3.66	3.87	4.03	4.17	4.29	4.40	4.58	4.79
30	2.40	3.02	3.39	3.65	3.85	4.02	4.16	4.28	4.38	4.56	4.77
35	2.39	3.00	3.36	3.62	3.82	3.99	4.12	4.24	4.34	4.52	4.73
40	2.38	2.99	3.35	3.61	3.80	3.96	4.10	4.22	4.32	4.49	4.69
45	2.38	2.98	3.34	3.59	3.79	3.95	4.08	4.20	4.30	4.47	4.67
50	2.37	2.97	3.33	3.58	3.77	3.93	4.07	4.18	4.28	4.45	4.65
60	2.36	2.96	3.31	3.56	3.76	3.91	4.04	4.16	4.25	4.42	4.62
70	2.36	2.95	3.30	3.55	3.74	3.90	4.03	4.14	4.24	4.40	4.60
80	2.35	2.95	3.29	3.54	3.73	3.89	4.01	4.13	4.22	4.39	4.58
90	2.35	2.94	3.29	3.53	3.72	3.88	4.01	4.12	4.21	4.38	4.57
100	2.35	2.94	3.28	3.53	3.72	3.87	4.00	4.11	4.20	4.37	4.56
110	2.35	2.93	3.28	3.52	3.71	3.86	3.99	4.10	4.20	4.36	4.55
120	2.35	2.93	3.28	3.52	3.71	3.86	3.99	4.10	4.19	4.35	4.54
∞	2.33	2.90	3.24	3.48	3.66	3.81	3.93	4.04	4.13	4.28	4.47

Critical values of the Studentized range statistic at $\alpha_{FW} = .05$

Number of means

df	2	3	4	5	6	7	8	9	10	12	15
2	6.10	8.34	9.81	10.89	11.74	12.44	13.04	13.55	14.00	14.76	15.66
3	4.51	5.91	6.83	7.50	8.04	8.48	8.86	9.18	9.47	9.95	10.52
4	3.93	5.04	5.76	6.29	6.71	7.05	7.35	7.60	7.83	8.21	8.67
5	3.64	4.61	5.22	5.68	6.04	6.33	6.58	6.80	7.00	7.33	7.72
6	3.46	4.34	4.90	5.31	5.63	5.90	6.12	6.32	6.50	6.79	7.14
7	3.35	4.17	4.68	5.06	5.36	5.61	5.82	6.00	6.16	6.43	6.76
8	3.26	4.04	4.53	4.89	5.17	5.40	5.60	5.77	5.92	6.18	6.48
9	3.20	3.95	4.42	4.76	5.03	5.25	5.43	5.60	5.74	5.98	6.28
10	3.15	3.88	4.33	4.66	4.91	5.13	5.31	5.46	5.60	5.83	6.12
12	3.08	3.77	4.20	4.51	4.75	4.95	5.12	5.27	5.40	5.62	5.88
14	3.04	3.70	4.11	4.41	4.64	4.83	4.99	5.13	5.25	5.46	5.72
16	3.00	3.65	4.05	4.33	4.56	4.74	4.90	5.03	5.15	5.35	5.59
18	2.97	3.61	4.00	4.28	4.50	4.67	4.83	4.96	5.07	5.27	5.50
20	2.95	3.58	3.96	4.23	4.45	4.62	4.77	4.90	5.01	5.20	5.43
22	2.93	3.55	3.93	4.20	4.41	4.58	4.72	4.85	4.96	5.15	5.37
24	2.92	3.53	3.90	4.17	4.37	4.54	4.69	4.81	4.92	5.10	5.32
26	2.91	3.52	3.88	4.14	4.35	4.51	4.65	4.77	4.88	5.06	5.28
28	2.90	3.50	3.86	4.12	4.32	4.49	4.63	4.75	4.85	5.03	5.24
30	2.89	3.49	3.85	4.10	4.30	4.47	4.60	4.72	4.83	5.00	5.21
35	2.87	3.46	3.82	4.07	4.26	4.42	4.56	4.67	4.77	4.95	5.15
40	2.86	3.44	3.79	4.04	4.23	4.39	4.52	4.64	4.74	4.90	5.11
45	2.85	3.43	3.77	4.02	4.21	4.36	4.49	4.61	4.71	4.87	5.07
50	2.84	3.42	3.76	4.00	4.19	4.34	4.47	4.58	4.68	4.85	5.04
60	2.83	3.40	3.74	3.98	4.16	4.31	4.44	4.55	4.65	4.81	5.00
70	2.82	3.39	3.72	3.96	4.14	4.29	4.42	4.53	4.62	4.78	4.97
80	2.82	3.38	3.71	3.95	4.13	4.28	4.40	4.51	4.60	4.76	4.95
90	2.81	3.37	3.70	3.94	4.12	4.27	4.39	4.50	4.59	4.75	4.93
100	2.81	3.37	3.70	3.93	4.11	4.26	4.38	4.48	4.58	4.73	4.92
110	2.80	3.36	3.69	3.92	4.10	4.25	4.37	4.48	4.57	4.72	4.91
120	2.80	3.36	3.69	3.92	4.10	4.24	4.36	4.47	4.56	4.72	4.90
∞	2.77	3.31	3.63	3.86	4.03	4.17	4.29	4.39	4.47	4.62	4.80

Critical values of the Studentized range statistic at $\alpha_{FW} = .01$

Number of means

df	2	3	4	5	6	7	8	9	10	12	15
2	14.25	19.21	22.52	24.90	26.81	28.38	29.75	30.92	31.93	33.64	35.69
3	8.31	10.66	12.22	13.36	14.28	15.03	15.69	16.25	16.75	17.57	18.57
4	6.54	8.15	9.21	9.99	10.61	11.13	11.57	11.96	12.30	12.87	13.56
5	5.73	7.00	7.83	8.44	8.93	9.34	9.69	10.00	10.27	10.72	11.27
6	5.27	6.35	7.05	7.57	7.99	8.34	8.63	8.89	9.12	9.50	9.97
7	4.97	5.93	6.56	7.02	7.39	7.69	7.95	8.18	8.38	8.72	9.14
8	4.76	5.65	6.22	6.64	6.97	7.25	7.49	7.69	7.88	8.19	8.56
9	4.61	5.44	5.97	6.36	6.67	6.92	7.14	7.34	7.51	7.79	8.14
10	4.49	5.28	5.78	6.15	6.44	6.68	6.88	7.06	7.22	7.49	7.82
12	4.33	5.06	5.51	5.84	6.11	6.33	6.51	6.68	6.82	7.07	7.36
14	4.22	4.90	5.33	5.64	5.89	6.09	6.27	6.42	6.55	6.78	7.05
16	4.14	4.79	5.20	5.50	5.73	5.92	6.09	6.23	6.36	6.57	6.83
18	4.08	4.71	5.10	5.39	5.61	5.79	5.95	6.09	6.21	6.41	6.66
20	4.03	4.65	5.02	5.30	5.52	5.69	5.84	5.98	6.09	6.29	6.53
22	4.00	4.59	4.96	5.23	5.44	5.61	5.76	5.89	6.00	6.19	6.42
24	3.96	4.55	4.91	5.18	5.38	5.55	5.69	5.81	5.92	6.11	6.33
26	3.94	4.52	4.87	5.13	5.33	5.49	5.63	5.75	5.86	6.04	6.26
28	3.92	4.49	4.83	5.09	5.28	5.45	5.58	5.70	5.81	5.99	6.20
30	3.90	4.46	4.80	5.05	5.25	5.41	5.54	5.66	5.76	5.94	6.15
35	3.86	4.41	4.74	4.99	5.17	5.33	5.46	5.57	5.67	5.84	6.04
40	3.83	4.37	4.70	4.94	5.12	5.27	5.40	5.51	5.60	5.77	5.97
45	3.81	4.34	4.67	4.90	5.08	5.22	5.35	5.46	5.55	5.71	5.91
50	3.79	4.32	4.64	4.87	5.05	5.19	5.31	5.42	5.51	5.67	5.86
60	3.77	4.29	4.60	4.82	5.00	5.14	5.26	5.36	5.45	5.60	5.79
70	3.75	4.26	4.57	4.79	4.96	5.10	5.22	5.32	5.41	5.56	5.74
80	3.74	4.25	4.55	4.77	4.94	5.07	5.19	5.29	5.38	5.52	5.70
90	3.73	4.23	4.53	4.75	4.92	5.05	5.17	5.26	5.35	5.50	5.67
100	3.72	4.22	4.52	4.73	4.90	5.04	5.15	5.25	5.33	5.48	5.65
110	3.71	4.21	4.51	4.72	4.89	5.02	5.13	5.23	5.32	5.46	5.63
120	3.71	4.20	4.50	4.71	4.88	5.01	5.12	5.22	5.30	5.45	5.62
∞	3.64	4.12	4.40	4.60	4.76	4.88	4.99	5.08	5.16	5.29	5.45

Note: These tables were calculated using the algorithm in Lund and Lund (1983).

A.7 Power Functions

Power for tests with $df_{\text{num}} = 1$

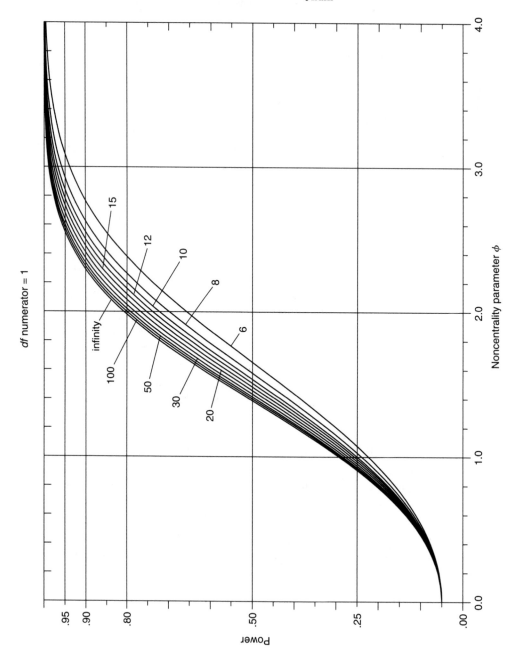

Power for tests with $df_{\text{num}} = 2$

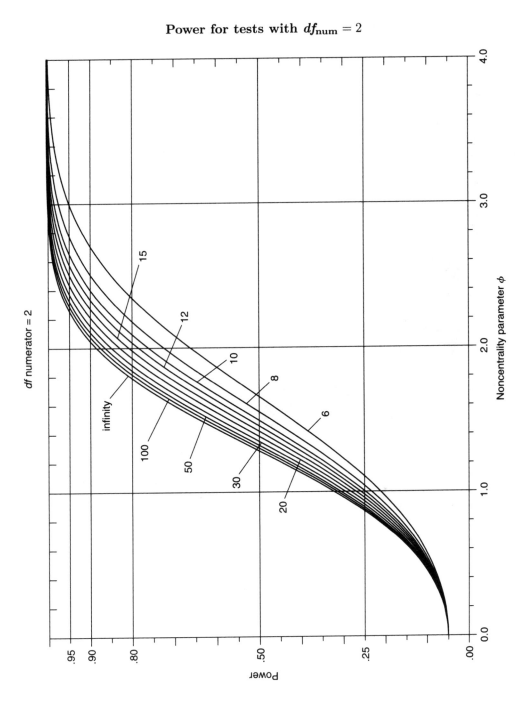

Power for tests with $df_{\mathrm{num}} = 3$

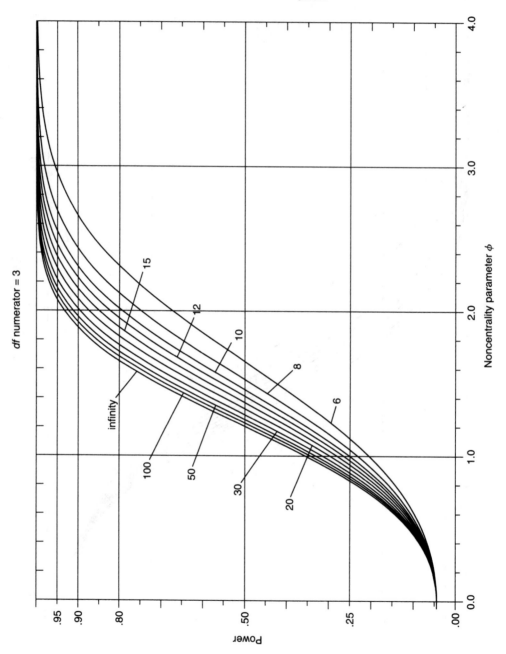

Power for tests with $df_{\mathrm{num}} = 4$

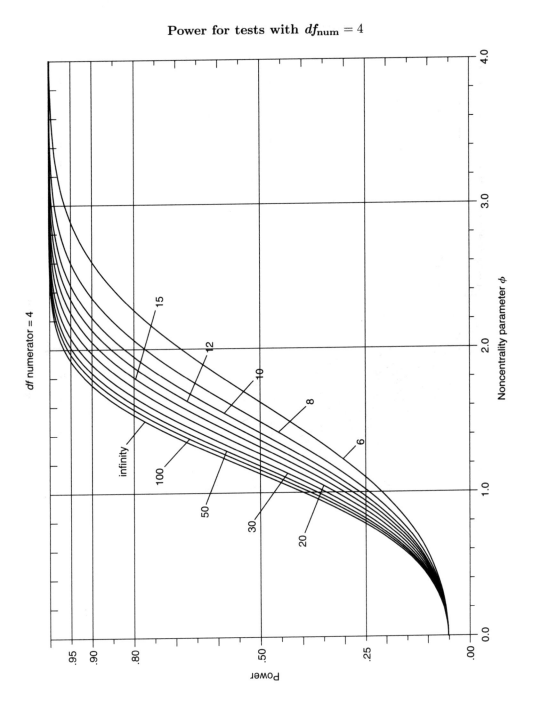

Power for tests with $df_{\text{num}} = 5$

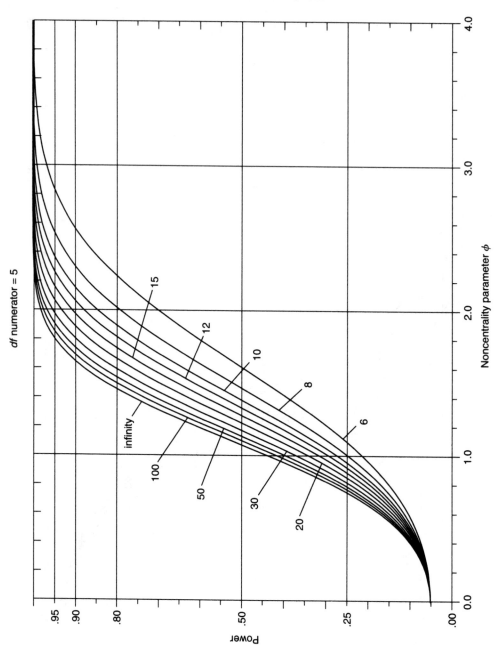

Power for tests with $df_{num} = 6$

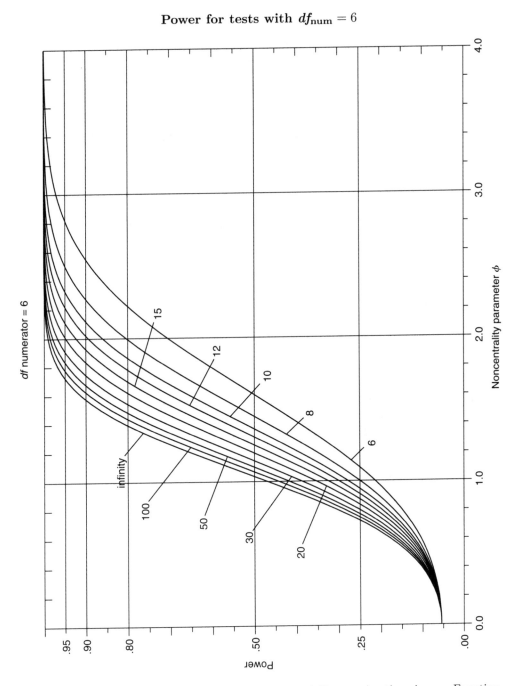

Note: These charts were drawn using the noncentral F approximation given as Equation 26.6.20 in Zelen and Severo (1964) and the incomplete beta algorithm given in Press et al. (1986).

B

Abbreviated Answers
to the Exercises

Answers to Chapter 2

2.1 a,b. $\bar{Y}_j$ ($\sum Y_{ij}^2$): 8.0 (684), 6.0 (426), 7.0 (600), 12.0 (1,524), 10.0 (1,096).
c. $SS_A = 232.00$; $SS_{S/A} = 400.00$; and $SS_T = 632.00$.
2.2 $SS_A = 40.500$; $SS_{S/A} = 217.375$; and $SS_T = 257.875$.

Answers to Chapter 3

3.1 a. 2.69; **b.** 11.38; **c.** 2.00; and **d.** 5.61.
3.2 a. Means (and standard deviations) are 24.00 (5.477), 33.00 (5.715), and 22.00 (7.528).
b. $21.262 \leq \mu_1 \leq 26.739$; $30.143 \leq \mu_2 \leq 35.858$; and $18.236 \leq \mu_3 \leq 25.764$. **c.** Using the value
of $t_{.10}(9) = 1.83$, $18.230 \leq \mu_1 \leq 29.770$; $27.230 \leq \mu_2 \leq 38.770$; and $16.230 \leq \mu_3 \leq 27.770$.
d. $F = 3.45$.[1]
3.3 For $\alpha = .10$, Type I error $= 0.133$ and Type II error $=0.511$; for $\alpha = .01$, the values are
0.022 and 0.800, respectively.
3.4 a. $F = 7.19^*$
3.5 Means (and standard deviations) are 4.6 (3.847), 6.0 (3.391), and 4.2 (3.114). $F = 0.37$.
3.6 $F = 6.52^*$.
3.7 a. $F = 3.15^*$. **b.** The 95% confidence interval for μ_1 is $0.967 \leq \mu_1 \leq 5.033$.
3.8 a. Means (and standard deviations): 15.0 (1.826), 10.0 (2.309), and 6.0 (3.391).
b. 15.0 ± 0.913; 10.0 ± 0.873; and 6.0 ± 1.517. **c.** $F = 13.30^*$. **d.** For the 95% confidence intervals, we used $t_{.05}(13) = \sqrt{F_{.05}(1, 13)} = 2.161$: $12.189 \leq \mu_1 \leq 17.811$; $7.876 \leq \mu_2 \leq 12.124$;
and $3.485 \leq \mu_3 \leq 8.515$.

Answers to Chapter 4

4.1 a. $F = 5.61^*$. **d.** $F_{\psi_1} = 0.02$; $F_{\psi_2} = 15.16^*$; $F_{\psi_3} = 3.18$; and $F_{\psi_4} = 4.07$.
4.2 a. $F_{\psi_1} = 11.29^*$; $F_{\psi_2} = 31.36^*$; $F_{\psi_3} = 16.00^*$; and $F_{\psi_4} = 4.33^*$.
4.3 a. $F = 1.50$. **b.** $F = 12.04$.
4.4 a. $F = 0.26$. **b.** $F = 5.48^*$. **c.** $F = 2.00$.
4.5 $F_{\text{fit}} = 74.90^*$. $F_{\text{failure}} = 2.10$.

---

[1]Throughout these answers, we will use an asterisk (*) to signify a significant effect at the 5%
level of significant

4.6 a. $SS_{\text{fit}} = 260.00$; $SS_{\text{failure}} = 0.00$. **b.** $SS_{\text{fit}} = 260.00$; $SS_{\text{failure}} = 0.00$. **c.** $SS_{\text{fit}} = 124.615$; $SS_{\text{failure}} = 2.052$. **d.** $SS_{\text{fit}} = 0.385$; $SS_{\text{failure}} = 259.615$.
4.7 a. $F = 88.95^*$. **b.** $c_j = \{2, 1, 1, 0, -1, -1, -2\}$. **c.** $F_{\text{fit}} = 508.80^*$. **d.** $F_{\text{failure}} = 4.98^*$.

Answers to Chapter 5

5.1 a. $F_{\text{lin}} = 3.55$; $F_{\text{quad}} = 5.44^*$. **b.** $\bar{Y}'_{j\,\text{lin}} = 0.488 + 0.229X_j$ and $\bar{Y}'_{j\,\text{quad}} = -22.424 + 4.1X_j - 0.164X_j^2$.
5.2 a. $F_{\text{lin}} = 38.80^*$; an upward linear trend is present. **b.** $F_{\text{quad}} = 29.86^*$.
5.3 a. $F = 7.53^*$. **b.** $F_{\text{lin}} = 19.29^*$ and $F_{\text{failure}} = 4.59^*$. $F_{\text{quad}} = 15.65^*$ and $F_{\text{failure}} = 0.90$.
c. $F_{\text{monotonic}} = 17.03^*$ and $F_{\text{failure}} = 5.16^*$.
5.4 a. $F = 3.22$ (not significant). **b.** $F_{\text{linear}} = 6.12^*$. $F_{\text{nonlinear}} = 0.32$.

Answers to Chapter 6

6.1 a. $F_{\text{crit}} = 6.20$. **b.** $t_{\text{crit}} = 2.49$ ($F_{\text{crit}} = 6.20$). **c.** $F_{\text{Scheffé}} = 9.44$.
6.2 a. $D_{\text{Dunnett}} = 8.80$. **b.** $D_{\text{Planned}} = 6.869$.
6.3 a. $D_{\text{Tukey}} = 10.05$. **b.** $D_{\text{FH}} = 9.368$. **c.** $F_{\text{Scheffé}} = 12.24$.
6.4 a. $t_{\text{SB}} = 2.79$. **b.** $D_{\text{Tukey}} = 2.449$. **c.** No tests permitted. **d.** The largest contrast is not significant against $D_{\text{NK}_4} = 2.449$.
6.5 a. $D_{\text{FH}} = 5.378$. **b.** $F_{\text{lin}} = 0.00$; $F_{\text{quad}} = 12.55$; $F_{\text{cubic}} = 1.36$; and $F_{\text{quartic}} = 4.10$. Because $F_{\text{SB}} = 7.508$, only the quadratic trend is significant.
6.6 a. $F_{.05}(1, 40) = 4.08$. **b.** $F_{\text{Scheffé}} = 8.52$.

Answers to Chapter 7

7.1 a. $F = 1.11$.
7.3 $t_{\text{lin}} = 6.53^*$ ($t_{.05}(7) = 2.36$); and $t_{\text{quad}} = 1.29$ ($t_{.05}(10) = 2.23$).

Answers to Chapter 8

8.1 a. $F = 2.03$. **b.** $d_{12} = -.713$; $R^2 = 0.127$; and $\hat{\omega}_A^2 = 0.060$.
8.2 a. $\hat{\omega}_A^2 = 0.290$. **b.** $\hat{\omega}_{\langle\psi_i\rangle}^2 = 0.277$; $\hat{\omega}_{\langle\psi_{ii}\rangle}^2 = 0.186$.
8.3 $R^2 = 0.135$ and $\hat{\omega}_A^2 = 0.087$; $R^2 = 0.066$ and $\hat{\omega}_A^2 = 0.016$.
8.4 $\omega_A^2 = 0.198$ and $n = 15$ (14.62); $\omega_\psi^2 = 0.315$ and $n = 12$ (11.50).
8.5 $\omega_A^2 = 0.20$; $\phi = 2.00$; and power is approximately .9.
8.6 A replication cannot be planned on the basis of this information ($\hat{\omega}_A^2 = -0.007$).
8.7 The values of $\hat{\omega}_A^2$ and sample size (using $\phi = 1.85$) are correct.

Answers to Chapter 10

10.1 a. A, B ; **b.** B, $A \times B$; **c.** B, $A \times B$; **d.** A, B, $A \times B$; **e.** B; **f.** A, $A \times B$; **g.** $A \times B$; **h.** B, $A \times B$; and **i.** B, $A \times B$.
10.3 a. A, B. **b.** A, B. **c.** A, B, $A \times B$. **d.** A, $A \times B$. **e.** A, B, $A \times B$. **f.** $A \times B$.
10.4 b. nonremovable. **c.** nonremovable. **d.** removable. **f.** nonremovable. **g.** nonremovable. **h.** nonremovable. **i.** nonremovable.

Answers to Chapter 11

11.1 a. $F_A = 10.55^*$; $F_B = 26.33^*$; and $F_{A \times B} = 3.55^*$. **b.** 5.80 ± 2.21; 11.133 ± 1.27; and 15.250 ± 1.10. **c.** $\hat{\omega}_A^2 = 0.185$; $\hat{\omega}_B^2 = 0.328$; and $\hat{\omega}_{A \times B}^2 = 0.099$. **d.** $\hat{\omega}_{\langle A \rangle}^2 = 0.323$; $\hat{\omega}_{\langle B \rangle}^2 = 0.458$; and $\hat{\omega}_{\langle A \times B \rangle}^2 = 0.203$.
11.2 a. $F_A = 81.80^*$; $F_B = 0.41$; and $F_{A \times B} = 3.74^*$. **b.** $\hat{\omega}_A^2 = 0.779$ and $\hat{\omega}_{\langle A \rangle}^2 = 0.818$; $\hat{\omega}_B^2 = -0.006$ and $\hat{\omega}_{\langle B \rangle}^2 = -0.034$ (report both as 0.00); $\hat{\omega}_{A \times B}^2 = 0.053$ and $\hat{\omega}_{\langle A \times B \rangle}^2 = 0.233$.
11.3 $MS_A = 24.00$; $MS_B = 56.00$; and $F_{A \times B} = 72.00$. Solving for $MS_{S/AB} = 18.32$, the rest of the table can be reconstructed.
11.4 a. $F_A = 8.79^*$; $F_B = 1.86$; and $F_{A \times B} = 1.76$.

11.5 a. $F_A = 2.05$; $F_B = 1.35$; and $F_{A \times B} = 1.34$. **b.** $\widehat{\omega}^2_{(B)} = 0.023$. From Table 8.1, $n = 80$ (79.5); using the power charts, $n = 77$ (76.7).
11.6 a. Using $\psi = 2.2$ for factor A, $n = 4$ (3.38). **b.** $n = 265$ (264.05).
11.7 $\sigma^2_{A \times B} = 0.16$, $n = 32$.

Answers to Chapter 12

12.1 a. $F = 17.69^*$. **b.** $F = 119.11^8$.
12.2 a. $F_{B \text{ at } a_1} = 6.98^*$; $F_{B \text{ at } a_2} = 0.44$; and $F_{B \text{ at } a_3} = 1.75$.
12.3 a. $F_{A \text{ at } b_1} = 15.85^*$; $F_{A \text{ at } b_2} = 1.20$; and $F_{A \text{ at } b_3} = 0.61$. **b.** $F = 36.62^*$. **c.** $F_{\psi_A} = 45.13^*$ and $F_{\text{residual}} = 1.22$.
12.4 a. $F_A = 25.65^*$; $F_B = 21.10^*$; and $F_{A \times B} = 3.05$. **b.** $F_{A \text{ at } b_1} = 7.60^*$ ($\widehat{\omega}^2 = 0.216$) and $F_{A \text{ at } b_2} = 21.10^*$ ($\widehat{\omega}^2 = 0.456$). **c.** $F_\psi = 0.20$ (report $\widehat{\omega}^2 = 0.00$).
12.5 a. $n = 27$ (26.95). **b.** Yes.

Answers to Chapter 13

13.1 a, b. $F_{\psi_{A_1 B_1}} = 4.23^*$; $F_{\psi_{A_2 B_1}} = 4.90^*$; and $F_{\psi_{A_3 B_1}} = 0.03$.
13.2 $F_{\psi_{AB}} = 1.96$.
13.3 a. $F_{\psi_{AB}} = 7.86^*$; $F_{\psi_A \text{ at } b_1} = 13.20^*$ and $F_{\psi_A \text{ at } b_2} = 0.11$. **b.** $F_{\psi_{AB}} = 1.96$. **c.** $F_{\psi_{AB}} = 5.89^*$; $F_{\psi_A \text{ at } b_1} = 11.78^*$ and $F_{\psi_A \text{ at } b_2} = 0$.
13.4 a. $F_{\psi_A \text{ at } b_2} = 1.59$; $F_{\psi_A \text{ at } b_3} = 1.04$. **b.** $F_{\psi_A \times B} = 10.39^*$.
13.5 a. $F_{\psi_{AB}} = 2.04$. **b.** $F_{\psi_{AB}} = 4.81$. **c.** $F_{\psi_A \text{ at } b_1} = 0.04$; $F_{\psi_A \text{ at } b_2} = 8.41^*$.
13.6 a. $F_{A \times \psi_B \text{ lin}} = 1.43$ and $F_{A \times \psi_B \text{ quad}} = 8.76^*$. **b.** $F_{\psi_B \text{ at } a_1} = 6.00^*$ and $F_{\psi_B \text{ at } a_2} = 3.01$.

Answers to Chapter 14

14.1 A difference of 1.497 based on scores and of 1.518 based on means.
14.2 b. $F = 30.29^*$.
14.3 a. $t_\psi = 2.25^*$. **b.** $t_\psi = -7.73^*$.
14.4 $F_A = 3.29$; $F_B = 0.01$; and $F_{A \times B} = 5.95^*$.
14.5 a. $t = -2.58^*$. **b.** $F = 8.36^*$ and 0.55. **c.** $t = -2.93^*$. **d.** $t = -0.04$.

Answers to Chapter 15

15.2 $SS_{\text{regression}} = 34.571$ ($df = 1$); $SS_{\text{error}} = 13.429$ ($df = 6$); and $F = 15.45^*$.
15.3 a. $F_X = 0.27$ **b.** $F_Y = 4.28^*$ **c.** $F_{\text{ancova}} = 8.56^*$.
15.4 a. From the analysis for part c in Problem 15.3, $SS^{H_0}_{\text{unexp}} = SS_{\text{error}} = 1{,}369.136$ ($df^{H_0}_{\text{unexp}} = 32$). A computer analysis using the individual X variables gives $SS^{H_1}_{\text{unexp}} = SS_{\text{error}} = 1{,}207.656$ ($df^{H_1}_{\text{unexp}} = 30$). We complete the analysis: $SS_{A \times X} = 1{,}369.136 - 1{,}207.656 = 161.480$ ($df_{A \times X} = 32 - 30 = 2$); $F = (161.480/2)/40.255 = 2.01$.
15.5 $F_{B \text{ at } a_1} = 1.77$; and $F_{B \text{ at } a_2} = 25.05^*$.
15.6 a. $\widehat{\omega}^2_A = 0.154$ and $\widehat{\omega}^2_{(A)} = 0.296$. **b.** $n = 11$ **c.** $n = 25$. **d.** Power is approximately 0.55.
15.7 a. $F_{\text{ancova}} = 22.88^*$.
15.8 $n = 16$ ($n = 20$ without covariate); $n = 27$ ($n = 33$ without covariate); and $n = 40$ ($n = 60$ without covariate).

Answers to Chapter 16

16.1 a. $F = 8.81^*$. **b.i.** $t = 0.60$. **b.ii.** $F = 0.23$. **b.iii.** $F = 11.27^*$. **c.** $F_{\text{crit}} = 9.34$. **d.** $n = 6$ (5.47); and $n = 15$ (14.59) per group.
16.2 a. $F = 10.31^*$. **c.** $F = 78.99^*$. **d.** $F_{\text{failure}} = 2.15$.
16.3 a. $F = 29.85^*$ **b.** $F_{\psi_{\text{lin}}} = 89.68^*$. **c.** $F_{\text{failure}} = 0.65$.

Answers to Chapter 17

17.1 a. $F_A = 1.19$. **b.** $F_A = 6.89^*$ and $F_P = 20.20^*$.
17.2 a. $F_{\psi_A} = 2.33$ and $F_{\text{set}} = 0.82$. **b.** $F_{\psi_A} = 81.09^*$ and $F_{\text{set}} = 3.74$.
17.3 $F_A = 28.83^*$; $F_{\psi_{\text{lin}}} = 49.11^*$; and $F_{\text{failure}} = 1.01$.
17.4 a. $\widehat{Y}_{63} = 741.800$. **b.** $F_A = 13.33^*$ ($df_{A \times S} = 10 - 1 = 9$). **c.** $\widehat{Y}_{31} = 728.061$ and $\widehat{Y}_{63} = 742.394$
17.5 $\widehat{Y}_{63} = 10.125$. $F_A = 6.45^*$; $F_P = 5.02^2$ ($df_{\text{residual}} = 8 - 1 = 7$).

Answers to Chapter 18

18.1 a. $F_A = 25.85^*$; $F_B = 29.12^*$; and $F_{A \times B} = 1.33$. **b.** $F_{\psi_{B_{\text{lin}}}} = 85.40^*$; and $F_{B_{\text{nonlinear}}} = 2.75$.
18.2 a. $F_A = 51.85^*$; $F_B = 8.03^*$; and $F_{A \times B} = 13.56^*$. **b.** $F_{B \text{ at } a_1} = 0.79$ and $F_{B \text{ at } a_2} = 359.21$. **c.** $F_{\psi_B \text{ at } a_2} = 342.25^*$. **d.** $F_{\psi_A \times \psi_B} = 39.51^*$.
18.3 $F_A = 625.00^*$; $F_B = 0.09$; and $F_{A \times B} = 171.88^*$.
18.4 a. $F_P = 9.86^*$; $F_B = 18.67^*$; and $F_{A \times B} = 0.69$. **b.** $F_A = 1.89$; $F_B = 18.67^*$; and $F_{A \times B} = 0.54$. **c.** $F_{\psi_A} = 2.75$.
18.5 The two estimates of partial effect size $\widehat{\omega}^2_{\langle A \rangle} = 0.172$ and 0.383; the corresponding sample sizes are $n = 7$ (6.37) and 3 (2.13).

Answers to Chapter 19

19.1 $F_A = 6.05^*$; $F_B = 14.43^*$; and $F_{A \times B} = 1.30$.
19.2 $F_A = 4.16^*$; $F_B = 104.04^*$; and $F_{A \times B} = 7.08^*$.

Answers to Chapter 20

20.1 a. For b_1, $F_{\text{w. cell}} = 0.15$ and $F_{\text{sep}} = 0.12$. For b_2, $F = 5.26$ and 4.81; and for b_3, $F = 8.85^*$ and 12.44^*. **b.** $F_{\text{w. cell}} = 6.01^*$ and $F_{\text{sep}} = 8.44^*$.
20.2 a. $F_{B \text{ at } a_1} = 9.08^*$; $F_{B \text{ at } a_2} == 58.17^*$; $F_{B \text{ at } a_3} = 57.31^*$. **b.** $F_{\psi_{B_1} \text{ at } a_3} = 134.49^*$; and $F_{\psi_{B_2} \text{ at } a_3} = 321.56^*$.
20.3 $F_A = 6.85^*$; and $F_{\psi_1} = 12.96^*$.
20.4 a. $F_{\psi_A \times B} = 2.03^*$. **c.** $F_{\text{within cell}} = 6.48^*$ and $F_{\text{sep}} = 7.30^*$.
20.5 a. $F_{\psi_B} = 189.19^*$; and $F_{A \times \psi_B} = 2.49$. **c.** $F_{\psi_B \text{ at } a_1} = 49.00^*$.
20.6 $F_{\psi_{AB}} = 2.40$.
20.7 a. $F_{A \times \psi_{B_{\text{lin}}}} = 13.47^*$. **b.i.** $F_{\psi_{AB}} = 2.72$. **b.ii.** $F_{\psi AB} = 24.23^*$.

Answers to Chapter 21

21.1 Note: An asterisk denotes an ambiguous main effect. **Ex.1:** A. **Ex.2:** A, B. **Ex.3:** A, B, C. **Ex.4:** $A \times B$. **Ex.5:** C, $A \times B$. **Ex.6:** A, C^*, $B \times C$. **Ex.7:** A^*, C^*, $A \times B$, $A \times C$. **Ex.8:** A^*, C^*, $A \times C$, $A \times B \times C$. **Ex.9:** All effects present and all main effects ambiguous. **Ex.10:** $A \times B$, $A \times B \times C$.
21.3 b. $F_A = 91.01^*$; $F_B = 59.72^*$; $F_C = 11.46^*$; $F_{A \times B} = 1.75$; $F_{A \times C} = 4.29^*$; $F_{B \times C} = 1.34$; $F_{A \times B \times C} = 1.96$. **c.** The main effect of B and the $A \times C$ interaction permit unambiguous interpretations. **d.** $\widehat{\omega}^2_{\langle A \rangle} = 0.714$; $\widehat{\omega}^2_{\langle B \rangle} = 0.620$; $\widehat{\omega}^2_{\langle C \rangle} = 0.127$; $\widehat{\omega}^2_{\langle A \times C \rangle} = 0.084$.
21.4 The researcher will need at least 14 subjects ($n = 13.23$) per group.
21.5 c, d. The sums of squares can be calculated by treating the group means $\overline{Y}_{jkl}$ as the results for an experiment with $n = 1$ observations, calculating the sums of squares for the effects SS_{means} (we used a computer), and then multiplying them by the sample size $n = 20$ to produce the actual sums of squares. From this information, we can solve for error term to produce the final analysis ($MS_{S/ABC} = 21.1800/29.83 = 0.7100$): $F_A = 29.83^*$; $F_B = 0.13$; $F_C = 0.02$; $F_{A \times B} = 0.85$; $F_{A \times C} = 0.13$; $F_{B \times C} = 0.85$; $F_{A \times B \times C} = 14.79^*$.

Answers to Chapter 22

22.2 a. Main effect of pilots; $SS_C = 293.486$. **b.** A contrast-by-factor interaction; $SS_{\psi_A \times B} = 22.762$. **c.** A main comparison; $SS_{\psi_A} = 53.366$. **d.** A main comparison; $SS_{\psi_B} = 922.925$. **e.** A two-way interaction contrast; $SS_{\psi_A \times \psi_C} = 88.443$.

22.3 a,b. A rough plot of the interaction suggests a dominant main effect of factor A ($\widehat{\omega}^2_{\langle A \rangle} = 0.714$) and a relatively small interaction ($\widehat{\omega}^2_{\langle A \times C \rangle} = 0.084$) and C main effect ($\widehat{\omega}^2_{\langle C \rangle} = 0.127$). **c.** All three pairwise effects are significant ($D_{FH} = 0.767$). **d.** $F_{\psi_{A_1} \times C} = 7.44^*$; $F_{\psi_{A_2} \times C} = 0.19$; and $F_{\psi_{A_3} \times C} = 5.25^*$.

22.4 b. $F_{\psi_{A_4} \times B_2 \times C_1} = 2.98$.

22.5 b. $\widehat{\psi}_{ABC} = -5.0 - (-5.0) = 0.0$.

22.6 a. $F_{\psi_{A \times B} \text{ at } c_1} = 11.36^*$; and $F_{\psi_{A \times B} \text{ at } c_2} = 4.28^*$. **b.** $F_{\psi_A \text{ at } b_2 c_1} = 28.00^*$; and $F_{\psi_A \text{ at } b_1 c_1} = 0.28$. **c.** $F_{\psi_A \text{ at } b_2 c_2} = 1.18$; and $F_{\psi_A \text{ at } b_1 c_2} = 16.13^*$.

Answers to Chapter 23

23.1 a. $F_{A \text{ at } b_1} = 9.23^*$; and $F_{A \text{ at } b_2} = 0.27$. **b.** $F_{\psi_{A_1} \text{ at } b_1} = 6.02^*$; and $F_{\psi_{A_2} \text{ at } b_1} = 12.43^*$. **c.** $F_{\psi_{AB}} = 4.93$.

23.2 a. $F_{\psi_{C_{\text{lin}}}} = 98.26^*$. **b.** $F_{\psi_{C_{\text{nonlinear}}}} = 4.48$.

23.3 a. $F_{B \text{ at } a_1} = 8.24^*$; and $F_{B \text{ at } a_2} = 0.74$. **b.** $F_{\psi_B \text{ at } a_1} = 35.56^*$. **c.** $F_{A \times \psi_B} = 6.70$.

Answers to Chapter 24

24.1 a. $F_A = 1.03$; $F_B = 9.44^*$; $F_C = 8.03^*$; $F_{A \times B} = 200.17^*$; $F_{A \times C} = 6.97^*$; $F_{B \times C} = 0.88$; and $F_{A \times B \times C} = 0.05$.

24.2

Source	Error term
A	$MS_{\text{error-}A} = MS_{A \times B} + MS_{A \times S} - MS_{A \times C \times S}$
B	$MS_{\text{error-}B} = MS_{B \times C} + MS_{B \times S} - MS_{B \times C \times S}$
C	$MS_{C \times S}$
$A \times B$	$MS_{\text{error-}A \times B} = MS_{A \times B \times C} + MS_{A \times B \times S} - MS_{A \times B \times C \times S}$
$A \times C$	$MS_{A \times C \times S}$
$B \times C$	$MS_{B \times C \times S}$
$A \times B \times C$	$MS_{A \times B \times C \times S}$

24.3

Source	Error term
A	$MS_{\text{error-}A} = MS_{A \times B} + MS_{A \times C} - MS_{A \times B \times C}$
B	$MS_{\text{error-}B} = MS_{B \times C} + MS_{B \times S} - MS_{B \times C \times S}$
C	$MS_{\text{error-}C} = MS_{B \times C} + MS_{C \times S} - MS_{B \times C \times S}$
$A \times B$	$MS_{\text{error-}A \times B} = MS_{A \times B \times C} + MS_{A \times B \times S} - MS_{A \times B \times C \times S}$,
$A \times C$	$MS_{\text{error-}A \times C} = MS_{A \times B \times C} + MS_{A \times C \times S} - MS_{A \times B \times C \times S}$
$B \times C$	$MS_{B \times C \times S}$
$A \times B \times C$	$MS_{A \times B \times C \times S}$

Answers to Chapter 25

25.1 $F_A = 32.36^*$. Nested analysis: $F_A = 5.32$ and $F_{B/A} = 39.89^*$.

25.2 $F' = 6.32$ ($df_{\text{error-}A} = 4.84$ or 4).

25.4 b. $F_A = 2.73$; $F_B = 1.74$; $F_{A \times B} = 2.17$; $F_{C/A} = 2.20$; $F_{B \times C/A} = 2.17$.

25.5 a. See upper part of Table 25.6 (p. 561). **b.** MS_A and $MS_{B/A}$ and test for the significance of factor A. **c.** $F_A = 21.81^*$.

Answers to Chapter 26

26.1 The one treatment source above the line is a between-subjects effect; the remaining are within-subject effects:

Effect	Error	Effect	Error
G.M.	S	$B \times C$	$B \times C \times S$
A	$A \times S$	$B \times D$	$B \times D \times S$
B	$B \times S$	$C \times D$	$C \times D \times S$
C	$C \times S$	$A \times B \times C$	$A \times B \times C \times S$
D	$D \times S$	$A \times B \times D$	$A \times B \times D \times S$
$A \times B$	$A \times B \times S$	$A \times C \times D$	$A \times C \times D \times S$
$A \times C$	$A \times C \times S$	$B \times C \times D$	$B \times C \times D \times S$
$A \times D$	$A \times D \times S$	$A \times B \times C \times D$	$A \times B \times C \times D \times S$

26.2 The two treatment sources above the line are between-subjects effects; the remaining are within-subject effects:

Effect	Error	Effect	Error
G.M.	S/A	$B \times C$	$B \times C \times S/A$
A	S/A	$B \times D$	$B \times D \times S/A$
B	$B \times S/A$	$C \times D$	$C \times D \times S/A$
C	$C \times S/A$	$A \times B \times C$	$A \times B \times C \times S/A$
D	$D \times S/A$	$A \times B \times D$	$A \times B \times D \times S/A$
$A \times B$	$A \times B \times S/A$	$A \times C \times D$	$A \times C \times D \times S/A$
$A \times C$	$A \times C \times S/A$	$B \times C \times D$	$B \times C \times D \times S/A$
$A \times D$	$A \times D \times S/A$	$A \times B \times C \times D$	$A \times B \times C \times D \times S/A$

References

Abelson, R. P. (1996). Vulnerability of contrast tests to simpler interpretations: An addendum to Rosnow and Rosenthal. *Psychological Science, 7*, 242–246.

Abelson, R. P., & Tukey, J. W. (1963). Efficient utilization of non-numerical information in quantitative analysis: General theory and the case of simple order. *Annals of Mathematical Statistics, 34*, 1347–1369.

Alexander, R. A., & Govern, D. M. (1994). A new and simpler approximation for ANOVA under variance heterogeneity. *Journal of Educational Statistics, 19*, 91–101.

American Psychological Association (Fifth edition). (2001). *Publication manual of the American Psychological Association.* Washington, DC.

Beyer, W. H. (1968). *Handbook of tables for probability and statistics* (Second ed.). Cleveland, OH: Chemical-Rubber.

Boik, R. J. (1981). A priori tests in repeated measures designs: Effects of nonsphericity. *Psychometrika, 46*, 241–255.

Bollen, K. A. (1989). *Structural equations with latent variables.* New York: Wiley.

Box, G. E. P. (1954a). Some theorems on quadratic forms applied to the study of analysis of variance problems: II. Effect of inequality of variance and correlation between errors in the two-way classification. *Annals of Mathematical Statistics, 25*, 484–498.

Box, G. E. P. (1954b). Some theorems on quadratic forms applied to the study of analysis of variance problems: I. Effect of inequality of variance in the one-way classification. *Annals of Mathematical Statistics, 25*, 290–302.

Braver, S. L., & Sheets, V. L. (1993). Monotonic hypotheses in multiple group designs: A Monte Carlo study. *Psychological Bulletin, 113*, 379–395.

Brown, M. B., & Forsythe, A. B. (1974a). Robust tests for equality of variance. *Journal of the American Statistical Association, 69*, 364–367.

Brown, M. B., & Forsythe, A. B. (1974b). The small sample behavior of some statistics which test the equality of several means. *Technometrics, 16*, 129–132.

Brown, M. B., & Forsythe, A. B. (1974c). The ANOVA and multiple comparisons for data with heterogeneous variances. *Biometrics, 30*, 719–724.

Carlin, B. P., & Louis, T. A. (2000). *Bayes and empirical Bayes methods for data analysis* (Second ed.). Boca Raton, FL: Chapman & Hall/CRC.

Clark, H. H. (1973). The language-as-fixed-effect fallacy: A critique of language statistics in psychological research. *Journal of Verbal Learning and Verbal Behavior, 12*, 335–359.

Clark, H. H. (1976). Reply to Wike and Church. *Journal of Verbal Learning and Verbal Behavior, 15*, 257–261.

Clinch, J. J., & Keselman, H. J. (1982). Parametric alternatives to the analysis of variance. *Journal of Educational Statistics, 7*, 207–214.

Cohen, J. (1962). The statistical power of abnormal-social psychological research. *Journal of Abnormal and Social Psychology, 65*, 145–153.

Cohen, J. (1988). *Statistical power analysis for the behavioral sciences* (Second ed.). Hillsdale, NJ: Erlbaum.

Cohen, J. (1992). The statistical power of abnormal-social psychological research. *Psychological Bulletin, 112*, 155–159.

Conover, W. J., Johnson, M. E., & Johnson, M. M. (1981). A comparative study of tests of homogeneity of variances, with applications to the outer continental shelf bidding data. *Technometrics, 23*, 351–61.

Coombs, W. A., Algina, J., & Oltman, D. O. (1996). Univariate and multivariate omnibus hypothesis tests selected to control type I error rates when population variances are not necessarily equal. *Review of Educational Research, 66*, 137–179.

Cooper, H., & Findley, M. (1982). Expected effect sizes: Estimates for statistical power analysis in social psychology. *Personality and Social Psychology Bulletin, 8*, 168–173.

Cornell, J. E., Young, D. M., Seaman, S. L., & Kirk, R. E. (1992). Power comparisons of eight tests for sphericity in repeated measures designs. *Journal of Educational Statistics, 17*, 233–249.

Cornfield, J., & Tukey, J. W. (1956). Average values of mean squares in factorials. *Annals of Mathematical Statistics, 27*, 907–949.

Cowles, M., & Davis, C. (1982). On the origins of the .05 level of statistical significance. *American Psychologist, 37*, 553–558.

Dempster, A. P., Laird, N. M., & Rubin, D. B. (1977). Maximum likelihood estimation from incomplete data via the EM Algorithm. *Journal of the Royal Statistical Society, Series B, B39*, 1–38. (Includes discussion)

Dodd, D. H., & Schultz, R. F., Jr. (1973). Computational procedures for estimating magnitude of effect for some analysis of variance designs. *Psychological Bulletin, 79*, 391–395.

Dunn, O. J. (1961). Multiple comparisons among means. *Journal of the American Statistical Association,* *56*, 52–64.

Dunnett, C. W. (1955). A multiple comparison procedure for comparing several treatments with a control. *Journal of the American Statistical Association, 50*, 1096–1121.

Dunnett, C. W. (1989). Algorithm AS251: Multivariate normal probability integrals with product correlation structure. *Applied Statistics, 38*, 564–579.

Einot, I., & Gabriel, K. R. (1975). A study of the powers of several methods of multiple comparisons. *Journal of the American Statistical Association, 70*, 574–584.

Elliott, J. A. (1976). Circadian rhythms and photoperiodic time measurement in mammals. *Federation Proceedings, 35*, 2,339–2,346.

Erdfelder, E., Faul, F., & Buchner, A. (1996). GPOWER: A general power analysis program. *Behavior Research Methods, Instruments, and Computers, 28*, 1–11.

Estes, W. K. (1997). On the communication of information by displays of standard errors and confidence intervals. *Psychonomic Bulletin and Review, 4*, 330–341.

Feldt, L. S. (1958). A comparison of the precision of three experimental designs employing a concomitant variable. *Psychometrika, 23*, 335–354.

Fisher, R. A. (1951). *The design of experiments.* Edinburgh: Oliver & Boyd.

Fisher, R. A., & Yates, F. (1953). *Statistical tables for biological, agricultural and medical researchers* (Fourth ed.). Edinburgh: Oliver & Boyd.

Forster, K. I., & Dickinson, R. G. (1976). More on the language-as-fixed-effect fallacy: Monte Carlo estimates of error rates for F_1, F_2, F' and min F'. *Journal of Verbal Learning and Verbal Behavior, 15*, 135–142.

Games, P. A., & Howell, J. F. (1976). Pairwise multiple comparison procedures with unequal N's and/or variances: A Monte Carlo study. *Journal of Educational Statistics, 1*, 113–125.

Garcia, J., McGowan, B. K., Ervin, F. R., & Koelling, R. A. (1968). Cues: Their relative effectiveness as a function of the reinforcer. *Science, 160*, 794–795.

Geisser, S., & Greenhouse, S. W. (1958). An extension of Box's results on the use of the F distribution in multivariate analysis. *Annals of Mathematical Statistics, 29*, 885–891.

Glass, C. V., Peckham, P. D., & Sanders, J. R. (1972). Consequences of failure to meet assumptions underlying the fixed effects analyses of variance and covariance. *Review of Educational Research, 42*, 237–288.

Grant, D. A. (1956). Analysis-of-variance tests in the analysis and comparison of curves. *Psychological Bulletin, 53*, 141–154.

Greenwald, A. G. (1976). Within-subject designs: To use or not to use? *Psychological Bulletin, 83*, 314–320.

Hand, D. J. (1996). Statistics and the theory of measurement. *Journal of the Royal Statistical Society, Series A, 159*, 445–492.

Harris, R. J. (1985). *A primer of multivariate statistics* (Second ed.). New York: Academic Press.

Harris, R. J. (2001). *A primer of multivariate statistics* (Third ed.). Mahwah, NJ: Erlbaum.

Hartley, H. O. (1950). The maximum F-ratio as a short-cut test for heterogeneity of variance. *Biometrika, 37*, 308–312.

Hayes-Roth, B. (1977). Evolution of cognitive structures and processes. *Psychological Review, 84*, 260–270.

Hays, W. L. (1994). *Statistics* (Fifth ed.). New York: Holt, Rinehart, & Winston.

Hayter, A. J. (1986). The maximum familywise error rate of Fisher's least significant difference test. *Journal of the American Statistical Association, 81*, 1000–1004.

Hedges, L. V., & Olkin, I. (1988). *Statistical methods for meta-analysis.* San Diego, CA: Academic Press.

Hoenig, J. M., & Heisey, D. M. (2001). The abuse of power: The pervasive fallacy of power calculations for data analysis. *American Statistician, 55*, 19–24.

Hollander, M., & Wolfe, D. A. (1999). *Nonparametric statistical methods.* New York: Wiley.

Huitema, B. E. (1980). *The analysis of covariance and alternatives.* New York: Wiley.

Hunka, S. (1995). Identifying regions of significance in ANCOVA problems having non-homogeneous regressions. *British Journal of Mathematical and Statistical Psychology, 48*, 161–188.

Huynh, H., & Feldt, L. S. (1976). Estimation of the Box correction for degrees of freedom from sample data in randomized blocks and split-plot designs. *Journal of Educational Statistics, 1*, 69–82.

James, G. S. (1951). The comparison of several groups of observations when the ratios of the population variances are unknown. *Biometrika, 38*, 324–329.

Johansen, S. (1980). The Welch-James approximation to the distribution of the residual sum of squares in a weighted linear regression. *Biometrika, 67*, 85–92.

John, S. (1971). Some optimal multivariate tests. *Biometrika, 58*, 123–127.

Johnson, N. F. (1986). On looking at letters within words: Do we "see" them in memory? *Journal of memory and language, 25*, 558–570.

Johnson, P. O., & Fay, L. C. (1950). The Johnson-Neyman technique, its theory and application. *Psychometrika, 15,* 249–367.

Johnson, P. O., & Neyman, J. (1936). Tests of certain hypotheses and their application to some education problems. *Statistical Research Memoirs, 1,* 57–93.

Keppel, G. (1973). *Design and analysis: A researcher's handbook.* Englewood Cliffs, NJ: Prentice-Hall.

Keppel, G. (1982). *Design and analysis: A researcher's handbook* (Second ed.). Englewood Cliffs, NJ: Prentice-Hall.

Keppel, G. (1991). *Design and analysis: A researcher's handbook* (Third ed.). Englewood Cliffs, NJ: Prentice-Hall.

Keppel, G., Postman, L., & Zavortink, B. (1968). Studies of learning to learn: VIII. the influence of massive amounts of training upon the learning and retention of paired-associate lists. *Journal of Verbal Learning and Verbal Behavior, 7,* 790–796.

Keselman, H. J., Algina, J., & Kowalchuk, R. K. (2001). The analysis of repeated measures designs: A review. *British Journal of Mathematical and Statistical Psychology, 54,* 1–20.

Keselman, H. J., Algina, J., & Kowalchuk, R. K. (2002). A comparison of data analysis strategies for testing omnibus effects in higher-order repeated measures designs. *Multivariate Behavioral Research, 37,* 331-357.

Keselman, H. J., Algina, J., Kowalchuk, R. K., & Wolfinger, R. D. (1999). A comparison of recent approaches to the analysis of repeated measurements. *British Journal of Mathematical and Statistical Psychology, 52,* 63–78.

Keselman, H. J., Carriere, K. C., & Lix, L. M. (1995). Robust and powerful nonorthogonal analyses. *Psychometrika, 60,* 395–418.

Keuls, M. (1952). The use of the studentized range in connection with the analysis of variance. *Euphytica, 1,* 112–122.

Kirk, R. E. (1995). *Experimental design: Procedures for the behavioral sciences* (Third ed.). Monterey, CA: Brooks-Cole.

Kramer, C. Y. (1956). Extension of multiple range test to group means with unequal numbers of replications. *Biometrics, 12,* 307–310.

Krzanovski, W. J., & Marriott, F. H. C. (1994). *Multivariate analysis. part 1: Distributions, ordination and inference.* London: Edward Arnold.

Levene, H. (1960). Robust tests for equality of variance. In I. Olkin (Ed.), *Contributions to probability and statistics: Essays in honor of Harold Hotelling.* Stanford, CA: Stanford University Press.

Levin, J. R., & Neumann, E. (1999). Testing for predicted patterns: When interest in the whole is greater than in some of its parts. *Psychological Methods, 4,* 44–57.

Little, R. J. A., & Rubin, D. B. (1987). *Statistical analysis with missing data.* New York: Wiley.

Little, R. J. A., & Rubin, D. B. (2002). *Statistical analysis with missing data* (Second ed.). New York: Wiley.

Lix, L. M., & Keselman, H. J. (1995). Approximate degrees of freedom tests: A unified perspective on testing for mean equality. *Psychological Bulletin, 117,* 547–560.

Loftus, G. R. (1978). On interpretation of interactions. *Memory and Cognition, 6,* 312–319.

Lord, F. M. (1967). A paradox in the interpretation of group comparisons. *Psychological Bulletin, 68,* 304–305.

Lord, F. M. (1969). Statistical adjustment when comparing preexisting groups. *Psychological Bulletin, 72,* 336–337.

Lund, R. E., & Lund, J. R. (1983). Algorithm AS190: Probabilities and upper quantiles for the Studentized range. *Applied Statistics, 32,* 204–210.

Mauchly, J. W. (1940). Significance test for sphericity of n-variate normal populations. *Annals of Mathematical Statistics, 11,* 37–53.

Maxwell, S. E., Delaney, H. D., & Dill, C. A. (1984). Another look at ANCOVA versus blocking. *Psychological Bulletin, 95,* 136–147.

Maxwell, S. E., O'Callaghan, M. F., & Delaney, H. D. (1993). Analysis of covariance. In L. K. Edwards (Ed.), *Applied analysis of variance in behavioral science* (pp. 63–104). New York: Marcel Dekker.

McGovern, J. B. (1964). Extinction of associations in four transfer paradigms. *Psychological Monographs: General and Applied, 78*(16), 1–21. (Whole number 593)

McKay, B. D., & Rogoyski, E. (1995). Latin squares of order 10. *Electronic Journal of Combinatorics, 2*(N2). (www.combinatorics.org)

Micceri, T. (1989). The unicorn, the normal curve, and other improbable creatures. *Psychological Bulletin, 105,* 156–166.

Milligan, G. W., Wong, D. S., & Thompson, P. A. (1987). Robustness properties of the nonorthogonal analysis of variance. *Psychological Bulletin, 101,* 464–470.

Morris, S. B., & DeShon, R. P. (2002). Combining effect size estimates in meta-analysis with repeated measures and independent-groups designs. *Psychological Methods, 7,* 105–125.

Myers, J. L., & Well, A. D. (1991). *Research design and statistical analysis*. New York: HarperCollins.

Newman, D. (1939). The distribution of range in samples from a normal population, expressed in terms of an independent estimate of standard deviation. *Biometrika, 31*, 20–30.

Nickerson, R. S. (2000). Null hypothesis significance testing: A review of an old and continuing controversy. *Psychological Methods, 5*, 251–301.

Olson, C. L. (1976). On choosing a test statistic in multivariate analysis of variance. *Psychological Bulletin, 83*, 579–586.

Pearson, E. S., & Hartley, H. O. (1951). Charts of the power function for analysis of variance tests, derived from the non-central *F*-distribution. *Biometrika, 38*, 112–130.

Pearson, E. S., & Hartley, H. O. (1970). *Biometrika tables for statisticians* (Vol. 1, Third ed.). London: Cambridge University Press.

Pearson, E. S., & Hartley, H. O. (1972). *Biometrika tables for statisticians* (Vol. 2). London: Cambridge University Press.

Pedersen, J. M. (1988). Laboratory observation of the function of tongue extrusion in the desert iguana (*Dipsosaurus dorsalis*). *Journal of Comparative Psychology, 102*, 193–196.

Pedhazur, E. J. (1997). *Multiple regression in behavioral research: Explanation and prediction* (Third ed.). Fort Worth, TX: Harcourt Brace College Publishers.

Petty, R. E., Cacioppo, J. T., & Heesacker, M. (1981). Effects of rhetorical questions on persuasion: A cognitive response analysis. *Journal of Personality and Social Psychology, 40*, 432–440.

Petty, R. E., Fabrigar, L. R., Wegener, D. T., & Priester, J. R. (1996). Understanding data when interactions are present or hypothesized. *Psychological Science, 7*, 247–252.

Pollard, P. (1993). How significant is "significance"? In G. Keren & C. Lewis (Eds.), *A handbook for data analysis in the behavioral sciences: Methodological issues* (pp. 449–460). Hillsdale, NJ: Erlbaum.

Postman, L., & Keppel, G. (1967). Retroactive inhibition in free recall. *Journal of Experimental Psychology, 74*, 203–211.

Prentice, D. A., & Miller, D. T. (1992). When small effects are impressive. *Psychological Bulletin, 112*, 160–164.

Press, W. H., Flannery, B. P., Teukolsky, S. A., & Vetterling, W. T. (1986). *Numerical recipes: The art of scientific computing*. Cambridge: Cambridge University Press.

Raaijmakers, J. G. W., Schrijnemakers, J. M. C., & Gremmen, F. (1999). How to deal with "The Language as Fixed Effect Fallacy": Common misconceptions and alternative solutions. *Journal of Memory and Language, 41*, 416–426.

Ramsey, P. H. (1981). Power of univariate pairwise multiple comparison procedures. *Psychological Bulletin, 90*, 352–366.

Ramsey, P. H. (1993). Multiple comparisons of independent means. In L. K. Edwards (Ed.), *Applied analysis of variance in behavioral science*. New York: Marcel Dekker.

Rasmussen, J. L., Heumann, K. A., Heumann, M., & Botzum, M. (1989). Univariate and multivariate groups by trial analysis under violation of variance-covariance and normality assumptions. *Multivariate Behavioral Research, 24*, 93–105.

Raudenbush, S. W., & Bryk, A. S. (2001). *Hierarchical linear models: Applications and data analysis methods* (Second ed.). Newbury Park, CA: Sage.

Richardson, J. T. E. (1996). Measures of effect size. *Behavior Research Methods, Instruments, and Computers, 28*, 12–22.

Roberts, F. S. (1979). *Measurement theory with applications to decision making, utility, and the social sciences* (Vol. 7). Reading, MA: Addison-Wesley.

Rogers, W. T., & Hopkins, K. D. (1988). Power estimates in the presence of a covariate and measurement error. *Educational and Psychological Measurement, 48*, 647–656.

Rosenthal, R. (1991). *Meta-analytic procedures for social research*. Newbury Park, CA: Sage.

Rosnow, R. L., & Rosenthal, R. (1989). Definition and interpretation of interaction effects. *Psychological Bulletin, 105*, 143–146.

Rosnow, R. L., & Rosenthal, R. (1995). "Some things you learn arn't so": Cohen's paradox, Asch's paradigm, and the interpretation of interaction. *Psychological Science, 6*, 3–9.

Rosnow, R. L., & Rosenthal, R. (1996). Contrasts and interactions redux: Five easy pieces. *Psychological Science, 7*, 253–257.

Rossi, J. S. (1990). Statistical power of psychological research: What have we gained in 20 years? *Journal of Consulting and Clinical Psychology, 58*, 646–656.

Ryan, T. A. (1960). Significance tests for multiple comparison of proportions, variance, and other statistics. *Psychological Bulletin, 57*, 318–328.

SAS Institute, Inc. (1998). *SAS/STAT* users guide, version 7-1*. Cary, NC: SAS Institute.

Satterthwaite, F. E. (1941). Synthesis of variance. *Psychometrika, 6*, 309–316.

Satterthwaite, F. E. (1946). An approximate distribution of estimates of variance components. *Biometrics Bulletin, 2,* 110–114.

Sawilowsky, S. S., & Blair, R. C. (1992). A more realistic look at the robustness and type II error properties of the *t* test to departures from population normality. *Psychological Bulletin, 111,* 352–360.

Scariano, S. M., & Davenport, J. M. (1987). The effects of violations of independence assumptions in the one-way ANOVA. *American Statistician, 41,* 123–129.

Schafer, J. L., & Graham, J. W. (2002). Missing data: Our view of the state of the art. *Psychological Methods, 7,* 147–177.

Scheffé, H. (1953). A method for judging all contrasts in the analysis of variance. *Biometrika, 40,* 87–104.

Scheffé, H. (1959). *The analysis of variance.* New York: Wiley.

Seaman, M. A., Levin, J. R., & Serlin, R. C. (1991). New developments in pairwise multiple comparisons: some powerful and practicable procedures. *Psychological Bulletin, 110,* 577–586.

Sedlmeier, P., & Gigerenzer, G. (1989). Do studies of statistical power have and effect on the power of studies? *Psychological Bulletin, 105,* 309–316.

Serlin, R. C., & Lapsley, D. K. (1985). Rationality in psychological research: The good-enough principle. *American Psychologist, 40,* 73–83.

Sheehe, P. R., & Bross, E. D. J. (1961). Latin squares to balance immediate residual, and other order, effects. *Biometrics, 17,* 405–414.

Šidák, Z. (1967). Rectangular confidence regions for the means of multivariate normal distributions. *Journal of the American Statistical Association, 62,* 636–633.

Siegel, S., & Castellan, N. J., Jr. (1988). *Nonparametric statistics for the behavioral sciences* (Second ed.). New York: McGraw-Hill.

Slobin, D. I. (1966). Grammatical transformations and sentence comprehension in childhood and adulthood. *Journal of Verbal Learning and Verbal Behavior, 5,* 219–227.

Speed, F. M., Hocking, R. R., & Hockney, O. P. (1978). Method of analysis of linear models with unbalanced data. *Journal of the American Statistical Association, 73,* 105–112.

SPSS, Inc. (1999). *SPSS Base 10.0 for Windows: User's guide.* Chicago, IL: SPSS, Inc.

Sternberg, S. (1966). High-speed scanning in human memory. *Science, 153,* 652–654.

Stevens, J. (2002). *Applied multivariate statistics for the social sciences* (Fourth ed.). Mahwah, NJ: Erlbaum.

Stevens, S. S. (1951). *Handbook of experimental psychology.* New York: Wiley.

Tabachnick, B. G., & Fidell, L. S. (2001). *Computer-assisted research design and analysis.* Boston: Allyn & Bacon.

Tan, W. Y. (1982). Sampling distributions and robustness of *t*, *F*, and variance-ratio in two samples and ANOVA models with respect to departures from normality. *Communications in Statistics: Theory and Methods, 11,* 2495–2411.

Timm, N. H. (1975). *Multivariate analysis with applications in education and psychology.* Monterey, CA: Brooks-Cole.

Toothaker, L. E. (1991). *Multiple comparisons for researchers.* Newbury Park, CA: Sage.

Tversky, A., & Kahneman, D. (1971). Belief in the law of small numbers. *Psychological Bulletin, 76,* 105–110.

Welch, B. L. (1938). The significance of the difference between two means when the population variances are unequal. *Biometrika, 29,* 350–361.

Welch, B. L. (1951). On the comparison of several mean values: An alternative approach. *Biometrika, 38,* 330–336.

Welsch, R. E. (1977). Stepwise multiple comparison procedures. *Journal of the American Statistical Association, 72,* 566–575.

Wickens, T. D. (1995). *The geometry of multivariate statistics.* Hillsdale, NJ: Erlbaum.

Wickens, T. D. (1998). Drawing conclusions from data: Statistical methods for coping with uncertainty. In D. Scarborough & S. Sternberg (Eds.), *An invitation to cognitive science. volume 4: Methods, models and conceptual issues* (pp. 585–634). Cambridge, MA: MIT Press.

Wickens, T. D., & Keppel, G. (1983). On the choice of design and of test statistic in the analysis of experiments with sampled materials. *Journal of Verbal Learning and Verbal Behavior, 22,* 296–309.

Wike, E. L., & Church, J. D. (1976). Comments on Clark's "The language-as-fixed-effect fallacy". *Journal of Verbal Learning and Verbal Behavior, 15,* 249–255.

Wilcox, R. R. (1987). New designs in analysis of variance. *Annual Review of Psychology, 32,* 29–60.

Wilcox, R. R. (1988). A new alternative to the ANOVA *F* and new results on James's second-order method. *British Journal of Mathematical and Statistical Psychology, 41,* 109–117.

Winer, B. J., Brown, D. R., & Michels, K. M. (1991). *Statistical principles in experimental design* (Third ed.). New York: McGraw-Hill.

Zelen, M., & Severo, N. C. (1964). Probability functions. In M. Abramowitz & I. A. Stegun (Eds.), *Handbook of mathematical functions with formulas, graphs, and mathematical tables.* Washington, D.C.: National Bureau of Standards.

Subject Index

Author Index